www.wadsworth.com

wadsworth.com is the World Wide Web site for Wadsworth Publishing Company and is your direct source to dozens of online resources.

At *wadsworth.com* you can find out about supplements, demonstration software, and student resources. You can also send e-mail to many of our authors and preview new publications and exciting new technologies.

wadsworth.com
Changing the way the world learns®

METAPHYSICS
Contemporary Readings

METAPHYSICS
Contemporary Readings

First Edition

Steven D. Hales

Bloomsburg University

Wadsworth Publishing Company

I(T)P ® An International Thomson Publishing Company

Belmont, CA • Albany, NY • Boston • Cincinnati • Detroit • Johannesburg • London • Madrid
Melbourne • Mexico City • New York • Pacific Grove, CA • Scottsdale, AZ • Singapore
Tokyo • Toronto

Philosophy Editor: Peter Adams
Assistant Editor: Kerri Abdinoor
Editorial Assistant: Mindy Newfarmer
Marketing Manager: Dave Garrison
Print Buyer: Stacey Weinberger
Permissions Editor: Robert Kauser
Production: Matrix Productions, Inc.
Copy Editor: Victoria Nelson
Cover Design: Cuttriss and Hambleton
Compositor: Cecelia G. Morales
Printer: Webcom

Printed in Canada
1 2 3 4 5 6 7 8 9 10

For more information, contact Wadsworth Publishing Company, 10 Davis Drive, Belmont, CA 94002, or electronically at http://www.wadsworth.com

International Thomson Publishing Europe
Berkshire House
168-173 High Holborn
London, WCIV 7AA, United Kingdom

Nelson ITP, Australia
102 Dodds Street
South Melbourne
Victoria 3205 Australia

Nelson Canada
1120 Birchmount Road
Scarborough, Ontario
Canada MIK 5G4

International Thomson Publishing Southern Africa
Building 18, Constantia Square
138 Sixteenth Road, P.O. Box 2459
Halfway House, 1685 South Africa

International Thomson Editores
Seneca, 53
Colonia Polanco
11560 México D.F. México

International Thomson Publishing Asia
60 Albert Street #15-01
Albert Complex
Singapore 189969

International Thomson Publishing Japan
Hirakawa-cho Kyowa Building, 3F
2-2-1 Hirakawa-cho, Chiyoda-ku
Tokyo 102 Japan

Library of Congress Cataloging-in-Publication Data
Metaphysics : contenporary readings / [edited by] Steven Hales. -- 1st ed.
p. cm.
Includes bibliographic references.
ISBN 0-534-55145-9 (alk. paper)
1. Metaphysics. I. Hales, Steven.
BD111.M573 1999
110--dc21 98-40779

This book is printed on acid-free recycled paper.

This work is dedicated to Roderick M. Chisholm, my first and best teacher of metaphysics.

Contents

Preface for Instructors

METAPHYSICS IS NOT ONLY ONE OF THE OLDEST, but also one of the most diverse fields in philosophy. No single volume could offer readings from every area of a field as multiplex as metaphysics, and in fact there has been a conspicuous dearth of anthologies that make any attempt at all. The selections in the present book represent those topics and viewpoints at the forefront of contemporary metaphysical inquiry. These are the seminal, cutting-edge articles that have advanced the frontiers of knowledge; indeed, the numerous original pieces in this book contribute to that advance. The volume in your hands presents precisely the issues with which advanced undergraduates and beginning graduate students need to be familiar in order to understand what metaphysicians care about and why. Some issues in metaphysics, such as modality and possible worlds semantics, have not been included here because an adequate treatment of them requires too much logical sophistication for undergraduates. Other topics, such as free will, causation, and personal identity, are not treated in this volume because in some respects they have become cul-de-sacs on the map of late twentieth-century metaphysics. Though they are important topics in their own right, they lack the interconnectedness that unifies the ontological core of metaphysics. It is this core that the current book attempts to capture.

One may think that it is too much to expect undergraduates to step up to the rarified realms of recent metaphysics. This is not so! The selections in this book were specifically selected for their accessibility and lack of logical formulæ, so that students with little or no background in symbolic logic can make sense of them. Even so, the language and background assumptions of some of the articles may be challenging for the philosophically uninitiated. That is why each of the nine parts of the book is introduced by a leading expert on the topic of the part. These parts are existence (introduced by Michael Burke), the realism/anti-realism debate (Simon Blackburn), truth (Frederick Schmitt), abstract objects (Bob Hale), secondary qualities (Edward Averill), events (Jonathan Bennett), substance (E. J. Lowe), dependent particulars (H. Scott Hestevold), and mereology (Peter Simons). In addition, there is a previously unpublished article by Michael Devitt defending realism, along with a postscript in which Devitt addresses the interpretation of his position that Simon Blackburn gives in the introduction to this part. These introductions provide the historical context of the issue they introduce, explain what the debate concerns and why it is important, and outline the major positions taken. They serve to bring students up to speed and provide an appetizer for students before they tackle the entrées.

In addition to the introductions, detailed study questions accompany each selection that will enable students to quickly apprehend the main points and argumentative structure of the articles they read. For more advanced students, or anyone wishing to delve more deeply into the topics of this book, extensive lists of further readings accompany each part.

I teach at a mid-sized comprehensive state university in rural Pennsylvania and have successfully used these readings with upper-division undergraduates. You can, too. And when you do, your students will really know what contemporary metaphysics is all about.

I wish to thank my colleagues in the philosophy department at Bloomsburg University for their support of this project, and the university for granting me release time to pursue it. I am also grateful to Stephanie Minnaugh, a work study student who diligently proofread the manuscript. The students who took Metaphysics with me in the Spring 1996 and Spring 1998 semesters were a fine testing ground for many of the essays in this book. I would also like to thank the authors who wrote original contributions to this anthology for their generosity, timeliness, and philosophical acumen. And finally, I wish to thank the reviewers for their comments: James Baillie, University of Portland; David Haugen, Western Illinois University; Richard Feldman, University of Rochester; David Newman, Western Michigan University; Lynn Pasquerella, University of Rhode Island; Thomas Ryckman, Lawrence University; Cindy Stern, California State University—Northridge; and Dean Zimmerman, University of Notre Dame.

Preface for Students

METAPHYSICS IS ONE OF THE OLDEST AND MOST CENTRAL divisions of philosophy, and its study is found in full flower among the Greeks of the fifth century B.C.E. The word *metaphysics* itself comes from a first-century B.C.E. edition of certain collected writings of Aristotle, assembled under the title *Ta Meta ta Phusika,* which means no more than "what comes after the writings on nature" (*ta phusika*). The topics treated by Aristotle in this posthumous edition became the focus of the specialty of metaphysics.

Aristotle set out three main tasks in *Ta Meta ta Phusika*. The first was the study of the first principles of logic and causation. The second chore was the reasoned investigation of the nature of divinity. The third was ontology: the exploration of being *qua* being, or the intrinsic nature of existence. In the past two thousand years, the first assignment has been divided variously among logicians, philosophers of science, and scientists. The second task has become the specialized subject of the philosophy of religion. It is the third task, that of ontology, which remains to metaphysics proper today.

Ontology has three primary objectives. The first is to establish the basic categories of what there is, or the taxonomy of the ultimate furniture of reality. In one respect, a kind of taxonomy is implied by the very divisions of this book, in which, for example, an entire part is devoted to one kind of thing (such as *truth*) and another whole part is devoted to another kind of thing (such as *events*). In another respect, debate about which entities are the real denizens of the ontological zoo and which are mere pretenders is a theme that runs throughout the selections. As you will see, in Part V, entitled "Secondary Qualities," some philosophers believe that colors are real things in the world and others maintain that colors are just illusions of the mind. In Part IV, "Abstracta," you will see a similar debate over properties, numbers, and propositions; in Part VIII, "Dependent Particulars," the same question is asked about holes, surfaces, and boundaries. In a very general way, Part II on "Realism/Anti-Realism" asks whether reality even has a determinate, mind-independent structure, thus putting the entire taxonomic enterprise on the table for debate.

The second task of ontology is to investigate the relations that hold among different types of things. This question too arises throughout the volume. What is the relationship between a true sentence and the nonlinguistic facts of the world? How about between properties and the predicates that express them (the relationship might be identity)? What is the real difference between substances (your eye) and events (your eye moving across this page)? In what way are surfaces dependent on the substances that have them? Could we remove only the surface from an object? If so, how?

The third objective of ontology is to delineate the relations that obtain among things in the same category. This is the focus of Part IX, "Mereology." How are parts related to their wholes? Are they essential, so that if a whole were to lose a part it would go out of existence? If you replace a tire on your car, is it a new car? How about if you replace the engine and half the body? Part I, "Existence," also addresses relations that obtain among things in the same category by focusing on the very broadest category—that of *entity.* Of everything there is, why does it exist rather than not? Are there facts about what exists that explain why there is something rather than nothing at all?

Though no single book could cover every issue in metaphysics, the volume you are holding surveys some of the most prominent topics in contemporary metaphysics. Each of the nine parts of the book is introduced by a leading scholar on the topic of that part, and each of the articles is accompanied by study questions to help you quickly grasp the key points of the article. In addition, extensive further readings at the end of each part allow you to delve more deeply. All study questions and further lists of readings have been written or compiled by the editor, with the exception of the study questions in Part VIII, which were written by H. Scott Hestevold.

Part I

Existence

MICHAEL B. BURKE

Introduction to Existence

THERE IS A UNIVERSE. And perhaps there is a God. But why? Why is there anything at all? Why is there something rather than nothing? This question, which acquired its modern formulation in the writings of the seventeenth-century German philosopher Gottfried Wilhelm Leibniz, is the main question addressed by the articles in this part.

Three points will help to clarify the question. First, it is arguable that abstract things, *abstracta,* such as numbers and properties, exist of absolute necessity. On this view, in which abstracta would have existed even if the universe and God had *not* existed, there would be no mystery about there being *something,* if mere abstracta counted as "something." But there would still be a mystery about the existence of concrete things, *concreta,* such as rocks, hurricanes, humans, and God. For this reason it is customary in discussions of Leibniz's question to understand 'something' to mean 'something concrete'. (To a first approximation, *concrete* things are things capable of interacting with other things. For more on abstracta and concreta, see Part IV.)

Second, in Leibniz's question, the verb 'is' does not bear its tensed sense. It does not mean 'is now'. If it did, the question could be answered easily: mass-energy is something; and its present existence is explained by its past existence, together with the principle of the conservation of mass-energy. Rather, 'is' bears its tenseless sense. The question is this: why is there something at least *one* time (or something concrete, such as God, "outside" time, if that makes sense) rather than nothing at *any* time (and nothing concrete outside time)?

Third, when we ask "why" there is something rather than nothing, we are asking for a reason, but not for any particular *kind* of reason. The sociobiologist Richard Dawkins[1] takes why-questions in general, and Leibniz's question in particular, to presuppose that the reason lies in a motive or *purpose.* Often, however, why-questions do *not* carry that presupposition. To ask why the car broke down is usually just to ask what mechanical problem caused the breakdown. In asking Leibniz's question, philosophers generally do not presuppose, even if they ultimately conclude, that the answer lies in something other than impersonal conditions, forces, or facts.

This essay was commissioned especially for this volume and appears here for the first time.

Leibniz's own answer, given in his essay "On the Ultimate Origin of Things" (1697), was this: There is something rather than nothing because there is a thing that exists of absolute necessity, namely God. It is part of God's essence that he exists, just as it is part of the essence of the number 4 that it is even. It is no more possible for God not to exist than for the number 4 to be odd. Thus it is impossible for there to be nothing, necessary for there to be something.

Leibniz inferred the existence and necessity of God from the existence of the universe. The latter, he held, does not exist of absolute or (as we say today) "logical" necessity: the supposition of its nonexistence, although false, is self-consistent. Accordingly, the universe does not contain within *itself* the reason for its existence. But by Leibniz's "principle of sufficient reason," there must *be* a reason for its existence. Leibniz concluded that the universe owes its existence to something outside the universe, to something that does exist of logical necessity, to God.

Perhaps the main doubt concerning this reasoning, one raised by the Scottish philosopher David Hume[2] concerns the intelligibility of the notion of a logically necessary God. It is easy to agree with Leibniz that there is nothing logically necessary about the universe. What is not so easy is to understand how *any* concretum could be logically necessary. It does seem inconceivable that *abstracta* should fail to exist, if we assume that abstracta (such as the number 4) do genuinely exist, and exist independently of persons and other concreta. But as noted by Hume, the nonexistence of God seems no more inconceivable than the nonexistence of the universe. Perhaps that is why logical necessity is not among the properties attributed to God in most of traditional theology. Still, there is no clear proof that God could *not* exist of logical necessity. So Leibniz' answer, even though it proposes to replace one mystery with another, remains an option.

One popular alternative is the answer Hume suggested (in the same part of the *Dialogues*), which was elaborated by the twentieth-century American philosopher Paul Edwards.[3] The answer relies on the principle that to explain each member of a set individually is to explain the members of the set collectively. The "Hume-Edwards" answer, as it has come to be called, may be stated thus: Matter (strictly speaking, mass-energy) can be neither created nor destroyed. Material objects come and go, but the matter that composes them is eternal. There is now, and always has been, matter. *Why* has there always been matter? Well, take any past time. The fact that matter existed at *that* time is explained by these two facts: (1) there was an *earlier* time at which matter existed; (2) it is a physical principle that matter is conserved, meaning that matter that exists at one time exists at all times. So, for every past time there is an explanation of why matter existed at that time. Collectively, those explanations provide an explanation of why matter has *always* existed. And since matter is *something,* they provide an explanation of why *something* has always existed.

In short, for each time up to now, the existence of something at that time has a straightforward explanation. By the Hume-Edwards principle, those straightforward explanations, taken collectively, constitute an explanation of the existence of something at *all* times up to now. They explain why there is, and always has been, something. We have the answer to Leibniz's question.

Or do we? Although some find the Hume-Edwards answer satisfying, some find it decidedly *un*satisfying, even on the assumption that the physical universe is eternal. Perhaps, say the critics, the principle of the conservation of matter explains why matter has existed at all times *rather than at just some.* What it does not explain, they say, is why matter has existed at all times *rather than at none.* Given that matter is conserved, matter exists at all times if it exists at any. But why does it exist at any? Why is it that matter has existed always rather than never? Critics of the Hume-Edwards approach think that this question has not been answered. Supporters of the approach think it has.

What makes it difficult to adjudicate this dispute is the absence of agreement concerning the necessary and sufficient conditions for the satisfactoriness of an explanation. Those wishing to pursue the dispute are referred, for criticism of the Hume-Edwards answer, to Michael Burke, and, for defense of the answer, to Quentin Smith.[4]

In recent decades, some have sought an answer to Leibniz's question in quantum cosmology. As reported by the English physicist Paul Davies,[5] the answer suggested by some current work in that field goes something like this: The universe began with an uncaused quantum transition, a transition from nothingness to a world, a cosmos, consisting of nothing but a tiny volume of space. Within that space, again as a spontaneous quantum transition, there appeared a "false vacuum," a region containing energy in the form of an explosive pressure. Because of the pressure, the false vacuum expanded, which resulted in an intensification of the pressure, which led to an ever faster expansion, and so on. This runaway "inflation" of the still massless cosmos, which produced huge amounts of explosive energy (precisely balanced, perhaps, by the negative gravitational energy also produced), terminated with another quantum transition, in which the false vacuum ended and its explosive pressure was converted, in a "big bang," into heat, light, matter, and antimatter. The hundreds of millions of outward flying galaxies that now comprise the universe (or the part of the universe that we know about) are condensations of the mass-energy released in that long-ago explosion. So, why is there something rather than nothing? It's because (in a fashionable formulation) "nothingness is unstable." The laws of quantum physics provide for spontaneous transitions within all physical systems, including vacuums. Extrapolating, it is reasonable to suggest that the same laws provide for spontaneous transitions within *nothingness,* which means transitions from nothing to something.

Much of this account, especially the final suggestion, is acknowledged by cosmologists to be highly speculative. And to those unaccustomed to the weirdness of quantum physics, much of it may seem preposterous. There are, however, two reasons that the account deserves serious consideration: (1) Quantum physics offers the only prospect we have for a naturalistic explanation of the origin of the universe. Quantum physics is the one physical science that countenances, and enables us to explain, untriggered events. If, as theory and observation both suggest, there was a *first* physical event, and if we hope to find a physical explanation for that event, quantum physics is currently the only place to look. It is true that quantum physical laws are probabilistic rather than deterministic and can never explain why an event occurred at the exact time it did. Still, in telling us that events of certain types occur spontaneously with certain average frequencies, quantum physical laws can explain, in a reasonably satisfying way, why a certain event *occurred.* They can tell us that the event was to be *expected,* sooner or later. (2) Not only does quantum physics countenance spontaneous changes within existing entities (such as the decay of a radioactive atom), it also countenances the spontaneous coming into *being* of entities—for example, the appearance (followed generally by the quick disappearance) of particles within strong fields. So the spontaneous transition from nothingness to a small volume of space, which is the part of the quantum cosmological account crucial to explaining why there is something rather than nothing, is similar in character, and hardly more incredible, than happenings already countenanced by quantum physicists.

Philosophically, however, there are reasons for doubting that quantum physical laws can provide a satisfying answer to Leibniz's question. One is that laws of nature could explain the existence of the world only if those laws were both objective, in the sense of being human discoveries rather than human inventions, and transcendent, in the sense of existing independently of the world. On one currently popular view, laws of nature are objective relations among properties. If we combine that view of laws with a Platonist view of properties (on which properties exist independently of their instantiations), then we can indeed attribute to laws the requisite objectivity and independence. But if, as some believe, laws of nature originated with the world, then laws of nature, quantum physical laws included, would be powerless to explain the world's existence.

Furthermore, even if the laws of nature do transcend the world, it is widely held that time does not. And if it doesn't, then the hypothesized transition from a state of nothingness to the initial state of the cosmos could not be explained by quantum physical laws, as those laws are standardly formulated. Typically, quantum physical laws assign probabilities to the occurrence, *within specified amounts of time,* of specified types of spontaneous transition. If certain quantum physical laws are to explain the origination of time itself, how are those laws to be formulated?[6]

Finally, even if we supposed that quantum physical laws transcend the world to which they apply, supposed also that they can obtain in the absence of time, and supposed as well that they account for the origin of the cosmos, one large question would remain: what accounts for the quantum physical *laws?* True, laws are not concreta, so we would indeed have an answer to our *original* question: why are there concreta? And that would be progress. But if there were no further progress, if the cosmos-generating laws were left as a brute fact, the quantum cosmological answer, like the theological answer, would replace one mystery with another.

Perhaps it will be suggested that there is no mystery about the quantum physical laws. Like all laws they are abstracta, whether propositions, relations, or abstracta of some other kind. And it is arguable that abstracta exist (or "subsist") of logical necessity. Unfortunately, the mystery cannot be dispelled that simply. To say that there are laws is to say that some abstracta are laws. When we ask *why* there are laws, and why there are the particular laws there are, we are not asking why those abstracta that are laws *exist.* (If all abstracta exist of logical necessity, that question would indeed have a simple answer.) We are asking why those abstracta, rather than other abstracta or no abstracta, *are laws.*

Occasionally we encounter the suggestion that there is only one self-consistent set of laws by which a universe might be governed, only one self-consistent "superunified theory" or "theory of everything." Physicist Paul Davies rejects that suggestion. He writes, "I believe it is demonstrably wrong that a superunified theory would be unique . . . theoretical physicists frequently discuss mathematically consistent "toy universes" which certainly do not correspond to our universe. . . . It seems to me that, to have any hope of uniqueness, one would need to demand not just self-consistency, but a host of contingent specifications, such as conformity with relativity, or the presence of certain symmetries, or the existence of three dimensions of space and one of time."[7] Anyway, even if the suggestion were correct, it would not answer the question of interest here: why are there laws at all? Even if there is only one comprehensive, self-consistent set of laws by which a universe might be governed, why is there a universe governed by those laws, rather than no laws and no universe?

The contributors to Part I, all of whom are prominent contemporary philosophers, advance none of the three answers we have considered. They advocate neither the theological answer, the Hume-Edwards answer, nor the quantum cosmological answer. They all take Leibniz's question seriously: they reject facile dismissals of the question, such as that no answer is needed because we wouldn't be here to ask the question if there *weren't* existing things. But none starts with the assumption that the question must *have* an answer. It seems clear nowadays that some why-questions do *not* have answers. Quantum theory, on its standard interpretation, denies that there are explanations of the exact timing of quantum transitions. And there are apparently conclusive philosophical arguments for the conclusion that there must be explanationless truths. Those arguments assume only what seems undeniable: that not all truths are logically necessary.[8] However, none of the contributors is willing to assume that the existence of something rather than nothing is a brute fact, an explanationless truth. All search vigorously for an explanation. Regardless of the merits of the explanations they ultimately suggest, there is much to be learned—and much inspiration to be drawn—from the seriousness, depth, and ingenuity of their inquiries.

The first selection, which is the initial chapter of Nicholas Rescher's *The Riddle of Existence,* begins with a historical survey, a classification of possible responses to Leibniz's question, and a discussion of each possible response. This helpful orientation is followed by Rescher's defense of what he calls the "nomological approach." Rescher believes that the world of (concrete) things owes its existence (not to say its origination) to the operation of the basic laws of nature, which he presumes to be field equations. If, as he hypothesizes, those field equations have no empty-world solutions, then their (transcendent) truth requires, and thus explains, the (eternal) existence of things. Rescher does a good job of spotlighting and challenging the assumption of "genetic homogeneity": the common assumption, generally unspoken, that cause and effect must belong to the same category and, in particular, that things can come only from things.

Well, if things exist because of the laws of nature, what accounts for the laws of nature? Rescher's response is that any world, even an empty world, must exhibit *some* lawful order. The question, he says, is not why there are laws at all, but why there are the particular laws there are. Rescher addresses this question in the following chapter (which is not reprinted here, because its main ideas are found also in the essay by Parfit), where he says that the laws of nature obtain because it's *good* for them to obtain, because it maximizes certain *values* for them to obtain. To modern ears this explanation sounds strange. But as documented by John Leslie,[9] there is abundant precedent in the philosophical tradition for assigning explanatory efficacy to values. Unlike Leslie, who also proposes a values-based response to Leibniz's question, Rescher believes that the operative values are "economic" rather than ethical. The laws of nature are as they are so as to yield a natural order exhibiting a maximum of simplicity, uniformity, continuity, harmony, and systemic elegance. Having explained the existence of things by the operation of laws, and the operation of those laws by reality's tendency toward the maximizing of certain values, Rescher addresses a further question: why does reality tend toward the maximizing of those values? His answer: its doing so maximizes those values. In short, the tendency is self-explanatory!

Derek Parfit, the author of the second selection, rejects the notion of self-explanation and allows that explanations of reality may ultimately have to terminate in some brute fact. But he thinks that there may well be a reason that there is something rather than nothing and that there is the particular something there is—in his language, a reason that the particular "global possibility" that obtains does, in fact, obtain. By a "global possibility" Parfit means a possibility with regard to which possible worlds actually exist. Parfit notes that there may be many worlds other than ours (that is, many worlds spatially unconnected to our world, such as worlds that originated in other big bangs) and that they may differ in any number of ways both from our world and from one another. The "null possibility," which we know to be unrealized, is that *no* worlds exist. The "all-worlds possibility" is the possibility that *all* possible worlds exist. And, of course, there are innumerable possibilities in between. Just one of the global possibilities—we don't know which—actually obtains. But whichever one it is, what conceivable explanation could there be of *why* it obtains? Parfit's idea is this: If the possibility that obtains has a certain special feature, such as being the best of the global possibilities, or the worst, or the fullest (the all-worlds possibility), or the emptiest (the null possibility), or the one featuring the most elegant laws, then probably that global possibility obtains precisely *because* it has that feature. It is unlikely that reality has that feature simply by chance. In Parfit's language, probably that feature is the "Selector." Parfit acknowledges that the kind of explanation he envisions may seem mysterious. But he defends it. And he points out that even ordinary causal explanation can come to seem mysterious when we try to analyze it.

Parfit does not, however, see a way of pushing explanation further. He sees no means of explaining why the Selector, if there indeed is one, is what it is. In particular, he does not think that a Selector could select itself. If, for example, the global possibility that obtained were the *best* of the global possibilities, and if it obtained *because* of its bestness, then bestness would the Selector. But unlike Rescher (and unlike Nozick), Parfit thinks that the efficacy of bestness would not be explained by the fact that it's *best* for bestness to be efficacious.

In the final selection, Robert Nozick suggests not just one but a variety of imaginative and intriguing responses to Leibniz's question. Although Nozick is not yet prepared to claim that any of the responses is fully satisfactory, he aims to show that there is more prospect than we might suppose of explaining why there is something rather than nothing.

One of the responses he suggests is this: there is only one way for there to be nothing, but there are many ways for there to be something. Furthermore, there is no good reason to think that nothingness is the "natural" or "default" state of reality. It is not at all surprising, therefore, that there is something rather than nothing.[10]

Also noteworthy is Nozick's tentative defense of a type of self-explanation he calls "explanatory self-subsumption." Nozick believes that much rides on the legitimacy of this type of explanation. Only if some facts explain themselves, he argues, can there be an ultimate explanation of reality.

NOTES

1. Richard Dawkins, *River Out of Eden* (New York: Basic Books, 1995), pp. 96–98.

2. David Hume, *Dialogues Concerning Natural Religion,* Part IX, 1779.

3. Paul Edwards, "The Cosmological Argument," *The Rationalist Annual,* 1959.

4. Michael Burke, "Hume and Edwards on 'Why Is There Something Rather than Nothing?'" *Australasian Journal of Philosophy* (December 1984); Quentin Smith, "Internal and External Explanations of the Universe," *Philosophical Studies* 79, 3 (September 1995): 283–310.

5. Paul Davies, *Superforce* (New York: Simon & Schuster, 1984), pp. 183–205.

6. For a possible answer, see Chris Mortensen, "Explaining Existence," *The Canadian Journal of Philosophy* 16 (December 1986): 713–722.

7. Paul Davies, *The Mind of God* (New York: Simon & Schuster, 1992), p. 166.

8. See, for instance, Peter van Inwagen, *Metaphysics* (Boulder, CO: Westview Press, 1993), pp. 104–7.

9. John Leslie, *Value and Existence* (Totowa, NJ: Rowman and Littlefield, 1979), chap. 13.

10. A similar argument is offered by Peter van Inwagen in "Why Is There Anything at All?" In *The Aristotelian Society,* 70 (supplement): 95–110. Van Inwagen's argument is criticized by Thomas Baldwin in "There Might Be Nothing" (*Analysis,* October 1996).

On Explaining Existence (Real Possibility as the Key to Actuality)

1

NICHOLAS RESCHER

"Utcunque regressus fueris in status anteriores, nunquam in slatibus rationem plenam repereris, cur scilicet aliquis sit potius Mundus, et cur talis." G. W. Leibniz, *Phil.* VII (Gerhardt), p. 302.

SYNOPSIS

(1) THE "RIDDLE OF EXISTENCE" poses the question of why anything exists at all. This question is often dismissed as improper—but on rather dubious grounds. (2) Various responses to the question are in principle available, including primarily the following six possibilities: the theological, necessitarian, rejectionist, nomological, mystificational, and acausal. (3) Mystificationism affords an unappealing prospect. (4) And the acausal approach is inherently problematic. (5) Nor is it appealing to invoke the supernatural for natural explanation. (6) Necessitarianism is too peremptory to provide an acceptable account. (7) The rejectionist approach is also questionable. (8) Despite its difficulties, the best available option is the nomological approach—which grounds natural existence not on the operation of *preexisting things* but rather in a *lawful principle* of some sort. (9) Such a principle is provided by the fundamental "protolaws" of nature, which draw the line of demarcation between mere possibility and real possibility. The fundamental laws can be conceptualized as representing conditions FOR existence rather than conditions OF existents: They are not so much laws OF nature as laws FOR nature. (10) If these laws take a suitable form—that of a "hylarchic principle" which *constrains* (rather than *causes*) the nonemptiness of the world—then they can provide an answer to the question of why things exist. (11) Appendix: One can in principle use this same approach to explain not only the *existence* of things but also their *character*—in other words, to explain the existence of *these particular* things. But the demands of such a position are so strong as to render it rather implausible.

1. THE RIDDLE OF EXISTENCE

On December 3, 1697 (November 23, O.S.), Gottfried Wilhelm Leibniz sat late (for he was generally a night-worker) in the large, book-filled workroom of his apartment in the large timbered house of the patrician widow von Anderten in the fashionable Leinstrasse in Hannover, close to the old ducal palace whose library was now partly housed in these quarters under his charge. Pausing occasionally to glance at the fire that kept the chill of the winter's night at bay, he composed a short Latin tract "On the Ultimate Origination of Things," (*De rerum origionatione radicali*).[1] In this essay, Leibniz addressed the ramifications of a metaphysical issue that occupied him on many occasions: Why is there something rather than nothing? Why are there physical (contingent) existents at all? Why does anything whatsoever exist in the world?

From Nicholas Rescher, The Riddle of Existence *(Lanham, MD: University Press of America, 1984). Reprinted by permission of Nicholas Rescher.*

Leibniz realized that the existence of *a* world is pretty much inevitable—that if one is prepared to count even the "empty world" as a world, then the existence of a world is categorically necessary.[2] But of course it does not follow (save by a wholly illicit process of reasoning) that a particular world (this world) necessarily exists.[3] Specifically, the existence of a world with *things* in it, a nonempty world, remains an open problem.

Moreover, Leibniz realized that this issue of the *existence* of a nonempty world is more fundamental than and conceptually prior to the issue of its *nature*. The question "Why is there a world with things in it at all?" is conceptually prior to the question "Why is the world as it is—why do its things have the character they do?"

Leibniz also recognized that it is not *creation* that is at issue. Whether the world is eternal (as Aristotle had taught) or created (as Christian theology had argued against him) is immaterial. The question of the character of the world—*why* it contains "things"—will arise either way.

For a long time after Leibniz, philosophers turned their back on this "riddle of existence." They inclined to construe it as a request for an explanation for everything-all-at-once, and followed Hume and Kant in thinking it is not rationally appropriate to ask for such global explanations.

But the question has refused to go away. In the manner typical of deep philosophical issues, it resists burial and keeps springing back to life.

It was Henri Bergson who revived the issue as a topic of 20th-century philosophy. In his classic *L'Évolution créatrice* he wrote:

> I want to know why the universe exists; and if I refer the universe to a Principle immanent or transcendent that supports it or creates it, my thought rests on this principle only a few moments, for the same problem recurs, this time in its full breadth and generality: Whence comes it, and how can it be understood, that anything exists? . . . Now, if I push these questions aside and go straight to what hides behind them, this is what I find:—Existence appears to me like a conquest over nought . . . If I ask myself why bodies or minds exist rather than nothing, I find no answer; but that a logical principle, such as A = A, should have the power of creating itself, triumphing over the nought throughout eternity, seems to me natural. . . . Suppose, then, that the principle on which all things rest, and which all things manifest, possesses an existence of the same nature as that of the definition of the circle, or as that of the axiom A = A: the mystery of existence vanishes. . . .[4]

Clearly, however, this idea of a "conquest over nothingness" along essentially logical lines is highly problematic. The "principle on which all things rest" simply cannot "possess an existence *of the same nature*" as that of a definition or logical axiom because (on the modern conception of the matter, at any rate) these are purely conceptual truths of reason ("analytic" truths) from which no factual juice can be extracted. Getting real existents from pure logic is just too much of a conjuring trick. That sort of hat cannot contain rabbits.

Martin Heidegger held that the question of "Why is there something rather than nothing?" is actually the most fundamental question of metaphysics, characterizing the entire subject as the "exfoliation" of this problem.[5] Heidegger, however, was much less concerned to find a solution to the problem than to explain why the desire for an answer is part of the human condition and in examining its implications for the nature of man. Heidegger's interest was not in answering the question, but in considering its significance for us as a creature who, in the (inevitable?) absence of understanding, confronts nothingness in the existential phenomenon of *Angst*. As one recent commentator observes: "So daunting is the question [of existence] that even a recent exponent of it, Heidegger, who terms it 'the fundamental question of metaphysics,' proposes no answer and does nothing towards showing how it might be answered."[6]

Ludwig Wittgenstein was also fascinated by this issue. He maintained that "Not *how* the world is, is the mystical, but *that* it is."[7] He told Norman Malcolm that he sometimes experienced "a certain feeling of amazement that anything should exist at all."[8] In *A Lecture on Ethics,* he returns to this theme: "it always happens that the idea of one particular experience presents itself to me . . . [and] the best way of describing it is to say that when I have it *I wonder at the existence of the world.* And I am then inclined to use such phrases as 'how extraordinary that anything should exist' or 'how extraordinary that the world should exist'."[9] Relegating the issue to the limbo of mysteries conveniently provided Wittgenstein with a plausible reason for not dealing with it seriously. He dismissed those aforementioned locutions he was "inclined to use" as nonsense, because "It is nonsense to say that I wonder at the existence of the world, because I cannot imagine its not existing."[10] The difficulty here lies in the ambiguity of "the world," which might just mean *some* world or other, possibly including the empty world (in which case the wonder should indeed diminish—and the interest of the issue with it), or *this* particular world (in which case Wittgenstein would emerge as very unimaginative indeed).

In recent days the problem has been the topic of an erudite but obscure book by Anna-Teresa Tymeniecka,[11] which grapples valiantly with the issues without any signal success in rendering them intelligible. It is also the subject of a long chapter in Robert Nozick's *Philosophical Explanations.* But this interesting and many-faceted discussion culminates in a recourse to a mystical understanding of nothingness that cannot, even on kindest interpretation, be said to throw much light on the subject. In fact, one usually good-natured reviewer was provoked by the tenor of Nozick's discussion to protest against

> its lack of restraint. By the time one has struggled through this wild and woolly attempt to find a category beyond existence and non-existence, and marvelled at such things as the graph showing "the amount of Nothingness Force it takes to nothing some more of the Nothingness Force being exerted," one is ready to turn logical positivist on the spot.[12]

One recent writer contemplates the prospect of making short shrift of the issue:

> "Why is there something rather nothing?"—"If there were nothing, you wouldn't be here to ask the question." Ask a silly question, get a silly answer. . . . [W]hat makes the answer silly is that it tells the questioner no more than he must have known already.[13]

Actually, what makes the answer silly it that it answers the wrong question. It's like responding "Because he's now in the room" to the question "Why did Smith go through the door?" We *know* that Smith went through the door because he's in the room, and we *know* that there's something in the world because here we are. These answers are perfectly good responses to "How do you know that . . . ?" questions. But they are miserably inept answers to "Why is it the case that . . . ?" questions. They reflect a posture that ignores the traditional and very useful distinction between knowledge-oriented *rationes cognoscendi* and fact-oriented *rationes essendi.*

In general, it might be said that those philosophers who do not evade the problem by rejecting it as meaningless or intractable are profoundly intimidated by it. Whatever good sense they may display in other contexts deserts them on this occasion. With the notable exception of Leibniz, philosophers who have struggled with this riddle of existence have always found it difficult to keep their discussion of the issue on this side of nonsense.

And yet, this issue of the existence of things is to all appearances, as fundamental, profound, and serious a problem as any that philosophy affords. Given that only one among alternative possible worlds exists—possibilities among which an empty world also figures—why should it be that the actually existing world is one of the nonempty ones—one with *things* in it? More generally, why should *this* world be actualized rather than *that* one? Such a question is not lightly got rid of. Certainly it is not resolved by the fact of being embarrassingly awkward to deal with.

To be sure, the question of why anything whatsoever exists in the world has its problematic side. The global, universalistic character of such a question is bound to be a source of difficulty. When we try to develop an answer by the usual device of explaining one thing in terms of another, the former immediately expands to swallow the latter up. The question of existence-in-general cannot be dealt with as one of the standard generative sort that asks for the existence of one thing to be explained in terms of the existence of another. We cannot say "Well there's X in the world, and X explains the existence of things" because this simply shifts the issue to X, which after all is itself an existent. If we want *global* explanations of existence of things in the world, we are going to have difficulty in getting them from existential premisses pertaining to what the world is like. Does this mean we cannot get them at all?

Clearly what is wanted represents a very tall order. If we cannot use existential inputs, then we are asking for a great deal—an account that explains the emergence from an existentially *empty* realm of a *nonempty* world, a domain of existents. The explanation has to pull off a very neat trick: it has to account for a "change of phase" of certain items from the condition of mere possibility to the condition of actuality.

Table 1 An Inventory of Possible Responses to the Question: "Why Is There Anything at All?"

I. The question is illegitimate and improper. [*Rejectionism*]
II. The question is legitimate
  1) but unanswerable: it represents a *mystery*. [*Mystificationism*]
  2) and answerable
    a) though only by the *via negativa* of an insistence that there really is no "answer" in the ordinary sense—no sort of explanatory rationale at all. The existence of things in the world is simply a brute fact. [The *no-reason* approach.]
    b) via a *substantival* route of roughly the following sort: "There is a substance [viz. God] whose position in the scheme of things is one that lies outside the world, and whose activity explains the existence of things in the world." [The *theological* approach.]
    c) via a *nonsubstantival* route of roughly the following sort: "There is a principle of creativity that obtains *in abstracto* (i.e., without being embedded in the characteristics of any substance and thus without a basis in any preexisting thing), and the operation of this principle accounts for the existence of things." (The *nomological* approach.]
    d) via the quasi-logical route of considerations of absolute necessity. [The *necessitarian* approach.]

2. ALTERNATIVE RESPONSES

The question of existence can, in theory, be handled by any of the various lines of response set out in Table 1. This inventory pretty well exhausts the range of available alternatives. We may refer to these six approaches as the *rejectionist, mystificational, arational, theological, nomological,* and *necessitarian* solutions, respectively. Let us examine the assets and liabilities of these various positions.

3. THE MYSTIFICATIONAL APPROACH

The mystificational position sees the "problem of existence" as genuine but unsolvable. It classifies the question as an authentic *insoluble* to which no satisfactory answer can be found.

This approach recognizes the problem of the existence of things in the world as legitimate and acknowledges that we have a real and pressing interest in this issue. But it insists that we cannot profitably pursue this interest. With sceptical philosophers and Barthian theologians, it poses the question: Have we a right to demand a reason for things? Can we avoid recognizing that this question is simply beyond the powers of human intelligence? Is it not untenably presumptuous to demand that reality should satisfy our intellect's demand for "natural explanations"? And can we suppose that an explanation so accessible that *we* would deem it plausible actually gets at the real truth of things? Mystificationism insists that, while the question is indeed appropriate, the attainment of any satisfactory solution to it nevertheless lies beyond our reach.

The clear advantage of such a noncommittal approach is that it spares us the daunting and difficult task of framing a serious proposal for answering the riddle—of trying to arrive at some definite resolution. But its obvious disadvantage is its leaving us in a state of suspended animation with regard to this challenging and intriguing problem. To see all prospect of solution as unattainable is to leave matters unresolved. It means that we can only contemplate possibilities for resolution but cannot settle the matter of deciding among them.

Now it is perfectly conceivable that this condition of indecision and suspension of judgment as between the alternatives (of indecisive *isostheneia*, as the ancient sceptics called it) is a position in which we will eventually find ourselves. It is altogether possible that, after determined but vain attempts at finding a satisfactory answer, we might be led to conclude in the end that no such answer can be validated. We may even eventually convince ourselves, Fox and Grapes fashion, that further effort is not worthwhile—that the game is not worth the candle. But this sort of thing is clearly a position of last resort. To speak of an intrinsic *mystery* here serves rather to highlight the difficulty than to remove it. We may conceivably find ourselves driven there eventually, but it is hardly the place to start. Indeed it seems plausible to clutch at any straw to avoid this result. Given the interest of the issue and its importance for the project of achieving a rational grasp on our place in the scheme of things, if there is any reasonable way to avoid agnosticism here, it seems well advised to avail ourselves of it.

The key point is this. The existence of the world is contingent: given that other alternative modes of world-arrangement are theoretically *possible* (in particular an empty world) we want to know why the world exists as it does (and in particular why it contains *things*). The recognition of this world's contingency—of its being one alternative among others—cries out for explanation so urgently that in its absence we cannot rest intellectually satisfied.[14] What is at issue here is not a metaphysical Principle of Sufficient Reason maintaining on grounds of general principle that every phenomena has an effective explanation, but a *methodological* principle to the effect that we should always do our utmost to find sensible explanations of phenomena so long as any hope of doing so remains.

Admittedly, we cannot preestablish that reality will indulge our demands for intelligibility. But we have no sensible alternative to proceeding on the supposition that our explanatory guest can prove successful—that there indeed is an explanation which might be found. We cannot win the race if we do not enter it—and one price of entry is the supposition that a finish line exists.

4. THE ARATIONAL APPROACH

The arational resolution in effect maintains that things exist "just because." It takes the stance that there simply is no particular reason for existence. This well-stocked universe of ours has somehow just happened into being—its existence is simply an irrationalizable brute fact. There really is no explanation for the world's nonemptiness: "That's just the way it is"—take it with no further questions asked. (Recall Carlyle's remark on being informed that some lady said she had learned to accept the world—"By God, she'd better!") The world's existence, as is, is simply a "brute fact."

But this is surely no more than a solution of last resort. It is like the explanation "on impulse" offered to account for someone's action. It is not so much an answer to the question of explanation as a concession of defeat—an indication that our efforts at finding a more adequate solution have failed. The arational approach verges on mystificationism.

Perhaps the world's existence is not a matter of brute (i.e., inexplicable) fact, but simply needs no explanation. Perhaps the request for an explanation of things-in-general rests on a mistaken basis. Perhaps only *particular* items need be explained and it is a sort of category-mistake to ask for explanations at the level of generality. This seems to be what Bertrand Russell argued against Father Copleston in their celebrated BBC debate on God as a first cause:

> I can illustrate what seems to me your fallacy. Every man who exists has a mother. And it seems to me that your argument is that therefore the human race must have a mother. But obviously the human race hasn't a mother—that's a different logical sphere.[15]

On such a view, there is—indeed there can be—no appropriate explanation of the world's existence or fundamental nature.

But Russell's reasoning is flawed. Granted, the fact that every individual member of the class C (humans) has a cause of type X (i.e., has parents) of course does not mean that the totality of the class C will have a cause *of this particular type*. But this does not imply that we should not look for a cause of C-as-a-whole—for example that once we know that children are born of parents we should cease trying to account for *homo sapiens* at large within the framework of evolutionary explanation. Russell's counter-example does not show that we should not ask for an explanation at all, just that we should not ask for one of a particular sort.

To be sure, theorists sometime maintain that when a whole has been explained via its parts, taken distributively, there is nothing left to explain regarding that whole, taken collectively. As David Hume's Cleanthes puts it:

> [E]ach part is caused by that which preceded it, and causes that which succeeds it. Where is the difficulty? But the whole, you say, wants a cause . . . Did I show you the particular cause of each individual in a collection of twenty particles of matter, I should think very unreasonable, should you afterwards ask me what was the cause of the whole twenty. This is sufficiently explained in explaining the cause of the parts.[16]

This Humean position holds that if we are in a position to explain any and every member of a series of events (even an infinite one) we are *thereby* in a position to explain the series as a whole.

This *sounds* good. But will it do? Each member of the team is present because he was invited. Does that explain why the team is present as a whole? When we ask for explanations about the team, we ask not just about its several members, but about the team as a team. The idea that we have accounted for the class as a whole when we have accounted for each one of its members is quite false. Even when we account for everyone of its members we have not explained the species as a whole. Explanation at the distributive level does not achieve explanation at the collective level—even when we have resolved the former issue, a genuine explanatory question still remains.

In explanatory contexts the move from parts to whole is highly problematic. Consider an example. We can explain for any time t of his lifespan why Kant never left Prussia roughly as follows. For every such t, there is a timespan e such that at $t - e$ he was at such-and-such a location in Prussia, and there simply was not enough time, given the available means of locomotion, for him to reach the boundary within the timespan e. That does it alright. But would anyone hold that this yields an *adequate* explanation of why, throughout his lifetime, Kant never left Prussia?[17] We must not be misled into thinking that we have explained the whole as such when we are in a position to account for its membership *seriatim*.

When we ask an explanatory question about a whole, we don't just want to know about it as a collection of parts, but want to know about it holistically qua whole. A seriatim explanation of why each and every dodo died is not thereby an explanation of why this type of bird died out as a species. When we know why each particular day was rain-free (there were no rain clouds about at that point) we still have not explained the occurrence of a drought. Here we need something deeper—something that accounts for the entire *Gestalt*.

Given a set S, we may have an explanation regarding each of its members:

$$(\forall x \in S)(\exists e)eEx$$

But this does not assure us of a single, all-encompassing explanation for the entire set:

$$(\exists e)(\forall x \in S)eEx$$

Only by indulging in an illicit quantifier inversion can one claim that a distributive explanation of parts yields a collective explanation of wholes.[18] Hume to the contrary notwithstanding, if we have a collection of explanations of the parts (even an exhaustive one!), we do not automatically have an answer to our explanatory questions about the whole. The existence of explanations for each-and-every member does *not* provide for an explanation of the group-as-a-whole. And we are perfectly entitled to ask for such an explanation. There must—surely—be some "reason why" for every fact about the world—aggregate facts included.[19]

To reject the arational approach we need not maintain a substantive Principle of Sufficient Reason—we need not preestablish that there indeed always is some sort of explanation for any fact about the world. It suffices to take the methodological line: proceed on the assumption that there always is an explanation; hew to this working hypothesis through thick and thin. For the issue is an important one and as rational beings we would like to settle it to our rational satisfaction. It makes good sense to operate on the principle that even when our best efforts at finding an explanation bear no fruit, this is so simply because we haven't looked far enough. From the methodological perspective, the no-reason approach appears not as a resolution of the issue, but as an excuse for not dealing with it with sufficient determination.

One could properly take the arational line only if there were good reasons based on appropriate positive information for holding that there cannot be an answer—that the line of "no possible explanation" is appropriate. (We can, for example, take this line in quantum theory: asked why this atom of a transurancic element disintegrated just when it did the response is to say that no causal explanation is *in principle* possible.) But this approach is not available to us in the case at hand. There is no earthly reason to think that this sort of situation obtains. Nobody had produced a good *argument* why the arational approach should be endorsed. Its sole recommendation is that it affords a convenient exit from difficulty.

5. THE THEOLOGICAL APPROACH

The ancient tradition of "the cosmological argument" resolves the question of world's existence (and nature) by recourse to the productive agency of a creator God.[20] This theological approach is so familiar that little need be said about it. It grounds the existence of the world's things in the machinations of a world-external creative being—a necessarily existing agent who is self-subsisting and, in turn, serves as causal ground of the existence of the things of this world. God is thus seen as creator (*causa mundi*), and as himself as uncaused (or self-caused, *causa sui*) to avert the regress threatened by the question: Why is there a Supreme Being rather than nothing?

For a long time in the history of human inquiry, people inclined to answer ultimate questions about the world with the response: God made it that way. Yet this approach to the issue has its problems. The presence of things in the world is a matter of natural fact, and the explanation of natural facts by theological means is hardly a satisfactory option. The point is not simply that the *odium theologicum* is too strong at this time of day for a supernatural grounding of natural existence to be deemed acceptable. It is that questions about the natural order should be addressed in nature-correlative terms of reference wherever this is at all possible. Kant's formulation of the point cannot be improved upon:

> To have recourse to God as the Creator of all things in explaining the arrangements of nature and their changes is at any rate not a scientific explanation, but a complete confession that one has come to the end of his philosophy, since he is compelled to assume something [supernatural]. . . to account for something he sees before his very eyes.[21]

The drawback of the theological solution to the problem of existence is that it uses a sledgehammer to crack a nut. It is unsatisfying to try to answer such questions, with Descartes, through recourse to the *mere will* or, with Leibniz, through recourse to the *good will* of the divine creator, because of the rational proprieties implicit in the scholastic dictum that scientific deliberations are not entitled to an explanatory recourse to God (*non in philosophia recurrere est ad deum*). Whatever be God's proper role in the scheme of things, it is not to solve our philosophical or scientific difficulties. Invoking a supernatural agency to solve our problems in understanding nature is inherently questionable etiquette.

No doubt a principle that can explain the existence of things in the world will have to invoke circumstances that are in some degree extraordinary and *preternatural* in being outside nature's common course, but it need not go so far as to invoke something *supernatural*—something as much "above" or remote from nature as the omnipotent deity of traditional monotheism. What is at issue here is simply a point of methodology, of explanatory economy, of accomplishing desired ends by the least complex means. If there is any prospect of resolving a question in a more straightforward way, we should avail ourselves of it.

6. THE NECESSITARIAN APPROACH

The necessitarian approach has it that the world exists as a matter of strict (or "logical") necessity. Its very nature requires its existence: like the God of traditional theology, it is something that cannot but exist. This approach was already encountered in the Bergson passage quoted above. It proposes to explain existence as somehow a matter of "logical principle." We are called on to take the stance that "the principle on which all things rest, and which all things manifest, possesses an existence of the same nature as that of the definition of the circle, or as that of the axiom $A = A$."

But such a way of addressing the problem of existence is simply too peremptory. Given that alternatives can readily be conceived, how can one possibly establish necessitarian inevitability? How could the constraints of logic alone possibly engender the arrangements of fact? Even to consider this alternative is to become persuaded of its unmanageability.

7. THE REJECTIONIST APPROACH

Questions like "Why is there anything at all?", "Why are things-in-general as they actually are?", and "Why is the law structure of the world as it is?" cannot be answered within the standard causal framework. For causal explanations need inputs: they are essentially *transformational* (rather than *formational* pure and simple). They can address themselves to specific issues distributively and seriatim, but not collectively and holistically. If we persist in posing the sorts of global questions at issue, we cannot hope to resolve them in orthodox causal terms. Does this mean that such questions are improper?

On the rejectionist approach, the entire question of obtaining the (or *a*) reason for the existence of things is simply dismissed as illegitimate. Even to inquire into the existence of the entire universe is held to be somehow illegitimate. It is just a mistake to ask for a causal explanation of existence *per se;* the question should be abandoned as improper—as not representing a legitimate issue. We are assured that in the light of closer scrutiny the explanatory "problem" vanishes as meaningless.

Dismissal of the problem as illegitimate is generally based on the idea that the question at issue involves an illicit presupposition. It looks to answers of the form "*Z* is the (or *an*) explanation for the existence of things." Committed to this response-schema, the question has the thesis "There is a ground for the existence of things—existence-in-general is the sort of thing that has an explanation." And this presumption—we are told—might well be false. In principle its falsity could emerge in two ways:

1. on grounds of deep general principle inherent in the conceptual "logic" of the situation; or
2. on grounds of a concrete doctrine of substantive metaphysics or science that precludes the prospect of an answer—even as quantum theory precludes the prospect of an answer to "Why did that atom of Californium decay at that particular time?"

Let us begin by considering if the question of existence might be invalidated by considerations of the first sort and root in circumstances that lie deep in the conceptual nature of things. Consider the following discussion by C. G. Hempel:

> Why is there anything at all rather than nothing? . . . But what kind of an answer could be appropriate? What seems to be wanted is an explanatory account which does not assume the existence of something or other. But such an account, I would submit, is a logical impossibility. For generally, the question "Why is it the case that *A*?" is answered by "Because *B* is the case" . . . [*A*]*n answer to our riddle which made no assumptions about the existence of anything cannot possibly provide adequate grounds*. . . . The riddle has been constructed in a manner that makes an answer logically impossible. . . .[22]

But this plausible line of argumentation has shortcomings. The most serious of these is that it fails to distinguish appropriately between the *existence of things* on the one hand and the *obtaining of facts* on the other,[23] and supplementarily also between specifically substantival facts regarding existing *things*, and nonsubstantival facts regarding *states of affairs* that are not dependent on the operation of preexisting things.

We are confronted here with a principle of hypostatization to the effect that the reason for anything must ultimately always inhere in the operations of things. And at this point we come to a prejudice as deep-rooted as any in Western philosophy: the idea that things can only originate from things, that nothing can come from nothing (*ex nihilo nihil fit*) in the sense that no *thing* can emerge from a thingless condition.[24] Now, this somewhat ambiguous principle is perfectly unproblematic when construed as saying that if the existence of something real has a correct explanation at all, then this explanation must pivot on something that is really and truly so. Clearly, we cannot explain one *fact* without involving other *facts* to do the explaining. But the principle becomes highly problematic when construed in the manner of the precept that "*things* must come from *things*," that *substances* must inevitably be invoked to explain the existence of *substances*. For we then become committed to the thesis that everything in nature has an efficient cause in some other natural thing that is its causal source, its reason for being.

This stance is implicit in Hempel's argument. And it is explicit in much of the philosophical tradition. Hume, for one, insists that there is no feasible way in which an existential conclusion can be obtained from nonexistential premisses.[25] And the principle is also supported by philosophers of a very different ilk on the other side of the channel—including Leibniz himself, who writes:

> [T]he sufficient reason [of contingent existence] . . . must be outside this series of contingent things, and *must reside in a substance which is the cause of this series* . . . .[26]

Such a view amounts to a thesis of genetic homogeneity which says (on analogy with the old but now rather obsolete principle that "life must come from life") that "things must come from things," or "stuff must come from stuff," or "substance must come from substance." What, after all, could be more plausible than the precept that only real (*existing*) causes can have real (*existing*) effects?

But despite its appeal, this principle has its problems. It presupposes that there must be a type-homogeneity between cause and effect on the lines of the ancient Greek principle that "like must come from like." This highly dubious principle of genetic homogeneity has taken hard knocks in the course of modern science. Matter can come from energy, and living organisms from complexes of inorganic molecules. If the principle fails with matter and life, need it hold for substance as such? The claim that it does so would need a very cogent defense. None has been forthcoming to date.

Is it indeed true that only *things* can engender things? Why need a ground of change always inhere in a *thing* rather than in a nonsubstantival "condition of things-in-general"? Must substance inevitably arise from *substance?* Even to state such a principle is in effect to challenge its credentials. For why must the explanation of facts rest in the operation of *things*? To be sure, fact-explanations must have inputs (*all* explanations must). Facts must root in facts. But why thing-existential ones? A highly problematic bit of metaphysics is involved here. Dogmas about explanatory homogeneity aside, there is no discernible reason why an existential fact cannot be grounded in nonexistential ones, and why the existence of substantival *things* cannot be explained on the basis of some nonsubstantival circumstance or principle whose operations can constrain existence in something of the way in which equations can constrain nonzero solutions. Once we give up the principle of genetic homogeneity and abandon the idea that existing things must originate in existing things, we remove the key prop of the idea that asking for an explanation of things in general is a logically inappropriate demand. The footing of the rejectionist approach is gravely undermined.

There are, of course, other routes to rejectionism. One of them turns on the doctrine of Kant's *Antinomy* that it is illegitimate to try to account for the phenomenal universe as a whole (the entire *Erscheinungswelt*). Explanation on this view is inherently partitive: phenomena can only be accounted for in terms of other phenomena, so that it is in principle improper to ask for an account of phenomena-as-a-whole. The very idea of an explanatory science of nature-as-a-whole is illegitimate. Yet this view is deeply problematic. To all intents and purposes, science strives to explain the age of the universe-as-a-whole, its structure, its volume, its laws, its composition, etc. Why not then its *existence* as well? The decree that explanatory discussion is by nature necessarily partial and incapable of dealing with the whole lacks plausibility. It seems a mere device for sidestepping embarrassingly difficult questions.

Rejectionism is not a particularly appealing course. Any alternative to rejectionism has the significant merit of retaining for rational inquiry and investigation a question that would otherwise be abandoned. The question of "the reason why" behind existence is surely important. If there is any possibility of getting an adequate answer—by hook or by crook—it seems reasonable that we would very much like to have it. There is nothing patently meaningless about this "riddle of existence." And it does not seem to rest in any obvious way on any particularly problematic presupposition—apart from the epistemically optimistic yet methodologically inevitable idea that there are always reasons why things are as they are (the "principle of sufficient reason"). To dismiss the question as improper or illegitimate is fruitless. Try as we will to put the question away, it comes back to haunt us.[27]

8. THE NOMOLOGICAL APPROACH

Consider the line of reasoning set out in the antinomy of causation formulated in Table 2. Since the assertions (A) and (B) squarely contradict each other, it is clear that theses (1)–(4) constitute an inconsistent group of propositions. In consequence, one member of this quartet, at least, must be rejected. Let us survey the options for resolving this antinomy.

Table 2 An Inconsistent Quartet

(1) Everything—that is, literally everything—that exists in nature has a causal explanation. (The Principle of Causality.)
(2) Natural-existence-as-a-whole must itself be counted as a natural thing: the universe itself qualifies as a thing or substance of some sort. (The Principle of Totalization: The entire universe that consists of things (substances) is itself a thing (substance).)
(A) The universe has a causal explanation. (From (1) and (2).)
(3) Causal explanations of existential facts require existential inputs to afford the requisite causes. (The Principle of Genetic Homogeneity.)
(4) No existential inputs are available to explain the existence of natural-existence-as-a-whole, the totality of things within the world (= the universe). For any existent invoked by the explanation would constitute part of the explanatory problem, thus vitiating the explanation on grounds of circularity. (The Principle of Causal Comprehension: Anything that stands in causally explanatory connection with the universe is thereby, *ipso facto,* a part of it.)
(B) No (adequate) causal explanation can be given for the universe. (From (3) and (4).)

(1)-rejection. One could abandon the Principle of Causality. This would pave the way for accepting the universe ("natural existence as a whole") as something whose existence just is uncaused. One would accordingly take roughly the following line:

> There are things in the world because once upon a time there was an alpha-event that was the origination of a world-with-things-in-it. And this event *just happened;* it was *uncaused.* And it had to be so. For it makes no sense to suppose a cause of the initiation (the beginning-to-be) of things-as-a-whole, because causal explanations require existential inputs to operate as causes.

The obvious shortcoming of this position is inherent in its commitment to the questionable idea that causation necessarily requires *preexisting things* to act as causes.

(2)-rejection. One could abandon the Principle of Totalization and maintain that the assimilation of the entire universe itself to particular things must be abandoned. Everything-as-a-whole is seen as *sui generis* and thus not as a literal *thing* that, along with particular things, can be expected to conform to thing-oriented principles such as the Principle of Causality. Accordingly, we would exempt the universe itself from membership in the class of things that have cause.

The difficulty with this approach lies in the problem of establishing the grounds of the purported impropriety. We unhesitatingly view galaxies as individual things whose origin, duration, and nature need explanation—why not then the cosmos as a whole? This synoptic question is, admittedly, more challenging and inconvenient. But why should that make it illegitimate?

(3)-rejection. One could reject (3) as we have in fact already proposed to do. Yet in dismissing genetic homogeneity one would (and should) not abandon it altogether, but rather subject it to a distinction. One could then say that there are *two different kinds* of causal explanation, those that proceed in terms of the causal agency of (preexisting) *things*—substance causality or efficient causality—and those that proceed in terms of the causal operation of lawful *principles*—law causality or nomological causality. The former, *efficient* mode of causality is clearly not up to the job. For someone who asks for a natural explanation of the world

in the order of efficient causality deserves to be told that "his explanandum is so global a feature of the world that it leaves no room for causes distinct from itself."[28] But this consideration does not put nomological causality *hors de combat.* This latter is not thing-based; it would not require that the causal principles at issue be rooted in the operations of "things." In its preparedness to let laws rather than things account for existence, the nomological principle that this mode of causal explanation envisages would not have any specifically *substantival* embodiment whatever.

Such an approach abandons the deep-rooted prejudice that efficient causality is the only mode of causality there is—that causal agency must always be hypostacized as the operation of a causal agent. Accordingly, this approach envisages a mode of "causality" whose operation can dispense with existential inputs. It recognizes that the orthodox terms of ordinary efficient causality are not the only ones available for developing explanations of existence. Thus while still retaining the Principle of Causality as per (1), this approach substantially alters its import.

(4)-rejection. This course commits us to the idea that existential inputs *are* available to explain the existence of natural-existence-as-a-whole. Standardly, this involves the introduction of a nature-external, literally supernatural being (viz. God) to serve as the once-and-for-all existential ground in explaining the existence of all natural things. On this *theological* alternative, one would then retain (1) intact by means of the principle that God is *causa sui.*

We have already remarked on the methodological shortcomings of this approach. A reasonable division of labor calls for leaving God to attend to the proper concerns of theology and refraining from importing him into the project of scientific explanation. It is surely not his proper job to help us out of theoretical difficulties in science or philosophy.

Each of these solutions exacts a price. Each calls on us to abandon a thesis that has substantial surface plausibility and appeal. And each requires us to tell a fairly complicated and in some degree unpalatable story to explain and justify the abandonment at issue.

The point to be emphasized, however, is that (3)-rejection—the recourse, in existence explanation, to a principle of lawfulness that does not itself have an existential grounding in a *thing* of some sort—emerges as *comparatively* optimal. The price it exacts, though real, is more affordable than that of its competitors. The consequences it engenders are on balance the least problematic—which is, of course, far from saying that they are not problematic at all. In the last analysis, we take recourse to nomological causality—to the creative operation of lawful principles—*faute de mieux,* because this is the contextually optimal alternative; no better one is in sight. While there indeed are alternatives, they are even more deeply problematic.

Accordingly, the idea of a hylarchic principle that grounds the existence of things not in preexisting *things* but rather in a functional principle of some sort—a specifically *nonsubstantival* state of affairs—becomes something one can at least entertain. The justification for resorting to this explanatory strategy is hypothetical in structure: "If you are going to explain existence at all, then you can do no better than to explain it along the lines of such a hylarchic principle." The justificatory rationale is not one of alternative-elimination ("this or nothing"), but of comparative optimization ("this or nothing better").

If we persist in posing these global questions, some extraordinary mechanism *must* be invoked because we cannot hope to resolve them in terms of ordinary efficient causality. For causal explanations require existential inputs to act as causes. And this vitiates their utility in the present context. As David Lewis has rightly noted, the question "Why is there something rather than nothing?" in the specifically *causal* sense invites the dismissive response of telling the questioner "that his explanandum is so global a feature of the world that it leaves no room for causes distinct from itself, and hence it cannot have any causal history."[29]

We confront the inconsistent triad:

(1) Existence-as-a-whole admits of no explanation in the order of efficient causality.

(2) The question "Why is there something rather than nothing?" must be treated in the order of efficient causality. If a

satisfactory answer is to be found at all, it will have to be a causal one.

(3) The question is a sensible one that in principle admits of a satisfactory answer.

It is tempting to resolve this inconsistency by rejecting (3) and dismissing our problem with it. (We "answer" the question by learning that it was a mistake to ask it.) But this particular way of resolving the inconsistency is not inevitable. A resolution predicated on (2)-rejection can certainly be contemplated. And just this is the root idea of a nomological approach that proceeds outside the order of efficient causality and sees the existence of the world as *constrained by lawful principles rather than produced by efficient causes.*

Consideration of the shortcomings of all available alternatives renders an approach made in terms of a lawful principle worthy of close and sympathetic attention. It has substantial advantages over its rivals. In particular, the explanation of existence in terms of a nomological principle is in the fortunate position of averting a problematic hypostatization. It avoids the basic defect of all versions of the cosmological argument of supposing that the world's existence must root in a *substance*—the only ultimately suitable substance being one that is self-generative *(causa sui)*, so that the project of an adequate explanation of existence leads inexorably to God. Nomological explanation enables us to address the "riddle of existence" without theological involvements.

9. PROTOLAWS AND METAPHYSICAL POSSIBILITY

But how might the existence of things possibly be accounted for through a lawful principle which operates wholly outside the existential arena? How can an explanation ever move from possibility to actuality by relatively unproblematic means? To deal sensibly with this question, it is necessary to make a brief excursus into the theory of possibility.

To begin with, there is the idea of a *spectrum* of possibility—an inventory of all distinct possibilities which, as such, is suitably exclusive and exhaustive. The question "Why are *any* possibilities realized? Why don't *all* of those possibilities just stay *mere* possibilities without *any* being actual?" is thus to be answered by the observation that some state of affairs must obtain—that if these possibilities indeed are mutually exclusive and exhaustive, then one or another of them *must* obtain in the "logical" nature of things. The difficulty of course is to get from the obtaining of a state of affairs to the existence of *things.*

The realm of the possible can be represented as a circle divided, target fashion, into three concentric rings—as per Figure 1. Moving inwards we encounter first (outermost) the domain of *mere logical* (or "purely hypothetical") possibility, and last (centrally) the domain of a *physical* possibility that reflects the mode of operation of the actual things of this world. Intermediate between them lies the realm of *real* (or "metaphysical") possible.[30] Mere possibility is a matter of abstract, logical consistency—of purely theoretical prospects. Physical possibility is a matter of the operation of things actually present on the world's existential stage. Real possibility is something intermediate between these two. It is a matter of genuine or "realistic" possibility, not in the sense of psychological imaginability, but in that of a "metaphysical" possibility which must eventually be cashed out through some substantive theory of possibility.

A "compatibility theory" of possibility is perfectly workable here. But we need to think of it in a three-stage way. As usual, mere *logical* possibility is a matter of compatibility with the laws of logic, and *physical* possibility is a matter of compatibility with the laws of nature. But *real* possibility is something intermediate between these, a matter of compatibility with the protophysical laws of nature that set the preconditions for its realization and determine

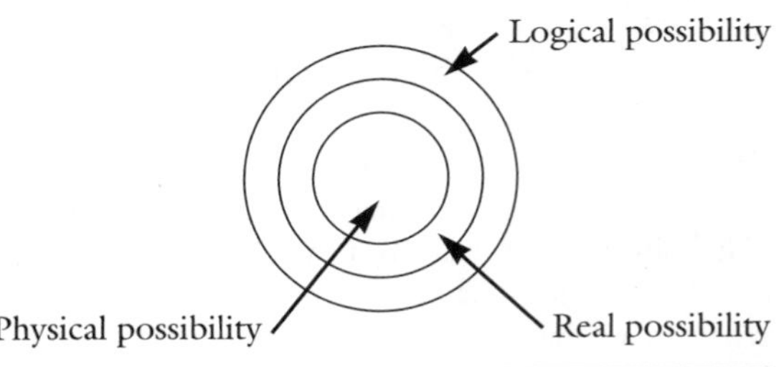

Figure 1 The Realm of Possibility

not *actualities* as such, but *realistic possibilities* for potential actualization.

Such protophysical laws will reflect the substance of our science in terms of its ability to implement the distinction between mere and real possibilities. They should be understood as laying down conditions of *real* possibility, ruling certain theoretical (logical) possibilities out as outside the realm of realizability. They "precede" nature and delineate among all the abstractly available possibilities certain ones as alone "real," ruling out the rest as unreal, remote, merely hypothetical or the like.

The root idea of this approach goes back to Leibniz, who—in distinguishing between "logical" and "metaphysical" necessity—first took explanatory recourse to a modality intermediate between physical and absolute ("logical") necessity. As he saw it, the arrangements of the world are neither absolutely nor logically necessary (à la Spinoza) nor wholly fortuitous (à la Epicurus) nor arbitrary (à la Descartes). Rather, they are necessary by a distinct mode of "metaphysical" necessity. Leibniz accordingly held that only by introducing a mode of necessity intermediate between absolute necessity and mere contingency can we cut the Gordian knot of reconciling the contingent with the necessary, seeing that that whose sufficient reason is *absolutely* necessary will itself be *absolutely necessary.*

The net effect of delineating such a range of "real possibility" is just this establishment of a new correlative mode of necessity. And this is the crux from the standpoint of our present discussion. For precisely this sort of necessity can furnish the answer to our question "Why does the world have such-and-such a feature—specifically, why is it nonempty?" For any feature that *all* the "really possible" worlds have is a feature that the existing world "has to" have—that it must necessarily have (in the "real" mode of necessity). The reasoning is simple and straightforward: the real world has a certain feature because it *has to,* since all "really" possible worlds do so.

Independently of, and, as it were, "prior" to the origination of existents there can be (and presumably is) a *nomically qualified framework of possibility* that sets the conditions, the "rules of the game" as it were, within which this origination of things comes to pass. The domain of real possibility constitutes a "receptacle" (in the manner of Plato's *Timaeus*)—a framework of possibility within which actuality must find its accommodation. But it is not, of course, one composed of physical or quasi-physical *dimensions* on the order of space and time, but one composed of lawful *principles*—a nomic framework of "laws of possibility." The salient idea is that such *protolaws* or "laws of possibility" can represent conditions FOR existents rather than conditions OF the operation of existing things and can thus exist independently of *things* of any sort.[31]

One can of course think of various laws of nature ("Copper conducts electricity") as entirely inherent in the make-up of the actual—that is, as merely representing the behavioral disposition of existing things. But the protolaws are not like that—they do not represent the behavioral dispositions of existents, but rather the *preconditions* to which something must conform if it is to become an existent at all. Such laws are not immanent in things but transcend their particular nature. They are "laws of nature" alright, but in the rather special way of being laws *for* nature—laws that set preconditions upon the realizability of possibilities. Such possibility-restrictive principles have an ontological footing that is independent of (because "prior" to) existing things. (If we are to explain the existence of things in terms of laws, we must of course refrain from thinking of laws as representing the dispositions of existing things.)

Accordingly, we can and should reject the thesis of genetic homogeneity with its insistence on the principle that: *All facts about the world's actualities must be grounded in existing things (or in their properties).* This thesis insists that every fact has a substantival embodiment—that facts must always root in the make-up of existents; that existence inevitably precedes essence. The nomological approach emphatically rejects this radical mode of metaphysical existentialism. It accounts for the real or actual (for "existence," that is), through a lawful principle which operates without being itself embodied in some existing thing or things. It denies that existence inevitably precedes essence. It is prepared to see some facts about the real world grounded in the nature of possibility rather than having to emerge from the operation of preexisting substances.

A protolaw which imposes conditions to which possibilities must answer to become *real* possibilities need not (and cannot always) root in the operations of real things. It can be thought of as *relational*—specifically, as invoking relations of requirement and exclusion between the subordinate elements of which possibilities are composed. Thus if there are three such elements, *A, B, C,* of which *A* requires *B,* and *C* precludes *B,* then certain "mere" possibilities would thereby become unreal, to wit those that have been starred in the following enumeration:

	A	B	C
*	+	+	+
	+	+	−
*	+	−	+
*	+	−	−
*	−	+	+
	−	+	−
	−	−	+
	−	−	−

The protolaws at issue can thus be thought of as principles of possibility-foreclosure. They represent constraints which simply exclude certain theoretically conceivable possibilities from the domain of *real* possibility. They are possibilities alright, but not "actualization-qualified" ones. They impute to the realm of *real* possibility a certain delimitative character—a structure that precludes some "theoretically available" possibilities from being accommodated within it.

Of course, every natural law rules out possibilities. ("Copper conducts electricity" means that we cannot have it both that something is made of copper and that it is a nonconductor.) The difference lies not in the common result, but in its variant rationale. A natural law is grounded in the make-up and dispositions of things; its electricity-conductivity roots in the make-up of copper. With protolaws the situation is different. That certain possibilities are "unreal"—that they are protolawfully unrealizable—lies not in the make-up of actual *things* but in "the nature of things." It is not a facet of actuality at all, but a feature of the realm of possibility itself.

These nomic principles that govern the realm of the possible need not have an *existential* footing—an ontological basis in some preexisting thing or collection of things. They need not—nay, must not—be hypostacized into features of things or into causal products of the operations of things. Our theory contemplates a mode of "being" independent of and prior to the existence of "things"—a nomic field which fixes the structure of possibility. This idea of a domain of "protolaws" rests on a firm refusal to locate the ground of the distinction between "mere" and "real" possibilities in the nature or the activities of things or existents of some sort. Such principles can and should be thought of as lacking a substantial basis—as conditioning possibilities without any foothold in the *modus operandi* of prior actualities.

Existence-explanation via a hylarchic principle of protolaw turns on a distinction between substantival explanations in terms of the operations of entities and process explanations in terms of primordial operational principles—principles that underlie rather than merely reflect the nature of the real. It is predicated on acknowledging that explanation in the case of existence-at-large cannot operate in the orthodox order of the efficient causation of preexisting things. In resorting to a hylarchic principle one can thus abandon altogether the hoary dogma that things can only come from things. A fundamental shift in explanatory methodology is at issue with this hylarchic approach—the shift to a nomological mode of explanation that operates in terms of laws which lack any and all "prior" embedding in an order of *things.* The fact of the world's nonemptiness is now accounted for as the consequence of a constraint by principles rather than as the product of the operation of causes.

This position does not, however, require us to reject the principle *ex nihilo nihil fit* totally and unqualifiedly. For one can distinguish between *nonexistence* and *nothingness.* The realm of mere possibility, as such, is a sphere of nonexistence in which no *thing* whatever exists. But it itself is not *nothing*—not totally devoid of character or structure. There is, after all, no reason why even the realm of mere possibility cannot have a structure of some sort. The fact that nothing *exists* within this realm does not preclude it from having a nature—indeed a nature such that a certain sort of possibility (and *only* a certain sort of possibility) is destined to emerge from it as actualized. Such a nomic "receptacle" realm is not a matter of mere nothingness; it can and must have a character of some sort (as per the old precept that *nihil sunt nullae proprietates*). We need to adopt the idea that existence precedes essence. The domain of the possible represents a state of affairs in which no *things* exist, but in which various conditions can certainly obtain—conditions that can, in particular, endow this realm with a possibility-restrictive nature. Possibilities can, as such, be subject to various laws, including those which separate them into "real" and "merely hypothetical" and thus provide for the operations of a hylarchic principle.

Real possibility accordingly need not—and should not—be rooted in the machinations of things. We must not attribute it to the inner nature or outer impetus of *substances* of some sort, or see it as the fruit of the productive efficacy of some existent or other. We must avoid taking the stance that the structure of possibility must root in an actuality of some type, *that* there is some*thing* that exerts a determinative agency in consequence of which real possibility is as it is. We can reject the "existentialist" thesis that possibility must be grounded in an actuality of some sort—or else modify it by taking the stance that the realm of possibility itself constitutes a (self-subsistent) actuality of sorts.

A protolaw accordingly does not root in the operations of preexisting things. It should be conceived of as an autonomous principle conditioning the sphere of (real) possibility without being emplaced in an actuality of some sort. These protolaws are not reality-reflecting at all, but possibility-determinative. They reflect the fact that a *field of possibility* is prior to and grounds any *physical* field—that there must be "laws of possibility" before there can be the powers and dispositions that encapsulate the "laws of things," the "laws of nature" as ordinarily understood. The "possibility-space" that encompasses the realm of the possible is seen as having a particular character in view of which certain conditions must be met by any *real* possibility that it can accommodate—a character which is encapsulated in the protolaws. To put it *very* figuratively, these protolaws brood over the realm of the possible like the primal logos over the waters.

10. EXPLAINING EXISTENCE BY MEANS OF A HYLARCHIC PRINCIPLE

A hylarchic principle explains the nonemptiness of the world by exploiting the distinction between *mere* possibilities ("merely logical" or "wholly hypothetical and imaginary" possibilities) and *real* possibilities based in suitable nomic principles. It does this by underwriting the minor (second) premiss of the argument:

—Argument A—

(1) If every *really possible* (R-possible) world has a certain feature *F*, then *F* will necessarily (i.e., R-necessarily) obtain in the actual world.

(2) Every R-possible world is nonempty: any R-possible worlds will contain certain things.

Therefore, it must (in the R-correlative sense of "must") be the case that the actual world is nonempty—that there is something rather than nothing.

This line of reasoning provides a scheme by which various conditions of the real (specifically, here, its being nonempty) can be explained in terms of an extremely simple necessitarian format. The existing world has feature *F* because this feature is R-necessary in that every R-possible world has feature *F*. It implements this generic scheme in the specific mode. *Only such worlds as are nonempty—that contain something or other, and have some sort of membership—can qualify as real possibilities.* The salient idea is the principle that the necessary must be actual (*a necesse ad esse valet consequentia*). The reasoning proceeds via the standard idea of all ontological arguments since Anselm—that the shift from possibility to actuality can be effected with the aid of a suitable mode of necessity. But—with Leibniz—it rejects the idea that the necessity at issue must be absolute (logical) necessity.

The role of a hylarchic principle is now clear. As a protophysical law of a characteristically *preexistential* kind, it reduces the range of real possibility so as to exclude from it (*inter alia*) those worlds that are existentially empty. A hylarchic principle is simply a particular sort of possibility-restricting condition—a rather special one that narrows the range of eligible cases down to nonempty worlds. And so the task of explaining why there is something rather than nothing can be discharged by relatively orthodox, direct and unproblematic means, since what is necessary must be actual. On such an approach it is not by chance that things exist in the world (that there is something rather than nothing) but by a natural (or, better, *proto*natural) necessity.

In accounting for a feature of the actual in this way, one can in principle explain a "change of phase" from the level of mere possibility to the level of actuality, maintaining that certain things *are* the case because they *must* be so—that their being otherwise lies outside the realm of (real) possibility. The "field of possibility" has a structure of such a sort that the existence of things of a certain sort is effectively necessitated. Such a field itself requires literally *nothing* for its "existence": like the God of scholastic demonstration, it is such that *nulla re indiget ad existendum.*

To be sure, the preceding course of reasoning does no more than carry the problem back one step further: For it now becomes incumbent upon us to secure premiss (2) of Argument A. How are we to do this—how can we establish that all "really" possible worlds will be nonempty?

This question can, in principle at least, be resolved along lines the following argumentation:

—Argument B—

(1) Possible worlds cannot represent *real* possibilities unless they have a certain feature *F.*
(2) No possible world which does not encompass existing things can have the feature *F.*

Therefore, it must be the case that every R-possible world is nonempty.

An argument of this format would enable us to establish our desired existential conclusion by reasoning that proceeds at the level of possibilities alone. It is in the implementation of this line of argumentation that the real task of a hylarchic principle lies.

The hylarchic approach to existence explanation thus has two components:

1. The existence of things in the world is accounted for by the fact that only real possibilities are also existential possibilities—that all of the really possible worlds are thing-populated worlds.
2. The nature of real possibility is accounted for in terms of a compatibility theory of possibility—by the circumstance that only those possibilities are "real" which are compatible with the world-determinative protolaws. (The only real possibilities are thus nomically authorized possibilities where it is the protolaws that do the authorization.)

The overall explanation of existence is thus fundamentally *nomological.* It pivots on the consideration that the protolaws require the existence of things—that they are in themselves such as to constrain an existential world.

But what manner of consideration could put flesh on the skeletal structure of this argument? The most plausible candidates for protolaws that could constrain the existence of things are the fundamental principles of physical nature—the basic cosmic equations (say the field equations of general relativity). For this sort of explanation to work, it would have to transpire that all of the possible (or all of the "available"—in some appropriate sense) solutions to these cosmic equations will accord to the key parameters values different from 0 (i.e., values which are existence-requiring). The only possible solutions to the fundamental equation which satisfy certain systemic requirements will have to be solutions that represent nonempty worlds.[32]

On such an approach, we would accordingly begin by looking to the fundamental field equations that delineate the operation of forces in nature: those which define the structures of the space-time continuum, say the basic laws of quantum mechanics and general relativity, and some fundamental structural principles of physical interaction. Principles of this sort characterizing the electromagnetic, gravitational, and metric fields provide the basic protolaws under whose aegis the drama of natural events will have to play itself out. And the existence of things would then be explained by noting that the fundamental equations themselves admit of no empty solutions—that any solution that satisfies them must incorporate the sorts of singularities we call "things."[33] The cosmic equations would be such as to *constrain* existence in nature: they admit of no empty states and only allow nonvacuous solutions. (As it were, they represent functions that take a nonzero value for *every* value of the variables—even when those "input" parameters themselves are set at zero.)[34] For such an approach to work, it would have to transpire that the only ultimately viable solutions to those cosmic equations are existential solutions.[35]

This explanatory strategy casts those "fundamental field equations" in a rather special light. They are not seen as ordinary laws of nature that can be construed as describing the *modus operandi* of real things that are already present in the world, but rather as preeconditions for the real—as delimiting the sorts of possibilities that can be realized. We thus have an account of the following structure: The fundamental field equations, seen to function not merely as laws OF nature, but as laws FOR nature, as *protolaws* in present terminology—delineate the domain of real possibility. And the nature of this domain is then, in its turn, such as to constrain the existence of things.

Such an explanation of existence is no doubt somewhat unorthodox. But there is nothing about it that is inherently unviable or somehow "unscientific." And it does have the substantial merit of enabling us to resolve the riddle of existence, answering Leibniz's question in a way that is conceptually cogent and wholly consonant with science as we know it.

To be sure, one big problem remains: How is one to account for the protolaws themselves? (And so—just what are the ultimate grounds of real possibility?) This question obviously presents a large nettle which our overall explanatory program must eventually grasp if it is to do its job in a satisfactory way.

11. APPENDIX: A SPECULATIVE QUESTION

Could one use the present approach to answer not merely the question "why is there anything at all?" but the obviously more demanding question "why is the existing order of things as it is—why do *these particular sorts of things* exist?" Can one continue to use a hylarchic principle on shifting from the question "why does a world of such-and-such-a-character exist?" to "why does *this* particular world exist?" Could the present approach accommodate the move from a generic necessitarianism (to the effect that the world must contain things of a certain sort) to a specific necessitarianism that the world must contain certain particular sorts of things (or perhaps even sundry particulars as such)?

This could perhaps be done. But it would require much more elaborate machinery than anything introduced in the preceding discussion. For we would again have to eliminate various theoretically available possibilities as unreal, but would now have to do this on a very grand scale indeed, by eliminating *all but one* particular sort of possibility. The protolaws would function as a Laplacean demon of sorts that in some respects constrains the world to its present character.

Proceeding in this way, we would arrive, in the end, at a collapse of modality: a world of the general type of the actual world (or indeed even the actual world itself) would emerge as alone realistically possible and thus as realistically necessary. We would then need a much stronger sort of hylarchic principle—a system of protolaws of nature (construed preexistentially) which narrows the range of *real* possibility down to a single case. This enormously demanding eventuation would require a system of cosmic equations that admit of only a single all-determinative solution. A thoroughgoing R-necessitarianism would now be upon us—an ultra-Leibnizian world whose character (in general and perhaps even in specific) is determined not (à la Spinoza) by logical but (à la Leibniz) by metaphysical necessity. Of course, to say that this sort of necessitarian position is possible and (in a sense) theoretically "available" is far from saying that it is correct. The pervasive necessitarianism that it envisages presumably lies outside the sphere of the plausible.[36]

NOTES

1. The tract is published in Gerhardt, *Phil.*, Vol. VII, pp. 302–08. An English translation is given in Loemker, pp. 480–91. For a useful recent study see

Diogenes Alien, "Mechanical Explanations and the Ultimate Origin of the Universe According to Leibniz," *Studia Leibnitiana,* Sonderheft 11 (Wiesbaden, 1983).

2. To be sure, it could be maintained that there is a difference between an "empty world" and "no world at all," in that even an empty world can have a *nature* of sorts *qua* world—by way of characterizing hypotheticals like "If there were things here, they would have to have such-and-such a nature." (Cf. sect. 9 below)

3. One cannot, that is, move from $N(\exists w)E!w$ to $(\exists w)NE!w$.

4. Henri Bergson, *Creative Evolution,* tr. by A. Mitchell (New York, 1944 [Modern Library]), pp. 299–301.

5. Martin Heidegger, *Was ist Metaphysik?* (Frankfurt, 1967); 2 tr., *Introduction to Metaphysics* (New Haven, 1959), Chap. I. Also tr. by D. F. Krell in *Martin Heidegger: Basic Writings* (New York, 1977), pp. 95–112.

6. Robert Nozick, *Philosophical Explanations* (Cambridge, Mass.; 1981), p. 115. As Heidegger sees it, such a metaphysical concern roots in *Seinsvergessenheit* and is accordingly *etwas, das ueberwunden werden muss,* although it is counterproductive to *strive* to overcome metaphysical worries instead of waiting, *gelassen,* for *das Geschick des Seins* to come to our aid.

7. Ludwig Wittgenstein, *Tractatus Logico-Philosophicus* (London, 1922), sect. 6.44 (p. 186).

8. Norman Malcolm, *Ludwig Wittgenstein: A Memoir* (Oxford, 1958), p. 20.

9. Ludwig Wittgenstein, "A Lecture on Ethics," in J. H. Gill (ed.), *Philosophy Today,* No. 1 (New York and London, 1968), pp. 4–14. Wittgenstein here describes a particularly profound experience as having the character "that when I have it *I wonder at the existence of the world.*" Gill's anthology also contains notes by Friedrich Waismann on a conversation with Wittgenstein on the same subject. Cf. also G. E. M. Anscombe, *An Introduction to Wittgenstein's Tractatus* (London, 1955), p. 173.

10. *Op. cit.,* p. 10.

11. Anna-Teresa Tymeniecka, *Why Is There Something Rather than Nothing?* (Assen, 1966).

12. Myles Burnyeat in the *Times Literary Supplement,* October 15, 1982, p. 1136.

13. David Lewis, *Philosophical Papers* (New York and Oxford, 1983), p. 23.

14. Regarding the "experience of contingency," see Paul Tillich, *Systematic Theology,* Vol. I (Chicago, 1958), pp. 110–13,163–64, and 186.

15. Reprinted in John Hick (ed.), *Classical and Contemporary Readings in the Philosophy of Religion,* 2nd ed. (Englewood Cliffs, 1970), pp. 288–289. Cf. also Diogenes Allen in *Studia Leibnitiana, op. cit.,* p. 34.

16. David Hume, *Dialogues Concerning Natural Religion and Posthumous Essays,* ed. by R. Popkin (Indianapolis, 1980), Pt. IX, p. 55. Cf. also William Rowe, *The Cosmological Argument* (Princeton, 1975), p. 153.

17. A strange object springs into being as of t_0; it does not exist at t_0 but does exist at any subsequent time. Now for any time t after t_0 we can explain its existence at t by noting that it existed at the prior time t-minus-epsilon and (so we may suppose) is self-preserving. But would anyone suppose that this *explains* its existence at large? (I owe this example to Michael B. Burke.) Cf. also the discussions of Chapter III of William Rowe, *The Cosmological Argument* (Princeton, 1975).

18. John Locke, for example, claimed that the facts that something exists now and that nothing cannot produce a real thing (*ex nihilo nihil*) imply that "something must have existed for eternity" meaning that these must be an *eternal being.* (*An Essay Concerning Human Understanding,* Bk. II, ch. X.) Locke thus commits exactly this quantifier confusion of moving from the distributive "Everything has a causal ground" to the collective "There is a (single) causal ground for everything."

19. See the interesting discussion of cognate issues in Diogenes Allen, *Mechanical Explanations of the Ultimate Origin of the Universe According to Leibniz* (Wiesbaden, 1983; *Studia Leibnitiana,* Sonderheft 11.)

20. See William Lane Craig, *The Cosmological Argument from Plato to Leibniz* (London, 1980), and William Rowe, *The Cosmological Argument* (Princeton, 1975). Some relevant texts are anthologized in Donald R. Burrill (ed.), *The Cosmological Argument* (Garden City, 1967).

21. Immanuel Kant, *C.Pr.R.,* p. 138 (Akad.).

22. Carl G. Hempel, '"Science Unlimited," *The Annals of the Japan Association for Philosophy of Science,* vol. 14 (1973), pp. 187–202. (See p. 200.) Our italics.

23. Note too that the question of the existence of facts is a horse of a very different color from that of the existence of things. There being no *things* is undoubtedly a possible situation, there being no *facts* is not (since if the situation were realized, this would itself constitute a fact).

24. Aristotle taught that every change must emanate from a '"mover," i.e., a substance whose machinations provide the cause of change. This commitment to causal reification is at work in much of the history of Western thought. That its pervasiveness is manifest at virtually every juncture is clear from William Lane Craig's interesting study of *The Cosmological Argument from Plato to Leibniz* (London, 1980).

25. David Hume, *Dialogues Concerning Natural Religion* (ed. N. K. Smith; London, 1922), p. 189.

26. G. W. Leibniz, "Principles of Nature and of Grace," sect. 8, italics supplied. Compare St. Thomas:

> Of necessity, herefore, anything in process of change is being changed by something else. (S.T., IA 2,3).

The idea that only substances can produce changes goes back to Thomas' master, Aristotle. In Plato and the Presocratics, the causal efficacy of *principles* is recognized (e.g., the love and strife of Empedocles).

27. For criticisms of ways of avoiding the question "Why is there something rather than nothing?" see Chap. III of William Rowe, *The Cosmological Argument* (Princeton, 1975). Cf. also Donald R Burrill (ed.), *The Cosmological Argument* (Garden City, 1967), esp. "The Cosmological Argument" by Paul Edwards.

28. David Lewis, *Philosophical Papers,* Vol. I (New York and Oxford, 1983), p. 24.

29. ibid.

30. In principle there might be more refinement here, with some actuality-departing possibilities being relatively more proximate or remote than others, depending on how radical the departures from existential reality. This would lead to gradations of more or less "real" possibility, depending how close one comes to the "real life" *modus operandi* of actual things. We shall for the time being ignore this prospect and abstract from such complications.

31. It might be this sort of thing that is darkly suggested in A.-T. Tymeniecka's tenebrous hints:

> [T]he world-order . . . indicates the necessity of a superior, universal order of planning according to which it is constructed. . . . This order is . . . an architectonic plan considering universal possibilities of beings and the principles of their selection. . . . [This] architectonic plan . . . must include consideration of all the elements involved in the possible existence of the world order. . . . (*Op. cit.,* pp. 90–91.)

This passage seems to point towards the idea of a duly ordered framework of possibility that underlies the real and conditions its nature.

32. It should be noted that *empty* should here be understood in the logical or set-theoretical sense, not just in the somewhat specialized physical sense in which physicists speak of empty-world solutions to the field equations of General Relativity—meaning worlds devoid of ordinary matter and all forms of non-gravitational energy, but which can be (and in non-trivial cases are) filled with sourceless gravitational waves carrying gravitational energy. One would not regard such worlds as metaphysically empty.

33. The emergence of an "existential" state is thus entirely independent of the initial boundary-value conditions—for *any* way of fixing these parameters, an existential state emerges.

34. A (clearly superable) complexity enters at this point through the fact that vacuity may be reflected in parameter-values other than zero. For example, consider the trivial empty-world solution of the field equations of General Relativity, i.e. the Minkowski metric. In its standard form it consists of sixteen real-valued functions of the coordinates, twelve of which vanish everywhere, while the other four "take a nonzero value for *every* value of the variables" (namely, the constant values –1, 1, 1, 1, respectively).

35. Or perhaps, even should "empty solutions" exist, they might be highly unstable; the protolaws would then be such that, under their aegis, an existentially empty state of things is inherently liable to undergo a phase transition, having a natural inclination to slip over into an "occupied" condition.

36. One possibility along these general lines is afforded by the "anthropic principle" which, in effect, maintains that the world must be pretty much as it is because only so is life possible. See George Gale, "The Anthropic Principle," *Scientific American,* vol. 245 (December, 1981), pp. 154–171.

Reading Questions

1. Rescher maintains that considering the fact that there is something rather than nothing to be a brute fact, admitting of no further explanation is "a solution of last resort." Is it just wishful thinking to suppose that a more substantial explanation is possible?
2. Rescher argues that the existence of explanations for why each member of a group has a certain property does not thereby give us an explanation of why the group as a whole has a certain property. "And we are perfectly entitled to ask for such an explanation," he writes. Why should we expect that such global explanations exist for every domain? For example, there is an explanation for why each person in this year's freshman class chose this school. Should we further expect that some fact exists that explains why the entire freshman class as a group chose this school?

3. In his second table, entitled "An Inconsistent Quartet," Rescher focuses on causal explanation as crucial to solving the riddle of existence. Should the requisite sort of explanation be causal? What other kinds of explanations are there?
4. Rescher thinks that there is a metaphysical structure of reality—that is, protolaws or laws of metaphysical possibility—that ensures that there is something rather than nothing. Assuming he is right, does the salient question then become: "Why are the protolaws such that they guarantee the actual world to be nonempty rather than empty?" Could this question be satisfactorily answered by appeal to protolaws?

2 Why Is Reality as It Is?

DEREK PARFIT

It might have been true that nothing ever existed: no minds, no atoms no space, no time. When we imagine this possibility, it can seem astonishing that anything exists. Why is there universe? And things might have been, in countless ways, different. So why is the Universe as it is?

These facts cannot be causally explained. No law of nature could explain why there are any laws of nature, or why these laws are as they are. And, if God created the world, there cannot be a causal explanation of why God exists.

Since our questions cannot have causal answers, we may wonder whether they make sense. But there may be other kinds of answers.

Consider, first, a more particular question. Many physicists believe that, for stars, planets and life to be able to exist, the initial conditions in the Big Bang had to be precisely as they were. Why were these conditions so precisely right? Some say: "If they had not been right, we couldn't even ask this question." But that is no answer. It could be baffling how we survived some crash even though, if we hadn't, we could not be baffled.

Others say: "There had to be some initial conditions, and those conditions were likely as any others. So there is nothing to be explained." To see what is wrong with this reply, we must distinguish two kinds of case. Suppose that, of a million people facing death, only one can be rescued. If there is a lottery to pick this one survivor, and I win, I would be very lucky. But there would be nothing to be explained. Someone had to win, and why not me? Consider next a second lottery. Unless my gaoler picks the longest of a million straws, I shall be beheaded. If I win this lottery, there *would* be something to be explained. It would not be enough to say, "That result was as likely as any other." In the first lottery, nothing special happened: whatever the result, someone's life would be saved. In this second lottery, the result *was* special. Of the million possible results, only one would save a life. Why was *this* what happened? Though this might be a coincidence, the chance of that is only one in a million. I could be almost certain that this lottery was rigged.

The Big Bang, it seems, was like the second lottery. For life to be possible, the initial conditions had to be selected with the kind of accuracy that would be needed to hit a bull's-eye in a distant galaxy. Since it is not arrogant to think life special, this appearance of fine-tuning needs to be explained. Of the countless possible initial conditions, why were the ones that allowed for life *also* the ones that actually obtained?

On one view, this was mere coincidence. That is conceivable, but most unlikely. On some estimates, the chance is below one in a billion billion. Others

From The Times Literary Supplement, *July 3, 1992. Reprinted by permission of the author.*

say: "The Big Bang *was* fine-tuned. It is not surprising that God chose to make life possible." We may be tempted to dismiss this answer, thinking it improbable that God exists. But should we put the chance as low as one in a billion billion? If not, this is a better explanation.

There is, however, a rival explanation. Our Universe may not be the whole of reality. Some physicists suggest that there are many other Universes—or, to avoid confusion, *worlds.* These worlds have the same laws of nature as our own world, and they emerged from similar Big Bangs, but each had slightly different initial conditions. On this *many-worlds hypothesis,* there would be no need for fine-tuning. If there were enough Big Bangs, it would be no surprise that, in a few of these, conditions were just right for life. And it would be no surprise that our Big Bang was one of these few.

On most versions of this theory, these many worlds are not causally related, and each has its own space and time. Some object that, since our world could not be affected by such other worlds, we have no reason to believe in them. But we do have such a reason, since their existence would explain an otherwise puzzling feature of our world: the appearance of fine-tuning.

How should we choose between these explanations? The many-worlds hypothesis is more cautious, since it merely claims that there is more of the kind of reality we know. But God's existence has been claimed to be intrinsically more plausible. By "God" we mean a being who is omnipotent, omniscient, and wholly good. The existence of such a being has been claimed to be both simpler, and less arbitrary, than the existence of many complicated and specific worlds.

If such a God exists, however, why is the Universe as it is? It may not be surprising that God chose to make life possible. But the laws of nature could have been different, so there are many possible worlds that would have contained life. It is hard to understand why, with all the possibilities, God chose to create *our* world. The greatest difficulty here is the problem of evil. There appears to be suffering which any good person, knowing the truth, would have prevented if he could. If there is such suffering, there cannot be a God who is omnipotent, omniscient, and wholly good.

One response to this problem is to revise our view of God. Some suggest that God is not omnipotent. But, with that revision, the hypothesis that God exists becomes less plausible. How could there be a being who, though able to create our world, cannot prevent such suffering? Others believe in a god who, whatever he is called, is not good. Though that view more easily explains the character of life on Earth, it may seem in other ways less credible.

As we shall see, there may be other answers to this problem. But we have larger questions to consider. I began by asking why things are as they are. We must also ask *how* things are. There is much about our world that we have not discovered. And, just as there may be other worlds like ours, there may be worlds that are very different.

It will help to distinguish two kinds of possibility. For each particular kind of possible world, there is the *local* possibility that such a world exists. If there is such a world, that leaves it open whether there are other worlds. *Global* possibilities, in contrast, cover the whole Universe, or everything that ever exists. One global possibility is that *every* conceivable world exists. That is claimed by the *all-worlds hypothesis.* Another possibility, which might have obtained, is that nothing ever exists. This we can call the *Null Possibility.* In each of the remaining possibilities, the number of possible worlds that exist is between none and all. There are countless of these possibilities, since there are countless combinations of particular possible worlds.

Of these different global possibilities, one must obtain, and only one can obtain. So we have two questions. Which obtains, and why? These questions are connected. If some possibility would be less puzzling, or easier to explain, we have more reason to think that it obtains. That is why, rather than believing that the Big Bang merely happened to be right for life, we should believe either in God or many worlds.

Is there some global possibility whose obtaining would be in no way puzzling? That might be claimed of the Null Possibility. It might be said that, if no one had ever existed, no one would have been puzzled. But that misunderstands our questions. Suppose that, in a mindless and finite Universe, an object looking like *Metaphysics: Contemporary Readings* spontaneously formed.

Even with no one to be puzzled, that would be, in the sense I mean, puzzling. It may next be said that, if there had never been anything, there wouldn't have been anything to be explained. But that is not so. When we imagine that nothing ever existed, what we imagine away are such things as minds and atoms, space and time. There would still have been truths. It would have been true that nothing existed, and that things might have existed. And there would have been other truths, such as the truth that 27 is divisible by 3. We can ask why these things would have been true.

These questions may have answers. We can explain why, even if nothing had ever existed, 27 would have been divisible by 3. There is no conceivable alternative. And we can explain the nonexistence of such things as two-horned unicorns, or spherical cubes. Such things are logically impossible. But why would *nothing* have existed? Why would there have been no stars or atoms, no minds or bluebell woods? How could *that* be explained?

We should not claim that, if nothing had existed, there would have been nothing to be explained. But we might claim something less. Perhaps, of all the global possibilities, this would have needed the least explanation. It is much the simplest. And it seems the easiest to understand. When we imagine there never being anything, that does not seem, as our own existence can, astonishing.

Here, for example, is one natural line of thought. It may seem that, for any particular thing to exist, its existence must have been caused by other things. If that is so, what could have caused them *all* to exist? If there were an infinite series of things, the existence of each might be caused by other members of that series. But that could not explain why there was this whole series, rather than some other series, or no series. In contrast, the Null Possibility raises no such problem. If nothing had ever existed, that state of affairs would not have needed to be caused.

Even if this possibility would have been the easiest to explain, it does not obtain. Reality does not take its simplest and least puzzling form.

Consider next the all-worlds hypothesis. That may seem the next least puzzling possibility. For one thing, it avoids arbitrary distinctions. If only one world exists, we have the question: "Out of all the possible worlds, why is *this* the one that exists?" On the many-worlds hypothesis, we have the question: Why are *these* the ones? But, if *all* possible worlds exist, there is no such question. Though the all-worlds hypothesis avoids that question, it is not as simple as it seems. Is there a sharp distinction between those worlds that are and are not possible? Must all worlds be governed by natural laws? Does each kind of world exist only once? And there are further complications.

Whichever global possibility obtains, we can ask why it obtains. All that I have claimed so far is that, with some possibilities, this question would be less puzzling. We should now ask: Could this question have an answer? Is there a theory that leaves nothing explained?

On one kind of view, it is logically necessary that God, or the whole Universe, exists. Though it may seem conceivable that there might never have been anything, that is not really logically possible. Some people even claim that there is only one coherent global possibility. If such a view were true, everything would be explained. But the standard objections to such views, which I shall not repeat, seem to me convincing.

Others claim that the Universe exists because its existence is good. This is the Platonic, or Axiarchic, View. Even if we think this view absurd, it is worth asking whether it makes sense. That may suggest other possibilities.

The Axiarchic View can take a theistic form. It can claim that God exists because His existence is good, and that the rest of the Universe exists because God caused it to exist. But in that explanation God is redundant. If God can exist because His existence is good, so can the whole Universe.

In its simplest form, the Axiarchic View makes three claims: (1) It would be best if reality were a certain way. (2) Reality is that way. (3) (1) explains (2).

(1) is an ordinary evaluative claim, like the claim that it would be better if there was no pointless suffering. The Axiarchic View assumes, in my opinion correctly, that such claims can be true. (2) is an ordinary descriptive claim, though of a sweeping kind. What is distinctive in this view is claim (3).

Can we understand (3)? To focus on this question, we should briefly ignore the world's evils.

Suppose that, as Leibniz claimed, the best possible Universe exists. Could this Universe exist *because* it is the best? That question might be confused with another. If God intentionally created the best possible world, that world would exist because it is the best. But, though God would not be part of the world that He creates, He would be part of the Universe, or the totality of what exists. And God cannot have created Himself. So an appeal to God cannot explain why the best Universe exists.

Axiarchists make a different claim. On their view, that there is a best way for reality to be explains *directly* why reality is that way. If God exists, that is because His existing is best. Truths about value are, in John Leslie's phrase, *creatively effective.*

This cannot be an ordinary causal claim. Ordinary causes are particular events, or facts about existing things. But the axiarchic claim may have some of the meaning of an ordinary causal claim.

When we believe that X caused Y, we usually believe that, without an X, there would have been no Y. A spark caused an explosion if, without a spark, there would have been no explosion. Axiarchists might make a similar claim. They might say that, if it had not been best if reality were a certain way, reality would not have been that way. But such a claim may not help to explain the Axiarchic View, since what it asks us to imagine could not have been true. Just as pointless suffering could not have been good, the best way for reality to be could not have failed to be the best.

In defending a causal claim, we may also appeal to a generalization. Certain conditions cause an explosion if, whenever there are such conditions, there is an explosion. It may seem that, with only one Universe, Axiarchists cannot appeal to a generalization. But that is not so. They could say that, whenever it would be better if the Universe had some particular feature, it *has* that feature.

Would that explain their claim that this is why the Universe has these features? That use of "why" may seem utterly mysterious. But we should remember that even ordinary causation is mysterious. At the most fundamental level, we have no idea why some events cause others. And it is hard to explain what causation is.

Axiarchy can be best explained as follows. We are now assuming that, of all the countless ways that reality might be, one is both the very best, and is the way that reality is. On the Axiarchic View, *that is no coincidence.* That claim makes, I believe, some kind of sense. And, on those assumptions, it would be a reasonable conclusion.

Compared with the appeal to God, the Axiarchic View has one advantage. God cannot have settled *whether,* as part of the best Universe, He himself exists, since He can only settle anything if He does exist. But even if nothing had ever existed, it would still have been true that it would be best if the best Universe existed. So that truth might explain why this Universe exists.

The main objection to this view is the problem of evil. Our world appears to be flawed.

If we appeal to a variant of the many-worlds hypothesis, this objection can be partly met. Perhaps, in the best Universe, *all* good possible worlds exist. We would then avoid the question why things are not much better than they are. Things *are*, on the whole, much better. They are better elsewhere.

Why are they not *also* better here? One answer might be as follows. If it is best that all good worlds exist, that implies that, even in the best Universe, many worlds would not be very good. Some would be only just good enough. Perhaps our world is one of these. It would then be good that our world exists, since a good niche is thereby filled. And we might be able to explain why our world is not better than it is. The Louvre would be a worse collection if its less good paintings were turned into copies of the *Mona Lisa*. In the same way, if our world were in itself better, reality as a whole might be less good. Since every other good niche is already filled, our world would then be a mere copy of some other world, and one good niche would be left unfilled.

Even on this view, however, each world must be good enough. The existence of each world must be better, even if only slightly, than its nonexistence. Can this be claimed of our world? It would be easier to make that claim on a broadly Utilitarian view. Our world's evils might then be outweighed by what is good. But, on some principles of justice, that would not be enough. If innocent beings suffer, in lives that are not worth living, that could not be morally outweighed by the happiness of other beings. For our world to be good enough, there must be future lives in which the sufferings of each being could, in the end, be made good. Even the burnt fawn in the forest fire must live again. Or perhaps these different beings are, at some level, one.

These replies may seem too weak. We may doubt that our world could be even the least good part of the best possible Universe.

If we reject the Axiarchic View, what conclusion should we draw? Is the existence of our world a mere brute fact, with no explanation? That does not follow. If we abstract from the optimism of this view, its claims are these. One global possibility has a special feature, this is the possibility that obtains, and it obtains because it has this feature. Other views can make such claims.

Suppose that our world were part of the worst possible Universe. Its bright days may only make its tragedies worse. If reality were as bad as it could be, could we not suspect that this was no coincidence?

Suppose next, more plausibly, that all possible worlds exist. That would also be grim, since the evil of the worst worlds could hardly be outweighed. But that would be incidental. If every conceivable world exists, reality has a different distinctive feature. It is *maximal:* as full and varied as it could possibly be. If this is true, is it a coincidence? Does it merely happen to be true that, of all the countless global possibilities, the one that obtains is at this extreme? As always, that is conceivable. Coincidences can occur. But it seems hard to believe. We can reasonably assume that, if all possible worlds exist, that is *because* that makes reality as full as it could be.

Similar remarks apply to the Null Possibility. If there had never been anything, would that have been a coincidence? Would it have merely happened that, of all the possibilities, what obtained was the *only* possibility in which nothing exists? That is also hard to believe. Rather, if the possibility had obtained, that would have been because it had that feature.

Here is another special feature. Perhaps reality is as it is because that makes its fundamental laws as mathematically beautiful as they could be. That is what many physicists believe.

If some possibility obtains because it has some feature, that feature selects what reality is like. Let us call it the *Selector.* A feature is a *plausible* Selector if we can reasonably believe that, were reality to have that feature, that would not merely happen to be true.

There are countless features which are not plausible Selectors. Suppose that fifty-seven worlds exist. Like all numbers, 57 has some special features. For example, it is the smallest number that is the sum of seven primes. But that could hardly be *why* that number of worlds exist.

I have mentioned certain plausible Selectors. A possibility might obtain because it is the best, or the simplest, or the least arbitrary, or because it makes reality as full as it could be, or because its fundamental laws are as elegant as they could be. There are, I assume, other such features, some of which we have yet to discover.

For each of these features, there is the *explanatory* possibility that this feature *is* the Selector. That feature then explains why reality is as it is. There is one other, special explanatory possibility: that there is *no* Selector. This is like the global possibility that nothing exists. If there is no Selector, it is random that reality is as it is. Events may be in one sense random, even though they are causally inevitable. That is how it is random whether a meteorite strikes the land or the sea. Events are random in a stronger sense if they have no cause. That is what most physicists believe about some facts at the quantum level, such as how some particles move. If it is random what reality is like, the Universe would not only have no cause, it would have no explanation of any kind. This we can call the *Brute Fact View.*

On this view, we should not expect reality to have very special features, such as being maximal, or best, or having very simple laws, or including God. In much the largest range of the global possibilities, there would exist an arbitrary set of messily complicated worlds. That is what, with a random selection, we should expect. It is unclear whether ours is one such world.

The Brute Fact View may seem hard to understand. It may seem baffling how reality could be even randomly selected. What kind of *process* could select whether time had no beginning, or whether anything ever exists? But this is not a real problem. It is logically necessary that one global possibility obtains. There is no conceivable alternative. Since it is necessary that it be settled which obtains. Even without any kind of process, logic ensures that a selection is made. There is no need for hidden machinery.

If reality were randomly selected, it would not be mysterious *how* the selection is made. It would be in one sense inexplicable why the Universe is as it is. But this would be no more puzzling than the random movement of a particle. If a particle can simply happen to move as it does, it could simply happen that reality is as it is. Randomness may even be *less* puzzling at the level of the whole Universe, since we know that facts at this level could not have been caused.

There would, however, be a further question. If there is no explanation why reality is as it is, why is *that* true?

Some reply that this, too, is logically necessary. On their view, the nature of the Universe must be a mere brute fact, since it could not conceivably be explained. But, as I have argued, that is not so. Though it is logically necessary that one global possibility obtain, it is not necessary that it be random which obtains. There are other explanatory possibilities.

Since it is not necessary that there be no explanation why reality is as it is, that truth might be another brute fact. There may be no explanation why there is no explanation. Perhaps both simply happen to be true. But why would *that* be true? Would it, too, simply happen to be true? And why should we accept this view? If it was randomly selected *whether* reality was selected randomly, and there are several other possibilities, why expect random selection to have been selected? Unless we can explain *why* it is random what reality is like, we may have no reason to believe that this *is* random.

Return now to the other explanatory possibilities. Each raises the same further question. Whichever possibility obtains, we can ask why it obtains. Consider first the Axiarchic View. Suppose that the best Universe exists because it is the best. Why is that true? Even if this view is true, its falsehood is at least logically conceivable. It may seem that Axiarchy could explain itself. On this view, claims about reality are true because their being true is best. It might be best if this view were true. Could that be why it *is* true? That is not possible. Even if this view is true, its being true could not be explained by its being true. Just as God cannot have caused His own existence, the truth of the Axiarchic View cannot be what makes this view true.

Consider next the Maximalist View. Suppose that all possible worlds exist, and that this is no coincidence. Suppose these worlds all exist because that makes reality as full as it could be. If that is true, why is it true? Perhaps this truth makes reality even more maximal. But, as before, this truth could not explain itself.

A similar claim may apply to every view. As we have seen, it is not logically necessary that, of the *global* possibilities, it is random which obtains. This possibility might be selected in other ways. But it may be logically necessary that, of the *explanatory* possibilities, it is random which obtains. Perhaps nothing could select between all the possible Selectors: If that were so, it would not be mysterious that a particular explanatory claim simply happened to be true. The randomness would be fully explained, since there would be no conceivable alternative.

It may be objected that, if some claim simply happens to be true, it cannot provide an explanation. Such a claim may seem to add nothing. To illustrate this objection, return to the Maximalist View. Consider first two global possibilities: (1) Only our world exists. (2) Every conceivable world exists. These possibilities are very different. Suppose next that (2) is true. There are then two explanatory possibilities. On the Brute Fact View, (2) simply happens to be true. On the Maximalist View, (2) is true because that makes reality as full as it could be. Here again, these seem to be different possibilities. But we are now supposing that, even if the Maximalist View is true, its truth is a brute fact, with no explanation. We may think that, if that is so, the Maximalist View could not *explain* (2). If this view simply happens to be true, it may seem not to differ from the Brute Fact View.

That reaction is a mistake. On the Brute Fact View, (2) would involve an extreme coincidence. There are countless global possibilities, and most of these, unlike (2), have no very special feature. It is hard to believe that, of this vast range of possibilities, it simply happens to be true that every conceivable world exists. That is implausible because, at this level, there is an alternative. If the

Maximalist View is true, the existence of all these worlds is no coincidence. At the next level, things are different. Of the plausible explanatory possibilities, all have special features. There is no possibility whose obtaining would be a coincidence. And, as we have seen, it may be logically necessary that, of *these* possibilities, one simply happens to obtain. At this level, there may be no alternative. It would then be in no way puzzling if the Maximalist View simply happens to be true.

We should not claim that, if an explanation rests on a brute fact, it is not an explanation. Scientific explanations all take this form. But we might claim something less. Any such explanation may, in the end, be merely a better description.

If that is true, there is a different answer. Even to discover how things are, we need explanations. And we may need explanations on the grandest scale. Our world may seem to have some feature that would be unlikely to be a coincidence. We might reasonably suspect that our world exists, not as a brute fact, but because it has this feature. That hypothesis might lead us to confirm that, as it seemed, our world does have this feature. We might then reasonably conclude either that ours is the only world, or that there are many other worlds, with the same or related features. We might reach truths about the whole Universe.

Even if all explanations must end with a brute fact, we should go on trying to explain why the Universe exists, and is as it is. The brute fact may not enter at the lowest level. If the Universe exists because it has some feature, to know *what* reality is like, we must ask *why*.

Reading Questions

1. Parfit starts by asking, "Why is the Universe as it is?" Is this just a version of the question "Why is there something rather than nothing?" or is Parfit asking something importantly different?
2. Parfit claims it is puzzling that the initial conditions of the universe were precisely those that permitted life, given long odds against it. Compare Parfit's claim with the following claim. Presumably there are certain initial conditions of our lives—decisions we made when we were young—such that if we had decided slightly differently, we would never have met our current mates. Is the following question a puzzle? *"Why were the decisions that I made precisely those that allowed me to meet my mate?"* This seems analogous to Parfit's question about the universe.
3. What does Parfit mean by "a plausible Selector"? Is there any possible Selector you would find to be explanatorily adequate?
4. Parfit thinks that the global possibility that obtains may not be random, even though that Selector which is the actual Selector is random. Why doesn't Selector arbitrariness produce arbitrariness all the way down?

Why Is There Something Rather than Nothing? 3

ROBERT NOZICK

THE QUESTION APPEARS impossible to answer.[1] Any factor introduced to explain why there is something will itself be part of the something to be explained, so it (or anything utilizing it) could not explain all of the something—it could not explain why there is *anything* at all. Explanation proceeds by explaining some things in terms of others, but this question seems to preclude introducing anything else, any explanatory factors. Some writers conclude from this that the question is ill-formed and meaningless. But why do they cheerfully reject the question rather than despairingly observe that it demarcates a limit of what we can hope to understand? So daunting is the question that even a recent urger of it, Heidegger, who terms it "the fundamental question of metaphysics", proposes no answer and does nothing toward showing how it might be answered.

This chapter considers several possible answers to the question. My aim is not to assert one of these answers as correct (if I had great confidence in any one, I wouldn't feel the special need to devise and present several); the aim, rather, is to loosen our feeling of being trapped by a question with no possible answer—one impossible to answer yet inescapable. (So that one feels the only thing to do is gesture at a Mark Rothko painting.) The question cuts so deep, however, that any approach that stands a chance of yielding an answer will look extremely weird. Someone who proposes a nonstrange answer shows he didn't understand this question. Since the question is not to be rejected, though, we must be prepared to accept strangeness or apparent craziness in a theory that answers it.

Still, I do not endorse here any one of the discussed possible answers as correct. It is too early for that. Yet it is late enough in the question's history to stop merely asking it insistently, and to begin proposing possible answers. Thereby, we at least show how it is possible to explain why there is something rather than nothing, how it is possible for the question to have an answer.

EXPLAINING EVERYTHING

The question "why is there something rather than nothing?" quickly raises issues about the limits of our understanding. Is it possible for everything to be explained? It often is said that at any given time the most general laws and theories we know (or believe) are unexplained, but nothing is unexplainable in principle. At a later time we can formulate a deeper theory to explain the previous deepest one. This previous theory wasn't unexplainable, and though the new deepest theory is unexplained, at least for the time being, it too is not unexplainable.

The question about whether everything is explainable is a different one. Let the relation E be the relation *correctly explains,* or *is the* (*or a*) *correct explanation of.* One partial analysis of E is the Hempelian analysis of deductive nomological and statistical explanation, which we may view as providing necessary but not sufficient conditions for two types of explanation. The explanatory relation E is irreflexive, asymmetrical, and transitive. Nothing explains itself; there is no X and Y such that X explains Y and Y explains X; and for all X, Y, Z, if X explains Y and Y explains Z then X explains Z. Thus, E establishes a strict partial ordering among all truths, or (alternatively) within the set of true sentences of English plus contemporary mathematics whose length is no more than 20,000,000 words. (I assume that anything of scientific interest can be expressed in such sentences, and shall treat their number as *in effect* infinite.) Notice that we are not talking only of what explanations are known to us, but rather of what explanatory relations actually hold within the set of truths.

How is the set of truths structured by the explanatory relation E? There appear to be only two possibilities. Either (1) there is some truth that no further truth stands in E to, or (2) there are infinite explanatory chains, and each truth has something else that stands in E to it. Either there are no foundations to science, no most fundamental or deep explanatory principles (the second possibility) or there are some truths without any explanation (the first possibility); these actually will be unexplainable in that *no* truths (known or not) explain them. About such truths *p* lacking further explanation, there also appear to be two possibilities. First, that such truths are necessarily true, and could not have been otherwise. (Aristotle, as standardly interpreted, maintained this.) But it is difficult to see how this would be true. It is not enough merely for it to be of the essence of the things which exist (and so necessarily true of them) that *p*. There would remain the question of why those and only those sorts of things (subject to *p*) exist; only if *p* must be true of everything possible would this question be avoided.

The second possibility is that *p* is a brute fact. It just happens that things are that way. There is no explanation (or reason) why they are that way rather than another way, no (hint of) necessity to remove this arbitrariness.

One way to remove some arbitrariness from the end of the explanatory chain is illustrated by the program of deriving moral content from the form of morality, a persistent attempt since Kant. Part of the motivation, no doubt, is the goal of convincing others of particular moral content: "If you accept any morality at all (the form), then you must accept this content." Apart from this interpersonal task, there is the desire to understand the structure of the realm of moral truths and, if that realm is autonomous and so underivable from nonmoral truths, to determine whether the fundamental moral truths or principles are arbitrary brute facts. If moral content could be gotten from moral form, that content would not be merely a brute fact; it would be the only possible moral content, holding true if any truths at all fit the form of morality. Particular moral content, thus, would be shown to be conditionally necessary: necessary given that there are any moral truths (of that form). To be sure, though that particular content would be rendered less arbitrary, the question would remain of why there were any truths exhibiting that form.

Within the factual realm, the parallel endeavor would derive particular empirical content from the form of facts, or more narrowly from the form of scientific laws or theories. This would show that if there are ultimate scientific laws, so nothing else does or can stand in the explanatory relation E to them, then these must have particular content. Such a project might formulate various symmetry and invariance conditions as holding of fundamental scientific laws, showing that only particular content satisfied all these conditions about form. This would render the particular contentless arbitrary, but the question would remain of why there were any ultimate scientific laws, any truths of that specified form. In any case, there will be the question of why there are any laws at all. This question is narrower than our title question but raises similar problems. If all explanation utilizes laws, then in the explanation of why there are any laws, some law will appear. Will not the question of why it holds, and hence of why any law holds, thereby go unanswered?[2]

Is there any way at all to remove these last unexplained bits? Since a fact that nothing explains is left dangling, while a fact explained by something else leaves the problem of explaining that something else, only one thing could leave nothing at all unexplained: a fact that explains itself. However, if anything has appeared obvious about explanation, it has been that the explanatory relation E is irreflexive. Explanations of the form "*p* because *p*" are inadequate and unsatisfactory. We want an explanation of *p* to provide a deeper reason why *p* is true; this is not provided by *p* itself. To answer "why is the sky blue?" by saying "because the sky is blue" would be taken as rejecting the question rather than answering it. A small literature exists that attempts to formulate precise conditions whereby circular explanations are excluded. Viewing the explanatory relation E as deductive but irreflexive, it must distinguish the legitimate ways a fact to be explained may "be contained in the (explanatory) premisses" from objectionable self-explanation.

The objectionable examples of explanatory self-deduction (total or partial) involve deductions that proceed via the propositional calculus. Would the explanation of a law be illegitimate automatically if instead the law was deduced from itself via quantification theory, as an instance of itself? If explanation is subsumption under a law, why may not a law be subsumed under itself?

Suppose a principle P presented sufficient conditions for a fundamental law's holding true; any lawlike statement that satisfies these conditions, such as invariance and symmetry, will hold true. P says: any lawlike statement having characteristics C is true. Let us imagine this is our deepest law; we explain why other fundamental laws hold true in accordance with the deep principle P, by their having the characteristic C. Those laws are true because they have C.

Next we face the question of why P holds true, and we notice that P itself also has characteristics C. This yields the following deduction.

> P: any lawlike statement having characteristic C is true.
> P is a lawlike statement with characteristic C.
> Therefore P is true.

This is not presented to justify P or as a reason for believing P. Rather, granting that P *is* true, the question is whether what explains its being true, is its having characteristics C (since everything with C is true). A general statement is not proven true simply by being susceptible to an inference of this form. Many false statements also are derivable from themselves in this way, for example

> S: Every sentence of exactly eight words is true.
> S has exactly eight words.
> Therefore S is true.

Although derivable as an instance of itself, S is false, nevertheless. Our question is not whether such self-subsumption as an instance of itself can constitute a proof, but whether it can constitute an explanation; *if* the statement is true, can the reason why be the very content it itself states?

Is self-subsuming explanation thwarted by the fact that explanations must be deeper than what they (purport to) explain? Within Tarski's framework, P would have to be assigned a fixed metalinguistic level of depth, and so could not be used to deduce itself as above; however, there could be a hierarchy of metalanguages, each one enabling a deduction of the next most superficial law of the family of similar P laws. Another theory recently has been presented by Saul Kripke, in which statements are not assigned fixed levels but each seeks its own appropriate level—the most superficial one wherein the statement applies to its referent(s). Hence, P when used in a deduction will be one level deeper than what instances it. In this spirit, a theory statement deduced as an instance of itself via quantification theory is deeper as subsuming than as subsumed. In contrast, when *p* is deduced from itself via the propositional calculus, both premiss and conclusion will have the same depth. A truth can go so deep that it holds in virtue of being subsumed under that very deep truth itself.

Explanatory self-subsumption, I admit, appears quite weird—a feat of legerdemain. When we reach the ultimate and most fundamental explanatory laws, however, there are few possibilities. Either there is an infinite chain of different laws and theories, each explaining the next, or there is a finite chain. If a finite chain, either the endmost laws are unexplainable facts or necessary truths or the only laws there can be if there are laws of a certain sort at all (the fact that there are laws of that sort is classified under one of the other possibilities)—or the endmost laws are self-subsuming.

We face two questions about such self-subsumption: does it reduce the arbitrariness and brute-fact quality of the endpoint at all? If so, does it remove that quality completely? It does reduce that quality, I believe, though I cannot quite say it removes it altogether. If a brute fact is something that cannot be explained by anything, then a self-subsumable principle isn't a brute fact; but if a brute fact is something that cannot be explained by anything *else,* such a principle counts as a brute fact. We normally have no need to distinguish these two senses of 'brute fact', and perhaps usually presume the second. However, we should not be too impressed by the literature's unanimity that explanation is irreflexive. Those writers were not considering explanatory self-subsumption, via quantification theory, of the most fundamental laws and principles. With these ultimate facts, explanatory self-subsumption seems illuminating and legitimate. What, after all, is the alternative?

INEGALITARIAN THEORIES

There is one common form many theories share: they hold that one situation or a small number of states N are natural or privileged and in need of no explanation, while all other states are to be explained as deviations from N, resulting from the action of forces F that cause movement away from the natural state. For Newton, rest or uniform rectilinear motion is the natural state requiring no explanation, while all other motions are to be explained by unbalanced forces acting upon bodies. For Aristotle, rest was the natural state, deviations from which were produced by the continual action of impressed forces. This pattern is not, however, restricted to theories of motion.

Let us call a theory of this sort an inegalitarian theory. An inegalitarian theory partitions states into two classes: those requiring explanation, and those neither needing nor admitting of explanation. Inegalitarian theories are especially well geared to answer questions of the form "why is there X rather than Y?" There is a non-N state rather than an N state because of the forces F that acted to bring the system away from N. When there is an N state, this is because there were no unbalanced forces acting to bring the system away from N.

Inegalitarian theories unavoidably leave two questions unanswered. First, why is it N that is the natural state which occurs in the absence of unbalanced external forces, rather than some other (type of) state N'? Second, given that N is a natural or privileged state, why is it forces of type F', not of some other type P, that produce deviations from N? If our fundamental theory has an inegalitarian structure, it will leave as brute and unexplained the fact that N rather than something else is a natural state, and that F rather than something else is the deviation force.

However special a state appears, to assume it is a natural state with an inegalitarian theory has significant content. We should be very suspicious of a priori arguments purporting to demonstrate that a state is a natural one, and we should search such arguments carefully for the covert assumption that the state is natural or that only certain types of forces can produce deviations from whatever the natural state happens to be.[3] We cannot assume any particular inegalitarian theory as our fundamental theory.

The question 'why is there something rather than nothing?' is posed against the background of an assumed inegalitarian theory. If there were nothing, then about this situation would there also be the question (though without anyone to ask it) of why there is nothing rather than something? To ask 'why is there something rather than nothing?' assumes that nothing(ness) is the natural state that does not need to be explained, while deviations or divergences from nothingness have to be explained by the introduction of special causal factors. There is, so to speak, a presumption in favor of nothingness. The problem is so intractable because any special causal factor that could explain a deviation from nothingness is itself a divergence from nothingness, and so the question seeks its explanation also.[4]

Is it possible to imagine nothingness being a natural state which itself contains the force whereby something is produced? One might hold that nothingness as a natural state is derivative from a very powerful force toward nothingness, one any other forces have to overcome. Imagine this force as a vacuum force, sucking things into nonexistence or keeping them there. If this force acts upon itself, it sucks nothingness into nothingness, producing something or, perhaps, everything, every possibility. If we introduced the verb "to nothing" to denote what this nothingness force does to things as it makes or keeps them nonexistent, then (we would say) the nothingness nothings itself. (See how Heideggerian the seas of language run here!) Nothingness, hoisted by its own powerful petard, produces something. In the Beatles' cartoon *The Yellow Submarine,* a being like a vacuum cleaner goes around sucking up first other objects, next the surrounding background; finally, turning upon itself, it sucks itself into nothingness, thereby producing with a pop a brightly colored variegated scene.

On this view, there is something rather than nothing because the nothingness there once was nothinged itself, thereby producing something. Perhaps it nothinged itself just a bit, though, producing something but leaving some remaining force for nothingness. Figure 1 graphs the amount of nothingness force it takes to nothing some part of a given nothingness force being exerted. Curve I begins above the 45° line x = y, and cuts across it at point *e*. If this curve holds true, then a certain amount of nothingness force *a*, to start with, will act upon itself and nothing some of itself, thereby reducing the amount remaining and also the amount necessary to nothing some of the remaining nothingness force. The situation moves down the curve I until it crosses the line x = y. Past that point *e*, to nothing some more nothingness force would require more than is being exerted and hence available. If the correct curve were II, however, then a nothingness force of *b*, to start with, would nothing some of itself and so would move down the curve to the origin, obliterating all of the nothingness force, leaving none remaining. On the other hand, if we start at a point below the 45° line x = y, for example point *n*, there is not being exerted enough nothingness force to nothing any of itself, and so the situation will remain just as is; there will be no movement down the curve from *n*.

Even if it were true, that there was an original nothingness force, the problem would remain of explaining the particular starting point and the shape of the curve that goes through it. Why was that the starting point, and in virtue of what did that curve hold? One possibility appears to leave nothing dangling: the curve is just the 45° line itself, and we start somewhere on it and move down to the origin. There will remain the problem of precisely where we start (is the only unarbitrary point infinitely far out?), but the curve itself may appear unarbitrary. The y axis measures the resistance being offered, so the curve x = y says it takes a force equal to the resistance to overcome some of it. This condition of symmetry, the 45° line, appears less arbitrary than any other. This appearance, however, is somewhat misleading. For why are we using this kind of graph paper? This 45° line would look very unsymmetrical on logarithmic graph paper, while the most symmetrical looking line there would stand for a very different phenomenon.

Thus far I have been considering the inegalitarian theory that assumes nothingness is the natural state. It is time to undermine the picture of nothingness as natural, first by imagining inegalitarian theories where it is not. We might imagine that some fullness of existence is the natural state, and that the actual situation deviates from this fullness because of special forces acting. Whether this theory allows nothingness to result eventually will

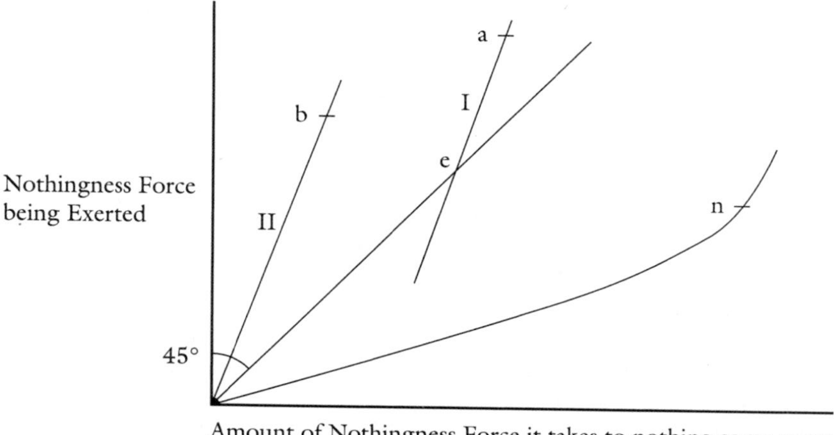

Figure 1

depend upon whether the force producing deviations from fullness, once it has performed the rest of its task, can act upon itself thereby annihilating itself, the very last vestige of any fullness. (Or perhaps several forces operate to diverge from fullness that, after the rest of their job is done, can simultaneously annihilate each other.) The western philosophical tradition tends to hold that existence is better or more perfect than nonexistence,[5] so it tends to view forces that cause divergence from fullness as malignant. But one can imagine another view, wherein the movement from thick and dense matter to more ethereal and spiritual modes of energy and existence is a movement of increasing perfection. The limit of such movement toward more and more insubstantial existence will be the most perfect: nothingness itself. Since reaching such perfection might take hard work and spiritual development, the answer to the question "why is there something rather than nothing?" might be that the universe is not yet spiritually developed enough for there to be nothing. The something is not enlightened yet. Perfection is not the natural state, and there is something rather than nothing because this is not the best of all possible worlds. Against the background of some such theory, the opposite question "why is there nothing rather than something?" (as applied to the appropriate situation) would make sense, and the correct answer would specify the forces that produced the deviation from somethingness, bringing about nothingness.

Apart from any such specific background theory, we should note a general reason or argument for *something's* being the natural state. (This argument was pointed out to me by Emily Nozick, then age twelve.) If something cannot be created out of nothing, then, since there is something, it didn't come from nothing. And there never was a time when there was only nothing. If ever nothing was the natural state, which obtained, then something could never have arisen. But there is something. So nothingness is not the natural state; if there is a natural state, it is somethingness. (If nothingness were the natural state, we never could have gotten to something—we couldn't have gotten here from there.)

It is possible to think that one cannot answer any question if one cannot answer the question of why there is something rather than nothing. How can we know why something is (or should be) a certain way if we don't know why there is anything at all? Surely this is the first philosophical question that has to be answered. It doesn't seem to assume anything (other than that there is something), while the answer to any other philosophical question is liable to be overturned or undermined or transformed by the answer to this one. However, to ask this question is to presume a great deal, namely, that nothingness is a natural state requiring no explanation, while all deviations from nothingness are in need of explanation. This is a very strong assumption, so strong that we cannot merely extrapolate from more limited contexts (such as argument, where the burden of proof is on the person who makes an existence claim[6]) and build the assumption into our fundamental theory, one not restricted within an understood wider context.

The first thing to admit is that we do not know what the natural state is; the second is that we do not know whether there is any fundamental natural state, whether the correct fundamental theory will have an inegalitarian structure. Any theory with such a structure will leave as unexplained brute facts N being the natural state, F being the deviation-producing forces, and also the laws of operation of F. Perhaps fewer things would be left dangling as brute facts by a fundamental theory that is egalitarian.

But won't the move away from an inegalitarian theory add to our explanatory tasks? If no state is privileged or natural, then for each state we shall have to explain why it rather than some other one exists. At least an inegalitarian theory didn't have to (try to) explain every state—so it faced fewer questions. To be sure, these questions it did not ask correspond to facts it left as brute. Still, to have to explain for each and every existing state why it exists seems to make the explanatory task even more unmanageable. The shift away from an inegalitarian theory seems to add to the explanatory task because now it seems that all existing states, not just some, will be in need of explanation. However, in thinking we have to explain why all existing states exist, we once again have slipped into treating nonexistence as the natural state. An egalitarian fundamental theory will not pick out existence as especially in need of explanation.

Questions of the form 'why X rather than Y?' find their home within a presumption or assumption that Y is natural. When this presumption is dropped, there is no fact of X rather than Y. Still, isn't there the fact of X to be explained, the question 'why X?' to be answered? But this is the question 'why does X exist rather than not?', 'why does X obtain rather than not?'. If we drop inegalitarian assumptions completely, we reject the view that when X exists or obtains, it exists or obtains rather than does not or rather than something else—we eliminate the "rather than".

EGALITARIANISM

One way to dissolve the inegalitarian class distinction between nothing and something, treating them on a par, is to apply a version of the principle of indifference from probability theory. There are many ways w_1, w_2, . . . for there to be something, but there is only one way w_0, for there to be nothing. Assign equal probability to each alternative possibility w_1, assuming it is a completely random matter which one obtains. The chances, then, are very great that there will be something, for "there is something" holds of every possibility except w_0. On some views of statistical explanation, by (correctly) specifying a random mechanism that yields a very high probability of there being something, we thereby would have explained why there is. ("Why is there something? It is just what you would expect that random mechanism to produce.")

In regard to the use of principles of indifference within probability theory, it often has been pointed out that much rests upon the initial partitioning into (what will be treated as equiprobable) states. A state that is single in one partition can encompass many states in another partition. Even the many ways of there being something might be viewed as just one state in the two-membered partition: there is nothing, there is something. Yet while we can shrink there being something down to only one alternative, we cannot, even artificially, expand there being nothing up to more than one alternative. If there is nothing(ness), there just are no aspects of it to use to divide it into two alternatives.[7]

So on the worst assumptions about how the partitioning goes, yielding the two-membered partition, there initially is a one-half chance that something exists. Since all other partitions are at least three-membered, on these other partitionings the initial chance of something's existing is at least two-thirds. Can we go up one level and assign probabilities to the different partitionings themselves? If we go up levels, assigning equal probabilities to the worst case partitioning and to all others (equally), then the probability of something existing increases, and tends toward the probability in the previous equal-chance large partitioning under the principle of indifference. The larger the number of alternatives partitioned, the closer the probability that something exists approaches to one.

This model of a random process with one alternative being that nothing exists (N), is illuminating. However, it does not sufficiently shake off inegalitarian assumptions. Though the model treats its possibilities on a par, it assumes a possibility will not be realized unless at random. It assumes that the natural state for a possibility is nonrealization, and that a possibility's being realized has to be explained by special factors (including, at the limit, random ones). At this deep level the presented model remains inegalitarian. What would a thoroughgoing egalitarian theory be like?

FECUNDITY

A thoroughgoing egalitarian theory will not treat nonexisting or nonobtaining as more natural or privileged, even for a possibility—it will treat all possibilities on a par. One way to do this is to say that all possibilities are realized.

For the most fundamental laws and initial conditions C of the universe, the answer to the question "why C rather than D?" is that *both* independently exist. We happen to find ourselves in a C universe rather than a D universe; perhaps this is no accident, for a D universe might not produce or support life such as ours. There is no explanation of why C rather than D, for there is no fact of C rather than D. All the possibilities exist in independent noninteracting realms, in "parallel universes". We might call this the fecundity assumption. It appears that only such an egalitarian view does not leave any question "why X rather than Y?" unanswered. No brute fact of X rather than Y is left unexplained, for no such fact holds.

Will the fecundity assumption serve to avoid inegalitarianism? Doesn't it, too, specify a natural state, one where all possibilities exist, while perhaps also countenancing deviations from this induced by various forces? Let X be the situation of every possibility obtaining, and Y one of all but two possibilities obtaining. There is no fact of X rather than Y, for both of these situations are realized. Each possibility countenanced by X obtains, as do the two fewer countenanced by Y; all together, these are merely the possibilities countenanced by X.

Y was described as admitting all but two possibilities, and so was compatible with X. Can there not be a Z that admits all but two possibilities and also excludes these remaining two as obtaining? Isn't there then a fact that has to be explained, of X rather than Z? I am tempted to answer that Z is not itself merely a description of possibilities obtaining. In attempting to exclude possibilities it becomes more than a description of possibilities; just as "only world number 3 exists and the fecundity assumption is false" is not merely a description of possibilities. Those to whom this appears lame can imagine the following. X and Z both exist in independent realms R_1 and R_2. In the realm of R_1, all possibilities exist, and in the realm of R_2 all possibilities except for two exist, and these two do not. These separate realms do not interact; also within a realm the possibilities realized are independent and noninteracting. Though not all possible worlds are realized in realm R_2, all of them are in the union of the two realms, written $R_1 \cup R_2$, which contains whatever is in either. Since R_1 already contains all possibilities, $R_1 \cup R_2 = R_1$. The (negative) fact that two possibilities do not obtain holds in the realm R_2, but not in the realm $R_1 \cup R_2$. (While all the worlds in R_2 also are in $R_1 \cup R_2$, not all the facts true of R_2 also are true of $R_1 \cup R_2$; for example, the predicate "$\neq R_1 \cup R_2$" holds of R_2 but not of its union with R_1.)

Consider the question "why isn't there nothing?" There *is* nothing—that is one of the separate possibilities which is realized. If the question means to ask why there isn't *only* nothing, with no other possibility also independently realized, it makes an unwarranted, inegalitarian assumption: that nothingness is the privileged and natural state. Why is there something rather than nothing? There isn't. There's both.

When a hypothesis avoids a fact's being left simply as a brute fact, this usually is taken to provide some reason for believing the hypothesis is true. The hypothesis of multiple independent possible worlds, too, enables us to avoid leaving something as a brute fact, in this case, the fact that there is something.

How does the principle of fecundity arise? Upon what is it based? What explains the fact that all possibilities are independently realized? That only with the principle of fecundity will no fact be left dangling as a brute fact, if true, is an insufficient explanation. It would remain to be explained why the cosmos is so structured that nothing (else) is left unexplained.

The principle of fecundity follows from the thoroughgoing rejection of inegalitarian theories. If no possibility has a privileged status, including nonexistence, then all possibilities independently exist or obtain. If the reason for an egalitarian theory is that only thus is nothing left dangling as a brute fact, we are left with the (metaphysical) question of why the universe is arranged in that epistemologically fortunate way. Why does a thoroughgoing egalitarian theory hold, rather than some inegalitarian one? The answer, of course, is that both hold in their own independent realms, while in the union of the realms all possibilities hold. But if such trickiness robs us of the ability to ask "why egalitarian rather than inegalitarian?", we still want to ask "why egalitarian?" We still want to understand the ground or basis of the realization of all possibilities.

The principle of fecundity is an invariance principle. Within general relativity, scientific laws are invariant with respect to all differentiable coordinate transformations. The principle of fecundity's description of the structure of possibilities is invariant across all possible worlds. There is no one specially privileged or preferred possibility, including the one we call actual. As David Lewis puts it, "actual" is an indexical expression referring to the possible world where the utterance containing it is located

(*Counterfactuals*, pp. 85–86). The actual world has no specially privileged status, it merely is the world where we are. Other independently realized possibilities also are correctly referred to by their inhabitants as actual. Invariance principles previously have removed the special status of particular portions of actuality: the (absolute) position and time of an event, the orientation, a particular state of motion (distinguished from its Lorentz transformations). The principle of fecundity extends this, denying special status to actuality itself. Yet, to point out that the principle of fecundity is an invariance principle does not explain why it holds or why a deep invariance of that sort obtains. What then is the basis or ground of the realization of all possibilities?

FECUNDITY AND SELF-SUBSUMPTION

As an ultimate and very deep principle, the principle of fecundity can subsume itself within a deductive explanation. It states that all possibilities are realized, while it itself is one of those possibilities. We can state the principle of fecundity F as

> All possible worlds obtain

or as

> For any *p*, if *p* states that some realm of possible worlds obtains, then *p* is true.

But F itself states that some realm of possible worlds obtains, namely, that of all possible worlds. So the principle F is just such a *p* as it describes. From this fact and from F it follows, via quantification theory, that F is true. The principle of fecundity F subsumes itself because it says that all possibilities obtain, and it itself is such a possibility. If it is a very deep fact that all possibilities obtain, then that fact, being a possibility, obtains in virtue of the deep fact that all possibilities do.[8]

Similarly we might try to formulate the full invariance condition that the principle of fecundity satisfies as a sufficient condition for something's holding true. Using that invariance property I, we have the invariance principle P: any (general law-like) statement with invariance feature I holds true. Now if this invariance principle P itself has the invariant property I, then it follows, via quantification theory, that P is true. If F and P are true ultimate explanatory principles, then they are subsumed under themselves. In this case, the principle of fecundity holds in virtue of being a possibility while it is a deep fact that all possibilities obtain, and the principle of invariance holds in virtue of having the property I, while it is a deep fact that every such thing holds true.

Thus, if F and P were true, they would subsume themselves and their arbitrary or brute fact quality would be (we have said) reduced or even removed. But apart from the initial difficulty that F countenances some independently existing parallel possible worlds, it makes a very strong claim, namely that all possible worlds independently exist. According to F there would obtain a world, for example, with 4,234 independent explanatory factors and laws, not to mention even more complicated possibilities. It then would be an accident that we inhabit a world with a high degree of explanatory unity. (True, any universe unified enough to contain knowers will possess a degree of explanatory unity they find striking; but ours exhibits more than the minimal amount needed to sustain knowers.) I view this consequence as highly unwelcome, even though I realize that if the full principle of fecundity were true there would be a world (among others) that realized a high degree of explanatory unity, yet whose inhabitants would find the principle of fecundity very implausible since it made the salient and striking cognitive feature of their world, explanatory unity, merely a happenstance.

This suggests that we limit or restrict the principle of fecundity to hold just that there obtain all possible worlds or realms of a certain sort S. There are two conditions we want satisfied by the sort S in the limited principle of fecundity LF: that our actual world be of sort S, and that the principle LF itself state a possibility of sort S. Moreover, if the limitation is to meet our previous objection to the unlimited principle of fecundity then also the sort S will (among other things) specify some high degree of explanatory unity. Such a limited principle of fecundity LF would explain the existence of the actual world, as well as explaining itself via explanatory self-subsumption, all without opening the door to every possibility's obtaining.

The more limited is the sort S, the less powerful is the principle of limited fecundity (as compared to the unlimited principle) and the narrower the range of worlds said to obtain. Which is the most limited sort S that satisfies the three conditions? Perhaps there is a sort S satisfying the three conditions that fits the actual world but no other possible world. The principle LF incorporating that sort would (potentially) explain why the actual world obtains, as well as why LF itself holds (via explanatory self-subsumption), without any reification of other possible worlds. Our claim is not that a (or the most) limited principle of fecundity that satisfied the three conditions must or would be true. The point, rather, is that given a true limited principle of fecundity satisfying the three conditions, there then will be an explanation of the world with nothing left dangling as an arbitrary or brute fact. Our aim is to describe how it could turn out that everything has an explanation.

One suggestion about the restrictive sort S is especially salient. Since the fundamental principle is to be self-subsuming, perhaps "self-subsuming" demarcates the sort itself. This specifies the following principle of limited fecundity:

> All self-subsuming principles hold true,
> All self-subsuming possibilities are realized.

There are two notions of self-subsumption to consider: a direct one wherein something subsumes itself in one step, and an indirect one where something x directly subsumes something else which directly subsumes something which . . . directly subsumes x. (Indirect subsumption is the ancestral of the direct subsumption relation.) The wider variant of this version of limited fecundity says that all indirectly self-subsuming possibilities are realized, the narrower one only that all directly self-subsuming possibilities are realized.

However, neither version limits the full principle of fecundity at all, for that full principle directly subsumes itself. (This also shows the wider version subsumes itself; it yields the full principle in one step, which yields the wider version in one or two more.) Thus the sort must be further specified: all self-subsuming possibilities of sort S are realized. Note, though, that this will raise the question of whether that principle itself is self-subsuming of sort S. Consider, for example, the narrower of the versions above of the principle of limited fecundity:

> All directly self-subsuming possibilities are realized;
> All directly self-subsuming principles hold true.

Is this principle itself directly self-subsuming? That seems undetermined by anything said thus far. If it directly subsumes itself—no contradiction follows from this supposition—then it does; while if it does not directly subsume itself—also a noncontradictory supposition—then it does not. Either supposition leads to a consistent theory.

Would a similar self-subsuming explanation be possible if only nothingness had existed instead? Some principle R would have to specify a property N which only two things satisfied: the possibility of nothing's existing, and R itself.

> R: Exactly what has feature N obtains.

R would hold in virtue of having N, while nothingness would obtain in virtue of being the only other N-satisfier, there being none further. Nothingness obtaining would not be an arbitrary and brute fact only if some deep true principle R explained itself via explanatory self-subsumption and yielded nothing (else). That is what would have to be the case if there was nothingness, unarbitrarily. However, since there is something, no such principle R holds true.

Different possible self-subsuming ultimate principles can be formulated, some yielding the actual world (and more), others not. That ultimate principle which is true will, I have suggested, explain itself by subsuming itself. (There need not be only one ultimate principle; the explanatory chains can terminate in several independent ones, each self-subsuming.) Being a deep fact, deep enough to subsume and to yield itself, the principle will not be left dangling without any explanation. A question seems to remain, however: why does that particular self-subsuming principle hold true rather than one of the other ones?[9] Can we merely answer: it holds in virtue of having the property it ascribes? If one of the others had held instead, it would have held in virtue of having the property it ascribed. So is it not still arbitrary that the particular self-subsuming principle that holds, does hold? Perhaps it is not a brute fact that it holds—for perhaps a brute fact is one without any explanation, while this principle is explained via self-subsumption. Yet though it is not a brute fact that the principle holds, still it seems arbitrary. Why couldn't one of the others have held just as well?

The principle LF that holds true is not a brute fact because it subsumes itself. It will not be arbitrary that this principle holds if it satisfies some deep invariance principle I, specifying an invariance feature that makes its possessors, including the principle LF, nonarbitrary. A principle that varied in the way I excludes would be, to that extent, arbitrary. However, I is not an explanatory factor; it holds because LF does. Self-subsuming, LF holds because LF does, so is no brute fact. It also has the feature I, so it is not arbitrary. What more remains to be explained?

Consider all those different self-subsuming ultimate principles (of which LF is one) that also satisfy some significant invariance feature or other. Why does the one of those that holds, LF say, hold? The holding of LF is not a brute fact (because of self-subsumption), nor is it arbitrary (because of I). However, some other self-subsuming principle LF" satisfies another invariance principle I"; and if LF" held it would not be arbitrary either (because of I"). So isn't it arbitrary that LF (with invariance feature I) holds rather than LF" (with invariance feature I")? Such problems would be avoided if there were a deepest invariance principle I_0, which, among the ultimate self-subsuming principles, was satisfied uniquely by LF. In that case, LF is not a brute fact (because it subsumes itself), it is not arbitrary (because it satisfies I_0); and it is not arbitrary that LF holds rather than some other self-subsuming principle LP", itself unarbitrary in virtue of satisfying I", because I_0, is deeper than I". It would be more arbitrary if LP" held.

We moved from the full principle of fecundity F to a more limited one LF in order to avoid the vast array of possible worlds, all obtaining, and the accompanying mere happenstance that our world has a high degree of explanatory unity. However, we seem to forgo the advantages of an egalitarian theory by restricting the possibilities that obtain to the sort S. In effect this makes of S a natural or privileged state in contrast to other possible ones, unless a deepest invariance principle can render this S-limitation unarbitrary.

If there is no such deepest invariance principle, however, merely alternates at the same level, each with its own version of nonarbitrariness, then although the particular self-subsuming principle LF which holds will not be a brute fact or completely arbitrary, still, it will hold merely in virtue of its holding, while other specifications of limited fecundity, satisfying different invariance conditions, also would have held if they had held, merely in virtue of their holding. This parity of status between different principles remains and disturbs.

Self-subsumption is a way a principle turns back on itself, yields itself, applies to itself, refers to itself. If the principle necessarily has the features it speaks of, then it necessarily will apply to itself. This mode of self-reference, whereby something refers to itself in all possible worlds where it refers, is like the Gödelian kind of the previous chapter. There we also discussed an even more restrictive mode of self-referring, reflexive self-referring. Can the fundamental explanatory principle(s) be not merely self-subsuming and necessarily self-applying, but also reflexively self-referring?

The fundamental explanatory principle will not contain an indexical term, it will not say: I am ________.[10] However, it can fit the general account of reflexive referring: the item refers or applies in virtue of a feature bestowed in that very token act of referring. A reflexive principle, then, will hold or self-apply in virtue of that very fact of holding or self-applying; it will hold in virtue of self-applying.

This puts the problems we have faced in a new guise. The specific principle of limited fecundity LF will be self-subsuming if it is, and will hold in virtue of being of the limited sort S. It will hold true as a fundamental principle *if* it holds, and in virtue of its holding. Other specifications or versions of limited fecundity also share these features. This presented the problem of explaining why one particular LF holds rather than those others, and it seemed insufficient to answer "it holds in virtue of its holding", since this also would have been true of any one of the others if it had held. Now we can see that this apparent insufficiency marks the fundamental principle as reflexive. A reflexive fundamental principle will hold merely in virtue of holding, it holds true "from the inside".[11]

To continue to press the question of why one self-subsuming principle LF holds rather than another assumes the ultimate self-subsuming explanatory principle will not be reflexive. But what else could it be?

ULTIMACY

Philosophers push or iterate a question, usually about justification, so far that they cannot find any acceptable deeper answer. Attempting to deduce, explain, or justify the principle or position already reached, they fail, or covertly reintroduce the very result to be gotten. Whereupon a crisis for philosophy or for reason is proclaimed: a surd has been reached which cannot be justified (or explained) further. Reason has been forced to halt.

What did they expect? Either the chain (of explanation or justification) goes on infinitely, or it goes in a circle, or it reaches an endpoint, either a simple point or a self-subsuming loop. What result would *not* constitute a crisis? It seems plausible that philosophy should seek to uncover the deepest truths, to find explanatory or (if that is its aim) justificatory principles so deep that nothing else yields them, yet deep enough to subsume themselves. Reaching these should be a goal of philosophy, so when that situation occurs with some topic or area, instead of a crisis we should announce a triumph.[12] One of philosophy's tasks is to probe so deeply as to uncover the fundamental truths, to list and identify these, and to trace out what they yield, including themselves. To succeed in this should occasion pride, not shame.

NOTES

1. That it is perhaps dangerous as well appears to be indicated in Hagigah 2:1 of the *Mishnah:* "Whosoever reflects on four things, it were better for him if he had not come into the world—what is above; what is beneath; what is before; and what is after." See also *Midrash Rabbah* (Soncino Press, London, 1939), 1:10, 8:2.

For Leibniz's discussion, see "On the Radical Origination of Things" in L. Loemaker, ed., *Leibniz Philosophical Papers and Letters* (2nd ed., Reidel, Dordrecht, 1969), pp. 486–491.

2. Could one try to show that if there are any truths at all, there must be ultimate scientific laws (of that form)?

3. See Ernest Nagel, *The Structure of Science* (Harcourt, Brace and World, New York, 1961), pp. 175–178. R. Harré recently has taken just such a suspicious position. He writes: "I come to the most fundamental and the most powerful of methodological principles. It is this. *Enduring is in no need of explanation.* We are not required to explain the fact that something remains the same; only if there is a change is an explanation called for." *(The Principles of Scientific Thinking,* Macmillan, 1970, p. 248.) But don't we need an explanation of why one thing counts as the same, for the purposes of the principle, while another does not? The principle is trivialized if whatever is thought to require no explanation will be said to endure relative to a set of concepts specially designed to fit.

In contrast to Harré's principle, consider the theory of the sixteenth century Kabbalist Meir ben Gabbai, according to whom only God's continuing production of the written and oral Torah maintains things in existence; "were it to be interrupted for even a moment, all creatures would sink back into their non-being." (Quoted in Gershom Scholem, *The Messianic Idea in Judaism,* Schocken Books, New York, 1971, p. 298.)

4. If a fundamental inegalitarian theory holds that everything not in N is a deviation from N, also that forces of type F are not in N, then the existence of any F force will be a deviation from N. Since according to the theory, all deviations from N are explainable only by the actions of F's, the fact that there are any F's at all (which fact is a deviation from N) can be explained only by the action of F's. According to the fundamental inegalitarian theory itself, though, there cannot be any explanation of why there are any F's at all that doesn't introduce some F's as explanatory factors. That necessarily leaves us, it seems, without an understanding of why there are any F's at all.

5. I am told (by Sidney Morgenbesser) that in a novel by Peter DeVries a minister is asked by a troubled parishioner whether God exists, and replies "God is so perfect he doesn't need to exist."

6. It is not clear even how to formulate this point about the burden of proof or argument. Why is an existence claim made by someone who says there is a God, whereas one is not made by someone who says there is a God-less cosmos or universe?

7. Can we say nothingness includes these two alternatives: nothingness up until and including now, and nothingness after now? First, if we treat everything symmetrically, then something also will get temporally divided similarly, preserving the ratio between the

number of somethingness and of nothingness alternatives. More to our point, time also is a "something", unavailable to partition nothing(ness) if there really be that.

8. Do all possibilities exist or obtain, including the one that not all possibilities do? If, to avoid contradiction, we restrict the principle of fecundity so that it speaks of and subsumes only first-level possibilities, those that neither entail nor exclude the existence of other possibilities, then it will not subsume itself. Thus, as before, we interpret it to speak of all possibilities in their own noninteracting realms. This includes, in its own separate realm, the possibility that not all possibilities obtain. However, in (set-theoretical) union there is strength.

9. Will there also remain the question of why *this* universe is one with the particular fundamental laws G (for example, general relativity and quantum electrodynamics)? Can we answer that different universes, all falling under LF, will be structured by different fundamental laws, each having those laws as part of its essence so that with different fundamental laws, it would be a different universe? Thus: Why does this universe satisfy G? It is part of its essence. Why does there exist any universe having that essence G? Because some such universe is given rise to under LF.

10. Theistic theories sometimes hold that the world or universe refers to God, is a name of God. Might it be a reflexive self-reference so the universe is one of God's tokenings of "I"? (Darker yet, can something be nothing's reflexive tokening?)

11. Is it a relevant disanalogy that in reflexive self-reference there is an act, independent of successful reference, that bestows the feature? The feature is not bestowed by successfully referring, is it? Is there a similar independent entity that bestows a feature in virtue of which a fundamental self-subsuming law holds?

12. Some may see this suggestion, as I myself sometimes do, as like that of the senator who during the war in Vietnam proposed that the United States should announce that it had *won,* and then leave.

Reading Questions

1. Nozick divides solutions to his title question into two types: inegalitarian and egalitarian. What is the difference between these two?
2. Nozick claims that explanation is normally assumed to be irreflexive—that is, nothing explains itself. Some epistemologists believe that some propositions are self-justifying. If they are right, why can't there be truths that are self-explaining?
3. Nozick tenders the following argument.

1. Something cannot be created out of nothing.	(premise)
2. There is something.	(premise)
3. Therefore there never was just nothing.	(from 1, 2)
4. If nothing were the natural state, then there must have been nothing.	(premise)
5. Thus nothing is not the natural state.	(3, 4 *modus tollens*)
6. Either something or nothing is the natural state.	(premise)
7. Thus something is the natural state.	(5, 6 disjunctive syllogism)
8. Thus we needn't explain why there is something—it is just what we should expect.	(from 7)

There seems to be a problem for premise (4). Newtonian mechanics considers rest to be the natural state. By analogy with (4), if rest were the natural state, then there must have been things at rest. Yet Newtonian mechanics maintains that rest is an idealization and that in fact everything is in motion. So why couldn't nothing be the natural state and there still always have been something? There also is a problem with the conclusion in (8). We may think that health is the natural state, but nevertheless it seems entirely sensible to ask why someone is so healthy. Thus even if something is the natural state, why is there nothing left to explain? How could Nozick answer these questions?

4. Would either a brute fact or a self-subsuming proposition be less worrying if it were necessarily true? Consider this question: why do all cubes have right angles? If it seems

nonpuzzling or inappropriate to ask, then perhaps we should hope that physicist Stephen Hawking is right in thinking that the initial conditions of the universe were necessarily what they were. Would Nozick object that this approach only pushes the question to either "why are there necessary truths rather than not?" or "why are the initial states and laws of the universe necessary rather than contingent?"

Further Readings

Books

Leslie, John. 1979. *Value and Existence.* Oxford: Blackwell.
Rescher, Nicholas. 1984. *The Riddle of Existence.* Lanham, MD: The University Press of America.
Tymieniecka, Anna-Teresa. 1966. *Why Is There Something Rather than Nothing?* Assen, Holland: Van Gorcum.

Articles

Archie, Lee. 1995. "The No-Alternative Paradox and the Possibility of Metaphysics." *Contemporary Philosophy* 17 (1): 13–20.
Brooks, David. 1992. "Why This World?" *Philosophical Papers* 21 (3): 259–273.
Benardete, Jose A. 1954. "On Being and Nothing." *Review of Metaphysics* 7: 363–367.
Ehman, Robert R. 1963. "On the Possibility of Nothing." *Review of Metaphysics* 17: 205–213.
Fleming, Noel. 1988. "Why Is There Something Rather than Nothing?" *Analysis* 48: 32–35.
Goldstick, D. 1979. "Why Is There Something Rather than Nothing?" *Philosophy and Phenomenological Research* 40: 265–271.
Knight, Thomas S. 1956. "Why Not Nothing?" *Review of Metaphysics* 10: 158–164.
Kusch, Martin. 1990. "On 'Why Is There Something Rather than Nothing?'" *American Philosophical Quarterly:* 253-257.
Lee, Martin. 1986. "Something Rather than Nothing." *Heythrop Journal* 27: 137–150.
Lowe, E. J. 1996. "Why Is There Anything at All?: II." *Proceedings of the Aristotelian Society* 70 (supplement): 111–120.
Mortensen, Chris. 1986. "Explaining Existence." *Canadian Journal of Philosophy* 16: 713–722.
Smith, Joseph Wayne. 1984. "Why Is There Something Rather than Nothing?" *Eidos* 3: 135–162.
Smith, Quentin. 1995. "Internal and External Causal Explanations of the Universe." *Philosophical Studies* 79 (3): 283–310.
Van Inwagen, Peter. 1996. "Why Is There Anything at All?: I." *Proceedings of the Aristotelian Society* 70 (supplement): 95–110.
Wedin, Michael V. 1984. "Nozick on Explaining Nothing." *Philosophy Research Archives* 10: 337–346.

Part II

Realism/Anti-Realism

SIMON BLACKBURN

Introduction to the Realism Debates

PHILOSOPHY IS ESSENTIALLY REFLECTIVE. It occurs when we reflect upon ourselves and our world, and ask questions about each. It also asks questions about the relation between ourselves and the world. 'Ourselves' here means our minds, as expressed in our thoughts and sayings; the world is that to which we direct our thoughts and sayings. The issue of 'realism' and its competitors is one about this relation.

Realism, we might say, wants to emphasize the world itself. The world has a nature, which, if all goes well, the mind can discover and reflect. This work of discovery is essentially obedient to the nature of the world. It is an attempt to get it right, to mirror or reflect the way things stand. The world is a vast totality of things, states of affairs, facts and events, and the task of the mind is to know which these are.

For realism, the mind is essentially responsive, receptive to a world which is objective, and largely independent of us. We live in a world whose nature and properties are just what they are, just 'there, anyway', and the mind reflects this world. Traditionally the competitor to realism is idealism. According to idealism, it is the human mind at a time that has a nature. This nature determines how it structures its response to the flux of data. The mind then builds its world in ways determined by that nature. For idealism, the mind is essentially creative, imposing its structures on the world, or at least upon the world as it is for us.

Each view, I want to emphasize, is at this point not so much a single doctrine as an invitation to sympathize with a range of doctrines. Realism is the disposition to insist that it is the world that shapes our responses and judgments, and that these responses and judgments have a goal, which is to reflect the way the world is. Idealism, correspondingly, is a disposition to insist on the contribution of the mind, which has organized and created its world. The tension between these two directions of thought comes up in many places, and not only when professional philosophy is involved. In the contemporary academy, postmodernism is a kind of celebration of the idealist sympathy, supposing that events and texts place little or no constraint on the interpreting historian or commentator. "Realism"

This essay was commissioned especially for this volume and appears here for the first time.

would here be the backlash that whatever latitude the interpreter has, his first responsibility is, in fact, to the events and the texts. Here, too, the realist emphasizes discovery where the idealist emphasizes creation.

Corresponding to the different sympathies, we expect to hear the realist insisting on one set of things, and the idealist insisting on others:

Realism. Facts are facts. The world is largely independent of us and the way we are; it has its things, facts, properties, events, and states of affairs that have their own objective nature; our responses are explained by the world and are intended to match the world; our judgments are supposed to reflect, or depict, or mirror, or correspond to the way the world is; success in judgment is a matter of getting the way of the world right, or successfully describing how things stand.

Idealism. There is no such thing as a view without a viewer. We perceive the world with a very specific set of sensory and interpretative mechanisms, including cultural lenses such as language, or the categories of our place and time. The world as it is for us, which means the world insofar as we can ever know about it or understand it, is shaped by those mechanisms; hence, there is an important sense in which we ourselves are the authors of the world as it is for us.

To use an example of Hilary Putnam's, we might say that when the realist looks at the sky, he sees the independent, eternal stars. The idealist sees patterns in the heavens, or constellations, and reflects that these patterns exist only from a viewpoint, and only for certain specific kinds of viewer.

Drawn with so broad a brush, the differences in emphasis between realism and idealism should be clear enough. But it remains most unclear how to sharpen the sympathies into distinct and competing theories and then how to conduct a debate between them. Let us consider a particular example. A realist theory of colors would claim that colors exist in reality and our visual systems enable us to perceive them. The sky is blue, and roses are red, and a human visual system in good order enables us to perceive them as they are. An idealist would make no sense of this assertion, but would claim instead that even if light exists, making up combinations of photons with different frequencies, colors themselves are the creation of our highly specific responses to this incoming energy. We have complex receptors and visual systems which translate that energy into colors, but there are no independent colors, just there anyway, which we are fortunate enough to get right. Take away the mind, and you take away colors with it.

In this example, the different sympathies of the realist and the idealist are again clear enough. But it is much less clear how to argue for the one emphasis rather than the other. For example, is it a good argument for realism about colors that the patterns of electromagnetic energy that correspond to colors are just 'there, anyway'? Would it be sensible to reduce or identify colors with these scientific properties, and claim a victory for realism? Or would this be a kind of cheat, sidestepping the idealist point that it takes the specific human (or primate) visual system to generate the patterns and boundaries of color in the flux of energies? And it might be less clear again whether arguments that ought to sway us in the case of colors would transfer to other domains where the same kind of debate could be mounted. Suppose, for example, we turn our attention to such things as rights or duties. A realist, again, will emphasize the way we think of these things as independent of our own opinions, objective. They are things that we can be right or wrong about, and that are matters of discovery. An idealist will emphasize the contingent and variable patterns of attitude that lead different people to respect different rights and duties and suggest that rather than reflecting an ethical reality, it is these responses that create it. Will a debate between these two sides be similar to the debate in the case of colors? Will it be the same arguments, or quite different ones? And how would anything applying to these cases translate to further examples: to issues of scientific realism, realism about possibilities, mathematical realism, realism about mental states, about causation or natural laws, about general as well as particular facts, about hypothetical as well as categorical facts, or about social as well as individual facts? For all these are areas in which the conflicting sympathies I have described come into collision.

As these examples suggest, the realism/idealism issue can crop up in many local areas. There is a line to be drawn, and some kinds of discourse fall within, and others fall outside it. A philosopher might, for instance, be a scientific realist, happy with the objective world revealed by physics, but not an ethical realist or color realist. The question then will be one of methodology: what determines which parts of our thought get the realist account, and which parts get a different account? We should not use the labels *realism* and *idealism* to suggest that there is one single, global debate, when local debates are in fact equally or more important.

Yet some philosophers have insisted on a global issue. A global account—for example, of our use of language in general—can be proffered in ways that accord better or worse with either sympathy. In recent philosophy of language this is illustrated in the debate between realists who put 'truth-conditions' at the center of their theory of the meaning of language, and their opponents, notably Michael Dummett, who work instead in terms of 'assertibility conditions', seeing meaning as answering to the epistemological situation of the language user, rather than answering to self-standing, independent facts about the world. This in turn is a sophisticated descendent of the difference between realists and verificationists in the first half of the twentieth century.

In local debates, it will be clear how a typical realist defense move will go: if the realist can show that no coherent line can be drawn where some particular kind of idealist wants to draw it, then this is a victory. Thus Berkeley tried to show that it is incoherent to be a realist about the shapes and sizes and other physical properties of things unless one is similarly a realist about colors and other 'secondary' qualities. Similarly people urge that there is no value-free neutral world, so that it is incoherent to be a realist about some things but not about values, or that there is no physical world without mathematical structure, so that it is incoherent to be a realist about physical reality but not about mathematics.

In the modern period few writers who oppose realism like to call themselves idealists. The term is used to describe Berkeley, Kant, and subsequent nineteenth-century philosophy and has too heavy an historical burden. The most general term of opposition is simply 'anti-realism'. It will cover various specific positions, of which we can distinguish two main families.

The most direct, and perhaps the ancestral family from which other anti-realisms are descended, is simply an ontological denial. There do not exist the objects or facts or properties that the realist takes us to have described. An anti-realist of this kind simply denies that there exist, for instance, possible worlds, or laws of nature, or colors, or whatever the contested discourse seems to describe. This denial may be motivated from a variety of sources, but again the most direct is that the world (or the world as we can conceive it) would be regarded as made up of some things but not others: things with physical properties in space and time, for instance, but no more. The realist will return that such ontological economy is mere prejudice: that properly regarded there is nothing mysterious about the things, or facts, or properties to which he is hospitable.

Having decided that there do not exist objects, or facts, or properties of some kind, ontological anti-realism is faced with a choice over what to say about discourses which seem to presuppose that there are. If there are indeed no numbers, what are we to make of the primary school doctrine that there is a number between 5 and 7? If there exist no duties, what of the reasonable doctrine that I have a duty to my children; if there are no colors, what are we to make of people who praise the deep vermilion in the rose?

One aggressive option is to urge that such sayings simply reflect mistakes, and should be eliminated. This is *eliminativism.* But in most areas the suggestion casts more discredit on the philosopher than on the discourse. It is far more likely that it is the philosopher who misunderstands the situation, than that we ought to give up primary school arithmetic, or love of duty or color. So more conciliatory attitudes are required. One is *reductionism:* say that the discourse is all right as it stands, but does not describe new or specific things, or facts or properties. Rather, it describes some old and respectable area in new terms (this would be the attitude of someone who thinks that discourse about color is discourse about electromagnetic energy, for example). Reductionism is more plausible than eliminativism; in fact, reductionism need not be called anti-realism at all. It allows that the discourse describes an aspect of the real world—only it was not the aspect that we naively thought it described. The problem with reductionism is making it credible, and one person's reduction is typically another person's elimination. To a realist about, for instance, social facts, it would not be welcome to suggest that they exist but are really all facts about individuals. The realist here is likely to be holding out for the specific self-standing nature of social facts, and reductionism fails to capture it.

A more subtle kind of anti-realist avoids head-on ontological battles. Instead it takes issue with the realist's view that a particular part of discourse seeks to represent a part of reality at all. Such a nondescriptive anti-realist might, for instance, urge that scientific theories do not describe an independent real world but are instead instruments of control or prediction of experience: this is *instrumentalism.* Some writers think that some of our theories should be regarded as useful fictions: *fictionalism.* Some think that sometimes (for instance, in ethics) we do not intend to describe an independent order of ethical facts but express attitudes and other practical stances, or even just tell each other what to do: *expressivism* and *prescriptivism.* Some think that describing and representing the world is something we manage to do only when we stick very close to the empirical given: this is *empiricism* or its cousin, *verificationism.*

In turn, this family can subdivide. One might hold these theses as true of the intentions with which people proffer doctrines in the contested areas. Or one might say that the real account of what they are doing is not reflected in their intentions, but is as it were hidden behind them. In turn, that might once more prompt the view that ordinary people are systematically in error about what they are doing as they use the relevant parts of language. But it need not go that way. One might hold that there is no error, unless indeed the ordinary speaker is tempted to theorize in a realist fashion. Rather, our discourse is quite in order as it stands, although true philosophy reveals what we are doing as we use it, and this turns out to be something other than describing a coordinated slice of reality. This position has been called *quasi-realism.*

Whenever philosophy clusters around an opposition, there is room for a third party who claims that the point at issue is badly formed, or even that no debate of the kind the opponents thought themselves to be engaged in is well founded. This reaction is very tempting in this case. If debates between realists and anti-realists grind to a halt, as they often seem to do, and if the methodology for conducting the debates remains obscure, and if the issue remains largely a matter of sympathies and prejudices rather than anything more scientific, then it becomes tempting to deny that the issue is a real one. Perhaps we cannot ascend to the metatheoretical position from which we can, as it were, survey in one view both our discourse, and the world, and decide upon their relationship. This is the view of ***minimalism***. The minimalist wants to turn his back on the whole reflective enterprise, doubting that anything except perhaps metaphors or images gives substance either to realism or anti-realism. Minimalism is attractively presented as the doctrine that areas of discourse are self-interpreting, needing no further metatheoretical commentary. The relationship between the world and the mind becomes just what first-order, untheoretical discourse says it is: we perceive colors, for example, or know that there is a number between 5 and 7.

Minimalism is sometimes confusingly presented as a kind of vindication of realism, whereas properly it is the denial that either the realist metatheory or any other is possible. The reason this point is often lost is that a *first-order* discourse may itself seem to make the kinds of claim that realism wanted. For example, it is just part of physical theory to say that the stars existed a long time before we did, so therefore we did not create them, and they are independent of us. It may just be part of our ethical outlook on the world that the wrongness of killing people does not depend upon what we happen to think about the wrongness of killing people, and is therefore independent of our attitudes and opinions. It is part of our common-sense doctrine of time that there are facts about what happened in the past that we cannot now know. If the original debate had been framed around these claims, then it looks as though minimalism, while apparently turning its back on the whole issue, in fact surreptitiously awards victory to the realist. It is as if realism is the default position certified simply by taking the original discourse at face value. The point is that the original discourse seems to speak enough of independent facts, or objectivity, to justify the realist emphasis. Thus in the present selection, Michael Devitt presents realism not as a claim about the relation between mind and the world, which would inevitably be a metatheoretical doctrine about such concepts as description, reflection, truth, and meaning, but simply as a conjunction of common-sense claims along the lines of 'rocks exist, and are independent of us'. Denial of such a truth seems absolutely outrageous—not a subtle philosophical position, but a simple ignorance of empirical and scientific fact. The position is minimalist, for it sees no reflective commentary as necessary beyond such first-order claims. But it presents itself as a vindication of common-sense realism.

It does not matter too much how we use the labels. What does matter is that we use them in perfect clarity. Minimalism is not an attempt to present a reflective theory about the relationship between ourselves and the world. It is the ***denial*** that such attempts are coherent. Hence, in particular, it is no vindication of one such attempt, the realist one. To suppose that it is such a vindication one would have to suppose that when this idealist talks of the mind making its world, he has a literal empirical claim in mind, as if someone is supposed to have made the planet Mars by accumulating enough rock and soil. But this is not what was intended, in the idealist direction.

The hard question in front of contemporary philosophy is whether minimalism is forced upon us. If it is, then not only does the reflective enterprise itself become impossible, but in a sense the history of philosophy does so too, since we could no longer maintain a grasp of what is at issue, for example between Berkeley and Locke, or Kant and Hegel. This is a higher intellectual, and cultural, price than many of us are prepared to pay without a battle.

4 Realism and Anti-Realism

MICHAEL DUMMETT

NEARLY THIRTY YEARS AGO, I first made a proposal concerning realism that took some time to evoke a response. The response, when it came, initially surprised me. My original intention had been to prompt what is called a 'research programme' in the form of a comparative study of disputes over realism. It had struck me that a variety of different traditional disputes within philosophy took the form of an opposition between a realist view of some particular subject-matter and a rejection of realism concerning that subject-matter; often one side in the dispute was conventionally labelled 'realist', though in other cases not. It appeared to me that no agreed method of settling these disputes was available, and that philosophers picked sides in them on the basis of predilection, not because they had discovered a means of resolving them. It further appeared to me that there was a striking parallelism in the arguments used on both sides in each of these disputes, so that, if one prescinded from the particular subject-matter, one could exhibit the abstract structure of the dispute. No two of the disputes seemed to me to be completely isomorphic, so as to have an identical abstract structure in common; but the structures were so similar that it seemed to me fruitful to propose that we should make a comparative study of them, from which, I hoped, principles would emerge for deciding in which cases the realist was in the right and in which cases his opponent.

I was understood, however, not as proposing a research programme, but as putting forward a specific philosophical thesis of great generality: not as suggesting a comparative study of a range of structurally similar problems case by case, but as advancing a single unitary thesis.

Delivered as a valedictory lecture in Oxford in Trinity Term, 1992.

On reflection, I concluded that this response was not wholly mistaken, but not wholly right, either. It was not wholly right, in that I viewed it, and still continue to view it, as a research programme, not the platform of a new philosophical party; I thus regarded the adversarial stance adopted by many who discussed the topic as inappropriate. That was precisely because I did not conceive myself as proposing for consideration, let alone sustaining, any precise thesis, to be accepted or rejected. I saw the matter, rather, as the posing of a question how far, and in what contexts, a certain generic line of argument could be pushed, where the answers "No distance at all" and "In no context whatever" could not be credibly entertained, and the answers "To the bitter end" and "In all conceivable contexts" were almost as unlikely to be right. Nevertheless, the common response was not wholly incorrect, either. What principally interested me, if it did not amount to a single overall thesis, was a fairly uniform *line* of argument, not a mere clutch of distinct theses about disparate subject-matters, united only by bearing a certain structural similarity to one another. I will try in this lecture to explain in more detail why the common response to my proposal strikes me as neither wholly right nor wholly wrong.

In attempting to delineate the common framework of the various disputes, I naturally labelled one side "realist"; for the other, I chose the deliberately colourless term "anti-realist". This was for two reasons. First, although in many cases the opponent of realism could be regarded as a species of idealist, this was not always so. For instance, one dispute that plainly exhibited the characteristic features common to others was that between realists about mental states and processes and behaviourists; and behaviourists are not naturally included under the generic characterization "idealists".

Secondly, the term "idealism" carried too many specific connotations, some of them irrelevant to the issue of realism, for my purpose. There is a sense of "idealism" in which it denotes the mirror-image of materialism: the doctrine that every truth is either included in, entailed by, or supervenient upon the totality of truths concerning what is immaterial. An idealist in this sense would be likely to reject a realist view of the physical universe, but would not be logically constrained to do so. If he did not, he would be a sophisticated, not a naïve, realist about it, just as, in the end, Berkeley was; but he would still be a realist. The term "idealist" was therefore unsuitable as a *general* label for the opponent of realism in each of these disputes. Moreover, I aimed at generality: I did not want to tie opposition to realism to any specific doctrine, but to consider any form that a rejection of realism might take.

In trying to describe the general form of disputes of the kind in which I was interested, I needed some generic means of referring to the particular subject-matter of any one such dispute. Very often, realism of a particular variety is referred to as realism about some particular class of putative entities—mental events, for example, or mathematical objects. I chose to speak instead of the "disputed class of statements", rather than of the "disputed class of objects". The motive was twofold.

1. In some cases—e.g., the dispute over realism concerning the future and that over realism concerning the past—there did not seem to be any objects in question; to count states of affairs as objects for this purpose would be mere sophistry, like the man imagined by Wittgenstein as saying that a ruler modifies our knowledge of length.

2. To characterize a type of realism as a thesis about (putative) objects of some kind focused attention, I thought, on the wrong issue. For example, a neo-Fregean platonist about mathematical objects, such as Wright or Hale, could still deny that they have any properties other than those we are capable of recognizing, whereas, conversely, a Dedekindian who maintained that mathematical objects are free creations of the human mind might nevertheless insist that, once created, they have properties independently of our capacity to recognize them. It appeared to me evident, and still appears to me evident, that, interesting as the questions about the nature of mathematical objects, and the ground of their existence, may be, the significant difference lies between those who consider all mathematical statements whose meaning is determinate to possess a definite truth-value independently of our capacity to discover it, and those who think that their truth or falsity consists in our ability to recognize it. Hence, from my standpoint, the Dedekindian would be a species of realist, and the neo-Fregean a species of constructivist. Put more generally, what reality consists in is not determined just by what objects there are, but by what propositions hold good: the world is the totality of facts, not of things. This was the reason for the concentration on acceptance or rejection of the principle of bivalence.

The formulation in terms of a class of statements, rather than of putative entities, and the emphasis on the underpinning of the logic that ought to be taken as governing those statements, made more plausible the strategy I recommended, of starting, not with the metaphysical status of the entities, but with the account to be given of the meanings of the statements. That was not the ground of the recommendation, however. Rather, since these metaphysical disagreements embodied divergent pictures of the reality to which the statements in question related, it seemed to me apparent that what underlay them were divergent pictures of the meanings of those statements. Since no means offered itself for deciding which picture of reality was correct, the more fruitful approach lay in determining which picture of meaning was, since in this case there was a theory of meaning to be constructed and a linguistic practice against which to check it.

What is a dispute of the relevant kind? A frequent philosophical move is to deny the status of statement to any member of a certain class of apparent assertables: on the one side, moral utterances (expressivists), and on the other conditionals (Ryle) and laws of nature (Ramsey). There is an important distinction between the two types. For expressivists, moral utterances express *attitudes* incapable of objective justification; but the proposal concerning conditionals and laws was that their content depended on what was required to justify them. Hilbert's account of unrestricted quantification over natural numbers provides the archetype of such a proposal: the speaker does not assert a state of affairs to obtain, but makes a *claim,* whose justification is perfectly objective; for instance, an unrestricted existential statement is justified if the one who makes it can produce an instance. The difference between utterances understood as embodying claims and statements proper is, on this view, that the latter have truth-conditions independent of the knowledge or abilities of the speaker, whereas the condition for a claim to be justified relates to what the speaker can do to vindicate his claim. The justification nevertheless concerns his *epistemic,* not his *affective* state; it is therefore wholly objective—he was right or wrong to make the claim.

Hilbert argued that, since utterances construed as making claims, such as arithmetical statements with unbounded quantifiers, are not understood as having truth-conditions, the sentential operators (Wittgenstein's 'calculus of truth-functions') could not be applied to them. The intuitionists denied this, however, proposing that all logical constants should be explained in terms of justification-conditions rather than truth-functionally. They thus rejected Hilbert's view that utterances embodying objectively assessable claims, but not possessing independent truth-conditions, could not qualify as statements; on the contrary, they proposed to interpret all mathematical statements in the former way, as embodying claims but not having independent truth-conditions. We need some terminology to distinguish these two types, or two interpretations, of assertoric utterances: let us call one embodying an objective claim a 'declaration', and one with independent truth-conditions an 'affirmation', using the term 'statement' to cover both.

Would a parallel reinterpretation of the logical constants be possible for expressivistically interpreted utterances? Peter Geach is famous for having argued that an expressivist interpretation of moral statements rules out the application to them of the sentential operators such as "if . . . then", and hence cannot account for such reasoning as "If telling lies is wrong, getting your little brother to tell lies must be wrong, too"; the argument is conclusive unless a suitable non-truth-functional reinterpretation of the sentential operators is to be found. Discussing the general category of what I called 'quasi-assertions', I once suggested that such a reinterpretation would be possible, a suggestion followed up by Blackburn. Even if it be so, the distinction between the subjectivist denial of statementhood to some utterance and the obectivist denial of the status of an affirmation to some statement would remain; all that would be gone is a simple knock-down argument against expressivism.

In the disputes about realism that interested me, the opponent of realism did not question fundamental objectivity: it has been common to both disputants that statements of the kind in dispute can, in favourable circumstances, be objectively established as true. Controversy between subjectivists and objectivists in ethics was therefore not an example of that kind of dispute. Crispin Wright, in recent lectures in Oxford, repudiated the strategy of declaring certain forms of utterance not to be genuine statements, maintaining that, in a thin sense of "statement", even expressivists, if they are to formulate their view correctly, ought to allow that moral utterances make statements. However this may be, the dispute between the subjectivist and the 'moral realist' is not one of those to which my comparative method was meant to apply: the issues in that dispute are different and *prior* to it.

Locating disputes over realism in the choice of a model for the meanings of statements of the disputed class tends to make the acceptance of bivalence a criterion for being a realist. More accurately, the criterion for having an anti-realist view becomes that of occupying a position that undercuts the ground for accepting bivalence. Phenomenalism is a case in point. Phenomenalists have not traditionally made any great objection to bivalence for material-object statements, and have sometimes overtly accepted it. I nevertheless wished to classify them as anti-realists, on the ground that their doctrine removed any rationale for accepting bivalence for such statements, and that, if they were consistent, they would reject it.

For all that, acceptance of bivalence should *not* be taken as a sufficient condition for realism: a generalization is required. For some time, I struggled to find a principled distinction between deep and shallow grounds for rejecting bivalence, the latter being compatible with realism and exemplified by the truth-value gap recognized, in different ways, by Frege and by Strawson, as induced by empty subject-terms. A plausible suggestion to this effect would be to make it a mark of the realist that he accepted, not bivalence, but the weaker principle that every unambiguous statement must be determinately either true or not true; let me dub this the principle of valence. This would allow the realist to favour a many-valued semantics which classified as false only a statement the application to which of what was recognized as a negation operator was true, and thereby flouted bivalence; for, after all, the use of more than two truth-values would merely systematize the effect of the sentential operators, and it would remain that the assertoric content of any statement was determined by the condition for it to be true. Moreover, the principle of valence would *allow* of the application of two-valued sentential operators, even if those actually existing in the language required a non-classical interpretation. A deep rejection of realism, by contrast, must have it that the classical logical constants would not even make sense.

It is undoubtedly correct that the distinction between one who accepts the principle of valence and one who rejects it is more profound than that between those who disagree about bivalence proper. Nevertheless, I came to think it mistaken to draw the line between realists and anti-realists at the former place rather than the latter. The admission of truth-value gaps in order to handle empty terms *was* a form of anti-realism—a rejection of Meinong's ultra-realism concerning possible objects. Russell indeed avoided being a realist about possible objects without impugning bivalence in the least degree. He did so by not countenancing definite descriptions as genuine singular terms, i.e., by interpreting sentences containing them otherwise than at face-value. I concluded that the true criterion for a realist interpretation of any given class of statements is an acceptance of classical two-valued semantics as applying to them in its entirety, where this includes construing apparent singular terms occurring in them at face-value, to be explained in terms of their referring to elements of the domain of quantification. This has the advantage of doing better justice to the intuition that realism has to do with the existence of objects, while retaining the insight, as I hope it to be, that rejection of bivalence is a salient feature of the deepest and most interesting forms of anti-realism.

The example shows that anti-realism can be manifested by a reinterpretation of statements of the disputed class, construing them not at face-value but as having a structure belied by their surface appearance; and this reinterpretation may serve to salvage bivalence. We should be aware that the descriptions 'realist' and 'anti-realist' are relative to what the philosophers to whom they are applied are being said to be, or not to be, realist about. Out of context, it would be wrong to deny that Frege, or Russell in 1905, was a realist: but, compared to Meinong, they were certainly both anti-realists concerning possible objects.

A formulation of bivalence must allow for vagueness. The thesis that every statement is determinately either true or false, even if it is vague, can be sustained only on the implausible supposition that our use of vague expressions confers on them meanings which determine precise applications for them that we ourselves do not know. A realist must therefore hold that, for every vague statement, there is a range of statements giving more precise information of which a determinate one is true and the rest false. An anti-realist may deny this, holding that reality may itself be vague, whereas, for the realist, vagueness inheres only in our forms of description.

The opinion is sometimes expressed that I succeeded in opening up a genuine philosophical problem, or range of problems, but that the resulting topic has little to do with traditional disputes concerning realism. That was certainly not my intention: I meant to apply a new technique to such wholly traditional questions as realism about the external world and about the mental questions which I continue to believe I characterized correctly. One immediately striking feature common to many traditional anti-realist arguments has been a reductionist account of statements of the disputed class. The anti-realist accuses the realist of interpreting those statements in the light of a conception of mythical states of affairs, not directly observable by us, rendering them true or false. According to the anti-realist, what makes them true or false are the observable states of affairs on the basis of which we judge of their truth-value. On the realist's interpretation, these merely provide *evidence* for the truth or falsity of the statements, or constitute an *indirect* means of judging them true or false; the anti-realist retorts that they are the most direct means there could be.

Behaviourism is typical. As Wittgenstein describes it, the realist conceives of mental events and mental processes on the analogy of physical events and processes, but in an immaterial medium, the individual's words and behaviour being evidence for these inner transactions; the behaviourist maintains that there is no such immaterial medium, and that the subject's words and behaviour, and, in certain cases, his physical condition, are what render our statements about his mental processes true.

Instrumentalism, the traditional alternative to a realist interpretation of the theoretical statements of science, likewise proposed to reduce them to statements about the grossly observable, such as readings of measuring devices. The same held good of radical formalism in mathematics, which proposed to reduce statements about mathematical entities such as real numbers, differential manifolds, groups, etc., to ones stating the derivability of individual formulae in a formal calculus—a reduction evidently vitiating bivalence whenever the calculus was incomplete. Phenomenalism, the traditional form of opposition to realism about the physical world, was equally obviously reductionist; but did it fit my characterization of the kind of anti-realism of which I proposed a comparative study? The issue of bivalence, for me central in all interesting cases, historically played little role in the debate over phenomenalism. To show that that debate nevertheless fitted my characterization, I argued that bivalence *ought* to have been an issue, since the phenomenalist had no principled reason to accept it; if he did so, that was mere logical inertia. Any reductionist thesis will lead to a repudiation of bivalence for statements of the disputed class, if there are occasions on which the (reductive) criterion for the truth neither of a given such statement nor of its negation is satisfied.

Philosophy abounds in anti-realist theses of this general form. It was the reductionist character of their traditional versions that made them so easy for the realists to refute. Phenomenalism proposed a reduction to a sense-datum language whose very intelligibility was shown by Wittgenstein's attack on the private ostensive definition to be unsustainable. The intelligibility of statements about behaviour and about formal calculi is not open to question; but, in both these cases, the proposed reduction showed itself implausible. Instrumentalism is the most interesting example. "The Sun" is not an indexical term in the ordinary sense: its denotation is constant from speaker to speaker. But it is indexical in an extended sense, in that its reference is fixed in terms of *our* position in the universe: it is the star that gives *us* light and heat. There is, at least as an ideal, a level of objectivity deeper than intersubjectivity: a form of description involving concepts that are not essentially dependent upon our perceptual abilities, position in space and time, and the like. The attainment of such a level of objectivity is the endeavour to describe the world as it is in itself; scientific realism credits science with striving for such an ideal, one to which it believes that we can approximate. The instrumentalist effort to repudiate this conception of the scientific endeavour is hampered, not merely by the gradual permeation of our 'common-sense' picture of the world by scientific concepts, but by the continuity of the striving of the scientist for an objective description with pre-scientific attempts to achieve greater objectivity in which we all engage—for example, with the transition from the concepts possessed by a child and their counterparts in an adult's understanding. This placed instrumentalists who were not, like Mach, also phenomenalists, in a delicate position; their problem was to discern where they must draw the line between what is unproblematically true and what, as purely theoretical, is a mere device for summarizing regularities exhibited by what is unproblematically true. No clear line presents itself between what they are proposing to reduce and what they are hoping to reduce it to; and so the reduction forfeits credibility.

This threatened that all the contests would end in victory for the realist before the comparative study had begin. There was, however, one form of anti-realism about mathematics, quite different from formalism, that was not reductionist: intuitionism (or, equally, the less adventurous version of constructivism advocated by Errett Bishop). Although intuitionists denied that we have any conception of truth for mathematical statements other than our possessing proofs of them, they did not postulate any language for describing proofs, to which the language of mathematics, taken as disjoint from it, could be reduced: they accepted mathematical concepts as indispensable, neither to be eliminated nor to be explained away. Instead, they propounded a new conception of what it is to understand a mathematical statement: not to know what it is for it to be true, independently of whether we are able to recognize its truth or falsity, but to know what is required to prove it. In the terms we used earlier, mathematical statements were to be interpreted as declarations, not as affirmations.

This means of rejecting a realist conception of mathematics appeared to me a prototype for a sustainable version of anti-realism in all other cases. The traditional anti-realist theories failed because of their reductionist form: but realism (including scientific realism) scored too easy a victory, because the reductive thesis was not essential to challenging realism. What was needed, therefore, was to undertake a comparative study, not of the disputes in their historical forms, but of versions of them in which the anti-realist view followed the intuitionist prototype in resting, not on a reduction of the disputed class of statements to those of some disjoint class, but on a non-realist, that is, non-truth-conditional, theory of meaning for them. It is a far from trivial matter to rebut the anti-realist arguments when divested of their reductionist guise, because it is at least highly plausible that a mastery of the use in practice of statements of the disputed class can be explained in terms of a grasp of what we take as establishing the truth of those statements; and since we accept mastery of use as confirming grasp of meaning, how can grasp of meaning involve more than mastery of use? The realist picture, though possibly faithful to our unreflective impression of what our understanding of statements of the disputed class consists in, will then fall away as superfluous, unless the anti-realist's challenge can be met; indignant expostulation is an inadequate response.

The charge that my enquiry did not concern realism as traditionally understood is thus mistaken: it concerned realism in precisely its traditional sense, but considered as facing, not the theories traditionally opposed to it, but emended versions of them.

Objectivity is an ingredient in the concept of truth, but does not of itself amount to it. An exponent of a sustainable anti-realism must have taken many strides in the direction of objectivity before his dispute with the realist begins; one reason why the traditional versions failed was their insufficient acknowledgement of this objectivity. The sense-datum language of the phenomenalists was an illusion because it was a solipsistic language, whereas human language, and hence the capacity for thoughts expressible in human language, is essentially communal, because essentially apt for communication. Thoughts are of their essence communicable; whether or not more than the most rudimentary thoughts are possible for those without language, *our* thought is shaped by the means for communicating it that we start to acquire in infancy. This means, not only that the experiential basis of knowledge must consist in *our* experience, not in *my* experience, but that experience can be characterized only as the experience of a common world inhabited by others as well as me; it is intrinsic to our grasp of our language that we take testimony as contributing to our stock of information.

Mathematics was the most propitious field for the development of an anti-realist theory of meaning precisely because the gap between the subjective and the objective is there at its narrowest. Brouwer was, notoriously, a solipsist, or something very close to one; but that did not vitiate his development of a theory of meaning for mathematical statements, and a consequent revisionist programme for mathematical practice. The reason is precisely the flagrant untruth of his solipsism. Far from its being the case, as Brouwer maintained, that mathematical constructions are only imperfectly communicable, the very opposite is true: they are *perfectly* communicable. Individual mathematicians may have different aptitudes, angles of attack, ranges of knowledge, etc., but they do not have different viewpoints on mathematical reality: whatever construction one mathematician discovers, any other is in a position to carry out. Just for this reason, it did not matter that Brouwer was conceiving his mathematical language solipsistically, as the analogue of a sense-datum language: by simply reversing the principle that mathematical language can only imperfectly convey mental constructions carried out by any one mathematician, it could without modification be interpreted as a language common to all mathematicians, and his theory of meaning understood in terms, not of individual mental constructions, but of constructions available to all.

As long as the disputes over realism concerning different subject-matters are treated as distinct, there is no reason to presume that all are to be resolved in the same sense: a realist about the physical world is under no compulsion to be a realist about mathematics or about mental events and states. The most a *general* argument for realism can do is to demonstrate its possibility in principle, never to show it to be correct in any particular case. By contrast, treating the topic as at bottom an issue about the representation of meaning does make possible a general argument for anti-realism, on the ground that a theory of meaning in terms of truth-conditions is never tenable.

This appears to yield a global form of anti-realism, of which the revised local anti-realisms would be merely particular applications. It would require displacing the notion of truth—of a statement's being true independently of our knowledge—from its central role in the explanation of meaning, substituting that of what we take as establishing truth: we should thus no longer be concerned with the criterion for the *truth* of a statement, but with the criterion for our recognizing it as true. That criterion would not be characterized as if each sentence had a meaning independently of the rest of the language: rather, a weak holism must be admitted, in accordance with Wittgenstein's dictum that to understand a sentence is to understand a language. The holism would only be weak, in that the language in question would not, in general, be the entire language to which the sentence belongs, but, rather, some fragment of it which could be, but was not, an entire language. The criterion for recognizing a statement as true would thus be whatever we actually count as establishing its truth, with no presumption that the process must be independent of language: it may well, and in general will, include inferences carried out in language.

The interpretation according to which I have been propounding a single philosophical thesis of very high generality seems thus to be vindicated. We appear to have arrived at a global anti-realism posing a challenge to realists as strong as, and more general than, those posed by the local anti-realisms, and rendering it unnecessary to pay any further attention to the purely local anti-realisms. This global anti-realism appears as a single unitary thesis, to the effect that a justificationist theory of meaning should supplant the generally received truth-conditional theory, on the ground that the obscurity of the general notion of a grasp of the condition for a statement to be true inhibits the received theory from yielding a plausible account of our understanding of language and our mastery of its use. The matter is then to be resolved by face-to-face combat between this general anti-realist theory of meaning and the truth-conditional theory, based on two-valued classical semantics, espoused by realists.

I have now to explain why this way of viewing the matter seems to me seriously mistaken. First, the thesis of global anti-realism has not merely to be *applied* to particular areas of language: it is no more than programmatic, and has to be *worked out* for different ranges of statement. Even a generalization of the constructive interpretation of the logical constants is far from straightforward. Ramsey long ago proposed an interpretation of conditionals as declarations rather than affirmations, virtually identical with the intuitionist understanding of them, and this is highly plausible as a representation of our use of conditionals in natural language. Negation, on the other hand, is highly problematic. In mathematics, given the meaning of "if . . . then", it is trivial to explain "Not *A*" as meaning "If *A*, then 0 = 1"; by contrast, a satisfactory explanation of "not," as applied to empirical statements for which bivalence is not, in general, taken as holding, is very difficult to arrive at. Given that the sentential operators cannot be thought of as explained by means of the two-valued truth-tables, the possibility that the laws of classical logic will fail is evidently open: but it is far from evident that the correct logical laws will always be the intuitionistic ones. More generally, it is by no means easy to determine what should serve as the analogue, for empirical statements, of the notion of proof as it figures in intuitionist semantics for mathematical statements. In mathematics, we may take as the property which a constructively valid proof is required to preserve from premisses to conclusion that of our having an effective means of devising a canonical proof. In the empirical case, however, a wholly constructive proof may lead from premisses that have been verified to a conclusion that cannot be directly verified, because its subject-matter is no longer accessible to observation. So, even where it makes sense to speak of a statement as having been conclusively established by direct means, we cannot without more ado take that property as the analogue of canonical proof for mathematical statements; and it is commonplace to observe that not all empirical statements can be conclusively established, even on the most generous reading of the term "conclusively".

A hostile critic might conclude from all this that the anti-realist theory of meaning is in at least as bad shape as the realist one, and hence that realism has nothing to fear until its opponents have clarified their views. This, however, is to insist on viewing the matter adversarially, to be fought out between two well-defined theories, whereas it remains, for me, a research programme. Justificationist and truth-conditional meaning-theories do not stand opposed to one another as rivals. Neither is a worked-out theory: the justificationist principle is an unavoidable starting point, the truth-conditional one no more than a hoped-for goal. Present-day truth-conditional meaning-theorists simply help themselves to what they have not earned. They ask neither what conception of truth is forced on us by the need to make sense of our linguistic practice—the practice we acquire as we grow to adulthood—nor what conception yields a credible account of that understanding which underlies out mastery of the practice. Their theories have the advantage that Russell famously called that of theft over honest toil, but make no serious contribution to philosophical comprehension of the functioning of language. We cannot hope to achieve any illumination by taking the notion of truth as given: we have to *win through* to that notion if we can, and in what form we can.

The notion of truth is not immediately given by the mere existence of a linguistic practice involving utterances of an assertoric character. That is sufficiently shown by the possibility, demonstrated by the intuitionists' way of construing mathematical statements in general, of interpreting a large range of statements, including ones of unlimited logical complexity, as declarations, rather than affirmations, that is, as embodying objective claims but not having independent truth-conditions. It is, indeed, open to doubt whether such an interpretation can be extended to non-mathematical statements; but it is a matter for investigation how far this can be done, and, if it cannot, what the obstacles are and just what notion of truth-conditions is called for.

A salutary lesson is provided by the controversy that has continued to surround indicative conditionals of natural language. Philosophers have continued to dispute what we should take the truth-conditions of such conditionals to be: in just which cases should an indicative conditional be considered true, and in which false? They asked this question because they were in the grip of a truth-conditional conception of meaning; and, if asked what they were investigating, they would have replied that it was the exact meaning of the indicative conditional form, as revealed by its truth-conditions. The fact was, however, that they were not in practice in the least doubt of its meaning. Philosophers who disagreed about the truth-conditions to be assigned to indicative conditionals did not, in ordinary converse, diverge in their understanding of particular conditional statements: they understood them in exactly the same way. The reason was that their understanding did not consist in any grasp of truth-conditions: in our terminology, they understood such utterances as declarations, embodying a certain claim on the part of the speaker, not as affirmations. Nothing in our use of indicative conditionals requires us to ascribe comprehensive truth-conditions to them; they therefore cannot be said to have truth-conditions, and any enquiry into what their truth-conditions are is doomed to futility.

We have therefore to start with an interpretation of the statements of our language as declarations, and enquire where and to what degree it falls short of being adequate. It is in this sense that a justificationist meaning-theory is an unavoidable starting-point. I am using the term "justificationist", which, to avoid misunderstanding, I have substituted for the word "verificationist" I have been accustomed to use, in the sense in which the intuitionist interpretation of mathematical statements may be termed 'justificationist': the meaning of a statement, on such a theory, is determined by what has to be done by a speaker to vindicate the claim that he makes by means of that statement.

We have, then, to start from that point and enquire how far it is necessary to move from it. To move from it can only mean that, in order to explain the meanings we attach to many of the forms of statement we employ, we find ourselves forced to adopt some notion of truth for them in terms of which we account for the principles underlying our use of them. The phrase "some notion of truth" is obviously exceedingly vague, and so I must provide some explanation of how I am understanding it. A stymie is laid by proponents of the minimalist theory of truth, who maintain that the sole notion of truth we have or can have is that for which the *whole* content of the term "true" is given by the fundamental equivalence between a statement *A* and the statement that *A* is true. Certainly, for any language that we already understand, it will almost always be possible to introduce a truth-predicate explained in this way; there is, for example, no difficulty about doing so for statements of intuitionistic mathematics. But such an explanation of "true" is plainly intended only for those who already know the language; unless I already understand the statement *A,* I cannot derive from the explanation the condition for it to be true, since that condition is stated by means of *A* itself. It follows at once that, if my grasp of the notion of truth had really been obtained in this way alone, my understanding of the language could not be explained in any manner that relied upon my grasp of it. That fits the language of intuitionistic mathematics very well, since it has a semantics not appealing to the notion of truth which can serve to explain the understanding of it I had before I was introduced to the truth-predicate as applying to it. It does not fit our ordinary employment of "true", however, for it fails to explain our knowledge that true statements can be made in every natural language (and many others), although we do not know all those languages. Paul Horwich, for example, refers, in a footnote, to someone ignorant of German who is told the condition for a certain German sentence to be true:[1] evidently, his understanding of the word "true", as applied to German sentences, cannot consist merely in his knowledge of the fundamental equivalence for English sentences. However this may be, in the present context we are concerned with notions that can be used to explain in what the meanings of statements framed in a natural language consist, and what constitutes a speaker's understanding of them; to such an explanation, the truth-predicate as interpreted by the minimalist is irrelevant.

What is at issue is the conception common to the speakers of a language of the contents of statements that can be made in it. The primary content of a statement is what is conveyed to a hearer who accepts an assertion of it as correct. We can also characterize it by what counts as the *ultimate* warrant for someone's assertion of it, that is, the ground of his knowledge when he first acquired it or the ground of the knowledge of the initiator of the information transmitted from one speaker to another (his *immediate* warrant may be merely that he remembers things as having been so or that he was told that things are so). Probably the best means of characterizing it is by appeal to that feature of statements which we require a valid argument to preserve from premisses to conclusion. Inferential reasoning (including non-deductive reasoning) may be direct or indirect. It is direct when it would be a step in the simplest means of warranting an assertion of the conclusion that accords with its composition out of its constituent words. For instance, the simplest means of warranting the assertion of a disjunctive statement is by whatever would warrant the assertion of one of its two clauses, followed by an application of the standard rule of "or"-introduction, which allows us to infer the statement "*A* or *B*" from the statement *A* or from the statement *B*. If we engaged only in direct inferential reasoning, then the property of a statement that a valid argument must preserve could be taken to be simply the existence of a direct warrant for asserting it; and the only notion of content it would be necessary to attribute to the statements of our language would be that determined by what we treated as such a warrant. In such a case, we should have a language whose statements could all be construed as declarations, in our sense: a theory of meaning for it would no more need any notion of truth going beyond that of the existence of a warrant for assertion than does the theory of meaning for intuitionistic mathematics.

Inferential reasoning has the value that it does, however, because it is usually indirect: a more direct warrant for the conclusion is conceivable, but not to hand. This has the effect that the property preserved by valid argument cannot be simply the existence of an ultimate warrant, since we draw conclusions for which there is in fact no such warrant from premisses that have them. Now is our practice justifiable, or is it simply what we do, without the need for any rationale? If it is simply what we do, then we need no notion of truth distinguishable from that of what, in accordance with our established practices, we treat as true; but we do not normally think in this nihilistic way. We take for granted that, in default of any demonstration that they are unreliable, our practices are faithful guides in a sense of "faithful" explicable without appeal to our engaging in them. In forming some conception of a property, weaker than our having a direct warrant, that a valid argument must preserve, we acquire an implicit grasp of a notion of truth.

This is not at all to say that the notion of truth required to account for our linguistic practice will be the full-blown realist conception. The realist helps himself to that conception by presuming that he has the right to use the notion of knowing what it is for something to be so without further explanation but, rather, as part of an explanation of what a speaker's understanding of a statement consists in; for instance, an understanding of the statement "There were once intelligent beings on Mars" will rest upon a knowledge of what it is for there once to have been intelligent beings on Mars. It is true that in everyday contexts we use the phrase "know what it is for . . . ", but here the direction of explanation is the opposite: "Don't you know what it is for *A* to be the case?" is simply a way of asking, "Don't you know what *A* means?" When it is required, conversely, as part of an explanation of understanding, however, the notion is *not* self-explanatory, and especially not in the context of a theory of meaning intended to explain in what our understanding of our mother tongue consists, so that the knowledge in question cannot be *verbalized* knowledge: if the notion is to be used at all, an account is required of what it is to have such knowledge, and it is quite obscure whether any can be given. Yet all proponents of a truth-conditional theory of meaning appeal to the notion of knowing what it is for . . . , save those who purport to explain meaning without attempting to explain understanding.

We cannot leap from a recognition that *some* notion of truth is needed for an account of our use of many of our statements to an embrace of full-fledged realism: rather, we have to undertake a research programme. We have to examine piecemeal which features of our linguistic practice call for a notion of truth, and what notion they call for, which is to say, how far that notion goes beyond the simple conception of the existence of a direct warrant. In the course of this investigation, we have, at each stage, to consider whether it is plausible to attribute to a speaker a grasp of such a notion of truth, and how his grasp of it is to be explained. All this is what I meant by saying that we have to *win through* to a notion of truth.

There is here a delicate balance to be maintained. Our object is to achieve a theory of meaning that accounts for our linguistic practice; but that practice is not sacrosanct when that object proves unattainable. Classical logic can be underpinned by other semantic theories than that which forms the base of truth-conditional meaning-theories, classical two-valued semantics: but such meaning-theories provide the most natural justification for our use of classical modes of reasoning that are not intuitionistically valid. Anyone who is prepared to say, "That is simply what we do", rejects all need for justification; and speaking of the complex web of theory and practice, within which neither can be distinguished from the other, is little more than a grandiose way of saying, "That is simply what we do". But one who cannot adopt this attitude, as I cannot, and who believes what I strongly suspect, that such meaning-theories are incapable of supplying a viable account of linguistic understanding, must either find an alternative semantics to justify our use of those modes of reasoning or declare our practice in this respect erroneous. I do not claim to have taken more than a few first steps in this research programme; my principal aim has been to convince my philosophical colleagues that such a programme is called for. That aim is frustrated when it is mistaken as the advocacy of a large and sharply defined philosophy.

NOTE

1. P. Horwich, *Truth* (Oxford, 1990), 73.

Reading Questions

1. Dummett claims that reality does not merely consist in what objects there are, but what propositions are true—that is, the world is a totality of facts, not of things. Why does he maintain this? How does this claim allow him to frame the realist/anti-realist debate in terms of sentences, statements, and meaning?
2. One traditional anti-realist strategy is to deny that certain sentences express propositions or make a statement. For example, moral expressivists deny that moral sentences express anything that could be objectively true or false. Dummett sets this stratagem aside as irrelevant to the realism issues he wants to address. He insists that both realists and anti-realists about some topic agree that sentences about that topic are meaningful ones. Why does he insist upon this? Is Dummett really offering a wholly general treatment of realism and anti-realism?
3. Bivalence is the principle that every statement is either true or false. Why does Dummett regard acceptance of this principle as a mark or indicator of realism? Why would allowing statements to have no truth value, or one other than *true* or *false,* be a form of anti-realism?
4. Dummett thinks that the rejection of bivalence is the heart of anti-realism. Thus he is at pains to show that traditional anti-realist arguments lead to a repudiation of bivalence. Exactly how does he argue that reductionism, as in the case of behaviorism or instrumentalism, fits this pattern?
5. Dummett contrasts two theories of meaning: (1) the justificationist theory, according to which the meaning of a statement is bound up with our criteria for recognizing the statement to be true, and (2) the truth-conditional theory, according to which the meaning of a statement is no more than the conditions under which the statement is true. The former is associated with anti-realism, and the latter with realism. Why does Dummett think that there is more to realism versus anti-realism than justificationism versus truth-conditionalism? What does he mean when he claims that these theories of meaning are "programmatic"?

Why There Isn't a Ready-Made World

5

HILARY PUTNAM

TWO IDEAS THAT HAVE BECOME a part of our philosophical culture stand in a certain amount of conflict. One idea, which was revived by Moore and Russell after having been definitely sunk by Kant and Hegel (or so people thought) is metaphysical realism, and the other is that there are no such things as intrinsic or 'essential' properties. Let me begin by saying a word about each.

What the metaphysical realist holds is that we can think and talk about things as they are, independently of our minds, and that we can do this by virtue of a 'correspondence' relation between the terms in our language and some sorts of mind-independent entities. Moore and Russell held the strange view that *sensibilia* (sense data) are such *mind-independent* entities: a view so dotty, on the face of it, that few analytic philosophers like to be reminded that this is how analytic philosophy started. Today material objects are taken to be paradigm mind-independent entities, and the 'correspondence' is taken to be some sort of causal relation. For example, it is said that what makes it the case that I refer to chairs is that I have causally interacted with them, and that I would not utter the utterances containing the word 'chair' that I do if I did not have causal transactions 'of the appropriate type' with chairs. This complex relationship—being connected with x by a causal chain of the appropriate type—between my word (or way of using the word) and x constitutes the relevant *correspondence* between my word and x. On this view, it is no puzzle that we can refer to physical things, but reference to numbers, sets, moral values, or anything not 'physical' is widely held to be problematical if not actually impossible.

This was a lecture delivered at the University of California, Berkeley, on 27 April 1981. It was the first of two Howison Lectures on "The Transcendence of Reason."

The second doctrine, the doctrine that there are no essential properties, is presaged by Locke's famous rejection of 'substantial forms'. Locke rejected the idea that the terms we use to classify things (e.g., 'man' or 'water') connote properties which are in any sense the 'real essences' of those things. Whereas the medievals thought that the real essence of water was a so-called substantial form, which exists both in the thing and *(minus* the matter) in our minds, Locke argued that what we have in our minds is a number of conventional marks (e.g., being liquid) which we have put together into a descriptive idea because of certain interests we have, and that any assumption that these marks are the 'real essence' of anything we classify under the idea is unwarranted.

Later empiricists went further and denied there was any place for the notion of an essence at all. Here is a typical way of arguing this case: 'Suppose a piece of clay has been formed into a statue. We are sure the piece of clay would not be what it is (a piece of clay) if it were dissolved, or separated into its chemical elements, or cut into five pieces. We can also say the *statue* would not be what it is *(that* statue) if the clay were squeezed into a ball (or formed into a different statue). But the piece of clay and the statue are *one* thing, not two. What this shows is that it only makes sense to speak of an "essential property" of something *relative to a description.* Relative to the description "that statue", a certain shape is an essential property of the object; relative to the description "that piece of clay", the shape is *not* an essential property (but being clay is). The question "what are the essential properties of the thing *in itself*" is a nonsensical one.'

The denial of essences is also a denial of intrinsic structure: an electron in my body has a certain electrical charge, but on the view just described it is a mistake to think that having that charge is an

From Realism and Reason: Philosophical Papers vol. 3 *by Hilary Putnam (Cambridge: Cambridge University Press, 1983). Reprinted by permission of Cambridge University Press and Professor Putnam.*

'intrinsic' property of the object (except *relative to the description* 'electron') in a way in which the property of being a part of my body is not. In short, it is (or was until recently) commonly thought that

> A thing is not related to any one of its properties (or relations) any more 'intrinsically' than it is to any of its other properties or relations.

The problem that the believer in metaphysical realism (or 'transcendental realism' as Kant called it) has always faced involves the notion of 'correspondence'. There are many different ways of putting the signs of a language and the things in a set S in correspondence with one another, in fact infinitely many if the set S is infinite (and a very large finite number if S is a large finite set). Even if the 'correspondence' has to be a reference relation and we specify which *sentences* are to correspond to *states of affairs which actually obtain,* it follows from theorems of model theory that there are still infinitely many ways of *specifying* such a correspondence.[1] How can we pick out any *one* correspondence between our words (or thoughts) and the supposed mind-independent things *if we have no direct access to the mind-independent things?* (German philosophy almost always began with a particular answer to this question—the answer 'we can't'—after Kant.)

One thing is clear: an act of will (or intention) won't work. I can't simply *pick* one particular correspondence C and *will* (or stipulate) that *C is to be* the designated correspondence relation, because in order to do that I would need *already* to be able to *think about* the correspondence C– and C, being a relation to things which are external and mind-independent, is itself something outside the mind, something 'external'! In short, if the mind does not have the ability to grasp external things or forms directly, then no *mental* act can give it the ability to single out a correspondence (or anything else external, for that matter).

But if the denial of intrinsic properties is correct, then no external thing or event is connected to any one relation it may have to other things (including our thoughts) in a way which is special or essential or intrinsic. If the denial of intrinsic properties is right, then it is not more essential to a mental event that it stand in a relation C_1, to any object x than it is that it stands in any other relation C_2 to any other object y. Nor is it any more essential to a non-mental object that it stand in a relation C to any one of my thoughts than it is that it stand in any one of a myriad other relations to any one of my other thoughts. On such a view, no relation C is metaphysically singled out as *the* relation between thoughts and things; reference becomes an 'occult' phenomenon.

The tension or incompatibility between metaphysical realism and the denial of intrinsic properties has not gone unnoticed by modern materialists. And for this reason we now find many materialists employing a metaphysical vocabulary that smacks of the fourteenth century: materialists who talk of 'causal powers', of 'built-in' similarities and dissimilarities between things in nature, even materialists who speak unabashedly of *essences.* In this lecture I want to ask if this modern mixture of materialism and essentialism *is consistent;* and I shall argue that it *isn't.*

WHY I FOCUS ON MATERIALISM

The reason I am going to focus my attack on materialism is that materialism is the only *metaphysical* picture that has contemporary 'clout'. Metaphysics, or the enterprise of describing the 'furniture of the world', the 'things in themselves' apart from our conceptual imposition, has been rejected by many analytic philosophers (though *not,* as I remarked, by Russell), and by all the leading brands of continental philosophy. Today, apart from relics, it is virtually only materialists (or 'physicalists', as they like to call themselves) who continue the traditional enterprise.

It was not always thus. Between the tenth and twelfth centuries the metaphysical community which included the Arabic Averroes and Avicenna, the Jewish Maimonides, and the Angelic Doctor in Paris disagreed on many questions, creation in particular. It was regarded as a hard issue whether the world always existed obeying the same laws (the doctrine ascribed to Aristotle), or was created from preexisting matter (the doctrine ascribed to Plato) or was created *ex nihilo* (the Scriptural doctrine). But the existence of a supersensible Cause of the contingent and moving sensible things was taken to be *demonstrable*. Speculative reason could *know* there was an Uncaused Cause.

When I was seven years old the question 'if God made the world, then who made God?' struck me one evening with vivid force. I remember pacing in circles around a little well for hours while the awful regress played itself out in my mind. If a medieval theologian had been handy, he would have told me that God was self-caused. He might have said God was the *ens necessarium*. I don't know if it would have helped; today philosophers would say that the doctrine of God's 'necessary' existence invokes a notion of 'necessity' which is incoherent or unintelligible.

The issue does, in a covert way, still trouble us. Wallace Matson (1967) ended a philosophic defense of atheism with the words, 'Still, why *is* there something rather than nothing?'. The doctrine that 'you take the universe you get' (a remark Steven Weinberg once made in a discussion) sounds close to saying it's some sort of metaphysical *chance* (we might just as well have *anything*). The idea of a supersensible Cause outside of the universe leads at once to the question that troubled me when I was seven. We don't even have the comfort of thinking of the universe as a kind of *ens necessarium: it* only came into existence a few billion years ago!

This situation was summed up by Kant: Kant held that the whole enterprise of trying to *demonstrate* the existence and nature of a supersensible world by speculation leads only to antinomies. (The universe *must* have a cause; but *that* cause would have to have a cause; but an infinite regress is no explanation and self-causation is impossible. . .) Today, as I remarked, only a few relics would challenge this conclusion, which put an end to rationalism as well as to the medieval synthesis of Greek philosophy with revealed religion.

This decline of medieval philosophy was a long process which overlapped the decline of medieval science (with its substantial forms). Here too Kant summed up the issue for our culture: the medievals (and the rationalists) thought the mind had an intellectual intuition (*intellektuelle Anschauung*), a sort of perception that would enable it to perceive essences, substantial forms, or whatever. But there is no such faculty. 'Nothing is in the mind that was not first in the senses *except the mind itself*', as Kant put it, quoting Leibniz.

Again, no one but a few relics challenge *this* conclusion. But Kant drew a bold corollary, and this corollary is hotly disputed to the present day.

The corollary depends upon a claim that Kant made. The claim can be illustrated by a famous observation of Wittgenstein's. Referring to the 'duck-rabbit' illusion (the figure that can be seen as either a duck or a rabbit), Wittgenstein remarked that while the physical image is capable of being seen either way, no 'mental image' is capable of being seen either way: the 'mental image' is always unambiguously a duck image or a rabbit image (*Philosophical Investigations* II, XI, 194–6). It follows that 'mental images' are really very different from physical images such as line drawings and photographs. We might express this difference by saying the interpretation is *built in* to the 'mental image'; the mental image is a *construction*.

Kant made the same point with respect to *memory*. When I have a memory of an experience this is not, contrary to Hume, *just* an image which 'resembles' the earlier experience. To be a memory the interpretation has to be 'built in': the interpretation that this is a *past* experience of *mine*. Kant (1933, Transcendental Deduction) argues that the notion of the *past* involves causality and that causality involves laws and objects (so, according to Kant, does the assignment of all these experiences to *myself*). Past experiences are not directly available; saying we 'remember' them is saying we have succeeded in constructing a version with causal relations and a continuing self in which they are located.

The corollary Kant drew from all this is that even experiences are in part constructions of the mind: I know what experiences I have and have had partly because I know what *objects* I am seeing and touching and have seen and touched, and partly because I know what *laws* these objects obey. Kant may have been over-ambitious in thinking he could specify the *a priori* constraints on the construction process; but the idea that all experience involves mental construction, and the idea that the dependence of physical object concepts and experience concepts goes *both* ways, continue to be of great importance in contemporary philosophy (of many varieties).

Since sense data and physical objects are interdependent constructions, in Kant's view, the idea that 'all we know is sense data' is as silly as the idea that we can have knowledge of objects that goes beyond experience. Although Kant does not put it this way, I have suggested elsewhere (Putnam, 1981, ch. 3) that we can view him as rejecting the idea of truth as correspondence (to a mind-independent reality) and as saying that the only sort of truth we can have an idea of, or use for, is *assertibility* (by creatures with our rational natures) *under optimal conditions* (as determined by our sensible natures). Truth becomes a radically epistemic notion.

However, Kant remarks that the *desire* for speculative metaphysics, the desire for a theory of the furniture of the world, is deep in our nature. He thought we should abandon the enterprise of trying to have speculative knowledge of the 'things in themselves' and sublimate the metaphysical impulse in the moral project of trying to make a more perfect world; but he was surely right about the strength of the metaphysical urge.

Contemporary materialism and scientism are a reflection of this urge in two ways. On the one hand, the materialist claims that physics is an approximation to a sketch of the one true theory, the true and complete description of the furniture of the world. (Since he often leaves out quantum mechanics, his picture differs remarkably little from Democritus': it's all atoms swerving in the void.) On the other hand, he meets the epistemological argument against metaphysics by claiming that we don't *need* an intellectual intuition to do *his* sort of metaphysics: his metaphysics, he says, is as open ended, as infinitely revisable and fallible, as science itself. In fact, it *is* science itself! (interpreted as claiming absolute truth, or, rather, claiming *convergence* to absolute truth). The appeal of materialism lies precisely in this, in its claim to be *natural* metaphysics, metaphysics within the bounds of science. That a doctrine which promises to gratify both our ambition (to know the noumena) and our caution (not to be unscientific) should have great appeal is hardly something to be wondered at.

This wide appeal would be reason enough to justify a critique of metaphysical materialism. But a second reason is this: metaphysical materialism has replaced positivism and pragmatism as the dominant contemporary form of scientism. Since scientism is, in my opinion, one of the most dangerous contemporary intellectual tendencies, a critique of its most influential contemporary form is a duty for a philosopher who views his enterprise as more than a purely technical discipline.

CAUSATION

What makes the metaphysical realist a *metaphysical* realist is his belief that there is somewhere 'one true theory' (two theories which are true and complete descriptions of the world would be mere notational variants of each other). In company with a correspondence theory of truth, this belief in one true theory requires a *ready-made* world (an expression suggested in this connection by Nelson Goodman): the world itself has to have a 'built-in' structure since otherwise theories with different structures might correctly 'copy' the world (from different perspectives) and truth would lose its absolute (non-perspectival) character. Moreover, as I already remarked, 'correspondence' between our symbols and something which has no determinate structure is hardly a well-defined notion.

The materialist metaphysician often takes *causal relations* as an example of built-in structure. Events have causes; objects have 'causal powers'. And he proudly proclaims his realism about these, his faith that they are 'in' the world itself, in the metaphysical realist sense. Well, let us grant him that this is so, for the sake of argument: my question for the moment is not whether this sort of realism is justified, but whether it is really compatible with materialism. Is *causation* a physical relation?

In this discussion, I shall follow the materialist in ignoring quantum mechanics since it has *no* generally acceptable interpretation of the kind the realist advocates:[2] the standard (Copenhagen) interpretation makes essential reference to *observers*, and the materialist wants to imagine a physics in which the observer is simply another part of the system, as seen from a God's eye view. Physics is then a theory whose fundamental magnitudes are defined at all points in space and time; a property or relation is physically definable if it is definable in terms of these.[3]

I shall also assume that the fundamental magnitudes are basically the usual ones: if no restraint at all is placed on what counts as a possible 'fundamental magnitude' in future physics, then *reference* or *soul* or *Good* could even be 'fundamental magnitudes' in future physics! I shall not allow the naturalist the escape hatch of letting 'future physics' mean we-know-not-what. Physicalism is only intelligible if 'future physics' is supposed to resemble what *we* call 'physics'. The possibility of natural metaphysics (metaphysics within the bounds of science) is, indeed, not conclusively refuted by showing that present-day materialism cannot be a correct sketch of the one true (metaphysical) theory: but present-day materialism is, as already remarked, the view with clout.

Now if '*A* causes *B*' simply meant 'whenever an *A*-type event happens, then a *B*-type event follows in time', 'causes' would be physically definable. Many attempts have been made to give such a definition of causation—one which would apply to genuine causal laws while not applying to sequences we would regard as coincidental or otherwise non-causal. Few philosophers believe today that this is possible.

But let us assume that 'causes' (in this sense) *is* somehow physically definable. A cause, in the sense this definition tries to capture, is a *sufficient* condition for its effect; whenever the cause occurs, the effect *must* follow (at least in a deterministic world). Following Mill, let us call such a cause a *total cause*. An example of a total cause at time t_0 of a physical event e occurring at a later time t_1, and a point x would be the entire distribution of values of the dynamical variables at time t_0 (inside a sphere S whose center is x and whose radius is sufficiently large so that events outside the sphere S could not influence events at x occurring at t_1 without having to send a signal to x faster than light, which I assume, on the basis of relativity, to be impossible).

Mill pointed out that in ordinary language 'cause' rarely (if ever) means 'total cause'. When I say 'failure to put out the campfire caused the forest fire', I do *not* mean that the campfire's remaining lit during a certain interval was the *total cause* of the forest fire. Many other things—the dryness of the leaves, their proximity to the campfire, the temperature of the day, even the presence of oxygen in the atmosphere—are part of the *total* cause of the forest fire. Mill's point is that we regard certain parts of the total cause as 'background', and refer only to the part of interest as 'the' cause.

Suppose a professor is found stark-naked in a girl's dormitory room at midnight. His being naked in the room at midnight—ε, where ε is so small that he could neither get out of the room or put on his clothes between midnight—ε and midnight without moving faster than light, would be a 'total cause' of his being naked in the girl's room at midnight; but no one would refer to this as the 'cause' of his presence in the room in that state. On the other hand, when it is said that the presence of certain bodies of H_2O in our environment 'causes' us to use the word 'water' as we do, it is certainly *not* meant that the presence of H_2O is the 'total cause'. In its ordinary sense, 'cause' can often be paraphrased by a locution involving *explain;* the presence of H_2O in our environment, our dependence on H_2O for life, etc., are 'part of' the *explanation* of our having a word which we use as we use the word 'water'. The forest fire is *explained* (given background knowledge) by the campfire's not having been extinguished; but the professor's state at midnight—ε is not what we consider an *explanation* of the state of affairs at midnight.

When it is said that a word refers to x just in case the (use of the) word is connected to x by a 'causal chain of the appropriate type', the notion of 'causal chain' involved is that of an *explanatory* chain. Even if the notion of 'total cause' *were* physically definable, it would not be possible to *use* it either in daily life or in philosophy; the notion the materialist really uses when he employs 'causal chain', etc., in his philosophical explications is the intuitive notion of an *explanation*.

But this notion is certainly not physically definable. To see that it isn't, observe, first, that 'explains' (and 'caused', when it has the force of 'explains why x happened') are abstract notions. Even when we imagine a possible world in which there are non-physical things or properties, we can conceive of these things and properties *causing* things to happen. A disembodied spirit would not have *mass* or *charge,* but (this is a conceptual question of course; I don't mean to suggest there *are* disembodied spirits) it could *cause* something (say, an emotional reaction in another spirit with which it communicated telepathically).

A definition of 'caused' (in this 'explanatory' sense) which was too 'first order', too tied to the particular magnitudes which are the 'fundamental magnitudes' of physics in *our* world, would make it *conceptually impossible* that a disembodied spirit (or an event involving magnitudes which are not 'physical' in *our* world) could be a cause. This is why the suggested Humean definition of *total* cause—*A* is the (total) cause of *B* if and only if an *A*-type event is always followed in time by a *B*-type event—contained no *specific* physical term (except 'time'): this definition *is* abstract enough to apply to possible worlds different from our own. (Although it fails even so.) Could there be an equally abstract (and more successful) definition of 'cause' in the explanatory sense?

Imagine that Venusians land on Earth and observe a forest fire. One of them says, '*I* know what caused that—the atmosphere of the damned planet is saturated with oxygen.'

What this vignette illustrates is that one man's (or extraterrestrial's) 'background condition' can easily be another man's 'cause.' What is and what is not a 'cause' or an 'explanation' depends on background knowledge and our reason for asking the question.

No purely *formal* relation between events will be sensitive to this relativity of explanatory arguments to background knowledge and interests.

Nelson Goodman has shown that no purely formal criterion can distinguish arguments which are intuitively sound inductive arguments from unsound arguments: for every sound inductive argument there is an unsound one of the very same form. The actual predicates occurring in the argument make the difference, and the distinction between 'projectible' and 'non-projectible' predicates is not a formal one. It is not difficult to show that the same thing is true of *explanations.* If we think of explanation as relation in 'the world', then to define it one would need a predicate which could sort projectible from non-projectible properties; such a predicate could not be purely formal for then it would run afoul of Goodman's result, but it could not involve the particular fundamental magnitudes in *our* world in an essential way for then it would be open to counterexamples in other possible worlds.

'NON-HUMEAN' CAUSATION

Richard Boyd (1980) has suggested that the whole enterprise of *defining* causation was a mistake: physicalists should simply take the notion as a primitive one. He may only mean that to insist on a definition of 'causes' (or anything else) in the standard formalism for mathematics and physics (which contains *names* for only countably many real numbers, etc.) is unreasonable: if so, this would not be an argument against expecting every *physical* property and relation to be definable in an *infinitary extension* of physics, a language which allows *infinitely long* names and sentences. (Indeed, if a property or relation is *not* physically definable even in this liberal sense, what is meant by calling it 'physical'?) But he may have meant that one should literally take 'causes' as an irreducible notion, one whose failure to be physically definable is not due to syntactic accidents, such as the limit on the length of formulas. But can a philosopher who accepts the existence of an irreducible phenomenon of *causation* call himself a materialist?

'Causes', we have just seen, is often paraphrasable as 'explains'. It rarely or never means 'is the total cause of'. When Boyd, for example, says that a certain micro-structure is a 'causal power' (the micro-structure of sugar is a 'causal power' in Boyd's sense, because it *causally explains* why sugar dissolves in water) he does not mean that the micro-structure in question is the *total cause* of the explained events (sugar will not dissolve in water if the water is *frozen,* for example, or if the water is already saturated with sugar, or if the water-cum-sugar is in an exotic quantum mechanical state). 'Causal powers' are properties that *explain* something, given background conditions and given standards of salience and relevance.

A metaphysical view in which 'causation' and 'causal explanation' are built into the world itself is one in which explanation is wrenched out of what

Professor Frederick Will (1974) has called 'the knowledge institution', the inherited tradition which defines for us what is a background condition and what a salient variable parameter, and projected into the structure of reality. Boyd would probably reply that the 'causal structure' of reality *explains* the success of the knowledge institution: our successful explanations simply copy the built-in causal structure.

Be that as it may, salience and relevance are attributes of thought and reasoning, not of nature. To project them into the realist's 'real world', into what Kant called the *noumenal* world, is to mix objective idealism (or, perhaps, medieval Aristotelianism) and materialism in a totally incoherent way. To say 'materialism is *almost* true: the world is completely describable in the language of physics *plus* the one little added notion that some events intrinsically *explain* other events' would be ridiculous. This would not be a 'near miss' for materialism, but a total failure. If events *intrinsically* explain other events, if there are saliencies, relevancies, standards of what are 'normal' conditions, and so on, built into the world itself independently of minds, then the world is in many ways *like* a mind, or infused with something very much like reason. And if *that* is true, then materialism *cannot* be true. One can try to revive the project of speculative metaphysics, if one wishes: but one should not pass *this* sort of metaphysics off as (future) *physics*.

COUNTERFACTUALS AND 'SIMILARITY'

Suppose I take a match from a new box of matches (in perfect condition), break it, and throw the pieces in the river. After all this, I remark, 'If I had struck that match (instead of breaking it, etc.) it would have lit'. Most of us would say, 'true', or 'probably true'. But what does the statement actually assert?

A first stab at an explication might go as follows: the statement is true if it follows from physical laws (assume these to be given by a list—otherwise there are further problems about 'laws') that if the match is struck (at an average [for me?] angle, with an average amount of force) against that striking surface, then it ignites. But this doesn't work: even if we describe the match down to the atomic level, and ditto for the striking surface and the angle and force involved, there are still many other relevant variables unmentioned. (Notice the similarity to the problem of 'cause' as 'total cause': the statement '*A* caused *B*', and the statement 'If *X* had happened, *Y* would have happened' have simple truth conditions when *all* the 'background conditions'—and all the 'laws'—are specified; but typically they *aren't* specified, and the speaker can't even conceive of *all* of them.) If no oxygen molecules happen to be near the top of the match, or if the entire match-cum-striking-surface-cum-atmosphere system is in a sufficiently strange quantum mechanical state, etc., then the match *won't* ignite (even if struck with that force, at that angle, etc.).

One is tempted to try: 'It follows from the physical laws that if the match is struck against that surface (at the specified force and angle) and everything is *normal* then the match ignites', but this brings the very strange predicate 'normal' into the story. Besides, maybe conditions *weren't* 'normal' (in the sense of 'average') at the time. (In infinitely many respects, conditions are *always* 'abnormal': a truism from statistical theory). Or one is tempted to say: 'It follows from the laws that if the match is struck against that surface (with the specified force and at the specified angle), and *everything else is as it actually was at the time,* then the match must ignite.' But, as Nelson Goodman (1947) pointed out in a celebrated paper on this logical question, *everything* else *couldn't* be as it was at the time if the match were struck. The gravitational fields, the quantum mechanical state, the places where there were oxygen molecules in the air, and infinitely many other things *couldn't have been* 'as they actually were at the time' if the match had been struck.

The reason I mention this is that David Lewis (in 'Causation', *Journal of Philosophy* LXX, 1973) proposed to analyze 'causes' using precisely this sort of contrary-to-fact conditional. The idea is that '*A* caused *B*' can be analyzed as 'if *A had not* happened, *B would not have* happened'.

Actually, this doesn't seem right. (Even if *A* caused *B*, there are situations in which it just isn't true that if *A* hadn't happened, *B* wouldn't have happened.[4] But suppose it were right, or that, if it isn't right, contrary-to-fact conditionals can at any rate be used to explicate the notions that we wanted to use the notion of causality to explicate. How are the truth conditions for contrary-to-fact conditionals *themselves* to be explicated?

One famous materialist, John Mackie (1974), thinks contrary-to-fact conditionals aren't true or false. He regards them as ways of indicating what inferences are allowable in one's knowledge situation, rather than as asserting something true or false in the realist sense, independently of one's knowledge situation. 'If I had struck that match it would have lit' indicates that my *knowledge situation* is such that (if I delete the information about what actually happened to the match) an inference from 'the match was struck' to 'the match ignited' would be *warranted*. The contrary-to-fact conditional signals the presence of what Wilfred Sellars calls a 'material rule of inference'. It has *assertibility conditions,* rather than truth conditions in the sense of absolute truth semantics.

Mackie, who follows Lewis in using counterfactuals to analyze 'causes', concludes that *causation* (in the ordinary sense) is something *epistemic,* and not something in the world at all. But he believes there is another notion of causation, 'mechanical causation', which is in the world. (It has to do with energy flow; as Mackie describes it, it is hard to see either what it is, or that it could be spelled out without using counterfactuals,[5] which would be fatal to Mackie's project of having a non-epistemic notion of causation.)

But Lewis, following Professor Robert Stalnaker, chooses to give *truth conditions* for contrary-to-fact conditionals. He postulates that there actually exist 'other possible worlds' (as in science fiction), and that there is a 'similarity metric' which determines how 'near' or how 'similar' any two possible worlds are (Lewis, 1973). A contrary-to-fact conditional, 'If *X* had happened, then *Y* would have happened', is true just in case *Y* is *actually* true in all the *nearest* 'parallel worlds' to the actual world in which *X* is actually true.

To me this smacks more of science fiction than of philosophy. But one thing is clear: a theory which requires an ontology of parallel worlds and a built-in 'similarity metric' certainly does not have a *materialist* ontology. More important, it does not have a *coherent* ontology: not only is the actual existence of parallel worlds a dotty idea, but the idea of an *intrinsic* similarity metric, a metric highly sensitive to what we regard as relevant conditions, or normal conditions, one which gives weight to what sorts of features *we* count as similarities and dissimilarities between states of affairs, is one which once again implies that the world is like a mind, or imbued with something very much like reason. And if *this is* true, then it must have a (suitably metaphysical) *explanation*. Objective idealism can hardly be a *little bit* true. ('It's all physics, except that there's this similarity metric' just doesn't make *sense.)*

ESSENCES AND OBJECTS

In this philosophical culture, the denial of intrinsic or 'essential' properties began with examples like the example of the thing whose shape is an 'essential' property under *one* description ('that statue') but not under a different description ('that piece of clay'). One philosopher who thinks a wholly wrong moral was drawn from this example is Saul Kripke.

According to Kripke, the statue and the piece of clay are two objects, not one. The fact that the piece of clay has a modal property, namely the property 'being a thing which *could have been* spherical in shape', which the statue lacks (I assume this is not one of those contemporary statues) already proves the two objects cannot be identical, in Kripke's view.

Now, this sounds very strange at first hearing. If I put the statue on the scale, have I put *two objects* on the scale? If the piece of clay weighs 20 pounds and the statue weighs 20 pounds, why doesn't the scale read 40 and not 20 if both objects are on it right now? But what Kripke has in mind is not silly at all.

First of all, it also sounds strange to be told that a human being is not identical with the aggregation of the molecules in his body. Yet on a moment's reflection each of us is aware that he was not *that* aggregate of molecules a day ago. Seven years ago, precious few of those molecules were in my body. If after my death that exact set of molecules is assembled and placed in a chemical flask, it will be the same aggregation of molecules, but it won't be *me.* David Lewis (1976) has suggested that I and the aggregation of molecules are 'identical for a period of time' in somewhat the way that Highway 2 and Highway 16 can be 'identical for a stretch'; as he points out, 'identity for a time' is not strict logical identity. If *A* and *B* are identical in the strict sense, every property of *A* is a property of *B;* but it is not the case that every property of the aggregation of molecules is a property of *me.*

Just as we can recognize that I am not the same object as the aggregation of molecules in my body without denying that I *consist* of those molecules right now (the difference between the objects lies in the different statements that are true of them, not in their physical distinctness), so, one can agree with Kripke that the statue is not the same object as the piece of clay without denying that the piece of clay is the matter of the statue; once again the difference between the objects lies in the different statements that are true of them, not in their physical distinctness.

But now it begins to look as if objects, properly individuated, *do* have essences, do have some properties in a special way. Can Kripke's doctrine be of aid to materialism? (Kripke himself is quite averse to materialism, as is well known.)

A materialist whose ontology includes 'possible worlds' might introduce suitable intensional objects by identifying them with functions taking possible worlds as arguments and space–time regions in those worlds as values. Thus, the statue would be the function defined on each possible world *Y* in which the statue exists, whose value on *Y* is the space–time region occupied by the statue in *Y.* This would, indeed, make the 'statue' and the 'piece of clay' different 'objects' (different logical constructions) even if they occupy the same space-time region in the actual world, since there are other possible worlds in which they do not occupy the same space–time region.

But functions of this kind are standardly used in modern semantics to represent *concepts.* No one doubts that the *concept* 'that statue' is a different *concept* from the *concept* 'that piece of clay'; the question is whether there is some *individual* in the actual world to which one of these concepts *essentially* applies while the other only accidentally applies. The space–time region itself is *not* such an individual; and it is hard to see how a materialist is going to find one in *his* ontology.

Moreover, clever logical constructions are no answer to the philosophical difficulty. Doubtless one can come up with as many 'objects' as one wants given 'possible worlds' plus the resources of modern set theory (the difficulty, indeed, is that one can come up with *too many).* Consider the metaphysical claim that my thoughts have some sort of intrinsic connection with external objects. If the events that take place in my brain are in a space–time region that has a set-theoretic connection with some abstract entity that involves certain external objects, then that same space–time region will have similar set-theoretic connections with some other abstract entities that involve some other external objects. To be sure, the materialist can say that my 'thoughts' *intrinsically* involve certain external objects by *identifying them* (the thoughts) with one abstract entity and not with another; but if this identification is supposed to be a feature of reality itself, then there must really *be* essences in the world in a sense which pure set theory can't hope to explicate.

The difficulty is that Kripke individuates objects *by their modal properties,* by what they (essentially) *could* and *could not* be. Kripke's ontology *presupposes* essentialism; it cannot be used to ground it. And modal properties are not, on the face of it, part of the materialist's furniture of the world.

But, I will be reminded, I have myself spoken of 'essential properties' elsewhere (see Putnam, 1975*a*). I have said that there are possible worlds (possible *states* of the world, that is, not parallel worlds à la Lewis) in which some liquid other than H_2O has the taste of water (we might have different taste buds, for example), fills the lakes and rivers, etc., but no possible world in which *water* isn't H_2O. Once we have discovered what water is in the actual world, we have discovered its *nature:* is this not essentialism?

It *is* a sort of essentialism, but not a sort which can help the materialist. For what I have said is that it has long been our *intention* that a liquid should *count* as 'water' only if it has the same composition as the paradigm examples of water (or as the majority of them). I claim that this was our intention even before we *knew* the ultimate composition of water. If I am right then, *given those referential intentions,* it was always impossible for a liquid other than H_2O to be water, even if it took empirical investigation to find it out. But the 'essence' of water in *this* sense is the product of our use of the word, the kinds of referential intentions we have: this sort of essence is not 'built into the world' in the way required by an *essentialist theory of reference itself* to get off the ground.

Similarly, Kripke has defended *his* essentialist theories by arguments which turn on speakers' referential intentions and practices; to date he has carefully refrained from trying to provide a metaphysical theory of reference (although he does seem to believe in mind-independent modal properties). I conclude that however one takes Kripke's theories (or mine); whether one takes them metaphysically, as theories of objective 'essences' which are somehow 'out there', or one takes them as theories of our referential practices and intentions, they are of no help to the materialist. On the metaphysical reading they are realist enough, but their realism is not of a materialist sort; on the purely semantical reading they *presuppose* the notion of reference, and cannot be used to support the metaphysical explanation of reference as intrinsic correspondence between thought and thing.

REFERENCE

Some metaphysical materialists might respond to what has been said by agreeing that '*A* causes *B*' does *not* describe a simple 'relation' between *A* and *B*. 'All you're saying is that causal statements *rest on* a distinction between background conditions and differentiating factors, and I agree that this distinction isn't built into the things themselves, but is a reflection of the way we think about the things', such a philosopher might say. But here he has used the words 'think about', i.e., he has appealed to the notion of *reference.*

The contemporary metaphysical materialist thinks about reference in the following way: the brain is a computer. Its computations involve *representations.* Some of these (perhaps all) are 'propositional': they resemble sentences in an internal *lingua mentis.* (They have been called 'sentence-analogs'.) Some of them could be sentences in a public language, as when we engage in interior monolog. A person refers to something when, for example, the person thinks 'the cat is on the mat' (the sentence-analog is 'subvocalized') and the entire organism-cum-environment situation is such that the words 'the cat' in the particular sentence-analog stand in a physical relation *R* (the relation of *reference*) to some cat and the words 'the mat' stand in the relation *R* to some mat.

But what is this relation *R*? And what on earth could make anyone think it is a *physical* relation?

Well, there is *one* way in which *no one,* to my knowledge, would try to define *R*, and that is by giving a list of all possible reference situations. It is useful, however, to consider why not. Suppose someone proposed to define reference (for some set of languages, including '*lingua mentis*') thus:

> *X refers to Y if and only if X is a (token) word or word-analog and Y is an object or event and the entire situation (including the organism that produced X and the environment that contains Y) is S_1 or S_2 or S_3 or . . . (infinite—possibly non-denumerably infinite—list of situations, described at the level of physics).*

There are (at least) three things wrong with this.

First, besides the fact that the list would have to be infinite, such a list would not tell us what the situations S_1, S_2, . . . *had in common.* To define a physical property or relation by *listing* the situations in which it is found is not to say what it *is.* In fact, the materialists themselves object to *Tarski's* definition of reference on just this ground: that Tarski defines primitive reference (for a fixed language), by a list of cases, and, as Hartry Field (1972a, p. 363) writes,

> Now, it would have been easy for a chemist, late in the last century, to have given a 'valence definition' of the following form:

(3) $(E)\ (n)\ (E$ has valence $n \equiv E$ is potassium and n is $+1$, or . . . or E is sulphur and n is $-2)$

where in the blanks go a list of similar clauses, one for each element. But, though this is an extensionally correct definition of valence, it would not have been an acceptable reduction; and had it turned out that nothing else was possible—had all efforts to explain valence in terms of the structural properties of atoms proved futile—scientists would have eventually had to decide either (a) to give up valence theory, or else (b) to replace the hypothesis of physicalism by another hypothesis (chemicalism?). It is part of scientific methodology to resist doing (b); and I also think it is part of scientific methodology to resist doing (a) as long as the notion of valence is serving the purposes for which it was designed (i.e., as long as it is proving useful in helping us characterize chemical compounds in terms of their valences). But the methodology is not to resist (a) and (b) by giving lists like (3); the methodology is to look for a real reduction. This is a methodology that has proved extremely fruitful in science, and I think we'd be crazy to give it up in linguistics. And I think we are giving up this fruitful methodology, unless we realize that we need to add theories of primitive reference to T_1 or T_2 if we are to establish the notion of truth as a physicalistically acceptable notion.

Secondly, it would be philosophically naïve to think that such a list could answer any *philosophical* question about reference. For example, one could hold Quine's view, that there are definite *true* and *false* sentences[6] in science, but *no* determinate reference relation (the true sentences have infinitely many models, and there is no such thing as *the* model, in Quine's view), and still accept the list. Quine would simply say that the terms used to describe the situations S_1, S_2, . . . etc., refer to different events in different models; thus the list, while correct in *each* admissible model, does not define a *determinate* reference relation (only a determinate reference relation *for each model*). Now Quine's view may be right, wrong, or meaningless; the question of the truth or falsity of metaphysical realism may be meaningful or meaningless (and if meaningful, may have a realist or a non-realist answer), but a list of cases (either this list or the one involved in the Tarskian truth definition referred to by Field), cannot speak to *this* issue. To think that it can is analogous to thinking (as G. E. Moore did) that one can refute Berkeley by holding up one's hand and saying 'This is a material object. Therefore matter exists.' This is, as Myles Burnyeat has put it, 'to philosophize as if Kant had never existed'. For better or worse, philosophy has gone second order.

Thirdly, the list is *too specific*. Reference is as 'abstract' as causation. In possible worlds which contain individual things or properties which are not physical (in the sense of 'physical$_2$':[7] not definable in terms of the fundamental magnitudes of the physics of the actual world), we could still *refer*: we could refer to disembodied minds, or to an emergent non-material property of Goodness, or to all sorts of things, in the appropriate worlds. But the relevant situations could not, by hypothesis, be completely described in terms of the fundamental magnitudes of the physics of *our* world. A definition of reference from which it followed that we could not refer to a non-physical magnitude if there were one is just *wrong*.

I know of only one realist who has sketched a way of defining reference which meets these difficulties, and that is David Lewis (1974). Lewis proposes to treat reference as a *functional* property of the organism-cum-environment-situation.

Typical examples of functional properties come from the world of computers. Having a particular program, for example, is a functional (or in computer jargon a 'software' property) as opposed to an ordinary first-order physical property (a 'hardware' property). Functional properties are typically defined in batches; the properties or 'states' in a typical batch (say, the properties that are involved in a given computer program) are characterized by a certain *pattern*. Each property has specified cause and effect relations to the other properties in the pattern and to certain non-functional properties (the 'inputs' and 'outputs' of the programs).

Lewis' suggestion is that *reference* is a member of such a batch of properties: not functional properties of the organism, but functional properties of the organism–environment system. If this could be shown, it would answer the question of what all the various situations in which something refers to something else 'have in common': what they would have in common is something as abstract as a program, a scheme or formal pattern of cause–effect relationships. And if this could be shown, it would characterize reference in a way that makes it sufficiently abstract; the definition would not require any particular set of magnitudes to be the fundamental ones any more than the abstract description of a computer program does. Whether the second difficulty I noted would be met, I shall not attempt to judge.

The crucial point is that functional properties are defined *using the notions of cause and effect.* This is no problem for Lewis; Lewis believes he can define cause and effect using counterfactuals, and, as already mentioned, he gives truth conditions for counterfactuals in terms of a primitive notion of 'similarity of possible worlds'. Since he has a non-physical primitive in his system, he does not have to show that any of the notions he uses is physically definable. But the notion of 'similarity of possible worlds' is not one to which the materialist is entitled; and neither is he entitled to counterfactuals or to the notion of 'functional organization'.

As Charles Fried remarked in his Tanner Lectures,[8] it is easy to *mistake* causality for a physical relation. *Act, smash, move,* etc., are causal verbs and describe events which are clearly physical ('Smashed', for example, conveys two kinds of information: the information that *momentum* was transferred from one thing to another, which is purely physical information, and the information that the *breaking* of the second thing was *caused* by the momentum transfer.) As Fried points out, the causal judgment may be quite complicated in cases when both objects were in motion before the collision. Once one has made the error of taking causality to be a physical relation, it is easy to think that functional properties are simply higher-order physical properties (an error I myself once committed), and then to think that reference (and just about anything else) may be a functional property and hence physical. But once one sees this is an error, there is no vestige of a reason that I know of to think reference is a physical relation.

If the materialist cannot *define* reference, he can, of course, just take it as *primitive.* But reference, like causality, is a flexible, interest-relative notion: what we count as *referring* to something depends on background knowledge and our willingness to be charitable in interpretation. To read a relation so deeply human and so pervasively intentional into the world and to call the resulting metaphysical picture satisfactory (never mind whether or not it is 'materialist') is absurd.

THE FAILURE OF NATURAL METAPHYSICS

As I've already pointed out, there are two traditional ways of attempting to overcome the obvious difficulties with a correspondence theory of truth. One way was to postulate a special mental power, an *intellektuelle Anschauung,* which gives the mind access to 'forms'. If the mind has direct access to the things in themselves, then there is no problem about how it can put them in correspondence with its 'signs'. The other way was to postulate a built-in structure of the world, a set of essences, and to say (what is certainly a dark saying) that this structure itself singles out *one* correspondence between signs and their objects. The two strategies were quite naturally related; if a philosopher believes in essences, he usually wants us to have epistemic access to them, and so he generally postulates an *intellektuelle Anschauung* to give us this access.

If all this is a failure, as Kant saw, where do we go from there? One direction, the only direction I myself see as making sense, might be a species of pragmatism (although the word 'pragmatism' has always been so ill-understood that one despairs of rescuing the term), 'internal' realism: a realism which recognizes a difference between '*p*' and 'I think that *p*', between being *right,* and merely thinking one is right without locating that objectivity in either transcendental correspondence or mere consensus. Nelson Goodman has done a wonderful job of 'selling' this point of view in *Ways of Worldmaking* (a book short enough to be read in an evening, and deep enough to be pondered for many). The other main direction—the one that does not make sense to me—is natural metaphysics, the tendency I have criticized here.

Goodman urges, shockingly, that we give up the notion of '*the* world'. Although he speaks of us as making *many* worlds, he does not mean that there are many worlds in the David Lewis (or science fiction) sense, but that rightness is relative to medium and message. We make many versions; the standards of rightness that determine what is right and what is wrong are corrigible, relative to task and technique, but not *subjective*. The question this tendency raises is whether a narrow path can indeed be found between the swamps of metaphysics and the quicksands of cultural relativism and historicism; I shall say more about this in the next chapter.

The approach to which I have devoted this paper is an approach which claims that there *is* a 'transcendental' reality in Kant's sense, one absolutely independent of our minds, that the regulative ideal of knowledge *is* to copy it or put our thoughts in 'correspondence' with it, *but* (and this is what makes it 'natural' metaphysics) we need no *intellektuelle Anschauung* to do this: the 'scientific method' will do the job for us. 'Metaphysics within the bounds of science alone' might be its slogan.

I can sympathize with the urge behind this view (I would not criticize it if I did not feel its attraction). I am not inclined to scoff at the idea of a noumenal ground behind the dualities of experience, even if all attempts to talk about it lead to antinomies. Analytic philosophers have always tried to dismiss the transcendental as nonsense, but it does have an eerie way of reappearing. (For one thing, almost every philosopher makes statements which contradict his own explicit account of what can be justified or known; this even arises in formal logic, when one makes statements about 'all languages' which are barred by the prohibitions on self-reference. For another, almost everyone regards the statement that there is *no* mind-independent reality, that there are *just* the 'versions', or there is just the 'discourse', or whatever, as itself intensely paradoxical.) Because one cannot talk about the transcendent or even deny its existence without paradox, one's attitude to it must, perhaps, be the concern of religion rather than of rational philosophy.

The idea of a coherent theory of the noumena; consistent, systematic, and arrived at by 'the scientific method' seems to me to be chimerical. True, a metaphysician could say 'You have, perhaps, shown that *materialist* metaphysics is incoherent. If so, let us assume some primitive notions of an "intentional" kind, say "thinks about", or "explains", and construct a scientific theory of *these* relations.' But what reason is there to regard this as a reasonable program?

The whole history of science seems to accord badly with such dreams. Science as we know it has been anti-metaphysical from the seventeenth century on; and not just because of 'positivistic interpretations'. Newton was certainly no positivist; but he strongly rejected the idea that his theory of universal gravitation could or should be read as a description of metaphysically ultimate fact. (*'Hypotheses non fingo'* was a rejection of metaphysical 'hypotheses', not of scientific ones.)

And Newton was certainly right. Suppose we lived in a Newtonian world, and suppose we could say with confidence that Newton's theory of gravity and Maxwell's theory of electromagnetism (referred to a privileged 'ether frame') were perfectly accurate. Even then, these theories admit of a bewildering variety of empirically equivalent formulations; formulations which agree on the equations while disagreeing precisely on their metaphysical interpretation. There are action-at-a-distance versions of *both* electromagnetism and gravity; there are versions of both in which an extended physical agent, the field, mediates the interactions between distant bodies; there are even *space–time* versions of *Newtonian* gravitational theory. Philosophers today argue about which of these would be 'right' in such a case; but I know of not a single first-rate physicist who takes an interest in such speculations.

The physics that has replaced Newton's has the same property. A theorist will say he is doing 'field theory' while his fingers are drawing Feynman diagrams, diagrams in which field interactions are depicted as exchanges of *particles* (calling the particles 'virtual' is, perhaps, a ghost of empiricist metaphysics). Even the statement that 'the electron we measure is not the bare electron of the theory, but the bare electron surrounded by a cloud of virtual *particles*' counts as a statement of *field* theory, if you please! What used to be the metaphysical question of atom or vortex has become a question of the choice of a notation!

Worse still, from the metaphysician's point of view, the most successful and most accurate physical theory of all time, quantum mechanics, has *no* 'realistic interpretation' that is acceptable to physicists. It is understood as a description of the world as *experienced by observers;* it does not even pretend to the kind of 'absoluteness' the metaphysician aims at (which is not to say that, given time and ingenuity, one could not come up with any number of empirical equivalents which *did* pretend to be observer independent; it is just that physicists refuse to take such efforts seriously).

There is, then, nothing in the history of science to suggest that it either aims at or should aim at one single *absolute* version of 'the world'. On the contrary, such an aim, which would require science itself to decide which of the empirically equivalent successful theories in any given context was 'really true', is contrary to the whole spirit of an enterprise whose strategy from the first has been to confine itself to claims with clear *empirical* significance. If metaphysics is ever revived as a culturally and humanly significant enterprise, it is far more likely to be along the lines of a Kurt Gödel or, perhaps, Saul Kripke—i.e., along the lines of those who *do* think, in spite of the history I cited, that we *do* have an *intellektuelle Anschauung*—than along the lines of natural metaphysics. But a successful revival along either line seems to be overwhelmingly unlikely.

NOTES

1. See chapter 1; in Putnam (1981) this result is extended to intensional logic; it is shown that even if we specify which sentences are to be true in each possible world, and not just in the actual world, the extensions of the extra-logical predicates are almost totally undetermined in almost all worlds.

2. I ignore here my *own* past attempts at a realist interpretation of quantum mechanics (using non-standard logic) for two reasons: they have never found much acceptance, and (more importantly) I no longer think quantum logic enables one to reconcile quantum mechanics with realism. (See chapter 14.)

3. Strictly speaking, 'if it is definable in terms of these, using, if necessary, constants for all real numbers and functions, infinite conjunctions and disjunctions, etc.': there is no philosophical significance to the question of whether a physical magnitude can be defined by a formula of finite length (or one containing a constant for some undefinable real number) from a metaphysical materialist's point of view.

4. These are situations in which *B* would have been produced by some other cause if *A* hadn't caused it. Another kind of counterexample: John and George are identical twins and have black hair. Is the following counterfactual true?

'If John hadn't had black hair, George wouldn't have had black hair either.' Everyone I've asked assures me it is. But then, on Lewis' theory it follows that

'John's having black hair *caused* George to have black hair too' which is absurd.

5. If 'mechanical causation' is simply momentum transfer, for example, then my flicking a virtually frictionless switch is *not* the 'mechanical cause' of the light going on. Similarly, my putting my hand in front of a light is not the 'mechanical cause' of the shadow. Such a narrow notion might be physical, but would be of no use in explicating *reference*. If, on the other hand, the switching case *is* a case of 'mechanical causation', how does one characterize it without using the clause 'the current *would not have* travelled to the light if the switch *had not been* moved', or some such subjunctive clause?

6. For Quine, this means true and false relative to our evolving doctrine; Quine rejects metaphysical realism and the idea of a unique 'correspondence' between our terms and things in themselves. Quine's views are discussed in chapter 13.

7. Paul Meehl and Wilfred Sellars (1956) introduced the terms 'physical$_1$' and 'physical$_2$'. 'Physical$_1$' properties are simply properties connected with space–time and with causal laws: thus a dualist could subscribe to the thesis 'all properties are physical$_1$'. 'Physical$_2$' properties are physical in the sense used here.

8. 'Is Liberty Possible?' *The Tanner Lectures on Human Values,* vol. 3, Cambridge 1982, pp. 89–135.

Reading Questions

1. How does Putnam define "metaphysical realism"? For Putnam, the doctrine is partly a linguistic one. In what way?
2. Is "materialist metaphysics" really metaphysics at all, or is it just another name for science?
3. Putnam discusses several things—causation, counterfactuals, essential properties, and reference—which he argues cannot be defined in the language of physics. This may bode ill for materialist metaphysics, but how is it relevant to metaphysical realism?

4. Why does a failure of science to define and explain reference show that science should not "aim at one single *absolute* version of 'the world'"? What would such an attempt even amount to?

Putnam's Pragmatic Realism 6

ERNEST SOSA

EXCEPTIONAL AMONG CONTEMPORARY PHILOSOPHERS, Hilary Putnam has long defended a philosophy sane enough to hold not only water, but also people and even values. Having once championed hard realism, he has moved steadily away from any scientism that would have physical science determine fully our world view and its ontology to the detriment of our lifeworld. In several fascinating papers and books, he has developed an alternative realism called first "internal" and more recently "pragmatic."

Putnam has been at pains to distinguish his view from Rortean relativism and from the excesses of recent French philosophy, but he has also warned repeatedly against naive belief in a ready-made world with "in-itself" categories. According to his own preferred *via media,* the mind and the world jointly constitute *both* the mind and the world. It is not immediately obvious what this amounts to in prosaic detail, however, and there is no better way to find out than to examine his arguments.

Putnam argues against "metaphysical realism" and in favor of his own "internal (or pragmatic) realism." Both the view and the arguments, however, have provoked much controversy. Donald Davidson,[1] for example, finds Putnam's version of antirealism objectionable, and indeed incoherent. By 'internal realism' Putnam seems to have in mind not just that the truth of sentences or utterances is relative to a language. That much is, as Davidson indicates, "familiar and trivially correct." But, Davidson continues, "Putnam seems to have more in mind—for example that a sentence of yours and a sentence of mine may contradict each other, and yet each be true 'for the speaker.' It is hard to think in what language this position can be coherently, much less persuasively, expressed" *(ibid.,* p. 307). What argument might lead to such a view?

Putnam has several arguments, actually, but four stand out. First, the "model-theoretic" argument; second, the argument from the nonobjectivity of reference and of the sort of causation involved in contemporary accounts of reference; third, the argument from the unlikelihood of scientific convergence on a finished science that provides an objective and absolute conception of reality; and, finally, the argument from the nonabsoluteness of objecthood and of existence.

The model-theoretic argument has been most extensively discussed and has elicited much criticism. It seems to me that on this argument we have reached an impasse. The critics charge that whatever it is that constitutes reference can on its own secure reference between our words and the pertinent items in the objective, independent world: for example, if a certain causal relation is what constitutes reference, then the existence of that causal relation between a word of ours and a

This paper grew (extensively) from one presented at a conference, *The Philosophy of Hilary Putnam,* organized by the Instituto de Investigaciones Filosóficas, National University of Mexico. I am very pleased to have been included in this conference on Hilary Putnam's work and in his honor.

certain item would be sufficient on its own to bring it about that the reference relation holds between the word and the item. Most emphatically, according to the critics, it is not required, as Putnam seems to believe, that we accept a theory about the relevant causal relation and about how it constitutes reference, a theory about which one could then with Putnam raise questions concerning how *its* words secure their reference, how the word 'causation' in it, for example, acquires its own reference. Putnam for his part accuses his critics of begging the question in supposing that the relevant causal relation can on its own, objectively and independently, secure reference relations between our words and corresponding items in ready-made reality. And he accuses his critics of superstitious belief in essentialism, and in a magical theory of reference.

Here I shall put that controversy aside, as one with little prospect of any new progress or insight beyond what is already contained in the extensive journal literature about it.[2] In what follows, I would like to discuss instead, and in turn, the other three arguments that sustain Putnam's pragmatic realism.

I. PERSPECTIVAL CAUSATION, REFERENCE, TRUTH, AND REALITY

One place where this argument is presented in detail by Putnam is in his paper "Why There Isn't a Ready-Made World."[3] Here is a thumbnail sketch:

P. 1. Truth depends on, and *is* constituted by, reference (at least in part).
2. Reference depends on, and is constituted by, causation (at least partly).
3. Causation is radically perspectival.
4. Reference is radically perspectival (from 2,3).
5. Truth is radically perspectival (from 1,4).
6. Reality is "internal" to one's perspective (from 5).

This can be spelled out a bit further as follows. When a belief or a sentence is true, that depends on and derives from what that belief or that sentence refers to. But when a belief or sentence refers to something, it does so, surely, in virtue of some appropriate causal relation holding between it and its referent. Causation is not an absolute relation, however, not a relation that holds in metaphysical reality independently of any perspective. For Earthians it may be a discarded cigarette that causes a forest fire, while for Martians it is the presence of oxygen. Strictly speaking '*X* causes *Y*' is true or false not absolutely, but only relative to perspective. At least that seems clear with regard to the less-than-total causation needed for an appropriate pairing of referents with referring terms. For example, we need to pair the term 'window' with windows and the term 'draft' with drafts, so we cannot stop with the *total* causation that relates, on one side, *both* the felt draft and the seen window (and much else) and, on the other, your utterance of 'Please close the window.'

If the sort of causation constitutive of reference is thus radically perspectival (perspective-relative), however, then reference is similarly perspectival, and so then must truth be, since reference is in turn constitutive of truth. But in that case reality itself must be also perspectival, also relative to perspective, and in that sense "internal" to perspective, and not wholly external.

What seems most questionable in that argument, put briefly and bluntly, is the move from the perspectival character of truth to the perspectival character of reality itself. Consider for comparison our vocabulary of indexicals and the associated perspectival concepts of oneself and of the temporal present. It may well be that these are important and ineliminable components of any adequate conceptual scheme (adequate for us limited humans, anyhow). Suppose that our *concepts* and our *conceptual scheme* are thus importantly perspectival. Would it follow that reality itself must be similarly perspectival? This seems implausible when we consider the following.

Take a world *W* defined by two people (Paul and Mary) and the postural state (standing, not-standing) of each, such that in *W* Paul is standing while Mary is sitting. In *W*, therefore, the sentence 'I am standing' is true relative to Paul, but false relative to Mary. And, more generally: whatever is true in a certain world *W* relative to a certain perspective and whatever is false in *W* relative to a certain perspective is as it is in that world as a necessary consequence of how things are in that world absolutely and nonperspectivally.

It is true that our talk and even, granted, our *thought* is in fact largely perspectival. It may well be, moreover, that the perspectival character of our thought is not eliminable except (at best) with a very high practical and intellectual cost. But from the fundamentally and ineliminably perspectival character of our thought it does not follow that reality itself is fundamentally perspectival. Everything that is true relative to a perspective and everything that is false relative to a perspective may be as it is as a necessary consequence of the absolute and nonperspectival character of things.

Perhaps it is true that our concepts of reference and truth are ineliminably perspectival. Even so, it still would not follow that reality itself could not be largely as it is independently of us and our thought, in the sense that plenty of reality could have existed propertied and interrelated very extensively just as it is in fact propertied and interrelated even if we had never existed to have any thoughts, and even if no other finite thinkers had taken our place. What is more, our perspectival references and truths may be seen to derive necessarily from absolute and unperspectival reality.

II. OBJECTIVITY, ABSOLUTENESS, AND THE MANY FACES OF REALISM

> What the metaphysical realist holds is that we can think and talk about things as they are, independently of our minds, and that we can do this by virtue of a 'correspondence' relation between the terms in our language and some sorts of mind-independent entities.[4]
>
> But reference, like causality, is a flexible, interest-relative notion [and so, therefore, is correspondence]: what we count as *referring* to something depends on background knowledge and our willingness to be charitable in interpretation. To read a relation so deeply human and so pervasively intentional into the world and to call the resulting metaphysical picture satisfactory (never mind whether or not it is 'materialist') is absurd (*ibid.*, p. 225).

But, again, why must the metaphysical realist "read into the world" any such relation of reference or of correspondence (or of causal explanation)? What the metaphysical realist is committed to holding is that there is an in-itself reality independent of our minds and even of our existence, and that we can talk about such reality and its constituents by virtue of correspondence relations between our language (and/or our minds), on one hand, and things-in-themselves and their intrinsic properties (including their relations), on the other. This does not commit the metaphysical realist to holding that reference itself (or correspondence, or causal explanation) is among the objective properties constitutive of in-itself reality.

Bernard Williams[5] apparently reaches just that conclusion and adopts the view that it opens up. Putnam responds as follows:

> . . . Williams's suggestion is that the intentional (or the "semantic") is itself perspectival, and the absolute conception will someday explain why this kind of talk is useful (as it explains why talk of "grass" and "green" is useful, even though "grass" and "green" are not notions that figure in the absolute conception of the world). But . . . the absolute conception of the world was *defined* in terms of the idea that some statements describe the world with a minimum of "distortion," that they describe it "as it is," that they describe it "independently of perspective"—and what does any of this talk mean, unless something like a correspondence theory of truth is in place? Williams tacitly assumes a correspondence theory of truth when he *defines* the absolute conception, and then forgets that he did this when he suggests that we do not need to assume that such semantic notions as the "content" of a sentence will turn out to figure in the absolute conception itself.[6]

It is hard to see this bit of reasoning as anything more than a fallacy. From the fact that the absoluteness that applies to conceptions is a perspectival concept, it simply does not follow that any absolute conception itself must include any perspectival concept, not even the concept of absoluteness. (My copy of *Principia Mathematica* is *mine*, and the concept of what is one's own is a perspectival concept, but it does not follow that my copy of PM must include the concept of what is one's own.)

Putnam does argue further that Williams must make room in his absolute conception itself for notions of reference and correspondence (and of absoluteness itself). Putnam writes that "if, as Williams believes, the fact that we are 'fated' to accept the sentence 'Snow is white' is *explained* by something 'out there', then the correspondence too must be 'out there'" (*ibid.*, pp. 172–3.) And his argument here seems to turn on an assumption that only an objective, nonperspectival correspondence could do the explanatory work that Williams requires. Only such an objective relation of correspondence could possibly explain why it is that we accept certain truths, and why it is that they are rightly assertible, when all this is so *because* the truths in question correspond to the way things (mind-independently) are. This seems inconclusive, however. Prima facie, it would seem I can explain why I return a book to you by saying that it is *yours.* I can explain why I reach for some water by saying that *I* am thirsty. And so on. Why assume that perspectival concepts have no legitimate place in explanations?

There is nevertheless an argument open to Putnam against Williams's view if the latter includes commitment to "objectivism," which is defined by Putnam in *The Many Faces of Realism*[7] (TMFR) as *the view that what really has a place in objective reality is only what is included in the ontology and the ideology of "finished science," only what the absolute conception recognizes* (TMFR, 4). It is not at all clear that Williams himself would accept objectivism, but in Putnam's own mind objectivism and absolutism are closely connected, as emerges clearly in TMFR. In any case, the argument against objectivism is as follows. The objectivist believes that only what would be reflected in finished science is truly real (the rest will amount at most to heuristically or practically valuable talk, and cannot truly represent reality). But, as we have seen, perspectival concepts like those of reference, correspondence, and causal explanation will not be reflected in finished science, in the science to be converged upon by all determined inquirers, whatever their perspective or context. So the objectivist seems committed by Putnam's reasoning to holding that he is not really thinking at all, nor referring to anything (assuming, again, that Putnam's reasoning about reference, correspondence, and causal explanation is correct). Thus Putnam's complaint in TMFR (16): "It's as if it were all right to say 'I don't deny that there is an external world; I just deny that we (truly really) *think* about it!'"

In TMFR, Putnam also returns to his argument against metaphysical realism via appeal to intentionality, aboutness, reference, and correspondence. And again his reasoning goes in outline like this:

a. The only viable form of metaphysical realism is objectivism (or materialism or scientific realism).

b. For objectivism only properties that figure in strict and exceptionless laws are real properties of things in themselves (and these are presumably laws that would be part of finished science)—though perhaps we might admit also properties based on strict laws in the way strict dispositional properties might be so based.

c. But clearly there is little prospect that the mind can be viewed as constituted or characterized by such properties. Sensa have no place in any actual science, much less in finished science (TMFR, 7–8). If we think of (some) mental properties in terms of dispositions, and of these in terms of conditionals, we find that the conditionals involved are all "in normal conditions," *ceteris paribus* sorts of conditionals; and none of these has a place in finished science (TMFR, 8–11). As for reference, aboutness, and correspondence, the most promising account of these acceptable to an objectivist (materialist, scientific realist) is in terms of causation. But the causation involved would be relative to interests and background conditions (in the way we have seen in earlier discussion) and hence perspectival in a way antithetical to finished science (TMFR, 11–6; 39–40; also 7 above).

Let us now consider this line of reasoning, which connects realism thus with objectivism.

In TMFR, four dichotomies are decisively rejected. First these three:

D1. Subjective (interest- and culture-relative) versus objective (interest- and culture-independent).

D2. Projection [property attributed falsely, etc.] versus property of the thing in itself.

D3. Power [dispositional property] versus property of the thing in itself (TMFR, 27–31).

About these we are told: "The rejection of these three dichotomies is the essence of . . . 'internal realism'" (TMFR, 28). And then a fourth dichotomy is also targeted:

D4. Statement possessing only assertibility conditions versus statement possessing truth conditions (TMFR, 31).

How are we to understand the technical terms used in the formulation of these four dichotomies? Here is a proposal:

i. ø is a subjective property = Df ø is postulated by a particular language or conceptual scheme.

ii. ø is a property of this thing in itself (an intrinsic, objective property) = Df ø is a property that is not just subjective but would be postulated by finished science.

iii. *x* is a subjective individual = Df *x* is among the individuals or is a member of a kind of individuals postulated by some particular language or conceptual scheme.

iv. *x* is a thing in itself (an objective individual) = Df *x* is among the individuals or is a member of a kind of individuals postulated by finished science.

v. Statement σ has assertibility conditions in a particular language or conceptual scheme L = Df L contains criteria or rules that specify conditions within which σ would be correctly assertible.

vi. Statement σ has truth conditions = Df σ has assertibility conditions within finished science (i.e., σ attributes an intrinsic, objective property with respect to things in themselves or objective individuals).

We can understand the emphasis that Putnam places on rejection of these dichotomies above, and on how that rejection defines his own internal or pragmatic realism, if we focus on how all four of them involve the notion of an intrinsic property of things-in-themselves, about which Putnam has this to say: "The deep systemic root of the disease [of objectivism or scientific realism, and hence of metaphysical realism], I want to suggest, lies in the notion of an 'intrinsic' property, a property something has 'in itself,' apart from any contribution made by language or the mind" (TMFR, 8).

Perhaps our definitions may help clarify Putnam's rationale for rejecting the four dichotomies, and the content and motivation for his own internal or pragmatic realism, as well as his emphasis on conceptual relativity, as put, for example, in the following passage: "The key to working out the program of preserving commonsense realism while avoiding the absurdities and antinomies of metaphysical realism in all its familiar varieties . . . is something I have called *internal realism*. (I should have called it pragmatic realism!) Internal realism is, at bottom, just the insistence that realism is *not* incompatible with conceptual relativity" (TMFR, 17).

Putnam's rejection of the dichotomies derives, on the present suggestion, from his rejection of the possibility that there are things-in-themselves with intrinsic properties. For if there is no possibility that there are any such things or properties, then there are no objective things-in-themselves, no intrinsic, objective properties of things-in-themselves, and no statements with truth conditions. All this may be seen through the definitions above. And it then follows that none of the dichotomies is real: they are all necessarily empty on one side.

But just how does Putnam refute the possibility that there are things-in-themselves with intrinsic, objective properties? He has argued explicitly as follows:

> [If] . . . it is simply a matter of how we formalize our language whether we say (with Saul Kripke) that stones, animals, persons, and so on are *not* identical with mereological sums at all, or say (as suggested by Lewis) that they *are* mereological sums (and take care of Kripke's difficulty by claiming that when we say that "the" stone consists of different particle-slices in different possible worlds, then what that means is that the various modal "counterparts" of the stone in different possible worlds consist of different particle slices, and not that the self-identical stone consists of

> different particle slices in different possible worlds)—and to me this certainly looks like a mere choice of a formalism, and not a question of fact—we will be forced to admit that it is partly a matter of our conceptual choice which scientific object a given common-sense object-a stone or a person-is identified with. . . . Nor is the situation any better in theoretical physics. At the level of space-time geometry, there is the well-known fact that we can take points to be individuals or we can take them to be mere limits. . . . Not only do single theories have a bewildering variety of alternative rational reconstructions (with quite different ontologies), but there is no evidence at all for the claim (which is essential to . . . an "absolute conception of the world") that science converges to a *single* theory. . . . We simply do not have the evidence to justify speculation as to whether or not science is "destined" to converge to some one definite theoretical picture. . . . Yet, without the postulate that science converges to a single definite theoretical picture with a unique ontology and a unique set of theoretical predicates, the whole notion of "absoluteness" collapses [and indeed is] . . . incoherent. Mathematics and physics, as well as ethics and history and politics, show our conceptual choices; the world is not going to impose a single language upon us, no matter what we choose to talk about.[8]

And that suggests the following argument against things-in-themselves with intrinsic properties.

a. There is no real possibility of a finished science.

b. Things-in-themselves are by definition the things in the ontology of finished science, and intrinsic, objective properties are by definition those in the ideology of finished science.

c. Hence, there is no possibility that there are things-in-themselves with intrinsic, objective properties.

When we take stock, now, we see that we must learn to view with unfinished science: when we affirm that there are certain things with certain properties, our affirmation must be viewed as relative to a particular language or conceptual scheme. It may then be viewed as one that, if correct, is correct by the assertibility rules or criteria of that language or scheme. I shall return to this form of reasoning below.

Putnam has further reasoning behind his rejection of objective or absolute reality, however; I mean his arguments from the nonabsoluteness of existence itself. To this reasoning I turn next.

III. NONABSOLUTE EXISTENCE AND CONCEPTUAL RELATIVITY

Suppose a world with just three individuals $x1$, $x2$, $x3$. Such a world is held by some "mereologists" to have in it a total of seven things or entities or objects, namely, $x1$, $x2$, $x3$, $x1 + x2$, $x1 + x3$, $x2 + x3$, $x1 + x2 + x3$. Antimereologists by contrast prefer the more austere ontology that recognizes only the three individuals as objects that *really* exist in that world. Talk of the existence of $x1 + x2$ and its ilk is just convenient abbreviation of a more complex discourse that refers to nothing but the three individuals. Thus, suppose $x1$ is wholly red and $x2$ is wholly black. And consider

1. There is an object that is partly red and partly black.
2. There is an object that is red and an object that is black.

For the antimereologist, statement 1 is not true, if we assume that $x3$ is also wholly red or wholly black. It is at best a convenient way of abbreviating the likes of 2.

Putnam has now joined Rudolf Carnap in viewing our controversy as follows:

> . . . the question is one of the choice of language. On some days it may be convenient to use [antimereological language]; . . . on other days it may be convenient to use [mereological] language.[9]

Take the question

> How many objects with a volume of at least 6 cubic centimeters are there in this container?

This question can have no absolute answer on the Carnap-Putnam view, even in a case where the container contains a vacuum except for three marbles each with a volume of 6 cubic centimeters. The antimereologist may say

3. There are three objects in the box.

But the mereologist will reply:

4. There are at least seven objects in the box.

The Carnap-Putnam line is now this: *which statement we accept—3 or 4—is a matter of linguistic convenience.* The language of mereology has criteria of existence and identity according to which sums of individuals are objects. The language of antimereology rejects such criteria, and may even claim that by its criteria only individuals are objects.

There is a valuable insight here, I believe, but I am puzzled by the linguistic wrapping in which it is offered. After all, none of 1–4 mentions any language or any piece of language, nor does any of them say that we shall or shall not or should or should not use any language or bit of language. So I do not see how our decision actually to use or not to use any or all of the sentences 1–4 can settle the question of whether what these sentences *say* is true or false. And if the point is that these sentences do not really *say* anything, then how can they be incompatible in the first place so that a conflict or problem can arise that requires resolution? Also, it is not clear how we gain by replacing questions about atoms (or the like) with questions about *sentences* and *our* relations to some specific ones of these sentences. This is all very puzzling, and we should pause to peer more closely.

What does the proposed linguistic relativity amount to? Can it be spelled out more fully and prosaically? Here, for a start, is a possibility:

LR1. In order to say *anything* you must adopt a language. So you must "adopt a meaning" even for so basic a term as 'object.' And you might have adopted another. Thus you might adopt Carnap-language (CL) or you might adopt Polish-logician-language (PL). What you say, i.e., the utterances you make, the sentences you affirm, are not true or false absolutely, but are true or false only relative to a given language. Thus, if you say "There are three objects in this box" your utterance or sentence may be true understood as a statement of CL while it is false understood as a statement in PL.

But under this interpretation linguistic relativity seems trivially true. Who could deny that inscriptions of shapes and emissions of sounds are not true or false independently of their meaning, independently of all relativization to language or idiolect? Of course, you must "adopt a language" in order to speak (though such "adoption" need not be a conscious and voluntary act), and indeed you might have adopted another. And it seems quite uncontroversial that an utterance of yours might be true relative to one language while it is false relative to another.

Perhaps then the point is rather this:

LR2. When we say 'There are 3 objects here, not 8' we are really saying: 'The following is assertible as true in our CL: "There are 3 objects here, not 8"'

This is indeed in the spirit of Carnap's philosophy, whose *Logical Syntax of Language,*[10] published in English in 1937, defends the following theses:

i. Philosophy, when cognitive at all, amounts to the logical syntax of scientific language.
ii. But there can be alternative such languages and we are to choose between them on grounds of convenience.
iii. A language is completely characterized by its formation and transformation rules.

In that book Carnap also distinguishes between:

*s*1. Object sentences: e.g., 'Five is a prime number,' 'Babylon was a big town.'

*s*2. Pseudo-object sentences: e.g., 'Five is not a thing but a number,' 'Babylon was treated of in yesterday's lecture.'

*s*3. Syntactical sentences: e.g., '"Five" is not a thing-word but a number-word,' '"Babylon" occurred in yesterday's lecture.'

And he defends the thesis that *s*2 sentences seem deceptively like *s*1 sentences but are really *s*3 sentences in "material mode" disguise.

It was W. V. Quine who in 1934 suggested 'material mode' to Carnap (as Quine himself reports in the section on "Semantic Ascent" in *Word and Object*[11]). Quine agrees that a kind of "semantic ascent" is possible, as when we shift from talk of miles to talk of 'mile,' but he thinks this kind of semantic ascent is *always* trivially available, not just in philosophy but in science generally and even beyond. Thus, we can paraphrase 'There are wombats in Tasmania' as '"Wombat" is true of some creatures in Tasmania.' Quine does grant that semantic ascent tends to be especially useful in philosophy. But he explains why as follows:

> The strategy of semantic ascent is that it carries the discussion into a domain where both parties are better

> agreed on the objects (viz., words) and on the main terms concerning them. Words, or their inscriptions, unlike points, miles, classes, and the rest, are tangible objects of the size so popular in the marketplace, where men of unlike conceptual schemes communicate at their best. . . . No wonder it helps in philosophy (*ibid*., p. 272).

The use of this strategy, however, is clearly limited to discourse about recondite entities of controversial status. No relevant gain is to be expected from semantic ascent when the subject matter is the inventory of the marketplace itself. Tables and chairs are no more controversial than words: in fact, they seem less so, by a good margin. No general internal realism, with its conceptual or linguistic relativity, can be plausibly supported by the semantic ascent strategy offered by Quine.

In addition, questions of coherence arise concerning LR2. When we say something of the form 'The following is assertible in our CL: . . .' can we rest with a literal interpretation that does not require ascent and relativization? If not, where does ascent stop? Are we then *really* saying 'The following is assertible in our CL: "The following is assertible in our CL: . . . ."' This way lies vicious regress. But if we *can* stop the regress with our metalinguistic reference to our sentences of CL (and to ourselves), why can we not stop it with our references to tables and chairs and other medium-sized dry goods?

An additional interpretation of Putnam's linguistic or conceptual relativism would have it say this:

LR3. When we see that finished science might well be a chimera, that our best attitude to it is that of agnosticism, we must not assert the claims of our present, unfinished science as if they amounted to truths about an in-itself reality and its intrinsic properties (which would require us to know that our claims would be found also in finished science—and who could possibly know about that?). Rather, we should rest content with the assertibility of our assertions in our unfinished conceptual or linguistic frameworks. But of course what is assertible in one framework may not be so in another. So we have to learn to live with our relativism. It is all pretty much like our claim that one must drive on the right, whose assertibility in the relevant American frameworks is not impugned by the fact that the opposite is assertible in the relevant British frameworks, nor by the absence of any "finished millenary legal system" that would include driving on the right as one of its requirements.

There is much to be discussed about this form of argument. But I would like to focus on one main presupposition required if it is put forward as a form of reasoning that would apply quite generally, whatever sphere may be involved. The argument, which I shall call *Putnam's master argument* (PMA) against realism, runs more simply as follows:

PMA: 1. Realism (in general) is acceptable only if scientific realism is acceptable.

2. Scientific realism is not acceptable, if only because of the history of science induction, which precludes any reasonable expectation of convergence on one final ontology and ideology.

3. Therefore, realism is unacceptable: we cannot accept that there are any things-in-themselves with intrinsic properties; we can accept at best a view of things constitutive of our present conceptual or linguistic framework, but we must not suppose that this would gain convergence among persistent, undefective inquirers, etc.

Here again there is much to be discussed, for example, about the relation between convergence and the existence of things-in-themselves, independently of the mind, with intrinsic properties in no way contributed by any speakers or thinkers. In any case, one premise of the argument that seems immediately dubious is the first. A large fragment of our common-sense view of ourselves and things around us seems quite safe from anything like the history of science induction. Surely, there is a great deal in our ordinary outlook that we share in common with groups widely divergent from us in place, time, and culture. Concerning all of that, nothing like the history of science induction stands in the way of convergence. Suppose we granted that the acceptability of (the certainty or at least the likelihood of) convergence *is* relevant to the acceptability of ordinary realism. And suppose we granted further that, given the history of science induction, we *cannot* plausibly expect that there would be any relevant sort of convergence in science: that here we must remain at best agnostic. Even so, that would not establish internal realism with its conceptual or linguistic relativity, as presently understood in line with interpretation L3 above.[12]

There is hence reason to doubt the linguistic turn taken by Carnap and now Putnam. We have found no very plausible way to conceive of the turn so that it discloses an attractive new direction in metaphysics. The only direction that seems certainly right and clearly defensible is that provided by our first interpretation above (interpretation LR1), but that also seemed trivially right, and not something anyone would deny, not even the most hard-line metaphysical realist. Nevertheless, it still seems to me that there is a valuable insight in Putnam's now repeated appeal to the contrast between the Carnapian conceptual scheme and that of the Polish logician. But, given our recent reflections, I would like to put the insight without appeal to language or to any linguistic relativity.

The artifacts and even the natural objects that we recognize as existing at a time are normally composed of stuff or of parts in certain ways, and those which we see as enduring for an interval are normally not only thus composed of stuff or of parts at each instant of their enduring; but also the stuff or parts thus composing them right up to *t*, must be related in certain restricted ways to the stuff or parts that compose them right after *t*, for any time *t* within the history of such an enduring object.

Thus, the existence of a snowball at a time *t* and location 1 requires that there be a round quantity of snow at 1 and *t* sufficiently separate from other snow, etc.; and for that snowball to endure through an interval *I*, it is required that for every division of *I* into a sequence of subintervals *I*1, *I*2, . . . , there must be a corresponding sequence of quantities of snow *Q*1, *Q*2, . . . , related in certain restricted ways. By all this I mean to point to our "criteria of existence and perdurance for snowballs."

I spoke of a snowball, its existence and perdurance, and what that requires of its sequence of constituent quantities of snow. In place of these, I might have talked of chains and constituent links, of boxes and constituent sides, or of a great variety of artifacts or natural entities such as hills or trees; or even—especially—of persons and their constituent bodies. In every case, there are criteria of existence and of perdurance for an entity of the sort in question such that necessarily an entity of the sort exists at *t* (perdures through *I*) if and only if its criteria of existence are satisfied at *t* (its criteria of perdurance are satisfied relative to *I*). Thus, necessarily a snowball exists at *t* if and only if at *t* a quantity of snow is round and separate from other snow; and a snowball perdures through *I* if and only if for any subdivision of *I* into a sequence of subintervals *I*1, *I*2, . . . , there must be a corresponding sequence of round, etc., quantities of snow *Q*1, *Q*2, . . . , such that, for all *i*, *Qi* satisfies the conditions for being successor of *Qi*-1 in the constitution of the "life" of a snowball. And similarly for chains, boxes, hills, trees, and persons.

I am supposing a snowball to be constituted by a certain piece of snow as constituent matter and the shape of (approximate) roundness as constituent form. That particular snowball exists at that time because of the roundness of that piece of snow. More, if at that time that piece of snow were to lose its roundness, then at that time that snowball would go out of existence.

Compare now with our ordinary concept of a snowball, the concept of a snowdiscall, defined as an entity constituted by a piece of snow as matter and as form any shape between being round and being discshaped. At any given time, therefore, any piece of snow that constitutes a snowball constitutes a snowdiscall, but a piece of snow might at a time constitute a snowdiscall without then constituting a snowball. For every round piece of snow is also in shape between discshaped and round (inclusive), but a discshaped piece of snow is of course not round.

Any snowball SB must hence be constituted by a piece of snow PS which also then constitutes a snowdiscall SD. Now, SB is distinct (a different entity) from PS, since PS would survive squashing and SB would not. By similar reasoning, SD also is distinct from PS. And, again by similar reasoning, SB must also be distinct from SD, since enough partial flattening of PS will destroy SB but not SD. Now, there are infinitely many shapes *S*1, *S*2, . . . , between roundness and flatness of a piece of snow, and, for each *i*, having a shape between flatness and *Si* would give the form of a distinctive kind of entity to be compared with snowballs and snowdiscalls. Whenever a piece of snow constitutes a snowball, therefore, it constitutes infinitely many entities all sharing its place with it.

Under a broadly Aristotelian conception, therefore, the barest flutter of the smallest leaf hence creates and destroys infinitely many things, and ordinary reality suffers a sort of "explosion."

We might perhaps resist this "explosion" of our ordinary world by embracing conceptual relativism. Constituted, supervenient entities do not just objectively supervene on their requisite, constitutive matters and forms, outside all conceptual schemes, with absolute independence from the categories recognized by any person or group. Perhaps snowballs do exist relative to all actual conceptual schemes ever, but not relative to all conceivable conceptual schemes, just as we are not willing to countenance the existence of snowdiscalls, just so another culture might have been unwilling to countenance snowballs. We do not countenance snowdiscalls, because our conceptual scheme does not give to the snowdiscall form (being in shape between round and discshaped) the status required for it to be a proper constitutive form of a separate sort of entity—at least not with snow as underlying stuff.

That would block the explosion of reality, but the price is conceptual relativity. Supervenient, constituted entities do not just exist or not in themselves, free of any dependence on or relativity to conceptual scheme. What thus exists relative to one conceptual scheme may not do so relative to another. In order for such a sort of entity to exist relative to a conceptual scheme, that conceptual scheme must recognize its constituent form as an appropriate way for a separate sort of entity to be constituted.

Must we now conceive of the existence even of the conceptual scheme itself and of its framers and users as also relative to that conceptual scheme? And are we not then caught in a vicious circle? The framers exist only relative to the scheme and this they do in virtue of the scheme's giving their constituent form-cum-matter the required status. But to say that the scheme gives to this form-cum-matter the required status—is that not just to say that the *framers* of that scheme do so? Yet are not the framers themselves dependent on the scheme for their existence relative to it?

Answer: existence *relative* to a conceptual scheme is *not* equivalent to existence *in virtue* of that conceptual scheme. Relative to scheme *C* the framers of *C* exist *in virtue* of their constitutive matter and form, and in virtue of how these satisfy certain criteria for existence and perdurance of such subjects (among whom happen to be the framers themselves). This existence of theirs is in that way relative to *C* but not in virtue of *C*. There is hence no vicious circularity.

The picture then is roughly this. Each of us acquires and develops a view of things that includes criteria of existence and perdurance for categories of objects. When we consider whether an object of a certain sort exists, the specification of the sort will entail the relevant criteria of existence and perdurance. And when we correctly recognize that an object of that sort does exist, our claim is elliptical for ". . . exists relative to *this* our conceptual scheme."

Again, this is *not* the only conceivable view of the matter. We could try to live with the explosion. And that does seem almost inevitable if we view it this way: a sort of object *O*—a constituted, supervenient sort—comes with a sort of constituent matter *M*, or sorts of constituent matters *M*1, *M*2, . . . , and a sort of constituent form *F*. These—*M* (or *M*1, *M*2, . . .), and *F*—we may take to be given independently of any acceptance by anyone of any criteria of existence or perdurance. For the sake of argument, then, we are accepting as given the sorts of items—*M*1, *M*2, . . .—that will play the role of constituent matters, and also the property or relation—*F*—that will play the role of constituent form. And presumably whether or not any particular sequence of matters [*m*1, *m*2, . . .] of sorts *M*1,

M2, . . . , respectively, does or does not satisfy form *F* is also generally independent of whether or not we accept any criteria of existence or perdurance, and indeed independent of whether ***anyone*** does so.

Suppose there is a time *t* when our conceptual scheme *C* first recognizes the appropriate criteria of existence and perdurance. According to our conceptual relativism, prior to that time *t* there were, relative to *C,* no objects of sort *O,* and in particular object *o* did not exist. But if there were no objects of sort *O,* such as *o,* relative to our scheme *C,* then why complicate our own scheme by supplementing it with criteria of existence and perdurance which do give standing to objects of sort *O*? After all, it is not as though we would fail to recognize the existence of something already in existence. By hypothesis ***there are no objects of sort*** *O,* not right up to that time *t,* anyhow.

On the other side, there is the threat of exploding reality, however. If we allow the satisfaction by any sequence *S* of any form *F* of the appropriate polyadicity and logical form to count as a criterion of existence for a corresponding sort of object, then reality right in us, before us, and all around us is unimaginably richer and more bizarre than we have ever imagined. And anyway we shall still face the problem of giving some explanation for why we focus so narrowly on the objects we do attend to, whose criteria of existence and perdurance we do recognize, to the exclusion of the plethora of other objects all around and even in the very same place.

A third option is a disappearance or elimination theory that refuses to countenance supervenient, constituted objects. But then most if not all of ordinary reality will be lost. Perhaps we shall allow ourselves to continue to use its forms of speech ". . . but only as a convenience or abbreviation." But in using those forms of speech, in speaking of snowballs, chains, boxes, trees, hills, or even people, we shall ***not*** believe ourselves to be seriously representing reality and its contents. "As a convenience": to ***whom*** and for what ***ends***? "As an abbreviation": of ***what***?

With alternatives so grim, we are encouraged to return to our relativistic reflections. Our conceptual scheme encompasses criteria of existence and of perdurance for the sorts of objects that it recognizes. Shall we say now that a sort of object *O* exists (has existed, exists now, or will exist) relative to a scheme *C* at *t* if and only if, at *t, C* recognizes sort *O* by allowing the corresponding criteria? But surely there are sorts of objects that our present conceptual scheme does not recognize, such as artifacts yet uninvented and particles yet undiscovered, to take only two obvious examples. Of course, we allow there might be and probably are many such things. Not that there could be any such entities relative to our ***present*** conceptual scheme, however, for by hypothesis it does not recognize them. So are there sorts of objects—constituted sorts among them, as are the artifacts at least—such that they exist but not relative to our present scheme *C*? In that case we are back to our problem. What is it for there to be such objects? Is it just the in-itself satisfaction of constitutive forms by constitutive matters? That yields the explosion of reality.

Shall we say then that a constituted, supervenient sort of object *O* exists relative to our present scheme *C* if and only if *O* is recognized by *C* directly or recognized by it indirectly through being recognized by some predecessor or successor scheme? That, I fear, cannot suffice, since there might be sorts of particles that always go undiscovered by us, and sorts of artifacts in long disappeared cultures unknown to us, whose conceptual schemes are not predecessors of ours.

Shall we then say that what exists relative to our present scheme *C* is what it recognizes directly, what it recognizes indirectly through its predecessors or successors, and what it ***would*** recognize if we had developed appropriately or were to do so now, and had been or were to be appropriately situated? This seems the sort of answer required, but it obviously will not be easy to say what appropriateness amounts to in our formula, in its various guises.

Regardless of whatever success may await any further specification of our formula, there is the following further objection. Take a sort of object *O* recognized by our scheme *C,* with actual instances o1, o2, . . . ; for example, the sort Planet, with various particular planets as instances: Mercury, Venus, etc. Its instances, say we, exist, which amounts to saying that they exist relative to our scheme. But if we had not existed there would have been no scheme of ours for anything to exist relative to; nor would there have been our actual scheme *C* either. For one thing, we may just assume the contingent existence of our actual scheme to depend on people's actually granting a certain status to certain constitutive forms. If we had not existed, therefore, the constitutive form for the sort Planet would not have had, relative to our conceptual scheme, the status required for it to be possible that there be instances of that sort, particular planets. And from this it apparently follows that if we had not existed there would have been no planets: no Mercury, no Venus, etc.

This objection conceptual relativism can rebut as follows. While existing in the actual world *x* we now have a conceptual scheme *Cx* relative to which we assert existence, when we assert it at all. Now, we suppose a possible world *w* in which we are not to be found, in which indeed no life of any sort is to be found. Still we may, in *x*: (a) consider alternative world *w* and recognize that our absence there would have no effect on the existence or course of a single planet or star, that Mercury, Venus, and the rest, would all still make their appointed rounds just as they do in *x*; while yet (b) this recognition, which after all takes place in *x*, is still relativized to *Cx*, so that the existence in *w* of whatever exists in *w* relative to *Cx* need not be affected at all by the absence from *w* of *Cx*, and indeed of every conceptual scheme and of every being who could have a conceptual scheme. For when we suppose existence in *w*, or allow the possibility of existence in *w*, *we* do so *in x*, and we do so there still relative to *Cx*, to our present conceptual scheme, and what it recognizes directly or indirectly, or ideally.

If I am right we have three choices:

Eliminativism: a disappearance view for which our ordinary talk is so much convenient abbreviation. Problem: we still need to hear: "abbreviation" of what, and "convenient" for what ends and whose ends? Most puzzling of all is how we are to take this "abbreviation"—not literally, surely.

Absolutism: snowballs, hills, trees, planets, etc., are all constituted by the in-itself satisfaction of certain conditions by certain chunks of matter, and the like, and all this goes on independently of any thought or conceptualization on the part of anyone. Problem: this leads to the "explosion of reality."

Conceptual relativism: we recognize potential constituted objects only relative to our implicit conceptual scheme with its criteria of existence and of perdurance. Problem: is there not much that is very small, or far away, or long ago, or yet to come, which surpasses our present acuity and acumen? How can we allow the existence of such sorts at present unrecognized by our conceptual scheme?

Right now I cannot decide which of these is least disastrous. But is there any other option?

IV. CONCLUSION

I have considered four lines of reasoning used by Putnam in favor of his pragmatic realism. Of these, the fourth seems to me deepest, most richly suggestive, and most effective. The first, the model-theoretic argument, we put aside. The interest of the second resides mainly in its exploration of (a) the sort of causation that is required for a realist account of reference, and (b) consequences of this for the perspectival nature of reference and of truth. My questions arise mainly with the last step of the argument, where the move is made from the perspectival status of truth to a correspondingly perspectival character of reality itself, its internality to conceptual scheme. As for the third line of reasoning, it merges with the second to some extent but is separable, and emphasizes a requirement of scientific convergence or absolutism. According to this line, the very idea of in-itself reality with intrinsic properties is tied together with the notion of an absolute conception of the world to be provided by finished science: an ontology and ideology that would attract convergence by all persistent and undefective inquirers, given sufficient time and resources. To the extent that we must remain agnostic with regard to the possibility or likelihood of such convergence, therefore, to that extent must we be equally agnostic with regard to the very idea of things-in-themselves with their mind-independent, intrinsic properties. There is much to discuss about this whole approach, but one main focus of serious doubt is its assumption that realism (in general, even common-sense realism about observable reality) can be upheld only if scientific realism can be upheld. This runs against a problem: *the history of science induction that feeds doubt against scientific convergence is inapplicable to our common-sense conception of ordinary reality or anyhow to a substantial enough portion of it.*

I also discussed a fourth line of reasoning used by Putnam, one that leads to a sort of conceptual relativity. I questioned the linguistic turn taken by Putnam's actual reasoning, since there seemed no good interpretation on which it would avoid both triviality and absurdity. Nevertheless, the considerations adduced by this line of reasoning contain important insights worth exploring. And in fact they eventually open a fascinating menu of ontological possibilities.[13] By extending Putnam's reasoning, we reach a set of options in contemporary ontology that presents us with a rather troublesome trilemma. Which shall we opt for: eliminativism, absolutism, or conceptual relativism? Putnam's own pragmatic realism is built around the case that he makes against both eliminativism and absolutism, and in favor of his special sort of conceptual relativism.

Of the four Putnamian arguments for pragmatic realism—the model-theoretic argument; the argument from the perspectival character of causation, reference, and truth; the argument from agnosticism regarding scientific convergence upon a finished science; and the argument for conceptual relativity—this fourth and last of them seems to me far the most powerful and persuasive. It raises a three-fold issue—the choice between eliminativism, absolutism, and relativism—still wide open on the philosophical agenda, and a most exciting issue before us today.

NOTES

1. "The Structure and Content of Truth," *Journal of Philosophy*, LXXXVII, 6 (June 1990): 279–328.

2. But see the excellent paper by James Van Cleve. "Semantic Supervenience and Referential Indeterminacy." *Journal of Philosophy*, LXXXIX, 7 (July 1992): 344–61.

3. In his *Realism and Reason* (New York: Cambridge, 1983), pp. 205–28. Similar reasoning may also be found in the more recent *Realism with a Human Face* (Cambridge: Harvard, 1991); see, e.g., ch. 11, "Objectivity and the Science/Ethics Distinction," and also ch. 5, "The Causal Structure of the Physical," on p. 88 of which we find: ". . . an *epistemic* distinction between a 'cause' and a 'background condition.' How does the mind get to be able to *refer* to the mind-independent world? Answer 'via the relation of causal connection,' and you have slipped back to treating causation as something 'out there' and not simply 'epistemic.'" Here again it is the last move that seems false, and in step with the misstep to be discussed here.

4. Putnam, "Why There Isn't A Ready-Made World," p. 205.

5. *Descartes: The Project of Pure Inquiry* (New York: Penguin, 1978) and *Moral Luck* (New York: Cambridge, 1981), esp. ch. 11.

6. "Objectivity and the Science/Ethics Distinction," p. 174.

7. La Salle, IL: Open Court, 1987.

8. "Objectivity and the Science/Ethics Distinction," pp. 170–1.

9. Putnam, "Truth and Convention: On Davidson's Refutation of Conceptual Relativism," *Dialectica*, XLI (1987): 69–77, p. 75.

10. New York: Harcourt Brace, 1937.

11. Cambridge: MIT, 1960.

12. To mention only one attractive possibility, one might, with Bas van Fraassen, combine both agnosticism toward theoretical science and common-sense realism toward observable reality; see, e.g., his *The Scientific Image* (New York: Oxford, 1980).

13. Closely related issues are explored in my "Subjects among Other Things: Persons and Other Beings," *Philosophical Perspectives*, I (1987): 155–89.

Reading Questions

1. Sosa argues against Putnam that even if truth is perspectival, this does not entail the perspectivity of reality. What does Sosa mean by "perspective" here? Is it really no more than indexicality, as he suggests? How could truth, or thought, be indexical in any important way?

2. Sosa rejects the first premise of Putnam's Master Argument (PMA). This premise states that realism (in general) is acceptable only if scientific realism is acceptable. However, scientific realism entails that the common-sense realism of tables and chairs is false, as Putnam himself notes. So why think that PMA is Putnam's main argument, as Sosa claims? Or if it is, why think that scientific realism is the only acceptable realism?
3. According to Sosa, we face a trilemma. First horn: scientific realism or eliminativism. Second horn: mereological absolutism or the "explosion of reality." Third horn: conceptual relativity. After you read James Van Cleve's "Mereological Essentialism, Mereological Conjunctivism, and Identity Through Time" in this volume, reconsider whether Sosa's second horn is really a problem after all.
4. The third horn of Sosa's trilemma, conceptual relativity, is problematic only if we assume, with Sosa, that we create conceptual schemes and thus that these CSs will be infected with our limitations and finitude. CSs are hence nonmaximal. Suppose instead that conceptual schemes are complete, maximal ways of filtering (or whatever) reality and exist in an abstract way apart from any particular human attitudes. They are maximal in this sense—they include or preclude every possible state of affairs. For every proposition, a CS either helps determine the truth of the proposition or the truth of its negation. Such a conceptual relativity would elude Sosa's criticisms. Is it a workable idea?

7 A Naturalistic Defense of Realism

MICHAEL DEVITT

ANTI-REALISM ABOUT THE PHYSICAL WORLD is an occupational hazard of philosophy. Most of the great philosophers have been anti-realists in one way or another. Many of the cleverest contemporary philosophers are also: Michael Dummett, Nelson Goodman, Hilary Putnam, and Bas van Fraassen. Yet anti-realism is enormously implausible on the face of it.

The defense of realism depends on distinguishing it from other doctrines and on choosing the right place to start the argument. And the defense of that choice depends on naturalism. In part I, I shall say what realism is, distinguishing it from semantic doctrines with which it is often confused. In part II, I shall consider the arguments for and against realism about observables. In part III, I shall consider the arguments for and against realism about unobservables, "scientific" realism. The discussion is based on my book, *Realism and Truth* (1997; unidentified references are to this work).

I. WHAT IS REALISM?

A striking aspect of the contemporary realism debate is that it contains almost as many doctrines under the name 'realism' as it contains participants.[1] However, some common features can be discerned in this chaos. First, nearly all the doctrines are, or seem to be, partly semantic. Consider, for example, Jarrett Leplin's editorial introduction to a collection of papers on scientific realism. He lists ten "characteristic realist claims" (1984b: 1–2). Nearly all of these are about the truth and reference of theories. Not one is straightforwardly metaphysical.[2] However, second, amongst all the semantic talk, it is usually possible to discern a metaphysical doctrine, a doctrine about what there is and what it is like. Thus 'realism' is now usually taken to refer to some combination of a metaphysical doctrine with a doctrine about truth, particularly with a correspondence doctrine.[3]

Professor Devitt's article was commissioned for this anthology and appears here for the first time.

The metaphysical doctrine has two dimensions, an existence dimension and an independence dimension (ch. 2 and sec. A.1). The existence dimension commits the realist to the existence of such common-sense entities as stones, trees and cats, and such scientific entities as electrons, muons and curved spacetime. Typically, idealists, the traditional opponent of realists, have not denied this dimension; or, at least, have not straightforwardly denied it. What they have denied is the independence dimension. According to some idealists, the entities identified by the first dimension are made up of mental items, "ideas" or "sense data," and so are not external to the mind. In recent times another sort of idealist has been much more common. According to these idealists, the entities are not, in a certain respect, "objective": they depend for their existence and nature on the cognitive activities and capacities of our minds. Realists reject all such mind dependencies. Relations between minds and those entities are limited to familiar causal interactions long noted by the folk: we throw stones, plant trees, kick cats, and so on.

Though the focus of the debate has mostly been on the independence dimension, the existence dimension is important. First, it identifies the entities that are the subject of the dispute over independence. In particular, it distinguishes a realism worth fighting for from what I call "Weak, or Fig-Leaf, Realism" (p. 23): a commitment merely to there being *something* independent of us. Second, in the discussion of unobservables—the debate about *scientific* realism—the main controversy has been over existence.

I capture the two dimensions in the following doctrine:

> *Realism:* Tokens of most common-sense, and scientific, physical types objectively exist independently of the mental.

This doctrine covers both the observable and the unobservable worlds. Some philosophers, like van Fraassen, have adopted a different attitude to these two worlds. So, for the purpose of argument, we can split the doctrine in two: *Common-Sense Realism* concerned with observables, and *Scientific Realism* concerned with unobservables.

In insisting on the objectivity of the world, Realists are not saying that it is unknowable. They are saying that it is not *constituted by* our knowledge, by our epistemic values, by our capacity to refer to it, by the synthesizing power of the mind, nor by our imposition of concepts, theories, or languages; it is not limited by what we can believe or discover. Many worlds lack this sort of objectivity and independence: Kant's "phenomenal" world; Dummett's verifiable world; the stars made by a Goodman "version"; the constructed world of Putnam's "internal realism"; Kuhn's world of theoretical ontologies[4]; the many worlds created by the "discourses" of structuralists and post-structuralists.

Realism accepts both the ontology of science and common sense as well as the folk epistemological view that this ontology is objective and independent. Science and common sense are not, for the most part, to be "reinterpreted." It is not just that our experiences are *as if* there are cats, there are cats. It is not just that the observable world is *as if* there are atoms, there are atoms. As Putnam once put it, Realism takes science at "face value" (1978: 37).

Realism is the minimal realist doctrine worth fighting for, once it is established, the battle against anti-realism is won; all that remains are skirmishes. Furthermore, Realism provides the place to stand in order to solve the many other difficult problems that have become entangled with it.

Any semantic doctrine needs to be disentangled from Realism (ch. 4 and sec. A.2). In particular, the correspondence theory of truth needs to be disentangled: it is in no way constitutive of Realism nor of any similarly metaphysical doctrine.[5]

On the one hand, Realism does not entail any theory of truth or meaning at all, as is obvious from our definition. So it does not entail the correspondence theory. On the other hand, the correspondence theory does not entail Realism. The correspondence theory claims that a sentence (or thought) is true in virtue of its structure, its relations to reality, usually reference relations, and the nature of reality. *This is compatible with absolutely any metaphysics.* The theory is often taken to require the objective mind-independent existence of the reality which makes sentences true or false. This addition of Realism's independence dimension does, of course, bring us closer to Realism. However, the addition seems like a gratuitous intrusion of metaphysics into semantics. And even with the addition, the correspondence theory is still distant from Realism, because it is silent on the existence dimension. It tells us what it is for a sentence to be true or false, but it does not tell us which ones are true and so *could* not tell us which particular entities exist.

Realism is about the nature of reality in general, about what there is and what it is like; it is about the largely inanimate impersonal world. If correspondence truth has a place, it is in our theory of only a small part of that reality: it is in our theory of people and their language.[6]

Not only is Realism independent of any *doctrine* of truth, we do not even need to use 'true' and its cognates to *state* Realism, as our definition shows. This is not to say that there is anything "wrong" with using 'true' for this purpose. Any predicate worthy of the name "truth" has a "disquotational" property captured by the "equivalence thesis." The thesis is that appropriate instances of

> *s* is true if and only if *p*

hold, where an appropriate instance is obtained by substituting for '*p*' a sentence which is the same as (or a translation of) the sentence referred to by the term substituted for '*s*.'[7] Because of this disquotational property, we can use 'true' to talk about *anything* by referring to sentences. Thus we can talk about the whiteness of snow by saying "'Snow is white' is true." And we can redefine the metaphysical doctrine Realism as follows:

> Most common-sense, and scientific, physical existence statements are objectively and mind-independently true.

This redefinition does not make Realism semantic (else every doctrine could be made semantic); it does not change the subject matter at all. It does not involve commitment to the correspondence *theory* of truth, nor to any other theory. Indeed, it is compatible with a *deflationary* view of truth according to which, roughly, the equivalence thesis captures all there is to truth.[8] This inessential redefinition *exhausts* the involvement of truth in constituting Realism.[8]

My view that realism does not involve correspondence truth flies so much in the face of entrenched opinion, and has received so little support, that I shall labor the point. I shall do so by considering a fairly typical contemporary statement of "Scientific Realism":

> *Contemporary Realism:* Most scientific statements about unobservables are (approximately) correspondence-true.

Why would people believe this? I suggest only because they believed something like the following two doctrines:

> *Strong Scientific Realism:* Tokens of most unobservable scientific types objectively exist independently of the mental and (approximately) obey the laws of science.

> *Correspondence Truth:* Sentences have correspondence-truth conditions.

These two doctrines, together with the equivalence thesis, imply Contemporary Realism. Yet the two doctrines have almost nothing to do with each other. *Contemporary Realism is an unfortunate hybrid.*

Strong Scientific Realism is stronger than my minimal doctrine, Scientific Realism, in requiring that science be mostly right not only about which unobservables exist but also about the properties of those unobservables. But the key point here is that both these doctrines are *metaphysical,* concerned with the underlying nature of the world in general. To accept Strong Scientific Realism, we have to be confident that science is discovering things about the unobservable world. Does the success of science show that we can be confident about this? Is inference to the best explanation appropriate here? Should we take skeptical worries seriously? These are just the sort of epistemological questions that have been, and still largely are, at the center of the realism debate. *Their home is with Strong Scientific Realism, not with Correspondence Truth.*

Correspondence Truth is a semantic doctrine about the pretensions of one small part of the world to represent the rest. The doctrine is the subject of lively debate in the philosophy of language, the philosophy of mind, and cognitive science. Do we need to ascribe truth conditions to sentences and thoughts to account for their roles in the explanation of behavior and as guides to reality? Do we need reference to explain truth conditions? Should we prefer a conceptual-role semantics? Or should we, perhaps, near enough eliminate meaning altogether? These are interesting and difficult questions (ch. 6 and secs. A.12–A.15), but they have no immediate bearing on scientific realism.

Semantic questions are not particularly concerned with the language of science. Even less are they particularly concerned with "theoretical" language "about unobservables." Insofar as the questions are concerned with that language, they have no direct relevance to the metaphysical *concerns of* Strong Scientific Realism. They bear directly on the sciences of language and mind and, via that, on the other human sciences. They do not bear directly on science in general. Many philosophers concerned with semantics and not in any way tainted by anti-realism are dubious of the need for a correspondence notion of truth.[10]

Are there atoms? Are there molecules? If there are, what are they like? How are they related to each other? Strong Scientific Realism says that we should take science's answers pretty much at face value. So there really are atoms and they really do make up molecules. That is one issue. Another issue altogether is about meaning. Do statements have correspondence-truth conditions? Correspondence Truth says that they do. This applies as much to 'Cats make up atoms' as to 'Atoms make up molecules'; indeed it applies as much to 'The Moon is made of green cheese.' Put the first issue together with the second and we get a third: Is 'Atoms make up molecules' correspondence-true? My point is that this issue is completely derivative from the other two. It arises only if we are wondering about, first, the meanings of sentences ranging from the scientific to the silly; and about, second, the nature of the unobservable world.

Suppose that we had established that Correspondence Truth was right for the familiar everyday language. Suppose further that we believed that atoms do make up molecules, and the like. Then, *of course,* we would conclude that Correspondence Truth applies to 'Atoms make up molecules,' and the like, and so conclude that such sentences are correspondence-true. What possible motive could there be for not concluding this? Scientific theories raise special metaphysical questions not semantic ones.

Strong Scientific Realism and Correspondence Truth have very different subject matters and should be supported by very different evidence. Underlying Contemporary Realism is a conflation of these two doctrines that has been detrimental to both.

It follows from this discussion that a metaphysical doctrine like Realism cannot be attacked *simply* by arguing against certain semantic theories of truth or reference; for example, against Correspondence Truth. As a result, much contemporary anti-Realist argument is largely beside the Realist point. I shall briefly consider two famous examples.[11]

(1) Dummett (1978) identifies realism with an evidence transcendent—in effect, correspondence—view of truth. He goes on to argue that this view is mistaken, that the notion of truth needed in our semantic theory must be an epistemic one based on verification. (2) Putnam has produced a model-theoretic argument (1978: 125–7; 1983: 1–25) against "metaphysical realism" and in favor of "internal realism." Putnam starts by arguing that there cannot be determinate reference relations to a mind-independent reality. As a result, there is no way in which the "ideal" theory—one meeting all operational and theoretical constraints—could be false. So metaphysical realism is "incoherent." The argument has generated a storm of responses.

Now whatever the rights and wrongs of these matters,[12] the arguments have no direct bearing on Realism. Dummett's argument is straightforwardly semantic, not metaphysical. Putnam's metaphysical realism is a hybrid of something like Realism with something like Correspondence Truth. The only part of this hybrid that *may* be directly affected by Putnam's argument about reference is Correspondence Truth.[13] Indeed, the challenge of Putnam's argument can be posed, and often seems to be posed, in a way that presupposes Realism: a representation is related by one causal relation to certain mind-independent entities and by another causal relation to other such entities; which relation determines reference?

I have emphasized that Realism is a metaphysical doctrine and hence different from semantic doctrines like Correspondence Truth. However, Realism is a little bit semantic in requiring that the world be independent of our semantic capacities. Similarly, it is a little bit epistemic in requiring that the world be independent of our epistemic capacities. But these are only minor qualifications to the metaphysical nature of Realism.

Why has the metaphysical issue been conflated with semantic issues? This is a difficult question, but part of the answer is surely the "linguistic turn" in twentieth-century philosophy. At its most extreme, this turn treats all philosophical issues as about language (sec. 4.5).

I claim that no semantic doctrine is in any way *constitutive* of Realism (or any metaphysical doctrine of realism). This is not to claim that there is no *evidential* connection between the two sorts of doctrines. Indeed, I favor the Quinean view that, roughly, everything is evidentially connected to everything else. So distinguishing Realism from anything semantic is only the first step in saving it. We have to consider the extent to which contemporary semantic arguments, once conflations are removed, might be used as evidence against Realism: although their conclusions do not *amount to* anti-Realism, they may *count in favor of* anti-Realism. Traditionally, philosophers started with an epistemological view and typically used this as evidence against Realism. We should reconstrue contemporary philosophers so that they are doing something similar: starting with a semantic view and using it as evidence against Realism.

In part II, I shall assess these arguments against Realism, claiming that they start in the wrong place. I shall first consider traditional arguments from epistemology and then, reconstrued contemporary arguments from semantics. The concern here is with realism about observables, Common-Sense Realism. Having established the case for this, I shall argue for Scientific Realism in part III.

II. WHY BE A COMMON-SENSE REALIST?

Realism about the ordinary observable physical world is a compelling doctrine. It is almost universally held outside intellectual circles. From an early age we come to believe that such objects as stones, cats, and trees exist. Furthermore, we believe that these objects exist even when we are not perceiving them, and that they do not depend for their existence on our opinions nor on anything mental. These beliefs about ordinary objects are central to our whole way of viewing the world. Common-Sense Realism is aptly named because it is the core of common sense.

What, then, has persuaded so many philosophers out of it? A clear answer emerges from the tradition before the linguistic turn (ch. 5). If we have knowledge of the external world, it is obvious that we acquire it through our sensory experiences. Yet how can we rely on these, Descartes (1641) asks? First, the Realist must allow that our senses sometimes deceive us: there are the familiar examples of illusion and hallucination. How, then, can we ever be justified in relying on our senses? Second, how can we be sure that we are not dreaming? Though we think we are perceiving the external world, perhaps we are only dreaming that we are. Finally, perhaps there is a deceitful demon causing us to have sensory experiences *as if* of an external world, when in fact there is no such world. If we are not certain that this is not the case, how can we know that Realism is correct? How can it be rational to believe Realism?

One traditional way of responding to the challenge of this extreme Cartesian skepticism is to seek an area of knowledge which is not open to skeptical doubt and which can serve as a "foundation" for all or most claims to knowledge. Since even the most basic common-sense and scientific knowledge—including that of the existence of the external world—is open to doubt, this search is for a special philosophical realm of knowledge outside science. The foundationalist has always found this realm in the same place. "In the search for certainty, it is natural to begin with our present experiences" (Russell 1912: 1). This natural beginning led traditionally to the view that we could not be mistaken about mental entities called "ideas." More recently, it has led to the similar view that we could not be mistaken about entities called "sense data." These entities are the "given" of experience. I shall talk of "sense data."

From this perspective, the justification of Realism can seem hopeless. The perspective yields what is sometimes called, anachronistically, "the movie-show model" of the mind. Sense data are the immediate objects of perception. They are like images playing on a screen in the inner theater of a person's mind. The person (a homunculus really) sits watching this movie and asks herself: (1) Is there anything outside the mind *causing* the show? (2) If so, does it *resemble* the images on the screen? To answer these questions "Yes," as Locke (1690) does with a qualification or two, is to be a "representative realist." But Locke's justification for his answers is desperately thin, as Berkeley (1710) shows: there seems to be no basis for the inference from the inner show to the external world. Certainly, there is no reason why a Cartesian skeptic should accept the inference.

The problem for Realism is the "gap" between the object known and the knowing mind. According to the Realist, the object known is external to the person's mind and independent of it. Yet the person has immediate knowledge only of her own sense data. She can never leave the inner theater to compare those sense data with the external world. So how could she ever know about such a world?

To save our knowledge, it seemed to Berkeley and many others, we must give up Realism and adopt idealism: the world is constructed, in some sense, out of sense data. The gap is closed by bringing objects, one way or another, "into the mind." But the problem is that even this desperate metaphysics does not save our knowledge. Idealism too is open to skeptical doubt.

First, consider the foundations of idealism: our allegedly indubitable knowledge of our own sense data. Why should the skeptic accept that there are any such mental objects as sense data? Even if there are, why should the skeptic accept that the person has indubitable knowledge of them? Why is this any more plausible than the view that we have indubitable knowledge of external objects?

Even if the foundations are granted, and Realism is abandoned, the task of building our familiar knowledge to Cartesian skeptical standards on these foundations has proved impossible.

The simplest part of this knowledge is singular knowledge of physical objects; for example, the knowledge that Nana is a cat. How can we get this knowledge from knowledge of sense data? This task might seem easy if Nana were literally constructed out of sense data, if she were nothing but a bundle of them. But then how could we explain the fact that Nana can exist unobserved? The obvious answer that *sense data* can exist unobserved is quite gratuitous from the skeptical viewpoint.

So idealists favored a different sort of construction, the "logical construction" proposed by "phenomenalism." Each statement about a physical object was to be translated, in some loose sense, into statements about sense data. Since the latter statements are the sort that the foundationalist thinks we know, it was hoped in this way to save our knowledge, albeit in a new form. However, the total failure of all attempts to fulfill this translation program over many years of trying is so impressive as to make it "overwhelmingly likely" that the program *cannot* be fulfilled (Putnam 1975b: 20).

From a Realist perspective, it is easy to see the problem for phenomenalism: there is a loose link between a physical object and any set of experiences we might have of it. As a result, no finite set of sense-datum statements is either necessary or sufficient for a physical-object statement.

In sum, the foundationalist anti-Realist cannot save physical objects. He cannot save even our singular knowledge of the world. We have already noted the failure of foundationalist Realism. The Cartesian skeptical challenge leaves the foundationalist no place to stand and no way to move: he is left, very likely, only with the knowledge that he is now experiencing, with "instantaneous solipsism." The foundationalist program is hopeless.[14]

Kant is responsible for another traditional idealist response to the skeptical challenge. Kant's way of saving knowledge is very different from foundationalism's. He closes the gap between the knowing mind and the object known with his view that the object is partly constituted by the cognitive activities of the mind. He distinguished objects as we know them—stones, trees, cats, and so on—from objects as they are independent of our knowledge. Kant calls the former "appearances" and the latter "things-in-themselves." Appearances are obtained by our *imposition* of *a priori* concepts; for example, causality, time and the Euclidian principles of spatial relations. Only things-in-themselves, forever beyond our ken, have the objectivity and independence required by Realism. Appearances do not, as they are partly our construction. And, it must be emphasized, the familiar furniture of the world are appearances not things-in-themselves. Although an idealist, Kant is a Weak Realist (p. 23).

How does this view help with skepticism? We can know about appearances because, crudely, we make them. Indeed, Kant thinks that we could not know about them unless we made them: it is a condition on the possibility of knowledge that we make them.

Many contemporary anti-Realisms combine Kantianism with relativism to yield what is known as "constructivism." Kant was no relativist: the concepts imposed to constitute the known world were common to all mankind. Contemporary anti-Realisms tend to retain Kant's ideas of things-in-themselves and of imposition, but drop the universality of what is imposed. Instead, different languages, theories, and world views are imposed to create different known worlds. Goodman, Putnam, and Kuhn are among the constructivists.

Constructivism is so bizarre and mysterious—how could we, literally, make dinosaurs and stars?—that one is tempted to seek a charitable reinterpretation of constructivist talk. But, sadly, charity is out of place here (13.1–13.3).[15]

Something has gone seriously wrong. The Cartesian skeptical challenge that has persuaded so many to abandon Realism has led us to disaster: either to a lack of any worthwhile knowledge or to knowledge at the expense of a truly bizarre metaphysics. It is time to think again.

The disaster has come from epistemological speculations about what we can know and how we can know it. But why should we have any confidence in these speculations? In particular, why should we have such confidence in them that they can undermine Realism? Over a few years of living people come to the conclusion that there are stones, trees, cats, and the like, existing largely independent of us. This Realism is confirmed day by day in their experience. It seems much more firmly based than the epistemological speculations. Perhaps, then, we have started the argument in the wrong place: rather than using the epistemological speculations as evidence against Realism, perhaps we should use Realism as evidence against the speculations.

Indeed, what support are these troubling speculations thought to have? Not the empirical support of the claims of science, for that sort of support is itself being doubted. The support is thought to be a priori, as is the support for our knowledge of mathematics and logic. Reflecting from the comfort of armchairs, foundationalists and Kantians decide what knowledge *must* be like, and from this, infer what the world *must* be like:

a priori epistemology → a priori metaphysics.

The disaster alone casts doubt on this procedure and the philosophical method it exemplifies, the a priori method of "First Philosophy." This doubt is confirmed by the sorts of considerations adduced by Quine (1952: Introduction; 1953: 42–46). These considerations should lead us to reject a priori knowledge and embrace "naturalism," the view that there is only one way of knowing, the empirical way that is the basis of science.16 From the naturalistic perspective, philosophy becomes continuous with science. And the troubling epistemological speculations have no special status: they are simply some among many empirical hypotheses about the world we live in. As such, they do not compare in evidential support with Realism. Experience has taught us a great deal about the world of stones, trees, and cats, but rather little about how we know about this world. So epistemology is just the wrong place to start the argument: the skeptical challenge should be rejected. Instead, we should start with an empirically based metaphysics and use that as evidence in an empirical study of what we can know and how we can know it: epistemology itself becomes part of science, "naturalized epistemology":

empirical metaphysics → empirical epistemology.

And when we approach our metaphysics empirically, Realism is irresistible.[17] Indeed, it faces no rival we should take seriously. Thus naturalism supports the order of procedure suggested tentatively in the last paragraph.

Quine is fond of a vivid image taken from Otto Neurath. He likens our knowledge—our "web of belief" to a boat that we continually rebuild while staying afloat on it. We can rebuild any part of the boat, but in so doing we must take a stand on the rest of the boat for the time being. So we cannot rebuild it all at once. Similarly, we can revise any part of our knowledge, but in so doing we must accept the rest for the time being. So we cannot revise it all at once. And just as we should start rebuilding the boat by standing on the firmest parts, so also should we start rebuilding our web.[18] Epistemology is one of the weakest parts to stand on. So also is semantics.

We noted in part I that semantics has been at the center of contemporary anti-Realist arguments. Setting aside the frequent conflation of semantics with metaphysics, I suggested that we reconstrue these arguments as simply offering evidence against Realism. So just as traditional philosophers argued for epistemological doctrines that show that we could not *know* the Realist world, we should see Dummett and Putnam as arguing for semantic doctrines that show that we could not *refer to* the Realist world. Since we obviously do know about and refer to the world, the arguments run, the world cannot be Realist. The objection to traditional arguments was that they started with a priori speculations on what knowledge *must* be like and inferred what the world *must* be like. The objection to contemporary arguments is that they start with *a priori* speculations on what meaning and reference *must* be like and infer what the world *must* be like:

a priori semantics → a priori metaphysics.

From the naturalistic perspective, this inference uses the wrong methodology and proceeds in the wrong direction. We should proceed:

empirical metaphysics → empirical semantics.

We should, as I like to say, "put metaphysics first."

Consider Dummett, for example (ch. 14). His case against Realism rests on an argument for a verificationist semantics. This argument rests entirely on claims about linguistic competence, about what meanings we could grasp and what concepts we could have. Why should we believe these claims? They are thought to be known a priori. Naturalism rejects that. As empirical claims, their support is very weak, far too weak to threaten something as plausible as Realism. Indeed, semantics as a whole is in such a poor state that it is just the wrong place to start in doing metaphysics. Rather, a Realist metaphysics is a firm place to start from—as firm as you could wish for—in doing semantics. With Realism as a base, I think the prospects of establishing a nonverificationist semantics based on Correspondence Truth are promising, although I would be the last to underestimate the dimensions of this task (ch. 6 and secs. A.12–A.15.)

Consider Kuhn, for another example (ch. 9). I have noted that Kuhn is a constructivist: he holds that the known world exists only relative to the imposition of concepts by our scientific theories. What drives him to this unlovely metaphysics? Implicitly, a "meta-induction"[19] against Realism along the following lines: past theories posited entities which, from the perspective of our current theories, we no longer think exist; so, probably, from the perspective of future theories we will come to think that the posits of our present theories do not exist. Kuhn has unobservables primarily in mind, but it is important to note that the argument applies even to the familiar observables. Why does Kuhn suppose that, from our current perspective, the posits of past theories do not exist? First, he starts with the semantic issue of whether the terms that purport to refer to those entities really do refer rather than with the metaphysical issue of whether the entities exist. Second, in considering the semantic issue, he takes for granted a "description" theory of reference. According to this theory, the reference of a term depends on the descriptions (other terms) associated with it in the theory: it refers to whatever those descriptions pick out. Now with theory change, particularly radical theory change, is likely to go the view that those descriptions do not pick anything out. So, from the new perspective, the term in the old theory does not refer. This will be true even of an "observational" term; think, for example, of descriptions associated with 'The Earth,' before the Copernican revolution. So the entities that the old terms purport to refer to do not exist.[20] The objection is, once again, that semantics is the wrong place to start. Set aside until part III the application of the meta-induction to unobservables. We should be much more confident of the continued existence of familiar observables, despite theory changes, than of any semantic theory. If a description theory of reference counts against that existence, so much the worse for the theory. Many ideas for other theories of reference compatible with Realism have emerged in recent times.[21]

The mistaken methodology is reflected in a certain caricature of Realism that tends to accompany contemporary anti-Realist polemics (sec. 12.6). Thus, according to Putnam, Realism requires a "God's Eye View" (1981: 74); that we have "direct access to a ready made world" (p. 146) and so can compare theories with "unconceptualized reality" (1979: 611); that we can make "a transcendental match between our representation and the world in itself" (1981: 134).[22] According to Richard Rorty, the Realist believes that we can "step out of our skins" (1982: xix) to judge, without dependence on any concepts, whether theories are true of reality.[23] But, of course, no sane person believes any of this. What Realists believe is that we can judge whether theories are true of reality, *the nature of which* does not depend on any theories or concepts.

What lies behind these views of Realism? The answer is clear: the Cartesian picture that leads to the skeptical challenge. According to this picture we are theorizing *from scratch,* locked in our mental theaters, trying to bridge the gap between our sense data and the external world. But we are not starting from scratch in epistemology and semantics. We can use well-established theories in physics, biology, and so forth; we already have the entities and relations which those theories posit. And if we were starting from scratch, skeptical doubts would condemn us to instantaneous solipsism. The picture puts the epistemic and semantic carts before the metaphysical horse.

To put the carts back where they belong, we take a naturalistic approach to epistemology and semantics. Reflection on our best science has committed us to the many entities of the largely impersonal and inanimate world. It has not committed us to sense data and so there is no gap between sense data and the world to be bridged. We go on to seek empirical explanations of that small part of the world in which there are problems of knowledge and reference: people and language. From the naturalistic perspective, the relations between our minds and reality are not, in principle, any more inaccessible than any other relations. Without jumping out of our skins, we can have well-based theories about the relations between, say, Michael and Scottie. Similarly, we can have such theories about our epistemic and semantic relations to Michael and Scottie.

In sum, objections to Common-Sense Realism have come from speculations in epistemology and semantics. From the naturalistic perspective, there can be no question of these speculations being known a priori. Once they are seen as empirical, they are far too ill-based to justify any metaphysical conclusion. We should put metaphysics first, and then Realism is the only doctrine that can be taken seriously.

III. WHY BE A SCIENTIFIC REALIST?

The argument for Scientific Realism—Realism about the unobservables of science—starts by assuming Common-Sense Realism. And, setting aside some deep and difficult problems in quantum theory, the issue is over the existence dimension, over whether these unobservables exist. For the independence dimension mostly goes without saying once Common-Sense Realism has been accepted.

The basic argument for Scientific Realism is simple (sec. 7.1). By supposing the unobservables of science exist, we can give good explanations of the behavior and characteristics of observed entities, behavior and characteristics which would otherwise remain completely inexplicable. Furthermore, such a supposition leads to predictions about observables which are well confirmed; the supposition is successful.

This argument should not be confused with one version of the popular and much discussed argument that "realism explains success" (sec. 7.3).[24] This version is most naturally expressed talking of truth. First we define success: for a theory to be successful is for its observational predictions to be true. Why is a theory thus successful? The Realist argument claims: because the theory is true. However, given the conflation of Realism with Correspondence Truth criticized in part I, it is worth noting that this talk exploits only the disquotational property of "true" and so does not require any robust notion of truth. This can be seen by rewriting the explanation without any talk of truth at all. Suppose a theory says that *S*. The rewrite defines success: for this theory to be successful is for the world to be observationally as if *S*. Why is the theory thus successful? The rewrite claims: because *S*. For example, why is the world observationally as if there are atoms? Why are all the observations we make just the sort we would make if there were atoms? Answer: because there *are* atoms. This Realist explanation has a trivial air to it because it is only if we suppose that *there aren't x's* that we feel any need to explain why it is *as if there are x's*. Still, it is a good explanation. And the strength of Scientific Realism is that the anti-Realist has no explanation of this success: if Scientific Realism were not correct, Realists are fond of saying, it would be "a miracle" that the observable world is as if it is correct.

This popular argument is good but it is different from my simple one and not as basic—Where the popular argument uses Realism to explain the observational success of theories, my simple one uses Realism to explain the observed phenomena, the behavior and characteristics of observed entities. This is not to say that observational success is unimportant to the simple argument: the explanation of observed phenomena, like any explanation, is *tested* by its observational success. So according to the simple argument, Scientific Realism *is* successful; according to the popular one, it explains success. There is not even an air of triviality about the simple argument.

I shall conclude by briefly considering three arguments against Scientific Realism. (1) The first is an influential empiricist argument. Richard Boyd, who does not agree with its conclusion, has nicely expressed the argument as follows:

> Suppose that *T* is a proposed theory of unobservable phenomena. . . . A theory is said to be empirically equivalent to *T* just in case it makes the same predictions about observable phenomena that *T* does. Now, it is always possible, given *T*, to construct arbitrarily many alternative theories that are empirically equivalent to *T* but which offer contradictory accounts of the nature of unobservable phenomena. . . . *T* and each of the theories empirically equivalent to it will be equally well confirmed or disconfirmed by any possible observational evidence. . . . scientific evidence can never decide the question between theories of unobservable phenomena and, therefore, knowledge of unobservable phenomena is impossible. (1984: 42–44)

One way of putting this is: we should not believe *T* because it is ***underdetermined by the possible evidence***. Commitment to the existence of the entities posited by *T*, rather than merely to the pragmatic advantages of the theory that talks of them, makes no evidential difference, and so is surely a piece of misguided metaphysics; it reflects super-empirical values, not hard facts.

Talk of "possible evidence" is vague (sec. 3.5). If it is construed in a restricted way, then theories may indeed be underdetermined by the possible evidence. Yet for underdetermination to threaten Scientific Realism, I argue (sec. 7.4), the talk of "possible evidence" must be construed in a very liberal way. And construed in this way, there is no reason to believe in underdetermination.

One sense of 'possible evidence' (see Quine 1970: 179; van Fraassen 1980: 12, 60, 64) is restricted in that it does not cover anything nonactual ***except acts of observation:*** it is restricted to all the points of ***actual*** space-time that we would have observed had we been around. Yet there are many things that we do not do, but could do, other than merely observing. If we had the time, talent, and money, perhaps we could invent the right instruments and conduct the right experiments to discriminate between *T* and its rival *T*'. There may be many differences between the theories which we would not have detected if we had ***passively observed*** each point of actual space-time but which we would have detected if we had ***actively intervened*** (Hacking 1983) to change what happened at points of space-time. In this liberal sense that allows for our capacity to ***create*** phenomena, the class of possible evidence seems totally open.

In the light of this consideration, given any *T*, what possible reason could there be for thinking ***a priori*** that we ***could not*** distinguish it empirically from any rival if we were ingenious enough in constructing experiments and auxiliary hypotheses? It is of course *possible* that we should be unable to distinguish two theories: we humans have finite capacities. The point is that we have no good reason for believing it in a particular case. Even less do we have a good reason for believing it in *all* cases; that is to say, for believing that *every* theory faces rivals that are not detectably different.

Behind these Realist doubts about underdetermination lies the following picture. *T* and *T'* describe different causal structures alleged to underlie the phenomena. We can manipulate the actual underlying structure to get observable effects. We have no reason to believe that we *could not* organize these manipulations so that, if the structure were as *T* says, the effects would be of one sort, whereas if the structure were as *T'* says, the effects would be of a different sort.

If the liberally interpreted underdetermination thesis were true, Realism might be in trouble. But why should the Realist be bothered by the restricted thesis? A consequence of that thesis is that we *do not,* as a matter of fact, ever conduct a crucial experiment for deciding between *T* and *T'*. This does not show that we *could not* conduct one. And the latter is what needs to be established for the empiricist argument against Realism (Boyd 1984: 50). The restricted empirical equivalence of *T* and *T'* does *not* show, *in any epistemologically interesting sense,* that they make "the same predictions about observable phenomena," nor that they "will be equally well confirmed or disconfirmed by any possible evidence." It does *not* show that "scientific evidence can never decide the question between theories of unobservable phenomena and [that], therefore, knowledge of unobservable phenomena is impossible." It does *not* show that commitment to *T* rather than *T'* is superempirical and hence a piece of misguided metaphysics.

(2) Van Fraassen (1980, 1985) has proposed a doctrine he calls "constructive empiricism." It is Common-Sense but not Scientific Realist. Suppose that a theory says that *S.* Van Fraassen holds that we may be justified in believing that the observable world is as if *S* but we are never justified in believing that *S.* So Scientific Realism is unjustified. From the Realist perspective, such a position amounts to an unprincipled selective skepticism against unobservables: it offends against unobservable rights.[25] An epistemology that justifies a belief in observables will also justify a belief in unobservables. An argument that undermines Scientific Realism, will also undermine Common-Sense Realism.

So the Realist has a simple strategy against such anti-Realism. First, she demands from the anti-Realist a justification of the knowledge that he claims to have about observables. Using this she attempts to show, positively, that the epistemology involved in this justification will also justify knowledge of unobservables. Second, she attempts to show, negatively, that the case for skepticism about unobservables produced by the anti-Realist is no better than the case for skepticism about observables. I claim that arguments along these lines work against van Fraassen (ch. 8).[26]

(3) Finally, perhaps the most influential recent argument against Scientific Realism arose from the revolution in the philosophy of science led by Kuhn (1962). It is the earlier-mentioned "meta-induction": past theories posited entities that, from the perspective of our current theories, we no longer think exist; so, probably, from the perspective of future theories we will come to think that the posits of our present theories do not exist. In part II I argued that the case offered for the premise of this meta-induction rests on two mistakes: first, the mistake of putting semantics before metaphysics; second, the mistake of taking a description theory of reference for granted. These arguments are enough to remove concern about the existence of past observables, but not of past unobservables. For, even without these mistakes there is plausibility to the idea that we no longer believe in the existence of past unobservables; phlogiston is a popular example. The meta-induction against Scientific Realism is a powerful argument. Still, I think that the Realist has a number of defenses against it which are jointly sufficient (sec. 9.4).

In conclusion, I have argued that the metaphysical issue of Realism about the external world is quite distinct from semantic issues about truth. Furthermore, we should not follow the tradition and argue the metaphysical issue from a perspective in epistemology, nor follow the recent linguistic turn and argue it from a perspective in semantics. Rather, we should adopt naturalism and argue the metaphysical issue first. When we do, the case for Common-Sense Realism is overwhelming and the case for Scientific Realism is very strong.

The realism dispute arises from the age-old metaphysical question, "What ultimately is there, and what is it like?" I am sympathetic to the complaint that Realism, as part of an answer to this question, is rather boring. Certainly it brings no mystical glow. Nevertheless, it needs to be kept firmly at the front of the mind to avoid mistakes in theorizing about other, more interesting, matters in semantics and epistemology where it makes a difference.[27]

REFERENCES

Berkeley, George. 1710. *Principles of Human Knowledge.*

Boyd, Richard N. 1984. "The Current Status of Scientific Realism." In Leplin 1984a: 41–82.

Brown, James Robert. 1994. *Smoke and Mirrors: How Science Reflects Reality.* New York: Routledge.

Churchland, Paul M. 1979. *Scientific Realism and the Plasticity of Mind.* Cambridge: Cambridge University Press.

Descartes, Rene. 1641. *Meditations on First Philosophy.*

Devitt, Michael. 1996. *Coming to Our Senses: A Naturalistic Defense of Semantic Localism.* New York: Cambridge University Press.

———. 1997. *Realism and Truth.* 2nd ed. with a new afterword (1st ed. 1984, 2nd ed. 1991). Princeton: Princeton University Press.

———. 1998. "Naturalism and the A Priori." *Philosophical Studies* 92: 45–65.

Dretske, Fred I. 1981. *Knowledge and the Flow of Information.* Cambridge, MA: MIT Press.

Dummett, Michael. 1978. *Truth and Other Enigmas.* Cambridge, MA: Harvard University Press.

Ellis, Brian 1979. *Rational Belief Systems.* Oxford: Basil Blackwell.

Fales, Evan. 1988. "How to be a Metaphysical Realist." In *Midwest Studies in Philosophy.* Vol. 12: *Realism and Antirealism,* ed. Peter A. French, Theodore E. Uehling, Jr., and Howard K. Wettstein. Minneapolis: University of Minnesota Press: 253–74.

Field, Hartry. 1978. "Mental Representation." *Erkenntnis* 13: 9–61.

Field, Hartry. 1998. "Epistemological Nonfactualism and the A Priority of Logic." *Philosophical Studies* 92:1–24.

Fine, Arthur. 1986a. *The Shaky Game: Einstein, Realism, and the Quantum Theory.* Chicago: University of Chicago Press.

Fine, Arthur. 1986b. "Unnatural Attitudes: Realist and Instrumentalist Attachments to Science." *Mind* 95: 149–77.

Goodman, Nelson. 1978. *Ways of Worldmaking.* Indianapolis: Hackett.

Haack, Susan. 1987. "'Realism.'" *Synthese* 73: 275–99.

Hacking, Ian. 1983. *Representing and Intervening: Introductory Topics in the Philosophy of Natural-Science.* Cambridge: Cambridge University Press.

Hesse, Mary. 1967: "Laws and Theories." In *The Encyclopedia of Philosophy,* ed. Paul Edwards. New York: Macmillan: vol. 4, pp. 404–10.

Hooker, Clifford A. 1974. "Systematic Realism." *Synthese,* 51, 409–97.

Jennings, Richard. 1989. "Scientific Quasi-Realism." *Mind,* 98, 223–45.

Kant, Immanuel. 1783. *Prolegomena to Any Future Metaphysics.*

Kitcher, Philip. 1993. *The Advancement of Science: Science without Legend, Objectivity without Illusions.* New York: Oxford University Press.

Kripke, Saul A. 1980. *Naming and Necessity.* Cambridge, MA: Harvard University Press.

Kuhn, Thomas S. 1962: *The Structure of Scientific Revolutions.* Chicago: Chicago University Press. 2nd ed. 1970.

Laudan, Larry. 1981. "A Confutation of Convergent Realism." *Philosophy of Science* 48: 19–49. Reprinted in Leplin 1984a.

Leeds, Stephen. 1978. "Theories of Reference and Truth." *Erkenntnis* 13: 111–29.

Leplin, Jarrett, ed. 1984a. *Scientific Realism.* Berkeley: University of California Press.

Leplin, Jarrett. 1984b. "Introduction." In Leplin 1984a: 1–7.

Locke, John. 1690. *An Essay Concerning Human Understanding.*

Luntley, Michael. 1988. *Language, Logic and Experience: The Case for Anti-Realism.* La Salle: Open court.

Matheson, Carl. 1989. "Is the Naturalist Really Naturally a Realist?" *Mind,* 98, 247–58.

Miller, Richard W. 1987. *Fact and Method: Explanation, Confirmation and Reality in the*

Natural and Social Sciences. Princeton: Princeton University Press.

Millikan, Ruth. 1984. *Language, Thought, and Other Biological Categories: New Foundations for Realism.* Cambridge, MA: MIT Press.

Papineau, David 1979: *Theory and Meaning.* Oxford: Clarendon Press.

Putnam, Hilary. 1975. *Mind, Language and Reality: Philosophical Papers,* vol. 2. Cambridge: Cambridge University Press.

______. 1978. *Meaning and the Moral Sciences.* London: Routledge & Kegan Paul.

______. 1979. "Reflections on Goodman's *Ways of World-Making.*" *Journal of Philosophy* 76: 603–18.

______. 1981. *Reason, Truth and History.* Cambridge: Cambridge University Press.

______. 1983. *Realism and Reason: Philosophical Papers,* vol. 3. Cambridge: Cambridge University Press.

______. 1985. "A Comparison of Something with Something Else." *New Literary History* 17: 61–79.

______. 1987. *The Many Faces of Realism.* La Salle: Open Court.

Quine, W. V. 1952. *Methods of Logic.* London: Routledge & Kegan Paul.

______. 1953. *From a Logical Point of View.* Cambridge, MA: Harvard University Press, 2nd ed. rev., 1st ed. 1953.

______. 1970. *Philosophy of Logic.* Cambridge, MA.: Harvard University Press.

Rey, Georges. 1998. "A Naturalistic A Priori." *Philosophical Studies* 92: 25–43.

Rorty, Richard. 1979. *Philosophy and the Mirror of Nature.* Princeton: Princeton University Press.

Rorty, Richard. 1982. *Consequences of Pragmaticism [Essays: 1972–1980].* Minneapolis: University of Minnesota Press.

Russell, Bertrand. 1912. *The Problems of Philosophy.* London: Oxford Paperbacks, 1967. [Original publ. 1912.]

Stich, Stephen P. 1983. *From Folk Psychology to Cognitive Science: The Case Against Belief.* Cambridge, MA: MIT Press.

Stove, David. 1991: *The Plato Cult and Other Philosophical Follies.* Oxford: Basil Blackwell.

Van Fraassen, Bas C. 1980. *The Scientific Image.* Oxford: The Clarendon Press.

______. 1985. "Empiricism in the Philosophy of Science." In *Images of Science: Essays on Realism and Empiricism, with a Reply from Bas C. van Fraassen,* ed. Paul M. Churchland and Clifford A. Hooker. Chicago: University of Chicago Press: 245–308.

______. 1989. *Laws and Symmetry.* Oxford: Clarendon Press.

Williams, Michael. 1993. "Realism and Scepticism." In *Reality. Representation, and Projection,* ed. John Haldane and Crispin Wright. New York: Oxford University Press: 193–214.

NOTES

1. Susan Haack (1987) distinguishes *nine* "senses" of "realism"!

2. Some other examples: Hesse 1967: 407; Hooker 1974: 409; Papineau 1979: 126; Ellis 1979: 28; Boyd 1984: 41–42; Miller 1987; Fales 1988: 253–54; Jennings 1989: 240; Matheson 1989; Kitcher 1993; Brown 1994.

3. Two examples are Putnam's "metaphysical realism" (1978, 123–25), and the account of realism by Arthur Fine (1986a: 115–16, 136–37).

4. For fairly accessible accounts of these worlds see, respectively: Kant 1783; Dummett 1978: preface and chs. 10 and 14; Goodman 1978; Putnam 1981; Kuhn 1962.

In characterizing the independence of the paradigm Realist objects, stones, trees, cats, and the like, we deny that they have *any* dependence on us except the occasional familiar causal one. Other physical objects that have a more interesting dependence on us—for example, hammers and money—pose more of a challenge to the characterization. But, with careful attention to the differences between this sort of dependence and the dependence that anti-realists allege, the challenge can be met (secs 13.5–13.7).

5. Cf. Putnam 1985: 78; 1987: 15–16. Most philosophers who tie realism to correspondence truth do not argue for their position. Dummett is one exception, criticized in my ch. 14. Michael Williams (1993: 212n) is another, criticized in my sec. A.2.

6. Note that the point is not a verbal one about how the word 'realism' should be used. The point is to distinguish two doctrines, whatever they are called (p. 40).

7. More needs to be said to allow for the paradoxes, ambiguity, indexicals, and truth-value gaps.

8. The utility of 'true' that comes from its disquotational property is much greater than the examples in this paragraph show. On this, and the idea of deflationary truth, see my sec. 3.4 and the works it draws on.

9. Some will object that we cannot assess Realism until we have *interpreted* it and this requires a semantic theory that talks of truth. I argue against this objection in secs. 4.6–4.9, A.2–A.11.

10. See, e.g., Leeds 1978, Field 1978, Churchland 1979, Stich 1983.

11. Two other examples are: Rorty 1979, discussed in my ch. 11; Laudan 1981, discussed in my ch. 9.

12. I argue that Dummett is wrong in ch. 14 and that Putnam is in ch. 12 and secs. A.16–A.19.

13. Putnam criticizes other views that he associates with metaphysical realism and that are also inessential to Realism. One example is the view that there is exactly one true and complete description of the world (1981: 49), a view that, with Correspondence Truth, is alleged to require "a *ready-made* world" (1983: 211; cf my sec. 13.4). Another example is a sort of individualistic essentialism (1983: 205–28). Even if Putnam's criticisms of these views were correct, they would leave Realism largely untouched.

14. Note that the program we are talking about attempts to answer the Cartesian skeptic by rebuilding our knowledge on the foundation of indubitable knowledge of sense data, mental entities that are the immediate objects of perception. Less demanding forms of foundationalism that do not make this attempt to answer the skeptic may well be promising; see note 18.

15. Because constructivism is so bizarre and mysterious, its popularity cries out for explanation. I have tried to offer some *rational* explanations (13.4–13.7). For some learned, and very entertaining, explanations of a different sort, see Stove 1991. Stove thinks that anti-Realism, like religion, stems from our need to have a *congenial* world. For some suggestions by Georges Rey along similar lines, see my p. 257, n. 11.

16. A particularly important consideration against the a priori, in my view (1996: 2.2), is that we lack anything close to a satisfactory *explanation* of a nonempirical way of knowing. We are told what this way of knowing is *not*—it is *not* the empirical way of deriving knowledge from experience—but we are not told what it *is*. Rey 1998 and Field 1998 have a more tolerant view of the a priori. My 1998 is a response.

17. Some people think that science itself undermines Realism. I think that this is a mistake (secs. 5.10, 7.9).

18. It is plausible to think that the firmest parts are our singular beliefs about the objects we observe. So we might hope for a new foundationalism built on these beliefs, one with no pretensions to answer the unanswerable Cartesian skeptic, and with no presumption that the beliefs are indubitable.

19. This apt term, and formulations of the argument along these lines, are due to Putnam (1978: 25).

20. A similar line of argument has been used by Stich (1983) and others to argue for various forms of eliminativism about the mind. Happily, Stich has recently recanted (1996: 3–90).

21. See, for example, Kripke 1980, Putnam 1975, Dretske 1981, and Millikan 1984.

22. Putnam attributes this view to realist friends "in places like Princeton and Australia" (1979: 611). The Dummettians have more bad news for Australians (particularly black ones): "there is no sense to supposing that [Australia] either determinately did or did not exist [in 1682]" (Luntley 1988: 249–50).

23. See also 1979: 293; Fine 1986a: 131–12; 1986b: 151–52.

24. I identify eight versions of the argument by distinguishing different senses of 'realism,' and 'success' (sec. 6.6).

25. This, not the legitimacy of "abduction," is the primary issue in the defense of Scientific Realism; cf. Laudan 1981: 45; Fine 1986a: 114–15; 1986b: 162.

26. However, it should be noted that my discussion does not take account of van Fraassen's radical nonjustificationist epistemology (1989).

27. My thanks to Steven Hales and Georges Rey for comments on a draft of this paper.

Reading Questions

1. Devitt's redefinition of the metaphysical doctrine of Realism is "most common-sense, and scientific, physical existence statements are objectively and mind-independently true." Notice that this statement says nothing about what exists. Instead it makes a claim about the truth-values of a certain class of statements. Is it a metaphysical view at all, or is it, say, epistemic?
2. Recall Sosa's argument in "Putnam's Pragmatic Realism" that scientific existence statements are ultimately eliminativist. On the scientific worldview, there aren't tables and chairs—they don't figure in the language of physics. But clearly common sense says that there are tables and chairs. So it is not obvious that most common-sense existence claims could be true at the same time that most scientific existence claims are true. If they can't, does this show that Devitt's redefinition of realism in terms of truth is inconsistent?

3. Devitt argues that we should have more confidence in realism than in the arguments for skepticism. Is this an appeal to common sense à la G. E. Moore? If so, how persuasive is it?
4. Devitt advocates the primacy of empirical metaphysics. How could he answer Putnam's argument in "Why There Isn't a Ready-Made World" that causation, counterfactuals, essential properties, and reference cannot be defined in the language of physics, and thus that the prospects for an "empirical metaphysics" are hopeless?

8 Postscript to "A Naturalistic Defense of Realism"

MICHAEL DEVITT

I AGREE WITH MOST of Simon Blackburn's "Introduction to the Realism Debates." He sees these debates as being about the mind independence of various realities: colors, morality, possibilities, and so on. My own account of the most fundamental of these debates, the debate over realism about "the external world," fits nicely into his picture: my "independence dimension" captures the mind independence and my "existence dimension" specifies the reality that is the concern of this particular debate. Idealists were the traditional opponents of this realism. Blackburn rightly says that contemporary opponents do not usually call themselves "idealists." However, I think that his account of the "two main families" of contemporary anti-realism misses *the* main one which is *in fact* close to one traditional idealism: this is constructivism, a combination of Kantian idealism with relativism. I have listed Goodman, Putnam, and Kuhn among the constructivists. I might have listed Benjamin Lee Whorf, many "sociologists of knowledge," the members of several radical political movements, and countless postmodernists.

Blackburn concludes by describing a position on the realism debate that he calls "minimalism." The minimalist "den[ies] that the issue is a real one . . . doubting that anything except perhaps metaphors or images gives substance either to realism or anti-realism." Something like this position is to be found in Richard Rorty (1979, 1982) and Arthur Fine (1986a, 1986b). Ironically, Blackburn himself once seemed to come close to embracing it (1993: 15–34). What is very surprising is that he attributes minimalism to me. Worse, he suggests that I confusingly present this minimalism "as a vindication of realism." He has gotten me all wrong.

According to Blackburn, minimalism denies that the realism issue is real by rejecting any ascent "to the metatheoretical position from which we can . . . survey in one view both our discourse, and the world, and decide upon their relationship." It denies that attempts "to present a reflective theory about the relationship between ourselves and the world . . . are coherent." This is not my view. There are two sorts of relationships between ourselves and the world that are the subject of "reflective theory": epistemic ones that are the concern of epistemology and semantic ones that are the concern of semantics. Epistemology and semantics can be as coherent as anything could be, and I am totally in favor of them, as part II of this paper demonstrates. (Indeed, I spend most of my life doing semantics!) *Where I differ from the tradition and, I infer, from Blackburn is in thinking that they should be done empirically, not a priori, and that they should not be the basis for a position on Realism.*

Blackburn alleges that I do not present realism "as a claim about the relation between mind and the world." This is plainly false, as part I demonstrates. The independence dimension of my Realism is precisely a claim about the relation between the mind and the world: it is the claim that

Professor Devitt's postscript was commissioned for this anthology and appears here for the first time.

the world does not depend on the mind in any of a variety of ways specified (and so, in this respect, Realism is a little bit semantic and epistemic). I see idealism's disagreement with Realism as being largely over this independence dimension.

Blackburn gets closer to me in suggesting that I take "the original discourse 'at face value.'" Realism does accept the folk view that there are stones, trees, cats, and the like, having natures independent of our minds. But I do not think that Realism is "certified" by these folk views, nor that Realism's denial is not "a subtle, philosophical, position." Realism has to be argued for, and I do argue for it in this paper (and in more detail in 1997).

Finally, Blackburn has a dark vision of what is at stake in the battle with minimalism: if "minimalism is forced upon us . . . not only does the reflective enterprise itself become impossible, but in a sense the history of philosophy does so too." Be that as it may, accepting my naturalistic defense of Realism will have no such dire consequences: the reflective enterprise can continue in epistemology and semantics; we can understand the history as an interesting, albeit mistaken, attempt to base metaphysics on epistemology and semantics.

What are we to make of Blackburn's misunderstandings? Why does he see my naturalistic defense as threatening the reflective enterprise, subtle philosophical positions, our history, and even our culture?

I think that the answer is that naturalism's empirical approach takes the philosophical fun out of the realism debate: it removes a lot of the debate's *excitement*, a lot of its *aura of significance*. D. C. Williams made the point nicely long ago:

> Dare I suggest at last that a kind of highmindedness and sportsmanship have conspired against the vulgar plethora of the evidence for realism to protect from bathos the "persistent problems" and the laborious ritual of our profession? To bring such gross implements as Mill's methods to the limpid regions of philosophic discourse is like dynamiting a trout stream. It gets the fish, but it misses all the exquisite impractical pleasure of angling with the thin line of dialectic. Besides, it depletes the game supply. These punctilios may, of course, mean simply a resolve that philosophy must be critical of the most obvious of mundane opinions and methods. But in so far as they are a mood of gratuitous superiority, the philosopher who does not think of philosophy as mere courtly pastime like parchesi will abandon them. The disclaimer of the earthier sorts of knowledge has isolated philosophy, made it a mystery or a jest, an escape from reality or a visionary interpretation. Philosophy is not higher and suprascientific. It is the lowest and grubbiest inquiry round the roots of things, and when it answers real questions about the world, it is and can only be an inductive science. (1966: 146–47)

ADDITIONAL REFERENCES

Blackburn, Simon. 1993. *Essays in Quasi-Realism.* New York: Oxford University Press.

Williams, D. C. 1966. *Principles of Empirical Realism: Philosophical Essays.* Editorial assistance by Harry Ruja. Springfield, IL: Charles C Thomas.

Further Readings

Books

Alston, William P. 1996. *A Realist Conception of Truth.* Ithaca: Cornell University Press.

Blackburn, Simon. 1993. *Essays in Quasi-Realism.* Oxford: Oxford University Press.

Devitt, Michael. 1984. *Realism and Truth.* Princeton: Princeton University Press.

French, Peter A., Theodore E. Uehling, and Howard K. Wettstein, eds. 1988. *Realism and Anti-Realism.* Vol. 12, Midwest Studies in Philosophy. Minneapolis: University of Minnesota Press.

Goodman, Nelson. 1978. *Ways of Worldmaking.* Indianapolis: Hackett.

Luntley, Michael. 1988. *Language, Logic, and Experience: The Case for Anti-Realism.* La Salle, IL: Open Court.

Putnam, Hilary. 1981. *Reason, Truth, and History.* Cambridge: Cambridge University Press.

———. 1983. *Realism and Reason.* Edited by H. Putnam. Vol. 3, *Philosophical Papers.* Cambridge: Cambridge University Press.

———. 1987. *The Many Faces of Realism.* La Salle, IL: Open Court.

———. 1990. *Realism With a Human Face.* Cambridge: Harvard University Press.

Vision, Gerald. 1988. *Modern Anti-Realism and Manufactured Truth.* London: Routledge.
Wright, Crispin. 1986. *Realism, Meaning, and Truth.* Oxford: Blackwell.
———. 1992. *Truth and Objectivity.* Cambridge: Harvard University Press.
Young, James 0. 1995. *Global Anti-Realism.* Brookfield: Ashgate.

Articles

Alston, William P. 1979. "Yes, Virginia, There Is a Real World." *The Proceedings and Addresses of the American Philosophical Association* 52 (6): 779–808.
Devitt, Michael. 1991. "Aberrations of the Realism Debate." *Philosophical Studies* 61: 43–63.
Dummett, Michael. 1982. "Realism." *Synthese* 52: 55–112.
Ellis, Brian. 1988. "Internal Realism." *Synthese* 76: 409–434.
Haack, Susan. 1987. "Realism." *Synthese* 73: 275–299.
Horwich, Paul. 1982. "Three Forms of Realism." *Synthese* 51: 181–201.
Millikan, Ruth Garrett. 1986. "Metaphysical Anti-Realism?" *Mind* 95: 417–431.
Plantinga, Alvin. 1982. "How to Be an Anti-Realist." *The Proceedings and Addresses of the American Philosophical Association* 56 (1): 47–70.
Smart, J. J. C. 1995. "A Form of Metaphysical Realism." *Philosophical Quarterly* 45 (180): 301–315.

Part III

Truth

FREDERICK SCHMITT

Introduction to Truth

THERE ARE FOUR HISTORICALLY IMPORTANT THEORIES of propositional or linguistic truth: the correspondence theory, the pragmatist theory, the coherence theory, and the deflationary theory.[1] The *correspondence theory* of truth holds that a proposition (or other bearer of truth-values—e.g., a sentence, utterance, statement, or belief) is true when it corresponds to reality. The correspondence theory has an ancient provenance and was endorsed, at least implicitly, by nearly all the philosophers before the year 1800 who had much to say about truth—philosophers as diverse as Aristotle, Spinoza, Hume, and Kant. The *pragmatist theory,* proposed by the American philosophers C. S. Peirce and William James, holds that a proposition is true just in case it is useful to believe the proposition. The *coherence theory* is associated with nineteenth- and twentieth-century idealism and claims that a proposition is true just in case it coheres with a specified system of belief. The *deflationary theory,* a twentieth-century reaction to earlier theories of truth, denies that there is anything more to truth than certain logical functions of the truth predicate "is true."

In this introduction, I will discuss these four historically important theories of truth, beginning with the pragmatist theory.[2] I will focus, in the case of the pragmatist and coherence theories, on the motivation for the theories. My reason for focusing on motivation here is that these theories are counterintuitive and thus need philosophical motivation. The deflationary and correspondence theories, by contrast, are intuitively attractive and need little antecedent motivation. Accordingly, I will concentrate on objections to these theories.

I will begin with the pragmatist theory of truth. In William James's version, the pragmatist theory of truth holds that the truth of a proposition turns on the utility of believing the proposition. As James put it, "The possession of true thoughts means everywhere the possession of invaluable instruments of action."[3] James held that "the true is only the expedient in our way of thinking, just as the right is only the expedient in our way of behaving."[4]

On one interpretation (ascribed to James by G. E. Moore[5]), the view is that a proposition is true just in case it is practically useful to believe it. This view is open to two objections. First, a proposition could be true but useless to believe—for example, propositions

This essay was commissioned especially for this volume and appears here for the first time.

about the precise temperature of small regions in the interior of stars outside of the light cone of any thinking being. Second, a proposition could be useful to believe but false. There are diverse and conflicting beliefs about the afterlife promulgated by various religions, and these beliefs make life easier to bear for many people; yet since they conflict, they cannot all be true. This account of truth as the practical utility of belief is quite implausible.

There is, however, an alternative, textually and philosophically more attractive interpretation of James (ascribed to him by Bertrand Russell and A. O. Lovejoy[6]), according to which a proposition is true just in case it is cognitively useful to believe it. Cognitive utility may be understood in either of two ways. On one understanding, it is the capacity of a belief to organize, predict, and explain experience (e.g., the belief that there is a mouse in the house organizes, explains, and predicts experiences about holes in the baseboard, the disappearance of cheese, etc.). So understood, the pragmatist theory is a version of the coherence theory of truth. Such a view would seem to face objections analogous to the useless true belief and useful false belief objections to the practical utility version of the pragmatist theory of truth just mentioned. However, the cognitive utility of a belief may also be understood differently, as Susan Haack suggests in her paper for this volume. The cognitive utility of a belief may be understood as the capacity of the belief to survive further experience: a proposition is true just in case a belief in the proposition would fail properly to survive all future actual (or, alternatively, possible) experience. On this pragmatist theory, James endorses something akin to C. S. Peirce's pragmatist theory of truth, according to which truth is the limit of inquiry: a proposition is true just in case belief in the proposition would result from repeated application of a proper method of inquiry in light of all actual (or possible) experience.[7] For Peirce, a method of inquiry is proper (my term for an unnamed status in Peirce) when it leads to stable belief, and scientific method is the only proper method because it alone among methods leads to stable belief. James replaces Peirce's account of a proper method as a method that yields stable beliefs with a more liberal account of proper belief revision in terms of conservative, consistent revision: a belief in a proposition properly survives an experience when it is retained under a revision of all beliefs in light of the experience, a revision that is conservative in retaining as many beliefs as possible while rendering beliefs consistent.[8] So understood, James's theory and Peirce's theory are both *epistemic* theories of truth: they characterize truth in terms of epistemically proper method or proper belief revision, where an epistemically proper method and epistemically proper belief revision lead to epistemically justified belief.

How might these pragmatist theories be motivated? One motivation for characterizing truth in epistemic terms is to guarantee that truth can be known. However, the definitions of truth offered by James and Peirce provide only the most tenuous guarantee that truth is knowable: they entail only that any given truth can be known in the limit of inquiry, not that it can be known in a finite span of time or effort. Yet many truths can be known intuitively right now. More importantly, one might question whether it is the job of a definition of truth to guarantee that truth is knowable. It would seem that whether truth is knowable should depend on the contingent cognitive capacities of knowers, not on the concept of truth alone.

Might there be a more successful motivation for a pragmatist theory of truth? Some writers (Misak,[9] and Haack in her contribution to this volume) have suggested that a pragmatist theory of truth can be motivated by another doctrine of American pragmatism, the pragmatist theory of concepts or meaning. Pragmatism broadly conceived is the idea, shared by Peirce, James, and John Dewey, that we should make sense of concepts by tying them to human practice and experience. As Peirce puts it:

> . . . consider what effects, which might conceivably have practical bearings, we conceive the object of our conception to have. Then our conception of those effects is the whole of our conception of the object.[10]

It is natural to interpret Peirce here as identifying a concept of *X* with the concept of the conceivable observable effects of *X*. This interpretation is confirmed by an example Peirce gives immediately following the quoted passage: the meaning of "hard" is that an object will not be scratched by many other substances and other such observable effects. If this pragmatist theory of meaning motivates a pragmatist theory of truth, then there is a motivation for the latter theory internal to pragmatism.

It is plausible to suppose that Peirce and James took the pragmatist theory of meaning to motivate their theories of truth, but I do not think the motivation succeeds. According to the pragmatist theory of meaning, the concept of the truth of a proposition is nothing but the concept of the conceivable observable effects of the truth of the proposition. This does not, however, motivate a pragmatist theory of truth. First, it does not entail that truth is the limit of inquiry, as Peirce claims. This is because the observable effects of the truth of a proposition include not just the consequence that belief in the proposition would result in the long run from scientific method; they also include the observable logical consequences of the proposition. Second, and for the same reason, the pragmatist theory of meaning does not entail that truth is what it is cognitively useful to believe in the sense of what survives further experiences.[11]

Might one interpret the pragmatist theory of meaning differently and in this way obtain support for a pragmatist theory of truth? One might suggest that the pragmatist theory of meaning claims that the concept of *X* is the concept, not of the conceivable observable effects of *X*, but rather of the conceivable effects of *X* on experience. The proposal would then be that the concept of the truth of a proposition is just the concept of the conceivable consequences of the proposition for experience. Might this support a pragmatist theory of truth? This interpretation conflicts with Peirce's own example of the meaning of "hard," which identifies that meaning with the observable effects of the object's being hard rather than with the effects on experience of the object's being hard. But apart from this textual objection to this reply, there is the philosophical point that even the effects of the truth of a proposition on experience outstrip the mere fact that the belief would result in the long run from scientific method or that the belief would survive further experiences. So the pragmatist theory of meaning does not motivate Peirce's and James's pragmatist theories of truth. Those theories have no compelling motivation internal to pragmatism.

Let us turn next to the coherence theory of truth. According to this theory, a true proposition is one that coheres with some specified coherent set of actual or ideal beliefs. The theory has roots in Hegelian idealism and may even be traced as far back to Spinoza. However, some writers in the Hegelian tradition endorse only a coherence theory of justification, not a coherence theory of truth. This is the case with F. H. Bradley.[12] Other writers endorse a coherence theory of truth, but do not oppose it to a correspondence theory of truth; on the contrary, they derive it from a correspondence theory under an idealist coherence account of reality. This appears to be true of Spinoza.[13] On this way of arguing for a coherence theory of truth, the theory is a substantive metaphysical theory of truth, rather than a basic account of the nature of truth; it is not a rival of the correspondence theory. However, one writer in the Hegelian tradition, Brand Blanshard, clearly distinguished the coherence theory of truth from the coherence theory of justification, endorsed both theories, and rejected the correspondence theory of truth.[14]

Blanshard offered the following argument for the coherence theory of truth on the basis of the coherence theory of justification—an argument embraced by Nicholas Rescher in his contribution to this volume. The argument begins with the premise that epistemic justification (or knowledge) and truth are essentially tied to one another: a justified belief is a belief that meets the test or criterion of truth—our means of judging the truth. But, as Rescher puts it, the criterion of truth must (in ideal circumstances) "identify real truths"—that is, identify a proposition as true only if it is true. If it does not do this, then it does not count as a genuine criterion. So justified beliefs must (in ideal circumstances) be true. But the coherence theory of justification is true, and according to this theory, a justified belief is a coherent belief. Thus, coherent beliefs must (in ideal circumstances) be true. Conversely, any true proposition must cohere with the set of ideally coherent (hence true) beliefs. So a proposition is true just in case it coheres with the ideally coherent set of beliefs.

Does this argument succeed in motivating the coherence theory of truth? We may waive the question whether the coherence theory of justification is correct.[15] Even with this waiver, there remain two obstacles to the success of the standard motivation. One obstacle is that Rescher's requirement that a genuine criterion of a kind *K* identifies real *K*s seems to be too strong. In the sense in which a justified belief is plausibly a belief that meets a criterion, the criterion must be one that enables us to acquire justified beliefs, and thus it must be a criterion that is practical in the sense that we are able to employ it to get justified beliefs. But we are not able to employ any criterion of truth that meets Rescher's requirement. Certainly it is not generally true that the tests we are able to employ, and think to be genuine criteria, for judging whether objects are of a given kind *K* meet Rescher's requirement. Consider, for example, a standard test we employ for judging whether a substance is an acid: it turns red litmus paper blue. This test is fallible and sometimes identifies nonacids as acids, even under ideal circumstances (unless ideal circumstances are simply defined, circularly, as circumstances in which the substance is an acid). Yet, I take it, this is a genuine criterion of being an acid, if criteria are tests that enable us to judge whether objects are of a given kind. The point generalizes: there are few if any practically useful criteria that meet Rescher's requirement. Insisting that the criterion of truth must identify real truths at the very least renders it doubtful whether the criterion will be one we are able to employ to judge whether propositions are true, and thus renders it doubtful that a justified belief is a belief that meets the criterion of truth. (This is not to say that a criterion of kind *K* need not *frequently* identify something as *K* only if it is *K*. It is plausible enough that a criterion of truth must identify real truths with high frequency. But that is not enough to motivate the coherence theory of truth, since the criterion will occasionally identify falsehoods as true and thus truth cannot be identified with meeting the criterion.)

There is a second obstacle to the standard motivation for the coherence theory of truth. It is doubtful that every true proposition must cohere with the ideally coherent set of beliefs. It seems possible that ideally coherent beliefs be generally false. At any rate, this is possible if the ideally coherent set of beliefs is the set of beliefs justified under ideal circumstances. For even under ideal circumstances, a justified coherent fantasy is possible. The coherentist might reply to this problem by imposing the requirement that the coherent set of beliefs coheres with a set of data describing actual or possible experiences (as Rescher does). But this requirement goes beyond the requirements imposed by a coherence theory of justification. Indeed, it seems that to avoid the problem, the coherentist would need to specify that the data are true propositions describing actual or possible experiences; for false propositions describing experiences would not rule out a coherent fantasy. But this specification would employ the notion of truth and thus introduce a circularity into the coherence theory of truth. Consequently, the standard motivation for the coherence theory of truth fails.

The third theory of truth we wish to examine is deflationism. Deflationists reject the view, common to pragmatist, coherence, and correspondence theories of truth, that truth is a normal property of propositions or other truth-bearers. Deflationists propose instead that there is nothing to the notion of truth but what is required by the logical, grammatical, or pragmatic functions of the truth predicate. On one version, the redundancy theory of truth, to say "'*p*' is true" (or "It is true that *p*") is not to attribute a property to the proposition expressed by "*p*," but simply to express "*p*."[16] On another version, to say "'*p*' is true" is simply to agree with, confirm, endorse, or concede what has already been said, "*p*."[17] However, I will focus on a third version of deflationism. According to this version, the point of truth predication is to be able to assent to propositions without expressing their exact content. Thus, we can assent to the proposition that $E = mc^2$, or Einstein's law, without saying "$E = mc^2$," by saying "Einstein's law is true." This logical function of "true" is indispensable for assenting to propositions when we are unable to express their exact content, as when we do not know the content or when the propositions can only be expressed by infinitely many sentences. Paul Horwich has proposed a simple and elegant version of deflationism, the minimal theory of truth, motivated by the idea that the nature of truth is given entirely by the function of truth predication in assent.[18] (I will follow Horwich in writing <*p*> for "the proposition that *p*.") For Horwich, the theory of truth consists simply of propositions like:

<<Snow is white> is true if and only if snow is white>.

In other words, it consists of all propositions of the form:

<*p*> is true if and only if *p*.

We may call propositions of this form T-equivalences.

Certainly deflationists are right that the truth-predicate does perform the logical function of enabling assent as just explained. I agree with the deflationist that if the truth predicate preformed only this logical function, and if the nature of truth were entirely captured by the logical function of the truth predicate, then deflationism would prevail. But neither of these assumptions is secure.

I will mention here four objections to Horwich's minimal theory of truth. First, the minimal theory entails bivalence, the principle that every proposition is either true or false. But bivalence is mistaken. To see that the minimal theory entails bivalence, suppose that, contrary to bivalence, some proposition <*p*> has no truth-value. Then the right-hand side of the T-equivalence for <*p*>, "*p*," would have no truth-value, while the left-hand side "<*p*> is true," would have the value false, since it is false that <*p*> is true (because <*p*> has no truth-value). So the T-equivalence fails. This reasoning shows that if bivalence fails, so does the minimal theory. But then, by contraposition, the minimal theory entails bivalence.

Now, the trouble is that bivalence is mistaken. For there are sentences that have no truth-value—such as sentences whose presuppositions fail ("The present king of France is tall") and propositions ascribing vague properties in borderline cases ("Joe is bald," when Joe's hairline is receding). Since the minimal theory entails bivalence, and bivalence is mistaken, the minimal theory is mistaken.

The deflationist might reply to this objection by insisting that when "*p*" has no truth-value, neither does "<*p*> is true" (Wright 92, 61–62). Alternatively, the deflationist might reply that sentences with failed presuppositions are simply false, while borderline vague sentences are either true or false; it is just that we cannot tell which truth-value they have. Whatever the merits of these replies, they do not answer a related objection to the minimal theory: that whether bivalence is correct or mistaken, a theory of truth ought not to entail that it is correct, or that sentences with failed presuppositions are false, or that borderline vague sentences are either true or false. The question whether sentences that fail their presuppositions are false or rather truth-valueless ought to be decided in part by the nature of presuppositions, not by the general nature of truth alone. Similarly, the question whether borderline vague sentences are truth-valueless should be decided in part by the theory of vagueness, not the general nature of truth alone. For example, a theory of truth ought to leave open the possibility that reality itself is vague in such a way that borderline vague sentences are neither true nor false.

A second objection to the minimal theory is that there are not enough T-equivalences to characterize truth for all propositions to which we can ascribe truth-values in English. Consider the sentence "What God believes is true." This seems to be a perfectly intelligible English sentence using our ordinary notion of truth. But the minimal theory cannot characterize the notion of truth here. There are not enough T-equivalences to define "true" in such a way as to cover this sentence. For presumably God believes many propositions that cannot be expressed in English. Yet all the T-equivalences are expressible in English; the minimal theory specifies the axioms of the theory of truth as precisely the T-equivalences expressible in English. But if a T-equivalence is expressible in English, so is the proposition <*p*> for which it defines truth. This problem arises because the minimal theory implicitly characterizes truth in a way that limits its application to propositions expressible in English. It makes truth implicitly a relation to a language.[19] Note, too, that on the minimal theory, one who uttered the sentence "What God believes is true" would thereby assert the propositions that God believes. But this seems very counterintuitive.

Similarly, we may object to the minimal theory on the ground that the sentence "God believes more true propositions than are expressible in English" is a consistent sentence, yet the minimal theory entails that it is self-contradictory. For on the minimal theory the sentence is equivalent to "There are true propositions expressible in English such that God believes them, but these propositions are not expressible in English"—a self-contradictory sentence. The minimal theorist would have to reply to this objection in one of two ways: either claim, implausibly, that all propositions are expressible in English, or insist, also implausibly, that the sentence "What God believes is true" is unintelligible or otherwise utilizes a nonstandard notion of truth.

A third objection to the minimal theory appeals to the nature of the truth-conditions we ascribe to beliefs and desires in our everyday explanations of human behavior.[20] We explain a human action (e.g., Skip's going to the grocer) by ascribing a belief (that by going to the grocer Skip will acquire food) and a desire (that Skip acquire food); and in ascribing the belief and desire, we ascribe propositions as contents of the belief and desire, and these propositions have truth-conditions. But the truth-conditions we ascribe here cannot be those the minimal theory ascribes. For ascribing such truth-conditions implicitly relates us, the explainers, to the belief and desire. This is because the minimal theory gives truth-conditions that are essentially related to the language of those ascribing the truth-conditions. Truth, and thus the truth-conditions for any given proposition, is defined by the T-equivalences, which are limited to the propositions expressible in the language of the ascriber. Thus, ascribing truth-conditions implicitly relates the agent's beliefs and desires to the ascriber. Indeed, on the minimal theory, a sentence has truth-conditions only if it is expressible in English. Yet it seems that we could explain an agent's behavior by ascribing beliefs and desires even though the beliefs and desires are not expressible in English. The objection to the minimal theory is that it makes the explanation of behavior implicitly a relation to the explainer when it should be a relation only between the agent's beliefs and desires and the action.

There is a fourth, related objection to the minimal theory. It begins with the observation that the notion of truth is employed in defining the notion of cognitive reliability (the tendency to believe truths on a given topic), and we ascribe cognitive reliability to explain people's success in various practices. We explain a cook's success in making tasty, nutritious food by ascribing cognitive reliability to the cook on the topic of cooking. This explanation involves ascribing truth-conditions to beliefs. But the explanation of the cook's success in cooking cannot involve a relation to us as explainers; it has solely to do with the capacities of the cook. Thus, the truth-conditions ascribed here are not those characterized by the minimal theory. So the minimal theory is mistaken.[21]

Let us turn, finally, to the correspondence theory of truth. The correspondence theory holds that a proposition is true just in case it corresponds to the way the world is. The view is customarily, and plausibly, attributed to Aristotle on the basis of his remark, "To say of what is not that it is *not* or of what is not that it *is,* is falsehood; and to say of what is that it is and of what is not that it is not, is true."[22] On one natural interpretation of this remark, it claims that a statement is true just when what it states to be the case is the case. So interpreted, Aristotle is clearly proposing a correspondence theory rather than a deflationary theory, since the right-hand side of the definition of truth employs the notion of what a statement states to be the case, and that notion is a semantical notion, one that refers to a kind of correspondence between statement and fact; but of course a deflationary definition of truth employs no semantical notions on its right-hand side. Similar correspondence theories were endorsed by writers as diverse as Plato, Spinoza, and Hume.[23]

Let us begin with the bare idea of the correspondence theory, that truth is correspondence between a proposition and the way the world is. A simple correspondence theory results from taking "the way the world is" to refer to facts:[24]

> A proposition is true is true just in case there is some fact to which it corresponds.
> A proposition is false just in case there is no fact to which it corresponds.

One might go on to define correspondence in a *logical* way:

> <*p*> corresponds only to the fact that *p*.

One difficulty with this simple correspondence theory is that it entails bivalence: every proposition is either true or false, since either there is some fact to which it corresponds, or there is no such fact. To get around this, one might introduce a distinction between negative and positive correspondence:

> A proposition is true just in case there is some fact to which it positively corresponds.
> A proposition is false just in case there is some fact to which it negatively corresponds.

One could then characterize positive and negative correspondence this way:

> <*p*> positively corresponds only to the fact that *p*.
> <*p*> negatively corresponds only to the fact that not-*p*.

On this reading of positive and negative correspondence, the theory avoids entailing bivalence if it can be that not-*p* while it is not a fact that not-*p*. The theory faces another problem, however: it is capable of defining correspondence only for propositions expressible in English (since it employs an English sentence, "*p*," to characterize the fact which corresponds to the proposition that *p*). Thus, the theory faces one of the objections that confronted deflationism: that it cannot define truth for propositions not expressible in English.

An alternative correspondence theory emerges from the idea, discussed by Marian David in this volume, that the correspondence relation is a representation relation: a proposition corresponds to whatever it represents (e.g., a possible fact). One value of employing the notion of representation here is that enables us to formulate a correspondence theory that applies to propositions not expressible in English. We might develop the idea by saying that[25]

> A proposition is true just in case it represents a possible fact, and the fact obtains.
> A proposition is false just in case it represents a possible fact, and the fact does not obtain.

This too avoids bivalence, if the negation of a proposition does not entail that the fact represented by the proposition fails to obtain. Note that on this account true and false propositions bear the same correspondence relation to reality, and the difference between them lies not in how they correspond to reality but in whether the possible facts to which they correspond obtain.

There is another way to develop the idea that the correspondence relation is a representation relation. Rather than saying that propositions represent facts, one might treat both propositions and facts as complex entities and treat representation as a complex relation between the constituents of a proposition and the constituents of a fact.[26] Such an account would have to characterize truth differently for propositions with different constituent structures. Consider the structurally simplest propositions, the atomic propositions—those of a sort typically expressed in English by a sentence of the form "*a* is *F*," where "*a*" names an object and "*F*" is a predicate. An atomic proposition consists of the concept *A* of an individual object and the predication *Pr* of a property of that object. For an atomic proposition *P* = <*A*,*Pr*>, the account of truth would read:

> *P* is true just in case *A* denotes some object *x*, *Pr* predicates some property *f* of *x*, and *x* belongs to the extension of *f*.
> *P* is false just in case *A* denotes some object *x*, *Pr* predicates some property *f* of *x*, and *x* does not belong to the extension of *f*.

(I will not address here what truth-value *P* gets when *A* fails to denote a real object.) The advantage of a compositional correspondence theory is that it can serve to account for the truth-conditions ascribed in explaining behavior, while theories that treat truth noncompositionally, referring to unitary facts, cannot do so. To explain behavior, it is necessary to treat the propositional contents of beliefs and desires compositionally, since parts of the content of belief (e.g., the subject concept) must be seen as repeating in the desire.

The compositional correspondence theory resembles Alfred Tarski's theory of the semantic conception of truth (as presented in his contribution to this volume). Tarski took himself to offer a correspondence account of truth (pp. 119, 130). However, Tarski was concerned to eliminate semantical notions from his characterization of truth. He replaced talk of representation, denotation, and the like with a list of identities that in effect associate terms and predicates with entities and properties. For this reason, his definition of truth resembles the deflationary theory in being unable to define truth for sentences that are not expressible in the language for which truth is defined.

I will mention here two chief objections to the correspondence theory. One objection is that it is impossible for propositions or other truth-bearers to correspond to facts (or objects and their properties). For propositions belong to the realm of ideas, while facts belong to the realm of things. But why should ideas not be able to correspond to things? If the correspondence relation is a representation relation, then it would seem that ideas can and do correspond to things, since they represent things.[27]

The second objection to the correspondence theory is that the theory makes truth unknowable, since true propositions must correspond to reality, and thus knowing whether a proposition is true requires knowing whether it corresponds to reality. But in reply, first, there is no objection hereto knowing *p*, for most propositions *p*. The objection is to knowing a certain kind of proposition—namely, of the form: a specified proposition is true. But once it conceded that we can know propositions not of this form, then it would seem that, for many propositions <*p*> we could infer that a proposition <*p*> is true, from the proposition <*p*> together with the T-equivalence <<*p*> is true if and only if *p*>. T-equivalences hold for many propositions, even on the correspondence theory, and indeed are derivable from the correspondence theory under certain assumptions, which we can generally know on the basis of semantical knowledge. Second, why should knowing that <*p*> corresponds to a fact be so difficult? On a representational approach to the correspondence relation, knowing that a proposition corresponds to reality requires knowing that it represents some fact and that the fact obtains. I take it that the correspondence theory puts up no special barrier to knowing that facts obtain, since whether we know such things has nothing to do with the nature of truth, only with the nature of facts and cognition. Thus, the difficulty would have to lie in our knowing that the proposition represents the fact. Whether this is difficult would presumably depend on just what representation involves. If, for example it involves a causal relation between the representation (or its mental correlate, a structure of concepts) and the fact represented, then we would have to know which such causal relations hold. But knowing which causal relations of this sort hold would not seem to be especially susceptible to skepticism. For this reason, the second objection to the correspondence theory does not seem persuasive.

This completes our review of the historically important theories of truth.[28]

NOTES

1. For an accessible, compact introduction to the theory of truth, see my *Truth: A Primer* (Boulder, CO: Westview, 1995). In this book, I develop many of the points made in this introduction. For a thorough, painstaking introduction to theories of truth, see Richard Kirkham, *Theories of Truth: A Critical Introduction* (Cambridge: MIT Press, 1992).

2. There are many important philosophical questions about truth besides the choice between these theories. Among these are: whether the bearers of truth-values are propositions, sentences, or statements (see Lawrence E. Johnson, *Focusing on Truth* [London: Routledge, 1992] for discussion); whether "true" is a predicate of sentences or a sentential operator; the relation between truth, assertion, reference, meaning, and information (see Michael Devitt and Kim Sterelny, *Language and Reality: An Introduction to the Philosophy of Language* [Cambridge: MIT Press, 1989]); "eternal" truths and indexicals; degrees of truth and quantity of information; and the semantical paradoxes such as the liar paradox (see Kirkham, ch. 9, for a good introductory review of the liar paradox).

3. William James, *Pragmatism* (Cambridge: Harvard University Press, 1975), p. 97.

4. William James, *The Meaning of Truth* (Cambridge: Harvard University Press, 1909), p. vii.

5. G. E. Moore, "Professor James' 'Pragmatism,'' in *Philosophical Studies* (London: Routledge, 1922).

6. Bertrand Russell, "James's Conception of Truth," in *Philosophical Essays* (London: Allen and Unwin, 1910); A. O. Lovejoy, "The Thirteen Pragmatisms II," *Journal of Philosophy* 5 (1908): 29–39.

7. C. S. Peirce, "The Fixation of Belief," in Justus Buchler, ed., *Philosophical Writings of Peirce* (New York: Dover, 1955).

8. Here I offer an alternative to Haack's view that James is merely *supplementing* Peirce's account of truth with a view of belief revision. I think it is more plausible to regard James as *replacing* Peirce's stability theory of proper method with a coherence theory of proper belief revision.

9. C. J. Misak, *Truth and the End of Inquiry* (Oxford: Clarendon Press, 1991).

10. C. S. Peirce, "How to Make Our Ideas Clear," in Justus Buchler, ed., *Philosophical Writings of Peirce* (New York: Dover, 1955): p. 31.

11. Perhaps the proponent of this motivation for the pragmatic theories of truth would reply that pragmatic theories of truth apply to beliefs, not to propositions, and the observable effects of the truth of a belief include only the effects of its truth on cognition. But even if this is granted, the effects of the truth of a belief on cognition outstrip the fact that the belief would result in the long run from scientific method.

12. F. H. Bradley, *Essays on Truth and Reality* (Oxford: Oxford University Press, 1914). See Susan Haack, *Philosophy of Logic* (Cambridge: Cambridge University Press, 1978), p. 95, for interpretation of Bradley on the coherence theory of justification.

13. Baruch Spinoza, *Ethics, The Collected Works of Spinoza,* vol. 1, ed. and trans. Edwin Curley (Princeton: Princeton University Press, 1985). For issues in interpreting Spinoza, see Ralph C. S. Walker, *The Coherence Theory of Truth* (London: Routledge, 1989).

14. See Brand Blanshard, *The Nature of Thought* (New York: Macmillan, 1941), pp. 260ff. For a useful historical review of coherence theories of truth, see Walker, *The Coherence Theory of Truth.* See also Gerald Vision, *Modern Anti-Realism and Manufactured Truth* (London: Routledge, 1988).

15. For coherence theories of justification, see Laurence BonJour, *The Coherence Theory of Empirical Knowledge* (Cambridge: Harvard University Press, 1985) and Keith Lehrer, *Theory of Knowledge* (Boulder, CO: Westview, 1990).

16. See F. P. Ramsey, "Facts and Propositions," *Proceedings of the Aristotelian Society,* supp. vol. 7 (1927): 153–170; and C. J. F. Williams, *What is Truth?* (Cambridge: Cambridge University Press, 1976).

17. See P. F. Strawson, "Truth," *Proceedings of the Aristotelian Society,* supp. vol. 24 (1950): 129–156. A related theory is the prosentential theory of truth of Dorothy Grover, Joe Camp, and Nuel Belnap, "A Prosentential Theory of Truth," *Philosophical Studies* 27 (1975): 72–124.

18. Paul Horwich, *Truth* (Oxford: Basil Blackwell, 1990).

19. Horwich says that it is possible to say what the T-equivalences are for propositions not expressible in English, though you cannot express these equivalences. Horwich seems to think that his theory can characterize truth as it applies to inexpressible propositions by saying what these T-equivalences are without expressing them—namely, by saying that they are propositions of the form <<*p*> is true if and only if *p*>. But this is mistaken. It is not possible to say what the T-equivalences

are for inexpressible propositions. For there are no such T-equivalences. The only T-equivalences there are are those expressible in English. The form <<*p*> is true if and only if *p*> has no content—adverting to the form does not tell us what the T-equivalence is for a given <*p*>—until "*p*" is specified, either by an English sentence or by a (substitutional) quantifier over English sentences. To see this, imagine that we refer to some proposition X that God believes that is inexpressible in English. We have no way of saying what the T-equivalence for X is, since we have no "*p*" that expresses X. Here is another way to put the point, for those familiar with substitutional quantification: the form <<*p*> is true if and only if *p*> is not the *form* of a proposition but the *name* of a proposition; yet the proposition it names is specified only when we specify "*p*," either by an English sentence or by a substitution quantifier (hence a quantifier restricted to English sentences).

20. Arguments of this sort were proposed by Hartry Field, "The Deflationary Conception of Truth," in G. MacDonald and C. Wright, eds., *Fact, Science and Morality: Essays on A. J. Ayer's Language Truth and Logic* (Oxford: Basil Blackwell, 1986). For a review of the arguments, see my *Truth: A Primer,* ch. 6.

21. Stephen Leeds ("Truth, Correspondence, and Success," *Philosophical Studies* 79 [1995]: 1–36) has suggested that this objection to the minimal theory fails because, on the minimal theory, the truth-conditions we appeal to in explaining behavior are no different from those we appeal to on the correspondence theory; it's just that on the minimal theory, we identify those truth-conditions in a way that relates them to a given language. According to Leeds, our explanation of behavior using the truth-conditions ascribed by the minimal theory no more implicitly refers to a language than our explanation of astronomical phenomena implicitly refers to Paris just because we refer in the explanation to the standard meter as defined by a meter bar in Paris. In my view, this reply to the objection to the minimal theory fails. There is an important difference between the example of the astronomical explanation and the explanation of behavior. In the case of the astronomical explanation, in referring to a meter we refer to a length that has its character independently of the existence of the meter bar in Paris to which we refer to designate that length. But in the case of the explanation of behavior, in referring to truth-conditions, we do not, on the minimal theory, refer to entities and properties that exist and have their character independently of the language to which we refer to designate these truth-conditions. We may take truth-conditions to be either of two items. We may take them to be T-equivalences or we may take them to be the propositions ascribed to beliefs (what is expressed by the right-hand side of the T-equivalences, "*p*"). Now, if truth-conditions are T-equivalences, then they involve the concept of truth. But on the minimal theory, the concept of truth is defined by the T-equivalences expressible in English, and so ascribing truth-conditions does implicitly relate the beliefs and desires to English (or, if you like, to the expressibility powers of English). On this way of understanding truth-conditions, the truth-conditions ascribed by the minimal theory are not the same as those ascribed by the correspondence theory. If, by contrast, truth-conditions are taken to be propositions, then ascribing truth-conditions does not itself ascribe a relation to English, even on the minimal theory. (However, the two theories still ascribe different truth-conditions in many cases. For example, in cases in which we cannot express the proposition in English, the minimal theory disallows ascribing a truth-condition, and so presumably disallows ascribing belief, while the correspondence theory does not.) But this does not save the minimal theory from the objection. For when we explain behavior, we ascribe not only truth-conditions in the sense of propositions; we also assume the T-equivalences, and we ascribe to the beliefs the satisfaction of analogous equivalences (<the belief that *p* is true if and only if *p*>). This assumption and this ascription of an equivalence figure in our explanation of behavior, at least in the case of explaining successful practices by appeal to T-reliability. Indeed, in the latter case, we ascribe not only the satisfaction of analogous equivalences to the beliefs; we also ascribe truth-values to many beliefs (in particular, the value true), and this clearly relates the beliefs to English, on the minimal theory.

22. Aristotle, *Metaphysics, The Basic Works of Aristotle* (New York: Random House, 1968), 1011b26.

23. Plato, *Sophist, Plato* 12 vols., trans. H. N. Fowler (Cambridge: Loeb Classical Library, Harvard University Press, 1921), 262E263D; Baruch Spinoza, *Ethics,* First Part, Axiom 6; David Hume, *A Treatise of Human Nature,* 2nd ed., L. A. Selby-Bigge and P. H. Nidditch (Oxford: Clarendon Press, 1978), p. 415.

24. For a correspondence theory along these lines, see G. E. Moore, *Some Main Problems in Philosophy* (London: Allen and Unwin, 1953). For a related account of truth, see William Alston, *A Realist Conception of Truth* (Ithaca: Cornell University Press, 1996).

25. For a correspondence theory of this sort, see J. L. Austin, "Truth," *Proceedings of the Aristotelian Society,* supp. vol. 24 (1950): 111–128. Lawrence Johnson develops and defends an Austinian theory of truth in *Focusing on Truth.*

26. For an account along these lines, see Hartry Field, "The Deflationary Conception of Truth." See also my *Truth: A Primer,* ch. 6.

27. For development of this response, see William Alston, *A Realist Conception of Truth,* ch. 3.

28. There are theories of truth that do not conform to any of the four theories we have discussed. Huw Price *(Facts and the Function of Truth* [Oxford: Basil Blackwell, 1988]) has proposed a theory of truth on which the truth predicate is not descriptive of propositions. Let it be noted that some have doubted or denied the value of ascriptions of truth. See William Alston, *A Realist Conception of Truth,* ch. 8, for a review of the issues.

9 The Semantic Conception of Truth and the Foundations of Semantics

ALFRED TARSKI

THIS PAPER CONSISTS OF TWO PARTS; the first has an expository character, and the second is rather polemical.

In the first part I want to summarize in an informal way the main results of my investigations concerning the definition of truth and the more general problem of the foundations of semantics. These results have been embodied in a work which appeared in print several years ago.[1] Although my investigations concern concepts dealt with in classical philosophy, they happen to be comparatively little known in philosophical circles, perhaps because of their strictly technical character. For this reason I hope I shall be excused for taking up the matter once again.[2]

Since my work was published, various objections, of unequal value, have been raised to my investigations; some of these appeared in print, and others were made in public and private discussions in which I took part. In the second part of the paper I should like to express my views regarding these objections. I hope that the remarks which will be made in this context will not be considered as purely polemical in character, but will be found to contain some constructive contributions to the subject.

In the second part of the paper I have made extensive use of material graciously put at my disposal by Dr. Maria Kokosyńska (University of Lwów). I am especially indebted and grateful to Professors Ernest Nagel (Columbia University) and David Rynin (University of California, Berkeley) for their help in preparing the final text and for various critical remarks.

I. EXPOSITION

1. THE MAIN PROBLEM—A SATISFACTORY DEFINITION OF TRUTH

Our discussion will be centered around the notion[4] of *truth*. The main problem is that of giving a *satis-*

From Philosophy *and* Phenomenological Research, *vol. 4, 1944, pp. 341–374. Reprinted by permission of the Tarski family.*

factory definition of this notion, i.e., a definition which is *materially adequate* and *formally correct.* But such a formulation of the problem, because of its generality, cannot be considered unequivocal, and requires some further comments.

In order to avoid any ambiguity, we must first specify the conditions under which the definition of truth will be considered adequate from the material point of view. The desired definition does not aim to specify the meaning of a familiar word used to denote a novel notion; on the contrary, it aims to catch hold of the actual meaning of an old notion. We must then characterize this notion precisely enough to enable anyone to determine whether the definition actually fulfills its task.

Secondly, we must determine on what the formal correctness of the definition depends. Thus, we must specify the words or concepts which we wish to use in defining the notion of truth; and we must also give the formal rules to which the definition should conform. Speaking more generally, we must describe the formal structure of the language in which the definition will be given.

The discussion of these points will occupy a considerable portion of the first part of the paper.

2. THE EXTENSION OF THE TERM "TRUE"

We begin with some remarks regarding the extension of the concept of truth which we have in mind here.

The predicate "true" is sometimes used to refer to psychological phenomena such as judgments or beliefs, sometimes to certain physical objects, namely, linguistic expressions and specifically sentences, and sometimes to certain ideal entities called "propositions." By "sentence" we understand here what is usually meant in grammar by "declarative sentence"; as regards the term "proposition," its meaning is notoriously a subject of lengthy disputations by various philosophers and logicians, and it seems never to have been made quite clear and unambiguous. For several reasons it appears most convenient to *apply the term "true" to sentences,* and we shall follow this course.[5]

Consequently, we must always relate the notion of truth, like that of a sentence, to a specific language; for it is obvious that the same expression which is a true sentence in one language can be false or meaningless in another.

Of course, the fact that we are interested here primarily in the notion of truth for sentences does not exclude the possibility of a subsequent extension of this notion to other kinds of objects.

3. THE MEANING OF THE TERM "TRUE"

Much more serious difficulties are connected with the problem of the meaning (or the intension) of the concept of truth.

The word "true," like other words from our everyday language, is certainly not unambiguous. And it does not seem to me that the philosophers who have discussed this concept have helped to diminish its ambiguity. In works and discussions of philosophers we meet many different conceptions of truth and falsity, and we must indicate which conception will be the basis of our discussion.

We should like our definition to do justice to the intuitions which adhere to the *classical Aristotelian conception of truth*—intuitions which find their expression in the well-known words of Aristotle's *Metaphysics:*

> To say of what is that it is not, or of what is not that it is, is false, while to say of what is that it is, or of what is not that it is not, is true.

If we wished to adapt ourselves to modern philosophical terminology, we could perhaps express this conception by means of the familiar formula:

> The truth of a sentence consists in its agreement with (or correspondence to) reality.

(For a theory of truth which is to be based upon the latter formulation the term "correspondence theory" has been suggested.)

If, on the other hand, we should decide to extend the popular usage of the term "designate" by applying it not only to names, but also to sentences, and if we agreed to speak of the designata of sentences as "states of affairs," we could possibly use for the same purpose the following phrase:

> A sentence is true if it designates an existing state of affairs.[6]

However, all these formulations can lead to various misunderstandings, for none of them is sufficiently precise and clear (though this applies much less to the original Aristotelian formulation than to either of the others); at any rate, none of them can be considered a satisfactory definition of truth. It is up to us to look for a more precise expression of our intuitions.

4. A CRITERION FOR THE MATERIAL ADEQUACY OF THE DEFINITION[7]

Let us start with a concrete example. Consider the sentence "snow is white." We ask the question under what conditions this sentence is true or false. It seems clear that if we base ourselves on the classical conception of truth, we shall say that the sentence is true if snow is white, and that it is false if snow is not white. Thus, if the definition of truth is to conform to our conception, it must imply the following equivalence:

> The sentence "snow is white" is true if, and only if, snow is white.

Let me point out that the phrase "snow is white" occurs on the left side of this equivalence in quotation marks, and on the right without quotation marks. On the right side we have the sentence itself, and on the left the name of the sentence. Employing the medieval logical terminology we could say that on the right side the words "snow is white" occur in *suppositio formalis,* and on the left in *suppositio materialis.* It is hardly necessary to explain why we must have the name of the sentence, and not the sentence itself, on the left side of the equivalence. For, in the first place, from the point of view of the grammar of our language, an expression of the form "*X* is true" will not become a meaningful sentence if we replace in it '*X*' by a sentence or by anything other than a name—since the subject of a sentence may be only a noun or an expression functioning like a noun. And, in the second place, the fundamental conventions regarding the use of any language require that in any utterance we make about an object it is the name of the object which must be employed, and not the object itself. In consequence, if we wish to say something about a sentence, for example that it is true, we must use the name of this sentence, and not the sentence itself.[8]

It may be added that enclosing a sentence in quotation marks is by no means the only way of forming its name. For instance, by assuming the usual order of letters in our alphabet, we can use the following expression as the name (the description) of the sentence "snow is white":

> the sentence constituted by three words, the first of which consists of the 19th, 14th, 15th, and 23rd letters, the second of the 9th and 19th letters, and the third of the 23rd, 8th, 9th, 20th, and 5th letters of the English alphabet.

We shall now generalize the procedure which we have applied above. Let us consider an arbitrary sentence; we shall replace it by the letter '*p*.' We form the name of this sentence and we replace it by another letter, say '*X*.' We ask now what is the logical relation between the two sentences "*X* is true" and '*p*.' It is clear that from the point of view of our basic conception of truth these sentences are equivalent. In other words, the following equivalence holds:

> (T) X is true if, and only if, p.

We shall call any such equivalence (with '*p*' replaced by any sentence of the language to which the word "true" refers, and '*X*' replaced by a name of this sentence) an "*equivalence of the form* (T)."

Now at last we are able to put into a precise form the conditions under which we will consider the usage and the definition of the term "true" as adequate from the material point of view: we wish to use the term "true" in such a way that all equivalences of the form (T) can be asserted, and *we shall call a definition of truth "adequate" if all these equivalences follow from it.*

It should be emphasized that neither the expression (T) itself (which is not a sentence, but only a schema of a sentence) nor any particular instance of the form (T) can be regarded as a definition of truth. We can only say that every equivalence of the form (T) obtained by replacing '*p*' by a particular sentence, and '*X*' by a name of this sentence, may be considered a partial definition of truth, which explains wherein the truth of this one individual sentence consists. The general definition has to be, in a certain sense, a logical conjunction of all these partial definitions.

(The last remark calls for some comments. A language may admit the construction of infinitely many sentences; and thus the number of partial definitions of truth referring to sentences of such a language will also be infinite. Hence to give our remark a precise sense we should have to explain what is meant by a "logical conjunction of infinitely many sentences"; but this would lead us too far into technical problems of modern logic.)

5. TRUTH AS A SEMANTIC CONCEPT

I should like to propose the name *"the semantic conception of truth"* for the conception of truth which has just been discussed.

Semantics is a discipline which, speaking loosely, *deals with certain relations between expressions of a language and the objects* (or "states of affairs") "*referred to*" by *those expressions.* As typical examples of semantic concepts we may mention the concepts of *designation, satisfaction,* and *definition* as these occur in the following examples:

> the expression "the father of his country" designates (denotes) George Washington;
>
> snow satisfies the sentential function (the condition) "x is white";
>
> the equation "2•x = 1" defines (uniquely determines) the number ½.

While the words "designates," "satisfies," and "defines" express relations (between certain expressions and the objects "referred to" by these expressions), the word "true" is of a different logical nature: it expresses a property (or denotes a class) of certain expressions, viz., of sentences. However, it is easily seen that all the formulations which were given earlier and which aimed to explain the meaning of this word (cf. sections 3 and 4) referred not only to sentences themselves, but also to objects "talked about" by these sentences, or possibly to "states of affairs" described by them. And, moreover, it turns out that the simplest and the most natural way of obtaining an exact definition of truth is one which involves the use of other semantic notions, e.g., the notion of satisfaction. It is for these reasons that we count the concept of truth which is discussed here among the concepts of semantics, and the problem of defining truth proves to be closely related to the more general problem of setting up the foundations of theoretical semantics.

It is perhaps worthwhile saying that semantics as it is conceived in this paper (and in former papers of the author) is a sober and modest discipline which has no pretensions of being a universal patent-medicine for all the ills and diseases of mankind, whether imaginary or real. You will not find in semantics any remedy for decayed teeth or illusions of grandeur or class conflicts. Nor is semantics a device for establishing that everyone except the speaker and his friends is speaking nonsense.

From antiquity to the present day the concepts of semantics have played an important role in the discussions of philosophers, logicians, and philologists. Nevertheless, these concepts have been treated for a long time with a certain amount of suspicion. From a historical standpoint, this suspicion is to be regarded as completely justified. For although the meaning of semantic concepts as they are used in everyday language seems to be rather clear and understandable, still all attempts to characterize this meaning in a general and exact way miscarried. And what is worse, various arguments in which these concepts were involved, and which seemed otherwise quite correct and based upon apparently obvious premises, led frequently to paradoxes and antinomies. It is sufficient to mention here the *antinomy of the liar,* Richard's *antinomy of definability* (by means of a finite number of words), and Grelling-Nelson's *antinomy of heterological terms.*[9]

I believe that the method which is outlined in this paper helps to overcome these difficulties and assures the possibility of a consistent use of semantic concepts.

6. LANGUAGES WITH A SPECIFIED STRUCTURE

Because of the possible occurrence of antinomies, the problem of specifying the formal structure and the vocabulary of a language in which definitions of semantic concepts are to be given becomes especially acute; and we turn now to this problem.

There are certain general conditions under which the structure of a language is regarded as *exactly specified*. Thus, to specify the structure of a language, we must characterize unambiguously the class of those words and expressions which are to be considered *meaningful*. In particular, we must indicate all words which we decide to use without defining them, and which are called "*undefined* (or *primitive*) *terms*"; and we must give the so-called *rules of definition* for introducing new or *defined terms*. Furthermore, we must set up criteria for distinguishing within the class of expressions those which we call "*sentences.*" Finally, we must formulate the conditions under which a sentence of the language can be *asserted*. In particular, we must indicate all *axioms* (or *primitive sentences*), i.e., those sentences which we decide to assert without proof; and we must give the so-called *rules of inference* (or *rules of proof*) by means of which we can deduce new asserted sentences from other sentences which have been previously asserted. Axioms, as well as sentences deduced from them by means of rules of inference, are referred to as "*theorems*" or "*provable sentences.*"

If in specifying the structure of a language we refer exclusively to the form of the expressions involved, the language is said to be *formalized*. In such a language theorems are the only sentences which can be asserted.

At the present time the only languages with a specified structure are the formalized languages of various systems of deductive logic, possibly enriched by the introduction of certain nonlogical terms. However, the field of application of these languages is rather comprehensive; we are able, theoretically, to develop in them various branches of science, for instance, mathematics and theoretical physics.

(On the other hand, we can imagine the construction of languages which have an exactly specified structure without being formalized. In such a language the assertability of sentences, for instance, may depend not always on their form, but sometimes on other, nonlinguistic factors. It would be interesting and important actually to construct a language of this type, and specifically one which would prove to be sufficient for the development of a comprehensive branch of empirical science; for this would justify the hope that languages with specified structure could finally replace everyday language in scientific discourse.)

The problem of the definition of truth obtains a precise meaning and can be solved in a rigorous way only for those languages whose structure has been exactly specified. For other languages—thus, for all natural, "spoken" languages—the meaning of the problem is more or less vague, and its solution can have only an approximate character. Roughly speaking, the approximation consists in replacing a natural language (or a portion of it in which we are interested) by one whose structure is exactly specified, and which diverges from the given language "as little as possible."

7. THE ANTINOMY OF THE LIAR

In order to discover some of the more specific conditions which must be satisfied by languages in which (or for which) the definition of truth is to be given, it will be advisable to begin with a discussion of that antinomy which directly involves the notion of truth, namely, the antinomy of the liar.

To obtain this antinomy in a perspicuous form,[10] consider the following sentence:

> The sentence printed in this book in the second column on p. 122, line 25 is not true.

For brevity we shall replace the sentence just stated by the letter 's.'

According to our convention concerning the adequate usage of the term 'true', we assert the following equivalence of the form (T):

> (1) 's' is true if, and only if, the sentence printed in this paper in the second column on p. 122, line 25 is not true.

On the other hand. keeping in mind the meaning of the symbol 's,' we establish empirically the following fact:

> (2) 's' is identical with the sentence printed in this paper in the second column on p. 122, line 25.

Now, by a familiar law from the theory of identity (Leibniz's law), it follows from (2) that we may replace in (1) the expression "the sentence printed in this paper in the second column on p. 122, lines 25–26" by the symbol 's.' We thus obtain what follows:

(3) 's' is true if, and only if, 's' is not true.

In this way we have arrived at an obvious contradiction.

In my judgment, it would be quite wrong and dangerous from the standpoint of scientific progress to depreciate the importance of this and other antinomies, and to treat them as jokes or sophistries. It is a fact that we are here in the presence of an absurdity, that we have been compelled to assert a false sentence [since (3), as an equivalence between two contradictory sentences, is necessarily false]. If we take our work seriously, we cannot be reconciled with this fact. We must discover its cause, that is to say, we must analyze premises upon which the antinomy is based; we must then reject at least one of these premises, and we must investigate the consequences which this has for the whole domain of our research.

It should be emphasized that antinomies have played a preeminent role in establishing the foundations of modern deductive sciences. And just as class-theoretical antinomies, and in particular Russell's antinomy (of the class of all classes that are not members of themselves), were the starting point for the successful attempts at a consistent formalization of logic and mathematics, so the antinomy of the liar and other semantic antinomies give rise to the construction of theoretical semantics.

8. THE INCONSISTENCY OF SEMANTICALLY CLOSED LANGUAGES[7]

If we now analyze the assumptions which lead to the antinomy of the liar, we notice the following:

(I) We have implicitly assumed that the language in which the antinomy is constructed contains, in addition to its expressions, also the names of these expressions, as well as semantic terms such as the term "true" referring to sentences (if this language; we have also assumed that all sentences which determine the adequate usage of this term can be asserted in the language. A language with these properties will be called *"semantically closed."*

(II) We have assumed that in this language the ordinary laws of logic hold.

(III) We have assumed that we can formulate and assert in our language an empirical premise such as the statement (2) which has occurred in our argument.

It turns out that the assumption (III) is not essential, for it is possible to reconstruct the antinomy of the liar without its help.[11] But the assumptions (I) and (II) prove essential. Since every language which satisfies both of these assumptions is inconsistent, we must reject at least one of them.

It would be superfluous to stress here the consequences of rejecting the assumption (II), that is, of changing our logic (supposing this were possible) even in its more elementary and fundamental parts. We thus consider only the possibility of rejecting the assumption (I). Accordingly, we decide not to *use any language which is semantically closed* in the sense given.

This restriction would of course be unacceptable for those who, for reasons which are not clear to me, believe that there is only one "genuine" language (or, at least, that all "genuine" languages are mutually translatable). However, this restriction does not affect the needs or interests of science in any essential way. The languages (either the formalized languages or—what is more frequently the case—the portions of everyday language) which are used in scientific discourse do not have to be semantically closed. This is obvious in case linguistic phenomena and, in particular, semantic notions do not enter in any way into the subject matter of a science; for in such a case the language of this science does not have to be provided with any semantic terms at all. However, we shall see in the next section how semantically closed languages can be dispensed with even in those scientific discussions in which semantic notions are essentially involved.

The problem arises as to the position of everyday language with regard to this point. At first blush it would seem that this language satisfies both assumptions (I) and (II), and that therefore it must be inconsistent. But actually the case is not so simple. Our everyday language is certainly not one with an exactly specified structure. We do not know precisely which expressions are sentences, and we know even to a smaller degree which sentences are to be taken as assertible. Thus the problem of consistency has no exact meaning with respect to this language. We may at best only risk the guess that a language whose structure has been exactly specified and which resembles our everyday language as closely as possible would be inconsistent.

9. OBJECT LANGUAGE AND METALANGUAGE

Since we have agreed not to employ semantically closed languages, we have to use two different languages in discussing the problem of the definition of truth and, more generally, any problems in the field of semantics. The first of these languages is the language which is "talked about" and which is the subject matter of the whole discussion; the definition of truth which we are seeking applies to the sentences of this language. The second is the language in which we "talk about" the first language, and in terms of which we wish, in particular, to construct the definition of truth for the first language. We shall refer to the first language as "the object language," and to the second as "the metalanguage."

It should be noticed that these terms "object language" and "metalanguage" have only a relative sense. If, for instance, we become interested in the notion of truth applying to sentences, not of our original object language, but of its metalanguage, the latter becomes automatically the object language of our discussion; and in order to define truth for this language, we have to go to a new metalanguage—so to speak, to a metalanguage of a higher level. In this way we arrive at a whole hierarchy of languages.

The vocabulary of the metalanguage is to a large extent determined by previously stated conditions under which a definition of truth will be considered materially adequate. This definition, as we recall, has to imply all equivalences of the form (T):

(T) X is true if, and only if, p.

The definition itself and all the equivalences implied by it are to be formulated in the metalanguage. On the other hand, the symbol '*p*' in (T) stands for an arbitrary sentence of our object language. Hence it follows that every sentence which occurs in the object language must also occur in the metalanguage; in other words, the metalanguage must contain the object language as a part. This is at any rate necessary for the proof of the adequacy of the definition—even though the definition itself can sometimes be formulated in a less comprehensive metalanguage which does not satisfy this requirement.

[The requirement in question can be somewhat modified, for it suffices to assume that the object-language can be translated into the metalanguage; this necessitates a certain change in the interpretation of the symbol '*p*' in (T). In all that follows we shall ignore the possibility of this modification.]

Furthermore, the symbol *X* in (T) represents the name of the sentence which '*p*' stands for. We see therefore that the metalanguage must be rich enough to provide possibilities of constructing a name for every sentence of the object language.

In addition, the metalanguage must obviously contain terms of a general logical character, such as the expression "if, and only if."[12]

It is desirable for the metalanguage not to contain any undefined terms except such as are involved explicitly or implicitly in the remarks above. i.e.: terms of the object language; terms referring to the form of the expressions of the object language, and used in building names for these expressions; and terms of logic. In particular, we desire *semantic terms* (referring to the object language) *to be introduced into the metalanguage only by definition*. For, if this postulate is satisfied, the definition of truth, or of any other semantic concept, will fulfill what we intuitively expect from every definition; that is, it will explain the meaning of the term being defined in terms whose meaning appears to be completely clear and unequivocal. And, moreover, we have then a kind of guarantee that the use of semantic concepts will not involve us in any contradictions.

We have no further requirements as to the formal structure of the object language and the metalanguage; we assume that it is similar to that of other formalized languages known at the present time. In particular, we assume that the usual formal rules of definition are observed in the metalanguage.

10. CONDITIONS FOR A POSITIVE SOLUTION OF THE MAIN PROBLEM

Now, we have already a clear idea both of the conditions of material adequacy to which the definition of truth is subjected, and of the formal structure of the language in which this definition is to be constructed. Under these circumstances the problem of the definition of truth acquires the character of a definite problem of a purely deductive nature.

The solution of the problem, however, is by no means obvious, and I would not attempt to give it in detail without using the whole machinery of contemporary logic. Here I shall confine myself to a rough outline of the solution and to the discussion of certain points of a more general interest which are involved in it.

The solution turns out to be sometimes positive, sometimes negative. This depends upon some formal relations between the object language and its metalanguage; or, more specifically, upon the fact whether the metalanguage in its logical part is *"essentially richer"* than the object language or not. It is not easy to give a general and precise definition of this notion of "essential richness." If we restrict ourselves to languages based on the logical theory of types, the condition for the metalanguage to be "essentially richer" than the object language is that it contain variables of a higher logical type than those of the object language.

If the condition of "essential richness" is not satisfied, it can usually be shown that an interpretation of the metalanguage in the object language is possible; that is to say, with any given term of the metalanguage a well-determined term of the object language can be correlated in such a way that the assertible sentences of the one language turn out to be correlated with assertible sentences of the other. As a result of this interpretation, the hypothesis that a satisfactory definition of truth has been formulated in the metalanguage turns out to imply the possibility of reconstructing in that language the antinomy of the liar; and this in turn forces us to reject the hypothesis in question.

(The fact that the metalanguage, in its nonlogical part, is ordinarily more comprehensive than the object language does not affect the possibility of interpreting the former in the latter. For example, the names of expressions of the object language occur in the metalanguage, though for the most part they do not occur in the object language itself; but, nevertheless, it may be possible to interpret these names in terms of the object language.)

Thus we see that the condition of "essential richness" is necessary for the possibility of a satisfactory definition of truth in the metalanguage. If we want to develop the theory of truth in a metalanguage which does not satisfy this condition, we must give up the idea of defining truth with the exclusive help of those terms which were indicated above (in section 8). We have then to include the term "true," or some other semantic term, in the list of undefined terms of the metalanguage, and to express fundamental properties of the notion of truth in a series of axioms. There is nothing essentially wrong in such an axiomatic procedure, and it may prove useful for various purposes.[13]

It turns out, however, that this procedure can be avoided. For *the condition of the "essential richness" of the metalanguage proves to be, not only necessary, but also sufficient for the construction of a satisfactory definition of truth;* i.e., if the metalanguage satisfies this condition, the notion of truth can be defined in it. We shall now indicate in general terms how this construction can be carried through.

11. THE CONSTRUCTION (IN OUTLINE) OF THE DEFINITION[14]

A definition of truth can be obtained in a very simple way from that of another semantic notion, namely, of the notion of *satisfaction.*

Satisfaction is a relation between arbitrary objects and certain expressions called *"sentential functions."* These are expressions like "x is white," "x is greater than y," etc. Their formal structure is analogous to that of sentences; however, they *may* contain the so-called free variables (like 'x' and 'y' in "x is greater than y"), which cannot occur in sentences.

In defining the notion of a sentential function in formalized languages, we usually apply what is called a "recursive procedure"; i.e., we first describe sentential functions of the simplest structure (which ordinarily presents no difficulty), and then we indicate the operations by means of which compound functions can be constructed from simpler ones. Such an operation may consist, for instance, in forming the logical disjunction or conjunction of two given functions, i.e., by combining them by the word "or" or "and." A sentence can now be defined simply as a sentential function which contains no free variables.

As regards the notion of satisfaction, we might try to define it by saying that given objects satisfy a given function if the latter becomes a true sentence when we replace in it free variables by names of given objects. In this sense, for example, snow satisfies the sentential function "*x* is white" since the sentence "snow is white" is true. However, apart from other difficulties, this method is not available to us, for we want to use the notion of satisfaction in defining truth.

To obtain a definition of satisfaction we have rather to apply again a recursive procedure. We indicate which objects satisfy the simplest sentential functions; and then we state the conditions under which given objects satisfy a compound function—assuming that we know which objects satisfy the simpler functions from which the compound one has been constructed. Thus, for instance, we say that given numbers satisfy the logical disjunction "*x* is greater than *y* or *x* is equal to *y*" if they satisfy at least one of the functions "*x* is greater than *y*" or "*x* is equal to *y*."

Once the general definition of satisfaction is obtained, we notice that it applies automatically also to those special sentential functions which contain no free variables, i.e., to sentences. It turns out that for a sentence only two cases are possible: a sentence is either satisfied by all objects, or by no objects. Hence we arrive at a definition of truth and falsehood simply by saying that *a sentence is true if it is satisfied by all objects, and false otherwise.*[15]

(It may seem strange that we have chosen a roundabout way of defining the truth of a sentence, instead of trying to apply, for instance, a direct recursive procedure. The reason is that compound sentences are constructed from simpler sentential functions, but not always from simpler sentences; hence no general recursive method is known which applies specifically to sentences.)

From this rough outline it is not clear where and how the assumption of the "essential richness" of the metalanguage is involved in the discussion; this becomes clear only when the construction is carried through in a detailed and formal way.[16]

12. CONSEQUENCES OF THE DEFINITION

The definition of truth which was outlined above has many interesting consequences.

In the first place, the definition proves to be not only formally correct, but also materially adequate (in the sense established in section 4); in other words, it implies all equivalences of the form (T). In this connection it is important to notice that the conditions for the material adequacy of the definition determine uniquely the extension of the term "true." Therefore, every definition of truth which is materially adequate would necessarily be equivalent to that actually constructed. The semantic conception of truth gives us, so to speak, no possibility of choice between various nonequivalent definitions of this notion.

Moreover, we can deduce from our definition various laws of a general nature. In particular, we can prove with its help the *laws of contradiction and of excluded middle,* which are so characteristic of the Aristotelian conception of truth; i.e., we can show that one and only one of any two contradictory sentences is true. These semantic laws should not be identified with the related logical laws of contradiction and excluded middle; the latter belong to the sentential calculus, i.e., to the most elementary part of logic, and do not involve the term "true" at all.

Further important results can be obtained by applying the theory of truth to formalized languages of a certain very comprehensive class of mathematical disciplines; only disciplines of an elementary character and a very elementary logical structure are excluded from this class. It turns out that for a discipline of this class *the notion of truth never coincides with that of provability;* for all provable sentences are true, but there are true sentences which are not provable.[17] Hence it follows further that every such discipline is consistent, but incomplete; that is to say, of any two contradictory sentences at most one is provable, and—what is more—there exists a pair of contradictory sentences neither of which is provable.[18]

13. EXTENSIONS OF THE RESULTS TO OTHER SEMANTIC NOTIONS

Most of the results at which we arrived in the preceding sections in discussing the notion of truth can be extended with appropriate changes to other semantic notions, for instance, to the notion of satisfaction (involved in our previous discussion), and to those of *designation* and *definition*.

Each of these notions can be analyzed along the lines followed in the analysis of truth. Thus, criteria for an adequate usage of these notions can be established; it can be shown that each of these notions, when used in a semantically closed language according to those criteria, leads necessarily to a contradiction;[19] a distinction between the object language and the metalanguage becomes again indispensable; and the "essential richness" of the metalanguage proves in each case to be a necessary and sufficient condition for a satisfactory definition of the notion involved. Hence the results obtained in discussing one particular semantic notion apply to the general problem of the foundations of theoretical semantics.

Within theoretical semantics we can define and study some further notions, whose intuitive content is more involved and whose semantic origin is less obvious, we have in mind, for instance, the important notions of *consequence, synonymity,* and *meaning*.[20]

We have concerned ourselves here with the theory of semantic notions related to an individual object language (although no specific properties of this language have been involved in our arguments). However, we could also consider the problem of developing *general semantics* which applies to a comprehensive class of object languages. A considerable part of our previous remarks can be extended to this general problem; however, certain new difficulties arise in this connection, which will not be discussed here. I shall merely observe that the axiomatic method (mentioned in section 10) may prove the most appropriate for the treatment of the problem.[21]

II. POLEMICAL REMARKS

14. IS THE SEMANTIC CONCEPTION OF TRUTH THE "RIGHT" ONE?

I should like to begin the polemical part of the paper with some general remarks.

I hope nothing which is said here will be interpreted as a claim that the semantic conception of truth is the "right" or indeed the "only possible" one. I do not have the slightest intention to contribute in any way to those endless, often violent discussions on the subject: "What is the right conception of truth?"[22] I must confess I do not understand what is at stake in such disputes, for the problem itself is so vague that no definite solution is possible. In fact, it seems to me that the sense in which the phrase "the right conception" is used has never been made clear. In most cases one gets the impression that the phrase is used in an almost mystical sense based upon the belief that every word has only one "real" meaning (a kind of Platonic or Aristotelian idea), and that all the competing conceptions really attempt to catch hold of this one meaning; since, however, they contradict each other, only one attempt can be successful, and hence only one conception is the "right" one.

Disputes of this type are by no means restricted to the notion of truth. They occur in all domains where—instead of an exact, scientific terminology—common language with its vagueness and ambiguity is used; and they are always meaningless, and therefore in vain.

It seems to me obvious that the only rational approach to such problems would be the following: We should reconcile ourselves with the fact that we are confronted, not with one concept, but with several different concepts which are denoted by one word; we should try to make these concepts as clear as possible (by means of definition, or of an axiomatic procedure, or in some other way); to avoid further confusions, we should agree to use different terms for different concepts; and then we may proceed to a quiet and systematic study of all concepts involved, which will exhibit their main properties and mutual relations.

Referring specifically to the notion of truth, it is undoubtedly the case that in philosophical discussions—and perhaps also in everyday usage—some incipient conceptions of this notion can be found that differ essentially from the classical one (of which the semantic conception is but a modernized form). In fact, various conceptions of this sort have been discussed in the literature, for instance, the pragmatic conception, the coherence theory, etc.[6]

It seems to me that none of these conceptions have been put so far in an intelligible and unequivocal form. This may change, however; a time may come when we find ourselves confronted with several incompatible, but equally clear and precise, conceptions of truth. It *will* then become necessary to abandon the ambiguous usage of the word "true," and to introduce several terms instead, each to denote a different notion. Personally, I should not feel hurt if a future world congress of the "theoreticians of truth" should decide—by a majority of votes—to reserve the word "true" for one of the nonclassical conceptions, and should suggest another word, say, "frue," for the conception considered here. But I cannot imagine that anybody could present cogent arguments to the effect that the semantic conception is "wrong" and should be entirely abandoned.

15. FORMAL CORRECTNESS OF THE SUGGESTED DEFINITION OF TRUTH

The specific objections which have been raised to my investigations can be divided into several groups; each of these will be discussed separately.

I think that practically all these objections apply, not to the special definition I have given, but to the semantic conception of truth in general. Even those which were leveled against the definition actually constructed could be related to any other definition which conforms to this conception.

This holds, in particular, for those objections which concern the formal correctness of the definition. I have heard a few objections of this kind; however, I doubt very much whether anyone of them can be treated seriously.

As a typical example let me quote in substance such an objection.[23] In formulating the definition we use necessarily sentential connectives, i.e., expressions like "if . . . , then," "or," etc. They occur in the definiens; and one of them, namely, the phrase "if, and only if" is usually employed to combine the definiendum with the definiens. However, it is well known that the meaning of sentential connectives is explained in logic with the help of the words "true" and "false"; for instance, we say that an equivalence, i.e., a sentence of the form "*p* if, and only if, *q*," is true if either both of its members, i.e., the sentences represented by '*p*' and '*q*,' are true or both are false. Hence the definition of truth involves a vicious circle.

If this objection were valid, no formally correct definition of truth would be possible: for we are unable to formulate any compound sentence without using sentential connectives, or other logical terms defined with their help. Fortunately, the situation is not so bad.

It is undoubtedly the case that a strictly deductive development of logic is often preceded by certain statements explaining the conditions under which sentences of the form "if *p*, then *q*," etc., are considered true or false. (Such explanations are often given schematically, by means of the so-called truth-tables.) However, these statements are outside of the system of logic, and should not be regarded as definitions of the terms involved. They are not formulated in the language of the system, but constitute rather special consequences of the definition of truth given in the metalanguage. Moreover, these statements do not influence the deductive development of logic in any way. For in such a development we do not discuss the question whether a given sentence is true, we are only interested in the problem whether it is provable.[24]

On the other hand, the moment we find ourselves within the deductive system of logic—or of any discipline based upon logic, e.g., of semantics—we either treat sentential connectives as undefined terms, or else we define them by means of other sentential connectives but never by means of semantic terms like "true" or "false." For instance, if we agree to regard the expressions "not" and "if . . . , then" (and possibly also "if, and only if") as undefined terms, we can define the term "*or*" by stating that a sentence of the form "*p* or *q*" is equivalent to the corresponding sentence of the form "if not *p*, then *q*." The definition can be formulated e.g., in the following way:

(p or q) if, and only if, (if not p, then q).

This definition obviously contains no semantic terms.

However, a vicious circle in definition arises only when the definiens contains either the term to be defined itself, or other terms defined with its help. Thus we clearly see that the use of sentential connectives in defining the semantic term "*true*" does not involve any circle.

I should like to mention a further objection which I have found in the literature and which seems also to concern the formal correctness, if not of the definition of truth itself, then at least of the arguments which lead to this definition.[25]

The author of this objection mistakenly regards scheme (T) (from section 4) as a definition of truth. He charges this alleged definition with "inadmissible brevity, i.e., incompleteness," which "does not give us the means of deciding whether by 'equivalence' is meant a logical-formal, or a nonlogical and also structurally nondescribable relation." To remove this "defect" he suggests supplementing (T) in one of the two following ways:

(T') X is true if, and only if, p is true.

or

(T") X is true if, and only if, p is the case (i.e., if what p states is the case).

Then he discusses these two new "definitions," which are supposedly free from the old, formal "defect," but which turn out to be unsatisfactory for other, nonformal reasons.

This new objection seems to arise from a misunderstanding concerning the nature of sentential connectives (and thus to be somehow related to that previously discussed). The author of the objection does not seem to realize that the phrase "if, and only if" (in opposition to such phrases as "are equivalent" or "is equivalent to") expresses no relation between sentences at all since it does not combine names of sentences.

In general, the whole argument is based upon an obvious confusion between sentences and their names. It suffices to point out that—in contradistinction to (T)—schemata (T') and (T") do not give any meaningful expressions if we replace in them 'p' by a sentence; for the phrases "p is true" and "p is the case" (i.e., "what p states is the case") become meaningless if 'p' is replaced by a sentence, and not by the name of a sentence (cf. section 4).[26]

While the author of the objection considers schema (T) "inadmissibly brief," I am inclined, on my part, to regard schemata (T') and (T") as "inadmissibly long." And I think even that I can rigorously prove this statement on the basis of the following definition: An expression is said to be "inadmissibly long" if (i) it is meaningless, and (ii) it has been obtained from a meaningful expression by inserting superfluous words.

16. REDUNDANCY OF SEMANTIC TERMS—THEIR POSSIBLE ELIMINATION

The objection I am going to discuss now no longer concerns the formal correctness of the definition, but is still concerned with certain formal features of the semantic conception of truth.

We have seen that this conception essentially consists in regarding the sentence "X is true" as equivalent to the sentence denoted by 'X' (where 'X' stands for a name of a sentence of the object language). Consequently, the term "true" when occurring in a simple sentence of the form "X is true" can easily be eliminated, and the sentence itself, which belongs to the metalanguage, can be replaced by an equivalent sentence of the object language; and the same applies to compound sentences provided the term "*true*" occurs in them exclusively as a part of the expressions of the form "X is true."

Some people have therefore urged that the term "true" in the semantic sense can always be eliminated; and that for this reason the semantic conception of truth is altogether sterile and useless. And since the same considerations apply to other semantic notions, the conclusion has been drawn that semantics as a whole is a purely verbal game and at best only a harmless hobby.

But the matter is not quite so simple.[27] The sort of elimination here discussed cannot always be made. It cannot be done in the case of universal statements which express the fact that all sentences of a certain type are true, or that all true sentences have a certain property. For instance, we can prove in the theory of truth the following statement:

All consequences of true sentences are true.

However, we cannot get rid here of the word "true" in the simple manner contemplated.

Again, even in the case of particular sentences having the form "X is true" such a simple elimination cannot always be made. In fact, the elimination is possible only in those cases in which the name of the sentence which is said to be true occurs in a form that enables us to reconstruct the sentence itself. For example, our present historical knowledge does not give us any possibility of eliminating the word "true" from the following sentence:

The first sentence written by Plato is true.

Of course, since we have a definition for truth and since every definition enables us to replace the definiendum by its definiens, an elimination of the term "true" in its semantic sense is always theoretically possible. But this would not be the kind of simple elimination discussed above, and it would not result in the replacement of a sentence in the metalanguage by a sentence in the object language.

If, however, anyone continues to urge that—because of the theoretical possibility of eliminating the word "true" on the basis of its definition—the concept of truth is sterile, he must accept the further conclusion that all defined notions are sterile. But this outcome is so absurd and so unsound historically that any comment on it is unnecessary. In fact, I am rather inclined to agree with those who maintain that the moments of greatest creative advancement in science frequently coincide with the introduction of new notions by means of definition.

17. CONFORMITY OF THE SEMANTIC CONCEPTION OF TRUTH WITH PHILOSOPHICAL AND COMMON-SENSE USAGE

The question has been raised whether the semantic conception of truth can indeed be regarded as a precise form of the old, classical conception of this notion.

Various formulations of the classical conception were quoted in the early part of this paper (section 3). I must repeat that in my judgment none of them is quite precise and clear. Accordingly, the only sure way of settling the question would be to confront the authors of those statements with our new formulation, and to ask them whether it agrees with their intentions. Unfortunately, this method is impractical since they died quite some time ago.

As far as my own opinion is concerned, I do not have any doubts that our formulation does conform to the intuitive content of that of Aristotle. I am less certain regarding the later formulations of the classical conception, for they are very vague indeed.[28]

Furthermore, some doubts have been expressed whether the semantic conception does reflect the notion of truth in its common-sense and everyday usage. I clearly realize (as I already indicated) that the common meaning of the word "true"—as that of any other word of everyday language—is to some extent vague, and that its usage more or less fluctuates. Hence the problem of assigning to this word a fixed and exact meaning is relatively unspecified, and every solution of this problem implies necessarily a certain deviation from the practice of everyday language.

In spite of all this, I happen to believe that the semantic conception does conform to a very considerable extent with the common-sense usage—although I readily admit I may be mistaken. What is more to the point, however, I believe that the issue raised can be settled scientifically, though of course not by a deductive procedure, but with the help of the statistical questionnaire method. As a matter of fact, such research has been carried on, and some of the results have been reported at congresses and in part published.[29]

I should like to emphasize that in my opinion such investigations must be conducted with the utmost care. Thus, if we ask a high-school boy, or even an adult intelligent man having no special philosophical training, whether he regards a sentence to be true if it agrees with reality, or if it designates an existing state of affairs, it may simply turn out that he does not understand the question; in consequence his response, whatever it may be, will be of no value for us. But his answer to the question whether he would admit that the sentence "it is snowing" could be true although it is not snowing, or could be false although it is snowing, would naturally be very significant for our problem.

Therefore, I was by no means surprised to learn (in a discussion devoted to these problems) that in a group of people who were questioned only 15% agreed that "true" means for them "agreeing with reality," while 90% agreed that a sentence such as "it is snowing" is true if, and only if, it is snowing. Thus, a great majority of these people seemed to reject the classical conception of truth in its "philosophical" formulation, while accepting the same conception when formulated in plain words (waiving the question whether the use of the phrase "the same conception" is here justified).

18. THE DEFINITION IN ITS RELATION TO "THE PHILOSOPHICAL PROBLEM OF TRUTH" AND TO VARIOUS EPISTEMOLOGICAL TRENDS

I have heard it remarked that the formal definition of truth has nothing to do with the philosophical problem of truth.[30] However, nobody has ever pointed out to me in an intelligible way just what this problem is. I have been informed in this connection that my definition, though it states necessary and sufficient conditions for a sentence to be true, does not really grasp the "essence" of this concept. Since I have never been able to understand what the "essence" of a concept is, I must be excused from discussing this point any longer.

In general, I do not believe that there is such a thing as "the philosophical problem of truth." I do believe that there are various intelligible and interesting (but not necessarily philosophical) problems concerning the notion of truth, but I also believe that they can be exactly formulated and possibly solved only on the basis of a precise conception of this notion.

While on the one hand the definition of truth has been blamed for not being philosophical enough, on the other a series of objections have been raised charging this definition with serious philosophical implications, always of a very undesirable nature. I shall discuss now one special objection of this type; another group of such objections will be dealt with in the next section.

It has been claimed that—due to the fact that a sentence like "snow is white" is taken to be semantically true if snow is *in fact* white (italics by the critic)—logic finds itself involved in a most uncritical realism.[31]

If there were an opportunity to discuss the objection with its author, I should raise two points. First, I should ask him to drop the words "in fact," which do not occur in the original formulation and which are misleading, even if they do not affect the content. For these words convey the impression that the semantic conception of truth is intended to establish the conditions under which we are warranted in asserting any given sentence, and in particular any empirical sentence. However, a moment's refection shows that this impression is merely an illusion; and I think that the author of the objection falls victim to the illusion which he himself created.

In fact, the semantic definition of truth implies nothing regarding the conditions under which a sentence like (1):

(1) snow is white

can be asserted. It implies only that, whenever we assert or reject this sentence, we must be ready to assert or reject the correlated sentence (2):

the sentence "snow is white" is true.

Thus, we may accept the semantic conception of truth without giving up any epistemological attitude we may have had; we may remain naive realists, critical realists or idealists, empiricists or metaphysicians—whatever we were before. The semantic conception is completely neutral toward all these issues.

In the second place, I should try to get some information regarding the conception of truth which (in the opinion of the author of the objection) does not involve logic in a most naive realism. I would gather that this conception must be incompatible with the semantic one. Thus, there must be sentences which are true in one of these conceptions without being true in the other. Assume, e.g., the sentence (1) to be of this kind. The truth of this sentence in the semantic conception is determined by an equivalence of the form (T):

> The sentence "snow is white" is true if, and only if, snow is white.

Hence in the new conception we must reject this equivalence, and consequently we must assume its denial:

> The sentence "snow is white" is true if, and only if, snow is not white (*or perhaps:* snow, in fact, is not white).

This sounds somewhat paradoxical. I do not regard such a consequence of the new conception as absurd; but I am a little fearful that someone in the future may charge this conception with involving logic in a "most sophisticated kind of irrealism." At any rate, it seems to me important to realize that every conception of truth which is incompatible with the semantic one carries with it consequences of this type.

I have dwelt a little on this whole question, not because the objection discussed seems to me very significant, but because certain points which have arisen in the discussion should be taken into account by all those who for various epistemological reasons are inclined to reject the semantic conception of truth.

19. ALLEGED METAPHYSICAL ELEMENTS IN SEMANTICS

The semantic conception of truth has been charged several times with involving certain metaphysical elements. Objections of this sort have been made to apply not only to the theory of truth, but to the whole domain of theoretical semantics.[32]

I do not intend to discuss the general problem whether the introduction of a metaphysical element into a science is at all objectionable. The only point which will interest me here is whether and in what sense metaphysics is involved in the subject of our present discussion.

The whole question obviously depends upon what one understands by metaphysics." Unfortunately, this notion is extremely vague and equivocal. When listening to discussions in this subject, sometimes one gets the impression that the term "metaphysical" has lost any objective meaning, and is merely used as a kind of professional philosophical invective.

For some people metaphysics is a general theory of objects (ontology)—a discipline which is to be developed in a purely empirical way, and which differs from other empirical sciences only by its generality. I do not know whether such a discipline actually exists (some cynics claim that it is customary in philosophy to baptize unborn children), but I think that in any case metaphysics in this conception is not objectionable to anybody, and has hardly any connections with semantics.

For the most part, however, the term "metaphysical" is used as directly opposed—in one sense or another—to the term "empirical"; at any rate, it is used in this way by those people who are distressed by the thought that any metaphysical elements might have managed to creep into science. This general conception of metaphysics assumes several more specific forms.

Thus, some people take it to be symptomatic of a metaphysical element in a science when methods of inquiry are employed which are neither deductive nor empirical. However, no trace of this symptom can be found in the development of semantics (unless some metaphysical elements are involved in the object language to which the semantic notions refer). In particular, the semantics of formalized languages is constructed in a purely deductive way.

Others maintain that the metaphysical character of a science depends mainly on its vocabulary and, more specifically, on its primitive terms. Thus, a term is said to be metaphysical if it is neither logical nor mathematical, and if it is not associated with an empirical procedure which enables us to decide whether a thing is denoted by this term or not. With respect to such a view of metaphysics it is sufficient to recall that a metalanguage includes only three kinds of undefined terms: (i) terms taken from logic, (ii) terms of the corresponding object language, and (iii) names of expressions in the object language. It is thus obvious that no metaphysical undefined terms occur in the metalanguage (again, unless such terms appear in the object language itself).

There are, however, some who believe that, even if no metaphysical terms occur among the primitive terms of a language, they may be introduced by definitions; namely, by those definitions which fail to provide us with general criteria for deciding whether an object falls under the defined concept. It is argued that the term "true" is of this kind, since no universal criterion of truth follows immediately from the definition of this term, and since it is generally believed (and in a certain sense can even be proved) that such a criterion will never be found. This comment on the actual character of the notion of truth seems to be perfectly just. However, it should be noticed that the notion of truth does not differ in this respect from many notions in logic, mathematics, and theoretical parts of various empirical sciences, e.g., in theoretical physics.

In general, it must be said that if the term "metaphysical" is employed in so wide a sense as to embrace certain notions (or methods) of logic, mathematics, or empirical sciences, it will apply a fortiori to those of semantics. In fact, as we know from part I of the paper, in developing the semantics of a language we use all the notions of this language, and we apply even a stronger logical apparatus than that which is used in the language itself. On the other hand, however, I can summarize the arguments given above by stating that in no interpretation of the term "metaphysical" which is familiar and more or less intelligible to me does semantics involve any metaphysical elements peculiar to itself.

I should like to make one final remark in connection with this group of objections. The history of science shows many instances of concepts which were judged metaphysical (in a loose, but in any case derogatory sense of this term) before their meaning was made precise; however, once they received a rigorous, formal definition, the distrust in them evaporated. As typical examples we may mention the concepts of negative and imaginary numbers in mathematics. I hope a similar fate awaits the concept of truth and other semantic concepts; and it seems to me, therefore, that those who have distrusted them because of their alleged metaphysical implications should welcome the fact that precise definitions of these concepts are now available. If in consequence semantic concepts lose philosophical interest, they will only share the fate of many other concepts of science, and this need give rise to no regret.

20. APPLICABILITY OF SEMANTICS TO SPECIAL EMPIRICAL SCIENCES

We come to the last and perhaps the most important group of objections. Some strong doubts have been expressed whether semantic notions find or can find applications in various domains of intellectual activity. For the most part such doubts have concerned the applicability of semantics to the field of empirical science—either to special sciences or to the general methodology of this field; although similar skepticism has been expressed regarding possible applications of semantics to mathematical sciences and their methodology.

I believe that it is possible to allay these doubts to a certain extent, and that some optimism with respect to the potential value of semantics for various domains of thought is not without ground.

To justify this optimism, it suffices I think to stress two rather obvious points. First, the development of a theory which formulates a precise definition of a notion and establishes its general properties provides *eo ipso* a firmer basis for all discussions in which this notion is involved; and, therefore, it cannot be irrelevant for anyone who uses this notion, and desires to do so in a conscious and consistent way. Secondly, semantic notions are actually involved in various branches of science, and in particular of empirical science.

The fact that in empirical research we are concerned only with natural languages and that theoretical semantics applies to these languages only with certain approximation, does not affect the problem essentially. However, it has undoubtedly this effect that progress in semantics will have but a delayed and somewhat limited influence in this field. The situation with which we are confronted here does not differ essentially from that which arises when we apply laws of logic to arguments in everyday life—or, generally, when we attempt to apply a theoretical science to empirical problems.

Semantic notions are undoubtedly involved, to a larger or smaller degree, in psychology, sociology, and in practically all the humanities. Thus, a psychologist defines the so-called intelligence quotient in terms of the numbers of *true* (right) and *false* (wrong) answers given by a person to certain questions; for a historian of culture the range of objects for which a human race in successive stages of its development possesses adequate *designations* may be a topic of great significance; a student of literature may be strongly interested in the problem whether a given author always uses two given words with the same *meaning*. Examples of this kind can be multiplied indefinitely.

The most natural and promising domain for the applications of theoretical semantics is clearly linguistics—the empirical study of natural languages. Certain parts of this science are even referred to as "semantics," sometimes with an additional qualification. Thus, this name is occasionally given to that portion of grammar which attempts to classify all words of a language into parts of speech, according to what the words mean or designate. The study of the evolution of meanings in the historical development of a language is sometimes called "historical semantics." In general, the totality of investigations on semantic relations which occur in a natural language is referred to as "descriptive semantics." The relation between theoretical and descriptive semantics is analogous to that between pure and applied mathematics, or perhaps to that between theoretical and empirical physics; the role of formalized languages in semantics can be roughly compared to that of isolated systems in physics.

It is perhaps unnecessary to say that semantics cannot find any direct applications in natural sciences such as physics, biology, etc.; for in none of these sciences are we concerned with linguistic phenomena, and even less with semantic relations between linguistic expressions and objects to which these expressions and objects which these expressions refer. We shall see, however, in the next section that semantics may have a kind of indirect influence even on those sciences in which semantic notions are not directly involved.

21. APPLICABILITY OF SEMANTICS TO THE METHODOLOGY OF EMPIRICAL SCIENCE

Besides linguistics, another important domain for possible applications of semantics is the methodology of science; this term is used here in a broad sense so as to embrace the theory of science in general. Independent of whether a science is conceived merely as a system of statements or as a totality of certain statements and human activities, the study of scientific language constitutes an essential part of the methodological discussion of a science. And it seems to me clear that any tendency to eliminate semantic notions (like those of truth and designation) from this discussion would make it fragmentary and inadequate.[33] Moreover, there is no reason for such a tendency today, once the main difficulties in using semantic terms have been overcome. The semantics of scientific language should be simply included as a part in the methodology of science.

I am by no means inclined to charge methodology and, in particular, semantics—whether theoretical or descriptive—with the task of clarifying the meanings of all scientific terms. This task is left to those sciences in which the terms are used, and is actually fulfilled by them (in the same way in which, e.g., the task of clarifying the meaning of the term "*true*" is left to, and fulfilled by, semantics). There may be, however, certain special problems of this sort in which a methodological approach is desirable or indeed necessary (perhaps, the problem of the notion of causality is a good example here); and in a methodological discussion of such problems semantic notions may play an essential role. Thus, semantics may have some bearing on any science whatsoever.

The question arises whether semantics can be helpful in solving general and, so to speak, classical problems of methodology. I should like to discuss here with some detail a special, though very important, aspect of this question.

One of the main problems of the methodology of empirical science consists in establishing conditions under which an empirical theory or hypothesis should be regarded as acceptable. This notion of acceptability must be relativized to a given stage of the development of a science (or to a given amount of presupposed knowledge). In other words, we may consider it as provided with a time coefficient; for a theory which is acceptable today may become untenable tomorrow as a result of new scientific discoveries.

It seems *a priori* very plausible that the acceptability of a theory somehow depends on the truth of its sciences, and that consequently a methodologist in his (so far rather unsuccessful) attempts at making the notion of acceptability precise, can expect some help from the semantic theory of truth. Hence we ask the question: Are there any postulates which can be reasonably imposed on acceptable theories and which involve the notion of truth? And, in particular, we ask whether the following postulate is a reasonable one:

> An acceptable theory cannot contain (or imply) any false sentences.

The answer to the last question is clearly negative. For, first of all, we are practically sure, on the basis of our historical experience, that every empirical theory which is accepted today will sooner or later be rejected and replaced by another theory. It is also very probable that the new theory will be incompatible with the old one; i.e., will imply a sentence which is contradictory to one of the sentences contained in the old theory. Hence, at least one of the two theories must include false sentences, in spite of the fact that each of them is accepted at a certain time. Secondly, the postulate in question could hardly ever be satisfied in practice, for we do not know, and are very unlikely to find, any criteria of truth which enables us to show that no sentence of an empirical theory is false.

The postulate in question could be at most regarded as the expression of an ideal limit for successively more adequate theories in a given field of research; but this hardly can be given any precise meaning.

Nevertheless, it seems to me that there is an important postulate which can be reasonably imposed on acceptable empirical theories and which involves the notion of truth. It is closely related to the one just discussed, but is essentially weaker. Remembering that the notion of acceptability is provided with a time coefficient, we can give this postulate the following form:

> As soon as we succeed in showing that an empirical theory contains (or implies) false sentences, it cannot be any longer considered acceptable.

In support of this postulate, I should like to make the following remarks.

I believe everybody agrees that one of the reasons which may compel us to reject an empirical theory is the proof of its inconsistency: a theory becomes untenable if we succeed in deriving from it two contradictory sentences. Now we can ask what are the usual motives for rejecting a theory on such grounds. Persons who are acquainted with modern logic are inclined to answer this question in the following way: A well-known logical law shows that a theory which enables us to derive two contradictory sentences enables us also to derive every sentence; therefore, such a theory is trivial and deprived of any scientific interest.

I have some doubts whether this answer contains an adequate analysis of the situation. I think that people who do not know modern logic are as little inclined to accept an inconsistent theory as those who are thoroughly familiar with it; and probably this applies even to those who regard (as some still do) the logical law on which the argument is based as a highly controversial issue, and almost as a paradox. I do not think that our attitude toward an inconsistent theory would change even if we decided for some reasons to weaken our system of logic so as to deprive ourselves of the possibility of deriving every sentence from any two contradictory sentences.

It seems to me that the real reason of our attitude is a different one: We know (if only intuitively) that an inconsistent theory must contain false sentences; and we are not inclined to regard as acceptable any theory which has been shown to contain such sentences.

There are various methods of showing that a given theory includes false sentences. Some of them are based upon purely logical properties of the theory involved; the method just discussed (i.e., the proof of inconsistency) is not the sole method of this type, but is the simplest one, and the one which is not frequently applied in practice. With the help of certain assumptions regarding the truth of empirical sentences, we can obtain methods to the same effect which are no longer of a purely logical nature. If we decide to accept the general postulate suggested above, then a successful application of any such method will make the theory untenable.

22. APPLICATIONS OF SEMANTICS TO DEDUCTIVE SCIENCE

As regards the applicability of semantics to mathematical sciences and their methodology, i.e., to metamathematics, we are in a much more favorable position than in the case of empirical sciences. For, instead of advancing reasons which justify some hopes for the future (and thus making a kind of pro-semantics propaganda), we are able to point out concrete results already achieved.

Doubts continue to be expressed whether the notion of a true sentence—as distinct from that of a provable sentence—can have any significance for mathematical disciplines and play any part in a methodological discussion of mathematics. It seems to me, however, that just this notion of a true sentence constitutes a most valuable contribution to metamathematics by semantics. We already possess a series of interesting metamathematical results gained with the help of the theory of truth. These results concern the mutual relations between the notion of truth and that of provability; establish new properties of the latter notion (which, as well known, is one of the basic notions of metamathematics); and throw some light on the fundamental problems of consistency and completeness. The most significant among these results have been briefly discussed in section 12.[34]

Furthermore, by applying the method of semantics we can adequately define several important metamathematical notions which have been used so far only in an intuitive way—such as, e.g., the notion of definability or that of a model of an axiom system; and thus we can undertake a systematic study of these notions. In particular, the investigations on definability have already brought some interesting results, and promise even more in the future.[35]

We have discussed the applications of semantics only to metamathematics, and not to mathematics proper. However, this distinction between mathematics and metamathematics is rather unimportant. For metamathematics is itself a deductive discipline and hence, from a certain point of view, a part of mathematics; and it is well known that—due to the formal character of deductive method—the results obtained in one deductive discipline can be automatically extended to any other discipline in which the given one finds an interpretation. Thus, for example, all metamathematical results can be interpreted as results of number theory. Also from a practical point of view there is no clearcut line between metamathematics and mathematics proper; for instance, the investigations on definability could be included in either of these domains.

23. FINAL REMARKS

I should like to conclude this discussion with some general and rather loose remarks concerning the whole question of the evaluation of scientific achievements in terms of their applicability. I must confess I have various doubts in this connection.

Being a mathematician (as well as a logician, and perhaps a philosopher of a sort), I have had the opportunity to attend many discussions between specialists in mathematics, where the problem of applications is especially acute, and I have noticed on several occasions the following phenomenon: If a mathematician wishes to disparage the work of one of his colleagues, say, A, the most effective method he finds for doing this is to ask where the results can be applied. The hard-pressed man, with his back against the wall, finally unearths the researches of another mathematician B as the locus of the application of his own results. If next B is plagued with a similar question, he will refer to another mathematician C. After a few steps of this kind we find ourselves referred back to the researches of A, and in this way the chain closes.

Speaking more seriously, I do not wish to deny that the value of a man's work may be increased by its implications for the research of others and for practice. But I believe, nevertheless, that it is inimical to the progress of science to measure the importance of any research exclusively or chiefly in terms of its usefulness and applicability. We know from the history of science that many important results and discoveries have had to wait centuries before they were applied in any field. And, in my opinion, there are also other important factors which cannot be disregarded in determining the value of a scientific work. It seems to me that there is a special domain of very profound and strong human needs related to scientific research, which are similar in many ways to aesthetic and perhaps religious needs. And it also seems to me that the satisfaction of these needs should be considered an important task of research. Hence, I believe, the question of the value of any research cannot be adequately answered without taking into account the intellectual satisfaction which the results of that research bring to those who understand it and care for it. It may be unpopular and out-of-date to say—but I do not think that a scientific result which gives us a better understanding of the world and makes it more harmonious in our eyes should be held in lower esteem than, say, an invention which reduces the cost of paving roads, or improves household plumbing.

It is clear that the remarks just made become pointless if the word "application" is used in a very wide and liberal sense. It is perhaps not less obvious that nothing follows from these general remarks concerning the specific topics which have been discussed in this paper; and I really do not know whether research in semantics stands to gain or lose by introducing the standard of value I have suggested.

NOTES

1. Compare Tarski [2] (see References following Notes). This work may be consulted for a more detailed and formal presentation of the subject of the paper, especially of the material included in sections 6 and 9–13. It contains also references to my earlier publications on the problems of semantics (a communication in Polish, 1930; the article Tarski [1] in French, 1931; a communication in German, 1932: and a book in Polish, 1933). The expository part of the present paper is related in its character to Tarski [3]. My investigations on the notion of truth and on theoretical semantics have been reviewed or discussed in Hofstadter [1], Juhos [1], Kokosyńska [1] and [2], Kotarbiński [2], Scholz [1], Weinberg [1], et al.

2. It may he hoped that the interest in theoretical semantics will now increase, as a result of the recent publication of the important work [by] Carnap [2].

3. This applies, in particular, to public discussions during the International Congress for the Unity of Science (Paris, 1935) and the Conference of International Congresses for the Unity of Science (Paris, 1937): cf., e.g., Neurath [1] and Gonseth [1].

4. The words "notion" and "concept" are used in this paper with all of the vagueness and ambiguity with which they occur in philosophical literature. Thus, sometimes they refer simply to a term, sometimes to what is meant by a term, and in other cases to what is denoted by a term. Sometimes it is irrelevant which of these interpretations is meant; and in certain cases perhaps none of them applies adequately. While on principle I share the tendency to avoid these words in any exact discussion, I did not consider it necessary to do so in this informal presentation.

5. For our present purposes it is somewhat more convenient to understand by "expressions," "sentences," etc., not individual inscriptions, but classes of inscriptions of similar form (thus, not individual physical things, but classes of such things).

6. For the Aristotelian formulation see Aristotle [1], γ, 7, 27. The other two formulations are very common in the literature, but I do not know with whom they originate. A critical discussion of various conceptions of truth can be found, e.g., in Kotarbiński [1] (so far available only in Polish), pp. 123ff., and Russell [1], pp. 362ff.

7. For most of the remarks contained in sections 4 and 8, I am indebted to the late S. Leśniewski who developed them in his unpublished lectures in the University of Warsaw (in 1919 and later). However, Leśniewski did not anticipate the possibility of a rigorous development of the theory of truth, and still less of a definition of this notion; hence, while indicating equivalences of the form (T) as premisses in the antinomy of the liar, he did not conceive them as any sufficient conditions for an adequate usage (or definition) of the notion of truth. Also the remarks in section 8 regarding the occurrence of an empirical premiss in the antinomy of the liar, and the possibility of eliminating this premiss, do not originate with him.

8. In connection with various logical and methodological problems involved in this paper the reader may consult Tarski [6].

9. The antinomy of the liar (ascribed to Eubulides or Epimenides) is discussed here in sections 7 and 8. For the antinomy of definability (due to J. Richard) see, e.g., Hilbert-Bernays [1], vol. 2. pp. 263ff.; for the antinomy of heterological terms see Grelling-Nelson [1], p. 307.

10. Due to Professor J. Lukasiewicz (University of Warsaw).

11. This can roughly be done in the following way. Let *S* be any sentence beginning with the words "Every sentence." We correlate with *S* a new sentence *S** by subjecting *S* to the following two modifications: we replace in *S* the first word. "Every," by "The"; and we insert after the second word, "sentence," the whole sentence *S* enclosed in quotation marks. Let us agree to

call the sentence S "(self-)applicable" or "non-(self-) applicable" dependent on whether the correlated sentence S^* is true or false. Now consider the following sentence:

Every sentence is nonapplicable.

It can easily be shown that the sentence just stated must be both applicable and nonapplicable; hence a contradiction. It may not be quite clear in what sense this formulation of the antinomy does not involve an empirical premiss; however, I shall not elaborate on this point.

12. The terms "logic" and "logical" are used in this paper in a broad sense, which has become almost traditional in the last decades; logic is assumed here to comprehend the whole theory of classes and relations (i.e., the mathematical theory of sets). For many different reasons I am personally inclined to use the term "logic" in a much narrower sense, so as to apply it only to what is sometimes called "elementary logic," i.e., to the sentential calculus and the (restricted) predicate calculus.

13. Cf. here, however, Tarski [3], pp. 5f.

14. The method of construction we are going to outline can be applied—with appropriate changes—to all formalized languages that are known at the present time; although it does not follow that a language could not be constructed to which this method would not apply.

15. In carrying through this idea a certain technical difficulty arises. A sentential function may contain an arbitrary number of free variables; and the logical nature of the notion of satisfaction varies with this number. Thus, the notion in question when applied to functions with one variable is a binary relation between these functions and single objects; when applied to functions with two variables it becomes a ternary relation between functions and couples of objects; and so on. Hence, strictly speaking, we are confronted, not with one notion of satisfaction, but with infinitely many notions; and it turns out that these notions cannot be defined independently of each other, but must all be introduced simultaneously.

To overcome this difficulty, we employ the mathematical notion of an infinite sequence (or, possibly, of a finite sequence with an arbitrary number of terms). We agree to regard satisfaction, not as a many-termed relation between sentential functions and an indefinite number of objects, but as a binary relation between functions and sequences of objects. Under this assumption the formulation of a general and precise definition of satisfaction no longer presents any difficulty; and a true sentence can now be defined as one which is satisfied by every sequence.

16. To define recursively the notion of satisfaction, we have to apply a certain form of recursive definition which is not admitted in the object-language. Hence the "essential richness" of the metalanguage may simply consist in admitting this type of definition. On the other hand, a general method is known which makes it possible to eliminate all recursive definitions and to replace them by normal, explicit ones. If we try to apply this method to the definition of satisfaction, we see that we have either to introduce into the metalanguage variables of a higher logical type than those which occur in the object language; or else to assume axiomatically in the metalanguage the existence of classes that are more comprehensive than all those whose existence can be established in the object-language. See here Tarski [2], pp. 393ff., and Tarski [5], p. 110.

17. Due to the development of modern logic, the notion of mathematical proof has undergone a far-reaching simplification. A sentence of a given formalized discipline is provable if it can be obtained from the axioms of this discipline by applying certain simple and purely formal rules of inference, such as those of detachment and substitution. Hence to show that all provable sentences are true, it suffices to prove that all the sentences accepted as axioms are true, and that the rules of inference when applied to true sentences yield new true sentences; and this usually presents no difficulty.

On the other hand, in view of the elementary nature of the notion of provability, a precise definition of this notion requires only rather simple logical devices. In most cases, those logical devices which are available in the formalized discipline itself (to which the notion of provability is related) are more than sufficient for this purpose. We know, however, that as regards the definition of truth just the opposite holds. Hence, as a rule, the notions of truth and provability cannot coincide; and since every provable sentence is true, there must be true sentences which are not provable.

18. Thus the theory of truth provides us with a general method for consistency proofs for formalized mathematical disciplines. It can be easily realized, however, that a consistency proof obtained by this method may possess some intuitive value— i.e., may convince us, or strengthen our belief, that the discipline under consideration is actually consistent—only in case we succeed in defining truth in terms of a metalanguage which does not contain the object language as a part (cf. here a remark in section 9). For only in this case the deductive assumptions of the metalanguage may be intuitively simpler and more obvious than those of the object-language—even though the condition of "essential richness" will be formally satisfied. Cf. here also Tarski [3], p. 7.

The incompleteness of a comprehensive class of formalized disciplines constitutes the essential content of a fundamental theorem of K. Gödel; cf. Gödel [1], pp. 187ff. The explanation of the fact that the theory of truth leads so directly to Gödel's theorem is rather simple. In deriving Gödel's result from the theory of truth we make an essential use of the fact that the definition of truth cannot be given in a metalanguage which is only as "rich" as the object language (cf. note 17); however, in establishing this fact, a method of reasoning has been applied which is very closely related to that used (for the first time) by Gödel. It may be added that Gödel was clearly guided in his proof by certain intuitive considerations regarding the notion of truth, although this notion does not occur in the proof explicitly; cf. Gödel [1], pp. 174f.

19. The notions of designation and definition lead respectively to the antinomies of Grelling-Nelson and Richard (cf. note 9). To obtain an antinomy for the notion of satisfaction, we construct the following expression:

The sentential function X does not satisfy X.

A contradiction arises when we consider the question whether this expression, which is clearly a sentential function, satisfies itself or not.

20. All notions mentioned in this section can be defined in terms of satisfaction. We can say, e.g., that a given term designates a given object if this object satisfies the sentential function "x is identical with T" where 'T' stands for the given term. Similarly, a sentential function is said to define a given object if the latter is the only object which satisfies this function. For a definition of consequence see Tarski [4], and for that of synonymity, Carnap [2].

21. General semantics is the subject of Carnap [2]. Cf. here also remarks in Tarski [2], pp. 388f.

22. Cf. various quotations in Ness [1], pp. 13f.

23. The names of persons who have raised objections will not be quoted here, unless their objections have appeared in print.

24. It should be emphasized, however, that as regards the question of an alleged vicious circle the situation would not change even if we took a different point of view, represented, e.g, in Carnap [2]; i.e., if we regarded the specification of conditions under which sentences of a language are true as an essential part of the description of this language. On the other hand, it may be noticed that the point of view represented in the text does not exclude the possibility of using truth-tables in a deductive development of logic. However, these tables are to be regarded then merely as a formal instrument for checking the provability of certain sentences; and the symbols 'T' and 'F' which occur in them and which are usually considered abbreviations of "true" and "false" should not be interpreted in any intuitive way.

25. Cf. Juhos [1]. I must admit that I do not clearly understand von Juhos' objections and do not know how to classify them; therefore, I confine myself here to certain points of a formal character. Von Juhos does not seem to know my definition of truth; he refers only to an informal presentation in Tarski [3] where the definition has not been given at all. If he knew the actual definition, he would have to change his argument. However, I have no doubt that he would discover in this definition some "defects" as well. For he believes he has proved that "on ground of principle it is impossible to give such a definition at all."

26. The phrases "*p* is true" and "*p* is the case" (or better "it is true that *p*" and "it is the case that *p*") are sometimes used in informal discussions, mainly for stylistic reasons; but they are considered then as synonymous with the sentence represented by '*p*'. On the other hand, as far as I understand the situation, the phrases in question cannot be used by von Juhos synonymously with '*p*'; for otherwise the replacement of (T) by (T') or (T") would not constitute any "improvement."

27. Cf. the discussion of this problem in Kokosyńska [1], pp. 161ff.

28. Most authors who have discussed my work on the notion of truth are of the opinion that my definition does conform with the classical conception of this notion; see, e.g., Kotarbiński [2] and Scholz [1].

29. Cf. Ness [1]. Unfortunately, the results of that part of Ness' research which is especially relevant for our problem are not discussed in his book; compare p. 148, footnote 1.

30. Though I have heard this opinion several times, I have seen it in print only once and, curiously enough, in a work which does not have a philosophical character—in fact, in Hilbert-Bernays [1], vol. II, p. 269 (where, by the way, it is not expressed as any kind of objection). On the other hand, I have not found any remark to this effect in discussions of my work by professional philosophers (cf. note 1).

31. Cf. Gonseth [1], pp. 187f.

32. See Nagel [1], and Nagel [2], pp. 471f. A remark which goes. perhaps, in the same direction is also to be found in Weinberg [1], p. 77; cf., however, his earlier remarks. pp. 75f.

33. Such a tendency was evident in earlier works of Carnap (see, e.g., Carnap [1], especially part V) and in writings of other members of Vienna Circle. Cf. Kokosyńska [1] and Weinberg [1].

34. For other results obtained with the help of the theory of truth see Gödel [2]; Tarski [2], pp. 401ff., and Tarski [5], pp. 111f.

35. An object—e.g., a number or a set of numbers—is said to be definable (in a given formalism) if there is a sentential function which defines it; cf. note 20. Thus, the term "definable," though of a metamathematical (semantic) origin, is purely mathematical as to its extension, for it expresses a property (denotes a class) of mathematical objects. In consequence, the notion of definability can be redefined in purely mathematical terms, though not within the formalized discipline to which this notion refers; however, the fundamental idea of the definition remains unchanged. Cf. here—also for further bibliographic references—Tarski [1]; various other results concerning definability can also be found in the literature, e.g., in Hilbert-Bernays [1], vol. I, pp. 354ff., 369ff., 456ff., etc., and in Lindenbaum-Tarski [1]. It may be noticed that the term "definable" is sometimes used in another, metamathematical (but not semantic), sense; this occurs, for instance, when we say that a term is definable in other terms (on the basis of a given axiom system). For a definition of a model of an axiom system see Tarski [4].

References

Aristotle [1]. *Metaphysica. (Works,* vol. VIII.) English translation by W. D. Ross. (Oxford: 1908).

Carnap, R. [1]. *Logical Syntax of Language* (London and New York: 1937).

——— [2]. *Introduction to Semantics.* (Cambridge: 1942).

Gödel, K. [1]. "Über formal unentscheidbare Sätze der *Principia Mathematica* und verwandter Systeme, I." *Monatshefte für Mathematik und Physik,* XXXVIII (1931), pp. 173–198.

——— [2]. "Über die Länge von Beweisen." *Ergebnisse eines mathematischen Kolloquiums,* vol. VII (1936), pp. 23–24.

Gonseth, F. [1]. "Le Congrès Descartes. Questions de Philosophie scientifique." *Revue thomiste,* vol. XLIV (1938), pp. 183–193.

Grelling, K., and Nelson, L. [1]. "Bemerkungen zu den Paradoxien von Russell und Burali-Forti." *Abhandlungen der Fries'schen Schule,* vol. II (new series), (1908), pp. 301–334.

Hofstadter, A. [1]. "On Semantic Problems." *The Journal of Philosophy,* vol. XXXV (1938), pp. 225–232.

Hilbert, D., and Bernays, P. [1]. *Grundlagen der Mathematik.* 2 vols. (Berlin: 1934–1939).

Juhos. B. von. [1]. "The Truth of Empirical Statements." *Analysis,* vol. IV (1937), pp. 65–70.

Kokosyńska, M. [1]. "Über den absoluten Wahrheitsbegriff und einige andcere semantische Begriffe." *Erkenntnis,* vol. VI (1936), pp. 143–165.

——— [2]. "Syntax, Semantik und Wissenschaftslogik." *Actes du Congrès International de Philosophie Scientifique,* vol. III (Paris: 1936), pp. 9–14.

Kotarbiński, T. [1]. *Elementary teorji poznania, logiki formalnej i metodologji nauk. (Elements of Epistemology, Formal Logic, and the Methodology of Sciences,* in Polish.) (Lwów: 1929).

——— [2]. "W sprawie pojęcia prawdy." (*"Concerning the Concept of Truth,"* in Polish.) *Przeglgd filozoficzny,* vol. XXXVII. pp. 85–91.

Lindenbaum, A., and Tarski, A. [1]. "Über die Beschränktheit der Ausdruccksmittel deduktiver Theorien." *Ergebnisse eines mathematischen Kolloquiums,* vol. VII, (1936), pp. 15–23.

Nagel. E. [1]. Review of Hofstadter [1]. *The Journal of Symbolic Logic,* vol. III, (1938), p. 90.

——— [2]. Review of Carnap [2]. *The Journal of Philosophy,* vol. XXXIX, (1942), pp. 468–473.

Ness. A. [1]. "'Truth' As Conceived by Those Who Are Not Professional Philosophers." *Skrifter utgitt av Det Norske VIdenskaps-Akademi i Oslo. II. Hist.-Filos. Klasse,* vol. IV (Oslo: 1938).

Neurath. 0. [1]. "Erster Internationaler Kongress für Einheit der Wissenschaft in Paris 1935." *Erkenntnis,* vol. V (1935), pp. 377–406.

Russell, B. [1]. *An Inquiry Into Meaning and Truth.* (New York: 1940).

Scholz, H. [1]. Review of *Studia philosophica,* vol. I. *Deutsche Literaturzeitung,* vol. LVIII (1937), pp. 1914–1917.

Tarski, A. [l]. "Sur les ensembles définissables de nombres réels, I." *Fundamenta mathematicae,* vol. XVII (1931), pp. 210–239.

——— [2]. "Der Wahrheitsbegriff in den formalisierten Sprachen." (German translation of a book in Polish, 1933.) *Studio philosophica,* vol. 1 (1935), pp. 261–405.

——— [3]. "Grundlegung der wissenschaftlichen Semantik." *Actes du Congrès International de Philosophie Scientifique,* vol. III (Paris: 1936), pp. 1–8.

——— [4]. "Über den Begriff der logischen Folgerung." *Actes du Congrès International de Philosophie Scientifique,* vol. VII (Paris: 1937), pp. 1–11.

——— [5]. "On Undecidable Statements in Enlarged Systems of Logic and the Concept of Truth." *The Journal of Symbolic Logic*, vol. IV, 1939, pp. 105–112.

——— [6]. *Introduction to Logic* (New York: 1941).

Weinberg, J. [1]. Review of *Studia philosophica*, vol. I. *The Philosophical Review*, vol. XLVII, pp. 70–77.

Reading Questions

1. Tarski states that a definition of truth is ***materially adequate*** if all T-sentences follow from it. What does he mean by this?
2. Tarski's semantic conception of truth defines truth in terms of certain linguistic expressions, namely, sentences. Is his optimism warranted that this definition can be exported to non-linguistic truth bearers like propositions or beliefs?
3. According to Tarski, "true" cannot be a predicate within an object language; it is definable only within a metalanguage. What is the problem that makes him want to banish "true"' from object languages?
4. What precisely is Tarski's definition of truth?
5. Tarski maintains that the semantic conception of truth is metaphysically neutral. One can adopt his definition while remaining "naïve realists, critical realists or idealists, empiricists or metaphysicians—whatever we were before." Is truth a metaphysical matter at all, then? If so, in what sense?

The Pragmatist Theory of Truth 10

SUSAN HAACK

1. INTRODUCTION

> How can the mere pragmatist feel any duty to think truly?
>
> (Royce)

> My failure in making converts to my conception of truth seems, if I may judge from what I hear, . . . almost complete. An ordinary philosopher would feel disheartened, and a common choleric sinner would curse God and die, after such a reception. But instead of taking counsel of despair, I make bold to vary my statements, in the faint hope that repeated drippings may wear upon the stone.
>
> (James, 'A Word More About Truth' in his [1909], p. 136)

JAMES'S PESSIMISM was amply justified; the unpopularity of the pragmatist theory of truth has persisted, at least on this side of the Atlantic, to the present day. The following passage is typical:

> William James, the originator of the [pragmatist] theory [of truth], took over the central idea from C. S. Peirce (*sic*), but altered it in the process. Peirce had put forward practical usefulness as a criterion of meaningfulness . . . James applied this idea (perhaps confusedly) to truth in the attempt to provide a down-to-earth substitute for certainty within the theory of knowledge. But merely to reject the search for certainty by putting something less in its place without diagnosis of the reasons for the demand for certainty in the first place is to some extent an abrogation of the

Reprinted by permission of Oxford University Press. Originally in The British Journal for the Philosophy of Science, *vol. 27, 1976, pp. 231–249.*

> philosopher's responsibility. The pragmatic theory cannot therefore be put on the same level as the . . . correspondence and coherence theories. I shall not discuss it further. (It would not be unfair to say that it is founded on a muddle.)
>
> (Hamlyn [1970], p. 119)

Every sentence of this passage, with the single exception of 'I shall not discuss it further', is either false or seriously misleading. Peirce, not James, originated the pragmatist theory of truth; Peirce's theory of meaning does not equate significance with practical usefulness, and neither does James's theory of truth straightforwardly equate truth with practical usefulness; Dewey provided in his [1929] a particularly acute diagnosis of the classical quest for certainty; and the pragmatist theory of truth contains substantial coherence and correspondence elements.

It would, I fear, be generous to describe Hamlyn's account as founded on a muddle; and I shall not discuss it, at least directly, further.

What I hope to do, though, is to convince you, by showing that the most influential criticisms have been based on a very inadequate understanding of the theory, that this kind of dismissive attitude is unjustified. The pragmatist theory of truth is not, to be sure, without difficulties; but there is, I think, a good deal to be learned from it, both from its strengths and from its weaknesses. It is, at any rate, of sufficient interest amply to repay the effort of setting the historical record straight.

2. SKETCH OF THE THEORY

By 'the pragmatist theory of truth' I shall understand a set of interlocking theses, to be found in the works of Peirce, Dewey and James, which may together be regarded as constituting a theory of truth. (I shall not consider the views of Schiller.) Not all these theses will be found in all three writers, but most of them will be found in at least two, though with varying emphasis. There are dangers, of course, in speaking of '*the* pragmatist theory of truth' at all, for there are interesting and important differences between the pragmatists on these issues. But I hope that a joint treatment will enable me to establish, first, that the theory originally offered by Peirce and subsequently adopted by Dewey was considerably extended by James, that it was upon James's version of the theory that the most influential criticisms fell, and that many of these criticisms can be seen to be misguided once James's views are placed in the context of the underlying Peircean theory; and second, that some of the differences between Peirce's and James's versions can be seen as resulting from *their different* reactions to an internal tension in the common part of their theory. I shall restrict myself to consideration of the truth of straightforwardly factual beliefs; the application of the theory to, for example, mathematical or metaphysical beliefs would require a detailed account of the pragmatic views on mathematics and metaphysics.

For Peirce, truth is the end of inquiry. Here 'end' is ambiguous, between 'aim' and 'final state'. This ambiguity gives rise to some difficulty, but for the present I leave it as it stands. Peirce's theory of inquiry goes, in outline, as follows: a person in a state of (real, not Cartesian) doubt, struggles to attain instead a state of fixed belief. Peirce argues that some methods of acquiring beliefs—the method of tenacity, the method of authority, and the *a priori* method—are unsatisfactory because they are inherently unstable. A person using one of these methods will acquire an opinion, but different people will thereby acquire different opinions, and the existence of rival opinions will raise doubt all over again. Only one method, the Scientific Method, is stable; enables one, that is, to acquire a belief that will not be shaken.

The Scientific Method, alone among methods of acquisition of beliefs, has this virtue, because it is constrained by Reality, which is independent of our beliefs about it. Beliefs acquired by the use of the Scientific Method are caused by Real Things; so the use of the Scientific Method cannot but lead, eventually, to a stable consensus.

Since inquiry is prompted by doubt, and ended only with the acquisition of a stable belief, and since the Truth is that stable consensus which the Scientific Method will eventually achieve, it follows that the true is, in a certain sense, satisfactory to believe; satisfactory because stable. (Since Peirce's theory of belief is behaviourist, this satisfactoriness is, in a way, 'practical'.)

James pays little attention to the theory of inquiry. He agrees that truth is correspondence with reality, but, even more vehemently than Peirce, insists on knowing what difference a belief's correspondence with reality might make. His major contribution is thus a substantial extension of the third thesis, that the truth is satisfactory to believe. The benefit of holding true beliefs, according to James, is that if what one believes is true one is, so to speak, guaranteed against recalcitrance on the part of experience. No doubt one could get along perfectly well, for a bit, holding false beliefs; but, James thinks, one would eventually be caught out.

This provides a sensible interpretation of those, perhaps, incautious remarks of James's which Moore found 'silly', that:

> The true is the name of whatever proves itself to be good in the way of belief . . .
>
> ('What Pragmatism Means', in [1907], p. 59)

and

> The true . . . is only the expedient in our way of thinking.
>
> ('Pragmatism's Conception of Truth' in [1907], p. 145)

By beliefs which are 'good' or 'expedient' or which 'pay' James means beliefs which are safe from the danger of inconsistency with subsequent experience. That this is a fair interpretation becomes clear from the following passages, the first appearing shortly after the identification of the true with the good to believe, the second immediately after the identification of the true with the expedient to believe:

> . . . what is better for us to believe is true *unless the belief incidentally clashes with some other vital benefit.* Now in real life what vital benefits is any particular belief most liable to clash with? What indeed except the vital benefits yielded by other benefits when these prove incompatible with the first ones?

> . . . expedient in the long run and on the whole of course; for what meets expediently all the experience in sight won't necessarily meet all farther experience equally satisfactorily. Experience, as we know, has ways of *boiling over,* and making us correct our present formulas.

So, for James as for Peirce, the true is satisfactory (useful, expedient, good) to believe, because it is safe from overthrow by subsequent experience. James, however, amplifies this thesis by an account of the way one modifies, in the face of inconsistency with a new experience, the beliefs one previously held true; one aims to maximise the conservation of the old belief set while restoring consistency. The likeness to Quine's epistemology ([1951]) is striking.

True beliefs, James frequently comments, are those which are verifiable. By this he means that those beliefs are true which, in the long run, are corroborated or confirmed by experience. (He does not distinguish corroboration from confirmation, as subsequent writers have done.) Most of the beliefs we take to be true are, James admits, actually verified at best only very indirectly. Our beliefs are like banknotes, they 'pass' so long as no-one challenges them; but, once again like the financial system, the system of beliefs would collapse were it not for actual direct verifications at some points.

I have so far stressed the similarities between Peirce's and James's view. But there is a difference of emphasis which it is important to consider. Peirce is preoccupied with the Truth, that is, the totality of individual truths. James, by contrast, is primarily interested in the individual truths, finding the Truth with a capital T a somewhat spectral and uninteresting abstraction. He is aware that one *could* say that some propositions just are true (or false) even though no-one has ever verified (or falsified) them or, indeed, even entertained them; but he finds this way of talking relatively *pointless.* (This view bears some resemblance to Dummett's rather stronger, Intuitionist view of truth in his [1959].) In fact James quite often insists that the Truth is growing corpus, that is, that new truths come into existence as human knowledge grows. This emphasis on the growth of truth can be understood as a consequence of James's switch of Peirce's emphasis on *the totality of truths in the long run* to an emphasis on *individual truths in the short run.* This difference of emphasis can probably be traced in its turn to the contrast between Peirce's realism and James's nominalism: Peirce did not share James's antipathy for abstractions. His nominalism also underlies James's tendency to prefer to speak of actual verifications, where possible, rather than verifiability (unactualised possible verifications being somewhat embarrassing to a nominalist). This tendency, as I shall argue subsequently, gets him into a serious difficulty.

The same difference of emphasis is reflected in another feature of James's presentation. At any particular time, James argues (short of the fictional Long Run, that is) the evidence available to us may be insufficient to decide between competing beliefs; and then our choice *will* be a matter of taste:

> . . . sometimes alternative theoretic formulas are equally compatible with all the truths we know, and then we choose between them for subjective reasons . . . we follow 'elegance' or 'economy'.
>
> ('Pragmatism's Conception of Truth', in his [1907], p. 142)

Indeed, in at least one place ('What Pragmatism Means', in his [1907], p. 44) James refers to the possibility that, even after *all* the data are in, alternative theories, between which we should choose on such 'aesthetic' grounds as simplicity, economy *etc.* may remain. Although the resemblance to Quine's epistemology is, once again, striking, two points of contrast should be noted. First, Quine takes it that there could be a real difference between two such theories, whereas James, I think, would rate the difference merely verbal; second, Quine would not, I think, so readily admit that considerations such as simplicity and economy are *purely* subjective. Both points will be relevant in later parts of the paper.

Dewey follows Peirce in stressing that truth is the end of inquiry, though he adds considerably to the theory of inquiry. In *Logic, the Theory Of Inquiry* ([1938], p. 345 n.) he simply quotes Peirce's as 'the best definition of truth'; Dewey prefers to replace the word 'truth' by 'warranted assertibility' to emphasise that the truth is precisely what the method of inquiry warrants us in asserting.

Dewey contributes to the theory an important insight into the role of truth. Truth, or warranted assertibility, characterises those beliefs to which we give the honorific title, 'knowledge'. It has subsequently been commonplace (though not, of course, uncontroversial) to analyse '*x* knows that *p*' along the lines of '*x* believes *p*, *p* is true and *x* has good reasons for his belief that *p*.' Dewey, interestingly enough, *merges* the truth with the warrant requirement.

The central thesis of the theory may be summarised thus:

Truth—			
is the end of inquiry	Peirce		Dewey
is correspondence with reality	Peirce	James	Dewey
is satisfactory to believe	Peirce	James	Dewey
is coherence with experience—verifiability [is a growing corpus]		James	Dewey
entitles belief to be called 'knowledge'.			Dewey

3 SOME REPLIES TO SOME CRITICS, AND SOME NEW CRITICISMS

(A) A DEFINITION OR A CRITERION OF TRUTH?

Some early critics suggested that the pragmatists had confusedly presented a criterion of truth as though it were a definition of truth; that their theory provided at best, a test of truth, but was offered as if it gave an analysis of the meaning of 'true':

> The test of truth and the meaning of truth are . . . completely identified
>
> (Pratt, What is Pragmatism? [1909], p. 80)

> . . . if pragmatists only affirmed that utility is a *criterion* of truth, there would be much less to be said against their view . . . The arguments of the pragmatists are almost wholly directed to proving that utility is a *criterion;* that utility is the *meaning* of truth is then supposed to follow.
>
> (Russell, 'James's Conception of Truth' [1908], p. 121)

Interestingly enough, the same distinction is used by Rescher in *The Coherence Theory of Truth* ([1973]), where he tries to give, as he thinks, a more sympathetic account of the pragmatist theory by presenting it as precisely, a criterion, but not a definition, of truth.

But these criticisms, and Rescher's attempted rehabilitation, are both inappropriate. For the pragmatists' view of meaning is such that a dichotomy between definitions and criteria would have been entirely unacceptable to them. It is a fundamental tenet of pragmatism (Peirce sometimes says, *the* fundamental tenet) that meaning is given by reference to experiential consequences. Thus, Peirce:

> . . . consider what effects, which might conceivably have practical bearings, we conceive the object of our conception to have. Then, our conception of those effects is the whole of our conception of the object.
>
> . . . let us ask what we mean by calling a thing *hard*. Evidently that it will not be scratched by many other substances. The whole conception of this quality, as of every other, lies in its conceived effects.
>
> ('How to Make Our Ideas Clear,' [1878], p. 124)

and James:

> There can *be* no difference that *makes* no difference
>
> ('What Pragmatism means,' in [1907], p. 45)

This view of meaning raises many interesting issues (its relation to Logical Positivism and Operationalism, for instance, and its role in persuading C. L. Lewis of the need for an implication relation stronger than the material conditional); but for present purposes it is sufficient to notice that it certainly does not allow a distinction between what 'true' means, and what difference it would make, whether a sentence were true or false. The pragmatists hoped to explain what 'true' means precisely by investigating what difference it makes whether one's beliefs are true or false. As James puts it:

> Pragmatism . . . asks its usual question. "Grant an idea or belief to be true", it says, "what concrete difference will its being true make in any one's actual life? How will the truth be realised? What experiences will be different from those which would obtain if the belief were false? What, in short, is the belief's cash-value in experimental terms?"
>
> ('Pragmatism's Conception of Truth,' in [1907], p. 133)

So the criticism that the pragmatists 'confuse' definition and criteria is totally inappropriate, since their theory of meaning quite deliberately equates the two; if this *is* a confusion, it must be shown, by a critique of their theory of meaning, *why* it is. I shall argue, later, however, that Peirce's equation of definitions and criteria does lead to a difficulty because of his fallibilist epistemology.

(B) TRUTH AND UTILITY[1]

Both Moore and Russell find James's equation of the true with the useful thoroughly unacceptable. They both assume that 'useful' has its usual, everyday sense, and proceed to argue, on the one hand, that some true beliefs can fail to be useful, and on the other, that some useful beliefs can fail to be true. It is notable that Moore and Russell are both assuming, in making this kind of criticism, some other, presumably plain correspondence, theory of truth.

> Is it not clear that we do actually sometimes have true ideas, at times when they are not useful, but positively in the way?
>
> (Moore, 'William James' "Pragmatism",' [1908], p. 110)

> It seems perfectly possible to suppose that the hypothesis that [other people] exist will always work, even if they do not in fact exist. It is plain . . . that it makes for happiness to believe that they exist . . . But if I am troubled by solipsism, the discovery that a belief in the existence of others is 'true' in the pragmatists' sense is not enough to allay my sense of loneliness.
>
> (Russell, 'James's Conception of Truth', [1908], p. 122)

I have argued in section 2 that when James says that true beliefs are 'useful' he should be understood to mean that they are so in the sense of being guaranteed against overthrow by subsequent experience. Neither Moore's nor Russell's criticisms are to the point if this *is* what James meant. And there are—besides the passages I have referred to as confirming my interpretation—also passages where James repudiates the thesis which Moore and Russell attribute to him. He observes, for example, that a belief in the Absolute would afford him a kind of 'moral holiday', that is, that it would be good, in the sense of congenial, to believe; but he rejects this belief, nevertheless, on the grounds that it would be inconsistent with 'other [*sic*] truths.' ('What Pragmatism Means' in [1907], p. 61). And compare this comment:

> Above all we find *consistency* satisfactory.
>
> ('The Pragmatist Account of Truth and its Misunderstanders', in [1909], p.192)

James perhaps comes closest to the view which Moore and Russell attribute to him in his discussions of religious belief, about which he is apt to say that that belief is true which best succeeds in making coherent both one's experiences and one's values. And even here, clearly, he is by no means straightforwardly maintaining that truth is a matter of taste or (in the ordinary sense) expediency; rather, he is extending his coherence view to moral as well as empirical beliefs.

The pragmatists' view of the truth as the satisfactory to believe has deep roots in Peirce's epistemology. Peirce's theory of inquiry rests, as I have reported, on the idea that the state of doubt, of not knowing, that is, whether *p*, is uncomfortable, that it prompts inquiry, and that the discomfort of doubt is ended by the acquisition of a stable belief. This idea in its turn is supported by definitions, due in essentials to Alexander Bain, of belief as a habit of action and of doubt as the interruption of such a habit by novel stimuli. I cannot enter, here, into the question of the adequacy or otherwise of these underlying views, except to comment that Peirce's theory of doubt does not seem to take much account of the fact that doubt or ignorance on some issues may occasion one much less discomfort than doubt or ignorance, on others with which one is—to put it, I fear, question beggingly as well as vaguely—concerned. Ironically, since the pragmatists are so often accused of excessive attention to the merely and vulgarly practical, this comment suggests that Peirce's theory may pay rather less attention to the practical than it should. And this difficulty suggests another: that the theory may be hard put to it to handle the question of the truth-value of propositions which have never been entertained. This, too, will turn out to be significant.

(C) TRUTH AND VERIFIABILITY

Since, as I have argued, they did not appreciate the relation between utility, in James's sense, and coherence with the totality of experience, it is not surprising that Moore and Russell also failed to appreciate the close connection between James's claim that the true is the useful, and his claim that the true is the verifiable. But, though they did not appreciate the connection between the two views, they objected to the identification of truth with verification nearly as vehemently as to the identification of truth with utility, and on similar grounds; a belief could be true but never verified. Now there is a view in James which is not straightforwardly vulnerable to this objection: the view, that is, that a belief is true just in case it is *verifiable*. If James is equating truth with verifiability, not with verification, the objection that there are true but unverified beliefs is irrelevant. And there are numerous passages where James concedes that plenty of true, that is to say *verifiable* beliefs, have not yet been verified (e.g. 'Pragmatism's Conception of Truth,' in [1907] pp. 136–7). Of course, there will still be room for argument about the identification of truth with verifiability, *à propos*, for example, undecidable mathematical or quantum mechanical sentences—argument which will not be made easier by James's rather vague gloss on 'verifiable': if *p* were to be tested it would, eventually, be verified; but at least this thesis does not fall to the simple objections of Moore and Russell. (There is, once again, a similarity to Dummett's views.)

However the matter is considerably more complicated than has yet appeared. As I reported in section 2, James's nominalistic embarrassment about the notion of possible verification in the long run leads him to try to replace 'verifiable' by 'verified' whenever he can, and, in consequence, to maintain that the Truth is a growing corpus, which individual truths join as they are verified. But if a belief is true just in case it is *verifiable,* all these individual truths are true *before* they are verified (which is what James plainly says in his [1909] p. 165); so the Truth consists always of the same truths, and does not, after all, grow. This is, I think, a simple inconsistency in James's view; that is why, on page 144, I relegated the thesis that the Truth is a growing corpus to brackets.

(D) THE PRAGMATIST THEORY AND THE T-SCHEMA

It seems worth observing that the admission of the thesis that the Truth grows—against which I have been arguing above—would make the pragmatist theory inconsistent with Tarski's material adequacy condition for theories of truth. Tarski requires (in [1931]) that any acceptable theory should entail all instances of

(T) *S* is true iff *p*
(where '*S*' names *p*).

In what follows I shall consider only the weaker condition, that any acceptable definition of truth should be consistent with the truth of all instances of (*T*); for it is in this form, rather than the stronger condition that all instances of (*T*) be deducible, that Tarski's material adequacy requirement can conveniently be applied to informal truth-definitions. It is not certain that this material adequacy requirement rules out what one might not too unfairly call 'bizarre' theories of truth—such as, say, 'true = asserted in the Bible'; since presumably a serious advocate of such a theory would maintain that *e.g.* 'Warsaw was bombed in 1940' is true iff Warsaw was bombed in 1940 holds, since if he agrees that the lefthand side is false, he will also maintain, if he is wise, that the righthand side is false too. But what the material adequacy condition *does* seem to rule out are theories which are not bivalent, which allow that some sentences are neither true nor false. Thus, if one supposed, as Łukasiewicz did (though I do not) that 'There will be a sea-battle tomorrow' is neither true nor false in advance of the outcome, then

'There will be a sea-battle tomorrow' is true iff there will be a sea-battle tomorrow

is presumably not true, since its lefthand side would be false and its righthand side neither true nor false.

One could, indeed, make the rejection of bivalence consistent with the acceptance of the *T*-schema if one envisaged the adoption of a nonbivalent metalanguage as well as a non-bivalent object language. Thus, if "*p*' is true' is neither true nor false if '*p*' is neither true or false, '*p*' is true iff '*p*' could be true even though '*p*' was truthvalueless. But to motivate this proposal some argument would be required why "*p*' is true' should be neither true nor false if '*p*' is neither true nor false. It seems doubtful whether, in the present case, one could find any very plausible argument to the desired effect. For that certain quantum mechanical sentences are neither verifiable nor falsifiable can itself be verified; so it would seem proper, if one identified 'true' with 'verifiable' at the metalinguistic level also, to admit that such sentences are true, is false.

Now if one took the view which James sometimes maintains, that a belief becomes true when it is verified, then since at any time there will be beliefs not yet verified or falsified, those beliefs will be, at that time, neither true nor false.

That version which replaces 'verified' by 'verifiable,' which, as I have argued, is to be preferred, may or may not be bivalent, depending upon whether or not it is so interpreted as to allow the possibility that some meaningful sentences may be neither verifiable nor falsifiable, and hence, neither true nor false. Some sentences are *practically* incapable of verification or falsification; but it would be possible to maintain that such sentences are nevertheless verifiable or falsifiable, on the grounds that if they *were to be* tested they *would* be verified or falsified. Other sentences are *theoretically* incapable of verification or falsification; for instance certain sentences of quantum mechanics are such that it follows from the theory that they are neither verifiable nor falsifiable. It would be harder, though not perhaps quite impossible, to maintain that such sentences are nevertheless in some weaker ('logical') sense verifiable or falsifiable; but it remains possible to retain bivalence by denying the meaningfulness of these sentences.

Since James is rather unspecific about exactly how he understands 'verifiable' it is not easy to say what view he would have adopted on these questions. However, his theory of meaning would presumably rule that whatever sentences he counted as unverifiable he would also count as meaningless. And only if some meaningful sentences are allowed to be neither true not false does the identification of truth with verifiability threaten to be inconsistent with Tarski's material adequacy requirement.

(E) A SUBJECTIVIST THEORY?

Moore's and Russell's fears that pragmatism would make truth a mere matter of taste are, as I have argued, unfounded. However, the questions whether, and if so in what sense, the pragmatist theory is subjectivist, require further attention.

It is clear, to begin with, that all the pragmatists agree that truth is correspondence with reality. Even James makes the point quite explicitly:

> [Truth] means [our ideas'] 'agreement' with 'reality'. Pragmatists and intellectualists both accept this definition as a matter of course.
>
> ('Pragmatism's Conception of Truth', in [1907], p. 133)

So far from denying the correspondence theory which their opponents championed, the pragmatists incorporate it as a part of their theory. But they are better aware than their opponents how inadequate, because unspecific, the formula of 'correspondence with reality' is as it stands.

Peirce frequently stresses that Reality is independent of human beliefs about it. Nonetheless, he manifests some embarrassment with his notion of Reality, since, as he is well aware, he can not prove that an external and independent Reality exists. As he puts it: since he uses the idea of Reality as the foundation for his theory of inquiry, he cannot use that theory to show that there is such a thing as Reality. However, he offers, in support of the hypothesis of Reality the following, rather less than conclusive considerations:

(i) Inquiry leads to no doubt of the existence of such a Reality: so the theory and its under-pinning are in harmony.

(ii) Doubt arises when one is undecided between a belief and its contradictory, which suggests that there is some *one* thing to which belief should conform.

(iii) The extraordinary success of the Scientific Method in leading to consensus can hardly be an accident, and would be explicable on the hypothesis of Reality.

(The last of these arguments has an independent interest, since it seems to support the hypothesis that Peirce took his theory of Scientific Method actually to describe the methods of practising scientists.) There are, though, some passages where Peirce apparently turns his theory on its head:

> . . . as what anything really is, is what it may finally come to be known to be in the ideal state of complete information . . . reality depends on the ultimate decision of the community . . .
>
> ('Some Consequences of Four Incapacities,' [1868], p. 72)

Although in 'The Fixation of Belief' [1877] he sounds confident about the view that agreement depends on Reality, not *vice-versa*, in 'How to Make Our Ideas Clear,' [1878] he comments that

> The opinion which is fated to be ultimately agreed by all who investigate is what we mean by the truth, and the object represented by this opinion is the real. *That is the way I would explain reality.*
>
> (p. 133, my italics)

James is less preoccupied with establishing the independence of reality, and more preoccupied with stressing that reality is experientially accessible:

> The only *real* guarantee we have against licentious thinking is the circumpressure of reality itself, which gets us sick of concrete errors, whether there be a trans-empirical reality or not.
>
> ('Humanism and Truth,' in his [1909], p. 72)

At this point it becomes essential to look, at least briefly, at the development of Peirce's view of reality. Although Peirce was an ontological realist at least since 1871, in his earlier work he did not accept epistemological realism, but subscribed, instead, to a kind of phenomenalism. His ontological realism allows a reality independent of our thought about it, which, as a constraint on Scientific Method, guarantees the eventual agreement of which it is the object. But his phenomenalism regards reality as merely a construction devised to order phenomena, which, since Peirce's doctrine that there are no incognisables ruled out appeal to possible but nonactual phenomena, could not allow there to be an 'object' of the final opinion unless and until that final opinion is reached. In the 1870s Peirce tried to resolve this conflict by appeal to the infinite future; by the 1890s he had resolved it by rejecting phenomenalism (see Murphey [1961], especially pp. 169, 376–7, O'Connor [1964], and Haack [1975], for more detailed discussion of this development). After about 1890, then, Peirce combined ontological with epistemological realism, a doctrine of direct perception. James's pragmatism, however, was always nominalistic. It will be apparent by now that I should disagree with Scheffler's suggestion that the way James goes beyond Peirce is in applying the pragmatic maxim to truth as well as meaning; I should locate an important difference between Peirce and James, rather, in their account of reality (*cf.* Scheffler [1974], Howard [1975]).

This, I think, supplies a better explanation of James's greater vulnerability to the charge of subjectivism.

Dewey's views have affinities with Peirce's later position. Dewey observes that pragmatism's opponents insist that truth is correspondence with reality, but then make that reality so remote and inaccessible that it becomes inexplicable how we should ever have the slightest reason to suppose that our beliefs correspond to it. A proper emphasis on the experiential character of reality will, Dewey thinks, serve to banish this mystery; correspondence with reality *is* coherence with the totality of experience.

The pragmatist theory of truth is certainly *not* subjectivist in the sense of identifying truth-for-me with whatever-I-happen-to-find-congenial-to-believe. The satisfactoriness of true beliefs consists in their correspondence with reality. But a further question then arises: how objective, on the pragmatist view, is reality?

It is here that an important tension in the theory begins to come to the surface. Peirce wishes to emphasise the externality and the independence of reality, for the sake of the objectivity of truth; but, though he would wish to hold that reality is independent of what anyone or everyone believes, he has difficulty in going beyond the weaker thesis that reality is independent of what any individual believes, but not of what the Scientific Community, as a whole and in the long run, believes. This tension arises because Peirce's theory of meaning identifies the sense of an expression with the criterion of its application, the meaning of 'true' in particular, with the criterion of truth. But Peirce doubts that we have certain ways of acquiring knowledge, or of knowing, if we do reach the truth, that we have done so; he is, in short, a fallibilist. This is why he feels the need to appeal to an independent—but, unfortunately, consequently inaccessible—reality, to close the gap which his fallibilism allows to open between the meaning of, and the criterion for, truth. (Though Popper's account of the pragmatists' views leave a good deal to be desired, some remarks in his [1960] suggest that he has noticed this tension.) This tension in Peirce also manifests itself in his shifts between the thesis that the truth is what the Scientific Community *will* in the long run agree on, and the thesis that the truth is what the Scientific Community *would* in the long run agree upon, if it *did* agree. These shifts will be examined in more detail in the next section. James, interestingly enough, reacts to this tension in a different way: he shuns the appeal to an independent but inaccessible reality, but then finds himself in a state of chronic embarrassment about those truths, which he cannot quite bring himself to deny to be truths, which, given the fallibility of our means of acquiring knowledge, may never be verified or falsified.

(F) TRUTH AS THE END OF INQUIRY

The thesis that the true is the satisfactory to believe has borne the brunt of criticism from opponents of pragmatism. The first thesis—truth as the end of inquiry—has received relatively less attention. In an article devoted to Dewey's views, however, Russell offers some counter-arguments. Russell points out that, on one interpretation, the thesis apparently entails that whatever beliefs are held by the last man on earth, are true. He comments, rather acidly:

> As, [the last man on earth) will presumably be entirely occupied in keeping warm and getting nourishment, it is doubtful whether his opinions will be any wiser than ours.
>
> ('Dewey's New Logic,' [19391], p. 145)

But the thesis may be more charitably interpreted, if it is understood to say that the truth is that opinion to which scientific inquiry tends as a limit, then the fact that science might come to an end before this terminal consensus is reached, is irrelevant.

This interpretation, however, is not without difficulties of its own. For it could still be questioned whether science manifests, as the thesis now seems to require, a tendency towards consensus. Peirce, it seems from at least some passages, *does* believe in such a tendency:

> There is a general *drift* in the history of human thought which will lead to one general agreement, one catholic consent.
>
> ([1931–58], IX, § 12)

Russell takes him severely to task for this faith:

> Is this an empirical generalisation from the history of research? Or is it an optimistic belief in the perfectibility of man? Does it contain any element of prophecy,

> or is it a merely hypothetical statement of what would happen if men of science grew continually cleverer? Whatever interpretation we adopt, we seem committed to some very rash assertion.
>
> ('Dewey's New Logic,' [1939], p. 146)

So it looks as if the thesis that the Truth is that consensus which use of the Scientific Method would if it continued sufficiently long, reach, may fail for want of an argument that there *is* any such end.

But this objection misses something. It has so far been left vague what, exactly, one is to understand by the 'Scientific Method.' The kind of objection just outlined takes for granted a rough-and-ready understanding in terms, presumably, of those methods which those we call 'scientists' use. Peirce, however, has a theory about Scientific Method, a theory which perhaps offers some explanation of his—as Russell supposed, quite unwarranted—optimism.

According to Peirce, the Scientific Method includes three types of argument: deductive, inductive and abductive. (Abduction Peirce defines as 'studying facts and devising a theory to explain them.') As so often, Peirce anticipates more recent philosophers of science, for his theory of scientific method strongly resembles the hypothetico-deductive.

What is important for present purposes is, specifically, Peirce's view of induction. Peirce thinks of inductive arguments as, roughly, those which extrapolate probabilities from given data. His view of probability is frequentist; the probability of *B* given *A* is given in terms of the proportion of *A*'s which are *B*'s, and, when the *A* series is infinite, the probability is the limiting frequency, if any. Peirce offers a justification depending upon the fact that induction, as he defines it, is a self-correcting proem. Once again, the argument anticipates a better known later version, Reichenbach's 'pragmatic justification' of the straight rule of induction.

Peirce's optimism about the eventual success of the Scientific Method is now more explicable. An essential element in Scientific Method is induction, and induction, Peirce thinks, is such as to yield the true probability, if there is one, eventually. This is not, of course, to say that Peirce's optimism is warranted; to show *that* one would have to devote considerably more detailed attention to his theory of induction than I have time to do. I claim only to have made his optimism explicable.

This suggestion leaves a question open: the question, whether Peirce's theory of scientific method is intended descriptively or prescriptively—as a description of the methods scientists do use, or as a prescription of the methods they should use. My impression is that Peirce is not wholly clear on this point. When he sounds confident that science progresses, it is perhaps because he is taking it to be the case that scientists do, in fact, use what he regards as the Scientific Method; when he seems less sure, it is perhaps because he is thinking of the theory of scientific method as prescriptive only. And sometimes he does sound much less confident than in the last passage quoted. For instance, in a letter of 1908 to Lady Welby he comments:

> I do not say that it is infallibly true that there is any belief to which a person would come if he were to carry his inquires far enough. I only say that that alone is what I call Truth. I cannot infallibly know that there is any truth.
>
> (p. 398)

Peirce's ambiguity on this point disguises a difficulty: if his theory of Scientific Method is intended prescriptively, he is not entitled to appeal to the alleged success of practising scientists in achieving consensus, as he does in his third argument for reality; if, on the other hand, the theory is intended descriptively, he is after all committed to some rather strong thesis about the progress of science, and so is vulnerable to some of Russell's criticisms.

Quine puts an objection which somewhat resembles Russell's. In *Word and Object* ([1960]) he objects to the proposed identification of the Truth with 'the ideal result of applying scientific method outright to the whole future totality of surface irritations', that there is no reason to suppose that there is any such unique result. Quine's objection is based, however, on his own theory of scientific method, which stresses that alternative theories, incompatible with each other, may be compatible with the totality of possible evidence. It is not certain that Peirce's theory of scientific method allows this possibility; and if not Quine's objection is not directly relevant to Peirce's position.

James, on the other hand, does seem to envisage such a possibility; but, taking seriously the principle that there can *be* no difference that *makes* no difference, he concludes that two such 'alternative' theories would not *really*, but, presumably, only *verbally* differ from each other. So his view too would avoid Quine's objection.

Both Russell's objection and Quine's objection bear on the supposed uniqueness of the end of inquiry. Even if Peirce's optimism that the Scientific Method will or would eventually yield a consensus can be justified by appeal to his theory of induction, however, there would remain another difficulty, which, curiously, Russell and Quine ignore. If truth is the end of inquiry, then, not only must all beliefs warranted, in the long run, by the Scientific Method, be true, but also, all truths must be, in the long run, warranted by the Scientific Method. But what reason is there to think that the Scientific Method would eventually yield all truths? Is it not likely, on the contrary, that some true propositions will never even be entertained? (On this point *cf.* Ayer [1968]). This difficulty relates to another feature of the pragmatists' views. The subject of 'true' in their writings is, usually, beliefs; and since they stress the importance of community, they clearly intend that different persons should be able to share the same belief. What is not clear, however, is whether 'belief' could be extended to cover propositions which have never been entertained, or whether, if it could not, the pragmatists would be willing to accept the consequence, that only propositions at some time entertained could be true or false. James, whom one might have expected to have been the most willing to admit this, in fact denies it:

> countless opinions 'fit' realities, and countless truths are valid, though no thinker ever thinks them.

But he finds such 'truths' of no consequence:

> . . . all discarnate truth is static, impotent and relatively spectral, full truth being the truth that energises and does battle.
>
> ('The Pragmatist Account of Truth and its Misunderstanders' in [1909], p. 204)

> . . . the truth with no-one thinking it, is like the coat that fits tho no one has ever tried it on . . .
>
> (p. 205)

This ambivalent attitude exactly parallels, of course, his attitude to 'truths' as yet unverified.

4 SOME CONCLUDING REMARKS

I shall end with some brief, but, I fear, rather vague, comments about what seem to me to be major strengths, and the major weaknesses, of the theory.

The theory is a cosmopolitan one, in that it includes substantial coherence and correspondence elements; and it thereby acquires some of the strengths of the coherence and correspondence theories while avoiding some of the weaknesses. Ironically, in view of the fact that the pragmatist theory has been available for a long time but has never enjoyed much popularity, Quinton commented as recently as 1966 that the direction from which progress in the theory of truth is to be expected is in 'the close interweaving of the coherence and correspondence theories' ('The Foundations of Knowledge,' [1966], p. 86). Furthermore, the pragmatist theory avoids that divorce of the theory of truth from epistemology—which is apt to make classical correspondence theories unsatisfying. By insisting that one ask what difference the truth or falsity of a belief would make, the pragmatists ensure that their theory of truth connects closely with their theory of knowledge. Russell, to be sure, found their stress on the experiential cash-value of true beliefs distasteful; he was apt to say that Pragmatism was an 'engineers' philosophy,' bound to lead to cosmic impiety, or at any rate to fascism. But this stress on the experiential cash-value of true beliefs can do us the important service of raising the neglected question, what, exactly, one should expect of a theory of truth.

Of course, the close connections between the pragmatist theory of truth and their theory of knowledge and theory of meaning mean that the former theory is vulnerable to criticisms directed, in the first instance, at the latter. The acceptability of the thesis that truth is the end of inquiry depends, for instance, on the thesis that the scientific method leads to consensus, and that in turn on a theory of induction, which may involve difficulties which would threaten the whole superstructure. Or again, objections to the pragmatist theory of meaning would be bound to involve consequent difficulties for the theory of truth. And, as I have suggested above, there are indeed tensions between Peirce's pragmatist theory of truth and his fallibilist epistemology. But it is to be hoped that recognition of such tensions may be useful in illuminating some real and important problems which a dogmatic separation of theory of truth and theory of knowledge is apt to disguise.

James once commented that theories generally run through three stages: first, the new theory is attacked as absurd; then it is admitted to be true, but obvious and insignificant; until finally it is seen to be so important that its former opponents claim that they discovered it. He hoped that *The Meaning of Truth,* published in 1909, would at least help the pragmatist theory of truth from the first into the second stage. Clearly, it did not. My object has been rather different: to ensure that if we reject the theory, we do so for the right reasons; and that, if there is anything of importance to be learned from it, we do not ignore the lesson.*

NOTES

1. *Cf.* Perkins [1952] and Hertz [1971].

REFERENCES

Ayer, A. J. [1968]: *The Origins* of *Pragmatism,* Macmillan.

Dewey, J. [1901]: 'A Short Catechism Concerning Truth,' in *The Influence of Darwin on Philosophy,* Henry Holt.

Dewey, J. [1929]: *Question or Certainty.* Capricorn Books, 1960.

Dewey. J. (1938]: *Logic, The Theory of Inquiry,* Henry Holt.

Dummett, M. A. E. [1959]: 'Truth,' *Proceedings of the Aristotelian Society* 1958–9, and in G. Pitcher (ed.) *Truth,* Prentice-Hall, 1964.

*I have been helped by comments made when an earlier version of this paper was read at the York conference on logic and semantics in 1974, and by the students, especially Ken Howse, who followed my course in Recent Anglo-Saxon Philosophy at Warwick in 1974–5.

Haack, S. [1975]: 'Pragmatism and Ontology: Peirce and James,' forthcoming in *Revue Internationale de Philosophie.*

Hamlyn, D. [1970]: *Theory of Knowledge,* Macmillan.

Hertz, R. A. [1971]: 'James and Moore: Two Perspectives on Truth,' *Journal of the History of Philosophy,* 9.

Howard, V. [1975]: 'The Pragmatic Maximum,' *British Journal for the Philosophy of Science,* 26, pp. 343–51.

James, W. [1907]: *Pragmatism,* Longman's Green. Page references to Meridian edition, 1955.

James, W. [1909]: *The Meaning of Truth,* Longman's Green. Page references to University of Michigan edition, 1970.

Moore, G. E. [1908]: 'Professor James' "Pragmatism".' *Proceedings of Aristotelian Society,* 8. And in *Philosophical Studies,* Routledge, 1922; page references to 1960 paperback edition of *Philosophical Studies.*

Murphy, M. [1961]: *The Development of Peirce's Philosophy,* Harvard University Press.

O'Connor, D. D. [1964]: 'Peirce's debt to F. E. Abbot,' *Journal of the History of Ideas,* 25.

Peirce, C. S. [1877]: 'The Fixation of Belief,' *Popular Science Monthly,* 12.

Peirce, C. S. [1878]: 'How to Make Our Ideas Clear,' *Popular Science Monthly,* 12.

Peirce, C. S. [1908]: Letter to Lady Welby, 1908. All in P. P. Wiener *(ed.)*: *Selected Writings.* Dover 1958; page references to Dover edition.

Peirce, C. S. [1931–58]: *The Collected Papers of Charles Saunders Peirce.* Harvard University Press.

Perkins, M. [1952]: 'Notes on the Pragmatic Theory of Truth,' *Journal of Philosophy,* 49.

Popper, K. R. [1960]: 'Truth, Rationality and the Growth of Scientific Knowledge,' in *Conjectures and Refutations,* Routledge & Kegan Paul, 1963.

Pratt, J. B. [1909]: *What is Pragmatism?* Macmillan, 1909.

Quine, W. V. O. [1951]: 'Two Dogmas of Empiricism,' *Philosophical Review,* 60 and in *From a Logical Point of View,* Harper Torchbooks, 1953.

Quine, W. V. O. [1960]: *Word and Object,* Wiley, 1960.

Quinton, A. [1966]: 'The Foundations of Knowledge' in B. A. O. Williams and A. Montifiore *(eds.): British Analytical Philosophy.* Routledge and Kegan Paul, 1966.

Rescher, N. [1973]: *The Coherence Theory of Truth.* Oxford University Press.

Russell, B. [1908]: 'James's Conception of Truth,' *Albany Review,* 3, and in *Philosophical Essays,* Allen and Unwin, 1910; references to 1966 revised edition of *Philosophical Essays.*

Russell, B. [1939]: 'Dewey's New Logic,' in P. A. Schiller *(ed.): The Philosophy Of John Dewey.* Tudor, 1939.

Scheffler, I. [1974]: *Four Pragmatists,* Routledge and Kegan Paul.

Tarski, A. [1931]: 'The Concept of Truth in Formalised Languages' in J. Woodger *(ed.): Logic, Semantics and Metamathematics,* Oxford University Press, 1956.

Reading Questions

1. In what way do Peirce and James consider the true to be useful or satisfactory to believe? Does truth consist in this usefulness, or is usefulness an external property of truth?
2. Why does James think that new truths come into existence as human knowledge increases? What does this imply for *discovery?*
3. For the pragmatic theory, are unexamined propositions devoid of truth value?
4. Suppose one criticizes the pragmatic theory by arguing that a proposition's being useful to believe is insufficient to secure its truth. For example, there may be beliefs such that no possible experience could overthrow them, but nevertheless these beliefs do not correspond with reality. (Keep in mind that Haack describes the pragmatic theory as incorporating a correspondence element.) Could this hypothesis be proven? If not, does it show that the pragmatic theory is unfalsifiable?

Truth as Ideal Coherence 11

NICHOLAS RESCHER

SUPPORTERS OF A COHERENTIST standard of truth must be able to establish that this criterion is duly consonant with the definitional nature of truth, for there ought rightfully to be a *continuity* between our evidential criterion of acceptability-as-true and the "truth" as definitionally specified. Any satisfactory criterion must be such as to yield the real thing—at any rate in sufficiently favorable circumstances. Fortunately for coherentism, it is possible to demonstrate rigorously that truth is tantamount to ideal coherence—that a proposition's being true is in fact *equivalent* with its being optimally coherent with an ideal data base. Given that the preceding continuity requirement is satisfied, the traditional view of truth as accord with fact *(adaequatio ad rem)* is thus also available to coherentists. However, the element of idealization at issue means that we cannot claim that coherence provides us with unqualified truth in actual practice. The coherence-based inquiries we actually carry out, can go only so far as to afford our best available *estimate* of the real truth.

Review of Metaphysics 38 (June 1985): 795–806.

I

The standard objection to the coherence theory of factual truth is that the linkage of coherence to truth is simply too loose for coherence to provide the definitive standard of truth. As Arthur Pap put it some years ago:

> It is quite conceivable that the coherence theory is a description of how the truth or falsehood of statements comes to be known rather than an analysis of the meaning of 'true'. . . . One might agree that a given statement is accepted as true in virtue of standing in certain logical relations to other statements; still it would not follow that in calling it true one *means* to ascribe to it those relations.[1]

Here then we have the standard reservations regarding a coherence theory of truth: "It may be suited as a *criterion* for the true, but certainly not as a *definitional standard* of truth." The aim of these deliberations is to show that this line of objection is untenable.

Our theme, then, is the much-debated question of whether the bearing of coherence is limited to its potential role as a mere *criterion of factual truth,* or whether coherence somehow inheres in the definition of truth by reflecting an *essential aspect of its nature.*[2] It will be shown here that if one is prepared to consider coherence in an *idealized* perspective—as *optimal* coherence with a *perfected* data base, rather than as a matter of apparent coherence with the imperfect data we actually have in hand—then an essential link between truth and coherence emerges.[3]

Such a linkage between criterion and definition is crucial to the viability of even a merely criteriological coherence theory, because the legitimating validation of a criterion of truth must be able to establish its consonance with the definitional nature of truth. A criterion of something cannot qualify as adequate unless one can establish that it must yield the real thing in appropriately benign circumstances. We shall refer to this requirement that true theses are coextensive with criteriologically justified beliefs in *ideal circumstances* as "the continuity condition."

A bit of symbolism will be helpful in providing a precise formulation to this condition:

> $C(S/f)$ is to stand for: the statement 'S' satisfies the truth-criterion C given that circumstances f obtain.
>
> $i(S)$ is to stand for: (epistemically) ideal circumstances with respect to the statement 'S.'

Given these specifications, the continuity condition now reads as follows:

> If C is to constitute an adequate criterion of truth, then it must be demonstrably the case that for any statement S, the truth of S is tantamount to its satisfying C under ideal evidential conditions with respect to S.
>
> 'S' is true iff $C(S/i(S))$

It is the demand for this sort of deep-rooted relationship which is at issue in Brand Blanshard's right-minded insistence that "a 'logical gap' so broad that a criterion and what it is supposed to indicate may each be present in the absence of the other surely falls short of the trustworthiness required of a criterion."[4]

This, then, is the thesis we have to demonstrate. To validate a coherence criteriology we must be able to show that, at least ideally, if we abstract from the imperfections of messy real-life situations, coherence does indeed get at "the real truth of things."

One preliminary point: If C is to serve as our criterion of truth, then we shall have it that C-satisfaction in the prevailing epistemic circumstances suffices to underwrite acceptance as true:

> If $C(S/a)$, when a are the actually prevailing circumstances, then 'S' is true.

Commitment to this implication follows at once from our adoption of C as a criterion *of truth.* But this condition of course only reflects a *practical policy* of ours, inherent in subscribing to C as a criterion of truth: it merely expresses our determination to accept 'S' as true when C is actually satisfied. What is at issue is not a relationship of abstract general principle, but only our adherence to a certain *modus operandi.* And there is of course the prospect of a slip between cup and lip here, since the actual circumstances a may be far from ideal for S. That "practical policy" at issue comes down to the rough and ready posture that the prevailing circumstances are good enough—that the "data on hand" are sufficient to permit us to decide the matter. On the other hand, the continuity criterion—'*S*' is true iff $C(S/i(S))$—represents a relationship that must be satisfied *as a matter of conceptual fact.* It must obtain demonstrably on the basis of "general principles" if the truth-condition *C* is to qualify as adequate.

II

Let us say that a factual proposition satisfies the condition of "ideal coherence" if it is *optimally* coherent with a *perfected* (or completed) data base. Given the nature of "coherence," such a proposition will fit more smoothly and consonantly with this idealized data base than does its negation (and consequently so fits better than any other proposition that is incompatible with it). The ensuing discussion will argue that, *when ideal coherence is construed in this way, then truth is demonstrably tantamount to ideal coherence.* It will endeavor to demonstrate that the linkage between these two factors then in fact becomes an essential one.

To establish this contention, it must be shown that two implication theses obtain with respect to any and all statements:

I. true ⇒ ideally coherent

II. ideally coherent ⇒ true

The idea of "ideal coherence" operative here should be understood as being a matter of *optimal coherence (c)* with a *perfected data base (B)*. Deploying these abbreviations, it is clear that the two principles at issue can now be formulated as follows:

(I) '*S*' is true → '*S*' c *B*

(II) '*S*' c *B* → '*S*' is true

Note that when the specific coherentist truth criterion stands in place of our earlier generic *C,* we have it that, by hypothesis, '*S*' c *B* is tantamount to: $C(S/i(S))$. Accordingly, these two principles simply restate the continuity condition.

If the coherence theory is to be adequate, the validation of these two principles will thus have to be grounded in the very nature of "optimal coherence (c) with a perfected data base (*B*)." To establish them we shall accordingly need to look more closely at the crucial ideas at issue: the conceptions of "optimal coherence" and of a "perfected data base."

First a word about *optimal* coherence. Just what is it "to cohere optimally with a data base"? What does "'*S*' c *B*" involve? The answer is provided by two conditions:

1. '*S*' represents a member of some family of mutually exclusive and exhaustive alternatives ($S_1, S_2, S_3, \ldots, S_n$).
2. '*S*' is more smoothly co-systematizable with *B* in this case than any of its alternatives, singly or in combination. (Note that this means specifically that '*S*' is more smoothly co-systematizable with *B* than is 'not-*S*'.)

To implement this second idea, we must have in hand some definite family of concrete principles of cognitive systematization which determines a standard of systemic connection according to which '*S*' is more smoothly coordinated with *B* than is the case with any (combination of) its available alternatives. But this is something into whose details we need not here enter further.[5]

Let us now turn to the idea of a "perfected data base." Perfection has two components: *completeness* (or comprehensiveness) and *adequacy* (or definitiveness). These have the following ramifications:

1. *Completeness:* If *D* is to be a *perfected* database, then it must be sufficiently complete and comprehensive that, for any thesis '*S*' within the domain of discussion at issue, either *S* itself or its negation 'not-*S*' will cohere optimally with *D:*

   If perf *(D)*, then: Either '*S*' c *D* or 'not-*S*' c *D*, for any and every statement '*S*' of the relevant domain.

2. *Adequacy.* To acknowledge *D* as a *perfected* data-base is to acknowledge it as actuality-determinative. And so we must endorse:

   If perf (*D*), then: if '*S*' c *D*, then *A(S)*.

Completeness requires *decisiveness;* adequacy requires *facticity.* These are conditions that inhere in the very notion of the "perfection" of a data base.

To be sure, all this is not to say that we can ever actually *find* such a perfected data base. We doubtless cannot. The very idea of such a data-base represents an idealization. What is being said is claimed in a strictly hypothetical mode: "If a perfected data base exists, then it must *ipso facto* have certain characteristics." We are, in effect, dealing with certain *meaning postulates* or definitional requirements for the idea of a "perfected data base"—certain explanatory stipulations for what the ideal of such a data base involves (in the context of "optimal coherence").

As a preliminary, let us first establish the effective *uniqueness* of such a perfected data base in point of optimal coherence. To demonstrate this, let us make the assumption that both B_1 and B_2 to answer to the characterization of a "perfected data base." We shall establish:

If 'S' c B_1 then 'S' c B_2, for any statement 'S'

This is accomplished by the following argument:

(1) Suppose: 'S' c B_1

(2) Suppose further that not: 'S' c B_2

(3) Then 'not-S' c B_2 follows from (2) by *Completeness*

(4) Then A(not-S) follows from (3) by *Adequacy*

(5) But $A(S)$ follows from (1) by *Adequacy*

(6) Since (4) and (5) are mutually contradictory given the Law of Excluded Middle, we must negate supposition (2), and hence have: 'S' c B_2. QED

The converse of course follows by exactly the same cause of reasoning. So with respect to "optimal coherence" there is in effect (at most) one perfected data base. Let us continue to designate this by B. By definition, then, B is the (unique) perfected data base, whose availability, as already observed, we can claim not as a matter of realizable fact but only as a matter of idealization.

It follows immediately from the two stipulated requirements of Completeness and Adequacy that B must satisfy the conditions represented by the following principles:

(P1) By the condition of Adequacy we have it that if 'S' does indeed optimally cohere with B, then this state of affairs must be actual:

'S' c $B \rightarrow A(S)$

(P2) By the condition of Completeness we have it that if 'S' coheres optimally with the perfected data base (B), then it follows that 'not-S' will be optimally coherent with the perfected data base B. Symbolically:

$\neg$('S' c B) $\rightarrow$ 'not-S' c B

These two principles, (P1) and (P2), will furnish the materials on whose basis our two focal implication theses (I) and (II) can be established. They are all we have; if the job is to be done, they must suffice to do it.

Before proceeding to show this, however, the idea of "actuality" reflected in our "$A(S)$" deserves some comment. The claim at issue is one of factuality, of "adequation to fact" *(adaequatio ad rem)*: to assert "$A(S)$" is to maintain that the state of affairs S is a constituent of the real world, that existing reality is (in part) characterized by this state of affairs. (Thus to assert "$A(S)$" is effectively to assert that S is a *"bestehender Sachverhalt,"* an *actual state of affairs,* in the language of Ludwig Wittgenstein's *Tractatus Logico-Philosophicus.*) The thesis at issue with "$A(S)$" is an *ontological* one: it claims that that's how things in fact are, whether or not people know or believe it. And this ontologically definitive aspect of A means that we must have the "law of the excluded middle" represented by a *tertium non datur* principle:

(LEM) $\neg A(S)$ iff A(not-S)

Actuality must "make up its mind" with respect to the $A(S)/A$(not-S) dichotomy. This condition inheres axiomatically in the very meaning of "actuality."

On this basis, let us now proceed to establish principles (I) and (II). The required demonstration is easily produced.

Given that truth is (by definition, as it were) subject to the ancient principle of accord with fact (*adaequatio ad rem*)

(A) 'S' is true $\leftrightarrow A(S)$

we have it that principle (P1) immediately entails:

$$\text{'}S\text{' c } B \rightarrow \text{'}S\text{' is true}$$

This provides for thesis (II), so that half of our task is already accomplished.

To obtain thesis (I), let us consider principle (P1) in the special case of the state of affairs not-*S*;

$$(1)\quad \neg A(\text{not-}S) \rightarrow \neg(\text{'not-}S\text{' c } B)$$

By the Law of Excluded Middle, namely

$$(\text{LEM})\qquad A(S) \rightarrow \neg A(\text{not-}S)$$

we have it that (1) yields

$$(2)\quad A(S) \rightarrow \neg(\text{'not-}S\text{' c } B)$$

Now in view of (P2), this yields

$$A(S) \rightarrow \text{'}S\text{' c } B$$

And given (A), this in turn yields

$$\text{'}S\text{' is true} \rightarrow \text{'}S\text{' c } B$$

We have thus also provided for thesis (I), thereby completing our task.

It follows from the resultant equivalence of truth-as-adequation with ideal coherence that an adequationist view of the nature of truth affords no insuperable obstacles to coherentism. The coordinative linkage between truth and (idealized) coherence is grounded in the fundamental general principles of the matter, and the coherentist standard thus meets the crucial continuity condition that is an adequacy requirement for any viable criterion of truth. The continuity condition is satisfied. As regards its theoretical eligibility, we may inscribe *nihil obstat* on the proposal to construe truth in terms of idealized coherence.

III

It remains to be shown, however, that the "ancient principle of accord with fact, of *adaequatio ad rem*"—namely, thesis (A) above—is also available to the coherentist who, after all, does not propose to *define* truth in this way, so that it is not available to him as a mere truism (as it is to the adequationist). Accordingly, we must show that this thesis is itself derivable on coherentist principles, given that these principles consist not of (PI) and (P2) alone, but also the favored truth-determinative axiom (or definition) that is obtained when we conjoin theses (I) and (II):

$$(\text{C})\qquad \text{'}S\text{' is true} \leftrightarrow \text{'}S\text{' c } B$$

Note that in view of this axiom, we have it that (P1) yields

$$\text{'}S\text{' is true} \rightarrow A(S)$$

To obtain the converse, consider the principle (P1) in the special case of the state of affairs not-*S*:

$$\neg A(\text{not-}S) \rightarrow -(\text{'not-}S\text{' c } B)$$

By the Law of Excluded Middle (LEM) this will entail:

$$A(S) \rightarrow -(\text{'not-}S\text{' c } B)$$

By (P2) this yields

$$A(S) \rightarrow \text{'}S\text{' c } B$$

By (C) this yields

$$A(S) \rightarrow \text{'}S\text{' is true}$$

Together with its converse, as derived above, this provides for (A). QED

It follows that an equating of "the (real) truth" with adequation to fact (with how matters actually stand in the world) is also an implicit consequence—in the idealized case—of a coherentist conception of the nature of truth. The coherentist accordingly has no need to renounce adequation. If he defines truth in terms of ideal coherence, the principle of adequation (A) remains available to the coherentist as reflecting an essential feature of truth. This circumstance that principle (A) characterizes the essence of truth is as available to him as to anyone else.

Let us recall that principle (A) encapsulates the *correspondentist* view of the nature of truth as adequation to fact:

$$(\text{A})\qquad \text{'}S\text{' is true} \leftrightarrow A(S)$$

On the other hand, principle (C) encapsulates the *coherentist* view of the nature of truth as ideal coherence:

$$(\text{C})\qquad \text{'}S\text{' is true} \leftrightarrow \text{'}S\text{' c } B$$

Note now that Part II has established:

{(LEM), (P1), (P2), (A)} entails (C)

And the opening discussion of Part III has established:

{(LEM), (PI), (P2), (C)} entails (A)

Noting these together, we arrive at:

{(LEM), (P1), (P2)} entails [(A) ↔ (C)]

Given the explication of "ideal coherence" at issue in the principles P1 and P2, (or, equivalently, in the conditions of *Completeness* and *Adequacy),* it emerges that adequationism and coherentism are effectively coordinated. The coherentist criteriology of truth is also available to the adequationist. The adequationist view of the nature of truth is also available to the coherentist. The two positions can (under plausible suppositions) be coordinated with one another as flatly equivalent.

The pivotal problem of Part I is thus resolved. The present deliberations indicate that the coherentist criterion of truth as optimal systematization is qualified to serve as a truth-criterion in virtue of satisfying the continuity condition. Authentic truth may be characterized essentialistically in terms of *idealized* coherence; putative truth may be identified criteriologically in terms of *manifest* coherence. And continuity is thereby assured.

And this is all to the good. Brand Blanshard's insistence on the continuity condition is very much in order. He urges, in effect, that "If you are seriously proposing to adopt coherence with 'the data' as a criterial standard of truth, then you should be able to show this proposal to be warranted through some sort of essential linkage between truth and coherence." As he puts it:

> If we accept coherence as our test, we must use it everywhere. We must therefore use it to test the suggestion that truth is other than coherence. But if we do, we shall find that we must reject the suggestion as leading to incoherence.[6]

And this point is well taken. A definition or interpretation of truth that did not meet this condition would thereby manifest its own inadequacy.

In showing that the coherentist criterion of truth is capable of meeting the continuity condition, the present deliberations accordingly manage to set aside one of the main traditional reservations about the acceptability of coherentism.

IV

To be sure, an important issue remains open. Given that "the real truth" is guaranteed only by *ideal* coherence—by optimal coherence with a perfected data base that we do not have, rather than by *apparent* coherence with the suboptimal data base we actually have in hand—we have no categorical assurance of the actual correctness of our coherence-guided inquiries, and no unqualified guarantee that their deliverances provide "the real truth" that we seek in matters of empirical inquiry. Quite the reverse: the history of science shows that our "discoveries" about how things work in the world secured through scientific coherentism constantly require adjustment, correction, replacement. We cannot say that our coherence-grounded inductive inquiries provide us with the real (definitive) truth, but just that they provide us with *the best estimate* of the truth that we can achieve in the circumstances at hand.

Definitive knowledge—as opposed to "merely putative" knowledge—is the fruit of *perfected* inquiry. Only here, at the idealized level of perfected science, could we count on securing the real truth about the world that "corresponds to reality" as the traditional phrase has it. Factual knowledge at the level of generality and precision at issue in scientific theorizing is akin to a *perfect* circle. Try as we will, we cannot quite succeed in producing it. We do our best and call the result knowledge, even as we call that carefully drawn "circle" on the blackboard a *circle*. But we realize deep down, as it were, that what we currently call scientific knowledge is no more authentic (perfected) knowledge than what we call a circle in that geometry diagram is an authentic (perfected) circle. Our "knowledge" is in such cases no more than our *best estimate* of the truth of things. Lacking the advantage of a God's eye view, we have no access to the world's facts save through the mediation of (potentially flawed) *inquiry*. All we can do—and what must suffice us because indeed it is *all* that we can do—is to do the best we can in the cognitive state of the art to *estimate* "the correct" answer to our scientific questions.

In subideal, real-life circumstances, an evidential gap indeed separates *presumptive* from *certifiable* truth. But, given an adequate criteriology of truth, this gap becomes closed in ideal circumstances. The continuity condition reflects the fact that inquiry aims at truth—that the real truth is the definitive aim and aspiration of the scientific enterprise.

The circumstance that what we achieve in our practice of scientific coherentism is not the real truth as such, but only our best estimate thereof, reflects the fact that we must pursue this cognitive enterprise amid the harsh realities and complexities of an imperfect world. In deliberating about the truth of our scientific claims, as elsewhere, the gap between the real and the ideal must be acknowledged.[7]

NOTES

1. Arthur Pap, *Elements of Analytic Philosophy* (New York: MacMillan, 1949), p. 356.

2. The definition vs. criterion dichotomy was the starting point of the author's *The Coherence Theory of Truth* (Oxford: Oxford University Press. 1973). It also provided the pivot for the critique of the coherentism of Blanshard's *The Nature of Thought* presented in Paul A. Schilpp, ed., *The Philosophy of Brand Blanshard* (La Salle, IL.: Open Court, 1980). Several subsequent publications have kept the pot boiling, in particular Scott D. Palmer, "Blanshard, Rescher, and the Coherence Theory of Truth," *Idealistic Studies,* 12 (1982): 211–30, and Robert Tad Lehe, "Coherence—Criterion and Nature of Truth," *ibid.* 13 (1983): 177–89.

3. This is an issue on which I have come to change my mind, largely owing to stimulating discussions held during the 1983–84 academic year, with Professor Lorenz Bruno Puntel of the University of Munich.

4. Brand Blanshard, "Reply to Nicholas Rescher," in Schilpp, ed., *The Philosophy of Brand Blanshard,* pp. 589–600 (see p. 596).

5. For a further development of these ideas, see the author's *The Coherence Theory of Truth* and *Cognitive Systematization* (Oxford: Blackwell, 1979).

6. Brand Blanshard, *The Nature of Thought,* 2 vols. (London: Allen & Unwin, 1939), vol. 2, pp. 267–68.

7. In revising this paper from an earlier version I have profited by discussion with Geo Siegwart.

Reading Questions

1. Rescher distinguishes between a *definition* of truth and a *criterion* of truth. What is this difference supposed to be?
2. Part of Rescher's theory requires the concept of a perfect database, and part of his characterization of perfection is the idea of adequacy. What is the adequacy condition? Rescher states that adequacy requires facticity. Is he slipping a notion of truth into his definition of a "perfect database"? If so, is Rescher's coherence theory circular?
3. Rescher states that 'S' is true $\leftrightarrow A(S)$. That is, proposition 'S' is true iff state of affairs S is actual. With this principle, is Rescher just pushing off the problem of truth onto the problem of explaining what it is for a state of affairs to be actual?
4. Just as Haack argued that the pragmatic theory of truth has a correspondence aspect, Rescher maintains that the coherence theory also has a correspondence component. What is this component in Rescher's theory?
5. Could all the coherence talk in Rescher's view just be window dressing on what is at heart a correspondence theory? Consider the role of his adequation condition.

12 The Deflationary View of Truth

PAUL HORWICH

THE CONCEPTION OF TRUTH to be defended in this essay is similar in spirit to other deflationary accounts that have appeared during the past hundred years or so, maintaining, in one way or another, that truth is not a normal property and that traditional investigations into its underlying nature have been misconceived. None of these accounts, however, has won over very many adherents, and the vast majority of philosophers either still subscribe to some form of correspondence, coherence, pragmatist or primitivist picture, or else think that no decent theory has yet been made available. One source of dissatisfaction with deflationary proposals in the literature is that they are not described fully or precisely enough to be properly evaluated. For instance, it isn't always said whether the theory concerns the nature of *truth itself*, or merely the meaning of the word "true." Second, and exacerbating the evaluation problem, is a tendency to omit explicit statement of what a decent account is supposed to do. The adequacy conditions for a theory of truth are left unclear. A third-place common defect of deflationary views is their commitment to certain blatantly implausible theses: for example, that *being true* is not a property at all, or that *every* instance of "'p' is true iff p" is correct. And, in the fourth place, objections are often left standing that could in fact be rebutted: for example, that the theory fails to say *what truth is*, and that it cannot be reconciled with the *desirability* of truth. The purpose of this chapter is to reach an exact characterization of the minimalist conception and, whilst doing so, to show how to deal with some of the problems that have notoriously afflicted previous deflationary proposals.

(1) *Of what kinds are the entities to which truth may be attributed?*

The list of candidates includes: (a) *utterances*—individual sounds and marks located in particular regions of space and time (e.g., Oscar's saying the words "I am hungry" at midday on the 1st January 1988); (b) *sentences*—types of expression in a language; syntactic forms that are exemplified by particular utterances (e.g., the English sentence "I am hungry"); (c) *statements, beliefs, suppositions, etc.*—individual, localised actions or states of mind (e.g., Oscar's state at midday of believing that he is hungry); (d) *propositions*—the things that are believed, stated, supposed, etc; the contents of such states (e.g., *that Oscar was hungry at midday on 1st January* 1988). I shall follow ordinary language in supposing that truth is a property of propositions.[1] Thus, if we agree with Oscar, we attribute truth to *what he said*, to the proposition he asserted. Presumably the *sentence-type of English* that he used is not true; for that very sentence-type is used on other occasions to make false statements. Nor would one normally characterize the noises he made, or his belief-state, as true. These entities are more naturally described as "expressing a truth" and "being *of* a true proposition." No doubt we do attribute truth to statements' beliefs, suppositions, and so on; but surely what we have in mind is that the propositional objects of these linguistic and mental acts are true, and not the acts themselves.

Most of the time I will conform to this way of speaking. To some extent this decision is non-trivial; for it involves a commitment to the existence of a breed of things called "propositions." However this commitment, though controversial and in need of some defence, is much less substantial than it might seem at first. For it presupposes very little about the *nature* of propositions. Granted, minimalism requires is that our conception of them not

This article originally appeared as Chapter 2 of Truth *(Oxford University Press, 2nd ed., 1998). Reprinted by kind permission of Prof. Horwich and Oxford University Press (UK).*

rely on the concept of truth. For the minimalist's direction of conceptual priority is the other way around: insofar as our concept of truth is constituted by our acceptance of instances of 'The proposition *that p* is true iff p,' we must already be capable of grasping propositions. But this leaves open many possibilities. As far as the minimal theory of truth is concerned, propositions could be composed of abstract Fregean senses, or of concrete objects and properties; they could be identical to a certain class of sentences in some specific language, or to the meanings of sentences, or to some new and irreducible type of entity that is correlated with the meanings of certain sentences. I am not saying that there is nothing to choose amongst these answers. The point is rather that the minimal theory does not require any particular one of them. So that someone who wishes to avoid commitment to 'propositions' of any specific sort need not on that score object to the conception of truth that will be elaborated here.

Moreover, the view that truth is not strictly speaking attributable to utterances, or to linguistic or mental acts, is not substantial and nothing of importance in what follows will depend on it. If someone holds that an utterance may be 'true,' in a certain sense, then he can simply regard my claims about the property of *expressing truth* as claims about 'truth' in his sense. Similarly for those who think that a truth predicate may be applied to acts of asserting, states of believing, etc.

(2) *What are the fundamental principles of the minimal theory of truth?*

The axioms of the theory are propositions like

(1) <<Snow is white> is true iff snow is white>

and

(2) <<Lying is wrong> is true iff lying is wrong>;

that is to say, all the propositions whose structure is

(E*) <<p> is true iff p>.[2]

In order to arrive at this 'propositional structure' we can begin with any one of the axioms and note that it may be divided into two complex constituents. First there is a part that is itself a proposition and which appears twice. In the case of (1), this is the constituent expressible by the English words

(3) "snow is white,"

i.e.,

(4) <Snow is white>.

And second there is the remainder of the proposition—a constituent expressed by the schematic sentence

(E) "<p> is true iff p"

i.e.,

(E*) <<p> is true iff p>[3]

This second constituent is a propositional structure. It is a function from propositions to propositions.[4] Thus if E* is applied to the proposition

(4) <Snow is white>

it yields the axiom

(1) <<Snow is white> is true iff snow is white>;

if it is applied to the proposition

(5) <Lying is wrong>

it yields

(2) <<Lying is wrong> is true iff lying is wrong>.

Indeed when applied to any proposition, y, this function yields a corresponding axiom of the minimal theory, MT. In other words the axioms of MT are given by the principle[5]

(6) For any object x: x is an axiom of the minimal theory if and only if, for some y, when the function E* is applied to y, its value is x.

Or in logical notation

(6*) $(\forall x)(x \text{ is an axiom of MT} \leftrightarrow (\exists y)(x = E^*(\forall y)))$

The minimal theory has several striking features—features that might at first be regarded as grounds for dissatisfaction with it.

In the first place it does not say explicitly *what truth is*; it contains no principle of the form, '(∀x)(x is true iff …x…).' And so one might suspect that certain general facts about truth could not be explained by the theory. Secondly, it does not mention phenomena such as reference, meaning, logical validity, assertion, and the aim of inquiry—notions whose relation to truth one might have thought any decent theory should describe. And, thirdly, although we have been able to characterize the axioms of MT (as the propositions of a certain form) we cannot explicitly formulate the theory—for two independent reasons. In the first place the number of *formulatable* axioms is too great; there are infinitely many and though each one of them can be expressed it is not possible to write down the whole collection. In the second place there are some propositions we cannot express. And for those the corresponding equivalence axioms are themselves inexpressible—although, as we have seen, it is *nonetheless* possible to say what they are.

In the following few sections we shall examine our justification for concluding that NIT is nevertheless the best theory of truth, and we shall see why the peculiar features of the theory should not be held against it.

(3) *It seems unlikely that instances of the equivalence schema could possibly suffice to explain all the great variety of facts about truth.*

The primary test of this (and any other) theory is its capacity to accommodate the phenomena in its domain. That is to say, if our theory is a good one, it will be able to account for all the facts about truth. Let me give three examples of the sort of explanation that minimalism can provide.

(I) From "What Smith said was true" and "What Smith said was that snow is white," it follows that "Snow is white." Given the minimal theory (MT) this fact can be explained as follows:

(1) What Smith said is true
(2) What Smith said = <snow is white>
∴ (3) <snow is white> is true [from 1,2]
(4) <snow is white> is true iff snow is white [MT]
∴ (5) snow is white [from 3,4][6]

(II) If one proposition (materially) implies another, and the first one is true, then so is the second. Here is a minimalist explanation:

1. Logic provides us with facts such [dogs bark & (dogs bark → pigs fly)] pigs fly; that is, with every fact of the form [p & (p→q)] → q
2. Therefore, given MT, we can then explain every fact of the form [<p> is true & (p→q)] → <q> is true
3. But from the meaning of "implies," we have all instances of <p>implies<q> → (p→q)
4. Therefore we can explain each fact of the form [<p> is true & <p>implies<q>] → <q> is true
5. And therefore, given MT, we get each fact of the form <[<p> is true & <p> implies <q>] → <q> is true> is true
6. But it is a peculiar property of propositions that any general fact about them—any characteristic of *all* propositions—is entailed by the infinite set of particular facts associating that characteristic with each individual proposition
7. Therefore, in light of (5) and (6), we can explain the general fact: Every proposition of the form, <[<p> is true & <p>implies <q>] → <q> is true>, is true

(III) We would be inclined to endorse the following thesis: "If all Bill wants is to have a beer, and he thinks that merely by nodding he will get one, then, if his belief is true, he will get what he wants." This fact would be explained as follows: We begin with the suppositions,

(1) Bill wants <Bill has a beer>
(2) Bill believes <Bill nods → Bill has a beer>

In addition, we can make the psychological assumption

(3) [Bill wants <Bill has a beer> & Bill believes <Bill nods → Bill has a beer>] → Bill nods [premise]
∴ (4) Bill nods [from 1,2,3]

Now let us assume for the sake of argument

(5) Bill's belief is true

That is to say

(6) <Bill nods → Bill has a beer> is true [from 2,5]

And we have

(7) <Bill nods → Bill has a beer> is true iff Bill nods → Bill has a beer [MT]
∴ (8) Bill nods → Bill has a beer [from 6,7]
∴ (9) Bill has a beer [from 4,8]

But again from the theory of truth,

(10) <Bill has a beer> is true iff Bill has a beer [MT]
∴ (11) <Bill has a beer> is true [from 9,10]
∴ (12) Bill gets what he wants [from 1,11]

This sort of explanation may be universalized to show in general how true beliefs engender successful action.

According to the minimalist thesis, all of the facts whose expression involves the truth predicate may be explained in such a way: namely, by assuming no more about truth than instances of the equivalence schema. Further explanations of this sort, dealing with a range of philosophically interesting facts about truth, will be given as we proceed. These explanations will confirm the minimalist thesis that no account of the *nature* of truth, no principle of the form '(∀x)(x is true iff ... x ...)' is called for.

(4) *The minimal theory must be incomplete, for it says nothing about the relationships between truth and affiliated phenomena such as verification, practical success, reference, meaning, logical validity and assertion.*

A theory of any phenomenon, X, is a collection of principles (i.e., axioms and/or rules); and the theory is *good* to the extent that it captures all the facts about that phenomenon in the simplest possible way. It won't do merely to produce some set of important facts about X and call that the theory. Nor would it suffice even if *every* fact about X were explicitly listed. Rather the understanding that we want requires some account of explanatory relationships. We have to locate the most basic facts regarding X, from which all the others may be explained.

Of course we don't expect our theory of X to do the explanatory work all by itself. It does not follow solely from the theory of electrons that electrons are smaller than elephants; we need a theory of elephants too. Our goal, then, is to find a simple theory of X, which together with our theories of other matters, will engender all the facts.

Now, sometimes it will turn out, for certain phenomena, X and Y, that we cannot separate two distinct theories, one for X and one for Y: the simplest adequate body of principles we can find concerns both X and Y. Consider, for example, a geometric theory about points, lines, angles, etc. This cannot be split up into a theory of points, a theory of lines, and so on. Sometimes we are forced to acknowledge that certain theoretical phenomena are, in this way, inextricably entangled with one another. And this is a significant fact about such phenomena. But when this is *not* so, where distinct theories of X and Y *can* be given, then they *should* be given. Otherwise, a misleading illusion of interdependence is conveyed and the cause of simplicity and explanatory insight is poorly served.

For this reason it seems to me not merely legitimate but important to separate, if we can, what we say about truth from our theories of reference, logic, meaning, verification, and so on. No doubt there are interesting relationships amongst these matters. But insofar as we want to *understand* truth and the other phenomena, then our task is to *explain* the relationships between them and not merely to recognize that they exist. We must discover the simplest principles from which they can all be deduced: and simplicity is promoted by the existence of separate theories of each phenomenon. Therefore it is quite proper to explain the properties of truth by conjoining the minimal theory with assumptions from elsewhere. (Note, for example, the use of extraneous premises in the explanations in the previous section—drawn, in those cases, from psychology, logic and the theory of propositions). The virtue of minimalism, I claim, is that *it provides a theory of truth that is a theory of nothing else, but which is sufficient, in combination with theories of other phenomena, to explain all the facts about truth.*

(5) *Even if the minimal theory is, in some sense, 'adequate' and 'pure,' it is nevertheless unsatisfactory, being so cumbersome that it cannot even be explicitly formulated.*

Presented with the minimal theory of truth, one's first instinct, no doubt, is to imagine that we can surely improve on it and capture the infinity of instances of the equivalence schema in a compact formulation. However, there does not *have* to be any succinct, non-trivial theory of truth, and I shall be arguing that in fact there isn't one. Such a theory would encapsulate the properties of truth in a *finite* body of principles which would generate everything true of truth, including, at the very least, infinitely many instances of '<p> is true iff p.' Moreover, if it is to be non-trivial, the theory would have to subsume all these facts without the use of notions that are themselves mysterious and unexplained. But how might this be done?

One natural suggestion is the single principle:

(7) $(\forall x)(x \text{ is true iff } \{\exists q\}(x=\langle q\rangle \;\&\; q))$

where the curly brackets indicate *substitutional quantification* over the sentences of English. But this idea fails for a couple of reasons.

In the first place, the use of substitutional quantification does not square with the *raison d'être* of our notion of truth, which is to enable use to do *without* substitutional quantification.[7] In the second place, the notion of susbstitutional quantification would itself require theoretical elucidation. But what kind of elucidation could be given? It would be circular to rely on the standard explanation which is couched in terms of truth.[8] Perhaps, alternatively, some specification of the rules of inference that govern substitutional quantification: for example, a version of 'universal instantiation,' which is the schematic rule:

(8) $$\frac{\{\forall q\}(\ \ldots\ q\ \ldots\ )}{\ldots\ p\ \ldots}$$

However, this cannot be formulated as a generalization over every sentence, "p": viz.

(9) $$\{\forall p\}\ \frac{\{\forall q\}(\ \ldots\ q\ \ldots\ )}{\ldots\ p\ \ldots}$$

For there would then be no way of getting from that principle to instances such as:

(10) $$\frac{\{\forall q\}(\ \ldots\ q\ \ldots\ )}{\ldots \text{ snow is white } \ldots}$$

Nor, again on pain of circularity, could we construe it as the claim that every instance of the schema preserves *truth*.

The only alternative would be to recognize that the apparently *single* rule, (8), is in fact an infinite collection of rules; one for each 'sentence in context' that can be put in place of "... p ...." But then we are embracing an unformulatable theory after all. Nothing has been gained; yet something (i.e., the use of truth to *dispense* with substitutional quantification) has been lost. Thus it seems that the best overall theory will not involve a definition of truth in terms of substitutional quantification.[9]

Another tempting approach, again designed to avoid the need for infinitely many axioms, is to formulate the theory of truth as the single proposition:

(11) Every instance of <<p> is true iff p> is true.

It is clear, however, that this will not do. For it would enable us to deduce, for example,

(12) <<Snow is white> is true iff snow is white> is true.

But we would have no license to get from there to the conclusion that

(1) <Snow is white> is true snow is white.

To do this we would need the schematic rule of inference:

(E#) $$\frac{\langle p\rangle \text{ is true}}{p}$$

which, as we have just seen, must be regarded as an infinite collection of separate rules.

Inspired by Tarski (1958), one might think that the solution to our difficulty is to be found by defining the truth of a whole proposition in terms of the reference of its parts and how these parts are put together. But this is a vain hope. Truth and reference are closely affiliated notions, and so a theory that characterized truth in terms of reference but gave no account of reference would be unsatisfactory. But any attempt to provide such a theory re-encounters precisely the problems with which we are now struggling. For just as the theory of truth must subsume everything like

(1) <Snow is white> is iff snow is white

so any decent theory of reference would have to subsume the fact that

(13) The propositional constituent with the word, "Aristotle," refers (if all) to Aristotle,

and so on. It might be thought that in the case of reference this problem may be solved easily—by simply listing the referents of each of the finitely many primitive terms in our language. But this is not so. Just as our understanding of truth goes beyond the list of presently formulable instances of the equivalence schema and tells us that any new sentences could also be instantiated, similarly, our conception of reference goes beyond a knowledge of the referents of our current primitive vocabulary.[10] It covers a potentially infinite number of new terms. Consequently, we are pushed into formulations such as

(14) $(\forall x)(\forall y)(x \text{ refers to } y \text{ iff } \{\exists d\}$ $(x = \text{“d”} \;\&\; y = d))$

where the substitutional variable, d, ranges over singular terms in possible extensions of our language. Thus we find ourselves relying again on substitutional quantification and the need to explain it with an infinite number of rules; so the reduction of truth to reference has turned out to be futile.

Let me emphasise four points about this line of thought. In the first place, exactly the same criticism applies to the project of explaining truth in terms of *predicate satisfaction*. We would need to add a theory of satisfaction that could encompass all facts like

(15) The predicate "blue" is satisfied by blue things;

and once again no list could suffice. An adequate theory would have to contain infinitely many propositions of the form,

(16) The propositional constituent associated with the predicate "F" is satisfied by, and only by, things that are F.

Therefore concern about the infinite character of the minimal theory of truth cannot be assuaged by explaining truth in terms of satisfaction.

Secondly, these conclusions do not tell against Tarski's *own* project, which was to explicate a notion of 'true-in-L' for certain highly artificial languages, L. Each of these languages has a fixed stock of primitives, so it is possible to explicate "refers-in-L" and "satisfies-in-L" with finite lists of principles. Our project, however, is in certain respects more ambitious than Tarski's. We are aiming for a theory of 'being true'—a property which is attributed to propositions regardless of how or whether they are expressed. Similarly we are looking for a theory of 'expressing truth'—a property we may attribute to an utterance regardless of the language in which it is couched. I have been considering the possibility that someone might hope, in defining "true," to exploit the strategy that Tarski used in his definition of "true-in-L"; but this will not work or so I have argued.

Thirdly, it might be thought that the difficulty in obtaining a finite, compositional theory of truth stems from the implicit assumption that propositions are constructed, as Frege said, from the *senses of words*—which are entities that require some theory of reference—and that such problems do not arise if propositions are instead constructed, as Russell proposed, from concrete objects and properties. For in that case we can say

(ET) $(\forall x)(\forall R)(\forall S)$[x is the consisting of the relation, R, and the sequence, S, of objects $\rightarrow$ (x is true $\leftrightarrow$ S exemplifies R)].

But although this may be fine as far as it goes, it does not go far enough. For it would have to be supplemented with a theory of *exemplification;* and here is where the old troubles will emerge. We will find that separate statements are needed to cover monadic properties, dyadic relations, triadic relations, and so on. In other words the theory would look roughly as follows:

(∃x) (S)(R)[S exemplifies R ↔
(∃ x)(S = <x> & Rx) ∨
(∃x)(∃y)(S = <x,y> & Rxy) ∨
(∃x)(∃y)(∃z)(S = <x,y,z> & Rxyz) ∨
. . . and so on . . .

And we are not yet dealing with logically very complex cases. Thus it isn't any easier to give a finite theory of truth if we focus on Russellian, 'concrete' propositions.

Finally, notice that no help is to be found by looking in the direction of traditional theories of truth such as the coherence and pragmatic approaches, or by entertaining some other way of identifying truth with a naturalistic property. For whatever property, F, is associated with truth, we will be able to explain instances of the equivalence schema only to the extent that we can explain instances of the schema,

(17) <p> is F iff p.

And *this* infinite theory will be no easier to encapsulate than the minimal theory.

I conclude that we should not expect to contain all instances of the equivalence schema within a finite formulation: an infinity of axioms is needed. And since this would seem to be an unavoidable feature of any adequate theory of truth, it should not be held against MT. Therefore we must acknowledge that the theory of truth cannot be explicitly formulated. The best we can do is to give an implicit specification of its basic principles.

(6) *If there were really no more to a complete theory of truth than a list of biconditionals like "The proposition that snow is white is true if and only if snow is white," then since one could always say "p" rather than "The proposition that p is true," it would be inexplicable that our language should contain the word "true": there would be no point in having such a notion.*

This argument has already been dealt with; but it is often raised against what are sometimes called 'redundancy' accounts of truth, so let me repeat my response. First, the fact that the only applications of truth expressly contained in the theory are within propositions of the form

(E*) <<p> is true iff p>,

does not imply that the theory covers only those cases in which truth is attributed to an articulated proposition. For suppose "Einstein's law" refers to the proposition, <E = mc²>. In other words,

(18) <E = mc^2> = Einstein's law.

In that case the theory of truth, which applies in the first instance to

(19) <E = mc^2> is true,

must apply indirectly to

(20) Einstein's law is true,

from which "is true" cannot be removed. And it is from its role in such sentences that the truth predicate gets is value. To see this, consider how we would manage without it. We would have to put the matter roughly as follows:

(21) (∀x)(If Einstein's law is the proposition *that x*, then x).

But this could not be construed in the usual manner. For, given the usual conventions of quantification, that sentence is ill-formed in two distinct ways: the second occurrence of "x" is in an opaque context, beyond the reach of normal quantification; and a variable that ranges over *objects* appears in sentential positions. In order to avoid these incoherences it would be necessary to introduce a new form of quantification—substitutional quantification—that *could* legitimately govern opaque contexts and sentence positions. That is to say, we need a quantifier

(22) {∀p}(... p ...)

whose meaning is not

(23) Every object, p, satisfies "... p ..."

but rather

(24) Every grammatical substitution of a declarative sentence of English in place of "p" in "... p ..." yields a truth.

But such a quantifier, with its special syntactic and semantic rules, would be a cumbersome addition to our language. The point of our notion of truth is that it provides a simple alternative to this apparatus. The truth predicate allows any sentence to be reformulated so that its entire content will be expressed by the new subject—a singular term open to normal objectual quantification. In other words, "p" becomes "<p> is true." Therefore instead of

(25) $\{\forall p\}(p \rightarrow p)$

we can say

(26) (∀x)(If x is a proposition of the form 'p → p,' then x is true).[11]

Instead of

(27) {∀p}(If Einstein's law is the proposition *that p,* then p)

we can say

(28) (∀x)(If x is a proposition of the form <If Einstein's principle is proposition that p, then p>, then x is true),

which is logically equivalent to

(29) (∀x)(If x = Einstein's principle, then x is true).

And, in general, instead of needing the substitutionally quantified

(22) {∀p}(… p …)

we can make do with the ordinary, objectually quantified

(30) (∀x)(If x is a proposition of the form < … p … >, then x is true),

I am not suggesting, of course, that the truth predicate was introduced *deliberately* to perform this useful function. But I *am* supposing that its usefulness, as just described, is what explains its presence. For if it were not valuable at all, it would presumably fall out of use; and as for alternative functions that it might have, there simply aren't any plausible candidates.

(7) *The minimal theory fails to specify what is meant by attributions of truth. It fails to provide necessary and sufficient conditions for the applicability of the truth predicate.*

The second part of this point is quite correct, but does not justify the initial complaint. For it is not the case that a satisfactory characterization of the meaning of a predicate must take the form of necessary and sufficient conditions for its correct application—i.e., an explicit, eliminative *analysis.* A definition of that sort is merely one particularly simple way of specifying the use of a word; but we should be open to more complex ways of doing it. So the present objection presupposes needless restrictions on what sort of definition of "true" is needed. Once these implicit constraints are loosened, the minimalist account will no longer seem inadequate.

I can perhaps clarify this response by distinguishing some different forms that a definition of "true" might be thought to take. In the first place one might offer an *atomic definition:* that is, a definition of the form,

(31) "true" means ". . . ,"

supplying a synonym that would permit us to eliminate the word "true" in a uniform way from every context in which it appears. An example of an atomic definition is the definition of "bachelor" as "unmarried man." The pragmatists' identification of truth with utility has this character.

In the second place, and a little more modestly, one might offer a *contextual definition:* that is, a set of rules that would allow the conversion of any sentence containing the word "true" into a synonymous sentence that does not contain it. A well known example of this style of definition is Russell's (1905) theory of definite descriptions:

(32) "The F is G" means "Some G is the same as every F,"

which reduces the definite article, "the," to the notions of predicate logic—specifically, "some," "every" and "the same as." A partial account of truth along these lines would be contained in the schema,

(E!) "It is true that p" means "p."

Thirdly, one might abandon the attempt to provide the sort of account that would enable the word "true" to be *eliminated*, and aim instead for *implicit definition:* that is, a set of principles involving the truth predicate, our commitment to which fixes its meaning. For example, it is sometimes said that the axioms of any geometry implicitly determine the meanings of the terms "point" and "line," at least as they are used when proving theorems of that geometry. An account of the meaning of "true" along these lines would be given by the substitutionally quantified principle,

(E+) $\{\forall p\}(\forall x)(x = \langle p \rangle \rightarrow (x \text{ is true} \leftrightarrow p))$.

Finally, one might deny that the meaning of the truth predicate can be captured in our commitment to any definite body of principles. One might hold that the use—hence the meaning—of "true" is given by regularities with a more complex structure than simply: *'We accept "A."'* An example of this sort of *use definition* is the idea that our conception of number is determined by the disposition to accept Peano's axioms, including infinitely many instance of the induction schema,

(33) $[F(0) \& (\forall n)[F(n) \rightarrow F(n+1)]] \rightarrow (\forall n)[F(n)]$.

Another example is provided by a certain account of the meaning of counterfactual implication: namely,

(34) "If p were true, then q would be true" is assertible to degree x *iff* it is known that x is the empirical tendency for q to be true in circumstances in which p is true and in which all the facts causally and conceptually independent of not p still obtain.

This rule characterizes a certain sense of "If . . . , then . . . " by specifying the appropriate level of confidence for any such conditional, and without involving and principles, in the material mode, relating counterfactual dependence to other aspects of reality.

I would suggest that the truth predicate belongs in this final category. Our understanding of the truth predicate, "is true"—our knowledge of its meaning—consists in the fact that the explanatorily basic regularity in our use of it is the disposition to accept instantiations of the schema,

(E) "The proposition *that p* is true and only if p,"

by declarative sentences[12] of English (including any extensions of English). Thus for a normal English speaker it consists in his disposition to accept

(MT) "The proposition *that snow is white* is true iff snow is white," "The proposition *that I am hungry* is true iff I am hungry," "The proposition *that Paris is beautiful* is true iff Paris is beautiful," . . . "[13]

The minimalist account of what it is to know the meaning of the truth predicate does not provide an *analysis* and does not enable us to specify in non-circular terms the *content* of attributions of truth. This is precisely what distinguishes it from traditional approaches. But it may be nonetheless a perfectly acceptable account of that in which our understanding consists, just so long as it is capable of explaining all pertinent linguistic behaviour—all our ways of deploying the term.[14] The question in other words is whether we can explain, on the hypothesis that MT governs some person's use of the truth predicate, why, for example, that person should endorse an inference from "What Oscar said is true" and "What Oscar said is that eels are good" to "Eels are good"; and, in general, why he uses the truth predicate in just the way that he does. This is the adequacy condition for a theory of the meaning of the truth predicate; and judging by the examples in the answers to question 3 the minimalist account would appear to satisfy it.[15]

(8) *Is the minimalist conception concerned with truth itself or with the word "true"?*

It is concerned with both—and other related entities as well. However it is important to separate the different questions it addresses. Specifically we should distinguish among

1 A theory of the *function* of the truth predicate
2 A theory of what it is for someone to *understand* the word "true"
3 A theory of the *meaning* of the word "true"

4 A theory of what it is to have, or grasp the *concept* of truth

5 A theory of *truth itself*

According to the minimalist conception the function of the truth predicate is to enable the explicit formulation of schematic generalizations. Our understanding of the word is constituted by the practice of using it to perform that function—a practice whose basic regularity is an inclination to accept instances of the equivalence schema, '<p> is true iff p.' The concept of truth (i.e., what is meant by the word "true") is that constituent of belief-states expressed in uses of the word by those who understand it. And the theory of truth itself—specifying the explanatorily fundamental facts about truth—is made up of instances of the equivalence schema. Thus, the minimal theory of truth will provide the basis for accounts of the meaning and function of the truth predicate, of our understanding it, and of our grasp upon the concept of truth.

(9) *Even if we grant that, as predicates go, the truth predicate is highly unusual—even if we grant that its special function is to enable us to say certain important things while avoiding new forms of quantification—it surely does not follow that being true is not a genuine property.*

Quite right. And it is not part of the minimalist conception to maintain that truth is not a property. On the contrary, "is true" is a perfectly good English predicate—and (leaving aside nominalistic concerns about the very notion of 'property') one might well take this to be a conclusive criterion of standing for a property of *some* sort. What the minimalist wishes to emphasize, however, is that truth is not a *complex* or *naturalistic* property but a property of some other kind. (Hartry Field suggests the term "*logical* property"). The point behind this jargon is that different kinds of property correspond to different roles that predicates play in our language, and that unless these differences are appreciated, we will be tempted to raise questions regarding one sort that can legitimately arise, only in connection with another sort. A familiar example of this phenomenon derives from the predicate "exists." Another, more controversial case is the conflation of normative and descriptive properties. According to minimalism, we should, for similar reasons, beware against assimilating *being true* to such properties as *being turquoise, being a tree*, or *being made of tin*. Otherwise we will find ourselves looking for its constitutive structure, its causal behavior, and its typical manifestations—features peculiar to what I am calling "*complex*" or "*naturalistic* properties." We will be puzzled when these expectations are inevitably frustrated, and incline to the conclusion that the nature of truth is profoundly obscure—perhaps even incomprehensible!

As I have indicated, some philosophers hold that *no* predicate refers and that properties do not exist; and, of course, from that nominalistic point of view the particular question 'whether *truth* is a property' does not arise—at least, in those words. However the underlying issue is still with us in the form of whether or not applications of the truth-predicate engender *statements* about the propositions to which it is applied. The thesis that they *do* distinguishes the present view from certain more radical formulations of deflationism—those according to which it is a grammatical illusion to think that

(35) X is true

makes a statement of *any* kind about the proposition X. For example, it was suggested by Frege (1891, 1918), Ramsey (1927) and Ayer (1935, 1936) that the forms

(36) p

and

(37) It is true *that p*

have the same sense no matter what English sentence is substituted for "p." This is appropriately referred to as "the redundancy theory of truth" and it evidently conflicts with the view advanced here which associates a definite propositional constituent to the truth predicate—a constituent which is part of one of these propositions but not of the other. Similarly, from the present perspective we are rejecting the idea due to Strawson (1950) and Ayer (1963) that the truth predicate is not used to give descriptions or make statements about the things to which it is applied, but that it is used instead to perform quite different speech acts: endorsing, agreeing, conceding, etc.

The trouble with the 'redundancy/performative' conception is that it cannot be squared with obvious facts about the character and function of truth. It addresses only cases like

(38) <Snow is white> is true,

in which the truth predicate is attached to an explicitly articulated proposition. And it maintains, with a certain *prima facie* plausibility, that the whole sentence has the same sense as the constituent

(39) Snow is white.

But notice that such uses of truth have no great value: we could easily do without them. And when we turn to genuinely useful attributions, as for example in

(40) Oscar's claim is true,

the theory has nothing to say about its sense, except that the logical form is *not* what it would seem to be: i.e., not

(41) X is F.

Consequently, the redundancy theory is quite unable to account for the inference from (40) and

(42) Oscar's claim = the proposition *that snow is white*

to

(38) The proposition *that snow is white* is true, and hence

to

(39) Snow is white,

—which is precisely the sort of reasoning on which the utility of our concept of truth depends.[16] Thus the redundancy/performative theory must be rejected. No doubt we do perform all kinds of speech act (such as *agreeing* and *conceding* with the truth predicate. But, as Warnock (1964) observed, it is best to say that we do so *by* (not *instead of*) making a statement—that is, *by* attributing the property, truth, to the proposition in question. Just as the assertion

(43) Your article is brilliant,

may be intended to achieve an effect beyond speaking the truth; so one might well have some ulterior purpose in mind in saying,

(40) Oscar's claim is true,

yet nonetheless be making a statement about Oscar's claim: i.e., attributing a property to it.

(10) *If the equivalence schema is relied on indiscriminately—if, for example, we instantiate "This proposition is not true"—then the notorious 'liar' paradoxes will result.*

Indeed—and for that reason we must conclude that permissible instantiations of the equivalence schema are restricted in some way so as to avoid paradoxical results.[17] We know that this restriction need not be severe. It need have no bearing on the propositions of science—the vast majority of which do not themselves involve the concept of truth. The problem of giving a *constructive* account of exactly how far one can push the equivalence principle without engendering paradox is the subject of a great deal of contemporary research (e.g. Tarski [1958], Kripke [1975)], Gupta [1982]) and will not be addressed in this essay. Given our purposes it suffices for us to concede that certain instances of the equivalence schema are not to be included as axioms of the minimal theory, and to note that the principles governing our selection of excluded instances are, in order of priority: (1) that the minimal theory not engender 'liar-type' contradictions; (2) that the set of excluded instances be as small as possible; and—perhaps just as important as (2)—(3) that there be a constructive specification of the excluded instances that is as simple as possible.[18]

I should emphasize that my intention in these remarks is not to disparage constructive attempts to deal with the paradoxes, or to suggest that our knowledge about truth is not deficient in the absence of such an account. My point is merely that there are manageable and philosophically fruitful problems of truth that are independent of the search for a constructive solution: first, to *outline* a theory of truth; second, to specify what we mean by the truth predicate; third, to explain its role in our conceptual scheme; and fourth, to say whether there is some theory of the underlying nature of truth. There is no reason to suppose that the minimalist answers that are advanced in this essay could be undermined by any particular constructive solution to the paradoxes—so we can temporarily set those problems aside.

The object of this chapter has been to specify the adequacy conditions for a complete account of truth, to suggest that these desiderata are satisfied by a certain deflationary conception of truth, called "minimalism," and to make sure that this proposal is not confused with various superficially similar views, such as Tarski's and the redundancy/performative account. The axioms of the minimal theory are all the propositions of the form, <<p> is true iff p>—at least, those that don't fall foul of the 'liar' paradoxes. We found some reason to believe that such a theory—weak as it is—is nevertheless strong enough to account for the conceptual utility of truth, and explain the facts in which truth is a constituent. And we saw that the single unattractive feature of the theory—its infinite list-like character—is not mitigated by accounts of truth in terms of reference or substitutional quantification. Thus we have gone some way towards justifying the minimalist conception: the view that the minimal theory is *the* theory of truth, to which nothing more should be added.

But many problems remain. For one thing, our entire discussion has taken for granted that truth is a property of *propositions;* and those philosophers suspicious of propositions will find it hard to swallow that aspect of the view.

Another widely felt objection to the deflationary view of truth is that it cannot be squared with the *explanatory role* of the notion of truth; and I shall attempt in [another] chapter to provide further support for minimalism by showing where this argument goes wrong. The basis for the objection is the idea that any law of nature relating various properties can be explained only by reference to theories that specify the underlying character of the properties involved. For example in order to say why *all emeralds are green* we need to know what it is to be an emerald and what it is to be green. And similarly, it is argued, insofar as the notion of truth is employed in the formulation of general laws, we are going to need a substantive theory of what truth is in order to explain these laws. I want to suggest on the contrary that truth appears in explanatory generalizations in precisely the role identified by the minimalist conception, and that the equivalence axioms are quite sufficient to account for them.

NOTES

1. In light of the locution, "It is true that p," it might be thought that a theory of the truth *predicate* would have to be supplemented with a separate theory of the truth *operator,* but this is not so. We can construe "It is true *that p,"* on a par with "It is true, *what Oscar said,"* as an application of the truth predicate to the thing to which the initial "It" refers, which is supplied by the subsequent noun phrase, *"that p."*

2. This claim will be modified slightly in the answer to question 10 in order to accommodate the 'liar' paradoxes.

3. Here I am employing the convention that surrounding any expression, e, with angled brackets, "<" and ">," produces an expression referring to *the propositional constituent corresponding to e.*

4. I am presupposing that if a complex expression results from the application of a schema to a sequence of terms, then the meaning of the expression is the result of applying the meaning of the schema to the sequence of the terms' meanings. In particular

(PR) <that p> = <that>(<p>)

and so the detailed semantic structure of each axiom of the minimal theory is

(EA) <iff>[<is true> [<that>(<p>)], <p>]

It might be argued that the two sentence-tokens in each MT axiom do not have the same content as one another (since the first occurs in an opaque context and the second does not) and, consequently, that these axioms cannot really be regarded as the results of applying one and the same propositional structure to the various propositions. If this is correct (which I doubt) then we must proceed differently.

One alternative is to characterize the axioms of the minimal theory as anything that is expressed by instances of the sentence schema,

(E) <p> is true iff p.

However, the theory cannot be restricted to instantiations of (E) by *English* sentences; for presumably there are propositions that are not expressible in current English, and the question of *their* truth must also be covered. So further 'equivalence axioms' are needed, one for each unformulatable proposition.

Although we cannot now *articulate* these extra axioms (any more than we can articulate the propositions they are about), we can nevertheless *identify* them. One way of doing this is by reference to *foreign* languages. We can suppose that the theory of truth includes whatever is expressed by instances of *translations* of the equivalence schema: e.g., instantiations of

(E-f) <p> est vrai ssi p

by French sentences, instantiations of

(E-g) <p> ist wahr gdw p

by German sentences, and so on, for all languages.

If it were assumed that every proposition is expressed in some language, then this would do. But we want to allow for the existence of propositions that are not yet expressible at all. To accommodate these we might suppose that every proposition, though perhaps not expressed by any *actual* sentence, is at least expressed by a sentence in some *possible* language. And we can then regard the theory of truth as whatever would be expressed by instances of translations of the equivalence schema into possible languages.

However, once the need to refer to possible languages has been acknowledged, we can see that there was no reason to have brought in *actual foreign languages.* For we can make do with our own language supplemented with possible extensions of it. In other words we can characterize the 'equivalence axioms' for unformulatable propositions by considering what would result if we *could* formulate them and *could* instantiate those formulations in our equivalence schema. Thus we may specify the axioms of the theory of truth as what are expressed when the schema,

(E) "<p> is true iff p"

is instantiated by sentences in any possible extension of English.

Alternatively, instead of identifying the axioms indirectly in terms of how they would be *expressed,* we can solve the problem by directly specifying the *propositional* structure which all and only the axioms have in common. This is the strategy adopted in the text.

5. Patrick Grim pointed out to me that the minimal theory cannot be regarded as *the set* of propositions of the form, <<p> is true iff p>; for there is no such set. The argument for this conclusion is that if there were such a set, then there would be distinct propositions regarding *each* of its subsets, and then there would have to be distinct axioms of the theory corresponding to those propositions. Therefore there would be a 1-1 function correlating the subsets of MT with some of its members. But Cantor's diagonal argument shows that there can be no such function. Therefore, MT is not a set. In light of this result, when we say things like "<A> follows from the minimal theory," we must take that to mean, not that the relation of *following from* holds between <A> and a certain entity, the minimal theory. But rather that it holds between <A> and *some part* of the minimal theory—i.e., between <A> and some set of propositions of the form, <<p> is true iff p>.

6. In order to explain why "*Possibly,* snow is white" follows from "What Smith said is *possibly* true" and "What Smith said is that snow is white" we must assume, not merely statement (4), but rather

Necessarily, <snow is white> is true iff snow is white.

Thus it might seem that the axioms of the theory of truth should be strengthened and taken to consist of modal propositions of the form

<*Necessarily,* <p> is true iff p>.

An alternative strategy, however—and one that I prefer—is to keep the theory of truth un-modal and simple, and instead *derive* the necessity of its axioms from a separate theory of necessity, specifying, in general, what makes a proposition not merely true but necessarily true. It might be supposed, for example, that the *necessary* truths are distinguished by being *explanatorily fundamental.* In that case, given our argument to the effect that MT is explanatorily basic, it would follow that its axioms are necessary. Thus we might obtain the necessity of instances of the equivalence schema without having to build it into the theory of truth itself.

Perhaps a similar strategy can be deployed in response to a point of Anil Gupta's ("Minimalism," *Philosophical Perspectives* Vols. 7–8, edited by James Tomberlin): namely that an axiom going beyond those in MT is needed to explain, for example, that *Julius Caesar is not true.* It might be possible to obtain this conclusion from the fact that MT is explanatorily basic. For it seems clear that nothing of the form 'x is true' could be derived from MT unless x were a proposition.

7. Cf. question 6.

8. "{∃p}(... p ...)" means "Some sentence formed by replacing the "p" in "... p ..." with a sentence of (some extension of) English is true."

9. For further discussion of the policy of explaining truth in terms of substitutional quantification see Grover, Camp & Belnap (1975), Baldwin (1989) and Brandom (1994) who embrace it, and Forbes (1986) who rejects it. Similar considerations apply to the prospect of explaining truth in terms of other forms of quantification into sentence positions.

10. This point is stressed by Max Black in his (1948) critique of Tarski's theory.

11. Anil Gupta rightly notes (in "A Critique of Deflationism," *Philosophical Topics,* vol. 21 No. 2, Spring 1993) that the instances of the generalizations that we need the concept of truth to formulate (e.g., "The proposition *that if dogs bark then dogs bark* is true") will not say exactly the same thing as what we wished to generalize (e.g., "If dogs bark then dogs bark") unless corresponding instances of "p" and "The proposition *that p* is true" express the very same proposition—which is not especially plausible. But this point does not undermine the deflationist story about the function of truth; for that function requires merely that the generalizations permit us to *derive* the statements to be generalized—which requires merely that the equivalence schema provide material equivalences. This isn't to deny that the instances so understood are not merely true but necessarily true (and a priori). The point is that their mere truth is enough to account for the generalizing function of truth.

12. Such sentences may be identified by their *meanings.* Moreover it is required that their two tokens express the same proposition. If meaning and propositions were then to be defined in terms of truth we would have a vicious circle. However, I argue in my answers to questions 22 and 32, and in section 3 of the Postscript [to *Truth*], that meaning and proposition may be explained in terms of aspects of use (including *assertibility)* that do not presuppose the notion of truth.

13. It might be objected that this condition is not strong enough to distinguish truth from various other concepts, since there are innumerable predicates, "F," other than "true," for which we would accept instantiations of

(F*) The proposition *that p* is F iff p

Consider, for example, "is true and 1+1=2." However, this objection (which was brought to my attention by Anil Gupta) overlooks the fact that although there are indeed many predicative expressions that satisfy schema (F*), it is not generally true that, for each such expression, (F*) gives the *full,* basic regularity governing its use. For example, our knowledge that "is true and 1 + 1 = 2" satisfies schema (F*) does not explain our inclination to deduce, from the premise that this predicate is true of an object, the conclusion that 1 + 1 = 2. And, in general, if a complex predicate satisfies schema (F*), then it will exhibit various use-relations to its constituents; and these facts will not be explained by its satisfaction of the schema. Thus, in the case of the truth predicate, the schema provides the complete, basic regularity for its use. In contrast, the predicates other than "true" that satisfy the schema are governed by additional regularities. And this is what distinguishes their meanings from that of "true."

14. Notice that since minimalism does not provide an explicit definition of truth, it superficially resembles Moore's (1899) view that truth is an 'inexplicable quality.' The important difference between the two accounts, however, is that minimalism, nevertheless purports to give, by means of the equivalence schema, a complete account of truth and of that in which our grasp of it consists, whereas on Moore's view it is impossible to shed any light on these matters (including why it is that the equivalence biconditionals hold) and truth remains impenetrably mysterious.

15. An objection made by Hartry Field [11] ("Critical Notice: Paul Horwich's *Truth," Philosophy of Science* 59 [1], 1992) is that the minimalist account could capture the meaning of "true" only in its application to statements that we are able to *formulate;* for only in those cases can we supply the relevant instance of the truth schemata. The idea is that if we take a statement, s, to say, for example, *that snow is white,* we might then suppose that the content of

s is true

is more or less

snow is white

whereas, if we don't know what "s" means, then we don't know the content of "s is true." Now this would indeed count against a theory that aimed, by means of the truth schemata, to provide a *reductive analysis* of each utterance containing the word "true." However, one need not, and should not, promise any such reductive analysis; indeed it is a central tenet of minimalism that there is no such thing. On the minimalist view, we aim to define the truth predicate, not by providing another expression with the same meaning (nor even by providing a rule transforming every sentence containing the word "true" into a content-equivalent sentence without it), but rather by specifying which property of the truth predicate constitutes its having the meaning it has; and to that end we must identify the property that best explains our overall use of the term. In particular, the minimalist thesis is that the meaning of "true" is constituted by our disposition to accept those instances of the truth schemata that we *can* formulate. In that way, the word is provided with a constant meaning wherever it appears—even when ascribed to untranslatable statements. And the justification for this thesis is that such a pattern of acceptance accounts for our entire use of the term—including its application to untranslatable utterances. Thus we might attribute truth to an untranslatable statement on the basis, for example, of a belief in the reliability of the person who made it; and we do, as Field suggests, need an account of truth that will explain this sort of attribution; but the minimalist proposal would do so perfectly well.

16. Similar objections to the redundancy theory have been made by Tarski (1943/44), Thomson (1948), Cohen (1950), Ziff (1962) and Ezorsky(1963). A redundancy theorist might attempt to explain the inference by first analysing "x is true" in terms of substitutional quantification as

(SB) {∃p}(x=<p> & <p> is true)

and then taking this to be synonymous with

(ST) {∃p}(x=<p> & p)]

However, although this strategy is clearly motivated by redundancy-theoretic intuitions, it departs from that theory in associating a definite content with the truth predicate. We should distinguish between the redundancy theory, according to which "x is true" says nothing about x, and theories according to which it says something—but something that is analysible in terms of substitutional quantification (theories which face their own set of difficulties, as we have seen in the answer to question 6).

17. To see this, let "#" abbreviate "THE PROPOSITION FORMULATED IN CAPITAL LETTERS IS NOT TRUE." Then assuming for the sake of argument that

<#> is true

and given the pertinent instance of the equivalence schema, namely

<#> is true iff #

we can infer

#

whose subject, said to be not true, turns out to be the proposition, <#>. Therefore we have

<#> is not true

contradicting our initial assumption. But the alternative fares no better. For if we suppose instead that

<#> is NOT true

then, given modus tollens applied to the equivalence schema, it follows that

¬#

which says of <#> that it is NOT not true. Therefore

<#> IS true

Thus we have deduced that

<#> is true iff <#> is not true

In order to block the derivation of this contradiction our options are either: (1) to deny classical logic specifically, either modus ponens, modus tollens, double-negation elimination, or Leibniz' Law (the indiscernibility of identicals); (2) to deny (à la Tarski) that the concept of truth can be coherently applied to propositions which themselves involve that concept; (3) to deny that there is any such proposition as the one formulated in capital letters; or (4) to reject certain instances of the equivalence schema—including the one obtained by substituting "#" into it.

But (1) cuts too deep; (2) also smacks of overkill; and (3) goes against the fact that one might well believe that the proposition meeting some condition C is not true—which (since any object of belief is a proposition) would imply that "The proposition meeting condition C is not true" expresses a proposition—even if it happens to turn out that the proposition it expresses is the one meeting C. Therefore the only acceptable solution is (4).

18. Anil Gupta argues that the need to restrict instantiation of the equivalence schema is somewhat in tension with the minimalist thesis about the function of our concept of truth—namely that it enables us to capture schematic generalizations. For insofar as "p" is not invariably equivalent to "<p> is true," then a generalization of the form "Every instance of schema S is true" will not invariably entail every instance of S; nor will it always be justified or explained on the basis of those instances. For example, "Everything he says is true" does not entail "If he says that #, then #," and is not partially justified or explained on the basis of that conditional. Luckily such problem cases are few and far between; so the utility of truth as a device of generalization is not substantially impaired by their existence.

REFERENCES

Ayer, A. J. (1935) "The Criterion of Truth," *Analysis*, 3.

______. (1936) *Language, Truth and Logic*. London, Gollanz.

______. (1963) "Truth," *The Concept of a Person and Other Essays*, London: MacMillan.

Baldwin, T. (1989) "Can There Be a Substantive Theory of Truth?" *Recherche sur la philosophie et le*

langage, 10. Grenoble: Université des Sciences Sociales de Grenoble.
Black, M. (1948) "The Semantic Definition of Truth," *Analysis,* 8.
Brandom, R. (1994) *Making It Explicit.* Cambridge: Harvard University Press.
Cohen, J. (1950) "Mr. Strawson's Analysis of Truth," *Analysis,* 10, 136–44.
Ezorsky, G. (1963) "Truth in Context," *Journal of Philosophy,* 60.
Field, Hartry. (1992) "Critical Notice: Paul Horwich's *Truth,*" *Philosophy of Science* 59(1).
Forbes, G. (1986) "Truth, Correspondence and Redundancy," *Fact, Science and Morality,* ed. G. MacDonald and C. Wright. Oxford: Blackwell.
Frege, G. (1891) "On Function and Concept," in *Translations from the Philosophical Writings of G. Frege,* by M. Black and P. Geach. London and New York, 1960.
Frege, G. (1918) "The Thought," trans. A. Quinton and M. Quinton, *Mind,* 65 (1956).
Grover, D., Camp, J., and Belnap, N. (1975) "A Prosentential Theory of Truth," *Philosophical Studies,* 27.
Gupta, A. (1982) "Truth and Paradox," *Journal of Philosophical Logic,* 11, 1–60. Reprinted in *Recent Essays on Truth and the Liar Paradox,* ed. R. L. Martin. Oxford: Clarendon Press (1984).
Kripke, S. (1975) "Outline of a Theory of Truth," *Journal of Philosophy,* 72.
Moore, G. E. (1899) "The Nature of Judgement," *Mind,* n.s. 8.
Ramsey, F. (1927) "Facts and Propositions," Proceedings of the Aristotelian Society, supplementary vol. 7.
Russell, B. (1905) "On Denoting," *Mind,* n.s. 14.
Strawson, P. (1950) "Truth," *Proceedings of the Aristotelian Society,* supplementary vol. 24.
Tarski, A. (1958) "The Concept of Truth in Formalized Languages," *Logic, Semantics, Metamathematics: Papers from 1923 to 1938.* Oxford: Oxford University Press, 152–278.
Tarski, A. (1943/44) "The Semantic Conception of Truth," *Philosophy and Phenomenological Research,* IV, pp. 341–75. Reprinted in this volume, pp. 118–141.
Thomson, J. F. (1948) "A Note On Truth," *Analysis,* 8, 67–72.
Ziff, P. (1962) *Semantic Analysis.* Ithaca: Cornell University Press.

Reading Questions

1. Horwich's account requires that there are propositions suitable as truth-value bearers but forbids arguing for the existence of propositions from the need to have something that is either true or false. He maintains that propositions are antecedent to our account of truth. Is this right? What is Horwich's argument for this claim?
2. Horwich argues that the deflationary view of truth requires an infinite number of axioms. Does this show that the theory relies essentially on mathematical induction in order for it to be known? Is this a problem with the view?
3. If there are an infinity of axioms for the theory, as Horwich argues, is it possible to derive *general* facts about truth? Or will we just have to rest content with a nongeneralizable infinite conjunction?
4. Horwich claims that it is important to separate what we say about truth from theories of reference, meaning, and verification. But does this attitude beg the question against those, for example, pragmatists, who view truth as ideally verified propositions at the end of inquiry?
5. Why does Horwich assert that the deflationary view of truth neither provides an analysis nor specifies in noncircular terms the content of truth attributions?

13 Truth as Correspondence

MARIAN DAVID

1. CORRESPONDING TO FACTS

"TRUTH IS A RELATION TO REALITY; therefore, truth has to be explained in terms of a relation to reality." This is the fundamental intuition underlying the accounts of truth that I shall discuss in this chapter. Of course, the idea that truth is a relation to reality does not provide a very informative answer to the question "What is truth?" It can only be regarded as a pattern for an answer. We may call it the *relation-to-reality* pattern. It is very unspecific. It needs to be filled in: What is the relation supposed to be? What are we to understand by reality?

The classical correspondence theory of truth attempts to answer these questions. Its central claim is the thesis that something is true just in case it *corresponds* to a *fact,* and false just in case it does not correspond to a fact. Since I am mainly interested in the correspondence theory insofar as it provides a contrast for the disquotational theory, and since the latter is a theory of sentence-truth, I shall apply the classical correspondence theory to sentences: the truth of a sentence consists in its correspondence to a fact. The thesis is motivated by intuitively plausible judgments of the following kind: The sentence 'Bats are mammals' is true because it corresponds to the fact that bats are mammals; the sentence 'Snow is white' is true because it corresponds to the fact that snow is white; the sentence 'Bats are birds' is false because it does not correspond to any fact. The central definition of the classical correspondence theory of truth for sentences is a straightforward generalization of such examples:

(C) x is a true sentence $=_{\mathrm{Df}} x$ is a sentence, and there is some fact y such that x corresponds to y;

x is a false sentence $=_{\mathrm{Df}} x$ is a sentence, and there is no fact y such that x corresponds to y.

The correspondence theory is sometimes traced back to Aristotle, but this ancestry is rather questionable.[1] Something very much in the spirit of the correspondence theory can be found in *De veritate,* Q.1., where Thomas Aquinas cites repeatedly, and with approval, a definition that he ascribes to Isaac Israeli: "*Veritas est adaequatio rei et intellectus*"—Truth is the adequation of thing and intellect. Although Aquinas does not use the notion of a fact—he uses related notions like "thing" or "being" instead—he quite clearly shares the correspondence intuition. Of course, the reference to the "intellect" in the definition indicates that it is intended as defining truth for cognitive mental states, like beliefs or thoughts, rather than for sentences. The classical version of the correspondence theory—again, typically applied to mental states rather than sentences—appears frequently and explicitly in the earlier writings of Russell and Moore: "Thus a belief is true when there is a corresponding fact, and is false when there is no corresponding fact" (Russell 1912, p. 129); "To say that this belief is true is to say that there is in the universe *a* fact to which it corresponds; and to say that it is false is to say that there is *not* in the universe any fact to which it corresponds" (Moore 1953, p. 277).[2]

The correspondence definition (C) satisfies the requirements that a definition is ordinarily expected

From Marian David, Correspondence and Disquotation: An Essay on the Nature of Truth *(Oxford University Press, 1994). Used by permission of Oxford University Press.*

to satisfy. The definition is not explicitly circular. It is clearly intelligible, even though it is expressed in what Dorothy Grover (1972, p. 47) has called "philosophers' English"—the mixture of English words and logical devices (quantifiers, variables, etc.) that philosophers use as a technical language. Its corresponding generalization (the universal biconditional that is entailed by the definition) is well formed and can be expressed in not-too-cumbersome, perfectly intelligible English: a sentence is true just in case it corresponds to a fact. The generalization has modal force, namely the force of a metaphysical necessity, which probably comes out better if it is read like this: For a sentence to be true *is* for it to correspond to a fact. I think it would be rather bold to maintain that (C) specifies what we mean when we apply the word 'true' to sentences, but fulfillment of this condition is optional anyway.

The correspondence definition, as given above, is not very specific. It does not, for example, tell us which sentences correspond to which facts. I think it is the desire for more information on this point that frequently leads proponents as well as adversaries of the correspondence theory to confuse (C) with the following schema:

(C*) 'p' is a true sentence iff 'p' corresponds to the fact that p.

This schema is incorrect when taken as a stab at a definition of sentence-truth. It derives from a flawed way of "generalizing" over the intuitive judgments that motivate the correspondence theory. These judgments do, of course, underwrite the idea that the correspondence of 'p' to the fact that p is a sufficient condition for 'p' being true: if 'Bats are mammals' corresponds to the fact that bats are mammals, then it is true. But they do not underwrite the idea that the correspondence of 'p' to the fact that p is a necessary condition for 'p' being true: if 'Bats are mammals' corresponds to the fact that snow is white, then it is true even if it does not correspond to the fact that bats are mammals. Clearly, it does not matter which fact a given sentence corresponds to; the sentence will be true as long as it corresponds to some fact or other. A correspondence theory of sentence-truth should, of course, tell us at some point which sentences correspond to which facts, but (C*) is a flawed attempt to address this concern. The idea that (C*) will somehow yield a definition is as mistaken as the idea that its instances are entailed by (C). Ultimately, I think, the mistake lies in the misguided attempt to make the definition do the work that should be done by an account of the correspondence relation.

The correspondence definition (C) will constitute the central definition of the classical correspondence theory as it applies to sentences, but the definition should not be confused with that theory. The definition is hardly satisfying when taken in isolation. Indeed, it is hardly more satisfying than the initial characterization of truth in terms of the relation-to-reality pattern. The mere thesis that truth is correspondence to a fact is awfully thin: all that has been done, so far, is that the word 'relation' has been replaced by 'correspondence' and reality has been made a little bit more specific by cutting it into sentence-like slices that make for a more convenient fit with sentences. A correspondence *theory*—even in a very loose sense of "theory"—should go beyond the mere definition; it should provide an account of the important notions that occur in the definiens. Without such an account we would have a definition but lack an explanation.

Using a terminology that is familiar from Quine, we may say that the correspondence definition is committed to an *ontology* of facts and an *ideology* of correspondence. That is, if one accepts the definition and maintains that there are true sentences, one has thereby committed oneself (ontologically) to the existence of facts; and by accepting the definition alone, one has already committed oneself (ideologically) to invoking the notion (idea, property) of correspondence as an explanatory resource of one's theory.[3] Quine's distinction between these two types of commitments allows us to discern two different but closely related tasks for the correspondence theorist who wants to offer more than just the definition. The ontological task will be to account for the notion of facts, that is, to answer the question "What is a fact?" The ideological task will be to account for the correspondence relation, that is, to answer the question "What is it for a sentence to correspond to a fact?"

This double task for a full-fledged correspondence theory is most naturally approached by construing correspondence as "congruence."[4] The basic idea behind this account is that sentences and facts are both complex structured entities: sentences are composed of words and phrases; facts are composed of things, properties, and relations, and maybe also of sets and functions. The account then proceeds by showing how sentence-to-fact correspondence can be constructed from further correspondence relations that obtain between the constituents of sentences and the constituents of facts. The specifically ideological part of the project will be concerned with these further correspondence relations and will, eventually, lead into a *semantic* theory that explains how names, predicates, and logical particles can *refer* to things, properties, relations, sets, and functions. The specifically ontological part of the project will have to explain how the simple constituents of facts combine into complex wholes, and it will have to identify the "glue" that keeps the constituents together. The latter part of the account should yield identity criteria for facts, that is, it should tell us when we are confronted with different names of one fact versus different names of different facts. Putting this together with the former part should yield an answer to the question of which sentences correspond to which facts.

Any straightforward way of working all of this out will inevitably be committed to various types of facts that are sometimes regarded with some amount of suspicion. People who have no problem with calling sentences true that concern mathematical, logical, modal, probabilistic, ethical, or aesthetical subject matter may balk at the idea that there are facts corresponding to all such sentences. Moreover, a straightforward congruence approach will also require all kinds of logically complex facts. It will require negative facts, conjunctive facts, disjunctive facts, conditional facts, subjunctive facts, and so on. Again, some people may find some or all of these "funny" facts rather appalling. The correspondence theorist might try to work around at least a limited number of such facts. Noticing that (C) by itself puts almost no constraints on the account of the correspondence relation, the correspondence theorist might try letting true sentences that apparently concern one subject matter correspond to facts concerning a quite different subject matter. For example, she might deny the existence of mathematical facts and suggest that the true sentences of mathematics really correspond to certain linguistic or psychological facts. However, this strategy is not very promising in the end. Setting up "surprising" sentence-to-fact correlations puts a heavy strain on the underlying semantics of the correspondence relation. Furthermore, even though it is true that the account of the correspondence relation is not much constrained by (C) itself, it seems to be quite narrowly constrained by the intuitive judgments that initially motivated the whole theory. An account of correspondence that does not honor the data of the correspondence theory pulls the rug from under itself. A better strategy would be to accept even those facts that one considers to be "funny" and to show that they can be "reduced" to other, more "serious" facts.[5]

Working out a correspondence theory will require an ontological account of facts and a semantic account of word-to-world relations: a rather daunting task. Could the correspondence theorist get around this task by maintaining that the notions of fact and correspondence are primitive and not in need of further explanations? She could try to stress that the notion of a fact is a rather ordinary, nontechnical notion. We all can give various examples of facts: that snow is white is a fact, that the earth is round is a fact, and so on. In general, fact talk is in no way alien to us. The frequency of such talk in ordinary discourse indicates that we all believe in facts—that facts belong to our "folk ontology." This makes it tempting to claim that facts are so fundamental to our thinking that we should be satisfied with a "thin" correspondence theory that takes them as primitive—and maybe a similar line could be tried with respect to the notion of correspondence. But the "primitivist" line is not very promising. It skirts all the important issues: funny facts, identity criteria for facts, and the question of which sentences correspond to which facts. These are precisely the issues that indicate that our ordinary intuitions, untutored, are not good enough for the correspondence definition. Our ordinary intuitions on these issues are so obscure and confused that one seems forced to admit that the terms 'fact' and 'correspondence'—as they appear in the definition—really invoke technical notions that overlap only partially with our ordinary notions.

Moreover, taking the "primitivist" line leaves the correspondence theorist wide open to deflationist attacks. The deflationist will typically start out with the claim that the notions of fact and correspondence are vacuous notions with zero explanatory import and that, therefore, the correspondence definition itself is pretty much vacuous—a string of words that creates an air of profundity while explaining nothing. As far as the deflationist is concerned, the correspondence theorist's facts are *fabricated* out of the notion of truth: take a *true* sentence 'p,' build a phrase of the form 'the fact that p,' declare that the latter phrase specifies an object, and you have all the facts you need for (C). But surely the notion in the driver's seat here is truth: the correspondence theorist's ontology is itself projected from the notion of sentence-truth, hence, it cannot fruitfully be employed to explain what it is for a sentence to be true. The deflationist will adopt a similar attitude towards the correspondence theorist's ideology. The term 'correspondence' is ordinarily used in various different ways to refer to different kinds of correspondence relations. In everyday situations we rely heavily on the context of our statements to make clear what kind of correspondence relation we have in mind. Since (C) does not specify what kind of correspondence relation is supposed to be responsible for truth, the definition invites the objection that it, too, relies on context to make clear what is meant. And in the absence of any further information, we have to take the definition itself as the relevant disambiguating context. But the only thing the definition tells us is that the correspondence relation in question must be one that has to obtain between a sentence and a fact in order for the sentence to be true. So the deflationist will charge that the notion of correspondence that appears in (C) is also a fabrication—that it has been invented for the sole purpose of binding the invented facts to the true sentences. According to the deflationist, the notion of truth is at the root of the correspondence theorist's ideology as it is at the root of her ontology. He sees nothing of explanatory value in correspondence and facts and suggests deflating the correspondence definition—to delete its vacuous ingredients and to work with the remainder.

A correspondence theorist who wants to get around the task of developing a full-fledged correspondence theory by leaving facts and correspondence unexplained will find it extremely difficult to answer these charges. She cannot really rely on our ordinary understanding of correspondence and facts because our ordinary understanding of these notions is far too nebulous to be of much help. To answer the charge of vacuousness, the correspondence theorist will have to develop an account of the nature of facts and the nature of correspondence; she will have to go beyond her definition and offer a full-fledged theory of truth.[6]

2. FALSEHOOD AND CONTENT

The classical correspondence definition of truth is, at best, a starting point—a point of departure for a much richer story. It is, however, rather questionable whether the classical definition can even be that much, for it is questionable whether the definition has the right structure to serve as an adequate way of spelling out the relation-to-reality pattern. The problem I have in mind is, at bottom, a problem with the notion of meaning, or content. Surely, the relation of correspondence should be connected somehow to meaning, for an account of that relation must eventually lead into an account of how sentences and their parts can stand for things in the world. Yet, so far, the connection between correspondence and meaning is somewhat obscure. What is quite clear, on the other hand, is that the connection cannot be completely straightforward: it would be a mistake to *identify* correspondence with meaning. According to (C), *false* sentences would not mean anything, which is absurd. It pays to look at how the classical correspondence definition treats *falsehood,* for its difficulty with falsehood is a symptom for its strained relations to the notion of content.

Shall we get falsehood for free as soon as we have truth? It is sometimes assumed that a theory of falsehood does indeed simply fall out of a theory of truth. But the assumption is far from innocuous—especially when it is sentence-truth that is at issue. Definition (C) defines a sentence as false just in case there is no fact that it corresponds to, that is, just in case the sentence is not true. This identification of falsehood with *un*truth is problematic. It leads to difficulties with sentences that are neither true nor false and it leads to difficulties with sentences that are both true and false.

SENTENCES THAT ARE NEITHER TRUE NOR FALSE

The most obvious examples are interrogative and imperative sentences. If we accept (C) and define falsehood as untruth, we shall have to say that interrogatives and imperatives are neither true nor not true, which is wrong because such sentences are not true. One might want to respond by pointing out that the objection is correct but somewhat pedantic. The correspondence definition, one might want to say, was not meant to be applicable to interrogatives and imperatives to begin with; it was supposed to be applicable only to *declarative* sentences. This seems a fair response; nevertheless, it would be a mistake to take the issues involved here too lightly. The response indicates that (C) does not express exactly what the correspondence theorist had in mind. What the correspondence theorist must have had in mind was an account of truth that is like (C) but conditional on the assumption that the set of sentences under consideration is restricted to the set of declarative sentences. In other words, it seems that the correspondence account should really be formulated like this:

> If x is a declarative sentence, then
>
> x is true iff there is some fact y such that x corresponds to y, and
>
> x is false iff there is no fact y such that x corresponds to y.

With this conditionalized account interrogatives and imperatives drop out of the picture. The hope is that the set of sentences that are false coincides exactly with the set of *declarative* sentences that are not true. If this is right, then the conditionalized account of falsehood as consisting in the absence of truth cannot get into trouble, because to say of a declarative that it is not true will entail that it is false. In other words, the revised approach assumes that declarativeness is sufficient for a sentence's being either true or false; the possession of this property by a sentence will amount to the same as its being susceptible to truth or falsehood. But so far we do not have a genuine definition; all we have is a conditional. However, it should be easy to turn the conditional into a definition. For, it seems that declarativeness is not only sufficient, it is also necessary for a sentence's being either true or false. A sentence that is not a declarative will be neither. So the correspondence definition should be rephrased in the following way:

> (C_D) x is a true sentence $=_{Df}$ x is a declarative sentence, and there is some fact y such that x corresponds to y;
>
> x is a false sentence $=_{Df}$ x is a declarative sentence, and there is no fact y such that x corresponds to y.[7]

This definition is better than the conditionalized account because it keeps the correspondence theorist honest. The notion of a declarative sentence plays an important role in the correspondence theory of sentence-truth. Yet, all we really know about this notion, so far, is that a declarative is a sentence that is either true or false, which raises the question of how declarativeness might be explicated without bringing in truth and falsehood. The new definition, (C_D), puts the notion of declarativeness right into the definiens. It thereby acknowledges explicitly that this notion requires explanation. If the conditionalized account serves any purpose not served by (C_D), it can only be the purpose of hiding the need for declarativeness. The very form of the conditionalized account creates the impression that the correspondence theorist can just help herself to this notion. The impression is misleading. The correspondence theorist cannot help herself to this notion as long as it is not settled whether declarativeness can be accounted for in terms other than truth and falsehood.

The new definition is not only better than the conditionalized account, it is also better than the original proposal (C). As soon as falsehood is distinguished from untruth it becomes clear that a simple definition like (C) cannot handle falsehood adequately. This is not, as it were, the fault of the correspondence relation but the fault of the structure of the definition: (C) simply does not have enough "degrees of freedom" to allow for a third possibility besides truth and untruth; it does not allow any room for the recognition that falsehood is not simply something negative but consists partly in the presence of a positive property. A true sentence and a false sentence share a positive property that is not present in a sentence that is merely not true. However, it is hard to avoid the suspicion that in trying to identify this common property (C_D) has latched on to a superficial grammatical feature. The deeper reason for why certain sentences are truth-evaluable at all should be found in their semantical rather than their grammatical properties: truth evaluability is a matter of the kind of content a sentence has. It may be that the semantical property that is responsible for truth evaluability typically manifests itself grammatically in the declarative sentence form—but this seems to be a relatively superficial regularity.

The suspicion that (C_D) does not really get at the heart of the matter is strengthened when one realizes that it is actually problematic to assume, as (C_D) does, that being a declarative is sufficient for being a sentence that is either true or false. The assumption faces at least two problems. First, according to Strawson (1950), declarative sentences like 'The present king of France is 30 years old' and 'Santa Claus is a nice guy' are associated with an unfulfilled presupposition, the fulfillment of which is necessary for them to be either true or false; hence, they are neither. Strawson's analysis of sentences like the above is controversial. So the correspondence theorist could side with Russell (1905) and hold that such sentences are false. The point is, however, that it does not seem quite right to decide the debate between Russellians and Strawsonians in favor of the former merely on the grounds that the position of the latter is not consistent with the "correct" definition of truth. A definition of truth should leave room for both positions. Second, it seems that vague declaratives are neither true nor false. I do not want to go into a discussion of vagueness here. I simply wish to note that vague declaratives constitute a problem for (C_D): they force the correspondence theorist to admit that a purely grammatical understanding of declarativeness will not be sufficient to make the definition work.

A further reason for thinking that (C_D) has mistakenly latched on to a superficial grammatical feature is that it still does not get falsehood right, because it cannot handle sentences that are both true and false. Such sentences give further support to the idea that there is a need for the notion of content in the definition of truth for sentences.

SENTENCES THAT ARE TRUE AND FALSE

What I have in mind here are sentences that are *ambiguous* and are true under one of their interpretations and false under the other. Examples are sentences that contain lexically ambiguous words (A broken seal was responsible for the Challenger disaster'); sentences that are ambiguous in syntactic structure ('Husbands are necessarily married'); and sentences that exhibit syntactical as well as lexical ambiguity ('Humans are flying planes'). Such sentences are best regarded as being true as well as false. But the above definition of falsehood does not allow us to evaluate such sentences in this way. Since (C_D) identifies false declaratives with declaratives that are untrue, it makes declaratives like the above come out both true and not true—an evaluation that is inconsistent.

Should we restrict the definiens of (C_D) to *un*ambiguous sentences? In other words, should we make the account of sentence-truth conditional on the assumption that the set of sentences under consideration is restricted to the set of unambiguous sentences? I do not think so. The suggestion would result in a conditionalized account of the form: If x is an unambiguous sentence, then x is true iff it is a declarative that corresponds to a fact and false iff it is a declarative that does not correspond to a fact. Notice that such an account does not tell us anything about sentences that do not satisfy the antecedent. If ambiguous sentences are taken to be either true or false (hence in some cases both), then the account is simply incomplete; it does not cover all the cases that need to be covered. If, contrary to what I have urged above, ambiguous sentences are taken to be neither true nor false, then the conditionalized account will merely serve to hide the fact that one is already committed to invoking nonambiguity in the definition of sentence truth, because the conditional in conjunction with the thesis that ambiguous sentences are neither true nor false is equivalent to an explicit definition that makes it a necessary condition of the truth as well as the falsehood of a sentence that it be unambiguous. Such a definition will simply confirm the main point that I am concerned with at the moment, for to require nonambiguity is to admit that the notion of content has to come up in the definitions of truth and falsehood for sentences: to require that a sentence is unambiguous is to require that it has only one content. But I also think that there is really no good reason for holding that ambiguous sentences are neither true nor false. The problem with ambiguous sentences is not that they lack truth-or-falsehood inducing interpretations; they have too many. I take it that is what 'ambiguous' means. Since ambiguous sentences have interpretations, there is no reason for thinking that they lack truth values.[8]

The correspondence definition in its present form cannot handle ambiguity. Ambiguity is a matter of having more than one interpretation—more than one content. Sentences that are both true and false are so because they are true under one of their interpretations and false under the other one. A definition of truth that can handle ambiguity will be one that acknowledges the need for content in the theory of truth; it will be one according to which the truth or falsehood of a sentence is due, in part, to its content.

3. REPRESENTING STATES OF AFFAIRS THAT OBTAIN

Let us take a look at another way of filling in the relation-to-reality pattern. It is natural to hold that what is distinctive about sentences that are true or false is that they *represent* reality as being a certain way. True ones represent it as it actually is, while false ones represent it as it is not. The ways reality can be represented as being are often called *states of affairs,* which are entities that are typically denoted by that-clauses. This makes for a natural way of talking. Instead of having to say that the sentence 'Snow is white' represents reality as being such that it has snow in it that is white, we can say that it represents the state of affairs that snow is white. A state of affairs can occur or fail to occur, or, as I shall say, it can *obtain* or fail to obtain. For example, the state of affairs that snow is white obtains, while the state of affairs that snow is green does not obtain. If a sentence represents a state of affairs that obtains, then it is true in virtue of representing that state of affairs and in virtue of that state's obtaining. If, on the other hand, a sentence represents a state of affairs that does not obtain, then it is false in virtue of representing that state and in virtue of that state's failing to obtain. If, finally, a sentence does not represent any state of affairs at all, then it is neither true nor false. The definition of sentence-truth that emerges from these considerations is the following:

(R) x is a true sentence $=_{\mathrm{Df}} x$ is a sentence, and there is state of affairs y such that x represents y and y obtains;

x is a false sentence $=_{\mathrm{Df}} x$ is a sentence, and there is a state of affairs y such that x represents y and y does not obtain.

I shall call (R)—or rather, the kind of theory in which (R) is the central definition—the *representation theory of truth.* It is rather popular among philosophers nowadays. This is not to say that many philosophers have explicitly put their views on truth and falsehood in the exact same words that I have used here. But one will frequently find philosophers talking about true sentences as sentences that represent, express, describe, refer to (etc.) states of affairs, situations, conditions (etc.) that obtain, occur, are realized, are actual (etc.). Such language indicates that an author thinks of truth along the lines of the representation theory. The terminology I have adopted here derives largely from Chisholm, with the only difference being that he uses 'expresses' where I use 'represents': "The following would be a simple account of the truth of sentences: A sentence is *true* provided only (i) it expresses a certain state of affairs and (ii) that state of affairs obtains. And a sentence is *false* provided only (i) it expresses a certain state of affairs and (ii) that state of affairs does not obtain" (Chisholm 1977, p. 89).[9]

Much of what I said earlier about the classical correspondence definition applies mutatis mutandis to the new definition. (R) satisfies the requirements that a definition is normally expected to satisfy: it is not explicitly circular; it is formulated in well-formed, intelligible "philosophers' English"; and it entails a universal generalization with the modal force of a metaphysical necessity. (R) should probably not be seen as specifying the meaning of 'true sentence,' and it should not be confused with the schema

(R*) 'p' is a true sentence iff 'p' represents the state of affairs that p, and the state of affairs that p obtains,

because this schema assumes that the sentence 'Bats are mammals' is true only if it represents the state of affairs that bats are mammals, whereas the sentence is true as long as it represents any state of affairs that obtains.

I shall regard (R) as a paradigmatic relation-to-reality definition of truth for sentences. By this I do not mean to imply that (R) does not need any further refinements; I am rather sure it does. I merely mean that (R) serves well as an illustration of a truth definition that conforms to the relation-to-reality pattern. It is free from cumbersome detail and it has a number of advantages over the classical correspondence definition. It accommodates the intuition that the notion of content should play a prominent role in this account of truth for sentences. I shall often circumscribe the notion of content that is operative here as *representational content:* a sentence has representational content just in case it represents a state of affairs; and a state of affairs that is represented by a sentence will count as its representational content. The correspondence theory tried to use the grammatical feature of declarativeness to distinguish the sentences that are either true or false from the sentences that are neither. The representation theory focuses instead on a semantic feature: representational content. The declarative sentence-form typically signals the presence of this semantic feature, but it does not have to. The cases that caused problems earlier can be accounted for because the representation theory is not committed to the claim that all declaratives represent states of affairs. Vague declaratives can be counted among the sentences that fail to represent states of affairs. Strawsonians can be understood as holding a theory of the representation relation according to which sentences like 'The present king of France is 30 years old' and 'Santa Claus is a nice guy' fail to represent states of affairs, whereas Russellians can be understood as favoring a theory of the representation relation according to which such sentences do represent states of affairs. The issue will be decided not by the definition of truth itself but by the underlying theory of the representation relation. Finally, definition (R) makes it easy to understand how there can be sentences that are true as well as false. They come out as sentences that represent more than one state of affairs, namely at least one that obtains and at least one that does not obtain.

Strictly speaking the representation theory competes with the classical correspondence theory. But from a slightly more broad-minded point of view the representation theory can also be regarded as a reconstruction of the classical correspondence theory—a revisionist reconstruction that gets a better grip on falsehood than its predecessor. To see how this would go one merely needs to ask, What is the relationship between obtaining states of affairs and facts? The answer appears to be quite simple: they are the same. After all, it is a fact that snow is white just in case the state of affairs that snow is white obtains. (Of course, only obtaining states of affairs are facts.) It seems, then, that a fact can simply be defined as an obtaining state of affairs.[10] This "simple" view of facts allows the representation theorist to vindicate the intuitive judgments that originally motivated the correspondence theory, hence it allows her to regain the classical correspondence definition of truth. For she can reinterpret 'correspondence' as 'representation' and 'fact' as 'state of affairs that obtains,' and she can say that, yes, a true sentence is one that corresponds to a fact. However, the classical correspondence definition of falsehood requires some structural change. Falsehood is not simply a lack of correspondence. Rather, a false sentence also corresponds to something: it corresponds to an "unfact," that is, it represents a state of affairs that does not obtain. This is why the representation definition should be seen as a revisionist reconstruction of the classical correspondence definition: truth as well as falsehood are relations to reality—of course, only truth is a relation to those parts of reality that we refer to as facts.

Definition (R) is superior to the classical correspondence definition; it is a better way of spelling out the relation-to-reality pattern. But it is not very informative. A satisfying representation *theory* of sentence-truth should go beyond the mere definition: it should offer an account of the definition's ideology (representation) as well as of its ontology (states of affairs). I shall not develop a specific version of the representation theory in any detail, nor shall I give anything like a complete catalogue of all the options available to a representation theorist. Instead, I want to indicate some areas in which representationalists are likely to encounter difficulties—or at least critical issues—of the sort that typically motivate deflationist disapproval of relation-to-reality accounts of sentence-truth.

Perhaps the most popular representational theories are *structural* accounts according to which states of affairs are complex entities whose ontological structure is reflected in the grammatical structure of the sentences that represent them. The ontological part of such an account will be concerned with the nature of the constituents of states of affairs and the mode of their composition into complex wholes. Logically complex (negative, conjunctive, disjunctive, conditional) states of affairs must be composed of logically simple states of affairs, which, in turn, must be composed of constituents that are not states of affairs. The ideological part of such an account will be concerned with spelling out how the representation relation that holds between sentences and states of affairs can be constructed out of further representation relations that hold between the constituents of sentences and the constituents of states of affairs, and it will be concerned with the nature of these subsentential representation relations. Proponents of such structural accounts will debate questions like "What types of entities are among the ultimate constituents of states of affairs?" "How do the constituents combine to build states of affairs?" "What types of sentence-constituents represent what types of constituents of states of affairs?" Answers to these questions should yield identity criteria for states of affairs and should tell us which sentences represent which states of affairs.[11]

Most proponents of structural accounts identify states of affairs with set-theoretic constructions on their constituents, more specifically, with ordered *n*-tuples of their constituents.[12] However, there are some difficulties when it comes to deciding what kinds of entities should be regarded as the ultimate constituents of these *n*-tuples. There is a family of well-known arguments—inspired by Frege (1892)—that can be used to raise troubles for about all the plausible candidates. These arguments assume that the referents of that-clauses, which are states of affairs according to the representation theory, are the bearers of modal properties and also the relata of psychological relations like belief and desire. The arguments then proceed by either one of the following recipes. Cleverly select two sentences 'p' and 'q' such that the account of the structure of states of affairs that one wants to get into trouble is forced to identify the state of affairs that p with the state of affairs that q while it is intuitively possible that the state of affairs that p and the state of affairs that q have contradictory modal properties (e.g., it is necessary that p but not necessary that q). If the modal version of the argument is unsuccessful against a given account, select the two sentences in such a way that the targeted account is again committed to identifying the relevant states of affairs while it is intuitively possible that they have contradictory psychological properties (e.g., John Doe believes that p but does not believe that q). Since it is not possible for one and the same thing to have contradictory properties, the Frege-inspired arguments will tend to raise rather serious worries whenever they are applicable. And they do seem to have a wide range of application. In their modal versions they have been used against the idea that the state of affairs constituents that are represented by predicates are the sets determined by those predicates and against the idea that the constituents represented by definite descriptions are the objects they describe. In their psychological versions they have been used against the idea that the state of affairs constituents that are represented by predicates are the properties or relations they express and against the idea that the constituents represented by proper names are the objects named. In fact, they have been used against all candidates for constituents of states of affairs that seem intuitively plausible. To avoid these arguments one might try to identify states of affairs with *n*-tuples of entities to which the arguments clearly fail to apply. The difficulty with this idea is to find entities that satisfy this requirement and are, at the same time, plausible candidates for constituents of states of affairs. This is especially difficult when it comes to the psychological versions of the Frege-inspired arguments. The alternative, and more popular, option is to identify states of affairs with *n*-tuples of entities to which the arguments initially appear to apply, at least in their psychological versions, but to find some good counterarguments that show why, contrary to appearances, the arguments are not successful after all. The difficulty with this idea is to find those good counterarguments.[13]

Some propose that states of affairs are unstructured entities, namely sets of possible worlds.[14] Proponents of this view have had some trouble with the objection that one cannot really make sense of possible worlds unless they are explained in terms of states of affairs. In addition, the proposal is also subject to the psychological versions of the Frege-inspired arguments mentioned above. If states of affairs are sets of possible worlds, then there is only one necessary state of affairs: the set of all possible worlds. This would seem to have the intuitively unacceptable consequence that a person who stands in the belief relation to one necessary state of affairs ipso facto stands in the belief relation to all necessary states of affairs.

Coming to terms with the various versions of the Frege-inspired arguments is perhaps the most pressing task for any account of states of affairs. An account that fails to provide an adequate reply to these arguments will fail to provide acceptable identity criteria for states of affairs and will fail to give a workable answer to the question of which sentences represent which states of affairs.

States of affairs are essentially such that they either obtain or fail to obtain. A satisfying representation theory should contain some account of what it is for a state of affairs to obtain. Our original question was, What is it for a sentence to be true or false? The representation theorist proposes to shift part of the burden of this question to her account of representation and her account of the nature of states of affairs. But they alone cannot carry the whole burden. The notion of obtaining carries a large share of the load. And since obtaining is a somewhat truth-like notion, the representation theorist can hardly afford to be silent about it. The account of obtaining will of course depend to a large extent on the presupposed account of the nature of states of affairs. I shall not discuss the various available options in any detail. However, there is a general issue that I want to mention. It concerns the question whether an account of what it is for a state of affairs to obtain will invoke a new relation between the state and another object—an object that is not among the constituents of the state in question. Take, for example, the state of affairs that Socrates is dead and assume that it is a structured complex whose constituents are Socrates and the property of being dead. One could hold that the state obtains just in case Socrates instantiates the property of being dead and fails to obtain just in case Socrates does not instantiate the property of being dead. (Of course, this idea would have to be expanded to cover all states of affairs.) Such an account would be relatively conservative: it does not mention any objects that are not already among the constituents of states of affairs and it makes do with the relation of property instantiation—a rather fundamental relation that goes hand in hand with the notion of a property. Alternatively, one could try to explain what it is for the state of affairs that Socrates is dead to obtain by relating it to yet further objects that are not among its constituents, for example, particular events, like Socrates' death, or Socrates' dying, or something like that. On such a view a state obtains just in case it is, say, "realized" by an event and fails to obtain just in case it is not realized by any event. The view is somewhat less conservative: it invokes explanatory resources (events, the relation of realization) that are not already covered by the presupposed theory of states of affairs. A satisfying account of obtaining will have to decide in favor of one of the two options.[15]

What about the ideology of the representation theory? A satisfying account of representation should explain what it is for a sentence to represent a state of affairs. Within the framework of a structural approach, for example, this will require spelling out how the representation relation that holds between sentences and states of affairs can be analyzed into further representation relations that hold between sentence constituents and constituents of states of affairs, and it will ultimately require some kind of explanation of these further subsentential representation relations. It is obvious that an account of the relation of representation belongs to what is usually regarded as *semantics*, that is, the theory that is concerned with linguistic meaning and with the question of how linguistic symbols relate to what they are about. It is equally obvious that the representation theorist, when working out her account of truth for sentences, will hardly be able to avoid the thorny problems that beset semantic theorizing.

The representation theorist should also clarify the connection between the notion of representation and other semantic notions, most prominently the notion of *meaning*. Most importantly, one would like to know whether the representation relation is supposed to coincide with the meaning relation. Are the states of affairs that are represented by sentences the meanings of those sentences? In other words, are representational contents meanings? Putnam's (1975) *Twin Earth* arguments are frequently taken to show that the answer to this question should be negative. Admittedly the notion of meaning is in some disarray. But it seems plausible that at least according to one intuitive understanding of 'meaning' the sentence 'Water is H_2O' has the same meaning on Earth as it has on Twin Earth. Yet, it also seems plausible that on Earth the sentence represents the state of affairs that H_2O is H_2O and is therefore true, while on Twin Earth the sentence represents the state of affairs that XYZ is H_2O and is therefore false. Arguments like this seem to establish that the meaning of a sentence should not be identified with its representational content, that is, with the state of affairs that it represents.[16] But even though meaning differs from representational content, it seems that the meaning of a sentence should at least help determine which state of affairs it represents. This raises the question of what other feature or features—besides meaning—contribute to the determination of the representational content of a sentence and also the question of how all the determining factors work together to fix the representational content of a sentence. No matter how exactly this is going to work out, it is quite clear that meaning and representation are closely connected and that it is part of the ideological task of the representation theorist to explain this connection.

The above remarks do not constitute anything like a complete catalogue of all the issues and difficulties that the representation theorist will have to address when working out the ontological and ideological parts of her theory. But they should give some idea of the rather daunting task that is involved in working out a full-fledged representation theory of truth for sentences. It will be helpful to keep this point in mind. For the very magnitude of the representationalist task with its inherent difficulties is certainly one of the factors that make it tempting to adopt deflationary theories of sentence-truth. After all, these theories contain the promise that we can account for the truth and falsehood of sentences without getting involved with any of the complicated issues that the representation theory has to address.

4. SOME REFINEMENTS

I have advertised the representation definition (R) as a good illustration of a relation-to-reality theory of truth for sentences. It should be noted that the definition is just that: a good illustration that should not be taken as the representation theorists' final word on the nature of truth and falsehood for sentences. The definition is overly simplistic and needs some refinements. Consider the following two cases.

Case 1: Imagine someone uttering the sentence 'Snow is white.' If asked, I would judge that the sentence is true because it represents a state of affairs that obtains. But a speaker of Korean who does not know any English and who has not had any significant contact with this language may say of the same sentence that it is not true. He may say that it does not have any content, maybe even that it is not a sentence at all. According to (R), the Korean and I contradict each other, so only one of us can be right. No sentence can be both true and not true. And it seems that I am right. After all, 'Snow is white' does have representational content and is true. Yet, it seems that this judgment does not do justice to the Korean. There should be some sense in which the Korean is right too, and hence some sense in which the sentence is both true and not true. Obviously, what we want to say here is that I am right because the sentence 'Snow is white' has a content in English in virtue of which it is true in English, while the Korean is right too because the sentence has no content in Korean and is therefore not true in Korean: no contradiction. But (R) does not allow us to say anything like that. It forces us to go against (healthy) intuitions and to judge harshly that only one of us, I or the Korean, but not both, can be right.

Case 2: Imagine someone utters the sentence 'Empedokles leaped.' Empedokles, of course, is a little kitten that just jumped out of the window but was never in love.[17] An English speaker who does not know German may judge that the sentence uttered is true, while a German speaker who does not know English may judge that the sentence uttered is false. And both may maintain that the sentence is not ambiguous. According to (R), both the Englishman and the German must be wrong, for the only way in which one sentence can be both true and false is by being ambiguous. But it seems that there should be a sense in which both of them are right. It seems that in some sense the sentence is unambiguous, while both true and false. Again, what we want to say here is quite clear. We want to say that both speakers are right because the uttered sentence in question has one content in English, in virtue of which it is true in English, and another content in German, in virtue of which it is false in German. But (R) leaves no room for such a conciliatory analysis and forces us to make a harsh judgment.

The two cases show that (R) does not always sit well with the way we are inclined to talk about truth and falsehood. They do not quite show that the definition is incorrect. For there is a sense in which the harsh judgments are right, even though they seem unnatural. The problem is rather that there is also a sense in which the much more natural lenient judgments are right, but the definition cannot capture this sense. A good explanation of truth should resolve these conflicting intuitions and show us their source.

The standard treatment of cases like the two described above is to suggest that the expression '*x* is a true sentence,' even though it looks like a one-place predicate, has the "deep structure," or "logical form," of a two-place predicate, namely the predicate '*x* is a true sentence of language *y*.' Truth for sentences, according to this suggestion, is a *relative* notion, and its relata are sentences and *languages*. Here relativization has to explain, and to get rid of, the appearance of contradiction in much the same way in which we explain and get rid of the appearance of contradiction between different "*x* is to the left of *y*"-judgers by proposing that being left is really a relative notion. The claim that *x* is to the left of *y* relative to *z* does not contradict the claim that *x* is not to the left of *y* relative to *v*. So, if the representation theorist wants to accommodate the intuitive judgments about cases 1 and 2, and she probably does, she can frame a revised definition for the relativized notion of ***truth for a sentence in a language***. Notice that 'true' will have to be regarded as a real two-place predicate, with the second variable ranging over languages. It will not do to go for a composite like '*x* is a sentence of language *y* and *x* is true.' A sentence may fulfill *that* condition by being a contentless sentence of one language and true in another language, which would give rise to case 1. It may also fulfill the condition by having an obtaining state of affairs as its content in one language and a nonobtaining state of affairs as its content in another language, which would give rise to case 2. So the definiens has to be '*x* is a true sentence of language *y*.' The refined definition goes like this:

(R_L) *x* is a true sentence of language $y =_{Df} x$ is a sentence of language *y*, and there is a state of affairs z such that x represents z in y and z obtains;

x is a false sentence of language $y =_{\text{Df}} x$ is a sentence of language y, and there is a state of affairs z such that x represents z in y and z does not obtain.

The somewhat awkward locution 'x represents z in y' will have to be spelled out in terms of x's representing z in accordance with the semantic rules of language y and/or in accordance with the intentions of the users of language y and the conventions they have adopted.

Given (R_L), the lenient judgments about the two cases can be easily accommodated by instantiating 'y' for different languages: English and Korean in case 1, English and German in case 2. And the source of the harsh judgments can now be explained too. They are based on the original definition (R) which, given the refined definition, is now seen to define the notion of truth (falsehood) *in some language or other.* That is, (R) defines the one-place predicate that results from existential generalization over the second variable of the two-place predicate defined in (R_L). What the Korean meant in case 1, or what he had better meant, was that 'Snow is white' is not true in Korean. If he did not mean that but used the unrelativized notion of truth defined in (R), then he was indeed wrong and I was right. Case 2 is handled accordingly. But in this case the operative idea is that the relativized notion of content in the definiens of (R_L) allows us to regard 'Empedokles leaped' as *unambiguous* in the ordinary sense of that term. The uttered sentence is unambiguous in English/German because it has only one representational content in English/German, so that its truth/falsehood in English/German does not entail that it is ambiguous. What was strange about (R) was that it treated *inter*language variations of content in the same way in which it treated *intra*language variations of content—as if there were ambiguity between languages as well as within languages. This does not fit with our intuitions about ambiguity. Ordinarily, only *intra*language variation of content is properly called "ambiguity." Ambiguity (proper) is handled nicely by (R). But the definition goes astray, or at least against our intuitions, when it treats variations in representational content between languages in the same way as it treats ambiguity.

There is another problem with (R) that is also a problem for (R_L) and hence calls for further refinement. (R) not only treats all variations of content in the same way, it also treats sentences whose truth or falsehood depends on contextual features as if they were ambiguous. Cases similar to cases 1 and 2 above can be construed with sentences containing indexical expressions or other elements that are in some way context-sensitive. And such cases will not be accounted for by (R_L). An indexical sentence of one and the same language may be judged to be both true and not true in that very language because it is uttered on different occasions, by different speakers, at different places, and so on. Context sensitivity arises *within* one language and cannot be accounted for by relativizing to languages. Considerations analogous to the ones above will lead the representation theorist to define a revised three-place predicate 'x is a true sentence of language y in context c.' I do not want to go into the complex question of what exact form such a definition will take. Relativization to "context" will have to do for now. The variable 'c' should be understood as ranging over some kind of "catch-all" relatum—maybe a sequence containing all "necessary" contextual features, like the time of utterance, the location of utterance, the utterer, the person referred to, and maybe more. The resulting revision of the revised representation definition will have the following form:

(R_{LC}) x is a true sentence of language y in context $c =_{\text{Df}} x$ is a sentence of language y, and there is a state of affairs z such that x represents z in y in c and z obtains;

x is a false sentence of language y in context $c =_{\text{Df}} x$ is a sentence of language y, and there is a state of affairs z such that x represents z in y in c and z does not obtain.

According to this definition, sentences containing indexical elements will represent different states of affairs in different contexts. The definition makes it the duty of the representation relation to take care not only of language relativity but also of context sensitivity. The representation theorist's account will have to include some rather more detailed remarks about how this language-relative and context-sensitive representation relation is supposed to work.[18] I do not wish to go any further into this topic. I brought it up to indicate that the definition (R) can be refined to handle complicated cases. The refinements that are required confirm once more that the attempt to develop a satisfying representation theory of sentence-truth will face a number of intricate questions about the nature of representation—questions that anything worthy of the name "theory" will have to address.

5. EXPRESSING TRUE PROPOSITIONS

Whenever truth is mentioned, propositions tend to come up soon. I have taken the liberty to hold back on propositions until now. I have done this partly because I wanted to make a general point about the form of a relation-to-reality theory of truth for sentences. Consider a definition of truth and falsehood for sentences in terms of propositions. Such a definition will assume that there are (at least) *two* notions of truth, *sentence-truth* and *proposition-truth,* and it will propose that the former can be defined and explained in terms of the latter:

(P) x is a true sentence $=_{Df} x$ is a sentence, and there is a proposition y such that x expresses y and y is true;

x is a false sentence $=_{Df} x$ is a sentence, and there is a proposition y such that x expresses y and y is false.

If one compares this definition with the representation definition (R) one will notice that the two definitions have the same structure. In fact, it looks as if they constitute two ways of filling in the relation-to-reality pattern that can be regarded as notational variants of each other. The definitions use different words at the same places, which indicates that they give different tags to elements that play analogous roles. They both relate a sentence via a semantic relation (representation or expression) to an object (a state of affairs or a proposition) that serves as the content of the sentence—"content" in the sense of "that kind of content in virtue of which a sentence is susceptible to truth or falsehood," that is, representational or propositional content. Assigning such contents to sentences serves a twofold role. Sentences are either true, false, neither, or both. By requiring that true as well as false sentences must have states of affairs, or propositions, as their contents, those sentences that are neither true nor false are excluded from the definiens, for states of affairs either obtain or fail to obtain and propositions are either true or false—that is part of their nature. Also, it is part of the nature of states of affairs that they cannot both obtain and fail to obtain, as it is part of the nature of propositions that they cannot be both true and false—for propositions, falsehood just is the absence of truth. Hence, relating sentences to states of affairs or propositions as their contents allows one to understand why some sentences are both true and false. A sentence is true and false only if it is ambiguous, that is, only if it has two different states of affairs, or propositions, as its contents, one of which obtains, or is true, and the other does not obtain, or is false. In short, the role played by propositions and the relation of expression in (P) is the same as the role played by states of affairs and the representation relation in (R). Obtaining and proposition-truth also serve the same role. They have the task to make sure that true sentences actually get related to those parts of reality that we refer to as facts, whereas nonobtaining and proposition-falsehood have the task to insure that false sentences do not get related to those parts of reality that we refer to as facts.

I think it is quite all right to regard (R) and (P) as notational variants of each other. The elements that play the same roles in the two definitions can simply be identified: representing = expressing; states of affairs = propositions; obtaining = truth for propositions; nonobtaining = falsehood for propositions. It follows from these identifications that (P) can be refined along the lines suggested with respect to (R) in the previous section. It also follows that the proposition theorist's work schedule coincides with the representation theorist's work schedule as sketched in section 3 of this chapter. Furthermore, if one accepts the "simple" view of facts, according to which a fact just is an obtaining state of affairs, it also follows that it is not incorrect to say that a proposition obtains, that a state of affairs is true, and that true propositions are facts. It might be somewhat strange to say such things. But this is merely strange in the same way in which it is strange to say that the morning star rises in the evening. Obtaining states of affairs, provided they are represented by sentences, are contents as well as facts. When we concentrate on their role as contents, we may find it more appropriate to call them "propositions" and to say that they are true. When we concentrate on their role as facts, we may find it more appropriate to call them "states of affairs" and to say that they obtain. But none of these terms has a precisely fixed meaning that can be determined before the representation theorist actually develops her theory. They serve as convenient labels that pick out the elements that are needed for an account of truth and falsehood of sentences. However, when the representation theorist actually spells out her theory, she may find that there are additional roles that need to be filled, additional elements that need to be labeled—a finding that may motivate some redistribution of her terminology.

Consider the following example: Assume that the representation relation is itself explained in terms of a further notion of content for which the term 'proposition' seems appropriate. That is, assume a sentence is said to represent a state of affairs in virtue of expressing a proposition that, say, determines, or helps determine, that state of affairs. Different sentences may express different propositions that determine the same state of affairs, hence, states of affairs ≠ propositions. If the representation relation is spelled out along these lines, a true proposition will be one that merely determines an obtaining state of affairs. Since, by the simple view of facts, a fact = an obtaining state of affairs, one could also say that a true proposition merely "corresponds to" but is not the same as a fact. In this scenario (P) and (R) would not be straightforward notational variants of each other. But they would still be very closely connected. They would be alternative formulations that emphasize different aspects of the same theory.

Consider another example: Assume that the representation theorist explains obtaining in terms of a further relation, say, "realization", that holds between states of affairs and some further entities, say, concrete events. Assume, furthermore, that the representation theorist wants to maintain that these concrete events, rather than the obtaining states of affairs, should be called "facts." So facts, in this sense, cannot simply be identified with obtaining states of affairs. Since she identifies propositions with states of affairs, the representation theorist would again say that a true proposition merely "corresponds to" but is not identical with a fact.[19] This is another scenario in which (P) and (R) would not be straightforward notational variants of each other but would still be very closely connected because they would constitute alternative formulations emphasizing different aspects of what is at bottom the same theory.

The two examples show that the representation theorist might ultimately want to drop the view that (R) and (P) are straightforward notational variants of each other and adopt a view according to which they are slightly different but equally good ways of formulating her definition of truth and falsehood for sentences. However, as long as one does not study the details of the representation theory, it is perfectly adequate—and far less confusing—to adopt the notational variant view. For many purposes—present purposes included—the notational variant view is good enough. Not much harm will be done if one uses the terms that occur in (P) and (R) interchangeably and does not bother to distinguish between the propositional and the representational accounts of sentence-truth.

We have seen that definitions (R) and (P) can be regarded as alternative formulations of the representation definition of sentence-truth. We have also seen that the classical correspondence definition can be reconstrued, albeit with some changes, in the light of the representation definition. It is fairly clear that all these definitions are different attempts at spelling out the relation-to-reality pattern. Since they share the same basic intuition, it would be nice to have a simple term that allows one to refer to them all at once. The label 'correspondence theory' is already used quite frequently in a rather broad sense to cover all theories that belong to the same general family as the theories that I have mentioned. So I think I shall not cause any serious confusions if I, too, adopt this terminology. From now on, I shall simply talk about correspondence theories whenever there is no need to bother about the more subtle differences between the various ways of spelling out the relation-to-reality pattern.

6. A GENERAL CORRESPONDENCE THEORY OF TRUTH

"What is sentence-truth?" is a rather limited question. It would be preferable to have an answer to Pilate's original, more general question, "What is truth?" To give an answer to this question would require developing not only a theory of sentence-truth but a general theory of truth for all the things that are normally said to be true or false. I want to conclude this chapter with a brief consideration of what a general correspondence theory of truth would look like.

Given what I have said in section 1.4 about the structure of a theory of truth, it is clear that a general correspondence definition of truth should take the form of the disjunctive definition

> x is true $=_{\mathrm{Df}}$ x is either a true sentence or a true statement or a true belief or a true proposition,

in which each of the disjuncts is in turn defined and explained in a manner that makes it appropriate to say that the resulting definition constitutes a correspondence definition of truth *simpliciter*. The first disjunct, sentence-truth, was the main topic of this chapter; it is defined in terms of representation, states of affairs, and obtaining. The last disjunct, proposition-truth, is identical with, or at least very closely related to, the notion of a state of affairs that obtains. Working out the representation theory of sentence-truth will automatically involve an account of the notion of proposition-truth. But what about the other two disjuncts?

It is somewhat tempting to suppose that belief-truth and statement-truth should be defined in strict analogy to the representational definition of sentence-truth. For a belief to be true, one might be tempted to think, is for it to represent a state of affairs that obtains—and analogously for statement-truth. However, on second thought, it seems rather unlikely that things could work out that smoothly. For one thing, it is rather unlikely that a representational definition of belief-truth will require all the refinements that gave rise to (R_{LC}). Maybe belief-truth needs to be relativized to contexts, but why relativize it to languages? One could maybe relativize truth for all bearers to contexts *and* languages and assign an empty element to the language variable in the case of truth for beliefs. But the resulting account would be somewhat artificial.

There is yet another, more serious, problem with the idea of defining belief-truth in strict analogy to the representational definition of sentence-truth. The representation relation that is involved in (R) is a *semantic* (word-to-world) relation. The representation relation involved in a definition of belief-truth would have to be a relation between mental states and the world; it would have to belong to the family of *intentional* relations (mind-to-world). If one tried to define belief-truth simply by substituting 'belief' for 'sentence' in (R), one would be committed to the view that the intentional relation of mental representation and the semantic relation of linguistic representation are one and the same. This seems implausible: linguistic representation is conventional, whereas mental representation is nonconventional.

However, even though it is a mistake to simply identify mental representation with linguistic representation, it is not at all implausible to assume that the two relations are closely connected. In fact, it is widely thought that semantic relations in general can be explained in terms of intentionality plus conventions. In addition, it is also plausible to think that the representation relation that applies to statements (speech acts) can be explained in terms of mental representation and linguistic representation. If all of this is on the right track and there really are such explanatory connections among the different notions of representation, the resulting correspondence theory of truth *simpliciter* will reveal that truth is not a merely disjunctive notion. The theory will take proposition-truth as its "bottom-level" explanandum: true propositions are (or determine) states of affairs that obtain. What it is for a state of affairs to obtain will have to be explained without bringing in any notion of truth. The "higher-level" explananda (sentence-truth, statement-truth, and belief-truth) will be defined in terms of "appropriate" representation relations—relations that relate sentences, statements, and beliefs to states of affairs and are also explanatorily connected to each other. A correspondence theory of this form promises an explanation of truth as a uniform concept. I would take this to be a definite virtue—a standard that other theories of truth have to live up to.

NOTES

1. Notice that Aristotle's famous definition in *Metaphysics* 1011^b25 has a rather deflationary flavor: "To say of what is that it is not, or of what is not that it is, is false, while to say of what is that it is, or of what is not that it is not, is true." This formulation does not invoke any correspondence-like relations, nor does it make any explicit reference to anything like facts.

2. The correspondence definition is sometimes interpreted as a statement of metaphysical realism, that is, the thesis that reality (or most of reality) is independent from consciousness. This interpretation betrays a confusion. Even though the "fact-correspondence" idiom is somewhat suggestive of realism, this suggestion can be cancelled without inconsistency: an antirealist may embrace the definition and add the thesis that all facts are mental, or mind-dependent, facts.

3. Quine explains ontological and ideological commitment in the following way: "Given a theory, *one* interesting aspect of it into which we can inquire is its ontology: what entities are the variables of quantification to range over if the theory is to hold true? Another no less important aspect into which we can inquire is its *ideology* . . . : What ideas can be expressed in it?" (Quine 1951, p. 14). Notice that, strictly speaking, (C) does not carry any ontological commitment to facts; it is the conjunction of (C) with the claim that there are some true sentences that carries such commitment. Notice also that a certain *formulation* of a theory might be ontologically or ideologically committed to certain objects or ideas while the theory itself might not be. This happens when the formulation in question is not the official, or final, or serious formulation of the theory. It will often be convenient to gloss over these niceties and to assume that the existence of true sentences is affirmed and that a given formulation of truth definition, or theory, represents its serious, final, rock-bottom version.

4. The terminology is suggested by Kirkham (1992, chap. 4). The best-known correspondence-as-congruence account is the one developed by Russell for belief-truth (1912). Russell's (1918) and (1921) also contain elements of this approach; unfortunately the latter works are not always quite clear on whether the account is supposed to apply to beliefs, propositions, or sentences.

5. Other strategies have been tried. The suggestion that sentences of a certain category (e.g., ethical sentences) are not truth-evaluable at all will simply remove any problems one may have with facts of that category. The suggestion that, say, logical sentences are truth-evaluable but do not correspond to any facts amounts to a serious restriction of the correspondence theory, for it will commit one to the thesis that there are at least two different notions of sentence-truth: nonlogical sentence-truth—defined by (C)—and logical sentence-truth—the latter will require a separate account. I should note that one might try to avoid commitment to logically complex facts by replacing (C) with a *recursive* definition of truth. I shall consider such theories later on.

6. Notice that the correspondence *definition* puts so few constraints on the correspondence *theory* that, as far as the definition by itself is concerned, one could have all true sentences correspond to one single fact. Davidson has argued (1969, p. 41f.) that the correspondence theory is bankrupt because it *cannot avoid* the consequence that all true sentences correspond to one fact, The Big Fact; and recently he has suggested that the argument provides the only good reason for rejecting that theory (cf. 1990, p. 303f.). One version of the argument goes like this: Assume that a given sentence, *s*, corresponds to the fact that p—abbreviate this as '*s*CFp.' Assume, furthermore, that 'p' and 'q' have the same truth value. Now: since "p" implies "$\{x: x = x \,\&\, p\} = \{x: x = x\}$," which implies "$\{x: x = x \,\&\, q\} = \{x: x = x\}$," which in turn implies "q"; "*s*CFp" implies "*s*CFq." Since the only restriction on 'q' was that is has the same truth value as 'p,' it would follow that a sentence corresponds to every fact, if it corresponds to one. The argument has been criticized again and again. It relies on the assumptions that (i) logically equivalent sentences can be substituted in the context '*s*CF_,' and (ii) if singular terms that refer to *or describe* the same thing can be substituted for each other in a given sentence, then they can still be so substituted if that sentence is embedded within the context '*s*CF_.' It is far from obvious why a correspondence theorist should be tempted by either one of these principles. See, for example, Gödel (1944), Mackie (1974, chap. 10), Barwise and Perry (1981), Taylor (1985, chap. 2), and Bennett (1988, sec. 16). Brandl (1991) also criticizes the further step needed to get from the conclusion of the argument to the conclusion that every true sentence corresponds to the same fact.

7. The conditional given earlier has the form of what Carnap (1936) called a "bilateral reduction sentence." One might regard it as a "conditional definition" of sentence-truth. (Notice, however, that the sign "$=_{Df}$" is usually reserved for unconditional definitions.) The conditional raises the question: What about sentences that do not satisfy the condition? If the correspondence theorist holds that some nondeclaratives are true or false, she has to admit that her definition of sentence-truth is incomplete: it does not cover all the cases. If she holds that nondeclaratives are never true or false—as I have assumed in the text—then her "conditional definition" is equivalent to (C_D).

8. It is sometimes said that ambiguous sentences require disambiguating contexts to provide them with interpretations that allow for evaluation in terms of truth and falsehood. This view confuses ambiguous sentences with sentences that contain *indexical* elements. The latter sentences do seem to possess "incomplete" contents that need to be supplemented by context before they can come up for evaluation in terms of truth and falsehood. But I see no reason for thinking that sentences exhibiting lexical or syntactical ambiguity have such "incomplete" contents. It is also said sometimes that a syntactical string like 'Husbands are necessarily married' should be counted as *two* sentences, rather than one, on the grounds that it has two different contents. The suggestion strikes me as odd, for it simply denies that there are any ambiguous sentences at all. The suggestion could be taken as a proposal for changing our terminology. But we shall see that it would be bad strategy to adopt this proposal when discussing disquotationalism: a terminology according to which sentences are symbol-plus-content units will completely obscure a number of issues that are relevant to the debate between disquotational and correspondence theories of sentence-truth.

9. Chisholm does not ultimately embrace this formulation. He suggests modifications similar to the ones I shall consider in the next section.

10. This simple account of facts is proposed by Chisholm (1977, p. 88), and adopted by Taylor (1976).

11. For three recent structural representation theories see Taylor (1976), (1985), Barwise and Perry (1983), and Forbes (1986).

12. One should be more comfortable with saying that states of affairs can be "modeled by," as opposed to "identified with," ordered *n*-tuples. I shall neglect this distinction for the sake of simplicity.

13. Many discussions of the force of Frege-inspired arguments focus on propositions rather than states of affairs. But since the arguments apply to whatever entities are identified as the referents of that-clauses, these discussions are equally relevant to the nature of states of affairs. Important contributions can be found in, for example, Carnap (1946), Kripke (1972), Kaplan (1976), Schiffer (1978), (1987), (1992), Evans (1982), Salmon (1986), Salmon and Soames (1988), and Devitt (1989a).

14. The possible worlds analysis of states of affairs is discussed and defended by Lewis (1986) and Stainaker (1984). Notice that the thesis that a state of affairs is simply a set of possible worlds should not be confused with the view according to which the state of affairs that is represented by a sentence is the set of possible worlds in which the sentence is true. The latter view is of little help to the representation theory of sentence-truth.

15. Austin (1950) seems to favor the less conservative view. He regards what I would call "states of affairs" as universals, or types, that can have instances, or tokens, which be calls "historic states of affairs" or "historic situations." He could have said that a state of affairs (type) obtains just in case it is instantiated or realized by a historic situation (token). Forbes (1986) holds a similar view. In general, since states of affairs are (or are made out of) abstract entities, or universals, many will be inclined toward a view that allows one to relate states of affairs to concrete entities, or particulars, like events or historic situations.

16. Twin Earth is exactly like earth in all respects, including the psychologies of its inhabitants, except that the liquid that looks exactly like water is XYZ instead of H_2O. As Richard Cartwright pointed out some time ago (1962), arguments like the one given in the text do not quite establish the desired conclusion. Strictly speaking, one can only infer that at least one of the representational contents of the sentence differs from the meaning of the sentence. The stronger claim that neither of the representational contents should be identified with the meaning of the sentence rests on a usually suppressed premise to the effect that, since there is no reason for identifying either one of the contents with the sentence's meaning, neither should be so identified.

17. This example is due to Davidson (1968).

18. (R_{LC}) keeps obtaining and nonobtaining of states of affairs free from context sensitivity because it relativizes the representation relation. There is an alternative definition that incorporates the opposite idea. One could define '*x* is a true (false) sentence of language *y* in context *c*' as '*x* is a sentence of language *y*, and there is a state of affairs *z* such that *x* represents *z* in *y* and *z* obtains in *c* (does not obtain in *c*).' Here contexts are used to relativize obtaining. This alternative definition treats the representation relation as stable and insensitive to contextual features and makes it the duty of the account of obtaining to take care of context sensitivity. According to this definition, a given state of affairs might obtain at some times, places, and so on, and fail to obtain at other times, places, and so on. The

alternative definition seems worthy of consideration. However, (R_{LC}) is closer to standard treatments of context sensitivity.

19. Such an account of truth for propositions is considered by Carnap (1946, pp. 28–32) and defended by Baylis (1949).

Reading Questions

1. David raises several objections to allowing the concepts of "correspondence" and "fact" to remain undefined primitives. What are his concerns?
2. David thinks that there are sentences which are both true and false, and that this is problematic for correspondence theories in which untrue = false. Could a defender of such a theory argue that David's problematic sentences express more than one proposition, and each such proposition is either true or false but not both? Therefore the problem sentence is both true and false only in a derivative, nonthreatening, way. Would this work?
3. What is the distinction David draws between a theory's ideology and its ontology?
4. David argues that obtaining states of affairs, true propositions, and facts are all the same thing, or at least, they probably are. His argument is a functional one: all three play the same functional role in a correspondence theory of sentence truth, therefore they are different ways of referring to the same entity. Is this functional argument persuasive? Or are there more general ontological reasons for distinguishing among the three?

Further Readings

Books

Alston, William P. 1996. A *Realist Conception of Truth.* Ithaca: Cornell University Press.

David, Marian. 1994. *Correspondence and Disquotation: An Essay on the Nature of Truth.* Oxford: Oxford University Press.

Davidson, Donald. 1984. *Inquiries Into Truth and Interpretation.* Oxford: Oxford University Press.

Dummett, Michael. 1978. *Truth and Other Enigmas.* Cambridge: Harvard University Press.

Horwich, Paul. 1990. *Truth.* Oxford: Basil Blackwell.

———, ed. 1994. *Theories of Truth.* Aldershot, England.

Grover, Dorothy. 1992. *A Prosentential Theory of Truth.* Princeton: Princeton University Press.

Gupta, Anil, and Nuel Belnap. 1993. *The Revision Theory of Truth.* Cambridge: MIT Press.

Kirkham, Richard L. 1992. *Theories of Truth.* Cambridge: MIT Press [A Bradford Book].

O'Connor, D. J. 1975. *The Correspondence Theory of Truth.* London: Hutchinson.

Rescher, Nicholas. 1973. *The Coherence Theory of Truth.* Oxford: Oxford University Press.

Schmitt, Frederick F. 1995. *Truth: A Primer.* Boulder: Westview.

Walker, Ralph C. S. 1989. *The Coherence Theory of Truth.* London: Routledge.

Articles

Austin, J. L. 1950. Truth. *Proceedings of the Aristotelian Society* 24 (supplement): 111–128.

Dauer, Francis W. 1974. "In Defense of the Coherence Theory of Truth." *The Journal of Philosophy* 71: 791–811.

David, Marian A. 1989. "Truth, Eliminativism, and Disquotationalism." *Noûs* 23 (5): 599–614.

Davidson, Donald. 1996. "The Folly of Trying to Define Truth." *The Journal of Philosophy* 93 (6): 263–278.

———. 1990. "The Structure and Content of Truth." *The Journal of Philosophy* 87 (6): 279–328.

Field, Hartry. 1972. "Tarski's Theory of Truth." *The Journal of Philosophy* 69: 347–375.

———. 1986. "The Deflationary Conception of Truth." In *Fact, Science, and Morality,* edited by Graham McDonald and Crispin Wright. Oxford: Blackwell.

Hamlyn, D. W. 1962. "The Correspondence Theory of Truth." *Philosophical Quarterly* 12:193-205.

James, William. 1981. Pragmatism's Conception of Truth. In *Pragmatism,* edited by W. James. Indianapolis: Hackett.

Kripke, Saul. 1975. "Outline of a Theory of Truth." *The Journal of Philosophy* 72: 690–716.

Rorty, Richard. 1991. "Solidarity or Objectivity." In *Objectivity, Relativism, and Truth,* edited by R. Rorty. Vol. 1, *Philosophical Papers.* Cambridge: Cambridge University Press.

Soames, Scott. 1984. "What Is a Theory of Truth?" *The Journal of Philosophy* 81: 411–429.

Strawson, Peter F. 1950. "Truth." *Proceedings of the Aristotelian Society* 24 (supplement): 129–156.

Tarski, Alfred. 1956. "The Concept of Truth in Formalized Languages." In *Logic, Semantics, Metamathematics,* edited by J. Corcoran. Indianapolis: Hackett.

Williams, Michael. 1986. "Do We (Epistemologists) Need a Theory of Truth?" *Philosophical Topics* 14 (1): 223–242.

Part IV

Abstracta: Properties, Numbers, and Propositions

BOB HALE

Introduction to Abstracta

1. Abstract Objects

BEFORE WE MAY PROFITABLY ARGUE about the existence of abstract objects, we need some account of how they are to be distinguished from concrete ones. An obvious starting point is that abstract objects can be neither seen nor heard, nor can they be tasted, felt or smelt (nor can we, therefore, point at them). But for several reasons it would be unsatisfactory to take inaccessibility to sense-perception as the basis of our distinction. Besides importing an unwanted relativity to human sensory faculties, it would fail to draw the distinction clearly, there being room for dispute over what should count as perceiving something. If the range of sense-perception is taken as including only what can be discerned with the naked organ, as it were, the condition for being concrete is clearly too restrictive, since it will exclude such things as subatomic particles and fields. The range might be extended to allow for detection via more or less remote effects, but once the criterion is loosened in this way, the proposal slides into taking capacity for involvement in causal interactions as the mark of the concrete. This suggestion avoids the difficulties with a sensory-access criterion, but even if it is extensionally correct, it does not go to the heart of the matter. We expect capacities in general to have some categorical basis. Why are concrete objects capable of causal interaction but abstract objects not? The answer, it would seem, should yield a more illuminating account of the distinction. Partly for this reason, a more promising account would be that what marks off abstract from concrete objects is *lack of location in space or time*. On this account, our other suggested marks of abstract objects, such as incapacity for involvement in causal interactions, and hence inaccessibility to sense-perception, will be consequential on their lack of spatio-temporal location. I shall assume the approximate correctness of this somewhat rough and ready account in what follows.[1]

This essay was commissioned especially for this volume and appears here for the first time.

Somewhat less obviously, we need also some account of the notion of *object* in terms of which the question whether there are abstract objects is to be understood. There is a familiar, everyday use of the term "object" in which we may speak of the objects found in the accused's pockets, for example. There are probably no very precise rules governing this use, but it seems clear that being extended in space and time is at least a necessary condition for its application (but probably not a sufficient condition, since holes, for example, are spatially located and persist through time, but would not be reckoned to be objects in the everyday sense). If "object" is so understood, the term "abstract object" is straightforwardly self-contradictory. We should infer, not that philosophers who have seriously disputed over the existence of abstract objects have been guilty of an obvious and elementary confusion, but that some other, less restrictive notion of object is in play. But if so, how should it be characterized? To avoid begging questions, it might be proposed that anything should be reckoned an object to which we may make reference. Arguably, however, this goes too far the other way. We employ many types of words—such as finite verbs, adverbs, and prepositions—which we should be unwilling to regard as standing for objects, without wishing to hold that they stand for nothing at all. If, when we assert "Nero fiddled," "fiddled" refers, like "Nero," to an object, then we should be hard put to it to explain how it is that our sentence differs from a mere list, like "Nero, Caligula, Augustus." A way forward that preserves this general approach is to take objects to be the referents of expressions of a certain restricted class—what logicians and philosophers of language usually call *singular terms*. Taking this step involves viewing the ontological categorization of entities as dependent upon a prior logical categorization of expressions.[2] Objects, properties, and relations, for example, are essentially the non-linguistic correlates of, respectively, singular terms (e.g., "Nero," "this lake," "the dome of St. Peter's," etc.), one-place predicates (e.g., ". . . fiddles," ". . . is deep") and two-or more-place predicates (e.g., ". . . loves . . .," ". . . is taller than . . ."). An object, on this account, is the referent of an actual or possible singular term.

If the general notion of object is to be explained in this way, an independent account is needed of which expressions should be reckoned singular terms. Surface grammatical form provides only a rough, uncertain, and sometimes misleading guide here, since there are many singular nouns or noun-phrases—e.g., "nobody," "any policeman," "the nick of time"—which it would be obviously wrong, or highly implausible, to regard as serving to convey reference to particular objects. However, it can be reasonably safely assumed that even when the needed refinements are supplied,[3] our account will recognize as singular terms various types of expression that may, with more or less plausibility, be regarded as standing for abstract objects, if for anything at all. Among such *abstract singular terms* we should certainly expect to find words for *numbers* and *classes*—ordinary numerals ("0," "1," "2," . . .), complex numerical terms like "the number of European capitals with populations exceeding 3 million" and "17^{17}," and class terms like "the class of tailless mammals." Other likely candidates are various expressions formed by the process known to linguists as nominalization, whereby expressions not themselves serving as names are transformed into others which can so serve. These include nominalized sentences, such as "that grass is green," which—along with more obviously namelike expressions such as "Euclid's Theorem" and "the proposition that there are infinitely many primes"—may be thought to make reference to *propositions*. They include, too, abstract nouns (such as "wisdom" and "redness"), corresponding to ordinary adjectives or predicates (such as ". . .(is) wise," ". . . (is) red"), which—along with complex terms such as "the property most commonly attributed to Socrates" and "the relation which every object bears to itself and to no other object"—may be thought to stand for general shareable *properties* (including relations, or relational properties), or *universals* in the traditional terminology.

Acknowledging the presence, in our language, of various types of abstract *terms* is one thing; accepting that such terms do in fact make reference to abstract *objects* is clearly quite another, if only because it is entirely possible that the presence of such terms is a potentially philosophically misleading feature of our language, to which nothing in reality corresponds. That is, we may ask, firstly and most generally, whether any abstract terms at all should be regarded as genuinely referential. And we may, secondly and more specifically, enquire whether particular types of abstract term really refer to abstract objects. In what follows, I shall say a little about the general question before proceeding to some remarks about the particular kinds of expression—numerical, propositional, and property terms—with the reference of which our selection of readings is concerned.

2. Realism and Nominalism

Philosophers who assert the existence of abstract objects of one or another kind are commonly labelled "Realists" or—in virtue of a generic similarity between their position and one standardly attributed to Plato—"Platonists." Proponents of the opposed view, that there are, in reality, no abstract objects at all, of any kind, are usually called "Nominalists." If the question ostensibly at issue—whether or not there exist abstract objects—is taken at face value, one of these positions must be right and the other wrong. I shall assume here, as nearly everyone else does, that that question is to be taken as genuine, in the sense that it is appropriate to muster philosophical arguments for, or against, an affirmative or negative answer to it. But it should be noted that the assumption is not uncontroversial. One notable dissenter is Carnap, who argues (in his essay "Empiricism, Semantics and Ontology," reprinted here) that, contrary to appearances, the question whether there are numbers and sets, propositions, or abstract objects of any other kind is not a genuine *theoretical* question at all, but a *practical* one, to be resolved, not by engaging in philosophical argument, but by taking a *decision* about what 'linguistic framework' it is most useful or convenient to employ. Once we decide to employ a linguistic framework including, say, numerals and quantifiers binding variables for which numerical terms are admissible substituends, the 'internal' question whether or not there are numbers is, Carnap claims, trivially answerable in the affirmative, but involves no philosophically suspect ontological thesis that might offend against nominalist scruples. I do not myself believe that Carnap's attempt to deflate the issue can succeed, in part because it is doubtful that his key distinction between 'external questions' (about what linguistic framework to adopt) and 'internal questions' (about what holds within a given framework) can ultimately be sustained—but I cannot digress to argue this here.[4]

Many philosophers, especially philosophers of broadly empiricist persuasion, have viewed claims about the existence of abstract objects as deeply suspect. If they have not always explicitly joined hands with nominalists in a blanket rejection of the abstract, they have at least evinced considerable sympathy with a methodological principle of ontological parsimony, known as Ockham's Razor,[5] to the effect that entities should not be postulated beyond necessity, and admitted abstract objects only grudgingly, when they could see no means of avoiding it. Why should this be?

Economy in theory, as measured by the range of irreducibly different types of entity the theory postulates, is undoubtedly a virtue, but it could hardly be a decisive consideration in the present case, if only because Platonists may argue that a theory that avoids reference to abstract objects either rests upon a prejudicial assessment of the facts to be accommodated or neglects some of them (e.g., facts about numbers). Probably the most important arguments against abstract objects are *epistemological.* One is that—in view of the presumed causal inertia of abstract objects—construing statements of some given kind as having their truth-conditions constituted by states of affairs essentially involving such objects puts those statements irretrievably beyond the reach of our knowledge. Crudely, if mathematical statements involved reference to abstract objects, such as numbers or sets, we could not possibly know them to be true; contraposing, since we do have mathematical knowledge, Platonism should be rejected as false. In its simplest, and earliest, versions, this argument relies upon a very exacting form of causal theory of knowledge, which takes it to be an invariably necessary condition for a thinker X to know that p, that X's true belief that p should itself be caused by, or otherwise suitably causally related to, the fact that p. A problem with this argument is that while such a strong condition (*modulo* the vagueness of 'suitable causal relation') may be satisfied in standard cases of perceptual and memory knowledge, it is very hard to see how it could be quite generally met, even when restricted in scope to ordinary empirical knowledge concerning perfectly concrete matters. Our inductively grounded belief that all aardvarks have bugs is, we may suppose, causally induced by inspection of a large and suitably varied contingent of bug-infested aardvarks—but there is no sort of causal relation, however complicated or attenuated, of which it may with any plausibility be claimed both that it holds between our general belief and the fact that all past, present, or future aardvarks have bugs and that its holding is epistemically significant. If knowledge does not demand a suitable causal link in every case, the argument against Platonism collapses, at least in its present form.

A related argument alleges that no satisfactory sense can be made of the idea that we are capable of identifying reference to or thought about abstract objects. And once again, the argument in its simplest form rests upon an eminently challengeable assumption—in this case, that identifying reference or thought about a particular object *always* requires a suitable causal link between the speaker/thinker (or their utterance/thought) and the object in question. Opponents of Platonism may hope to fashion more sophisticated causal analyses of knowledge and reference which are strong enough to sustain versions of these objections without being so strong as to be independently objectionable, but none has yet come forth.

A more powerful epistemological objection appeals to the thought that even if knowledge is not to be *analyzed* in specifically causal terms, we should expect to be able to provide a naturalistic explanation of our tendency to get things right significantly more often than not, in any area where we are disposed to credit ourselves with a capacity for knowledge. In the absence of causal or other natural relations between ourselves and abstract objects, it is hard to see how any credible such explanation might run for any region of discourse whose statements are supposed to carry Platonistic truth-conditions. Formulated in this way, the objection relies on the much weaker and more plausible assumption that ontological views are tenable only to the extent that they leave space for a credible epistemology. The arguments reviewed here confront Platonism with a strong challenge, even if they could not, by their very nature, tell decisively against it.[6]

3. *Numbers*

Since abstract objects are, by their very nature, inaccessible to sense-perception, we cannot have direct, experiential grounds to believe in their existence. Nor, in view of their acausality, can we infer their existence as the unobservable causes of observed effects, as we might infer the existence of a magnetic field from the observed behaviour of iron filings. It is, accordingly, a pressing question what grounds we *can* have to believe in them. The general form of what appears to be the Platonist's best answer is that abstract singular terms figure in many statements which we have—or at least take ourselves to have—good reason to believe true. If the logical form of those statements is as their surface grammar suggests, they involve at least purported references to abstract objects. If, in addition, those statements are indeed true, then those purported references must be successful—that is, there must be abstract objects of the kinds to which their ingredient abstract terms refer.

Let us see in more detail how an argument of this general kind might run in a particular case. As applied to numbers, the premisses are:

1. There are statements—both statements of pure arithmetic, like "2 + 3 = 5," and applied statements of numbers, such as "The number of natural satellites of Earth = 1"—in which numerical expressions function as singular terms,
2. Statements of this kind are often true.

From these premisses, the number-theoretic Platonist infers that there are objects—numbers—to which terms of the kind mentioned in the first premiss make reference. The principles underlying the inference are that singular terms are terms whose function is to make reference to particular objects, and that a statement incorporating such terms cannot be true unless those terms actually do discharge their referential function successfully. Since these principles do no more than spell out uncontroversial aspects of the semantics of singular terms and statements involving them, the Platonist can reasonably expect us to concede the *validity* of his argument. Assuming he is right on that point, resistance to the argument must take the form of challenging one or other of its premisses.

Most opponents of Platonism have concentrated their fire on the first premiss, denying that the surface grammatical form of statements of the kinds illustrated is a reliable guide to their real, logical form. Such a denial might be motivated by appeal to difficulties with the very notion of abstract reference of the sort alluded to in the preceding section. If taking this course is not to involve simply giving up pure and applied arithmetic, the nominalist needs to supply an alternative account, eliminating apparent reference to numbers, of what is truly—but misleadingly, in his view—said by statements like "2 + 3 = 5" and "The number of natural satellites of Earth = 1." As far as applied statements of number go, he can make some progress by pointing out that their content can be re-expressed, without using terms for numbers, in the language of first-order quantification logic with identity. Thus our second statement is equivalent to: "Something is a natural satellite of Earth and not more than one thing is." It is true that this still appears to employ the numerical term "one," but this appearance can be dispelled by making its quantificational structure more explicit: "$\exists x$(x is a natural satellite of Earth & $\forall y$(y is a natural satellite of Earth $\rightarrow y = x$))." More generally, numerically definite quantifiers—"Exactly 1 object x is such that . . . x . . . ," "Exactly 2 objects x are such that . . . x . . . ," etc., may be recursively defined by setting:

$$\exists_1 xPx \quad = \text{def. } \exists x(Px \;\&\; \forall y(Py \rightarrow y = x))$$

$$\exists_{n+1} xPx \quad = \text{def. } \exists x(Px \;\&\; \exists_n y(Py \;\&\; y \neq x))$$

With these at his disposal, the nominalist can make a plausible stab at reconstruing some purely arithmetic statements too. For example, he may reconstrue "2 + 3 = 5" as asserting that if exactly 2 objects are F and exactly 3 objects are G and no object is both F and G, then exactly 5 objects are F or G, for any properties F and G. But nominalist celebrations would be somewhat premature, for at least two reasons. First, even to deal with so simple an equality as "2 + 3 = 5," we have had to invoke higher-order quantification ("for any properties F and G"), which nominalists have generally sought to avoid because it appears to carry a commitment to properties. Second, and more decisively, there remain many statements of pure number theory—centrally, those involving quantification over numbers—which will not yield to nominalistic reconstruction along these lines. A simple example is Euclid's theorem, mentioned earlier, that there are infinitely many primes.

Paul Benacerraf's highly influential paper "What Numbers Could Not Be," besides advancing a powerful argument for the conclusion that (natural) numbers are not objects (or at least, not objects of any independently specifiable kind), offers the nominalist a different way of reconstruing arithmetic. His proposal is that, instead of construing it at face value, as a theory about a particular infinite sequence of (abstract) objects named by the successive numerals "1," "2," "3," . . . , it should be seen as a purely structural theory, about progressions in general—that is, about any sequences, if such there be, which have a first element, and for every element a unique predecessor and a unique successor (save the first, of course, which has no predecessor).

What about the nominalist's other option, of resisting the argument for numbers by rejecting its second premiss? Since, on the face of it, arithmetic is a body of true statements, this is likely to seem an implausible and unattractive course. It has, nevertheless, been pursued in at least one recent, and somewhat unorthodox, defence of nominalism. Hartry Field claims[7] that the nominalist has no need to reinterpret mathematics in order to render it nominalistically acceptable, because he can accept and use mathematical theories as they stand, without accepting them as *true*. Field takes it that the only really strong reason for thinking that mathematical theories *are* true derives from the fact that the natural sciences, and physics especially, require substantial use of arithmetic and analysis, and the latter in turn draws fairly heavily on set theory. This argument—known as the Quine-Putnam Indispensability Argument[8]—provides, if accepted, a strong *indirect* reason for believing in numbers and sets at least: scientific theories require acceptance of mathematical theories, so that whatever reasons we have to believe our best scientific theories true is reason to accept mathematical theories, and so to believe in the abstract objects of which they speak. Against this, Field argues that there is, contrary to appearances, no need for mathematical theories to be true for their use in science to be justified. It is enough that such theories should have a certain strong kind of consistency property, which he calls 'conservativeness.' Roughly, a mathematical theory is conservative if combining it with a nonmathematical (e.g., physical) theory yields no nonmathematical consequences which are not consequences of the nonmathematical theory by itself (so that math provides a very useful shortcut, but a theoretically dispensable one, since it adds nothing to the nonmathematical content of our other theories). Since a theory can have this property without its theorems being true, this leaves the nominalist free to deny that they are literally true, thereby avoiding commitment to the abstract objects their truth would require. We cannot here go into the difficulties confronting this approach, but one important assumption Field makes is worth highlighting. Field takes the Quine-Putnam argument to offer the only ground worth taking seriously for holding mathematical theories to be true, so that if he is able to undermine it, there remains no pressure to take on the ontological commitments they import. If Field's assessment were correct, the best grounds we could have for believing mathematics and the like, would be indirect and *a posteriori*. But this assessment rests upon the challengeable assumption that the only statements we may justifiably accept on other than indirect *a posteriori* grounds are those directly ascertainable as true by observation. Perhaps we should take seriously, as he does not, the possibility that belief in the truth of mathematical statements and acceptance of their ontology may be warranted *a priori*.[9]

4. *Propositions*

When Pierre, Helmut and Henry, who happen all to be in Rome on the same afternoon, assert, respectively: "Il pleut," "Es regnet," and "It's raining," there appears to be a clear sense in which they all say the same thing, even though they use different sentences to say it. This suggests we should distinguish between the sentences we speak and what we say by means of them. When Henry hopes, but Mary fears, that the Conservatives will be returned to power in the forthcoming election, they have distinct attitudes with something in common—what Henry hopes *is* what Mary fears. Many philosophers have employed the term "proposition" to stand for the common content which may be expressed by (suitably related) different sentences, and which may be the object of different psychological attitudes, such as belief and hope. Precisely because propositions are to serve as the common contents of different sayings and thinkings, they must, it seems, lack spatio-temporal location, and thus be abstract objects.[10]

For this reason, we may expect philosophers of nominalist leanings to argue that the phenomena that have led their less parsimonious colleagues to talk of propositions can be adequately handled without bringing them in. One strategy here would be to try to make do with just sentences—or more precisely, with particular, spatio-temporally located, utterances or inscriptions. The point here is that in what is usually called the *type*, as opposed to *token*, sense of 'sentence'—in which, if I write: "It's raining. It's raining," I have written one sentence twice—sentences, as distinct from particular utterances or inscriptions (i.e., token sentences), are themselves abstract objects. Church's paper in the present selection criticizes one attempt to avoid propositions by making do with sentences instead.

Objections to propositions, though they may have their source in a blanket rejection of abstract entities, need not do so. Quine's is a case in point. His central objection, presented in the selection reprinted here, appeals rather to the idea that if apparent singular terms are properly to be viewed as standing for objects, it should be possible to give what Frege called a criterion of identity for the objects in question.[11] That is, roughly, we must be able to formulate a condition necessary and sufficient for terms of the kind in question to refer to one and the same object. This requirement (expressed by Quine in his slogan "No entity without identity") is arguably met in case of some kinds of abstract object. Classes, for example, are the same if and only if they have the same members. So Quine has no objection, on this score, to admitting classes. But the requirement is not, he argues, met for propositions. There is, he claims, no satisfactory way of saying when two sentences stand for, or express, the same proposition, because any such account must appeal to philosophically suspect notions of meaning and sameness of meaning. His hostility to propositions thus derives from his rejection of the traditional analytic-synthetic distinction and his thesis of the indeterminacy of translation.[12]

5. *Properties*

In identifying nominalism with the rejection of abstract entities, I have given prominence to a well-entrenched modern usage, somewhat at the expense of a much older tradition in which the nominalist is one of the protagonists in the dispute—initiated principally by Plato and Aristotle and running through the medieval period—over *universals*. This older dispute has been continued in the modern period, without always being as clearly separated as it probably should be from the more general issue of the existence of abstract objects with which my introductory remarks have been mainly concerned. The issue can be briefly, if somewhat opaquely, put as whether there exist universals as well as particulars, and if so, what kind of thing universals are. Plato held—or was at least taken by his critics, including Aristotle, to have held—that where a particular object, such as this man or that act, is characterized by a certain general property, such as being wise or being just, this is to be understood in terms of that particular object's standing in a special relation (of participation or resemblance) to what he called a Form or Idea, which he denoted 'wisdom' or 'the wise itself,' 'justice,' or 'the just itself,' or the like. Plato appears to have conceived of wisdom, justice, and the like as abstract entities, somehow more real than any of their imperfect manifestations in the world of appearance (i.e., than anything perceivable by means of the senses). Although everyone who can use language must have at least some vague 'recollection' of these entities, they are fully and graspable only by the philosophically schooled intellect.[13]

As against this, Aristotle[14] argued that while there do indeed exist universals (general properties and relations), they have no freestanding, independent existence, as Plato had maintained, but exist only in the particulars that instantiate them. So his position is realist in so far as it accepts that there are universals as well as particulars, but it is a moderate form of realism as contrasted with the extreme realism of Plato in that it denies the existence of abstract universals. (The contrast is often made by saying that Aristotle advocates *universalia in rebus,* as opposed to Plato's *universalia ante rem.* Rejecting realism of either of these kinds, the medieval nominalists such as Peter Abelard and William of Ockham insisted that everything in the nonlinguistic world is particular, arguing that talk of universals is merely talk of words which have general application. A further, distinct position in this debate is the so-called 'conceptualist' view, which agrees with nominalists that everything in the world of which we speak and think is particular, not universal, but holds that words having general application do so by virtue of standing for general ideas or concepts. This view is medieval in origin, but finds its best known implementation in John Locke's theory of abstract general ideas,[15] so-called because they are supposed to be formed by a process of abstraction from the wholly particular ideas we obtain by sense-perception, by 'removing' in thought those features peculiar to the particulars in question (such as their particular size, color, etc.), leaving only what is common to all of them (such as their shape, e.g., triangularity). Locke's doctrine of abstraction was savagely criticized by his empiricist successors, Berkeley and Hume,[16] who argued that the ideas corresponding to general words are fully determinate and particular, and that their generality of application is a matter of a particular idea's being used as a representative of many distinct particular ideas of the same sort.

Recent work in this tradition has seen something of a revival of Aristotle's moderate realism about universals. Thus David Armstrong—one of the principal modern realists about universals—insists, with Aristotle, that universals must satisfy a *principle of instantiation*, to the effect that a universal (property or relation) exists only if it is instantiated (at some time or other, not necessarily the present time). Armstrong's position involves some significant departures from older versions of realism. In particular, he does not think that every well-formed and meaningful general predicate or relational expression has a universal corresponding to it. And he denies that it is, in general, an *a priori* matter what universals there are—this is, rather, something to be determined, *a posteriori,* by empirical scientific investigation. Although Armstrong argues against various positions he calls 'nominalist,' he would probably agree that his own position need involve no departure from nominalism in the sense of a general rejection of abstract objects.

NOTES

1. For a searching examination of the distinction, see Dummett (1973), ch. 14. Other useful discussion may be found in Quine (1960), ch. 7 and Lewis (1987), ch. 2. See also Hale (1987), ch. 3, and further references given there.
2. See Frege (1884, 1892); Dummett (1973), ch. 4.
3. See Dummett (1973), ch. 4, Wright (1983) §ix, Hale (1987), ch. 2. This approach is criticized in Wetzel (1990), some of whose criticisms are dealt with in Hale (1990).
4. For fuller discussion see Hale (1987), ch. 1.
5. So named after the fourteenth-century nominalist philosopher and logician William of Ockham, who is supposed to have asserted, "Entia non sunt multiplicanda praeter necessitatem."
6. For further discussion of broadly epistemological difficulties for Platonism, see Benacerraf (1973), Steiner (1973, 1975), Kitcher (1978), Wright (1983), §§11,12, Hale (1987), ch. 4 (1994), Field (1989), essay 7.
7. See Field (1980) and the essays collected in Field (1989).
8. For what is probably the fullest and most explicit presentation, see Putnam (1971).
9. Field's position has attracted a good deal of critical discussion. See, for example, Chihara (1990), ch. 8, Maddy (1990), ch. 5, Hale (1987), ch. 5, Hale & Wright (1993), (to which Field (1993) replies; and (1994).
10. The use of the term 'proposition' described here is a comparatively modern one. In scholastic and traditional logic, a proposition was usually taken to be a declarative sentence with a certain meaning. For a helpful, concise account, see Church (1971).
11. See Frege (1884), §62.
12. See Quine (1951; 1960, ch. 2; 1968; 1970).
13. Plato presents the theory of forms in several of his works. See *Phaedo* 64d–67b, 72e–77a, 78b–80a, 102a–105b; *Republic* 474c–480a, 506e–521b, 596a–598d; *Parmenides* 126–137.
14. See Aristotle *Metaphysics* book M, chs. 4, 5 1078b6–1080a10, ch. 9 1086a24–b13; *Nicomachean Ethics* book I, ch. 6 1096a11–1097a14, and also the fragments of Aristotle's *On Ideas,* published in G. Fine, *On Ideas* (Oxford, 1993).
15. For which see Locke's *Essay Concerning Human Understanding* Book III, ch. 3.
16. See Berkeley's *Principles of Human Knowledge,* Introduction, and Hume's *Treatise of Human Nature* book I, part I, section vii.

REFERENCES

Benacerraf, Paul. 1973. "Mathematical Truth," *Journal of Philosophy* 70: 661–679.
Berkeley, George. 1710. *A Treatise Concerning the Principles of Human Knowledge.*
Chihara, Charles. 1990. *Constructibility and Mathematical Existence.* Oxford: Oxford University Press.
Church, Alonzo. 1971. '"Proposition." *Encyclopedia Britannica,* vol. 18, p. 640.
Dummett, Michael. 1973. *Frege: Philosophy of Language.* London: Duckworth.
Field, Hartry. 1980. *Science Without Numbers.* Oxford: Blackwell.
———. 1989. *Realism, Mathematics and Modality.* Oxford: Blackwell.
———. 1993. "The Conceptual Contingency of Mathematical Objects." *Mind* 102: 285–299.
Frege, Gottlob. 1884, [1953]. *The Foundations of Arithmetic.* Oxford: Blackwell.
———. 1892 [1970]. "On Concept and Object" in Peter Geach and Max Black, *Translations from the Philosophical Writings of Gottlob Frege.* Oxford: Blackwell.
Hale, Bob. 1987. *Abstract Objects.* Oxford: Blackwell.

———. 1990. "Singular terms." In Brian McGuinness and Gianluigi Oliveri, eds., *The Philosophy of Michael Dummett*. Dordrecht, Holland: Kluwer.
———. 1994. "Is Platonism Epistemologically Bankrupt?" *Philosophical Review* 103: 299–325.
Hale, Bob, and Wright, Crispin. 1993. "Nominalism and the Contingency of Abstract Objects." *Journal of Philosophy* 89: 111–135.
———. 1994. "A reductio ad surdum? Field on Contingency of Mathematical Objects." *Mind* 103: 169–184.
Hume, David. 1739. *A Treatise of Human Nature.*
Kitcher, Philip. 1978. "The Plight of the Platonist." *Noûs* 12: 119–136.
Lewis, David. 1987. *On the Plurality of Worlds.* Oxford: Blackwell.
Locke, John. 1690. *An Essay Concerning Human Understanding.*
Maddy, Penelope. 1990. *Realism in Mathematics.* Oxford: Oxford University Press.
Putnam, Hilary. 1971 [1979]. "Philosophy of logic," in *Mathematics. Matter and Method: Philosophical Papers,* vol. 1, 2nd ed., pp. 323–357. Cambridge: Cambridge University Press.
Quine, W. V. 1951. "Two Dogmas of Empiricism." *Philosophical Review* 60. Reprinted in Quine's *From a Logical Point of View,* pp. 20–46 (New York: Harper Torchbooks, 1953).
———. 1960. *Word and Object.* Cambridge, MA: MIT Press.
———. 1968. "Ontological Relativity." *Journal of Philosophy* 65. Reprinted in Quine's *Ontological Relativity,* pp. 26–68. (New York: Columbia University Press, 1969).
———. 1970. "On the Reasons for the Indeterminacy of Translation." *Journal of Philosophy* 67: 178–183.
Steiner, Mark. 1973. "Platonism and the Causal Theory of Knowledge." *Journal of Philosophy* 70: 57–66.
———. 1975. *Mathematical Knowledge.* Ithaca, NY: Cornell University Press.
Wetzel, Linda. 1990. "Dummett's Criteria for Singular Terms." *Mind* 99: 239–254.
Wright, Crispin. 1983. *Frege's Conception of Numbers as Objects.* Aberdeen: Aberdeen University Press.

14 On What There Is

W. V. Quine

A CURIOUS THING ABOUT the ontological problem is its simplicity. It can be put in three Anglo-Saxon monosyllables: 'What is there?' It can be answered, moreover, in a word—'Everything'—and everyone will accept this answer as true. However, this is merely to say that there is what there is. There remains room for disagreement over cases; and so the issue has stayed alive down the centuries.

Suppose now that two philosophers, McX and I, differ over ontology. Suppose McX maintains there is something which I maintain there is not. McX can, quite consistently with his own point of view, describe our difference of opinion by saying that I refuse to recognize certain entities. I should protest, of course, that he is wrong in his formulation of our disagreement, for I maintain that there are no entities, of the kind which he alleges, for me to recognize; but my finding him wrong in his formulation of our disagreement is unimportant, for I am committed to considering him wrong in his ontology anyway.

When *I* try to formulate our difference of opinion, on the other hand, I seem to be in a predicament. I cannot admit that there are some things

Originally published in the Review of Metaphysics, *vol. 2, no. 1 (September 1948). Reprinted with permission of the publisher.*

which McX countenances and I do not, for in admitting that there are such things I should be contradicting my own rejection of them.

It would appear, if this reasoning were sound, that in any ontological dispute the proponent of the negative side suffers the disadvantage of not being able to admit that his opponent disagrees with him.

This is the old Platonic riddle of nonbeing. Nonbeing must in some sense be, otherwise what is it that there is not? This tangled doctrine might be nicknamed *Plato's beard;* historically it has proved tough, frequently dulling the edge of Occam's razor.

It is some such line of thought that leads philosophers like McX to impute being where they might otherwise be quite content to recognize that there is nothing. Thus, take Pegasus. If Pegasus *were* not, McX argues, we should not be talking about anything when we use the word; therefore it would be nonsense to say even that Pegasus is not. Thinking to show thus that the denial of Pegasus cannot be coherently maintained, he concludes that Pegasus is.

McX cannot, indeed, quite persuade himself that any region of space-time, near or remote, contains a flying horse of flesh and blood. Primed for further details on Pegasus, then, he says that Pegasus is an idea in men's minds. Here, however, a confusion begins to be apparent. We may for the sake of argument concede that there is an entity, and even a unique entity (though this is rather implausible), which is the mental Pegasus-idea; but this mental entity is not what people are talking about when they deny Pegasus.

McX never confuses the Parthenon with the Parthenon-idea. The Parthenon is physical; the Parthenon-idea is mental (according anyway to McX's version of idea, and I have no better to offer). The Parthenon is visible; the Parthenon-idea is invisible. We cannot easily imagine two things more unlike, and less liable to confusion, than the Parthenon and the Parthenon-idea. But when we shift from the Parthenon to Pegasus, the confusion sets in—for no other reason than that McX would sooner be deceived by the crudest and most flagrant counterfeit than grant the nonbeing of Pegasus.

The notion that Pegasus must be, because it would otherwise be nonsense to say even that Pegasus is not, has been seen to lead McX into an elementary confusion. Subtler minds, taking the same precept as their starting point, come out with theories of Pegasus which are less patently misguided than McX's, and correspondingly more difficult to eradicate. One of these subtler minds is named, let us say, Wyman. Pegasus, Wyman maintains, has his being as an unactualized possible. When we say of Pegasus that there is no such thing, we are saying, more precisely, that Pegasus does not have the special attribute of actuality. Saying that Pegasus is not actual is on a par, logically, with saying that the Parthenon is not red; in either case we are saying something about an entity whose being is unquestioned.

Wyman, by the way, is one of those philosophers who have united in ruining the good old word 'exist.' Despite his espousal of unactualized possibles, he limits the word 'existence' to actuality—thus preserving an illusion of ontological agreement between himself and us who repudiate the rest of his bloated universe. We have all been prone to say, in our common-sense usage of 'exist,'[1] that Pegasus does not exist, meaning simply that there is no such entity at all. If Pegasus existed he would indeed be in space and time, but only because the word 'Pegasus' has spatio-temporal connotations, and not because 'exists' has spatio-temporal connotations. If spatio-temporal reference is lacking when we affirm the existence of the cube root of 27, this is simply because a cube root is not a spatio-temporal kind of thing, and not because we are being ambiguous in our use of 'exist.' However, Wyman, in an ill-conceived effort to appear agreeable, genially grants us the nonexistence of Pegasus and then, contrary to what *we* meant by nonexistence of Pegasus, insists that Pegasus *is.* Existence is one thing, he says, and subsistence is another. The only way I know of coping with this obfuscation of issues is to *give* Wyman the word 'exist.' I'll try not to use it again; I still have 'is.' So much for lexicography; let's get back to Wyman's ontology.

Wyman's overpopulated universe is in many ways unlovely. It offends the aesthetic sense of us who have a taste for desert landscapes, but this is not the worst of it. Wyman's slum of possibles is a breeding ground for disorderly elements. Take, for instance, the possible fat man in that doorway; and, again, the possible bald man in that doorway. Are they the same possible man, or two possible men? How do we decide? How many possible men are there in that doorway? Are there more possible thin ones than fat ones? How many of them are alike? Or would their being alike make them one? Are no *two* possible things alike? Is this the same as saying that it is impossible for two things to be alike? Or, finally, is the concept of identity simply inapplicable to unactualized possibles? But what sense can be found in talking of entities which cannot meaningfully be said to be identical with themselves and distinct from one another? These elements are well-nigh incorrigible. By a Fregean therapy of individual concepts, some effort might be made at rehabilitation; but I feel we'd do better simply to clear Wyman's slum and be done with it.

Possibility, along with the other modalities of necessity and impossibility and contingency, raises problems upon which I do not mean to imply that we should turn our backs. But we can at least limit modalities to whole statements. We may impose the adverb 'possibly' upon a statement as a whole, and we may well worry about the semantical analysis of such usage; but little real advance in such analysis is to be hoped for in expanding our universe to include so-called *possible entities.* I suspect that the main motive for this expansion is simply the old notion that Pegasus, for example, must be because otherwise it would be nonsense to say even that he is not.

Still, all the rank luxuriance of Wyman's universe of possibles would seem to come to naught when we make a slight change in the example and speak not of Pegasus but of the round square cupola on Berkeley College. If, unless Pegasus were, it would be nonsense to say that he is not, then by the same token, unless the round square cupola on Berkeley College were, it would be nonsense to say that it is not. But, unlike Pegasus, the round square cupola on Berkeley College cannot be admitted even as an unactualized *possible.* Can we drive Wyman now to admitting also a realm of unactualizable impossibles? If so, a good many embarrassing questions could be asked about them. We might hope even to trap Wyman in contradictions, by getting him to admit that certain of these entities are at once round and square. But the wily Wyman chooses the other horn of the dilemma and concedes that it is nonsense to say that the round square cupola on Berkeley College is not. He says that the phrase 'round square cupola' is meaningless.

Wyman was not the first to embrace this alternative. The doctrine of the meaninglessness of contradictions runs away back. The tradition survives, moreover, in writers who seem to share none of Wyman's motivations. Still, I wonder whether the first temptation to such a doctrine may not have been substantially the motivation which we have observed in Wyman. Certainly the doctrine has no intrinsic appeal; and it has led its devotees to such quixotic extremes as that of challenging the method of proof by *reductio ad absurdum*—a challenge in which I sense a *reductio ad absurdum* of the doctrine itself.

Moreover, the doctrine of meaninglessness of contradictions has the severe methodological drawback that it makes it impossible, in principle, ever to devise an effective test of what is meaningful and what is not. It would be forever impossible for us to devise systematic ways of deciding whether a string of signs made sense—even to us individually, let alone other people—or not. For it follows from a discovery in mathematical logic, due to Church [2], that there can be no generally applicable test of contradictoriness.

I have spoken disparagingly of Plato's beard, and hinted that it is tangled. I have dwelt at length on the inconveniences of putting up with it. It is time to think about taking steps.

Russell, in his theory of so-called singular descriptions, showed clearly how we might meaningfully use seeming names without supposing that there be the entities allegedly named. The names to which Russell's theory directly applies are complex descriptive names such as 'the author of *Waverley,*' 'the present King of France,' 'the round square cupola on Berkeley College.' Russell analyzes such phrases systematically as fragments of the whole sentences in which they occur. The sentence 'The author of *Waverley* was a poet,' for example, is explained as a whole as meaning 'Someone (better: something) wrote *Waverley* and was a poet, and nothing else wrote *Waverley*.' (The point of this added clause is to affirm the uniqueness which is implicit in the word 'the,' in '*the* author of *Waverley*.') The sentence 'The round square cupola on Berkeley College is pink' is explained as 'Something is round and square and is a cupola on Berkeley College and is pink, and nothing else is round and square and a cupola on Berkeley College.

The virtue of this analysis is that the seeming name, a descriptive phrase, is paraphrased *in context* as a so-called incomplete symbol. No unified expression is offered as an analysis of the descriptive phrase, but the statement as a whole which was the context of that phrase still gets its full quota of meaning—whether true or false.

The unanalyzed statement 'The author of *Waverley* was a poet' contains a part, 'the author of *Waverley*,' which is wrongly supposed by McX and Wyman to demand objective reference in order to be meaningful at all. But in Russell's translation, 'Something wrote *Waverley* and was a poet and nothing else wrote *Waverley*,' the burden of objective reference which had been put upon the descriptive phrase is now taken over by words of the kind that logicians call bound variables, variables of quantification, namely, words like 'something,' 'nothing,' 'everything.' These words, far from purporting to be names specifically of the author of *Waverley*, do not purport to be names at all; they refer to entities generally, with a kind of studied ambiguity peculiar to themselves. These quantificational words or bound variables are, of course a basic part of language, and their meaningfulness, at least in context, is not to be challenged. But their meaningfulness in no way presupposes there being either the author of *Waverley* or the round square cupola on Berkeley College or any other specifically preassigned objects.

Where descriptions are concerned, there is no longer any difficulty in affirming or denying being. 'There *is* the author of *Waverley*' is explained by Russell as meaning 'Someone (or, more strictly, something) wrote *Waverley* and nothing else wrote *Waverley*.' 'The author of *Waverley* is not' is explained, correspondingly, as the alternation 'Either each thing failed to write *Waverley* or two or more things wrote *Waverley*.' This alternation is false, but meaningful; and it contains no expression purporting to name the author of *Waverley*. The statement 'The round square cupola on Berkeley College is not' is analyzed in similar fashion. So the old notion that statements of nonbeing defeat themselves goes by the board. When a statement of being or nonbeing is analyzed by Russell's theory of descriptions, it ceases to contain any expression which even purports to name the alleged entity whose being is in question, so that the meaningfulness of the statement no longer can be thought to presuppose that there be such an entity.

Now what of 'Pegasus'? This being a word rather than a descriptive phrase, Russell's argument does not immediately apply to it. However, it can easily be made to apply. We have only to rephrase 'Pegasus' as a description, in any way that seems adequately to single out our idea; say, 'the winged horse that was captured by Bellerophon.' Substituting such a phrase for 'Pegasus,' we can then proceed to analyze the statement 'Pegasus is,' or 'Pegasus is not,' precisely on the analogy of Russell's analysis of 'The author of *Waverley* is' and 'The author of *Waverley* is not.'

In order thus to subsume a one-word name or alleged name such as 'Pegasus' under Russell's theory of description, we must, of course, be able first to translate the word into a description. But this is no real restriction. If the notion of Pegasus had been so obscure or so basic a one that no pat translation into a descriptive phrase had offered itself along familiar lines, we could still have availed ourselves of the following artificial and trivial-seeming device: we could have appealed to the *ex hypothesi* unanalyzable, irreducible attribute of *being Pegasus*, adopting, for its expression, the verb 'is-Pegasus,' or 'pegasizes.' The noun 'Pegasus' itself could then be treated as derivative, and identified after all with a description: 'the thing that is-Pegasus,' 'the thing that pegasizes.'[2]

If the importing of such a predicate as 'pegasizes' seems to commit us to recognizing that there is a corresponding attribute, pegasizing, in Plato's heaven or in the minds of men, well and good. Neither we nor Wyman nor McX have been contending, thus far, about the being or nonbeing of universals, but rather about that of Pegasus. If in terms of pegasizing we can interpret the noun

'Pegasus' as a description subject to Russell's theory of descriptions, then we have disposed of the old notion that Pegasus cannot be said not to be without presupposing that in some sense Pegasus is.

Our argument is now quite general. McX and Wyman supposed that we could not meaningfully affirm a statement of the form 'So-and-so is not,' with a simple or descriptive singular noun in place of 'so-and-so,' unless so-and-so is. This supposition is now seen to be quite generally groundless, since the singular noun in question can always be expanded into a singular description, trivially or otherwise, and then analyzed out *à la* Russell.

We commit ourselves to an ontology containing numbers when we say there are prime numbers larger than a million; we commit ourselves to an ontology containing centaurs when we say there are centaurs; and we commit ourselves to an ontology containing Pegasus when we say Pegasus is. But we do not commit ourselves to an ontology containing Pegasus or the author of *Waverley* or the round square cupola on Berkeley College when we say that Pegasus or the author of *Waverley* or the cupola in question is *not*. We need no longer labor under the delusion that the meaningfulness of a statement containing a singular term presupposes an entity named by the term. A singular term need not name to be significant.

An inkling of this might have dawned on Wyman and McX even without benefit of Russell if they had only noticed—as so few of us do—that there is a gulf between *meaning* and *naming* even in the case of a singular term which is genuinely a name of an object. The following example from Frege [3] will serve. The phrase 'Evening Star' names a certain large physical object of spherical form, which is hurtling through space some scores of millions of miles from here. The phrase 'Morning Star' names the same thing, as was probably first established by some observant Babylonian. But the two phrases cannot be regarded as having the same meaning; otherwise that Babylonian could have dispensed with his observations and contented himself with reflecting on the meanings of his words. The meanings, then, being different from one another, must be other than the named object, which is one and the same in both cases.

Confusion of meaning with naming not only made McX think he could not meaningfully repudiate Pegasus; a continuing confusion of meaning with naming no doubt helped engender his absurd notion that Pegasus is an idea, a mental entity. The structure of his confusion is as follows. He confused the alleged *named object* Pegasus with the *meaning* of the word 'Pegasus,' therefore concluding that Pegasus must be in order that the word have meaning. But what sorts of things are meanings? This is a moot point; however, one might quite plausibly explain meanings as ideas in the mind, supposing we can make clear sense in turn of the idea of ideas in the mind. Therefore Pegasus, initially confused with a meaning, ends up as an idea in the mind. It is the more remarkable that Wyman, subject to the same initial motivation as McX, should have avoided this particular blunder and wound up with unactualized possibles instead.

Now let us turn to the ontological problem of universals: the question whether there are such entities as attributes, relations, classes, numbers, functions. McX, characteristically enough, thinks there are. Speaking of attributes, he says: "There are red houses, red roses, red sunsets; this much is prephilosophical common sense in which we must all agree. These houses, roses, and sunsets, then, have something in common; and this which they have in common is all I mean by the attribute of redness." For McX, thus, there being attributes is even more obvious and trivial than the obvious and trivial fact of there being red houses, roses, and sunsets. This, I think, is characteristic of metaphysics, or at least of that part of metaphysics called ontology: one who regards a statement on this subject as true at all must regard it as trivially true. One's ontology is basic to the conceptual scheme by which he interprets all experiences, even the most commonplace ones. Judged within some particular conceptual scheme—and how else is judgment possible?—an ontological statement goes without saying, standing in need of no separate justification at all. Ontological statements follow immediately from all manner of casual statements of commonplace fact, just as—from the point of view, anyway, of McX's conceptual scheme—'There is an attribute' follows from 'There are red houses, red roses, red sunsets.'

Judged in another conceptual scheme, an ontological statement which is axiomatic to McX's mind may, with equal immediacy and triviality, be adjudged false. One may admit that there are red houses, roses, and sunsets, but deny, except as a popular and misleading manner of speaking, that they have anything in common. The words 'houses,' 'roses,' and 'sunsets' are true of sundry individual entities which are houses and roses and sunsets, and the word 'red' or 'red object' is true of each of sundry individual entities which are red houses, red roses, red sunsets; but there is not, in addition, any entity whatever, individual or otherwise, which is named by the word 'redness,' nor, for that matter, by the word 'househood,' 'rosehood,' 'sunsethood.' That the houses and roses and sunsets are all of them red may be taken as ultimate and irreducible, and it may be held that McX is no better off, in point of real explanatory power, for all the occult entities which he posits under such names as 'redness.'

One means by which McX might naturally have tried to impose his ontology of universals on us was already removed before we turned to the problem of universals. McX cannot argue that predicates such as 'red' or 'is-red,' which we all concur in using, must be regarded as names each of a single universal entity in order that they be meaningful at all. For we have seen that being a name of something is a much more special feature than being meaningful. He cannot even charge us—at least not by *that* argument—with having posited an attribute of pegasizing by our adoption of the predicate 'pegasizes.'

However, McX hits upon a different strategem. "Let us grant," he says, "this distinction between meaning and naming of which you make so much. Let us even grant that 'is red,' 'pegasizes,' etc., are not names of attributes. Still, you admit they have meanings. But these *meanings,* whether they are *named* or not, are still universals, and I venture to say that some of them might even be the very things that I call attributes, or something to much the same purpose in the end."

For McX, this is an unusually penetrating speech; and the only way I know to counter if is by refusing to admit meanings. However, I feel no reluctance toward refusing to admit meanings, for I do not thereby deny that words and statements are meaningful. McX and I may agree to the letter in our classification of linguistic forms into the meaningful and the meaningless, even though McX construes meaningfulness as the *having* (in some sense of 'having') of some abstract entity which he calls a meaning, whereas I do not. I remain free to maintain that the fact that a given linguistic utterance is meaningful (or *significant,* as I prefer to say so as not to invite hypostasis of meanings as entities) is an ultimate and irreducible matter of fact; or, I may undertake to analyze it in terms directly of what people do in the presence of the linguistic utterance in question and other utterances similar to it.

The useful ways in which people ordinarily talk or seem to talk about meanings boil down to two: the *having* of meanings, which is significance, and *sameness* of meaning, or synonomy. What is called *giving* the meaning of an utterance is simply the uttering of a synonym, couched, ordinarily, in clearer language than the original. If we are allergic to meanings as such, we can speak directly of utterances as significant or insignificant, and as synonymous or heteronymous one with another. The problem of explaining these adjectives 'significant' and 'synonymous' with some degree of clarity and rigor—preferably, as I see it, in terms of behavior—is as difficult as it is important. But the explanatory value of special and irreducible intermediary entities called meanings is surely illusory.

Up to now I have argued that we can use singular terms significantly in sentences without presupposing that there are the entities which those terms purport to name. I have argued further that we can use general terms, for example, predicates, without conceding them to be names of abstract entities. I have argued further that we can view utterances as significant, and as synonymous or heteronymous with one another, without countenancing a realm of entities called meanings. At this point McX begins to wonder whether there is any limit at all to our ontological immunity. Does *nothing* we may say commit us to the assumption of universals or other entities which we may find unwelcome?

I have already suggested a negative answer to this question, in speaking of bound variables, or variables of quantification, in connection with Russell's theory of descriptions. We can very easily involve ourselves in ontological commitments by saying, for example, that *there is something* (bound variable) which red houses and sunsets have in common; or that *there is something* which is a prime number larger than a million. But this is, essentially, the *only* way we can involve ourselves in ontological commitments: by our use of bound variables. The use of alleged names is no criterion, for we can repudiate their namehood at the drop of a hat unless the assumption of a corresponding entity can be spotted in the things we affirm in terms of bound variables. Names are, in fact, altogether immaterial to the ontological issue, for I have shown, in connection with 'Pegasus' and 'pegasize,' that names can be converted to descriptions, and Russell has shown that descriptions can be eliminated. Whatever we say with the help of names can be said in a language which shuns names altogether. To be assumed as an entity is, purely and simply, to be reckoned as the value of a variable. In terms of the categories of traditional grammar, this amounts roughly to saying that to be is to be in the range of reference of a pronoun. Pronouns are the basic media of reference; nouns might better have been named propronouns. The variables of quantification, 'something,' 'nothing,' 'everything,' range over our whole ontology, whatever it may be; and we are convicted of a particular ontological presupposition if, and only if, the alleged presupposition has to be reckoned among the entities over which our variables range in order to render one of our affirmations true.

We may say, for example, that some dogs are white and not thereby commit ourselves to recognizing either doghood or whiteness as entities. 'Some dogs are white' says that some things that are dogs are white; and, in order that this statement be true, the things over which the bound variable 'something' ranges must include some white dogs, but need not include doghood or whiteness. On the other hand, when we say that some zoölogical species are cross-fertile we are committing ourselves to recognizing as entities the several species themselves, abstract though they are. We remain so committed at least until we devise some way of so paraphrasing the statement as to show that the seeming reference to species on the part of our bound variable was an avoidable manner of speaking.

Classical mathematics, as the example of primes larger than a million clearly illustrates, is up to its neck in commitments to an ontology of abstract entities. Thus it is that the great mediaeval controversy over universals has flared up anew in the modern philosophy of mathematics. The issue is clearer now than of old, because we now have a more explicit standard whereby to decide what ontology a given theory or form of discourse is committed to: a theory is committed to those and only those entities to which the bound variables of the theory must be capable of referring in order that the affirmations made in the theory be true.

Because this standard of ontological presupposition did not emerge clearly in the philosophical tradition, the modern philosophical mathematicians have not on the whole recognized that they were debating the same old problem of universals in a newly clarified form. But the fundamental cleavages among modern points of view on foundations of mathematics do come down pretty explicitly to disagreements as to the range of entities to which the bound variables should be permitted to refer.

The three main mediaeval points of view regarding universals are designated by historians as *realism, conceptualism,* and *nominalism.* Essentially these same three doctrines reappear in twentieth-century surveys of the philosophy of mathematics under the new names *logicism, intuitionism,* and *formalism.*

Realism, as the word is used in connection with the mediaeval controversy over universals, is the Platonic doctrine that universals or abstract entities have being independently of the mind; the mind may discover them but cannot create them. *Logicism,* represented by Frege, Russell, Whitehead, Church, and Carnap, condones the use of bound variables to refer to abstract entities known and unknown, specifiable and unspecifiable, indiscriminately.

Conceptualism holds that there are universals but they are mind-made. *Intuitionism,* espoused in modern times in one form or another by Poincaré,

Brouwer, Weyl, and others, countenances the use of bound variables to refer to abstract entities only when those entities are capable of being cooked up individually from ingredients specified in advance. As Fraenkel has put it, logicism holds that classes are discovered while intuitionism holds that they are invented—a fair statement indeed of the old opposition between realism and conceptualism. This opposition is no mere quibble; it makes an essential difference in the amount of classical mathematics to which one is willing to subscribe. Logicists, or realists, are able on their assumptions to get Cantor's ascending orders of infinity; intuitionists are compelled to stop with the lowest order of infinity, and, as an indirect consequence, to abandon even some of the classical laws of real numbers. The modern controversy between logicism and intuitionism arose, in fact, from disagreements over infinity.

Formalism, associated with the name of Hilbert, echoes intuitionism in deploring the logicist's unbridled recourse to universals. But formalism also finds intuitionism unsatisfactory. This could happen for either of two opposite reasons. The formalist might, like the logicist, object to the crippling of classical mathematics; or he might, like the *nominalists* of old, object to admitting abstract entities at all, even in the restrained sense of mind-made entities. The upshot is the same: the formalist keeps classical mathematics as a play of insignificant notations. This play of notations can still be of utility—whatever utility it has already shown itself to have as a crutch for physicists and technologists. But utility need not imply significance, in any literal linguistic sense. Nor need the marked success of mathematicians in spinning out theorems, and in finding objective bases for agreement with one another's results, imply significance. For an adequate basis for agreement among mathematicians can be found simply in the rules which govern the manipulation of the notations—these syntactical rules being, unlike the notations themselves, quite significant and intelligible.[3]

I have argued that the sort of ontology we adopt can be consequential—notably in connection with mathematics, although this is only an example. Now how are we to adjudicate among rival ontologies? Certainly the answer is not provided by the semantical formula "To be is to be the value of a variable"; this formula serves rather, conversely, in testing the conformity of a given remark or doctrine to a prior ontological standard. We look to bound variables in connection with ontology not in order to know what there is, but in order to know what a given remark or doctrine, ours or someone else's, *says* there is; and this much is quite properly a problem involving language. But what there is is another question.

In debating over what there is, there are still reasons for operating on a semantical plane. One reason is to escape from the predicament noted at the beginning of this essay: the predicament of my not being able to admit that there are things which McX countenances and I do not. So long as I adhere to my ontology, as opposed to McX's, I cannot allow my bound variables to refer to entities which belong to McX's ontology and not to mine. I can, however, consistently describe our disagreement by characterizing the statements which McX affirms. Provided merely that my ontology countenances linguistic forms, or at least concrete inscriptions and utterances, I can talk about McX's sentences.

Another reason for withdrawing to a semantical plane is to find common ground on which to argue. Disagreement in ontology involves basic disagreement in conceptual schemes; yet McX and I, despite these basic disagreements, find that our conceptual schemes converge sufficiently in their intermediate and upper ramifications to enable us to communicate successfully on such topics as politics, weather, and, in particular, language. In so far as our basic controversy over ontology can be translated upward into a semantical controversy about words and what to do with them, the collapse of the controversy into question-begging may be delayed.

It is no wonder, then, that ontological controversy should tend into controversy over language. But we must not jump to the conclusion that what there is depends on words. Translatability of a question into semantical terms is no indication that the question is linguistic. To see Naples is to bear a name which, when prefixed to the words 'sees Naples,' yields a true sentence; still there is nothing linguistic about seeing Naples.

Our acceptance of an ontology is, I think, similar in principle to our acceptance of a scientific theory, say a system of physics: we adopt, at least insofar as we are reasonable, the simplest conceptual scheme into which the disordered fragments of raw experience can be fitted and arranged. Our ontology is determined once we have fixed upon the over-all conceptual scheme which is to accommodate science in the broadest sense; and the considerations which determine a reasonable construction of any part of that conceptual scheme, for example, the biological or the physical part, are not different in kind from the considerations which determine a reasonable construction of the whole. To whatever extent the adoption of any system of scientific theory may be said to be a matter of language, the same—but no more—may be said of the adoption of an ontology.

But simplicity, as a guiding principle in constructing conceptual schemes, is not a clear and unambiguous idea; and it is quite capable of presenting a double or multiple standard. Imagine, for example, that we have devised the most economical set of concepts adequate to the play-by-play reporting of immediate experience. The entities under this scheme—the values of bound variables—are, let us suppose, individual subjective events of sensation or reflection. We should still find, no doubt, that a physicalistic conceptual scheme, purporting to talk about external objects, offers great advantages in simplifying our over-all reports. By bringing together scattered sense events and treating them as perceptions of one object, we reduce the complexity of our stream of experience to a manageable conceptual simplicity. The rule of simplicity is indeed our guiding maxim in assigning sense data to objects: we associate an earlier and a later round sensum with the same so-called penny, or with two different so-called pennies, in obedience to the demands of maximum simplicity in our total world-picture.

Here we have two competing conceptual schemes, a phenomenalistic one and a physicalistic one. Which should prevail? Each has its advantages; each has its special simplicity in its own way. Each, I suggest, deserves to be developed. Each may be said, indeed, to be the more fundamental, though in different senses: the one is epistemologically, the other physically, fundamental.

The physical conceptual scheme simplifies our account of experience because of the way myriad scattered sense events come to be associated with single so-called objects; still there is no likelihood that each sentence about physical objects can actually be translated, however deviously and complexly, into the phenomenalistic language. Physical objects are postulated entities which round out and simplify our account of the flux of experience, just as the introduction of irrational numbers simplifies laws of arithmetic. From the point of view of the conceptual scheme of the elementary arithmetic of rational numbers alone, the broader arithmetic of rational and irrational numbers would have the status of a convenient myth, simpler than the literal truth (namely, the arithmetic of rationals) and yet containing that literal truth as a scattered part. Similarly, from a phenomenalistic point of view, the conceptual scheme of physical objects is a convenient myth, simpler than the literal truth and yet containing that literal truth as a scattered part.[4]

Now what of classes or attributes of physical objects, in turn? A platonistic ontology of this sort is, from the point of view of a strictly physicalistic conceptual scheme, as much a myth as that physicalistic conceptual scheme itself is for phenomenalism. This higher myth is a good and useful one, in turn, in so far as it simplifies our account of physics. Since mathematics is an integral part of this higher myth, the utility of this myth for physical science is evident enough. In speaking of it nevertheless as a myth, I echo that philosophy of mathematics to which I alluded earlier under the name of formalism. But an attitude of formalism may with equal justice be adopted toward the physical conceptual scheme, in turn, by the pure aesthete or phenomenalist.

The analogy between the myth of mathematics and the myth of physics is, in some additional and perhaps fortuitous ways, strikingly close. Consider, for example, the crisis which was precipitated in the foundations of mathematics, at the turn of the century, by the discovery of Russell's paradox and other antinomies of set theory. These contradictions had to be obviated by unintuitive, *ad hoc* devices; our mathematical myth-making became deliberate and evident to all. But what of physics? An antinomy arose between the undular and the corpuscular accounts of light; and if this was not as out-and-out a contradiction as Russell's paradox, I suspect that the reason is that physics is not as out-and-out as mathematics. Again, the second great modern crisis in the foundations of mathematics—precipitated in 1931 by Gödel's proof [2] that there are bound to be undecidable statements in arithmetic—has its companion piece in physics in Heisenberg's indeterminacy principle.

In earlier pages I undertook to show that some common arguments in favor of certain ontologies are fallacious. Further, I advanced an explicit standard whereby to decide what the ontological commitments of a theory are. But the question what ontology actually to adopt still stands open, and the obvious counsel is tolerance and an experimental spirit. Let us by all means see how much of the physicalistic conceptual scheme can be reduced to a phenomenalistic one; still, physics also naturally demands pursuing, irreducible *in toto* though it be. Let us see how, or to what degree, natural science may be rendered independent of Platonistic mathematics; but let us also pursue mathematics and delve into its Platonistic foundations.

From among the various conceptual schemes best suited to these various pursuits, one—the phenomenalistic—claims epistemological priority. Viewed from within the phenomenalistic conceptual scheme, the ontologies of physical objects and mathematical objects are myths. The quality of myth, however, is relative; relative, in this case, to the epistemological point of view. This point of view is one among various, corresponding to one among our various interests and purposes.

NOTES

1. The impulse to distinguish terminologically between existence as applied to objects actualized somewhere in space-time and existence (or subsistence or being) as applied to other entities arises in part, perhaps, from an idea that the observation of nature is relevant only to questions of existence of the first kind. But this idea is readily refuted by counter-instances such as 'the ratio of the number of centaurs to the number of unicorns.' If there were such a ratio, it would be an abstract entity, viz. a number. Yet it is only by studying nature that we conclude that the number of centaurs and the number of unicorns are both 0 and hence that there is no such ratio.

2. For further remarks on such assimilation of all singular terms to descriptions see also Quine [2], pp. 218–224.

3. See Goodman and Quine. For further discussion of the general matters touched on in the past two pages, see Bernays [1], Fraenkel, Black.

4. The arithmetical analogy is due to Frank, pp. 108f.

Reading Questions

1. McX argues as follows:
    1. Suppose "Pegasus does not exist" is true.
    2. If Pegasus does not exist, then "Pegasus" is meaningless—it doesn't refer to anything.
    3. If "Pegasus" is meaningless, then any sentence containing "Pegasus" is meaningless.
    4. Thus any sentence containing "Pegasus" is meaningless.
    5. Thus "Pegasus does not exist" is meaningless.
    6. This contradicts our assumption in (1) that the sentence is true (true sentences can't be meaningless).
    7. By *reductio,* Pegasus exists.

    Quine claims that when we press McX for an explanation of what "Pegasus" refers to, and whether it refers to some mass of flying horse flesh in some region of space-time, McX agrees that there is no such object. So what does "Pegasus" refer to, according to Quine?
2. In what way does Quine treat proper names as disguised definite descriptions?

3. Quine offers this criterion for reality: to be is to be the value of a bound variable. His interlocutor McX relies on this criterion to defend universals as follows:
   1. There are red houses, red roses, and red sunsets.
   2. There is something they all have something in common.
   3. What they have in common is the attribute or property of *redness* or *being red*.
   4. Thus there is redness. (from 2,3).
   5. By Quine's Criterion for Reality, redness is real.

   Quine denies premise (2) of McX's argument. But why? What is his argument? He claims that their redness is ultimate and irreducible. Yet do they *really* lack anything in common?
4. McX also moots this argument:
   1. Predicates like "is red" are meaningful.
   2. Thus there is something that "is red" means.
   3. This meaning is the attribute redness, or something very like it.
   4. Thus there is redness. (from 2,3).
   5. By Quine's Criterion for Reality, redness is real.

   Here Quine denies the move from (1) to (2). What is his reasoning?
5. Quine seems quite concerned with limiting how many entities we have in our overall global ontology. Yet he seems at least tempted by realism about numbers, a position committed to at least an infinity of abstract objects. Since $\aleph_0$ (numbers) + $\aleph_0$ (properties) = $\aleph_0$ objects, allowing property realism adds no more entities to our ontology than we already have once we countenence numbers. In fact, $\aleph_0$ is just the number of the natural numbers; there are more numbers than $\aleph_0$. Indeed, there is no highest bound, no number of the numbers. So why isn't number realism dynamiting Quine's plans for a minimalist ontology?

15 Empiricism, Semantics, and Ontology

RUDOLF CARNAP

1. THE PROBLEM OF ABSTRACT ENTITIES

EMPIRICISTS ARE IN GENERAL rather suspicious with respect to any kind of abstract entities like properties, classes, relations, numbers, propositions, etc. They usually feel much more in sympathy with nominalists than with realists (in the medieval sense). As far as possible they try to avoid any reference to abstract entities and to restrict themselves to what is sometimes called a nominalistic language, i.e., one not containing such references. However, within certain scientific contexts it seems hardly possible to avoid them. In the case of mathematics, some empiricists try to find a way out by treating the whole of mathematics as a mere calculus, a formal system for which no interpretation is given or can be given. Accordingly, the mathematician is said to speak not about numbers, functions, and infinite classes, but merely about meaningless

I have made here some minor changes in the formulations to the effect that the term "framework" is now used only for the system of linguistic expressions, and not for the system of the entities in question.

From Revue Internationale de Philosophie, *vol. 4 (1950), pp. 20–40. Reprinted by permission of The University of Chicago Press.*

symbols and formulas manipulated according to given formal rules. In physics it is more difficult to shun the suspected entities, because the language of physics serves for the communication of reports and predictions and hence cannot be taken as a mere calculus. A physicist who is suspicious of abstract entities may perhaps try to declare a certain part of the language of physics as uninterpreted and uninterpretable, that part which refers to real numbers as space-time coordinates or as values of physical magnitudes, to functions, limits, etc. More probably he will just speak about all these things like anybody else but with an uneasy conscience, like a man who in his everyday life does with qualms many things which are not in accord with the high moral principles he professes on Sundays. Recently the problem of abstract entities has arisen again in connection with semantics, the theory of meaning and truth. Some semanticists say that certain expressions designate certain entities, and among these designated entities they include not only concrete material things but also abstract entities, e.g., properties as designated by predicates and propositions as designated by sentences.[1] Others object strongly to this procedure as violating the basic principles of empiricism and leading back to a metaphysical ontology of the Platonic kind.

It is the purpose of this article to clarify this controversial issue. The nature and implications of the acceptance of a language referring to abstract entities will first be discussed in general; it will be shown that using such a language does not imply embracing a Platonic ontology but is perfectly compatible with empiricism and strictly scientific thinking. Then the special question of the role of abstract entities in semantics will be discussed. It is hoped that the clarification of the issue will be useful to those who would like to accept abstract entities in their work in mathematics, physics, semantics, or any other field; it may help them to overcome nominalistic scruples.

2. LINGUISTIC FRAMEWORKS

Are there properties, classes, numbers, propositions? In order to understand more clearly the nature of these and related problems, it is above all necessary to recognize a fundamental distinction between two kinds of questions concerning the existence or reality of entities. If someone wishes to speak in his language about a new kind of entities, he has to introduce a system of new ways of speaking, subject to new rules; we shall call this procedure the construction of a linguistic *framework* for the new entities in question. And now we must distinguish two kinds of questions of existence: first, questions of the existence of certain entities of the new kind *within the framework;* we call them *internal questions;* and second, questions concerning the existence or reality *of the system of entities as a whole,* called *external questions.* Internal questions and possible answers to them are formulated with the help of the new forms of expressions. The answers may be found either by purely logical methods or by empirical methods, depending upon whether the framework is a logical or a factual one. An external question is of a problematic character which is in need of closer examination.

The world of things. Let us consider as an example the simplest kind of entities dealt with in the everyday language: the spatio-temporally ordered system of observable things and events. Once we have accepted the thing language with its framework for things, we can raise and answer internal questions, e.g., "Is there a white piece of paper on my desk?", "Did King Arthur actually live?", "Are unicorns and centaurs real or merely imaginary?", and the like. These questions are to be answered by empirical investigations. Results of observations are evaluated according to certain rules as confirming or disconfirming evidence for possible answers. (This evaluation is usually carried out, of course, as a matter of habit rather than a deliberate, rational procedure. But it is possible, in a rational reconstruction, to lay down explicit rules for the evaluation. This is one of the main tasks of a pure, as distinguished from a psychological, epistemology.) The concept of reality occurring in these internal questions is an empirical, scientific, non-metaphysical concept. To recognize something as a real thing or event means to succeed in incorporating it into the system of things at a particular space-time position so that it fits together with the other things recognized as real, according to the rules of the framework.

From these questions we must distinguish the external question of the reality of the thing world itself. In contrast to the former questions, this question is raised neither by the man in the street nor by scientists, but only by philosophers. Realists give an affirmative answer, subjective idealists a negative one, and the controversy goes on for centuries without ever being solved. And it cannot be solved because it is framed in a wrong way. To be real in the scientific sense means to be an element of the system; hence this concept cannot be meaningfully applied to the system itself. Those who raise the question of the reality of the thing world itself have perhaps in mind not a theoretical question as their formulation seems to suggest, but rather a practical question, a matter of a practical decision concerning the structure of our language. We have to make the choice whether or not to accept and use the forms of expression in the framework in question.

In the case of this particular example, there is usually no deliberate choice because we all have accepted the thing language early in our lives as a matter of course. Nevertheless, we may regard it as a matter of decision in this sense: we are free to choose to continue using the thing language or not; in the latter case we could restrict ourselves to a language of sense-data and other "phenomenal" entities, or construct an alternative to the customary thing language with another structure, or, finally, we could refrain from speaking. If someone decides to accept the thing language, there is no objection against saying that he has accepted the world of things. But this must not be interpreted as if it meant his acceptance of a *belief* in the reality of the thing world; there is no such belief or assertion or assumption, because it is not a theoretical question. To accept the thing world means nothing more than to accept a certain form of language, in other words, to accept rules for forming statements and for testing, accepting, or rejecting them. The acceptance of the thing language leads, on the basis of observations made, also to the acceptance, belief, and assertion of certain statements. But the thesis of the reality of the thing world cannot be among these statements, because it cannot be formulated in the thing language or, it seems, in any other theoretical language.

The decision of accepting the thing language, although itself not of a cognitive nature, will nevertheless usually be influenced by theoretical knowledge, just like any other deliberate decision concerning the acceptance of linguistic or other rules. The purposes for which the language is intended to be used, for instance, the purpose of communicating factual knowledge, will determine which factors are relevant for the decision. The efficiency, fruitfulness, and simplicity of the use of the thing language may be among the decisive factors. And the questions concerning these qualities are indeed of a theoretical nature. But these questions cannot be identified with the question of realism. They are not yes-no questions but questions of degree. The thing language in the customary form works indeed with a high degree of efficiency for most purposes of everyday life. This is a matter of fact, based upon the content of our experiences. However, it would be wrong to describe this situation by saying: "The fact of the efficiency of the thing language is confirming evidence for the reality of the thing world"; we should rather say instead: "This fact makes it advisable to accept the thing language."

The system of numbers. As an example of a system which is of a logical rather than a factual nature let us take the system of natural numbers. The framework for this system is constructed by introducing into the language new expressions with suitable rules: (i) numerals like "five" and sentence forms like "there are five books on the table"; (2) the general term "number" for the new entities, and sentence forms like "five is a number"; (3) expressions for properties of numbers (e.g., "odd," "prime,"), relations (e.g., "greater than"), and functions (e.g., "plus"), and sentence forms like "two plus three is five"; (4) numerical variables ("*m*," "*n*," etc.) and quantifiers for universal sentences ("for every *n*, . . .") and existential sentences ("there is an *n* such that . . .") with the customary deductive rules.

Here again there are internal questions, e.g., "Is there a prime number greater than a hundred?"

Here, however, the answers are found, not by empirical investigation based on observations, but by logical analysis based on the rules for the new expressions. Therefore the answers are here analytic, i.e., logically true.

What is now the nature of the philosophical question concerning the existence or reality of numbers? To begin with, there is the internal question which, together with the affirmative answer, can be formulated in the new terms, say, by "There are numbers" or, more explicitly, "There is an *n* such that *n* is a number." This statement follows from the analytic statement "five is a number" and is therefore itself analytic. Moreover, it is rather trivial (in contradistinction to a statement like "There is a prime number greater than a million," which is likewise analytic but far from trivial), because it does not say more than that the new system is not empty; but this is immediately seen from the rule which states that words like "five" are substitutable for the new variables. Therefore nobody who meant the question "Are there numbers?" in the internal sense would either assert or even seriously consider a negative answer. This makes it plausible to assume that those philosophers who treat the question of the existence of numbers as a serious philosophical problem and offer lengthy arguments on either side, do not have in mind the internal question. And, indeed, if we were to ask them: "Do you mean the question as to whether the framework of numbers, *if* we were to accept it, would be found to be empty or not?", they would probably reply: "Not at all; we mean a question *prior* to the acceptance of the new framework." They might try to explain what they mean by saying that it is a question of the ontological status of numbers; the question whether or not numbers have a certain metaphysical characteristic called reality (but a kind of ideal reality, different from the material reality of the thing world) or subsistence or status of "independent entities." Unfortunately, these philosophers have so far not given a formulation of their question in terms of the common scientific language. Therefore our judgment must be that they have not succeeded in giving to the external question and to the possible answers any cognitive content. Unless and until they supply a clear cognitive interpretation, we are justified in our suspicion that their question is a pseudo-question, that is, one disguised in the form of a theoretical question while in fact it is non-theoretical; in the present case it is the practical problem whether or not to incorporate into the language the new linguistic forms which constitute the framework of numbers.

The system of propositions. New variables, "*p*," "*q*," etc., are introduced with a rule to the effect that any (declarative) sentence may be substituted for a variable of this kind; this includes, in addition to the sentences of the original thing language, also all general sentences with variables of any kind which may have been introduced into the language. Further, the general term "proposition" is introduced. "*p* is a proposition" may be defined by "*p* or not *p*" (or by any other sentence form yielding only analytic sentences). Therefore, every sentence of the form ". . . is a proposition" (where any sentence may stand in the place of the dots) is analytic. This holds, for example, for the sentence:

(*a*) "Chicago is large is a proposition."

(We disregard here the fact that the rules of English grammar require not a sentence but a that-clause as the subject of another sentence; accordingly, instead of (*a*) we should have to say "That Chicago is large is a proposition.") Predicates may be admitted whose argument expressions are sentences; these predicates may be either extensional (e.g., the customary truth-functional connectives) or not (e.g., modal predicates like "possible," "necessary," etc.). With the help of the new variables, general sentences may be formed, e.g.,

(*b*) "For every *p*, either *p* or not-*p*."

(*c*) "There is a *p* such that *p* is not necessary and not-*p* is not necessary."

(*d*) "There is a *p* such that *p* is a proposition."

(*c*) and (*d*) are internal assertions of existence. The statement "There are propositions" may be meant in the sense of (*d*); in this case it is analytic (since it follows from (*a*)) and even trivial. If, however, the statement is meant in an external sense, then it is non-cognitive.

It is important to notice that the system of rules for the linguistic expressions of the propositional framework (of which only a few rules have here been briefly indicated) is sufficient for the introduction of the framework. Any further explanations as to the nature of the propositions (i.e., the elements of the system indicated, the values of the variables "*p*," "*q*," etc.) are theoretically unnecessary because, if correct, they follow from the rules. For example, are propositions mental events (as in Russell's theory)? A look at the rules shows us that they are not, because otherwise existential statements would be of the form: "If the mental state of the person in question fulfills such and such conditions, then there is a *p* such that. . . ." The fact that no references to mental conditions occur in existential statements (like (*c*), (*d*), etc.) shows that propositions are not mental entities. Further, a statement of the existence of linguistic entities (e.g., expressions, classes of expressions, etc.) must contain a reference to a language. The fact that no such reference occurs in the existential statements here, shows that propositions are not linguistic entities. The fact that in these statements no reference to a subject (an observer or knower) occurs (nothing like: "There is a *p* which is necessary for Mr. *X*"), shows that the propositions (and their properties, like necessity, etc.) are not subjective. Although characterizations of these or similar kinds are, strictly speaking, unnecessary, they may nevertheless be practically useful. If they are given, they should be understood, not as ingredient parts of the system, but merely as marginal notes with the purpose of supplying to the reader helpful hints or convenient pictorial associations which may make his learning of the use of the expressions easier than the bare system of the rules would do. Such a characterization is analogous to an extra-systematic explanation which a physicist sometimes gives to the beginner. He might, for example, tell him to imagine the atoms of a gas as small balls rushing around with great speed, or the electromagnetic field and its oscillations as quasi-elastic tensions and vibrations in an ether. In fact, however, all that can accurately be said about atoms or the field is implicitly contained in the physical laws of the theories in question.[2]

The system of thing properties. The thing language contains words like "red," "hard," "stone," "house," etc., which are used for describing what things are like. Now we may introduce new variables, say "*f*," "*g*," etc., for which those words are substitutable and furthermore the general term "property." New rules are laid down which admit sentences like "Red is a property," "Red is a color," "These two pieces of paper have at least one color in common" (i.e., "There is an *f* such that *f* is a color, and . . ."). The last sentence is an internal assertion. It is of an empirical, factual nature. However, the external statement, the *philosophical statement* of the reality of properties—a special case of the thesis of the reality of universals—is devoid of cognitive content.

The systems of integers and rational numbers. Into a language containing the framework of natural numbers we may introduce first the (positive and negative) integers as relations among natural numbers and then the rational numbers as relations among integers. This involves introducing new types of variables, expressions substitutable for them, and the general terms "integer" and "rational number."

The system of real numbers. On the basis of the rational numbers, the real numbers may be introduced as classes of a special kind (segments) of rational numbers (according to the method developed by Dedekind and Frege). Here again a new type of variables is introduced, expressions substitutable for them (e.g., "$\sqrt{2}$"), and the general term "real number."

The spatio-temporal coordinate system for physics. The new entities are the space-time points. Each is an ordered quadruple of four real numbers, called its coordinates, consisting of three spatial and one temporal coordinates. The physical state of a spatio-temporal point or region is described either with the help of qualitative predicates (e.g., "hot") or by ascribing numbers as values of a physical magnitude (e.g., mass, temperature, and the like). The step from the system of things (which does not contain space-time points but only extended objects with spatial and temporal relations between them) to the physical coordinate system is again a matter of decision. Our choice of certain features, although itself not theoretical, is suggested by theoretical knowledge, either logical or factual. For example, the choice of real numbers rather than rational numbers or integers as coordinates is not much influenced by the facts of experience but mainly due to considerations of mathematical simplicity. The restriction to rational coordinates would not be in conflict with any experimental knowledge we have, because the result of any measurement is a rational number. However, it would prevent the use of ordinary geometry (which says, e.g., that the diagonal of a square with the side 1 has the irrational value $\sqrt{2}$) and thus lead to great complications. On the other hand, the decision to use three rather than two or four spatial coordinates is strongly suggested, but still not forced upon us, by the result of common observations. If certain events allegedly observed in spiritualistic séances, e.g., a ball moving out of a sealed box, were confirmed beyond any reasonable doubt, it might seem advisable to use four spatial coordinates. Internal questions are here, in general, empirical questions to be answered by empirical investigations. On the other hand, the external questions of the reality of physical space and physical time are pseudo-questions. A question like "Are there (really) space-time points? " is ambiguous. It may be meant as an internal question; then the affirmative answer is, of course, analytic and trivial. Or it may be meant in the external sense: "Shall we introduce such and such forms into our language?"; in this case it is not a theoretical but a practical question, a matter of decision rather than assertion, and hence the proposed formulation would be misleading. Or finally, it may be meant in the following sense: "Are our experiences such that the use of the linguistic forms in question will be expedient and fruitful?" This is a theoretical question of a factual, empirical nature. But it concerns a matter of degree; therefore a formulation in the form "real or not?" would be inadequate.

3. WHAT DOES ACCEPTANCE OF A KIND OF ENTITIES MEAN?

Let us now summarize the essential characteristics of situations involving the introduction of a new kind of entities, characteristics which are common to the various examples outlined above.

The acceptance of a new kind of entities is represented in the language by the introduction of a framework of new forms of expressions to be used according to a new set of rules. There may be new names for particular entities of the kind in question; but some such names may already occur in the language before the introduction of the new framework. (Thus, for example, the thing language contains certainly words of the type of "blue" and "house" before the framework of properties is introduced; and it may contain words like "ten" in sentences of the form "I have ten fingers" before the framework of numbers is introduced.) The latter fact shows that the occurrence of constants of the type in question—regarded as names of entities of the new kind after the new framework is introduced—is not a sure sign of the acceptance of the new kind of entities. Therefore the introduction of such constants is not to be regarded as an essential step in the introduction of the framework. The two essential steps are rather the following. First, the introduction of a general term, a predicate of higher level, for the new kind of entities, permitting us to say of any particular entity that it belongs to this kind (e.g., "Red is a *property,*" "Five is a *number*"). Second, the introduction of variables of the new type. The new entities are values of these variables; the constants (and the closed compound expressions, if any) are substitutable for the variables.[3] With the help of the variables, general sentences concerning the new entities can be formulated.

After the new forms are introduced into the language, it is possible to formulate with their help internal questions and possible answers to them. A question of this kind may be either empirical or logical; accordingly a true answer is either factually true or analytic.

From the internal questions we must clearly distinguish external questions, i.e., philosophical questions concerning the existence or reality of the total system of the new entities. Many philosophers regard a question of this kind as an ontological question which must be raised and answered *before* the introduction of the new language forms. The latter introduction, they believe, is legitimate only if it can be justified by an ontological insight supplying an affirmative answer to the question of reality. In contrast to this view, we take the position that the introduction of the new ways of speaking does not need any theoretical justification because it does not imply any assertion of reality. We may still speak (and have done so) of "the acceptance of the new entities" since this form of speech is customary; but one must keep in mind that this phrase does not mean for us anything more than acceptance of the new framework, i.e., of the new linguistic forms. Above all, it must not be interpreted as referring to an assumption, belief, or assertion of "the reality of the entities." There is no such assertion. An alleged statement of the reality of the system of entities is a pseudo-statement without cognitive content. To be sure, we have to face at this point an important question; but it is a practical, not a theoretical question; it is the question of whether or not to accept the new linguistic forms. The acceptance cannot be judged as being either true or false because it is not an assertion. It can only be judged as being more or less expedient, fruitful, conducive to the aim for which the language is intended. Judgments of this kind supply the motivation for the decision of accepting or rejecting the kind of entities.[4]

Thus it is clear that the acceptance of a linguistic framework must not be regarded as implying a metaphysical doctrine concerning the reality of the entities in question. It seems to me due to a neglect of this important distinction that some contemporary nominalists label the admission of variables of abstract types as "Platonism."[5] This is, to say the least, an extremely misleading terminology. It leads to the absurd consequence, that the position of everybody who accepts the language of physics with its real number variables (as a language of communication, not merely as a calculus) would be called Platonistic, even if he is a strict empiricist who rejects Platonic metaphysics.

A brief historical remark may here be inserted. The non-cognitive character of the questions which we have called here external questions was recognized and emphasized already by the Vienna Circle under the leadership of Moritz Schlick, the group from which the movement of logical empiricism originated. Influenced by ideas of Ludwig Wittgenstein, the Circle rejected both the thesis of the reality of the external world and the thesis of its irreality as pseudo-statements[6]; the same was the case for both the thesis of the reality of universals (abstract entities, in our present terminology) and the nominalistic thesis that they are not real and that their alleged names are not names of anything but merely *flatus vocis.* (It is obvious that the apparent negation of a pseudo-statement must also be a pseudo-statement.) It is therefore not correct to classify the members of the Vienna Circle as nominalists, as is sometimes done. However, if we look at the basic anti-metaphysical and pro-scientific attitude of most nominalists (and the same holds for many materialists and realists in the modern sense), disregarding their occasional pseudo-theoretical formulations, then it is, of course, true to say that the Vienna Circle was much closer to those philosophers than to their opponents.

4. ABSTRACT ENTITIES IN SEMANTICS

The problem of the legitimacy and the status of abstract entities has recently again led to controversial discussions in connection with semantics. In a semantical meaning analysis certain expressions in a language are often said to designate (or name or denote or signify or refer to) certain extra-linguistic entities.[7] As long as physical things or events (e.g., Chicago or Caesar's death) are taken as designata (entities designated), no serious doubts arise. But strong objections have been raised, especially by some empiricists, against abstract entities as designata, e.g., against semantical statements of the following kind:

(1) "The word 'red' designates a property of things";

(2) "The word 'color' designates a property of properties of things";

(3) "The word 'five' designates a number";

(4) "The word 'odd' designates a property of numbers";

(5) "The sentence 'Chicago is large' designates a proposition."

Those who criticize these statements do not, of course, reject the use of the expressions in question, like "red" or "five"; nor would they deny that these expressions are meaningful. But to be meaningful, they would say, is not the same as having a meaning in the sense of an entity designated. They reject the belief, which they regard as implicitly presupposed by those semantical statements, that to each expression of the types in question (adjectives like "red," numerals like "five," etc.) there is a particular real entity to which the expression stands in the relation of designation. This belief is rejected as incompatible with the basic principles of empiricism or of scientific thinking. Derogatory labels like "Platonic realism," "hypostatization," or "'Fido'-Fido principle" are attached to it. The latter is the name given by Gilbert Ryle to the criticized belief, which, in his view, arises by a naive inference of analogy: just as there is an entity well known to me, viz. my dog Fido, which is designated by the name "Fido," thus there must be for every meaningful expression a particular entity to which it stands in the relation of designation or naming, i.e., the relation exemplified by "Fido"-Fido. The belief criticized is thus a case of hypostatization, i.e., of treating as names expressions which are not names. While "Fido" is a name, expressions like "red," "five," etc., are said not to be names, not to designate anything.

Our previous discussion concerning the acceptance of frameworks enables us now to clarify the situation with respect to abstract entities as designata. Let us take as an example the statement:

(*a*) "'Five' designates a number."

The formulation of this statement presupposes that our language L contains the forms of expressions which we have called the framework of numbers, in particular, numerical variables and the general term "number." If L contains these forms, the following is an analytic statement in L:

(*b*) "Five is a number."

Further, to make the statement (*a*) possible, L must contain an expression like "designates" or "is a name of" for the semantical relation of designation. If suitable rules for this term are laid down, the following is likewise analytic:

(*c*) "'Five' designates five."

(Generally speaking, any expression of the form "'. . .' designates . . ." is an analytic statement provided the term ". . ." is a constant in an accepted framework. If the latter condition is not fulfilled, the expression is not a statement.) Since (*a*) follows from (*c*) and (*b*), (*a*) is likewise analytic.

Thus it is clear that *if* someone accepts the framework of numbers, then he must acknowledge (*c*) and (*b*) and hence (*a*) as true statements. Generally speaking, if someone accepts a framework for a certain kind of entities, then he is bound to admit the entities as possible designata. Thus the question of the admissibility of entities of a certain type or of abstract entities in general as designata is reduced to the question of the acceptability of the linguistic framework for those entities. Both the nominalistic critics, who refuse the status of designators or names to expressions like "red," "five," etc., because they deny the existence of abstract entities, and the skeptics, who express doubts concerning the existence and demand evidence for it, treat the question of existence as a theoretical question. They do, of course, not mean the internal question; the affirmative answer to *this* question is analytic and trivial and too obvious for doubt or denial, as we have seen. Their doubts refer rather to the system of entities itself; hence they mean the external question. They believe that only after making sure that there really is a system of entities of the kind in question are we justified in accepting the framework by incorporating the linguistic forms into our language. However, we have seen that the external question is not a theoretical question but rather the practical question whether or not to accept those linguistic forms. This acceptance is not in need of a theoretical justification (except with respect to expediency and fruitfulness), because it does not imply a belief or assertion. Ryle says that the "Fido"-Fido principle is "a grotesque theory." Grotesque or not, Ryle is wrong in calling it a theory. It is rather the practical decision to accept certain frameworks. Maybe Ryle is historically right with respect to those whom he mentions as previous representatives of the principle, viz. John Stuart Mill, Frege, and Russell. If these philosophers regarded the acceptance of a system of entities as a theory, an assertion, they were victims of the same old, metaphysical confusion. But it is certainly wrong to regard my semantical method as involving a belief in the reality of abstract entities, since I reject a thesis of this kind as a metaphysical pseudo-statement.

The critics of the use of abstract entities in semantics overlook the fundamental difference between the acceptance of a system of entities and an internal assertion, e.g., an assertion that there are elephants or electrons or prime numbers greater than a million. Whoever makes an internal assertion is certainly obliged to justify it by providing evidence, empirical evidence in the case of electrons, logical proof in the case of the prime numbers. The demand for a theoretical justification, correct in the case of internal assertions, is sometimes wrongly applied to the acceptance of a system of entities. Thus, for example, Ernest Nagel in asks for "evidence relevant for affirming with warrant that there are such entities as infinitesimals or propositions." He characterizes the evidence required in these cases—in distinction to the empirical evidence in the case of electrons—as "in the broad sense logical and dialectical." Beyond this no hint is given as to what might be regarded as relevant evidence. Some nominalists regard the acceptance of abstract entities as a kind of superstition or myth, populating the world with fictitious or at least dubious entities, analogous to the belief in centaurs or demons. This shows again the confusion mentioned, because a superstition or myth is a false (or dubious) internal statement.

Let us take as example the natural numbers as cardinal numbers, i.e., in contexts like "Here are three books." The linguistic forms of the framework of numbers, including variables and the general term "number," are generally used in our common language of communication; and it is easy to formulate explicit rules for their use. Thus the logical characteristics of this framework are sufficiently clear (while many internal questions, i.e., arithmetical questions, are, of course, still open). In spite of this, the controversy concerning the external question of the ontological reality of the system of numbers continues. Suppose that one philosopher says: "I believe that there are numbers as real entities. This gives me the right to use the linguistic forms of the numerical framework and to make semantical statements about numbers as designata of numerals." His nominalistic opponent replies: "You are wrong; there are no numbers. The numerals may still be used as meaningful expressions. But they are not names, there are no entities designated by them. Therefore the word "number" and numerical variables must not be used (unless a way were found to introduce them as merely abbreviating devices, a way of translating them into the nominalistic thing language)." I cannot think of any possible evidence that would be regarded as relevant by both philosophers, and therefore, if actually found, would decide the controversy or at least make one of the opposite theses more probable than the other. (To construe the numbers as classes or properties of the second level, according to the Frege-Russell method, does, of course, not solve the controversy, because the first philosopher would affirm and the second deny the existence of the system of classes or properties of the second level.) Therefore I feel compelled to regard the external question as a pseudo-question, until both parties to the controversy offer a common interpretation of the question as a cognitive question; this would involve an indication of possible evidence regarded as relevant by both sides.

There is a particular kind of misinterpretation of the acceptance of abstract entities in various fields of science and in semantics, that needs to be cleared up. Certain early British empiricists, (e.g., Berkeley and Hume) denied the existence of abstract entities on the ground that immediate experience presents us only with particulars, not with universals, e.g., with this red patch, but not with Redness or Color-in-General; with this scalene triangle, but not with Scalene Triangularity or Triangularity-in-General. Only entities belonging to a type of which examples were to be found within immediate experience could be accepted as ultimate constituents of reality. Thus, according to this way of thinking, the existence of abstract entities could be asserted only if one could show either that some abstract entities fall within the given, or that abstract entities can be defined in terms of the types of entity which are given. Since these empiricists found no abstract entities within the realm of sense-data, they either denied their existence, or else made a futile attempt to define universals in terms of particulars. Some contemporary philosophers, especially English philosophers following Bertrand Russell, think in basically similar terms. They emphasize a distinction between the data (that which is immediately given in consciousness, e.g., sense-data, immediately past experiences, etc.) and the constructs based on the data. Existence or reality is ascribed only to the data; the constructs are not real entities; the corresponding linguistic expressions are merely ways of speech not actually designating anything (reminiscent of the nominalists' *flatus vocis*). We shall not criticize here this general conception. (As far as it is a principle of accepting certain entities and not accepting others, leaving aside any ontological, phenomenalistic and nominalistic pseudo-statements, there cannot be any theoretical objection to it.) But if this conception leads to the view that other philosophers or scientists who accept abstract entities thereby assert or imply their occurrence as immediate data, then such a view must be rejected as a misinterpretation. References to space-time points, the electromagnetic field, or electrons in physics, to real or complex numbers and their functions in mathematics, to the excitatory potential or unconscious complexes in psychology, to an inflationary trend in economics, and the like, do not imply the assertion that entities of these kinds occur as immediate data. And the same holds for references to abstract entities as designata in semantics. Some of the criticisms by English philosophers against such references give the impression that, probably due to the misinterpretation just indicated, they accuse the semanticist not so much of bad metaphysics (as some nominalists would do) but of bad psychology. The fact that they regard a semantical method involving abstract entities not merely as doubtful and perhaps wrong, but as manifestly absurd, preposterous and grotesque, and that they show a deep horror and indignation against this method, is perhaps to be explained by a misinterpretation of the kind described. In fact, of course, the semanticist does not in the least assert or imply that the abstract entities to which he refers can be experienced as immediately given either by sensation or by a kind of rational intuition. An assertion of this kind would indeed be very dubious psychology. The psychological question as to which kinds of entities do and which do not occur as immediate data is entirely irrelevant for semantics, just as it is for physics, mathematics, economics, etc., with respect to the examples mentioned above.[8]

5. CONCLUSION

For those who want to develop or use semantical methods, the decisive question is not the alleged ontological question of the existence of abstract entities but rather the question whether the use of abstract linguistic forms or, in technical terms, the use of variables beyond those for things (or phenomenal data), is expedient and fruitful for the purposes for which semantical analyses are made, viz. the analysis, interpretation, clarification, or construction of languages of communication, especially languages of science. This question is here neither decided nor even discussed. It is not a question simply of yes or no, but a matter of degree. Among those philosophers who have carried out semantical analyses and thought about suitable tools for this work, beginning with Plato and Aristotle and, in a more technical way on the basis of modern logic, with C. S. Peirce and Frege, a great majority accepted abstract entities. This does, of course, not prove the case. After all, semantics in the technical sense is still in the initial phases of its development, and we must be prepared for possible fundamental changes in methods. Let us therefore admit that the nominalistic critics may possibly be right. But if so, they will have to offer better arguments than they have so far. Appeal to ontological insight will not carry much weight. The critics will have to show that it is possible to construct a semantical method which avoids all references to abstract entities and achieves by simpler means essentially the same results as the other methods.

The acceptance or rejection of abstract linguistic forms, just as the acceptance or rejection of any other linguistic forms in any branch of science, will finally be decided by their efficiency as instruments, the ratio of the results achieved to the amount and complexity of the efforts required. To decree dogmatic prohibitions of certain linguistic forms instead of testing them by their success or failure in practical use, is worse than futile; it is positively harmful because it may obstruct scientific progress. The history of science shows examples of such prohibitions based on prejudices deriving from religious, mythological, metaphysical, or other irrational sources, which slowed up the developments for shorter or longer periods of time. Let us learn from the lessons of history. Let us grant to those who work in any special field of investigation the freedom to use any form of expression which seems useful to them; the work in the field will sooner or later lead to the elimination of those forms which have no useful function. *Let us be cautious in making assertions and critical in examining them, but tolerant in permitting linguistic forms.*

NOTES

1. The terms "sentence" and "statement" are here used synonymously for declarative (indicative, propositional) sentences.

2. In my book *Meaning and Necessity* (Chicago, 1947) I have developed a semantical method which takes propositions as entities designated by sentences (more specifically, as intensions of sentences). In order to facilitate the understanding of the systematic development, I added some informal, extra-systematic explanations concerning the nature of propositions. I said that the term "proposition" "is used neither for a linguistic expression nor for a subjective, mental occurrence, but rather for something objective that may or may not be exemplified in nature. . . . We apply the term 'proposition' to any entities of a certain logical type, namely, those that may be expressed by (declarative) sentences in a language" (p. 27). After some more detailed discussions concerning the relation between propositions and facts, and the nature of false propositions, I added: "It has been the purpose of the preceding remarks to facilitate the understanding of our conception of propositions. If, however, a reader should find these explanations more puzzling than clarifying, or even unacceptable, he may disregard them" (p. 31) (that is, disregard these extra-systematic explanations, not the whole theory of the propositions as intensions of sentences, as one reviewer understood). In spite of this warning, it seems that some of those readers who were puzzled by the explanations, did not disregard them but thought that by raising objections against them they could refute the theory. This is analogous to the procedure of some laymen who by (correctly) criticizing the ether picture or other visualizations of physical theories, thought they had refuted those theories. Perhaps the discussions in the present paper will help in clarifying the role of the system of linguistic rules for the introduction of a framework for entities on the one hand, and that of extra-systematic explanations concerning the nature of the entities on the other.

3. W. V. Quine was the first to recognize the importance of the introduction of variables as indicating the acceptance of entities. "The ontology to which one's use of language commits him comprises simply the objects that he treats as falling . . . within the range of values of his variables." "Notes on Existence and Necessity," *Journal of Philosophy,* 40 (1943), 113–127.

4. For a closely related point of view on these questions tions see the detailed discussions in Herbert Feigl, "Existential Hypotheses," *Philosophy of Science,* 17 (1950), 35–62.

5. Paul Bernays, "Sur le platonisme dans les mathématiques" (*L'Enseignement math.,* 34 (1935), 52–69). W. V. Quine, see previous footnote and a recent paper "On What There Is," in this volume. Quine does not acknowledge the distinction which I emphasize above, because according to his general conception there are no sharp boundary lines between logical and factual truth, between questions of meaning and questions of fact, between the acceptance of a language structure and the acceptance of an assertion formulated in the language. This conception, which seems to deviate considerably from customary ways of thinking, will be explained in his article "Semantics and Abstract Objects," *Proceedings of the American Academy of Arts and Sciences,* 80 (1951), 90–96. When Quine classifies my logicistic conception of mathematics (derived from Frege and Russell) as "platonic realism" (p. 212 in this volume), this is meant (according to a personal communication from him) not as ascribing to me agreement with Plato's metaphysical doctrine of universals, but merely as referring to the fact that I accept a language of mathematics containing variables of higher levels. With respect to the basic attitude to take in choosing a language form (an "ontology" in Quine's terminology, which seems to me misleading), there appears now to be agreement between us: "the obvious counsel is tolerance and an experimental spirit" (p. 215 in this volume).

6. See Carnap, *Scheinprobleme in der Philosophie; das Fremdpsychische und der Realismusstreit,* Berlin, 1928.

Moritz Schlick, *Positivismus und Realismus,* reprinted in *Gesammelte Aufsätze,* Wien, 1938.

7. See [I]; *Meaning and Necessity* (Chicago, 1947). The distinction I have drawn in the latter book between the method of the name-relation and the method of intension and extension is not essential for our present discussion. The term "designation" is used in the present article in a neutral way; it may be understood as referring to the name-relation or to the intension-relation or to the extension-relation or to any similar relations used in other semantical methods.

8. Wilfrid Sellars ("Acquaintance and Description Again," in *Journal of Philosophy,* 46 (1949), 496–504; see pp. 502f.) analyzes clearly the roots of the mistake "of taking the designation relation of semantic theory to be a reconstruction of *being present to an experience.*"

Reading Questions

1. Is this question an internal one or an external one: "Is the internal/external question dichotomy legitimate?"
2. Carnap states that external questions are a matter of practical decision and are not theoretical issues. Therefore if the internal/external dichotomy is external, we can choose to accept it or not on pragmatic grounds. Is this a problem for Carnap?
3. Does Carnap propose a test procedure for distinguishing which questions are internal ones and which external? If so, what is it?
4. At times Carnap states that it is an illegitimate question to ask whether there really are abstract objects or not. It would be analogous to asking whether, apart from the framework of any map, Canada is *really* above the United States. The question is sensible only as an internal question, relative to some particular system of cartography. At other points, Carnap implies that the existence of abstract objects ought to be considered a pseudo-question until all disputants agree as to what kind of evidence would be relevant to deciding. Then it becomes a meaningful question. Are these two Carnapian positions consistent? If not, which one is his considered view?

On Carnap's Analysis of Statements of Assertion and Belief 16

ALONZO CHURCH

I

FOR STATEMENTS SUCH AS (1) *Seneca said that man is a rational animal* and (A) *Columbus believed the world to be round,* the most obvious analysis makes them statements about certain abstract entities which we shall call 'propositions' (though this is not the same as Carnap's use of the term), namely the proposition that man is a rational animal and the proposition that the world is round; and these propositions are taken as having been respectively the object of an assertion by Seneca and the object of a belief by Columbus. We shall not discuss this obvious analysis here except to admit that it threatens difficulties and complications of its own, which appear as soon as the attempt is made to formulate systematically the syntax of a language in which statements like (1) and (A) are possible. But our purpose is to point out what we believe may be an insuperable objection against alternative analyses that undertake to do away with propositions in favour of such more concrete things as sentences.

From Analysis, *vol. 10 (1950), pp. 97–99. Reprinted by permission of the estate of Alonzo Church.*

As attempts which have been or might be made to analyze (1) in terms in sentences we cite: (2) *Seneca wrote the words 'Man is a rational animal'*; (3) *Seneca wrote the words 'Rationale enim animal est homo'*; (4) *Seneca wrote words whose translation from Latin into English is 'Man is a rational animal'*; (5) *Seneca wrote words whose translation from some language S′ into English is 'Man is a rational animal'*; (6) *There is a language S′ such that Seneca wrote a sentence of S′ words whose translation from S′ into English is 'Man is a rational animal.'* In each case, 'wrote' is to be understood in the sense, "wrote with assertive intent." And to simplify the discussion, we ignore the existence of spoken languages, and treat all languages as written.

Of these proposed analyses of (1), we must reject (2) on the ground that it is no doubt false although (1) is true. And each of (3)–(6), though having the same truth-value as (1), must be rejected on the ground that it does not convey the same information as (1). Thus (1) conveys the content of what Seneca said without revealing his actual words, while (3) reproduces Seneca's words without saying what meaning was attached to them. In (4) the crucial information is omitted (without which (1) is not even a consequence) that Seneca intended his words as a Latin sentence, rather than as a sentence of some other language in which conceivably the identical words 'Rationale enim animal est homo' might have some quite different meaning. To (5) the objection is the same as to (4), and indeed if we take 'language' in the abstract sense of Carnap's 'semantical system' (so that it is not part of the concept of a language that a language must have been used in historical fact by some human kindred or tribe), then (5) is L-equivalent merely to the statement that Seneca once wrote something.

(5) and (6) are closely similar to the analysis of belief statements which is offered by Carnap in "Meaning and Necessity," and although he does not say so explicitly it seems clear that Carnap must have intended also such an analysis as this for statements of assertion. However, (6) is likewise unacceptable as an analysis of (1). For it is not even possible to infer (1) as a consequence of (6), on logical grounds alone—but only by making use of the item of factual information, not contained in (6), that 'Man is a rational animal' means in English that man is a rational animal.

Following a suggestion of Langford we may bring out more sharply the inadequacy of (6) as an analysis of (1) by translating into another language, say German, and observing that the two translated statements would obviously convey different meanings to a German (whom we may suppose to have no knowledge of English). The German translation of (1) is (1′) *Seneca hat gesagt, dass der Mensch ein vernünftiges Tier sei*. In translating (6), of course 'English' must be translated as 'Englisch' (not as 'Deutsch') and "Man is a rational animal" must be translated as "Man is a rational animal" (not as "Der Mensch ist ein vernünftiges Tier").

Replacing the use of translation (as it appears in (6)) by the stronger requirement of intensional isomorphism, Carnap would analyze the belief statement (A) as follows: (B) *There is a sentence* $\mathfrak{I}_i$ *in a semantical system S′ such that (a) is intensionally isomorphic to 'The world is round' and (b) Columbus was disposed to an affirmative response to* $\mathfrak{I}_i$. However, intensional isomorphism, as appears from Carnap's definition of it, is a relation between ordered pairs consisting each of a sentence and a semantical system. Hence (B) must be rewritten as: (c) *There is a sentence* $\mathfrak{I}_i$ *in a semantical system S′ such that (a)* $\mathfrak{I}_i$ *as sentence of S′ is intensionally isomorphic to 'The world is round' as English sentence and (b) Columbus was disposed to an affirmative response to* $\mathfrak{I}_i$ *as sentence of S′*.

For the analysis of (1), the analogue of (C) would seem to be: (7) *There is a sentence* $\mathfrak{I}_i$ *in a semantical system S′ such that (a)* $\mathfrak{I}_i$ *as sentence of S′ is intensionally isomorphic to 'Man is a rational animal' as English sentence and (b) Seneca wrote* $\mathfrak{I}_i$ *as sentence of S′*.

Again Langford's device of translation makes evident the untenability of (C) as an analysis of (A), and of (7) as an analysis of (1).

II

The foregoing assumes that the word 'English' in English and the word 'Englisch' in German have a sense which includes a reference to matters of pragmatics (in the sense of Morris and Carnap)-something like, e.g., "the language which was current in Great Britain and the United States in 1949 A.D."

As an alternative we might consider taking the sense of these words to be something like "the language for which such and such semantical rules hold," a sufficient list of rules being given to ensure that there is only one language satisfying the description. The objection would then be less immediate that (1) is not a logical consequence of (6) or (7), and it is possible that it would disappear.

In order to meet this latter alternative without discussing in detail the list of semantical rules which would be required, we modify as follows the objection to (7) as an analysis of (1). Analogous to the proposal, for English, to analyze (1) as (7) we have, for German, the proposal to analyze (1') as (7') *Es gibt einen Satz* $\mathfrak{S}_i$ *auf einem semantischen System S', so dass (a)* $\mathfrak{S}_i$ *als Satz von S' intensional isomorph zu 'Der Mensch is ein vernünftiges Tier' als deutscher Satz ist, und (b) Seneca* $\mathfrak{S}_i$ *als Satz von S' geschrieben hat.* Because of the exact parallelism between them, the two proposals stand or fall together, yet (7') in German and (7) in English are not in any acceptable sense translations of each other. In particular, they are not intensionally isomorphic. And if we consider the English sentence (α) *John believes that Seneca said that man is a rational animal* and its German translation (α'), we see that the sentences to which we are led as supposed analyses of (α) and (α') may even have opposite truth-values in their respective languages; for John, though knowing the semantical rules of both English and German, may nevertheless fail to draw certain of the logical (or other) consequences.

Reading Questions

1. Church considers whether "Seneca said that man is a rational animal" can be paraphrased into "Seneca said words whose translation from Latin into English is 'man is a rational animal.'" He argues that this is an inadequate paraphrase since it omits the information that Seneca intended his words as a Latin sentence. But how is a propositional account superior? Neither "Seneca expressed the proposition that man is a rational animal" nor "Seneca expressed the proposition that man is a rational animal by saying the Latin words *rationale enim animal est homo*" show anything about what Seneca intended. Should a semantic account of sentence meaning include the speaker's intentions?
2. Church states that the English sentence A: "Seneca said that man is a rational animal" means the same as the German sentence B: "*Seneca hat gesagt das der Mensch ein vernünftiges Tier sei.*" Put another way, B is a translation of A. Carnap's theory provides an analysis of A (call it A*) and an analysis of B (call it B*). Church argues that Carnap's theory is adequate only if B* is a translation of A*. Why does Church think B* cannot translate A*? Is his translation requirement correct?

17 Meaning and Truth

W. V. Quine

OBJECTION TO PROPOSITIONS

When someone speaks truly, what makes his statement true? We tend to feel that there are two factors: meaning and fact. A German utters a declarative sentence: 'Der Schnee ist weiss.' In so doing he speaks truly, thanks to the happy concurrence of two circumstances: his sentence means that snow is white, and in point of fact, snow *is* white. If meanings had been different, if 'weiss' had meant green, then in uttering what he did he would not have spoken truly. If the facts had been different, if snow had been red, then again he would not have spoken truly.

What I have just said has a reassuring air of platitude about it, and at the same time it shows disturbing signs of philosophical extravagance. The German utters his declarative sentence; also there is this white snow all around; so far so good. But must we go on and appeal also to intangible intervening elements, a meaning and a fact? The *meaning* of the *sentence* is that snow is white, and the *fact* of the *matter* is that snow is white. The meaning of the sentence and the fact of the matter here are apparently identical, or at any rate they have the same name: that snow is white. And it is apparently because of this identity, or homonymy, that the German may be said to have spoken truly. His meaning matches the fact.

This has the ring of a correspondence theory of truth, but as a theory it is a hollow mockery. The correspondence holds only between two intangibles that we have invoked as intervening elements between the German sentence and the white snow.

Someone may protest that I am being too severely literalistic about this seeming invocation of intervening elements. He may protest that when we speak of meaning as a factor in the truth of what the German said, we are merely saying, somewhat figuratively, what nobody can deny; namely, that if, for instance, the word 'weiss' were applied in German to green things instead of white ones, then what the German said about snow would have been false. He may protest likewise that the seeming reference to a fact, as something over and above the snow and its color, is only a manner of speaking.

Very well; as long as we can view matters thus, I have no complaint. But there has long been a strong trend in the philosophy of logic that cannot be thus excused. It is on meanings of sentences, rather than on facts, that this trend has offended most. Meanings of sentences are exalted as abstract entities in their own right, under the name of *propositions*. These, not the sentences themselves, are seen as the things that are true or false. These are the things also that stand in the logical relation of implication. These are the things also that are known or believed or disbelieved and are found obvious or surprising.

Philosophers' tolerance toward propositions has been encouraged partly by ambiguity in the term 'proposition.' The term often is used simply for the sentences themselves, declarative sentences; and then some writers who do use the term for meanings of sentences are careless about the distinction between sentences and their meanings. In inveighing against propositions in ensuing pages, I shall of course be inveighing against them always in the sense of sentence meanings.

Some philosophers, commendably diffident about positing propositions in this bold sense, have taken refuge in the word 'statement.' The opening question of this chapter illustrates this evasive use. My inveterate use of 'statement' in earlier books does not; I there used the word merely to refer to declarative sentences, and said so. Later I gave up the word in the face of the growing tendency at

From Philosophy of Logic, *by W. V. Quine. Englewood Cliffs: Prentice Hall, 1970. Reprinted by permission of the author.*

Oxford to use the word for acts that we perform in uttering declarative sentences. Now by appealing to statements in such a sense, instead of to propositions, certainly no clarity is gained. I shall say no more about statements, but will go on about propositions.

Once a philosopher, whether through inattention to ambiguity or simply through an excess of hospitality, has admitted propositions to his ontology, he invariably proceeds to view propositions rather than sentences as the things that are true and false. He feels he thereby gains directness, saving a step. Thus let us recall the German. He spoke truly, we saw, inasmuch as (1) 'Der Schnee ist weiss' means that the snow is white and (2) snow *is* white. Now our propositionalist saves step (1). The proposition, that snow is white, is true simply inasmuch as (2) snow *is* white. The propositionalist bypasses differences between languages; also differences of formulation within a language.

My objection to recognizing propositions does not arise primarily from philosophical parsimony—from a desire to dream of no more things in heaven and earth than need be. Nor does it arise, more specifically, from particularism—from a disapproval of intangible or abstract entities. My objection is more urgent. If there were propositions, they would induce a certain relation of synonymy or equivalence between sentences themselves: those sentences would be equivalent that expressed the same proposition. Now my objection is going to be that the appropriate equivalence relation makes no objective sense at the level of sentences. This, if I succeed in making it plain, should spike the hypothesis of propositions.

PROPOSITIONS AS INFORMATION

It is commonplace to speak of sentences as alike or unlike in meaning. This is such everyday, unphilosophical usage that it is apt to seem clearer than it really is. In fact it is vague, and the force of it varies excessively with the special needs of the moment. Thus suppose we are reporting a man's remark in indirect quotation. We are supposed to supply a sentence that is like his in meaning. In such a case we may be counted guilty of distorting his meaning when we so much as substitute a derogatory word for a neutral word having the same reference. Our substitution misrepresents his attitude and, therewith, his meaning. Yet on another occasion, where the interest is in relaying objective information without regard to attitudes, our substitution of the derogatory word for the neutral one will not be counted as distorting the man's meaning. Similar shifting of standards of likeness of meaning is evident in literary translation, according as our interest is in the poetic qualities of the passage or in the objective information conveyed.

The kind of likeness of meaning that is relevant to our present concerns, namely sameness of proposition, is the second of the alternatives mentioned in each of these examples. It is sameness of objective information, without regard to attitudes or to poetic qualities. If the notion of objective information were itself acceptably clear, there would be no quarrel with propositions.

The notion of information is indeed clear enough, nowadays, when properly relativized. It is central to the theory of communication. It makes sense relative to one or another preassigned matrix of alternatives—one or another checklist. You have to say in advance what features are going to count. Thus consider the familiar halftone method of photographic illustration. There is a screen, say six by six inches, containing a square array of regularly spaced positions, say a hundred to the inch in rows and columns. A halftone picture is completely determined by settling which of these 360,000 points are black. Relative to this screen as the matrix of alternatives, information consists in saying which places are black. Two paintings give the same information, relative to this matrix, when they determine the same points as black. Differences in color are, so to speak, purely stylistic relative to this matrix; they convey no information. The case is similar even for differences in shape or position, when these are too slight to be registered in the dots of the halftone. Relative to this matrix, furthermore, a verbal specification of the dots gives the same information as did the painting. (This is the principle of transmitting pictures by telegraph.) And of course two verbal accounts can give the information in very different phrasing; one of them might give the information by saying which positions are white instead of black.

Sameness of information thus stands forth clear against a preassigned matrix of black and white alternatives. But a trouble with trying to equate sentences in real life, in respect of the information they convey is that no matrix of alternatives is given; we do not know what to count. There is no evident rule for separating the information from stylistic or other immaterial features of the sentences. The question when to say that two sentences mean the same proposition is consequently not adequately answered by alluding to sameness of objective information. This only rephrases the problem.

Ideally, a particle physics does offer a matrix of alternatives and therewith an absolute concept of objective information. Two sentences agree in objective information, and so express the same proposition, when every cosmic distribution of particles that would make either sentence true would make the other true as well. Each distribution of elementary particles of specified kinds over total space-time may be called a possible world; and then two sentences mean the same proposition when they are true in all the same possible worlds. The truths of pure mathematics and logic stand at an extreme, true in *all* possible worlds. The class of possible worlds in which a sentence comes out true is, we might say, the sentence's objective information—indeed, its proposition. But still this idea affords us no general way of equating sentences in real life. For surely we can never hope to arrive at a technique for so analyzing our ordinary sentences as to reveal their implications in respect of the distribution of particles.

A different way of reckoning objective information is suggested by the empiricist tradition in epistemology. Say what difference the truth or falsity of a sentence would make to possible experience, and you have said all there is to say about the meaning of the sentence; such, in substantially the words of C. S. Peirce, is the verification theory of meaning. This theory can be seen still as identifying the proposition or meaning of a sentence with the information conveyed; but the matrix of alternatives to be used in defining information is now the totality of possible distinctions and combinations of sensory input. Some epistemologists would catalog these alternatives by introspection of sense data. Others, more naturalistically inclined, would look to neural stimulation; the organism's triggered nerve endings are the analogues of the halftone's black dots. Either way, however, a doctrine of propositions as empirical meanings runs into trouble. The trouble comes, as we shall now see, in trying to distribute the sensory evidence over separate sentences.

DIFFUSENESS OF EMPIRICAL MEANING

Suppose an experiment has yielded a result contrary to a theory currently held in some natural science. The theory comprises a whole bundle of conjoint hypotheses, or is resoluble into such a bundle. The most that the experiment shows is that at least one of those hypotheses is false; it does not show which. It is only the theory as a whole, and not any one of the hypotheses, that admits of evidence or counter-evidence in observation and experiment.

And how wide is a theory? No part of science is quite isolated from the rest. Parts as disparate as you please may be expected to share laws of logic and arithmetic, anyway, and to share various common-sense generalities about bodies in motion. Legalistically, one could claim that evidence counts always for or against the total system, however loose-knit, of science. Evidence against the system is not evidence against any one sentence rather than another, but can be acted on rather by any of various adjustments.

An important exception suggests itself: surely an observation is evidence for the sentence that reports that very observation, and against the sentence that predicted the contrary. Our legalist can stand his ground even here, pointing out that in an extreme case, where beliefs that have been supported overwhelmingly from time immemorial are suddenly challenged by a single contrary observation, the observation will be dismissed as illusion. What is more important, however, is that usually observation sentences are indeed individually responsive to observation. This is what distinguishes observation sentences from theoretical sentences.

It is only through the responsiveness of observation sentences individually to observation, and through the connections in turn of theoretical sentences to observation sentences, that a scientific theory admits of evidence at all.

Why certain sentences are thus individually responsive to observations becomes evident when we think about how we learn language. Many expressions, including most of our earliest, are learned *ostensively;* they are learned in the situation that they describe, or in the presence of the things that they describe. They are conditioned, in short, to observations; and to publicly shared observations, since both teacher and learner have to see the appropriateness of the occasion. Now if an expression is learned in this way by everyone, everyone will tend uniformly to apply it in the presence of the same stimulations. This uniformity affords, indeed, a behavioral criterion of what to count as an observation sentence. It is because of this uniformity, also, that scientists who are checking one another's evidence gravitate to observation sentences as a point where concurrence is assured.

We learn further expressions contextually in ways that generate a fabric of sentences, complexly interconnected. The connections are such as to incline us to affirm or deny some of these sentences when inclined to affirm or deny others. These are the connections through which a theory of nature imbibes its empirical substance from the observation sentences. They are also the connections whereby, in an extremity, our theory of nature may tempt us to ignore or disavow an observation, though it would be regrettable to yield often to this temptation.

The hopelessness of distributing empirical information generally over separate sentences, or even over fairly large bundles of sentences, is in some sense widely recognized, if only by implication. For, look at it this way. It will be widely agreed that our theory of nature is under-determined by our data; and not only by the observations we actually have made and will make, but even by all the unobserved events that are of an observable kind. Briefly, our theory of nature is under-determined by all "possible" observations. This means that there can be a set H of hypotheses, and an alternative set H' incompatible with H, and it can happen that when our total theory T is changed to the extent of putting H' for H in it, the resulting theory T' still fits all possible observations just as well as T did. Evidently then H and H' convey the same empirical information, as far as empirical information can be apportioned to H and H' at all; but still they are incompatible. This reflection should scotch any general notion of propositions as empirical meanings of sentences.

Why then is the notion so stubborn? Partly because the separate sentences of science and common sense do in practice seem after all to carry their separate empirical meanings. This is misleading, and explicable. Thus suppose that from a combined dozen of our theoretical beliefs a scientist derives a prediction in molecular biology, and the prediction fails. He is apt to scrutinize for possible revision only the half dozen beliefs that belonged to molecular biology rather than tamper with the more general half dozen having to do with logic and arithmetic and the gross behavior of bodies. This is a reasonable strategy—a maxim of minimum mutilation. But an effect of it is that the portion of theory to which the discovered failure of prediction is relevant seems narrower than it otherwise might.

Probably, moreover, he will not even confront the six beliefs from molecular biology impartially with the failure of prediction; he will concentrate on one of the six, which was more suspect than the rest. Scientists are indeed forever devising experiments for the express purpose of testing single hypotheses; and this is reasonable, insofar as one hypothesis has been fixed upon as more tentative and suspect than other parts of the theory.

It would be a mistake, however, to see the scientist's move as one of questioning a single hypothesis while keeping *all* else fixed. His experiment is prompted by suspicion of one hypothesis, yes; and if the test proves negative he is resolved to reject that hypothesis, but not quite it alone. Along with it he will reject also any which, as he says, imply it. I must not myself now lean on a notion of implication, for I am challenging that notion (or the associated notion of equivalence, which is simply mutual implication). But we do have to recognize that sentences are interconnected by means of associations entrenched in behavior.

There are the complex interconnections lately remarked upon: connections of varying strengths that incline us to affirm or deny some sentences when affirming or denying others. Whoever rejects one hypothesis will be led by these habit patterns to reject other sentences with it.

The scientist's strategy of dividing and conquering serves science well, but it does not show how to allocate separate empirical evidence to separate sentences. We can allocate separate evidence to each observation sentence, but that is about the end of it.

PROPOSITIONS DISMISSED

The uncritical acceptance of propositions as meanings of sentences is one manifestation of a widespread myth of meaning. It is as if there were a gallery of ideas, and each idea were tagged with the expression that means it; each proposition, in particular, with an appropriate sentence. In criticism of this attitude I have been airing the problem of individuation of propositions. In this connection a passing attraction of an empirical theory of meaning was the fairly clear individuation enjoyed by the domain of sensory evidence. However, we have since been finding reason to despair of this line.

The question how to individuate propositions is the question how to define equivalence of sentences—if not empirical equivalence, at any rate "cognitive" equivalence geared somehow to truth conditions. It may be well now to note and reject another inviting idea in this direction, an idea other than empirical equivalence, just to enhance our appreciation of the problem. We can define, it would seem, a strong synonymy relation for single words simply by requiring that they be interchangeable *salva veritate*. That is, putting the one word for the other always preserves the truth value of the context, turning truths into truths and falsehoods into falsehoods. More generally a word and a phrase, for example, 'bachelor' and 'unmarried man,' may be called synonymous when always interchangeable *salva veritate*. Afterward we can turn about and call two sentences equivalent, in a strong sense, when they are built up of corresponding parts which are pairwise synonymous in the above sense.

Here, evidently, is a tricky way of promoting a weak relation, mere sameness of truth value, into a strong equivalence relation by sheer force of numbers. The equivalent sentences are parallel structures whose corresponding parts are related each to each by the strong relation of being interchangeable *salva veritate* in *all* sentences. The equivalence relation thus obtained has the drawback of requiring parallel structure; but this limitation can be eased somewhat by listing also some allowable grammatical transformations.

Let us now think critically about the synonymy of words to words and phrases. Consider the terms 'creature with a heart,' briefly 'cordate,'[1] and 'creature with kidneys,' briefly 'renate.' All four terms are true of just the same creatures, but still of course we should not like to call them synonymous. They invite the title of synonymy only in pairs, 'cordate' with 'creature with a heart' and 'renate' with 'creature with kidneys.' Now how, in these cases, does our contemplated definition of synonymy fare—namely, interchangeability *salva veritate*? Can we show interchangeability of 'cordate' with 'creature with a heart,' and yet failure of interchangeability of 'cordate' with 'renate'?

Perhaps we can, perhaps not; it all depends on what resources of contextual material we suppose to be available elsewhere in our language. If, for instance, the context:

(1) Necessarily all cordates are cordates

is available in the language, then the desired contrast seems to work out. Interchangeability of 'cordate' with 'renate' fails, as desired; for, putting 'renates' for the second occurrence of 'cordates' in the true sentence (1), we get a falsehood. At the same time, as desired, 'cordate' remains interchangeable with 'creature with a heart,' at least in the example (1); for necessarily all cordates, by definition, have hearts.

But this successful contrast depends oddly on the resources of the language. If the adverb 'necessarily' had not been available, and in such a sense as to fail for 'all cordates are renates' and hold for 'all cordates have hearts,' then this particular contrast between synonymy and failure of synonymy would have been denied us. And the unsatisfactory thing about this dependence is that the adverb 'necessarily,' in the needed sense, is exactly as obscure as the notions of synonymy and equivalence that we are trying in the end to justify. If we had been content with this adverb, we could have defined equivalence in a moment: sentences are equivalent if, necessarily, they are either both true or both false.

True, other examples could be cited. The example:

(2) Tom thinks all cordates are cordates

serves as well as (1), since Tom might well not think that all cordates are renates, while still recognizing that all cordates have hearts. And (2) has the advantage of being couched in more innocent language than (1) with its cooked-up sense of necessity. However, innocence is one thing, clarity another. The 'thinks' idiom in (2), for all its ordinariness, is heir to all the obscurities of the notions of synonymy and equivalence and more.

Anyway, the 'thinks' idiom can scarcely be said to be more ordinary than the notion of equivalence. It is not as though equivalence were a new and technical notion, needing still to be paraphrased into ordinary language. On the contrary, the term is itself ordinary, for all its obscurity. The idea of equivalence, "cognitive" equivalence, seems to make sense as it stands, until scrutinized. It is only mutual implication, after all, and implication is only deducibility. The complaint against these notions is not lack of familiarity, but lack of clarity.

Are all these notions to be dispensed with in serious science? In large part I think they are. [Elsewhere the author examines and defends certain narrowly logical notions of equivalence and deducibility. -ed.] Also there are relativized usages that account for much of the everyday utility of these terms; we speak of equivalence or deducibility relative to one or another tacitly accepted corpus of background information. But none of those uses, of which fair sense can be made, is of any evident avail in individuating propositions.

The doctrine of propositions seems in a way futile on the face of it, even if we imagine the individuation problem solved. For, that solution would consist in some suitable definition of equivalence of sentences; why not then just talk of sentences and equivalence and let the propositions go? The long and short of it is that propositions have been projected as shadows of sentences, if I may transplant a figure of Wittgenstein's. At best they will give us nothing the sentences will not give. Their promise of more is mainly due to our uncritically assuming for them an individuation which matches no equivalence between sentences that we see how to define. The shadows have favored wishful thinking.

TRUTH AND SEMANTIC ASCENT

Philosophers who favor propositions have said that propositions are needed because truth only of propositions, not of sentences, is intelligible. An unsympathetic answer is that we can explain truth of sentences to the propositionalist in his own terms: sentences are true whose meanings are true propositions. Any failure of intelligibility here is already his own fault.

But there is a deeper and vaguer reason for his feeling that truth is intelligible primarily for propositions. It is that truth should hinge on reality not language; sentences are language. His way of producing a reality for truth to hinge on is shabby, certainly: an imaginary projection from sentences. But he is right that truth should hinge on reality, and it does. No sentence is true but reality makes it so. The sentence 'Snow is white' is true, as Tarski has taught us, if and only if real snow is really white. The same can be said of the sentence 'Der Schnee ist weiss'; language is not the point. In speaking of the truth of a given sentence there is only indirection; we do better simply to say the sentence and so speak not about language but about the world. So long as we are speaking only of the truth of singly given sentences, the perfect theory of truth is what Wilfrid Sellars has called the disappearance theory of truth.

Truth hinges on reality; but to object, on this score, to calling sentences true, is a confusion. Where the truth predicate has its utility is in just those places where, though still concerned with reality, we are impelled by certain technical complications to mention sentences. Here the truth predicate serves, as it were, to point through the sentence to the reality; it serves as a reminder that though sentences are mentioned, reality is still the whole point.

What, then, are the places where, though still concerned with unlinguistic reality, we are moved to proceed indirectly and talk of sentences? The important places of this kind are places where we are seeking generality, and seeking it along certain oblique planes that we cannot sweep out by generalizing over objects.

We can generalize on 'Tom is mortal,' 'Dick is mortal,' and so on, without talking of truth or of sentences; we can say 'All men are mortal.' We can generalize similarly on 'Tom is Tom,' 'Dick is Dick,' '0 is 0,' and so on, saying 'Everything is itself.' When on the other hand we want to generalize on 'Tom is mortal or Tom is not mortal,' 'Snow is white or snow is not white,' and so on, we ascend to talk of truth and of sentences, saying 'Every sentence of the form '*p* or not *p*' is true,' or 'Every alternation of a sentence with its negation is true.' What prompts this semantic ascent is not that 'Tom is mortal or Tom is not mortal' is somehow about sentences while 'Tom is mortal' and 'Tom is Tom' are about Tom. All three are about Tom. We ascend only because of the oblique way in which the instances over which we are generalizing are related to one another.

We were able to phrase our generalization 'Everything is itself' without such ascent just because the changes that were rung in passing from instance to instance—'Tom is Tom,' 'Dick is Dick,' '0 is 0'—were changes in names. Similarly for 'All men are mortal.' This generalization may be read '*x* is mortal for all *men x*'—all things *x* of the sort that 'Tom' is a name of. But what would be a parallel reading of the generalization of 'Tom is mortal or Tom is not mortal'? It would read '*p* or not *p* for all things *p* of the sort that sentences are names of.' But sentences are not names, and this reading is simply incoherent; it uses '*p*' both in positions that call for sentence clauses and in a position that calls for a noun substantive. So, to gain our desired generality, we go up one step and talk about sentences: 'Every *sentence* of the *form* '*p* or not *p*' is *true*.'

The incoherent alternative reading might of course be expressly accorded meaning, if there were anything to gain by so doing. One could cause sentences to double as names, by specifying what they were to be names of. One might declare them to be names of propositions. In earlier pages, when propositions were still under advisement, I represented propositions as the meanings of sentences rather than as things named by sentences; still one could declare them to be named by sentences, and some there are who have done so. Until such a line is adopted, the letter '*p*' is no variable ranging over objects; it is only a schematic letter for sentences, only a dummy to mark a position appropriate to a component sentence in some logical form or grammatical construction. Once the sentences are taken as names of propositions, on the other hand, the letter '*p*' comes to double as a variable ranging over objects which are propositions. Thereafter we can coherently say '*p* or not *p* for all propositions *p*.'

However, this move has the drawback of reinstating propositions, which we saw reason not to welcome. Moreover, the move brings no visible benefit; for we already saw how to express generalizations of the desired sort without appeal to propositions, by just going up a step and attributing truth to sentences. This ascent to a linguistic plane of reference is only a momentary retreat from the world, for the utility of the truth predicate is precisely the cancellation of linguistic reference. The truth predicate is a reminder that, despite a technical ascent to talk of sentences, our eye is on the world. This cancellatory force of the truth predicate is explicit in Tarski's paradigm:

> 'Snow is white' is true if and only if snow is white.

Quotation marks make all the difference between talking about words and talking about snow. The quotation is a name of a sentence that contains a name, namely 'snow,' of snow. By calling the sentence true, we call snow white. The truth predicate is a device of disquotation. We may affirm the single sentence by just uttering it, unaided by quotation or by the truth predicate; but if we want to affirm some infinite lot of sentences that we can demarcate only by talking about the sentences, then the truth predicate has its use. We need it to restore the effect of objective reference when for the sake of some generalization we have resorted to semantic ascent.

Tarski's paradigm cannot be generalized to read:

'*p*' is true if and only if *p*,

since quoting the schematic sentence letter '*p*' produces a name only of the sixteenth letter of the alphabet, and no generality over sentences. The truth predicate in its general use, attachable to a quantifiable variable in the fashion '*x* is true,' is eliminable by no facile paradigm. It can be defined, Tarski shows, in a devious way but only if some powerful apparatus is available. . . .

TOKENS AND ETERNAL SENTENCES

Having now recognized in a general way that what are true are sentences, we must turn to certain refinements. What are best seen as primarily true or false are not sentences but events of utterance. If a man utters the words 'It is raining' in the rain, or the words 'I am hungry' while hungry, his verbal performance counts as true. Obviously one utterance of a sentence may be true and another utterance of the same sentence be false.

Derivatively, we often speak also of inscriptions as true or false. Just as a sentence may admit of both a true and a false utterance, so also it may admit of both a true and a false inscription. An inscription of the sentence 'You owe me ten dollars' may be true or false depending on who writes it, whom he addresses it to, and when.

We speak yet more derivatively when we speak of sentences outright as true or false. This usage works all right for *eternal* sentences: sentences that stay forever true, or forever false, independently of any special circumstances under which they happen to be uttered or written. Under the head of eternal sentences ones thinks first of the sentences of arithmetic, since time and place are so conspicuously irrelevant to the subject matter of arithmetic. One thinks next of the laws of physics; for these, though occupied with the material world in a way that the laws of pure number are not, are meant to hold for all times and places. The general run of eternal sentences, however, are not so august as their name and these examples suggest. Any casual statement of inconsequential fact can be filled out into an eternal sentence by supplying names and dates and cancelling the tenses of verbs. Corresponding to 'It is raining' and 'You owe me ten dollars' we have the eternal sentence 'It rains in Boston, Mass., on July 15, 1968' and 'Bernard J. Ortcutt owes W. V. Quine ten dollars on July 15, 1968,' where 'rains' and 'owes' are to be thought of now as tenseless.

In Peirce's terminology, utterances and inscriptions are *tokens* of the sentence or other linguistic expression concerned; and this linguistic expression is the *type* of those utterances and inscriptions. In Frege's terminology, truth and falsity are the two *truth values*. Succinctly, then, an eternal sentence is a sentence whose tokens all have the same truth value.

Conceivably, by an extraordinary coincidence, one and the same string of sounds or characters could serve for '$2 < 5$' in one language and '$2 > 5$' in another. When we speak of '$2 < 5$' as an eternal sentence, then, we must understand that we are considering it exclusively as a sentence in our language, and claiming the truth only of those of its tokens that are utterances or inscriptions produced in our linguistic community. By a less extraordinary coincidence, for that matter, an eternal sentence that was true could become false because of some semantic change occurring in the continuing evolution of our own language. Here again we must view the discrepancy as a difference between two languages: English as of one date and English as of another. The string of sounds or characters in question is, and remains, an eternal sentence of earlier English, and a true one; it just happens to do double duty as a falsehood in another language, later English.

When we call a sentence eternal, therefore, we are calling it eternal relative only to a particular language at a particular time.[2] Because of this awkward relativity there remains a theoretical advantage in assigning truth values to tokens, since in that quarter there is normally no question of choosing among languages and language stages; we are concerned simply with the language of the speaker or writer as of the time of speaking or writing. But in practice it can be convenient to talk simply of truth values of eternal sentences, tacitly understanding these as relativized to our present-day English language habits.

Let us now sum up our main conclusions. What are best regarded as true and false are not propositions but sentence tokens, or sentences if they are eternal. The desire for a non-linguistic truth vehicle comes of not appreciating that the truth predicate has precisely the purpose of reconciling the mention of linguistic forms with an interest in the objective world. This need of mentioning sentences, when interested rather in things, is merely a technical need that arises when we seek to generalize along a direction that cannot be swept out by a variable.

NOTES

1. Not to be confused with 'chordate.'
2. This point worried L. J. Cohen, *The Diversity of Meaning* (London: Methuen, 1962), p. 19.

Reading Questions

1. Quine criticizes the view that we need propositions to be the meanings of sentences with his meaning holism argument:
   1. Theories are large bundles of statements and hypotheses.
   2. Experimental counterevidence only shows that at least one of these hypotheses is false, but it does not show which one. (Consider: $(p \;\&\; q \;\&\; r) \rightarrow s; \neg s; \therefore \neg(p \;\&\; q \;\&\; r)$. This means that at least one of these must be false, but we don't know which one).
   3. Thus observation statements generally refute whole sets of (disjunctive) theoretical statements, not any particular disjunct.
   4. The same works in reverse: observation statements tend to support or confirm whole sets of theoretical statements, not any specific one.
   5. Thus meaning is essentially a feature of whole theories, not of particular sentences.
   6. Thus (theoretical) sentences in isolation don't have a determinate meaning and so don't express a proposition.

   Quine seems to allow that observation sentences have determinate meanings apart from a whole theory. Is this right? If it is, do observation sentences express propositions? How is this consistent with meaning holism?
2. Suppose that Quine is right and theoretical sentences do not acquire meanings, or cannot have them, apart from whole theories of which they are a part. Wouldn't a theoretical sentence within some given meaningful theory express a proposition?
3. Quine criticizes the view that we can explain propositions in terms of sameness of meaning with an *obscurum per obscuras* argument:
   1. Two sentences that are synonymous express the same proposition. (realist premise)
   2. Two sentences are synonymous iff they are logically equivalent; i.e., they have parallel structures with synonymous terms. (Quine's definition)
   3. Two terms are synonymous iff they are interchangeable in all sentences *salva veritate.* (Quine's definition)
   4. There are types of sentences in which coextensive terms are not interchangeable *salva veritate*. Let us call these opaque contexts. (premise)
   5. Opacity is no less mysterious than propositions. (premise)
   6. Thus we have explained the obscure (propositions) only in terms of something equally obscure (opacity).
   7. Thus we have not yet adequately explained propositions.

   Imagine that someone like Church were to respond to this argument by saying that we still know that there must be propositions, even though they are perhaps mysterious. We know that photons exhibit the properties of both particles and waves, even though it is mysterious how they could do so. Propositions are no different. How could Quine reply?

4. What is the semantic ascent argument designed to show? How could a defender of propositions reply?

What Numbers Could Not Be 18

PAUL BENACERRAF

The attention of the mathematician focuses primarily upon mathematical structure, and his intellectual delight arises (in part) from seeing that a given theory exhibits such and such a structure, from seeing how one structure is "modelled" in another, or in exhibiting some new structure and showing how it relates to previously studied ones. . . . But . . . the mathematician is satisfied so long as he has some "entities" or "objects" (or "sets" or "numbers" or "functions" or "spaces" or "points") to work with, and he does not inquire into their inner character or ontological status.

The philosophical logician, on the other hand, is more sensitive to matters of ontology and will be especially interested in the kind or kinds of entities there are actually . . . . He will not be satisfied with being told merely that such and such entities exhibit such and such a mathematical structure. He will wish to inquire more deeply into what these entities are, how they relate to other entities . . . . Also he will wish to ask whether the entity dealt with is sui generis *or whether it is in some sense* reducible *to (or* constructible *in terms of) other, perhaps more fundamental entities.*

—R. M. MARTIN, *Intension and Decision*

We can . . . by using . . . [our] . . . definitions say what is meant by

"the number 1 + 1 belongs to the concept F"

and then, using this, give the sense of the expression

"the number 1 + 1 + 1 belongs to the concept F"

and so on; but we can never . . . decide by means of our definitions whether any concept has the number Julius Caesar belonging to it, or whether that same familiar conqueror of Gaul is a number or not.

—G. FREGE, *The Foundation of Arithmetic*

From The Philosophical Review, *vol. 74 (1965). Reprinted by permission of the author and publisher.*

I. THE EDUCATION

IMAGINE ERNIE AND JOHNNY, sons of two militant logicists—children who have not been taught in the vulgar (old-fashioned) way but for whom the pedagogical order of things has been the epistemological order. They did not learn straight off how to count. Instead of beginning their mathematical training with arithmetic as ordinary men know it, they first learned logic—in their case, actually set theory. Then they were told about the numbers. But to tell people in their position about the numbers was an easy task—very much like the one which faced Monsieur Jourdain's tutor (who, oddly enough, was a philosopher). The parents of our imagined children needed only to point out what aspect or part of what the children already knew, under other names, was what ordinary people called "numbers." Learning the numbers merely involved learning new names for familiar sets. Old (set-theoretic) truths took on new (number-theoretic) clothing.

The way in which this was done will, however, bear some scrutiny and re-examination. To facilitate the exposition, I will concentrate on Ernie and follow his arithmetical education to its completion. I will then return to Johnny.

It might have gone as follows. Ernie was told that there was a set whose members were what ordinary people referred to as the (natural) numbers, and that these were what he had known all along as the elements of the (infinite) set N. He was further told that there was a relation defined on these "numbers" (henceforth I shall usually omit the shudder quotes), the *less-than* relation, under which the numbers were well ordered. This relation, he learned, was really the one, defined on N, for which he had always used the letter "R." And indeed, speaking intuitively now, Ernie could verify that every nonempty subset of N contained a "least" element—that is, one that bore R to every other member of the subset. He could also show that nothing bore R to itself, and that R was transitive, antisymmetric, irreflexive, and connected in N. In short, the elements of N formed a progression, or series, under R.

And then there was 1, the smallest number (for reasons of future convenience we are ignoring 0). Ernie learned that what people had been referring to as 1 was really the element a of N, the first, or least, element of N under R. Talk about "successors" (each number is said to have one) was easily translated in terms of the concept of the "next" member of N (under R). At this point, it was no trick to show that the assumptions made by ordinary mortals about numbers were in fact theorems for Ernie. For on the basis of his theory, he could establish Peano's axioms—an advantage which he enjoyed over ordinary mortals, who must more or less take them as given, or self-evident, or meaningless-but-useful, or what have you.[1]

There are two more things that Ernie had to learn before he could truly be said to be able to speak with the vulgar. It had to be pointed out to him which operations on the members of N were the ones referred to as "addition," "multiplication," "exponentiation," and so forth. And here again he was in a position of epistemological superiority. For whereas ordinary folk had to introduce such operations by recursive definition, a euphemism for postulation, he was in a position to show that these operations could be *explicitly* defined. So the additional postulates assumed by the number people were also shown to be derivable in his theory, once it was seen which set-theoretic operations addition, multiplication, and so forth really are.

The last element needed to complete Ernie's education was the explanation of the *applications* of these devices: counting and measurement. For they employ concepts beyond those as yet introduced. But fortunately, Ernie was in a position to see what it was that he was doing that corresponded to these activities (we will concentrate on counting, assuming that measurement can be explained either similarly or in terms of counting).

There are two kinds of counting, corresponding to transitive and intransitive uses of the verb "to count." In one, "counting" admits of a direct object, as in "counting the marbles"; in the other it does not. The case I have in mind is that of the preoperative patient being prepared for the operating

Much of the work on this paper was done while the author held a Procter and Gamble Faculty Fellowship at Princeton University. This is gratefully acknowledged.

room. The ether mask is placed over his face and he is told to count, as far as he can. He has not been instructed to count anything at all. He has merely been told to count. A likely story is that we normally learn the first few numbers in connection with sets having that number of members—that is, in terms of *transitive* counting (thereby learning the use of numbers)—and then learn how to generate "the rest" of the numbers. Actually, "the rest" always remains a relatively vague matter. Most of us simply learn that we will never run out, that our notation will extend as far as we will ever need to count. Learning these words, and how to repeat them in the right order, is learning *intransitive* counting. Learning their use as measures of sets is learning *transitive* counting. Whether we learn one kind of counting before the other is immaterial so far as the initial numbers are concerned. What is certain, and not immaterial, is that we will have to learn some recursive procedure for generating the *notation* in the proper order before we have learned to count transitively, for to do the latter is, either directly or indirectly, to correlate the elements of the number series with the members of the set we are counting. It seems, therefore, that it is possible for someone to learn to count intransitively without learning to count transitively. But not vice versa. This is, I think, a mildly significant point. But what *is* transitive counting, exactly?

To count the members of a set is to determine the cardinality of the set. It is to establish that a particular relation C obtains between the set and one of the numbers—that is, one of the elements of N (we will restrict ourselves to counting finite sets here). Practically speaking, and in simple cases, one determines that a set has k elements by taking (sometimes metaphorically) its elements one by one as we say the numbers one by one (starting with 1 and in order of magnitude, the last number we say being k). To count the elements of some k-membered set b is to establish a one-to-one correspondence between the elements of b and the elements of N less than or equal to k. The relation "pointing-to-each-member-of-*b*-in-turn-while-saying-the-numbers-up-to-and-including-*k*" establishes such a correspondence.

Since Ernie has at his disposal the machinery necessary to show of any two equivalent finite sets that such a correspondence exists between them, it will be a theorem of his system that any set has k members if and only if it can be put into one-to-one correspondence with the set of numbers less than or equal to k.[2]

Before Ernie's education (and the analysis of number) can be said to have been completed, one last condition on R should be mentioned: that R must be at least recursive, and possibly even primitive recursive. I have never seen this condition included in the analysis of number, but it seems to me so obviously required that its inclusion is hardly debatable. We have already seen that Quine denies (by implication) that this constitutes an additional requirement: "The condition upon all acceptable explications of number . . . can be put . . . : any *progression*—i.e., any infinite series each of whose members has only finitely many precursors—will do nicely" (see note 3). But suppose, for example, that one chose the progression $A = a_1, a_2, a_3, \ldots a_n, \ldots$ obtained as follows. Divide the positive integers into two sequences B and C, within each sequence letting the elements come in order of magnitude. Let B (that is, $b_1, b_2, \ldots$) be the sequence of Gödel numbers of valid formulas of quantification theory, under some suitable numbering, and let C (that is, $c_1, c_2, \ldots$) be the sequence of positive integers which are not numbers of valid formulas of quantification theory under that numbering (in order of magnitude in each case). Now in the sequence A, for each n let $a_{2n-1} = b_n$ and $a_{2n} = c_n$. Clearly A, though a progression, is not recursive, much less primitive recursive. Just as clearly, this progression would be unusable as the numbers—and the reason is that we expect that if we know which numbers two expressions designate, we are able to calculate in a finite number of steps which is the "greater" (in this case, which one comes later in A).[3] More dramatically, if told that set b has n members, and that c has m, it should be possible to determine in a finite number of steps which has more members. Yet it is precisely that which is not possible here. This ability (to tell in a finite number of steps which of two numbers is the greater) is connected with (both transitive and intransitive) counting, since its possibility is equivalent to the possibility of generating ("saying") the numbers in order of magnitude (that is, in their order in A). You could not know that you were saying them in order of magnitude since, no recursive rule existing for generating its members, you could not know what their order of magnitude should be. This is, of course, a very strong claim. There are two questions here, both of which are interesting and neither of which could conceivably receive discussion in this paper. (1) Could a human being be a decision procedure for nonrecursive sets, or is the human organism at best a Turing machine (in the relevant respect)? If the latter, then there could not exist a human being who could generate the sequence A, much less *know* that this is what he was doing. Even if the answer to (1), however, is that a human being *could* be (act or be used as) such a decision procedure, the following question would still arise and need an answer: (2) could he *know* all truths of the form $i < j$ (in A)? And it seems that what constitutes knowledge might preclude such a possibility.

But I have digressed enough on this issue. The main point is that the "<" relation over the numbers must be recursive. Obviously I cannot give a rigorous proof that this is a requirement, because I cannot prove that man is at best a Turing machine. That the requirement is met by the usual "<" relation among numbers—the paradigm of a primitive recursive relation—and has also been met in every detailed analysis ever proposed constitutes good evidence for its correctness.[4] I am just making explicit what almost everyone takes for granted. Later in this paper, we will see that one plausible account of why this is taken for granted connects very closely with one of the views I will be urging.

So it was thus that Ernie learned that he had really been doing number theory all his life (I guess in much the same way that *our* children will learn this surprising fact about themselves if the *nouvelle vogue* of mathematics teachers manages to drown them all).

It should be clear that Ernie's education is now complete. He has learned to speak with the vulgar, and it should be obvious to all that my earlier description was correct. He had at his disposal all that was needed for the concept of number. One might even say that he already possessed the concepts of number, cardinal, ordinal, and the usual operations on them, and needed only to learn a different vocabulary. It is my claim that there is nothing having to do with the task of "reducing" the concept of number to logic (or set theory) that has not been done above, or that could not be done along the lines already marked out.

To recapitulate: It was necessary (1) to give definitions of "1," "number," and "successor," and "+," "×," and so forth, on the basis of which the laws of arithmetic could be derived; and (2) to explain the "extramathematical" uses of numbers, the principal one being counting—thereby introducing the concept of *cardinality* and cardinal number.

I trust that both were done satisfactorily, that the preceding contains all the elements of a correct account, albeit somewhat incompletely. None of the above was essentially new; I apologize for the tedium of expounding these details yet another time, but it will be crucial to my point that the sufficiency of the above account be clearly seen. For if it is sufficient, presumably Ernie *now* knows which sets the numbers are.

II. THE DILEMMA

The story told in the previous section could have been told about Ernie's friend Johnny as well. For his education also satisfied the conditions just mentioned. Delighted with what they had learned, they started proving theorems about numbers. Comparing notes, they soon became aware that something was wrong, for a dispute immediately ensued about whether or not 3 belonged to 17. Ernie said that it did, Johnny that it did not. Attempts to settle this by asking ordinary folk (who had been dealing with numbers *as* numbers for a long time) understandably brought only blank stares. In support of his view, Ernie pointed to his theorem that for any two numbers, x and y, x is less than y if and only if x belongs to y and x is a proper subset of y. Since by common admission 3 is less than 17 it followed that 3 belonged to 17. Johnny, on the other hand, countered that Ernie's "theorem" was mistaken, for given two numbers, x and y, x belongs to y if and only if y is the successor of x. These were clearly incompatible "theorems."

Excluding the possibility of the inconsistency of their common set theory, the incompatibility must reside in the definitions. First "less-than." But both held that x is less than y if and only if x bears R to y. A little probing, however, revealed the source of the trouble. For Ernie, the successor under R of a number x was the set consisting of x and all the members of x, while for Johnny the successor of x was simply [x], the unit set of x—the set whose only member is x. Since for each of them 1 was the unit set of the null set, their respective progressions were

(i) [∅], [∅,[∅]], [∅,[∅],[∅,[∅]]], . . . for Ernie

and

(ii) [∅], [[∅]], [[[∅]]], . . . for Johnny.

There were further disagreements. As you will recall, Ernie had been able to prove that a set had n members if and only if it could be put into one-to-one correspondence with the set of members less than or equal to n. Johnny concurred. But they disagreed when Ernie claimed further that a set had n members if and only if it could be put into one-to-one correspondence with the number n itself For Johnny, every number is single-membered. In short, their cardinality relations were different. For Ernie, 17 had 17 members, while for Johnny it had only one.[5] And so it went.

Under the circumstances, it became perfectly obvious why these disagreements arose. But what did not become perfectly obvious was how they were to be resolved. For the problem was this:

If the conclusions of the previous section are correct, then both boys have been given correct accounts of the numbers. Each was told by his father which set the set of numbers really was. Each was taught which object—whose independent existence he was able to prove—was the number 3. Each was given an account of the meaning (and reference) of number words to which no exception could be taken and on the basis of which all that we know about or do with numbers could be explained. Each was taught that some particular set of objects contained what people who used number words were really referring to. But the sets were different in each case. And so were the relations defined on these sets—including crucial ones, like cardinality and the like. But if, as I think we agreed, the account of the previous section was correct—not only as far as it went but correct in that it contained conditions which were both necessary and *sufficient* for any correct account of the phenomena under discussion, then the fact that they disagree on which particular sets the numbers are is fatal to the view that each number is some particular set. For if the number 3 is in fact some particular set b, it cannot be that two correct accounts of the meaning of "3"—and therefore also of its reference—assign two different sets to 3. For if it is true that for some set b, $3 = b$, then it cannot be true that for some set c, different from b, $3 = c$. But if Ernie's account is adequate in virtue of satisfying the conditions spelled out in Section I, so is Johnny's, for it too satisfies those conditions. We are left in a quandary. We have two (infinitely many, really) accounts of the meaning of certain words ("number," "one," "seventeen," and so forth) each of which satisfies what appear to be necessary and sufficient conditions for a correct account. Although there are differences between the two accounts, it appears that both are correct in virtue of satisfying common conditions. If so, the differences are incidental and do not affect correctness. Furthermore, in Fregean terminology, each account fixes the *sense* of the words whose analysis it provides. Each account must also, therefore, fix the *reference* of these expressions. Yet, as we have seen, one way in which these accounts differ is in the referents assigned to the terms under analysis. This leaves us with the following alternatives:

(A) Both are right in their contentions: each account contained conditions each of which was necessary and which were jointly sufficient. Therefore 3 = [[[∅]]], and 3 = [∅,[∅],[∅,[∅]]].

(B) It is not the case that both accounts were correct; that is, at least one contained conditions which were not necessary and possibly failed to contain further conditions which, taken together with those remaining, would make a set of sufficient conditions.

(A) is, of course, absurd. So we must explore (B).

The two accounts agree in over-all structure. They disagree when it comes to fixing the referents for the terms in question. Given the identification of the numbers as some particular set of sets, the two accounts generally agree on the relations defined on that set; under both, we have what is demonstrably a recursive progression and a successor function which follows the order of that progression. Furthermore, the notions of cardinality are defined in terms of the progression, insuring that it becomes a theorem for each *n* that a set has *n* members if and only if it can be put into one-to-one correspondence with the set of numbers less than or equal to *n*. Finally, the ordinary arithmetical operations are defined for these "numbers." They do differ in the way in which cardinality is defined, for in Ernie's account the fact that the number *n* had *n* members was exploited to define the notion of having *n* members. In all other respects, however, they agree.

Therefore, if it is not the case that both 3 = [[[∅]]] and 3 = [∅,[∅],[∅,[∅]]], which it surely is not, then at least one of the corresponding accounts is incorrect as a result of containing a condition that is not necessary. It may be incorrect in other respects as well, but at least that much is clear. I can distinguish two possibilities again: either all the conditions just listed, which both of these accounts share, are necessary for a correct and complete account, or some are not. Let us assume that the former is the case, although I reserve the right to discard this assumption if it becomes necessary to question it.

If all the conditions they share are necessary, then the superfluous conditions are to be found among those that are not shared. Again there are two possibilities: either at least one of the accounts satisfying the conditions we are assuming to be necessary, but which assigns a definite set to each number, is correct, or none are. Clearly no two different ones can be, since they are not even extensionally equivalent, much less intensionally. Therefore exactly one is correct or none is. But then the correct one must be the one that picks out which set of sets is *in fact* the numbers. We are now faced with a crucial problem: if there exists such a "correct" account, do there also exist arguments which will show it to be the correct one? Or does there exist a particular set of sets *b*, which is *really* the numbers, but such that there exists no argument one can give to establish that it, and not, say, Ernie's set *N*, is really the numbers? It seems altogether too obvious that this latter possibility borders on the absurd. If the numbers constitute one particular set of sets, and not another, then there must be arguments to indicate which. In urging this I am not committing myself to the decidability by proof of every mathematical question—for I consider this neither a mathematical question nor one amenable to proof. The answer to the question I am raising will follow from an analysis of questions of the form "Is *n* = . . . ?" It will suffice for now to point to the difference between our question and

> Is there a greatest prime *p* such that *p* + 2 is also prime?

or even

> Does there exist an infinite set of real numbers equivalent with neither the set of integers nor with the set of all real numbers?

In awaiting enlightenment on the true identity of 3 we are not awaiting a proof of some deep theorem. Having gotten as far as we have without settling the identity of 3, we can go no further. We do not know what a proof of that *could* look like. The notion of "correct account" is breaking loose from its moorings if we admit of the possible existence of unjustifiable but correct answers to questions such as this. To take seriously the question "Is 3 = [[[∅]]]?" *tout court* (and not elliptically for "in Ernie's account?"), in the absence of any way of settling it, is to lose one's bearings completely. No, if such a question has an answer, there are arguments supporting it, and if there are no such arguments, then there *is* no "correct" account that discriminates among all the accounts satisfying the conditions of which we reminded ourselves a couple of pages back.

How then might one distinguish *the* correct account from all the possible ones? Is there a set of sets that has a greater claim to be the numbers than any other? Are there reasons one can offer to single out that set? Frege chose as the number 3 the extension of the concept "equivalent with some 3-membered set"; that is, for Frege a number was an equivalence class—the class of all classes equivalent with a given class. Although an appealing notion, there seems little to recommend it over, say, Ernie's. It has been argued that this is a more fitting account because number words are really class predicates, and that this account reveals that fact. The view is that in saying that there are *n* *F*'s you are predicating *n*-hood of *F*, just as in saying that red is a color you are predicating colorhood of red. I do not think this is true. And neither did Frege.[6] It is certainly true that to say

(1) There are seventeen lions in the zoo

is not to predicate seventeen-hood of each individual lion. I suppose that it is also true that if there are seventeen lions in the zoo and also seventeen tigers in the zoo, the classes of lions-in-the-zoo and tigers-in-the-zoo are in a class together, though we shall return to that. It does not follow from this that (1) predicates seventeen-hood of one of those classes. First of all, the grammatical evidence for this is scanty indeed. The best one can conjure up by way of an example of the occurrence of a number word in predicative position is a rather artificial one like

(2) The lions in the zoo are seventeen.

If we do not interpret this as a statement about the ages of the beasts, we see that such statements do not predicate anything of any individual lion. One might then succumb to the temptation of analyzing (2) as the noun phrase "The lions in the zoo" followed by the verb phrase "are seventeen," where the analysis is parallel to that of

(3) The Cherokees are vanishing

where the noun phrase refers to the class and the verb phrase predicates something of that class. But the parallel is short-lived. For we soon notice that (2) probably comes into the language by deletion from

(4) The lions in the zoo are seventeen in number,

which in turn probably derives from something like

(5) Seventeen lions are in the zoo.

This is no place to explore in detail the grammar of number words. Suffice it to point out that they differ in many important respects from words we do not hesitate to call predicates. Probably the closest thing to a genuine class predicate involving number words is something on the model of "seventeen-membered" or "has seventeen members." But the step from there to "seventeen" being itself a predicate of classes is a long one indeed. In fact, I should think that pointing to the above two predicates gives away the show—for what is to be the analysis of "seventeen" as it occurs in those phrases?

Not only is there scanty grammatical evidence for this view, there seems to be considerable evidence against it, as any scrutiny of the similarity of function among the number words and "many," "few," "all," "some," "any," and so forth will immediately reveal. The proper study of these matters will have to await another context, but the nonpredicative nature of number words can be further seen by noting how different they are from, say, ordinary adjectives, which do function as predicates. We have already seen that there are really no occurrences of number words in typical predicative position (that is, in "is (are) . . ."), the only putative cases being along the lines of (2) above, and therefore rather implausible. The other anomaly is that number words normally outrank *all* adjectives (or all other adjectives, if one wants to class them as such) in having to appear at the head of an adjective string, and not inside. This is such a strong ranking that deviation virtually inevitably results in ungrammaticalness:

(6) The five lovely little square blue tiles

is fine, but any modification of the position of "five" yields an ungrammatical string; the farther to the right, the worse.[7]

Further reason for denying the predicative nature of number words comes from the traditional first-order analysis of sentences such as (1), with which we started. For that is usually analyzed as:

$$(7)\ (\exists x_1) \ldots (\exists x_{17})\ (Lx_1 \cdot Lx_2 \cdot \ldots \cdot Lx_{17} \cdot x_1 \neq x_2 \cdot x_1 \neq x_3 \cdot \ldots \cdot x_{16} \neq x_{17} \cdot (y)\ (Ly \supset . y = x_1 \vee y = x_2 \vee \ldots y = x_{17})).$$

The only predicate in (1) which remains is "lion in the zoo," "seventeen" giving way to numerous quantifiers, truth functions, variables, and occurrences of "=," unless, of course, one wishes to consider these also to be predicates of classes. But there are slim grounds indeed for the view that (1) or (7) predicates seventeen-hood of the class of lions in the zoo. Number words function so much like operators such as "all," "some," and so forth, that a readiness to make class names of them should be accompanied by a readiness to make the corresponding move with respect to quantifiers, thereby proving (in traditional philosophic fashion) the existence of the one, the many, the few, the all, the some, the any, the every, the several, and the each.[8]

But then, what support *does* this view have? Well, this much: if two classes each have seventeen members, there probably exists a class which contains them both in virtue of that fact. I say "probably" because this varies from set theory to set theory. For example, this is not the case with type theory, since the two classes have both to be of the same type. But in no consistent theory is there a class of all classes with seventeen members, at least not alongside the other standard set-theoretical apparatus. The existence of the paradoxes is itself a good reason to deny to "seventeen" this univocal role of designating the class of all classes with seventeen members.

I think, therefore, that we may conclude that "seventeen" *need* not be considered a predicate of classes, and there is similarly no necessity to view 3 as the set of all triplets. This is not to deny that "is a class having three members" is a predicate of classes; but that is a different matter indeed. For that follows from all of the accounts under consideration.[9] Our present problem is to see if there is one account which can be established to the exclusion of all others, thereby settling the issue of which sets the numbers really are. And it should be clear by now that there is not. Any purpose we may have in giving an account of the notion of number and of the individual numbers, other than the question-begging one of proving of the right set of sets that *it* is the set of numbers, will be equally well (or badly) served by any one of the infinitely many accounts satisfying the conditions we set out so tediously. There is little need to examine all the possibilities in detail, once the traditionally favored one of Frege and Russell has been seen not to be uniquely suitable.

Where does that leave us? I have argued that at most one of the infinitely many different accounts satisfying our conditions can be correct, on the grounds that they are not even extensionally equivalent, and therefore at least all but one, and possibly all, contain conditions that are not necessary and that lead to the identification of the numbers with some particular set of sets. If numbers are sets, then they must be *particular sets,* for each set is some particular set. But if the number 3 is really one set rather than another, it must be possible to give some cogent reason for thinking so; for the position that this is an unknowable truth is hardly tenable. But there seems to be little to choose among the accounts. Relative to our purposes in giving an account of these matters, one will do as well as another, stylistic preferences aside. There is no way connected with the reference of number words that will allow us to choose among them, *for the accounts differ at places where there is no connection whatever between features of the accounts and our uses of the words in question.* If all the above is cogent, then there is little to conclude except that any feature of an account that identifies 3 with a set is a superfluous one—and that therefore 3, and its fellow numbers, could not be sets at all.

III. WAY OUT

In this third and final section, I shall examine and urge some considerations that I hope will lend plausibility to the conclusion of the previous section, if only by contrast. The issues involved are evidently so numerous and complex, and cover such a broad spectrum of philosophic problems, that in this paper I can do no more than indicate what I think they are and how, in general, I think they may be resolved. I hope nevertheless that a more positive account will emerge from these considerations.

A. IDENTITY

Throughout the first two sections, I have treated expressions of the form

(8) $n = s$,

where n is a number expression and s a set expression as if I thought that they made perfectly good sense, and that it was our job to sort the true from the false.[10] And it might appear that I had concluded that all such statements were false. I did this to dramatize the kind of answer that a Fregean might give to the request for an analysis of number—to point up the kind of question Frege took it to be. For he clearly wanted the analysis to determine a truth value for each such identity. In fact, he wanted to determine a sense for the result of replacing s with any name or description whatsoever (while an expression ordinarily believed to name a number occupied the position of n). Given the symmetry and transitivity of identity, there were three kinds of identities satisfying these conditions, corresponding to the three kinds of expressions that can appear on the right:

(a) with some arithmetical expression on the right as well as on the left (for example, "$2^{17} = 4{,}892$," and so forth);

(b) with an expression designating a number, but not in a standard arithmetical way, as "the number of apples in the pot," or "the number of *F*'s" (for example, 7 = the number of the dwarfs);

(c) with a referring expression on the right which is of neither of the above sorts, such as "Julius Caesar," "[[∅]]" (for example, 17 = [[[∅]]]).

The requirement that the usual laws of arithmetic follow from the account takes care of all identities of the first sort. Adding an explication of the concept of cardinality will then suffice for those of kind (b). But to include those of kind (c), Frege felt it necessary to find some "objects" for number words to name and with which numbers could be identical. It was at this point that questions about which set of objects the numbers *really* were began to appear to need answering for, evidently, the simple answer "numbers" would not do. To speak from Frege's standpoint, there is a world of objects—that is, the designata or referents of names, descriptions, and so forth—in which the identity relation had free reign. It made sense for Frege to ask of *any* two names (or descriptions) whether they named the same object or different ones. Hence the complaint at one point in his argument that, thus far, one could not tell from his definitions whether Julius Caesar was a number.

I rather doubt that in order to explicate the use and meaning of number words one will have to decide whether Julius Caesar was (is?) or was not the number 43. Frege's insistence that this needed to be done stemmed, I think, from his (demonstrably) inconsistent logic (interpreted sufficiently broadly to encompass set theory). All items (names) in the universe were on a par, and the question whether two names had the same referent always presumably had an answer—yes or no. The inconsistency of the logic from which this stems is of course *some* reason to regard the view with suspicion. But it is hardly a refutation, since one might grant the meaningfulness of all identity statements, the existence of a universal set as the range of the relation, and still have principles of set existence sufficiently restrictive to avoid inconsistency. But such a view, divorced from the naïve set theory from which it stems .. loses much of its appeal. I suggest, tentatively, that we look at the matter differently.

I propose to deny that all identities are meaningful, in particular to discard all questions of the form of (c) above as senseless or "unsemantical" (they are not totally senseless, for we grasp enough of their sense to explain why they are senseless). Identity statements make sense only in contexts where there exist possible individuating conditions. If an expression of the form "$x = y$" is to have a sense, it can be only in contexts where it is clear that both x and y are of some kind or category C, and that it is the conditions which individuate things *as the same* C which are operative and determine its truth value. An example might help clarify the point. If we know x and y to be lampposts (possibly the same, but nothing in the way they are designated decides the issue) we can ask if they are *the same lamppost*. It will be their color, history, mass, position, and so forth which will determine if they are indeed the same lamppost. Similarly, if we know *z* and *w* to be numbers, then we can ask if they are *the same number.* And it will be whether they are prime, greater than 17, and so forth which will decide if they are indeed the same number. But just as we cannot individuate a lamppost in terms of these latter predicates, neither can we individuate a number in terms of its mass, color, or similar considerations. What determines that something is a *particular lamppost* could not individuate it as a *particular number.* I am arguing that questions of the identity of a particular "entity" do not make sense. "Entity" is too broad. For such questions to make sense, there must be a well-entrenched predicate *C,* in terms of which one then asks about the identity of a *particular C,* and the conditions associated with identifying *C*'s as *the same C* will be the deciding ones. Therefore, if for two predicates *F* and *G* there is no third predicate *C* which subsumes both and which has associated with it some uniform conditions for identifying two putative elements as the same (or different) *C*'s, the identity statements crossing the *F* and *G* boundary will not make sense.[11] For example, it will make sense to ask of something *x* (which is in fact a chair) if it is the same . . . as *y* (which in fact is a table). For we can fill the blank with a predicate, "piece of furniture," and we know what it is for *a* and *b* to be the same or different pieces of furniture. To put the point differently, questions of identity contain the presupposition that the "entities" inquired about both belong to some general category. This presupposition is normally carried by the context or theory (that is, a more systematic context). To say that they are both "entities" is to make no presuppositions at all—for everything purports to be at least that. "Entity," "thing," "object" are words having a role in the language; they are place fillers whose function is analogous to that of pronouns (and, in more formalized contexts, to variables of quantification).

Identity *is* id-entity, but only within narrowly restricted contexts. Alternatively, what constitutes an entity is category or theory dependent. There are really two correlative ways of looking at the problem. One might conclude that identity is systematically ambiguous, or else one might agree with Frege, that identity is unambiguous, always meaning sameness of object, but that (contra-Frege now) the notion of an *object* varies from theory to theory, category to category—and therefore that his mistake lay in failure to realize this fact. This last is what I am urging, for it has the virtue of preserving identity as a general logical relation whose application in any given well-defined context (that is, one within which the notion of object is univocal) remains unproblematic. Logic can then still be seen as the most general of disciplines, applicable in the same way to and within any given theory. It remains the tool applicable to all disciplines and theories, the difference being only that it is left to the discipline or theory to determine what shall count as an "object" or "individual."

That this is not an implausible view is also suggested by the language. Contexts of the form "the same *G*" abound, and indeed it is in terms of them that identity should be explained, for what will be counted as the same *G* will depend heavily on *G.* The same *man* will have to be an individual man; "the same *act*" is a description that can be satisfied by many individual acts, or by only one, for the individuating conditions for acts make them sometimes types, sometimes tokens. Very rare in the language are contexts open to (satisfiable by) any kind of "thing" whatsoever. There are some—for example, "Sam referred to . . . ," "Helen thought of . . ."—and it seems perfectly all right to ask if what Sam referred to on some occasion was what Helen thought of. But these contexts are very few, and they all seem to be intensional, which casts a referentially opaque shadow over the role that identity plays in them.

Some will want to argue that identities of type (c) are not senseless or unsemantical, but simply false—on the grounds that the distinction of categories is one that cannot be drawn. I have only the following argument to counter such a view. It will be just as hard to explain how one *knows* that they are false as it would be to explain how one knows that they are senseless, for normally we know the falsity of some identity "$x = y$" only if we know of *x* (or *y*) that it has some characteristic that we know *y* (or *x*) *not* to have. I know that $2 \neq 3$ because I know, for example, that 3 is odd and 2 is not, yet it seems clearly wrong to argue that we know that

3 ≠ [[[∅]]] because, say, we know that 3 has no (or seventeen, or infinitely many) members while [[[∅]]] has exactly one. We know no such thing. We do not know that it does. But that does not constitute knowing that it does not. What is enticing about the view that these are all false is, of course, that they hardly seem to be open questions to which we may find the answer any day. Clearly, all the evidence is in; if no decision is possible on the basis of it, none will ever be possible. But for the purposes at hand the difference between these two views is not a very serious one. I should certainly be happy with the conclusion that all identities of type (c) are either senseless or false.

B. EXPLICATION AND REDUCTION

I would like now to approach the question from a slightly different angle. Throughout this paper, I have been discussing what was substantially Frege's view, in an effort to cast some light on the meaning of number words by exposing the difficulties involved in trying to determine which objects the numbers really are. The analyses we have considered all contain the condition that numbers are sets, and that therefore each individual number is some individual set. We concluded at the end of Section II that numbers could not be sets at all—on the grounds that there are no good reasons to say that any particular number is some particular set. To bolster our argument, it might be instructive to look briefly at two activities closely related to that of stating that numbers *are* sets—those of explication and reduction.

In putting forth an explication of number, a philosopher may have as part of his explication the statement that 3 = [[[∅]]]. Does it follow that he is making the kind of mistake of which I accused Frege? I think not. For there is a difference between *asserting* that 3 *is* the set of all triplets and *identifying* 3 with that set, which last is what might be done in the context of some explication. I certainly do not wish what I am arguing in this paper to militate against identifying 3 with anything you like. The difference lies in that, normally, one who identifies 3 with some particular set does so for the purpose of presenting some theory and does not claim that he has *discovered* which object 3 really is. We might want to know whether some set (and relations and so forth) would do as number surrogates. In investigating this it would be entirely legitimate to state that making such an identification, we can do with that set (and those relations) what we now do with the numbers. Hence we find Quine saying:

> Frege dealt with the question "What is a number?" by showing how the work for which the objects in question might be wanted could be done by objects whose nature was presumed to be less in question.[12]

Ignoring whether this is a correct interpretation of Frege, it is clear that someone who says this would not claim that, since the answer turned out to be "Yes," it is now clear that numbers were really sets all along. In such a context, the adequacy of some system of objects to the task is a very real question and one which can be settled. Under our analysis, *any* system of objects, sets or not, that forms a recursive progression must be adequate. It is therefore obvious that to discover that a system will do cannot be to discover which objects the numbers are . . . . Explication, in the above reductionistic sense, is therefore neutral with respect to the sort of problem we have been discussing, but it does cast some sobering light on what it is to be an individual number.

There is another reason to deny that it would be legitimate to use the reducibility of arithmetic to set theory as a reason to assert that numbers are really sets after all. Gaisi Takeuti has shown that the Gödel-von Neumann-Bernays set theory is in a strong sense *reducible to* the theory of ordinal numbers less than the least inaccessible number.[13] No wonder numbers are sets; sets are really (ordinal) numbers, after all. *But now, which is really which?*

These brief comments on reduction, explication, and what they might be said to achieve in mathematics lead us back to the quotation from Richard Martin which heads this paper. Martin correctly points out that the mathematician's interest stops at the level of structure. If one theory can be modeled in another (that is, reduced to another) then further questions about whether the individuals of one theory are really those of the second just do not arise. In the same passage, Martin goes on to point out (approvingly, I take it) that the philosopher is not satisfied with this limited view of things. He wants to know more and does ask the questions in which the mathematician professes no interest. I agree. He does. And mistakenly so. It will be the burden of the rest of this paper to argue that such questions miss the point of what arithmetic, at least, is all about.

C. CONCLUSION: NUMBERS AND OBJECTS

It was pointed out above that any system of objects, whether sets or not, that forms a recursive progression must be adequate. But this is odd, for any recursive set can be arranged in a recursive progression. So what matters, really, is not any condition on the *objects* (that is, on the set) but rather a condition on the relation under which they form a progression. To put the point differently—and this is the crux of the matter—that any recursive sequence whatever would do suggests that what is important is not the individuality of each element but the structure which they jointly exhibit. This is an extremely striking feature. One would be led to expect from this fact alone that the question of whether a particular "object"—for example, [[[∅]]]—would do as a replacement for the number 3 would be pointless in the extreme, as indeed it is. "Objects" do not do the job of numbers singly; the whole system performs the job or nothing does. I therefore argue, extending the argument that led to the conclusion that numbers could not be sets, that numbers could not be objects at all; for there is no more reason to identify any individual number with any one particular object than with any other (not already known to be a number).

The pointlessness of trying to determine which objects the numbers are thus derives directly from the pointlessness of asking the question of any individual number. For arithmetical purposes the properties of numbers which do not stem from the relations they bear to one another in virtue of being arranged in a progression are of no consequence whatsoever. But it would be only these properties that would single out a number as this object or that.

Therefore, numbers are not objects at all, because in giving the properties (that is, necessary and sufficient) of numbers you merely characterize an *abstract structure*—and the distinction lies in the fact that the "elements" of the structure have no properties other than those relating them to other "elements" of the same structure. If we identify an abstract structure with a system of relations (in intension, of course, or else with the set of all relations in extension isomorphic to a given system of relations), we get arithmetic elaborating the properties of the "less-than" relation, or of all systems of objects (that is, *concrete* structures) exhibiting that abstract structure. That a system of objects exhibits the structure of the integers implies that the elements of that system have some properties not dependent on structure. It must be possible to individuate those objects independently of the role they play in that structure. But this is precisely what cannot be done with the numbers. To *be* the number 3 is no more and no less than to be preceded by 2, 1, and possibly 0, and to be followed by 4, 5, and so forth. And to *be* the number 4 is no more and no less than to be preceded by 3, 2, 1, and possibly 0, and to be followed by . . . . *Any* object can *play the role of* 3; that is, any object can be the third element in some progression. What is peculiar to 3 is that it defines that role—not by being a paradigm of any object which plays it, but by representing the relation that any third member of a progression bears to the rest of the progression.

Arithmetic is therefore the science that elaborates the abstract structure that all progressions have in common merely in virtue of being progressions. It is not a science concerned with particular objects—the numbers. The search for which independently identifiable particular objects the numbers really are (sets? Julius Caesars?) is a misguided one.

On this view many things that puzzled us in this paper seem to fall into place. Why so many interpretations of number theory are possible without any being uniquely singled out becomes obvious: there is no unique set of objects that are the numbers. Number theory is the elaboration of the properties of *all* structures of the order type of the numbers. The number words do not have single referents. Furthermore, the reason identification of numbers with objects works wholesale but fails utterly object by object is the fact that the theory is elaborating an abstract structure and not the properties of independent individuals, any one of which could be characterized without reference to its relations to the rest. Only when we are considering a particular sequence as being, not the numbers, but *of the structure of the numbers* does the question of which element is, or rather *corresponds to,* 3 begin to make any sense.

Slogans like "Arithmetic is about numbers," "Number words refer to numbers," when properly urged, may be interpreted as pointing out two quite distinct things: (1) that number words are not names of special nonnumerical entities, like sets, tomatoes, or Gila monsters; and (2) that a purely formalistic view that fails to assign any meaning whatsoever to the statements of number theory is also wrong. They need not be incompatible with what I am urging here.

This last formalism is too extreme. But there is a modified form of it, also denying that number words are names, which constitutes a plausible and tempting extension of the view I have been arguing. Let me suggest it here. On this view the sequence of number words is just that—a sequence of words or expressions with certain properties. There are not two kinds of things, numbers and number words, but just one, the words themselves. Most languages contain such a sequence, and any such sequence (of words or terms) will serve the purposes for which we have ours, provided it is recursive in the relevant respect. In counting, we do not correlate sets with initial segments of the numbers as extralinguistic entities, but correlate sets with initial segments of the sequence of number *words.* The central idea is that this recursive sequence is a sort of yardstick which we use to measure sets. Questions of the identification of the referents of number words should be dismissed as misguided in just the way that a question about the referents of the parts of a ruler would be seen as misguided. Although any sequence of expressions with the proper structure would do the job for which we employ our present number words, there is still some reason for having one, relatively uniform, notation: ordinary communication. Too many sequences in common use would make it necessary for us to learn too many different equivalences. The usual objection to such an account—that there is a distinction between numbers and number words which it fails to make will, I think, not do. It is made on the grounds that "two," "*zwei,*" "*deux,*" "2" are all supposed to "stand for" the same number but yet are *different* words (one of them not a word at all). One can mark the differences among the expressions in question, and the similarities as well, without conjuring up some extralinguistic objects for them to name. One need only point to the similarity of function: within any numbering system, what will be important will be what place in the system any particular expression is used to mark. All the above expressions share this feature with one another—and with the binary use of "10," but not with its decimal employment. The "ambiguity" of "10" is thus easily explained. Here again we see the series-related character of individual numbers, except that it is now mapped a little closer to home. One cannot tell what number a particular expression represents without being given the sequence of which it forms a part. It will then be from its place in that sequence—that is, from its relation to other members of the sequence, *and from the rules governing the use of the sequence in counting*—that it will derive its individuality. It is for this last reason that I urged, contra Quine, that the account of cardinality must explicitly be included in the account of number (see note 2).

Furthermore, other things fall into place as well. The requirement, discussed in Section I, that the "less-than" relation be recursive is most easily explained in terms of a recursive notation. After all, the whole theory of recursive functions makes most sense when viewed in close connection with notations rather than with extralinguistic objects. This makes itself most obvious in three places: the development of the theory by Post systems, by Turing machines, and in the theory of constructive ordinals, where the concern is frankly with recursive notations for ordinals. I do not see why this should not be true of the finite ordinals as well. For a set of *numbers* is recursive if and only if a machine of a particular sort could be programmed to generate them in order of magnitude—that is, to generate the standard or canonical notations for those numbers following the (reverse) order of the "less-than" relation. If that relation over the notation were not recursive, the above theorem would not hold.

It also becomes obvious why every analysis of number ever presented has had a recursive "less-than" relation. If what we are generating is a notation, the most natural way for generating it is by giving recursive rules for getting the next element from any element you may have—and you would have to go far out of your way (and be slightly mad) to generate the notation and then define "less than" as I did on pages 241–242 in discussing the requirement of recursiveness.

Furthermore, on this view, we learn the elementary arithmetical operations as the cardinal operations on small sets, and, extend them by the usual algorithms. Arithmetic then becomes cardinal arithmetic at the earlier levels in the obvious way, and the more advanced statements become easily interpretable as *projections* via truth functions, quantifiers, and the recursive rules governing the operations. One can therefore be this sort of formalist without denying that there is such a thing as arithmetical truth other than derivability within some given system. One can even explain what the ordinary formalist apparently cannot—why these were chosen and which of two possible consistent extensions should adopt in any given case.

But I must stop here. I cannot defend this view in detail without writing a book. To return in closing to our poor abandoned children, I think we must conclude that their education was badly mismanaged—not from the mathematical point of view, since we have concluded that there is no mathematically significant difference between what they were taught and what ordinary mortals know, but from the philosophical point of view. They think that numbers are really sets of sets while, if the truth be known, there are no such things as numbers; which is not to say that there are not at least two prime numbers between 15 and 20.[14]

NOTES

1. I will not bore the reader with the details of the proofs.

2. It is not universally agreed that these last two parts of our account (defining the operations and defining cardinality) are indeed required for an adequate explication of number. W. V. Quine, for one, explicitly denies that anything need be done other than provide a progression to serve as the numbers. In *Word and Object* (London, 1960), pp. 262–263, he states: "The condition upon all acceptable explications of number . . . can be put . . . : *any progression*—i.e., any infinite series each of whose members has only finitely many precursors will do nicely. Russell once held that a further condition had to be met, to the effect that there be a way of applying one's would-be numbers to the measurement of multiplicity: a way of saying that (1) There are *n* objects *x* such that F*x*. This, however, was a mistake, for any progression can be fitted to that further condition. For (1) can be paraphrased as saying that the numbers less than *n* [Quine uses o as well] admit of correlation with the objects *x* such that F*x*. This requires that our apparatus include enough of the elementary theory of relations for talk of correlation, or one-one relation; but it requires nothing special about numbers except that they form a progression." I would disagree. The explanation of cardinality—i.e., of the use of numbers for "transitive counting," as I have called it—is part and parcel of the explication of number. Indeed, if it may be excluded on the grounds Quine offers, we might as well say that there are *no* necessary conditions, since the only one he cites is hardly necessary, provided "that our apparatus contain enough of the theory of sets to contain a progression." But I will return to this point.

3. There is, of course, a difficulty with the notion of "knowing which numbers two expressions designate." It is the old one illustrated by the following example. Abraham thinks of a number, and so does Isaac. Call Abraham's number *a* and Isaac's *i*. Is *a* greater than *i*? I know which number *a* refers to: Abraham's. And similarly with *i*. But that brings me no closer to deciding which is the greater. This can be avoided, however, by requiring that numbers be given in canonical notation, as follows. Let the usual (recursive) definition of the numbers serve to define the *set* of "numbers," but not to establish their order. Then take the above definition of *a* as defining the *less-than* relation among the members of that set, thus defining the *progression*. (The fact that the nonrecursive progression that I use is a progression of *numbers* is clearly inessential to the point at issue. I use it here merely to avoid the elaborate circumlocutions that would result from doing everything set-theoretically. One could get the same effect by letting the "numbers" be formulas of quantification theory, instead of their Gödel numbers, and using the formulas autonomously.)

4. Needless to say, it is trivially met in any analysis that provides an effective correlation between the names of the "numbers" of the analysis and the more common names under which we know those numbers.

5. Some of their type-theoretical cousins had even more peculiar views—for to be of cardinality 5 a set had to *belong* to one of the numbers 5. I say "some of" because others did not use that definition of cardinality, or of numbers, but sided either with Ernie or with Johnny.

6. Cf. Frege, *The Foundation of Arithmetic* (New York, 1950), sec. 57.

7. It might be thought that constructions such as

(i) The hungry five went home

constitute counterexamples to the thesis that number words must come first in an adjective string. But they do not. For in (i) and similar cases, the number word occurs as a noun, and not as an adjective, probably deriving from

(ii) The five hungry NP_{pl} went home

by the obvious transformation, and should be understood as such. There are certain genuine counterexamples, but the matter is too complicated for discussion here.

8. And indeed why not "I am the one who gave his all in fighting for the few against the many"?

9. Within the bounds imposed by consistency.

10. I was pleased to find that several of the points in my discussion of Frege have been made quite independently by Charles Parsons in a paper entitled "Frege's Thesis that Numbers Are Objects," unpublished. I am indebted to his discussion for a number of improvements.

11. To give a precise account, it will be necessary to explain "uniform conditions" in such a way as to rule out the obvious counterexamples generated by constructed *ad hoc* disjunctive conditions. But to discuss the way to do this would take us too far afield. I do not pretend to know the answer in any detail.

12. Quine, *op. cit.*, p. 262.

13. Takeuti, "Construction of the Set Theory from the Theory of Ordinal Numbers," *Journal of the Mathematical Society of Japan*, 6 (1954).

14. I am indebted to Paul Ziff for his helpful comments on an earlier draft.

Reading Questions

1. Benacerraf argues that the following argument is unsound:
   1. The linguistic string "being a lion," if meaningful, expresses a property.
   2. The linguistic string "Leo is a lion," if meaningful, expresses a proposition.
   3. Thus the linguistic string "3"—a numeral—expresses the number 3.

   He maintains that number-words are importantly different from predicates and sentences. Why are they different?
2. Benacerraf offers this argument to show why numbers are not sets:
   1. Either the number 3 is identical with the set [∅,[∅],[∅,[∅]]] (as Ernie believes), or the number 3 is identical with the set [[[∅]]] (as Johnny believes).
   2. These sets are not identical with each other, since they contain different elements.
   3. Thus at most one is right.
   4. If either one is right, then there will be a way (at least in principle) of deciding which one.
   5. There is no way of deciding between them.
   6. Thus neither one is right.
   7. Thus numbers are not sets.

   What do you think of the fourth premise of this argument? Could there be undecidable or unprovable truths? There are mathematical truths that are unprovable from a finite set of consistent axioms, as Kurt Gödel showed. Why not unprovable philosophical truths?
3. According to Benacerraf, certain ostensible identity statements are meaningless. Particularly, he thinks that these are meaningless:

   3 = [[[∅]]]
   3 = Julius Caesar

   He thinks they are meaningless because there is no context in which there are possible individuating conditions that would enable a decision about whether these equivalences are true. We can't make decent enough sense out of them to determine their truth value. Thus there is no reason to think that they have one, or that they mean anything. Compare Benacerraf's claim that the notion of an object varies from theory to theory to Carnap's distinction between internal and external questions. Is Benacerraf a Carnapian?

4. One of Benacerraf's key arguments is the Argument from Structure:
    1. Any set that forms a recursive progression can define the numbers.
    2. Thus it is *structure* that is important, not what elements are in the sets.
    3. Thus numbers are not objects.

    Assuming that the first premise is true, does this establish mathematical nominalism?

19 Universals as Attributes

DAVID M. ARMSTRONG

I. UNINSTANTIATED UNIVERSALS?

IF WE ABANDON THE IDEA that particulars are nothing but bundles of universals but still want to recognize universals, then we must return to the traditional view that particulars, tokens, *instantiate* universals: having properties and standing to each other in relations. If we do this, then there are a number of controversial questions that have to be settled. One key question is this. Should we, or should we not, accept a Principle of Instantiation for universals? That is, should we, or should we not, demand that every universal be instantiated? That is, for each property universal must it be the case that it is a property of some particular? For each relation universal must it be the case that there are particulars between which the relation holds?

We certainly should not demand that every universal should be instantiated *now.* It would be enough if a particular universal was not instantiated now, but was instantiated in the past, or would be instantiated in the future. The Principle of Instantiation should be interpreted as ranging over all time: past, present, and future. But should we uphold the principle even in this relatively liberal form?

This is a big parting of the ways. We can call the view that there are uninstantiated universals the Platonist view. It appears to have been the view held by Plato, who was also, apparently, the first philosopher to introduce universals. (He spoke of Forms or Ideas—but there was nothing psychological about the Ideas.)

Once you have uninstantiated universals you need somewhere special to put them, a "Platonic heaven," as philosophers often say. They are not to be found in the ordinary world of space and time. And since it seems that any instantiated universal might have been uninstantiated—for example, there might have been nothing past, present, or future that had that property—then if uninstantiated universals are in a Platonic heaven, it will be natural to place all universals in that heaven. The result is that we get two realms: the realm of universals and the realm of particulars, the latter being ordinary things in space and time. Such universals are often spoken of as *transcendent.* (A view of this sort was explicitly held by Russell in his earlier days

It is suggested that Chapter 11 of D. M. Armstrong's *Nominalism and Realism* and Chapters 13–17 of his *A Theory of Universals* be used as companion readings to this essay.

From David M. Armstrong, Universals: An Opinionated Introduction. *Boulder, CO: Westview Press, 1989. Reprinted by permission of Westview Press.*

before he adopted a bundle-of-universals view. See his introductory book *The Problems of Philosophy,* 1912, Chs. 9 and 10.) Instantiation then becomes a very big deal: a relation between universals and particulars that crosses realms. The Latin tag used by the Scholastics for a theory of this sort is *universalia ante res,* "universals before things." Such a view is unacceptable to Naturalists, that is, to those who think that the space-time world is all the world that there is. This helps to explain why Empiricists, who tend to be sympathetic to Naturalism, often reject universals.

It is interesting to notice that a separate-realm theory of universals permits of a blob as opposed to a layer-cake view of particulars. For on this view, what is it for a thing to have a property? It is not the thing's having some internal feature, but rather its having a relationship, the instantiation relationship, to certain universals or Forms in another realm. The thing itself could be bloblike. It is true that the thing could also be given a property structure. But then the properties that make up this structure cannot be universals but must be particulars. They would have to be tropes. . . . The particular involves property tropes, but these property tropes are put into natural classes by their instantiating a certain universal in the realm of the universals. At any rate, without bringing in tropes in addition it seems that Platonic theories of universals have to treat particulars as bloblike rather than layer-caked. I think that this is an argument against Platonic theories.

If, however, we reject uninstantiated universals, then we are at least in a position, if we want to do it, to bring the universals down to earth. We can adopt the view whose Latin tag is *universalia in rebus,* "universals in things." We can think of a thing's properties as constituents of the thing and think of the properties as universals. This may have been the position of Aristotle. (The scholars differ. Some make him a Nominalist. Some think he believed in this-worldly universals. Certainly, he criticized Plato's otherworldly universals.) *Universalia in rebus* is, of course, a layer-cake view, with properties as universals as part of the internal structure of things. (Relations will be *universalia inter res,* "universals between things" [Abbott 1886].)

There are difficulties in this position, of course, objections that can be brought, as with every other solution to the Problem of Universals. One thing that has worried many philosophers, including perhaps Plato, is that on this view we appear to have multiple location of the same thing. Suppose *a* is F and *b* is also F, with F a property universal. The very same entity has to be part of the structure of two things at two places. How can the universal be in two places at once? I will come back to this question later in this chapter.

First to round things off I will mention the third Scholastic tag: *universalia post res,* "universals after things." This was applied to Nominalist theories. It fits best with *Predicate* or *Concept Nominalism,* where properties, et cetera, are as it were created by the classifying mind: shadows cast on things by our predicates or concepts.

But our present task is to decide whether or not we ought to countenance uninstantiated universals. The first point to be made is that the onus of proof seems to be firmly on the side of the Platonists. It can hardly be doubted that there is a world of space and time. But a separate realm of universals is a mere hypothesis, or postulation. If a postulation has great explanatory value, then it may be a good postulation. But it has to prove itself. Why should we postulate uninstantiated universals?

One thing that has moved many philosophers is what we may call the argument from the meaning of general terms. Plato, in his *Republic,* had Socrates say, "shall we proceed as usual and begin by assuming the existence of a single essential nature or Form for every set of things which we call by the same name?" (595, trans. F. M. Cornford). Socrates may have been thinking along the following lines. Ordinary names, that is, proper names, have a bearer of the name. If we turn to general terms—words like 'horse' and 'triangular' that apply to many different things—then we need something that stands to the word in the same general sort of relation that the bearer of the proper name stands to the proper name. There has to be an object that constitutes or corresponds to the meaning of the general word. So there has to be something called horseness, and triangularity. But now consider a general word that applies to nothing particular at all, a word like 'unicorn' for instance. It is perfectly meaningful. And if it is meaningful, must there not be something in the world that constitutes or corresponds to the word? So there must be uninstantiated universals.

This "argument from meaning" is a very bad argument. (In fairness to Socrates, it is not clear whether he was using it. Other philosophers have, though, often at a rather unselfconscious level.) The argument depends on the assumption that in every case where a general word has meaning, there is something in the world that constitutes or corresponds to that meaning. Gilbert Ryle spoke of this as the 'Fido'-Fido fallacy. Fido corresponds to the word 'Fido,' but there does not have to be some single thing corresponding to a general word.

To go along with the argument from meaning is to be led into a very promiscuous theory of universals. If it is correct, then we know a priori that for each general word with a certain meaning, there exists a universal. This lines up predicates and properties in a nice neat way, but it is a way that we ought to be very suspicious of. Is it that easy to discover what universals there are?

Plato had another line of thought that led him toward uninstantiated universals. This is the apparent failure of things in the ordinary world to come up to exact standards. It seems that nothing in the world is perfectly straight or circular, yet in geometry we discuss the properties of perfectly straight lines or perfect circles. Again, no thing is perfectly changeless. Yet again, it may well be that no act is perfectly just. Certainly no person is perfectly virtuous and no state is perfectly just. Yet in ethical and political discussion (e.g., in the *Republic*) we can discuss the nature of virtue and justice. In general, we perceive the world as falling short of certain standards. This can be explained if, whether we know it or not, we are comparing ordinary things to Forms, which the ordinary things can never fully instantiate. (This can lead one, and perhaps led Plato, to the difficult notion of degrees of instantiation, with the highest degree never realized.)

It is interesting to notice that this argument did not quite lead Plato where he wanted to go in every case. Consider geometry. In geometry one might wish to consider the properties of, say, two intersecting circles. These circles will be perfectly circular. But also, of course, there is only *one* Form of the circle. So what are these two perfect circles? Plato, apparently, had to introduce what he called the Mathematicals. Like the mathematical Forms they were perfect and thus were unlike ordinary things. But unlike the Forms, there could be many tokens of the same type, and in this they were like ordinary things. They were particulars, although perfect particulars. But if this is so, though perhaps the falling away from standards gave Plato an argument for the Mathematicals, it is not clear that it is any argument for the Forms.

But in any case, cannot ideal standards simply be things that we merely think of? We can quite knowingly form thoughts of that which does not exist. In the case of ideal standards nothing comes up to the standard, but by extrapolating from ordinary things that approximate to the standard in different degrees, we can form the thought of something that does come up to the standard. It turns out to be useful to do so. Why attribute metaphysical reality to such standards? They could be useful fictions. As a matter of fact, in the geometrical case it appears that such notions as that of a perfectly straight line or a perfectly circular object may be acquired directly in experience. For cannot something look perfectly straight or perfectly circular, even if it is not in fact so?

One should note that one thing that seems to keep a theory of uninstantiated universals going is the widespread idea that it is sufficient for a universal to exist if it is merely possible that it should be instantiated. I have found in discussion that this idea has particular appeal if it is empirically possible (that is, compatible with the laws of nature) that the alleged universal should have actual instances. Suppose, for instance, that somebody describes a very complex pattern of wallpaper but does not ever sketch the pattern or manufacture the wallpaper. Suppose nobody else does either in the whole history of the universe. It is clear that there was nothing in the laws of nature that prevented the pattern's ever having an instance, from ever having a token of the type. But is not that pattern a monadic universal, a complex and structural universal to be sure, but a universal nonetheless?

In this way, apparently, it is natural for philosophers to argue. But for myself I do not see the force of the argument. Philosophers do not reason that way about particulars. They do not argue that it is empirically possible that present-day France should be a monarchy and therefore that the present king of France exists, although, unfortunately for French royalists, he is not instantiated. Why argue in the same way about universals? Is it that philosophers think that universals are so special that they can exist whether or not particular things, which are contingent only, exist? If so, I think that this is no better than a prejudice, perhaps inherited from Plato.

There is one subtle variation of the argument to uninstantiated universals from their empirical possibility that I think has more weight. It has been developed by Michael Tooley (1987, 3.1.4 and 3.2). However, it depends upon deep considerations about the nature of the laws of nature, which cannot be discussed here. And in any case, the argument depends upon the laws' being found to have a very special structure, which it is unlikely that they actually have. As a result, it seems that the best that the argument shows is that uninstantiated universals are possible rather than actual. And even this conclusion may be avoidable (see Armstrong 1983, Ch. 8).

It may also be thought that considerations from mathematics, and the properties and relations postulated by mathematicians, push toward the recognition of uninstantiated universals. However, the whole project of bringing together the theory of universals with the disciplines of mathematics, although very important, cannot be undertaken here. I have sketched out, rather broadly, the way that I think it ought to go in a book on the nature of possibility (1989, Chapter 10).

From this point on, therefore, I am going to assume the truth of the Principle of Instantiation. As already noted, this does not compel one to abandon a two-realm doctrine. It does not compel one to bring the universals down among ordinary things. But it does *permit* one to do this, and to do so seems the natural way to develop the theory once one rejects uninstantiated universals.

II. DISJUNCTIVE, NEGATIVE, AND CONJUNCTIVE UNIVERSALS

For simplicity, in this section I will consider property universals only. But the points to be made appear to apply to relations also. We have already rejected uninstantiated universals. But it seems that the potential class of universals needs to be cut down a great deal further if we are to get a plausible theory. I will begin by giving reasons for rejecting disjunctive property universals. By a disjunctive property I mean a disjunction of (property) universals. Let us assume that particular electric charges and particular masses are universals. Then having charge C or having mass M (with C and M dummies for determinate, that is, definite values) would be an example of a disjunctive property. Why is it not a universal? Consider two objects. One has charge C but lacks mass M. The other lacks charge C but has mass M. So they have the disjunctive property having charge C or having mass M. But surely that does not show that, in any serious sense, they thereby have something identical? The whole point of a universal, however, is that it should be identical in its different instances.

There is another reason to deny that a disjunction of universals is a universal. There is some very close link between universals and causality. The link is of this nature. If a thing instantiates a certain universal, then, in virtue of that, it has the power to act in a certain way. For instance, if a thing has a certain mass, then it has the power to act upon the scalepan of a balance, or upon scales, in a certain way. Furthermore, different universals bestow different powers. Charge and mass, for instance, manifest themselves in different ways. I doubt if the link between universals and powers is a necessary one, but it seems real. Moreover, if, as seems abstractly possible, two different universals bestowed the very same powers, how could one ever know that they were two different universals? If they affect all apparatus, including our brains, in exactly the same way, will we not judge that we are dealing with one universal only?

Now suppose that a thing has charge C but lacks mass M. In virtue of charge C, it has certain powers to act. For instance, it repels things with like charge. Possession of the disjunctive property

C or M adds nothing to its power. This suggests that while C may be a genuine universal, C or M is not.

So I think that we should reject disjunctive universals. A similar case seems to hold against negative universals: the lack or absence of a property is not a property. If having charge C is the instantiation of a universal, then not having C is not the instantiating of a universal.

First, we may appeal to identity again. Is there really something in common, something identical, in everything that lacks charge C? Of course, there might be some universal property that just happened to be coextensive with lacking charge C. But the lack itself does not seem to be a factor found in each thing that lacks charge C.

Second, causal considerations seem to point in the same direction. It is a strange idea that lacks or absences do any causing. It is natural to say that a thing acts in virtue of positive factors alone. This also suggests that absences of universals are not universals.

It is true that there is some linguistic evidence that might be thought to point the other way. We do say things like 'lack of water caused his death.' At the surface, the statement says that a lack of water caused an absence of life. But how seriously should we take such ways of expressing ourselves? Michael Tooley has pointed out that we are unhappy to say 'lack of poison causes us to remain alive.' Yet if the surface way of understanding the first statement is correct, then the second statement should be understood in the same way and thought to be true. Certain counterfactual statements are true in both cases: If he had had water, then he would (could) have still been alive; if we had taken poison, we would have been dead now. These are causal truths. But they tell us very little about the actual causal factors operative in the two cases. We believe, I think, that these actual causal factors could be spelled out in purely positive terms.

It is interesting to notice that conjunctions of universals (having both charge C and mass M) escape the two criticisms leveled against disjunctive and negative universals. With conjunctions we do have identity. The very same conjunction of factors is present in each instance. There is no problem about causality. If a thing instantiates the conjunction, then it will have certain powers as a consequence. These powers will be different from those that the thing would have had if it had had just one of the conjuncts. It may even be that the conjunction can do more than the sum of what each property would do if each was instantiated alone. (As scientists say: There could be synergism. The effect could be more than the sum of each cause acting by itself.)

But there is one condition that ought to be put on conjunctive universals. Some thing (past, present, future) must actually have both properties and at the same time. This, of course, is simply the Principle of Instantiation applied to conjunctive universals.

III. PREDICATES AND UNIVERSALS

What has been said about uninstantiated universals, and also about disjunctions and negations of universals, has brought out a most important point. It is that there is no automatic passage from predicates (linguistic entities) to universals. For instance, the expression 'either having charge C or having mass M' is a perfectly good predicate. It could apply to, or be true of, innumerable objects. But as we have seen, this does not mean that there is a universal corresponding to this predicate.

Wittgenstein made a famous contribution to the Problem of Universals with his discussion of *family resemblances*. Wittgenstein was an antimetaphysician, and his object was to dissolve rather than to solve the Problem of Universals. He seems to have thought that what he said about family resemblances was (among other things) a step toward getting rid of the problem. But I think that the real moral of what he said is only that predicates and universals do not line up in any simple way.

In his *Philosophical Investigations* (1953, Secs. 66 and 67) he considered the notion of a *game*. He had this to say about it:

> 66. Consider for example the proceedings that we call "games." I mean board-games, card-games, ball-games, Olympic games, and so on. What is common to them all?—Don't say: "There *must* be something common, or they would not be called 'games'"!—but

look and see whether there is anything common to all.—For if you look at them you will not see something that is common to *all*, but similarities, relationships, and a whole series of them at that. To repeat: don't think, but look!—Look for example at board-games, with their multifarious relationships. Now pass to card-games; here you find many correspondences with the first group, but many common features drop out, and others appear. When we pass next to ball-games, much that is common is retained, but much is lost.—Are they all 'amusing'? Compare chess with noughts and crosses. Or is there always winning and losing, or competition between players? Think of patience. In ball games there is winning and losing; but when a child throws his ball at the wall and catches it again, this feature has disappeared. Look at the parts played by skill and luck; and at the games like ring-a-ring-a-roses; here is the element of amusement, but how many other characteristic features have disappeared! And we can go through the many, many other groups of games in the same way; we can see how similarities crop up and disappear.

And the result of this examination is: we see a complicated network of similarities overlapping and criss-crossing: sometimes overall similarities, sometimes similarities of detail.

67. I can think of no better expression to characterize these similarities than "family resemblances"; for the various resemblances between members of a family: build, features, colour of eyes, gait, temperament, etc. etc. overlap and crisscross in the same way—And I shall say: 'games' form a family.

This has been a very influential passage. Wittgenstein and his followers applied the point to all sorts of notions besides those of a game, including many of the central notions discussed by philosophers. But what should a believer in universals think that Wittgenstein has shown about universals?

Let us agree, as we probably should, that there is no universal of gamehood. But now what of this "complicated network of similarities overlapping and criss-crossing" of which Wittgenstein speaks? All the Realist has to do is to analyze each of these similarities in terms of common properties. That analysis of similarity is not a difficult or unfamiliar idea, though it is an analysis that would be contested by a Nominalist. But there will not be any property that runs through the whole class and makes them all games. To give a crude and oversimplified sketch, the situation might be like this:

Particulars:	*a*	*b*	*c*	*d*	*e*
Their properties:	FGHJ	GHJK	HJKL	JKLM	KLMN

Here F to N are supposed to be genuine property universals, and it is supposed that the predicate "game" applies in virtue of these properties. But the class of particulars [*a* . . . *e*], which is the class of all tokens of games, is a family in Wittgenstein's sense. Here, though, I have sketched an account of such families that is completely compatible with Realism about universals.

However, Wittgenstein's remarks do raise a big question. How does one decide whether one is or is not in the presence of a genuine property or relation? Wittgenstein says of games, "don't think, but look." As a general recipe, at least, that seems far too simple.

I do not think that there is any infallible way of deciding what are the true universals. It seems clear that we must not look to semantic considerations. As I said in section I of this essay, those who argue to particular universals from semantic data, from predicates to a universal corresponding to that predicate, argue in a very optimistic and unempirical manner. I call them *a priori realists*. Better, I think, is *a posteriori realism*. The best guide that we have to just what universals there are is total science.

For myself, I believe that this puts physics in a special position. There seem to be reasons (scientific, empirical, a posteriori reasons) to think that physics is *the* fundamental science. If that is correct, then such properties as mass, charge, extension, duration, space-time interval, and other properties envisaged by physics may be the true monadic universals. (They are mostly ranges of quantities. Quantities raise problems that will need some later discussion.) Spatio-temporal and causal relations will perhaps be the true polyadic universals.

If this is correct, then the ordinary types—the type red, the type horse, in general, the types of the manifest image of the world—will emerge as preliminary, rough-and-ready, classifications of reality. For the most part they are not false, but they are rough-and-ready. Many of them will be family affairs, as games appear to be. To the one type will correspond a whole family of universals and not always a very close family. And even where the ordinary types do carve the beast of reality along its true joints, they may still not expose those joints for the things that they are. But let it be emphasized that any identification of universals remains rather speculative. In what I have just been saying I have been trying to combine a philosophy of universals with Physicalism. Others may have other ideas.

IV. STATES OF AFFAIRS

In the Universals theory that we are examining, particulars instantiate properties, pairs of particulars instantiate (dyadic) relations, triples of particulars instantiate (triadic) relations, and so on as far as is needed. Suppose that *a* is F, with F a universal, or that *a* has R to *b*, with R a universal. It appears that we are required to recognize *a*'s being F and *a*'s having R to *b* as items in our ontology. I will speak of these items as *states of affairs*. Others have called them facts (e.g., Wittgenstein 1961, Skyrms 1981).

Why do we need to recognize states of affairs? Why not recognize simply particulars, universals (divided into properties and relations), and, perhaps, instantiation? The answer appears by considering the following point. If *a* is F, then it is entailed that *a* exists and that the universal F exists. However, *a* could exist, and F could exist, and yet it fails to be the case that *a* is F (F is instantiated, but instantiated elsewhere only). *a*'s being F involves something more than *a* and F. It is no good simply adding the fundamental tie or nexus of instantiation to the sum of *a* and F. The existence of *a*, of instantiation, and of F does not amount to *a*'s being F. The something more must be *a*'s being F—and this is a state of affairs.

This argument rests upon a general principle, which, following C. B. Martin, I call the truth-maker principle. According to this principle, for every contingent truth at least (and perhaps for all truths contingent or necessary) there must be something in the world that makes it true. "Something" here may be taken as widely as may be wished. The "making" is not causality, of course: Rather, it is that in the world in virtue of which the truth is true. Gustav Bergmann and his followers have spoken of the "ontological ground" of truths, and I think that this is my "something in the world" that makes truths true. An important point to notice is that different truths may all have the same truth-maker, or ontological ground. For instance, that this thing is colored, is red, and is scarlet are all made true by the thing's having a particular shade of color.

The truth-maker principle seems to me to be fairly obvious once attention is drawn to it, but I do not know how to argue for it further. It is to be noted however that some of those who take perfectly seriously the sort of metaphysical investigation that we are here engaged upon nevertheless reject the principle (e.g., David Lewis).

Accepting the truth-maker principle will lead one to reject Quine's view (1961) that *predicates* do not have to be taken seriously in considering the ontological implications of statements one takes to be true. Consider the difference between asserting that a certain surface is red and asserting that it is green. An upholder of the truth-maker principle will think that there has to be an ontological ground, a difference in the world, to account for the difference between the predicate 'red' applying to the surface and the predicate 'green' so applying. Of course, what that ontological ground is, is a further matter. There is no high road from the principle to universals and states of affairs.

Returning now to states of affairs, it may be pointed out that there are some reasons for accepting states of affairs even if the truth-maker principle is rejected. First, we can apparently refer to states of affairs, preparatory to saying something further about them. But it is generally, if not universally, conceded by philosophers that what can be referred to exists. Second, states of affairs are plausible candidates for the terms of causal relations. The state of affairs of *a*'s being F may be the cause of *b*'s being G. Third, as we shall see in Section VIII of this chapter, states of affairs can help to solve a fairly pressing problem in the theory of universals: how to understand the multiple location of property universals and the nonlocation of relation universals.

It is interesting to see that states of affairs seem not to be required by a Class Nominalist or a Resemblance Nominalist, and of course that is an important economy for their respective theories. The Class Nominalist analyzes *a*'s being F as *a*'s being a member of a class (or natural class) containing {*a, b, c,* . . . }. But here we have simply *a* and the class. The class-membership relation is internal, dictated by the nature of the terms. So we need not recognize it as something additional to the terms. The terms by themselves are sufficient truth-makers. Hence we do not need states of affairs.

The Resemblance Nominalist analyzes *a*'s being F as a matter of resemblance relations holding between *a* and, say, suitable paradigm Fs. But that relation is also internal, dictated by what I called the particularized nature of *a* and the paradigm objects. Once again, states of affairs are not needed.

(But it seems that a Predicate Nominalist *will* require states of affairs. *a*'s being F is analyzed as *a*'s falling under the predicate F. But how can the falling under be dictated simply by *a* and the linguistic object F? Falling under is an external relation.)

Now for something very important. States of affairs have some rather surprising characteristics. Let us call *a, b,* F, R, et cetera, the constituents of states of affairs. It turns out that it is possible for there to be two different states of affairs that nevertheless have *exactly the same constituents.*

Here is a simple example. Let R be a nonsymmetrical relation (for instance, loves). Let it be the case, contingently, that *a* has R to *b* and *b* has R to *a*. Two distinct states of affairs exist: *a*'s having R to *b*, and *b*'s having R to *a* (*a*'s loving *b* and *b*'s loving *a*). Indeed, these states of affairs are *wholly* distinct, in the sense that it is possible for either state of affairs to fail to obtain while the other exists. Yet the two states of affairs have exactly the same constituents.

You can get the same phenomenon with properties as well as relations (as pointed out by Lewis 1986c). Assume, as I think it is correct to assume, that a conjunction of states of affairs is itself a state of affairs. Then consider (1) *a*'s being F and *b*'s being G; and (2) *a*'s being G and *b*'s being F. Two wholly distinct states of affairs, it may be, but the very same constituents.

At this point, it is worth realizing that states of affairs may be required not simply by those who recognize universals but also by any philosophy that recognizes properties and relations, whether as universals or as particulars. This is very important, because we saw in examining Natural Class and Resemblance theories what difficulties there are in denying properties and relations (in espousing a blob view).

Suppose that *a* has R_1 to *b*, with R_1 a particular, but a nonsymmetrical, relation. If *b* has 'the same' relation to *a,* then, on a philosophy of tropes, we have *b*'s having R_2 to *a:* two states of affairs with different (though overlapping) constituents. For the loving that holds between *a* and *b* is a different object from the loving that holds between *b* and *a*. Nevertheless *a*'s having R_1 to *b* entails the existence of constituents *a,* R_1, and *b,* but the existence of these constituents does not entail that *a* has R_1 to *b*. So states of affairs still seem to be something more than their constituents.

With tropes, you never get different states of affairs constructed out of exactly the same constituents. But given just one set of constituents, more than one state of affairs having just these constituents is *possible*. From *a*, trope R_1, and *b,* for instance, we could get *a*'s having R_1 to *b* or *b*'s having R_1 to *a*. There is a way for a philosophy of tropes to avoid having to postulate states of affairs. But let us leave that aside until the next chapter.

I have spoken of the constituents of states of affairs. Could we also think and speak of them as *parts* of states of affairs? I think that it would be very unwise to think and speak of them in this way. Logicians have paid some attention to the notions of whole and part. They have worked out a formal calculus for manipulating these notions, which is sometimes called the calculus of individuals or, better, *mereology* (in Greek *meros* means a part). One philosopher who helped to work this out was Nelson Goodman, and in his book *The Structure of Appearance,* 1966, an account of mereology is given. There is one mereological principle that is very important for us here: If there are a number of things, and if they have a sum, that is, a whole of which they are parts, then they have just one sum.

I say *if* they have a sum, because it is controversial whether a number of things *always* have a sum. Do the square root of 2 and the Sydney Opera House have a sum? Philosophers differ on how permissive a mereology should be, that is, on whether there are limits to what you can sum, and if there are limits, where the limits fall. I myself would accept total permissiveness in summing. But all that is needed here is something that is agreed by all: where things can be summed, for each collection of things there is just one sum. We have just seen, however, that the complete constituents of a state of affairs are capable of being, and may actually even be, the complete constituents of a different state of affairs. Hence constituents do not stand to states of affairs as parts to whole.

It is worth noticing that complex universals have constituents rather than parts. At any rate this is so if we accept the Principle of Instantiation. Consider, for instance, conjunctive universals. If being P and Q is a conjunctive universal, then there must exist some particular, *x*, such that *x* is both P and Q. But to say that is to say that there exists at least one state of affairs of the form *x* is P and *x* is Q. For the conjunctive universal to exist is for there to be a state of affairs of a certain sort. As a result, it is misleading to say that P and Q are *parts* of the conjunctive universal, a thing that I myself did say in the past (1978b, Ch. 15, Sec. 11).

A very important type of complex universal is a structural property. A *structural* property involves a thing instantiating a certain pattern, such as a flag. Different parts (mereological parts) of the thing that instantiates the structural Property will have certain properties. If the structural property involves relations, as a flag does, some or all of these parts will be related in various ways. It is easy to see that states of affairs must be appealed to. If *a* has P, and *b* has Q, and *a* has R to *b*, then and only then the object [*a* + *b*] has the structural property that may be presented in a shorthand way as P-R-Q.

A final point before leaving this particularly important section. The fact that states of affairs, if they exist, have a nonmereological mode of composition may have consequences for the theory examined in the previous chapter: the view that particulars are no more than bundles of universals. (I understand that this point comes from Mark Johnston.) We have seen that different states of affairs can have exactly the same constituents (*a*'s loving *b*, and *b*'s loving *a*). We have previously argued against the Bundle theory that two bundles containing exactly the same universals are impossible. They would be the very same bundle. Yet, considering the matter independently of the Bundle theory, why should not two different particulars be exactly alike? But now suppose that, as is plausible, we treat a bundling of universals as a state of affairs. Why should not exactly the same universals be bundled up in different ways?

In reply, I think it must be admitted that this is conceivable. But it would depend upon the Bundle theorist's working out a scheme that allowed for different bundling of the very same things. This is not provided for in the actual Bundle theories that have been developed. So if they want to take this path, then the onus is on Bundle theorists to try to develop their theory in a new way.

V. A WORLD OF STATES OF AFFAIRS?

In the previous section it was argued that a philosophy that admits both particulars and universals ought to admit states of affairs (facts), which have particulars and universals as constituents (not as parts). As a matter of fact we saw that to introduce properties and relations at all, even as particulars, would apparently involve states of affairs. But our present concern is with universals.

The suggestion to be put forward now is that we should think of the world as a world of states of affairs, with particulars and universals only having existence within states of affairs. We have already argued for a Principle of Instantiation for universals. If this is a true principle, then the way is open to regard a universal as an identical element present in certain states of affairs. A particular that existed outside states of affairs would not be clothed in any properties or relations. It may be called a *bare* particular. If the world is to be a world of states of affairs we must add to the Principle of Instantiation a Principle of the Rejection of Bare Particulars.

This second principle looks plausible enough. In a Universals theory, it is universals that give a thing its nature, kind, or sort. A bare particular would not instantiate any universals, and thus would have no nature, be of no kind or sort. What could we make of such an entity? Perhaps a particular need not have any relations to any other particular—perhaps it could be quite isolated. But it must instantiate at least one property.

VI. THE THIN AND THE THICK PARTICULAR

Here is a problem that has been raised by John Quilter (1985). He calls it the "Antinomy of Bare Particulars." Suppose that particular *a* instantiates property F. *a* is F. This 'is' is obviously not the 'is' of identity, as in *a* is *a* or F is F. *a* and F are different entities, one being a particular, the other a universal. The 'is' we are dealing with is the 'is' of instantiation—of a fundamental tie between particular and property. But if the 'is' is not the 'is' of identity, then it appears that *a* considered in itself is really a bare particular lacking any properties. But in that case *a* has not got the property F. The property F remains outside *a*—just as transcendent forms remain outside the particular in Plato's theory.

I believe that we can at least begin to meet this difficulty by drawing the important distinction . . . between the *thin* and the *thick* particular. The thin particular is *a*, taken apart from its properties (substratum). It is linked to its properties by instantiation, but it is not identical with them. It is not bare because to be bare it would have to be not instantiating any properties. But though clothed, it is thin.

However, this is not the only way that a particular can be thought of. It can also be thought of as involving its properties. Indeed, that seems to be the normal way that we think of particulars. This is the thick particular. But the thick particular, because it enfolds both thin particulars and properties, held together by instantiation, can be nothing but a state of affairs.

Suppose that *a* instantiates F, G, H, . . . They comprise the totality of *a*'s (nonrelational) properties. Now form the conjunctive property F&G&H. . . . Call this property N, where N is meant to be short for *a*'s nature. *a* is N is true, and *a*'s being N is a (rather complex) state of affairs. It is also the thick particular. *The thick particular is a state of affairs.* The properties of a thing are "contained within it" because they are constituents of this state of affairs. (Notice that states of affairs, such as *a*'s being N, are not repeatable. So, along with thin particulars, they can be called particulars also.)

Therefore, in one sense a particular is propertyless. That is the thin particular. In another sense it enfolds properties within itself. In the latter case it is the thick particular and is a state of affairs. I think that this answers the difficulty raised by the Antinomy of Bare Particulars.

Two points before leaving this section: First, the distinction between thin and thick particulars does not depend upon a doctrine of properties as universals. It does presuppose a substance-attribute account of a particular, rather than a bundle view. But we have already seen that it is possible to take a substance-attribute view with the attributes as particulars, that is, as tropes. The thin particular remains the particular with its attributes abstracted away. The thick particular is again a state of affairs: the thin particular's having the (particular) attributes that it has.

Second, the thin and the thick particular are really the two ends of a scale. In between is the particular clothed with some, but only some, of its properties. They may be properties that are, for one reason or another, particularly important. This intermediate particular will, of course, be a state of affairs, but a less comprehensive one than the state of affairs that is the thick particular.

VII. UNIVERSALS AS WAYS

The discussion in the previous section is not entirely satisfactory as it stands. It still leaves us with a picture of the thin particular and its properties as distinct metaphysical nodules that are linked together in states of affairs to form the thick particular. This makes the Principles of Instantiation and of the Rejection of Bare Particulars seem a bit arbitrary. Why must the nodules occur together? Could they not come apart? But would they then not be those unwanted creatures: uninstantiated universals and bare particulars?

Here I turn to a suggestion that has often been in the air, but had not, I think, been expounded systematically before David Seargent's book on Stout's theory of universals (1985). Unlike Stout, Seargent accepts universals, and in Chapter 4 he argues that we should think of them as *ways*. Properties are ways things are. The mass or charge of an electron is a way the electron is (in this case, a way that any electron is). Relations are ways things stand to each other.

If a property is a way that a thing is, then this brings the property into very intimate connection with the thing, but without destroying the distinction between them. One can see the point of thinking of instantiation as a fundamental connection, a tie or nexus closer than mere relation. Nor will one be much tempted by the idea of an uninstantiated property. A way that things are could hardly exist on its own.

Again, one will not be tempted by the idea that the way a thing stands to other things, a relation, could exist on its own, independent of the things. (Not that the idea was ever very tempting! It is easier to substantialize properties than relations.)

It may be objected that the phrases "ways things are" and "ways things stand to each other" beg the question against uninstantiated universals. Should I not have spoken of ways things could be and ways things could stand to each other, thus cancelling the implication that the ways must be the ways of actual things?

However, my argument is not attempting to take advantage of this semantic point. My contention is that once properties and relations are thought of not as things, but as ways, it is profoundly unnatural to think of these ways as floating free from things. Ways, I am saying, are naturally construed only as ways actual things are or ways actual things stand to each other. The idea that properties and relations can exist uninstantiated is nourished by the idea that they are not ways but things.

Before concluding this section, I should like to note that the conception of properties and relations as ways does not depend upon taking them as universals. We can still think of *a*'s property as a way that *a* is, even if the property is particular, a trope. It will just be the case that no other thing besides *a* can be that way. Similarly, a relation holding between *a* and *b* can still be a way *a* and *b* stand to each other, even if this way is nonrepeatable.

It is very important to realize that the notions of states of affairs and their constituents, the distinction between the thin and the thick particular, and the conception of properties and relations as ways things are and ways things stand to other things are available, if desired, to a philosophy of tropes as much as to a philosophy of universals.

VIII. MULTIPLE LOCATION

To bring universals from a platonic realm down to earth, down to space-time, seems to involve saying something rather strange. It seems to follow that universals are, or may be, multiply located. For are they not to be found wherever the particulars that instantiate them are found? If two different electrons each have charge *e*, then *e*, one thing, a universal, is to be found in two different places, the places where the two electrons are, yet entirely and completely in each place. This has seemed wildly paradoxical to many philosophers.

Plato appears to be raising this difficulty in the *Philebus*, 15b–c. There he asked about a Form: "Can it be as a whole outside itself, and thus come to be one and identical in one thing and in several at once,—a view which might be thought to be the most impossible of all?" (trans. A. E. Taylor). A theory that kept universals in a separate realm from particulars would at least avoid this difficulty!

You might try just accepting the multiple location of universals. Some philosophers have. But then a difficulty can be raised: What about relations? Perhaps one can give *properties* a multiple location. But just where will you locate the "multiply located" relations? In the related things? That does not sound right. If *a* precedes *b* is the relation in both *a* and *b*? Or in the thing [*a* + *b*]? Neither answer sounds right. But if it is not in the things, where is it?

I am inclined to meet the difficulty by saying that talk of the location of universals, while better than placing them in another realm, is also not quite appropriate. What should be said first, I think, is that the world is a world of states of affairs. These states of affairs involve particulars having properties and standing in relations to each other. The properties and relations are universals, which means both that different particulars can have the very same property and that different pairs, triples, . . . , of particulars can stand in the very same relation to each other. I do not think that all that is too startling a claim.

But if Naturalism is true, then the world is a single spatio-temporal manifold. What does this come to in terms of the states of affairs theory? That is, how do we reconcile Naturalism with the view sketched in the previous paragraph? It would be an enormous undertaking, presumably involving both fundamental science and philosophy, to give an answer involving even the sketchiest detail. All that can be said here is that the space-time world would have to be an enormous plurality or conjunction of states of affairs, with all the particulars that feature in the states of affairs linked up together (in states of affairs) by spatio-temporal relations.

To talk of locating universals in space-time then emerges as a crude way of speaking. Space-time is not a box into which universals are put. Universals are constituents of states of affairs. Space-time is a conjunction of states of affairs. In that sense universals are "in" space-time. But they are in it as helping to constitute it. I think that this is a reasonable understanding of *universalia in rebus,* and I hope that it meets Plato's objection. (For more on this topic see my "Can a Naturalist Believe in Universals?" [1988a], together with critical comment in the same volume by Gilead Bar-Elli 1988.)

IX. HIGHER-ORDER TYPES

We have seen that Class Nominalism and Resemblance Nominalism are in some difficulty with higher-order types: types whose tokens are themselves types. The difficulty is largely caused by the fact that these theories try to account for our talk about properties and relations without actually allowing that there are any properties or relations. There is no such difficulty for a theory, such as the Universals theory, that admits properties and relations. But once we have properties and relations, possibilities open up. For now it is possible that these first-order properties and relations themselves have properties and relations.

Is it then being suggested that we should introduce *higher-order* properties and relations in order to explain higher-order types? Here we have to be very careful. Consider:

> Redness is more like orange than it is like yellow.

One might take this as a second-order relation, of being more like than, which holds between three first-order universals. (Assuming they are universals, which can be disputed.) We have seen, however, that resemblance is an *internal* relation, one that flows necessarily from the nature of the terms. (Most philosophers would take the proposition above to be a necessary truth.)

[Elsewhere] I have suggested that where we have internal relation, there we do not have anything ontologically extra over and above the related terms. The relation supervenes upon the terms: In every possible world that contains those terms, the relation holds. That, I think, makes the relation an ontological free lunch. But if that is so, we do not have any need to postulate a genuine higher-order relation.

Now many of the things that we want to say about properties and relations seem to be necessary truths. Consider red is a color, a meter is longer than a yard, being a mile distant from is a symmetrical relation. They all seem to be necessary truths. I am inclined to treat this necessity as giving us a clue that when we have a perspicuous account or analysis of these truths (no easy matter!), we shall not find any need to postulate higher-order properties and relations.

One very interesting internal relation that can hold between universals depends on these universals' being *complex.* We have noted that it is unwise to speak of universals having parts, because that suggests the part-whole relations studied by mereology. But complex universals do have constituents, and different universals may nevertheless contain the same constituent. A simple example is the complex properties P&Q and Q&R. Q is a common constituent of the two different properties. In virtue of these common constituents some complex universals may be said to be incompletely identical with each other.

I believe that these relations of incomplete identity between universals are of immense importance.

In particular, they can be used to explain what *quantities* are. Consider the whole range of a quantity such as mass (an ounce in mass, a ton in mass, etc.). What unifies this class of universals, I suggest, are the incomplete identities holding between any two members of the class. But I leave development of this point aside for the present.

So do we ever need to postulate genuinely higher-order properties and relations of first-order properties and relations? For myself I believe that we do. In particular, we require relations between universals in order to give a satisfactory account of laws of nature. These should not be thought of, in the tradition of Hume, as mere regularities in the behavior of things. Rather, laws of nature are a matter of the presence of one property ensuring, or probabilifying, the presence of another. These are relations of external relations, contingent relations, holding between the one property and the other.

What of higher-order properties? I think that there may be need to postulate such properties in connection with the analysis of *functional* laws. But I cannot discuss this here. (See Armstrong 1983 for an account of laws of nature as relations between universals. Functional laws are discussed in Chapter 7 of that book.)

I will leave the topic of higher-order relations and properties of universals with this brief mention. What does require further discussion is the topic of the resemblance of universals. I will preface this, however, with a discussion of the formal properties of the relation of resemblance. We shall find that the Universals theory is very well placed to explain these formal properties.

X. THE FORMAL PROPERTIES OF RESEMBLANCE

It will be remembered that the Resemblance Nominalist, for whom resemblance is a primitive notion, requires a series of special axioms for the characteristics of resemblance, axioms that he cannot justify but only state. (The Natural Class Nominalist equally requires special axioms for degrees of naturalness of classes.)

First, resemblance is symmetrical. If *a* resembles *b* to a certain degree, then *b* resembles *a* to just that degree. The upholder of universals can give a straightforward reductive explanation of this symmetry: It is simply the symmetry of identity. In the simplest case of resemblance, it is just a matter of common, that is, identical properties. However, a less simple case, it may be that *a* and *b* have no identical properties, yet have one or more *resembling* properties. I shall argue in the next section that in such a case the properties have common, that is, identical constituents. If that is correct, then the symmetry of resemblance of properties is again explained by the symmetry of identity.

If *a* is exactly like *b*, and *b* exactly like *c*, then *a* must be exactly like *c*. Exact resemblance is not merely symmetrical: It is transitive. The Universals theory analyzes this situation by saying that *a, b,* and *c* have exactly the same, the identical, properties. Identity is transitive.

We saw that the transitivity of exact resemblance is only a particular application of something more general. If *a* resembles *b* to some degree, and if *b* exactly resembles *c,* then *a* resembles *c* to just the same extent that *a* resembles *b*. Resemblance of any degree is conserved under the substitution of exactly resembling objects. It is easy to see that this formal property will hold if resemblance always involves some identity of properties and that exact resemblance is identity of all properties.

Less than exact resemblance is not transitive. *a* can resemble *b* to a certain degree, *b* resemble *c* to the same degree, yet *a* fail to resemble *c* to that degree. Again the Universals theory explains the situation without the least difficulty. *a* and *b* have something identical, as have *b* and *c*. But because the identity is partial (incomplete) only, it need not be in the same *(identical)* respect. So transitivity fails for some, though not all, cases.

The Universals theory also explains why the notion of degrees of resemblance is so rough-and-ready. If resemblance is a matter of different identities in different cases, it is easy to see that degrees of resemblance will be a partially subjective matter, depending upon what particular properties we happen to be interested in, in the particular context. A Resemblance theory, on the contrary, just has to accept the rough-and-ready nature of resemblance as a primitive fact.

XI. RESEMBLANCE BETWEEN UNIVERSALS

Particulars, tokens, resemble each other in different degrees. The Universals theory begins, at least, by trying to analyze this in terms of common properties. But it seems that properties themselves resemble each other. Red, orange, and yellow all resemble each other: We group them together as colors. Triangularity and squareness resemble each other: They are both shapes. The ounce, the kilo, and the ton all resemble each other: They are all masses. Just as with resemblance of particulars, resemblance of properties admits of degree. Red is more like orange than it is like yellow. An ounce is more like a kilo than it is like a ton. These resemblances at the property level transfer themselves down to the first-order level of particulars. Other things being equal, a red thing is more like an orange thing than it is like a yellow thing.

In Section III of this essay I discussed Wittgenstein's reflections on the word 'game' and other family-resemblance notions. I presented the following schematic picture of how a Universals theory might analyze such a situation:

Particulars:	*a*	*b*	*c*	*d*	*e*
Their properties:	FGHJ	GHJK	HJKL	JKLM	KLMN

We can now see this picture quite seriously underdescribes the typical situation. What contributes to resemblance-without-identity of the different sorts of thing covered by the one general word are resemblances-without-identity in the properties F, G, H, . . . For instance, all the objects falling under a certain general word may do so in virtue of having shape or mass. But they may have rather different sorts of shape and mass, so that the properties involved in applying the word are different in different cases, yet still have a likeness.

Here is an attractive preliminary way to think of the resemblance of universals. Many properties (colors, shapes, masses, etc.) fall into *orders*. (The orders may or may not be one dimensional.) The orders, which by and large are objective and not just a way that we happen to like arranging properties, are *resemblance* orders. Two properties that are close together in a certain order resemble each other closely. To be a color, say, is to be a property that lies in a certain resemblance order. Similarly for being a shape or a mass. You can work your way from one color to another via the close resemblance of intermediates. That is what makes the colors *colors*. It explains what we mean by saying, for instance, red is a color. The same goes for the shapes and masses, and so on.

Now because the relations involved are resemblance relations, they are internal relations, dictated by the nature of their terms. (I should argue that they are not something additional to the terms.) How shall we analyze the resemblance relations involved?

An analysis in the spirit of a Universals theory would be to appeal to common properties of the resembling things. This would involve common properties of properties: higher-order properties. However, although there seems to be no objection in principle to such a move, it is hard to see how such an analysis can be applied to the present cases. If the order considered contains many different properties to be ordered, as in the case of most quantities, huge numbers of higher-order properties would be required. We seem to have no independent grip on these properties besides their role in solving our present problem.

Perhaps then we should walk a bit towards a Resemblance theory? . . . But that was because it rejected properties at the first-order level. We have got first-order properties now. Should we say that some of these first-order properties stand in unanalyzable resemblance relations to each other? Though unanalyzable, these relations of resemblance will have varying degrees of closeness. The resemblances will flow from the nature of the resembling universals. (Remember the particularized nature that I introduced in order to make Resemblance Nominalism as plausible as possible. But now we are appealing to the nature of universals.)

Such unanalyzable, primitive, resemblance of universals I regard as a fall-back position for the Realist about universals. It may in the end have to be accepted, at least for some cases. But it is an uncomfortable compromise, true to the superficial appearances, but lacking the deep attractiveness of a theory that always takes resemblance to involve some degree of identity.

A certain phenomenon noticed by one or two philosophers may provide us with encouragement. If we consider ordinary, first-order, particulars, then, two things, while remaining two, can resemble exactly. At least exact resemblance is possible (assuming that the Identity of Indiscernibles is not a necessary truth). In the limit, resemblance of particulars does not give identity. But now consider the resemblance of universals. As resemblance of properties gets closer and closer, we arrive in the limit at identity. Two become one. This suggests that as resemblance gets closer, more and more constituents of the resembling properties are identical, until all the constituents are identical and we have identity rather than resemblance.

Here is a working out of this idea in a simple case: Consider the property of being just five kilograms in mass. For something to have that property the thing must consist of two parts, parts with no overlap between them, such that one part is just four kilos in mass, the other just one. It is a simple form of structural property, simple because no special relations are needed between the two parts: The parts can be scattered parts. We can use the language of states of affairs. The state of affairs of something's being a five-kilo object is the conjunction of two states of affairs: something's being four kilos plus something else's (nonoverlapping something else) being a one-kilo state of affairs.

We can now understand the (reasonably close) resemblance between the properties being five kilos in mass and being four kilos in mass. (We can also see clearly, incidentally, why no object can have both these properties at the same time.) Being five kilos in mass involves the five-kilo thing having a part, a proper part to put it technically, that is four kilos in mass. (Moreover, a thing that is four kilos in mass can never be more than a proper part of a five-kilo object.) The properties resemble because a four-kilo object is a large proportion of a five-kilo object. The bigger the part, the closer to identity, and so the closer the resemblance.

My idea is that in this or similar ways, the resemblances holding between properties can be explained. Resembling properties are never simple properties. Different simple properties never resemble, at any rate in the absence of common higher-order properties. Resembling properties are complex properties, their complexity established by logical analysis or, more likely, empirical, scientific, identification. The complexity will regularly involve structures, with the parts of the things having the property themselves having properties and, perhaps, standing in relations to other parts. Thus, the "soundiness" of sound is to be identified with a suitable wave structure of a suitable medium. Resemblances between sounds are to be spelled out in terms of resemblances between their wave structures, ultimately getting down to such things as length, which can be treated in the same way as that indicated for mass.

(Hume thought that different simple properties *can* resemble. In the *Treatise,* Bk. I, Pt. 1, Sec. VII, note, he wrote:

> 'Tis evident, that even different simple ideas may have a similarity or resemblance to each other; nor is it necessary, that the point or circumstance of resemblance should be distinct or separable from that in which they differ. *Blue* and *green* are different simple ideas, but are more resembling than *blue* and *scarlet;* tho' their perfect simplicity excludes all possibility of separation or distinction.

Hume, in effect, is here upholding primitive resemblance between properties. I would argue against him that the color properties have a concealed complexity, a complexity that nevertheless operates upon us to produce an awareness of resemblance. Hume's view that "simple ideas" must be as they appear to be, namely, simple, would prevent him from accepting this.)

Whether this program can be carried through or not, it is an appealing idea that we can get rid of primitive resemblances between universals. But there are some quite formidable difficulties. A recent attempt of mine to advance the program can be found in my paper "Are Quantities Relations?".

XII. THE FUNDAMENTAL TIE

What of the need for a fundamental tie—the tie or nexus of instantiation? Many people have thought it an overwhelming difficulty for a theory of universals. I do not think that the problem of characterizing the nature of the tie should detain us. This was Plato's concern in the first part of his *Parmenides.*

There he showed conclusively that the relation of particular to form cannot be either "participation" or "imitation." But it is perfectly reasonable for an upholder of universals to claim that instantiation is a primitive that cannot be explicated by any analysis, definition, or metaphor. Nevertheless, the upholder of universals can go on to say, we all understand what it is to judge or even just to perceive that a particular has a property or that a relation holds between two or more terms. After all, the Natural Class theory takes the notion of a natural class as primitive and the Resemblance Nominalist does the same with the relation of resemblance. Why not instantiation as a directly apprehended primitive?

The problem is rather the regress that seems to be involved. The particular *a* instantiates property F. Prima facie, however, instantiation is a universal, found wherever there are things having properties. So this state of affairs, *a*'s instantiating property F, is a token of the type ***instantiation*** (but dyadic instantiation now). The state of affairs instantiates instantiation. But here we have another token of instantiation. So the state of affairs (that state of affairs instantiating instantiation) also instantiates instantiation. And so on ad infinitum. The regress that results is either vicious or at least viciously uneconomical.

This regress I have called in the past the relation regress. It could also be called the fundamental tie regress or nexus regress. It takes the fundamental tie patronized by particular solutions to the Problem of Universals. It then applies that solution to the particular tie and attempts to deduce a regress.

The Natural Class theory uses class membership as the nexus; the Resemblance Nominalist uses primitive resemblance. [Elsewhere] I tried to answer the nexus-regress argument as it was deployed by Russell against the Resemblance theory. I suggested that what saved the Resemblance theory was that resemblance is an internal relation, dictated by the nature of its terms, the resembling things. Internal relations, it is plausible to hold, are nothing over and above their terms. The same holds for resemblances between resemblance situations, and so on. But if so, I argued, the regress is as harmless as, say, the truth regress.

The same holds for class membership. Given *a* and given {*a*, . . . } the relation of class membership supervenes. Hence, it seems, the regress is not to be feared. No ontological regress, no need to postulate an infinity of extra entities (with each bringing up the same old problem).

But in general at least and perhaps in every case, the fact that an object instantiates a certain property does not flow from the nature of the object and the nature of the universal that are involved. The connection is contingent. And if an object is related to another object and that relation is external, the same point holds. So it may seem that, unlike the cases of resemblance and class membership, the regress of instantiation goes through.

However, my idea is that the instantiation regress can be halted after one step. We have to allow the introduction of a fundamental tie or nexus: instantiation. But suppose that we have that *a* instantiates F or that *a* and *b* in that order instantiate R. Do we have to advance any further? I do not think that we do. For note that the alleged advance is now, as it was not at the first step, logically determined by the postulated states of affairs. If *a* instantiates F and instantiation is a universal-like entity, then we are logically forced to say that *a*, F, and instantiation instantiate instantiation, and so on. But perhaps we can allow this while denying that to "*a*, F, and instantiation instantiating instantiation" any extra state of affairs in the world corresponds. As we go on expanding the regress, our statements remain true, but no new truth-maker, or ontological ground, is required for all these statements to be true.

I do not feel totally secure about this answer. But suppose that it is unsatisfactory. Will not that unsatisfactoriness also reopen the question of the other two regresses, the class and the resemblance regress? If the obtaining of instantiation must be analyzed in terms of instantiation, will it not be fair to insist that the holding of class membership must be analyzed in terms of classes and the relation of resemblance must be analyzed in terms of resemblances? And what theory then will escape the whipping? As Berkeley pointed out on a number of occasions, what is an objection to all theories equally does nothing to favor some over others.

A very important final point. In Section IV of this chapter we encountered the notion of states of affairs, with (thin) particulars and universals as the constituents of states of affairs. But we said that *a*'s being F is something more than just its constituents *a* and F. It may now be seen that in talking about states of affairs and talking about instantiation, we are talking about the same phenomenon. The state of affairs of *a*'s being F exists if and only if *a* instantiates F because these are two ways of talking about the same thing. Similarly, if R is a symmetrical relation, then *a*'s having R to *b* is the same thing as *a* and *b* instantiating R. If R is nonsymmetrical or asymmetrical, then the situation is a little more complex. There are two possible states of affairs that can both be rendered as *a* and *b* instantiating R: *a*'s having R to *b* and *b*'s having R to *a*. That, indeed, suggests that talking about states of affairs is a simpler and more perspicuous way of talking than talking about instantiation. The *fundamental tie,* or *nexus,* in a Universals theory is nothing but the bringing together of particulars and universals in states of affairs.

XIII. THE APPARATUS OF AN ATTRIBUTE THEORY OF UNIVERSALS

The Universals theory, in its subject-attribute form, requires a reasonably comprehensive ontology to account for the objective existence of natural classes. First, it countenances properties and relations. However, in view of the great difficulties posed by theories that try to construct properties and relations out of other materials, this is perhaps prudence rather than extravagance. Second, it accepts the existence of states of affairs. These are complex entities having constituents, but these constituents differ from the parts of wholes treated by the calculus of whole and part. It is true that any recognition of properties and relations, even as particulars, as tropes, will apparently involve states of affairs. But the rules of composition for possible states of affairs that involve only tropes are somewhat nearer to the rules for whole and part. (For instance, if R is a nonsymmetrical relation, a Universals theory has the possibility of two wholly distinct states of affairs: *a*R*b* and *b*R*a* composed of the very same constituents. With tropes the two Rs could not be identical. Given *a,* trope R', and *b,* one might have *a*R'*b* or *b*R'*a* but not both, although one could have, for example, *a*R'*b* and *b*R''*a*.)

The Universals theory requires the notion of the instantiation of a property, the instantiation of a dyadic relation, or a triadic relation, . . . or of an n-adic relation. (If what universals there are is a contingent matter, not to be settled a priori, then not all these sorts of instantiation need actually exist.) But notice that the trope theory, in its subject-attribute form, also requires monadic, dyadic, triadic, . . . fundamental ties. By contrast, a Bundle theory of tropes does not require a monadic tie (it substitutes the dyadic compresence of properties), but it still requires dyadic, triadic, . . . relations *between* bundles.

But as we have noticed, a Universals theory does not require both states of affairs and a set of fundamental ties. To have one is to have the other. The Universals theory may require a primitive notion of degrees of resemblance holding between universals. This seems a quite heavy extra commitment for the theory. As a result, a good deal may hang on whether this sort of resemblance can be analyzed in terms of overlap of constituents of the resembling universals.

Reading Questions

1. What is the difference between *universalia ante res* and *universalia in rebus*?
2. Armstrong asserts that Plato's "'argument from meaning' is a very bad argument." In defense of this claim, Armstrong maintains that there does not have to be some single thing corresponding to a general word. Since the argument from meaning denies this very thing, is Armstrong merely begging the question against Plato?
3. One of Armstrong's goals is to combine a philosophy of universals with physicalism. But what is the motivation for this goal? Is it an *a priori* dogma that all truths are physical truths? How could Armstrong square this with pure mathematics?

4. Armstrong considers the idea that properties are ways things are, and states that a proponent of this view would not be tempted by the idea of an uninstantiated property. "A way that things are could hardly exist on its own," he writes. Consider the (alleged) property of *being a square circle.* This "property" is not only uninstantiated, but uninstantiable—nothing could be a square circle. That is, being a square circle is a way that nothing could be. Why doesn't this show *universalia ante res* to be consistent with properties as ways things are?

Further Readings

Books

Armstrong, David M. 1978. *A Theory of Universals.* 2 vols. Cambridge: Cambridge University Press.

———. 1989. *Universals: An Opinionated Introduction.* Boulder: Westview Publishing Co.

Bacon, John. 1995. *Universals and Property Instances: The Alphabet of Being.* Oxford: Blackwell.

Bealer, George. 1983. *Quality and Concept.* Oxford: Oxford University Press.

Bigelow, John. 1988. *The Reality of Numbers: A Physicalist's Philosophy of Mathematics.* Oxford: Oxford University Press.

Bonevac, Daniel A. 1982. *Reduction in the Abstract Sciences.* Indianapolis: Hackett.

Burgess, John, and Gideon Rosen. 1997. *Subject with No Object: Strategies for Nominalistic Interpretation of Mathematics.* Oxford: Oxford University Press.

Campbell, Keith. 1990. *Abstract Particulars.* Oxford: Blackwell.

Cocchiarella, Nino B. 1986. *Logical Investigations of Predication Theory and the Problem of Universals.* Napoli, Italy: Bibliopolis.

Field, Hartry. 1989. *Realism, Mathematics, and Modality.* Oxford: Blackwell.

Hale, Bob. 1988. *Abstract Objects.* Oxford: Blackwell.

Katz, Jerrold J. 1981. *Language and Other Abstract Objects.* Totowa: Rowman and Littlefield.

Lewis, David. 1986. *On the Plurality of Worlds.* Oxford: Blackwell.

Loux, Michael J., ed. 1979. *The Possible and the Actual: Readings in the Metaphysics of Modality.* Ithaca, NY: Cornell University Press.

Maddy, Penelope. 1990. *Realism in Mathematics.* Oxford: Oxford University Press.

Mellor, D. H., and Alex Oliver, eds. 1997. *Properties.* Oxford: Oxford University Press.

Moreland, James Porter. 1985. *Universals, Qualities, and Quality-Instances: A Defense of Realism.* Lanham: University Press of America.

Newman, Andrew. 1992. *The Physical Basis of Predication.* Oxford: Blackwell.

Schoedinger, Andrew B., ed. 1991. *The Problem of Universals.* Atlantic Highlands, NJ: Humanities Press.

Zalta, Edward N. 1983. *Abstract Objects: An Introduction to Axiomatic Metaphysics.* Dordrecht, Holland: D. Reidel.

Articles

Armstrong, David M. 1986. "In Defence of Structural Universals." *Australasian Journal of Philosophy* 64: 85–88.

Bealer, George. 1993. "Universals." *The Journal of Philosophy* 90 (1): 5–32.

Chisholm, Roderick M. 1992. "Identity Criteria for Properties." *Harvard Review of Philosophy* 2 (1): 14–17.

Creath, Richard. 1980. "Nominalism by Theft." *American Philosophical Quarterly* 17: 311–318.

Elder, Crawford L. 1996. "Realism and Determinable Properties." *Philosophy and Phenomenological Research* 56 (1): 149–159.

Hazen, Allen. 1985. "Nominalism and Abstract Entities." *Analysis* 45: 65–68.

Jubien, Michael. 1989. "Straight Talk about Sets." *Philosophical Topics:* 91–107.

Lewis, David. 1984. "New Work for a Theory of Universals." *Australasian Journal of Philosophy* 62: 343–377.

Lewis, David. 1986. "Against Structural Universals." *Australasian Journal of Philosophy* 64: 25–46.

Loux, Michael J. 1986. "Toward an Aristotelian Theory of Abstract Objects." In *Studies in Essentialism,* ed. P. A. French, T. E. Uehling, and H. K. Wettstein. Vol. 2, *Midwest Studies in Philosophy.* Minneapolis: University of Minnesota Press.

Lowe, E. J. 1995. "The Metaphysics of Abstract Objects." *The Journal of Philosophy* 92 (10): 509–524.

Mellor, D. H. 1993. "Properties and Predicates." In *Ontology, Causality and Mind: Essays in Honour of D. M. Armstrong,* ed. J. Bacon. Cambridge: Cambridge University Press.

Mortensen, Chris. 1987. "Arguing for Universals." *Revue Internationale de Philosophie* 41: 97–111.

Oddie, Graham. 1982. "Armstrong on the Eleatic Principle and Abstract Entities." *Philosophical Studies* 41: 285–295.

Oliver, Alex. 1996. "The Metaphysics of Properties." *Mind* 105 (417): 1–80.

Oldfield, Edward. 1981. "Reference to Abstract Entities." *Canadian Journal of Philosophy* 11: 425–438.

Tymoczko, Thomas. 1991. "Mathematics, Science, and Ontology." *Synthèse:* 201–228.

Part V

Secondary Qualities

EDWARD W. AVERILL

Introduction to Secondary Qualities

THE ENGLISH PHILOSOPHER JOHN LOCKE (1632–1704) is famous for, among other things, his explanation and defense of the primary-secondary quality distinction. He thought the properties of objects could be divided into perceiver-dependent properties, the *secondary qualities,* and perceiver-independent properties, the *primary qualities.* Those who accept Locke's distinction usually include, as Locke did, colors, tastes, smells, sounds, and warmth and coldness among the secondary qualities; and size, shape, weight (or mass), and electrical charge among the primary qualities. Most contemporary philosophers think that Locke's original arguments for his distinction are unsuccessful. So this introduction begins by sketching a modern argument for Locke's distinction as it applies to colors and shapes, and then moves on to other accounts of color.[1] (In discussions of colors as secondary qualities, black, white, and gray count as colors.)

To get a feel for Locke's distinction, consider property dependency in a nonperceptual case. At one time DDT had the property of being poisonous to mosquitoes. Because a change in mosquitoes, but not in DDT, DDT is no longer poisonous to them. This shows that being poisonous to mosquitoes is not an inherent property of DDT but depends on the characteristics of both mosquitoes and DDT. In other words, being poisonous to mosquitoes is a relational property; that is, "*x* is poisonous to mosquitoes" is short for "*x* is poisonous to normal mosquitoes in population *y*." DDT is poisonous to normal mosquitoes in the population of mosquitoes that existed in 1950, but DDT is not poisonous to normal mosquitoes in the population of mosquitoes that exists in 1999. Could yellowness be similarly dependent upon humans? Could the human perceptual system change (like mosquitoes changed) so that, say, gold things (like DDT) that were yellow (were poisonous) would no longer be yellow (would not be poisonous)?

Here in rough outline is an argument for the claim that yellowness is a perceiver-dependent property. There are three types of cone cells in the retina at the back of the human eye; the S cells (short wavelength receptors), the M cells (middle wavelength receptors), and L cells (long wavelength receptors). Each type of cone cell has a pigmented tip that absorbs light in a specific band of wavelengths. These three bands of wavelengths overlap—both the L and M cells are sensitive to light between 587 nm and

This essay was commissioned especially for this volume and appears here for the first time.

590 nm in the lower yellow part of the spectrum. Furthermore, within its band a cone cell is more sensitive to some wavelengths than to others. The relative rates of light absorption by the S, M, and L cells form the initial basis for color perception. (There are more details in the essay by Hardin.) So, if the sensitivities of these cells to light at specific wavelengths were to change, objects would appear to have different colors. Suppose, for example, that the pigment of the L and M cone cells were to change slightly so that L cells were more sensitive to light between 587 nm and 590 nm and M cells were less sensitive to such light. The pigment change does not change the way the excitations of the S, M, and L cells is processed by the optic nerve and the brain. The pigment change does effect the reactions of the M and L cells in a narrow band of the spectrum, and so the change affects the relative rates at which the S and M and L cells absorb light in this band. Since only light from a narrow band of the spectrum is affected, the change will not affect the apparent color of most objects. Indeed, many yellow objects do not reflect light from this part of the spectrum, and so they would continue to look yellow. However, gold reflects light between 587 nm and 590 nm and from the red part of the spectrum. So, after the change, lumps of the metal gold look red to normal observers (normal after the change) under normal viewing conditions. Thus gold, which was yellow before the change, would be red after the change, although none of the nonrelational properties of gold have changed. (Note that this last step moves from a claim about a property gold appears to have to a claim about a property gold does have.)

Here is another argument for the same conclusion. Imagine that the air changed so that one of the gases in our atmosphere absorbed light between 587 nm and 590 nm. Like the imagined change in our eyes, this change in the atmosphere would make gold look red instead of yellow. So gold would be red after the change.

Supposing for the moment that these *gold-could-be-red* arguments are sound, three Lockean assumptions about the nature of color and color perception explain this soundness.[2] Before and after the change, a physical object that looks red to a person looks a certain distinctive way to that person. To capture this point in terms of properties, assume that when a physical object looks red to a person, the person visually represents the object as having a distinctive color property. Call this property "sensuous-red." *First Assumption:* a physical object looks red to a person if and only if the person visually represents the physical object as being sensuous-red. (Similarly for other colors.)[3]

Second Assumption: besides sensuous-redness there is a relational concept of redness; that is, a physical object is red-for-population-*x*-in-environment-*y*. So when we say "John's car is red" we imply that John's car is red-for-our-population-in-our-environment. Given the gold-could-be-red argument, gold is yellow for one population (in its environment) and it is red for another population (in the same environment).

Third Assumption: relational-redness is logically constructed from sensuous-redness. Locke spelled out this construction in terms of dispositions, or powers, of objects to look red:

(1) Necessarily, for any physical object *O*, whose surfaces are not intricately curved or very small, *O* is red-for-population-*x*-in-environment-*y* if and only if normal members of *x* would visually represent *O* as sensuous-red if they were to perceive *O* under normal conditions for *y*. (Similarly for other colors.)

(1) does not apply to afterimages, and (1) does not apply to all physical objects. (The color of objects that cannot be seen easily is derivative from the color of objects that can be seen easily. Explaining how this derivation goes amounts to filling out the Third

Assumption farther than [1] does.) (1) says that there is a logical connection between looking red and being red. If such a connection exists, it would justify the last move in the gold-could-be-red arguments that goes from gold looks red under normal conditions to gold is red.[4] Notice that in a normal perceptual case observers will see a gold ring as having two color properties: it will look sensuous-yellow and it will look relational-yellow. (An object that looks relational-yellow looks like it would appear sensuous-yellow under normal conditions.) A red afterimage, by contrast, merely looks sensuous-red.

Squareness is not like yellowness. Given the gold-could-be-red arguments, a change in our nervous systems could change the yellow color of gold objects. But no change in the human nervous system would change the squareness of an object; that is, if the squareness of an object changes then the object itself changes, because the squareness is not a relational property of an object. The reason yellowness is different from squareness in this way is that looking square is not tightly tied to being square but looking yellow is tightly tied to being yellow. Yellowness is associated with a characteristic appearance that is unique to easily perceived yellow physical objects; that is, yellow objects, seen under normal conditions, appear sensuous-yellow. By contrast, having an electrical charge is not associated with any distinctive appearance. However, there is a distinctive "square look" that all square objects have, when seen under normal conditions. If all humans developed bad curvatures in the lenses of their eyes, it might happen that square objects no longer had this square look. But square objects would not cease to be square, although it might happen that a new distinctive sort of look came to be associated with looking square. In short, gold rings could change color in virtue of a change in the way they look to us, but square table tops could not change shape by virtue of a change in the way they look to us. The conclusion is that the shape of an object is perceiver independent, but color of an object is perceiver dependent. This is the point that Locke's primary-secondary quality distinction seeks to capture.

Locke thought that the primary-secondary quality distinction has its basis in another distinction. He thought that the primary qualities, but not the-secondary qualities, are causally explanatory; that is, size, shape, mass, electrical charge, and molecular structure are all causally explanatory properties of objects. Consider how this applies to the look of things. That an object is square is part of the causal explanation of why it looks square. But that an object is yellow does not causally explain its looking yellow under normal circumstances, because being yellow is logically constructed from looking yellow.

To get a sense of what a full Lockean account of color amounts to, consider what has not been explained in the above sketch. (1) depends on the concepts of normal-observer-for-population-x and normal-viewing-conditions-for-population-x. But, "normal" needs to be defined and, as Hardin's essay shows, this is difficult to do.[6] On the First Assumption, a physical object that looks red is visually represented as being sensuous-red. There is a difficulty in extending this assumption to afterimages, as the Boghossian and Velleman essay points out. So an account of looks red must explain the sense in which an afterimage can look red, and why looking red is different for sensations than it is for perceptions. Since the Third Assumption accounts for relational-red in terms of sensuous-red, to show how colors fit into the causal structure of the world it must show how sensuous-red fits into the world's causal structure. Clearly, spelling out a Lockean account of color is a very big undertaking.

As the preceding paragraph suggests, there are several ways of criticizing a Lockean account of color. One famous criticism notes that a surface made up of tiny red and green dots looks yellow under normal conditions. So looking red and green under normal conditions is not a necessary condition for being red and green; and looking yellow under normal conditions is not sufficient for being yellow. (The argument from microscopes, explained in Armstrong's essay, carries this criticism further.) But even if one or more of the three Lockean assumptions about color is incorrect, how could the gold-could-be-red arguments be answered? One reply holds that these arguments only show that our use of the terms "red" and "yellow" could change; that is, the color of gold would not change but the way we use color terms would change. After the change, gold would still be yellow and not red, given our present use of "yellow" and "red"; but gold would also be red and not yellow, given our new use of "yellow" and "red." (This criticism does not accept the last step in the gold-could-be-red argument that goes from gold looks red under normal conditions [after the change] to gold is red after the change. Filling out this criticism is a matter of explaining the principles of linguistic change on which it is based, and how those principles apply to "poisonous to mosquitoes.")

Accounts of color that are not perceiver-dependent accounts divide into two large categories. First, the colors of physical objects are perceiver-independent properties of physical objects. (For example, see the essay by Armstrong.) Second, colors are not properties of physical objects; that is, physical objects have no color. (This view is defended by Boghossian and Velleman and by Hardin.)

Accounts of color that take the first approach usually hold that the colors of objects are identical to physical properties of those objects. To understand how this might work, consider the spectral reflectance of an object. When light of a specific wavelength and a specific intensity hits an object, some of the light is reflected, some is transmitted, and some is absorbed. For most opaque surfaces the following law holds: for each wavelength λ of the light hitting the surface, the ratio of the intensity of the incident light at λ to the intensity of the reflected light at λ is a constant. For any given surface, a list of these ratios for each wavelength characterizes the way the surface of the object reflects light. This list is the spectral reflectance of the object. Most opaque objects are visible because they reflect some of the light that strikes them diffusely. (Mirrors reflect light without diffusing it.) So it may seem plausible to hold that the color of a physical object, which diffuses the light it reflects, is identical to its spectral reflectance. But this cannot be quite right. A surface that only reflects light at a wavelength of 580 nm looks yellow. But some surfaces that only reflect light at 540 nm and 670 nm look exactly the same shade of yellow as a surface that only reflects light at 580 nm. Many surfaces appear to be the same shade of the same color, but have different spectral reflectances. So it cannot be that a specific color shade is identical to a specific spectral reflectance.

One way of handling this problem is to hold that a specific color shade is identical to a disjunction of specific spectral reflectances. For example, the shade of yellow mentioned above is identical to either a spectral reflectance near 100% at 580 nm and near 0% at other wavelengths, or a spectral reflectance of near 100% at 540 nm and 670 nm and near 0% at other wavelengths, or a spectral reflectance of . . . . More generally:

(2) If x is a shade of color, then there exists a set of spectral reflectances $s-1 \ldots s-n$ such that x is identical to $s-1$ or $s-2$ or . . . $s-n$. So, necessarily, a physical object is the color x if and only if its spectral reflectance is $s-1$ or $s-2$ or . . . $s-n$.

Given (2), after the change imagined in the gold-could-be-red arguments gold is still yellow because the change does not change the spectral reflectance of gold. (The Boghossian and Velleman essay and the Hardin essay contain criticisms of [2].)

Some non-Lockean accounts of color hold that physical objects have no color. We can imagine conditions under which things would not seem to have any stable color. Suppose that the pigments of the cone cells in human eyes varied dramatically from person to person so that some people saw gold as blue, others as red, still others as green. Suppose further that human eyes adapted to small changes in the level of light intensity slowly, over hours, and during this time the colors of things appeared to change a good deal. Surely there would be no point in assigning colors to things. The Hardin essay plays up the similarities of our present condition to this extreme condition, and concludes (or merely suggests?) that physical objects have no colors. Gold is not yellow! Snow is not white! To put the point another way, Hardin holds that human color perception is so varied that we cannot logically construct the concepts of red-physical-object out of our color experiences along the lines of (1). So Hardin's challenge to the modern Lockean is to show how the Third Assumption can be carried out.

Boghossian and Velleman also hold that physical objects have no color, but they reach this conclusion by a different argument. They argue that some color properties are intrinsic to visual fields and that physical objects are seen as having these color properties. If it is further assumed that the color properties of visual fields are the only color properties physical objects are seen as having (and that physical objects have no unseen color properties), it follows that physical objects have no color properties. The implicit assumption that red physical objects are not seen as having more than one sort of red property is not obvious. (See the remarks under [1].) To support their assumption Boghossian and Velleman argue against content-dispositionalism; that is, there is no dispositional property of redness that physical objects are seen as having, which is defined in terms of some more basic property of redness (like sensuous-red, or in their terminology red* or red') that physical objects are also seen as having. Like Hardin, Boghossian and Velleman argue against the Third Assumption by arguing against some form of (1).

NOTES

1. Jonathan Bennett's contemporary interpretation and defense of Locke's view of secondary qualities is highly regarded. (*Locke, Berkeley, Hume: Central Themes* [Oxford: Clarendon Press, 1972].) Bennett's new argument for the perceiver dependence of secondary qualities was criticized by Margaret D. Wilson ("The Primary-Secondary Quality Distinction: Against Two Recent Defenses" [unpublished manuscript, Princeton University, 1979]) and by Edward Wilson Averill ("The Primary-Secondary Quality Distinction," *The Philosophical Review*, vol. 91, no. 3 [July 1982], 343–361). Later Averill developed another argument for the perceiver dependency of color, which is sketched here. ("The Relational Nature of Color," *The Philosophical Review*, vol. 101, no. 3, [July 1992], 551–588.) Boghossian and Velleman criticize Bennett's interpretation of Locke (see note 16 in their essay) and suggest a different interpretation. On their interpretation, what distinguishes primary from secondary qualities is that primary, but not secondary, qualities are uninstantiated in physical objects.

2. The three assumptions set out are similar to three assumptions Bennett attributes to Locke, op. cit., p. 103.

3. This assumption about looking red is limited to the perception of physical objects. In the terminology of the Boghossian and Velleman essay it is a limited form of the intentionalist assumption about color perception.

4. In terms of the Boghossian and Velleman essay, (1) is something like the first version of content-dispositionalism. For this version, Boghossian and Velleman distinguish two concepts of red; the one they call "red" roughly corresponds to relational-red, and the one they call "red*" roughly corresponds to sensuous-red.

5. There are other problems with (1). (1) implies that "looks the same in relational-color" is a transitive relation, which is false. (1) also fails to cover all physical objects. For a way of spelling out the Third Assumption that does not use (1), see Averill, op. cit., 1992. On that account sensuous-red, but not relational-red, is an uninstantiated property.

20 The Secondary Qualities

DAVID M. ARMSTRONG

I. THE PROBLEM OF THE SECONDARY QUALITIES

IN WHAT WE HAVE SAID SO FAR, it has been assumed that the 'secondary qualities'—colour, sound, taste, smell, heat and cold—are objective properties of physical objects or physical processes. We discover the colour of an object, or its taste, in just the same way that we discover its shape or its texture. But, it may be argued, such a naïvely realistic attitude to these qualities is indeed naïve. For modern science finds no room for such properties in its account of the physical world.

Some properties of physical objects and processes are susceptible of logical analysis in terms of other properties. Thus, we might give an analysis of hardness in terms of a disposition in the hard object not to change its shape or break up easily when under pressure. But colour, sound, taste, smell, heat and cold, even if no other qualities, seem to resist any such analysis. They seem to be *irreducible* qualities. Any connection that they have with other properties of physical objects seems to be a contingent one.

However, as is well-known, the conception of the secondary qualities as irreducible or unanalysable properties of physical objects or processes has led to the greatest problems. The difficulties have been with us at least since the time of Galileo, and have only become more pressing with every advance in physical knowledge. How are we to fit such irreducible properties into the physical world as it is conceived by physicists? For instance, modern physics pictures an ordinary macroscopic object as an indefinitely large swarm of 'fundamental particles' moving in a space that is, despite the numbers of these particles, relatively empty. Only in the densest stars, where matter exists in a 'collapsed' state, are the fundamental particles packed in at all closely. Now what can we predicate the secondary qualities of? They surely cannot be predicable of individual 'fundamental particles.' Are they, then, 'emergent' properties of the whole area or surface of the area 'occupied' by the particles? Perhaps this is a barely possible line to take, but it is not one that a physicist, or, I think, anyone else, could look upon with much enthusiasm.

In the excellent terminology of Wilfrid Sellars, there is a *prima facie* contradiction between the 'manifest image' of the physical world that ordinary perception presents us with, and the 'scientific image' of the world that physicists are gradually articulating for us. If the secondary qualities are taken to be irreducible properties of physical objects, they can be fitted into the manifest, but not the scientific, image of the world.

Some philosophers and scientists have sought to remove the contradiction by arguing that the 'scientific image' of the world proposed by physics is a mere *manner of speaking*. The real world is the world of the manifest image, and the 'scientific image' is an abstraction of certain features from the manifest world, or is a fiction that has only heuristic and predictive value. I have said what I have to say in criticism of this view in *Perception and the Physical World,* Chapter 12, Section 2. There is very forceful criticism in J. J. C. Smart's *Philosophy and Scientific Realism* (Routledge, 1963), Chapter 2. Here I will say only that I think the scientific image of the world has to be taken seriously. It has to be taken ontologically. If this is so, there is still a problem of how the secondary qualities can be fitted into the physical world.

But most philosophers and scientists who have tried to tackle this problem have reached a different conclusion. They have concluded that the

From David M. Armstrong, A Materialist Theory of the Mind *(London: Routledge and Kegan Paul, 1968). Reprinted by permission of the publisher.*

irreducible *qualia* cannot really qualify the physical objects they appear to qualify. The *qualia* qualify items in the mind of the perceiver. To say that a physical surface is coloured cannot truly imply anything more than that this surface has the power of producing items having a certain irreducible quality in the mind of a normal perceiver.

But from this conclusion further conclusions follow.

In the first place, Berkeley was surely right in arguing that if the secondary qualities qualify mental items, then the other directly perceived properties are also properties of mental, not physical, objects. Colour and visible extension, for instance, are inextricably bound up with each other. If colour qualifies something mental, so does visible extension. And so we are led to the view that what we are non-inferentially aware of in perception is never a physical situation but a situation in our own mind: our own current sense-impressions, perhaps. We are forced to accept a Representative theory of perception, with all its difficulties, unless, indeed, we accept the still more desperate doctrine of Phenomenalism.

In the second place, we are back in that bifurcation of mental and physical reality which it is the object of a physicalist doctrine of man to overcome. Man's mind becomes a quite different sort of object from physical objects because it is qualified by, or in some way linked with, qualities that physical science need take no account of. To accept the view that the secondary qualities are irreducible *qualia* of mental items would be to abandon the whole programme of this work.

It is clear, then, that a Materialist account of the mind must offer some new account of the secondary qualities. In this chapter, therefore, I put forward the view that they are nothing but *physical* properties of physical objects or processes. Colours of surfaces, on this view, will be simply physical properties of those surfaces. And by 'physical properties' is meant the sort of properties a physicist would be prepared to attribute to those surfaces, the sort of properties that would figure in the 'scientific image' of the world.

Notice that it is a physical surface's *being* red that is being identified with physical properties of that surface, and not that surface's *looking* red. Something looking red is a matter of a person or persons having certain perceptions as a result of the causal action of that surface on their eyes. These perceptions, we have argued, are not themselves red, and so do not necessitate the postulating of any *qualia* at all. The perceptions are acquirings of belief, or 'potential belief,' that something physical *is* red; or, at a deeper level of analysis, they are acquirings of capacities for selective behaviour towards particular red objects, capacities characteristically brought into existence by the red object. As we may put it, red objects are red, but red sensations are not red, save *per accidens*.

In what follows I will concern myself chiefly with the colours of surfaces. There are other physical things that are coloured, such as transparent cubes of coloured glass. There are also other secondary qualities. But in the case of colours of surfaces various problems for our identification come up in an especially acute form. So I do not think that this concentration of attention will involve any evasion of issues.

I will proceed by considering in turn two sorts of objection to a physicalist account of the secondary qualities: *a priori* objections, and empirical objections.

II. *A PRIORI* OBJECTIONS TO IDENTIFYING SECONDARY QUALITIES WITH PHYSICAL PROPERTIES

Objection 1. We knew what redness was long before we knew what physical properties are necessary and sufficient for redness of physical surface. So redness is not a physical property of surfaces.

Reply. The claim that redness is a purely physical property of surfaces is not intended to be a logical analysis of the concept of red. It is not a necessary truth that redness is a purely physical property of that surface. We have argued in this work that, as a contingent matter of fact, mental states are purely physical states of the central nervous system. In just the same way, it is now being claimed that, as a matter of contingent fact, redness is a purely physical property of surfaces.

Objection 2. The secondary qualities of things might be imagined to change completely, although the physical characteristics with which they are correlated did not change at all. (What is being imagined here is a change in quality that everybody *noticed.*) So the secondary qualities cannot be identified with physical characteristics.

Reply. The objection depends upon covertly treating the connection between the secondary qualities and physical characteristics as if it were necessary, and not contingent. It is perfectly possible, in the logician's sense of 'possible,' that the redness of surfaces is not a physical property of the surface. And, if this is so, it is perfectly possible that the redness of a surface should begin to vary independently of the physical properties of the surface. Now to imagine a migration of the secondary qualities is simply to imagine that both these conditions are fulfilled.

Consider a parallel case. It is logically possible that the morning star is not the evening star. And if the morning star is not the evening star, it is also possible that one day the two should appear in the sky side-by-side. But, of course, *given that the morning star is in fact the evening star,* it is not possible that the two should appear in the sky side-by-side. In the same way, it is possible that redness of surface is not a physical property of the surface. If this is so, it is further possible that redness of surface should vary independently of the physical properties of the surface. But, of course, *given that redness of surface is in fact a physical property of that surface,* it is not possible that redness of surface should vary independently of the physical properties of the surface.

Objection 3. But if the identity of redness with some physical property of surfaces is a contingent one, then it must be possible to give an account of the meaning of the word 'red' in terms logically independent of any reference to the physical properties of objects or their surfaces. This explanation of meaning can only take the form of saying that 'red' stands for a unique, irreducible, property: redness.

Reply. I grant that we must give an account of the meaning of the word 'red' in terms that involve no reference to the physical properties of surfaces. But I deny that this explanation must take the form of saying that 'redness' stands for an irreducible property.

But before going on to develop my own account of the meaning of the word 'red,' I will say that I think that this is *the* critical objection to the identification of secondary qualities with physical properties. If the identification is incorrect, this is the reason that it is incorrect. When the contingent identification of mental states with states of the central nervous system was proposed in Chapter 6, we considered the objection that this required a characterization of the meaning of the phrase 'mental state' in terms quite independent of any reference to physical states of the brain. This objection was taken to be an objection of crucial importance, and, indeed, our account of the concept of a mental state as a state of the person apt for the production of certain sorts of behaviour grew out of the attempt to answer this objection. Now the objection we are currently considering to the proposed account of the secondary qualities is essentially the same objection. We may suspect that it is an objection of peculiar importance.

A mental state is a state of the person apt for the production of certain sorts of behaviour, but the further nature of this state of the person is not given by our concept of a mental state. This blank or gap in the formula enables us to make sense of the assertion that these states are purely physical states of the brain. Physical states can, as it were, be plugged into the gap. Now if we want to make a contingent identification of redness with some physical property, must not our account of what redness is involve some similar blank or gap? There seems to be no other way to carry through a reductive programme.

But at this point it may seem that in the case of colour there is no hope of working the same trick that was worked with the concept of a mental state. It is plausible to say that the concept of a mental state is a complex concept, and so that the phrase 'mental state' admits of definition or unfolding. The blank or gap then appears within the definition. But a word like 'red' seems to be indefinable except by synonyms. In Lockean terms, the concept of red is a 'simple idea.' And so there is, as it were, no room for any blank or gap within our concept of redness.

But this line of thought has overlooked one possibility. Suppose that our concept of red is *all* blank or gap? May it not be that we know *nothing* about what redness is in its own nature? May it not be that we only know contingent truths about redness—such truths as that it is a property detected by the eye and possessed, or apparently possessed, by such things as the surface of ripe tomatoes and Jonathan apples? Then it would be possible to go on to a contingent identification of redness with a physical property of the red thing.

But if the concept of redness is all blank or gap, would it not follow that the word 'red' lacks a meaning, a conclusion which is manifestly false? By no means. Consider the following imaginary situation. Let us suppose that there is an indefinitely large group of people who fall into a number of quite distinct subgroups: 'families' that do not overlap. Members of the same 'family' all have certain subtleties of feature and behaviour in common that set them off from the members of the other 'families.' Normal observers can be fairly easily taught to sort members of the group as a whole into these mutually exclusive subgroups. Normal observers spontaneously agree that individuals picked at random belong in a particular sub-group. Nevertheless, because the differences between the sub-groups are very subtle, such observers can make no comment on, and, indeed, have no knowledge of, the way that they sort out these people. They simply sort individuals into groups in a spontaneous way as the result of the action of these individuals upon the perceiver's sense-organs.

Now under such circumstances, I suggest, observers would be entitled to talk about the differentiating properties, and bestow names upon these properties, *although they would know nothing at all about the intrinsic nature of the properties.* Certain persons are all put into one group. They can then be said to have a certain property *P* not possessed by those who are put in other groups. *P* is given the name '*p*.' But what can the observers say about *P*? Only that it attaches to certain individuals and no others. But that it attaches to these individuals is surely only a contingent fact about *P*.

I suggest that this imaginary situation will serve as a model for our knowledge of redness. Red objects all have a property in common which all normal observers can detect. But we normal observers are not aware of the nature of this property. We can only identify the property by reference to the way it is detected (by the eyes) and by mentioning objects that happen to be red. What principally stands in the way of our accepting this solution is the illusion that perception gives us a through-and-through knowledge of, or acquaintance with, such qualities as redness. (There is also the objection that we seem to have a greater knowledge of the intrinsic nature of redness than this account would allow, an objection that will be considered and answered shortly.)

Our imaginary case can easily be developed so that it will parallel the various things that we want to say about redness. Here are two important parallels. It was argued in the previous chapter that an object, or class of objects, that normal observers in normal conditions take to be red, may not be red in fact but only appear so. This possibility can be duplicated in the imaginary model. A certain individual, or class of individuals, may look to everybody to belong to sub-group A. But investigators might discover that the objective physical characteristics of this individual or individuals are those of sub-group B, although, for some further reason, these characteristics, when they attach to these individuals, have the effects upon perceivers that members of sub-group A normally have. Here we have individuals that look to be A's but are in fact B's. And, because they look to be A's they would be just as useful as real A's in teaching somebody what an A was.

It was also argued in the previous chapter that it was meaningful to say that different observers might have 'inverted spectra' with respect to each other, so that one man's 'red' should be the other's 'green,' and *vice-versa,* and so for all other colours, although this inversion is behaviourly undetectable. Again, this possibility can be duplicated in our model. Suppose investigators discover that individuals in group A affect some people in manner *x.* The objects stimulate their sense-organs, and then bring about processes in their brain, associated with perception of the sort *x.*

Individuals in group B affect the same perceivers in manner *y*. But suppose there are other perceivers who are affected by individuals in group A in manner *y*, and by individuals in group B in manner *x*, although this inversion is behaviourly undetectable. It would follow that A's look to one group as B's look to the other group, and *vice-versa*.

Here, then, is an account of the concept of redness, and so of the meaning of the word 'red.' Now, if the account is correct, then, just as there arises the question what, as a contingent matter of fact, a mental state is, so there arises the question what, as a contingent matter of fact, the property of redness actually is. And here, just as in the case of mental states, various answers seem to be in good logical order. It is an intelligible hypothesis that redness is an irreducible property that is quite different from the properties considered by physicists. But, from the standpoint of total science, the most ***plausible*** answer is that redness is a purely physical property. In this way we solve the difficulties raised in the first section of this chapter.

If properties such as redness are not identified with purely physical properties, then, presumably they will have to be correlated with the physical properties. But every consideration of economy speaks in favour of the identification. If we take a Realistic view of the entities of physics, then we have the physical properties on our hands in any case. So why not identify the secondary qualities with the physical properties?

Objection 4. The attempt we have given to characterize redness as an ***unknown*** property of certain surfaces and objects, breaks down when we remember that redness is seen to have something in common with blue, green, orange, etc. They are all *colours*. If our eyes became sensitive to ultra-violet and infra-red radiation we might become aware of hitherto unperceived visual qualities. Yet we might recognize at once that they were colours, that is, that they resembled the known colours. How could we do this if perception gave us no acquaintance with the nature of colours? Again, we recognize that the colours resemble and differ from each other in certain complex ways. For instance, red is more like orange than it is like yellow. Does not this imply some acquaintance with the nature of the three colours?

Reply. This objection shows that there has been an omission in our account of redness in particular and colour-concepts in general. It is true that we recognize that red, green, blue, orange, etc., have something in common. To be precise, what we recognize is that they are all determinates falling under a common determinable. Calling them all 'colours' is a verbal acknowledgement of this recognition. But this does not mean that we have any concrete knowledge of what this determinable, colour, is. We simply recognize that red, green, blue, orange and the other colours are determinates falling under a single determinable, ***without having any visual awareness of what that determinable is.*** The particular colours are identified as visually detected properties of certain surfaces and objects. We recognize further that these properties are determinates falling under a common determinable. But further than this, perception fails to inform us.

In defence of this view, we may recall the notorious difficulty that philosophers have found in saying what it is that all the colours have in common. Any alternative view of the nature of colours, or other 'ranges' of secondary qualities, may be challenged to give an account of the uniting principle of such ranges. I am proposing to solve the problem by saying that, although we perceive that the individual colours, etc., have something in common, we do not perceive what it is.

Now we also recognize further similarities and differences between the colours besides the fact that they are all determinates falling under the one determinable. The perceived relationship between red, orange and yellow is a case in point. On our account, this is interpreted as a recognition that red things are more like orange things than they are like yellow things in a certain respect, unaccompanied by any awareness of what that respect is.

Our account is also able to give a solution of the problem of colour-incompatibilities. (It will be assumed here that the colour-incompatibilities are logical incompatibilities, that it is logically impossible for two different colours both to characterize the whole of a surface at the same time. If the incompatibility is empirical, then a similar line of solution applies, ***mutatis mutandis.***)

Consider first a more straightforward case of the perceptual recognition of an incompatibility.

Suppose I can see that a line is of a certain length. In bringing the line under the concept of length *x* (which, let us say, I do simply by using my eyes) it is automatically given that the line is not of another length. If I failed to realize this, to this extent my concept of length would be defective. So in perceiving that the line is of a certain length I perceive that it cannot be of another length.

Now, in perceiving that a certain surface is red, I perceive that it cannot be another colour. Just as different lengths are incompatible, so are different colours. But if my account of our perceptual acquaintance with colour is correct, then, unlike the case of length, vision does not inform us what colours are. All that we know is that they are incompatible. So the perception that a red surface cannot simultaneously have another colour is a perception that it has an unknown property, a property incompatible with certain other similar unknown properties possessed by other surfaces. The solution of the colour-incompatibility problem is simply to recognize that, in this case, the awareness of the incompatibility of certain properties is unaccompanied by any knowledge of the nature of the properties.

But suppose that the contingent identification of colours of surfaces with purely physical properties of the surfaces were correct. Suppose, to make a simplifying assumption, that the physical property of the surface that constituted redness of surface was a relatively fine-grained grid, while the physical property of the surface that constituted greenness of surface was a relatively coarse-grained grid. A grid cannot be fine-grained and coarse-grained all over at the same time, and so the incompatibility would *turn out* to be a quite unmysterious incompatibility of physical properties. Perception, of course, does not inform us that the incompatibility is an incompatibility of this simple sort. It simply informs us that the properties are incompatible.

The position may be illustrated by a somewhat fanciful analogy. Suppose that pairs of statements are put in separate envelopes, and suppose that some of the pairs are incompatible statements, although some are not. Now suppose that a clairvoyant has certain non-inferential knowledge concerning these statement-pairs. He always knows infallibly whether any given envelope contains a compatible or an incompatible pair of statements. But he never knows what the content of the statements is. This may serve as a picture of our knowledge derived from perception of the compatibilities and incompatibilities of the secondary qualities.

If the traditional view is accepted that properties such as redness and greenness are irreducible qualities whose whole nature is perceptually given, then some *other* account of how colour-incompatibilities are possible must be produced. The history of philosophical discussions of this problem shows that a satisfactory account is not easily found. It is a powerful argument for our view that it solves the problem.

Notice, finally, before moving on to consider the next objection, that the fact that colours are recognized to be different determinables falling under a common determinate enables a physicalist theory of colour to give worthy hostages to fortune. If the physical properties connected with the colour of surfaces did not turn out to be determinates falling under a determinable physical property, this would count against this theory of colour.

In the same way, we can predict that the physical properties connected with red, orange and yellow surfaces will be such that in some respect they form a scale, a scale on which the physical property connected with orange is the intermediate member. Such a prediction might be falsified.

Objection 5. Colour-surfaces are homogeneous. It is part of the essence of what it is to be a red surface that *each* part of that surface is also red. Contrast this with 'shaped like a grid.' Not every part of a grid-shaped thing is itself grid-shaped. Gridded surfaces are not homogeneous in this respect. Now the physical property of the surface with which the redness of the surface is to be putatively identified may not be a homogeneous property. But how can something homogeneous be identified with something that is not homogeneous?

Reply. May we not distinguish between relative and complete homogeneity? Consider a uniformly coloured surface. Now consider any ***minimum visible*** in that surface, by which is meant here any smallest portion of the surface that we are able to discern in the conditions of observation then prevailing. This ***minimum*** must be coloured. But need we say that any proper part of this ***minimum*** is necessarily coloured? I do not think we need.

Consider a parallel case. The larger parts of a quantity of water are themselves quantities of water. But when we get down to the molecular level we finally reach parts which are not quantities of water. Why should it not be the same with coloured surfaces?

The objection that can be brought against this answer, and which I used to think conclusive, is that proper parts of a coloured *minimum* can lack colour only if colour is a structural, or nonhomogeneous, property of surfaces. We cannot divide water forever, and still reach quantities of water, because, it turns out, water is made up of water-molecules which have a certain complex structure: hydrogen and oxygen atoms linked together. But colour of surface seems to be something that lacks any such complexity of structure: in this respect it is a simple property.

On the view of colour being put forward here, however, we can evade this point by arguing that the 'simplicity' of colour is epistemological, not ontological. Colour may in fact be a 'structural' property of physical surfaces, but this is a fact that is not given to us in perception. *All* we are given in the perception of a uniform coloured surface is that the *minima* do not differ in colour-property. So, for all perception tells us, the property is a simple one as opposed to a structural one. But since, on our view, the property of colour is like an iceberg—the greater part of its nature is hidden from us—it *also* remains possible that colour is a structural property, not a simple one. Perception fails to inform us. What hinders us from seeing this possibility is the belief that perception gives us a through-and-through acquaintance with colour.

Objection 6. Colour, sound, taste, smell, heat and cold are the paradigms of *qualities*. Yet the proposed analysis is reducing them to mere theoretical concepts, mere 'that whiches' whose nature must be determined by further scientific research. Surely this is a topsy-turvey account of the secondary qualities?

Reply. On the view being argued for, it is part of the notion of a quality such as red that it has certain resemblances to, and differences from, other properties. Thus, in perception we are directly aware that all the colours are determinates falling under a single determinable. Again, we are directly aware that red is more like orange than it is like yellow. And so on. We are aware of many resemblances and differences between red and the other colours. So we are not completely in the dark as to the intrinsic nature of a secondary quality, even if all we perceive of this nature is its resemblance to, and difference from, other qualities. This, I hope, preserves the distinction between our concepts of the secondary qualities, on the one hand, and mere theoretical concepts, on the other.

Objection 7. If we 'reduce' the secondary qualities of objects to purely physical properties of objects, then it seems that we will not be able to form a coherent conception of a physical object. This is an argument I myself advanced in the last chapter of *Perception and the Physical World*. It is to be found in embryo form in Berkeley, and was very carefully worked out by Hume in a brilliant section of the *Treatise* (Bk. I, Pt. IV, Sect. 4).

I put the argument in the form 'How can we differentiate a physical object from empty space?' Mere spatial properties are insufficient, because physical objects share these with empty space. But if we look at the properties of physical objects that physicists are prepared to allow them, such as mass, electric charge, or momentum, these show a distressing tendency to dissolve into *relations* that one object has to another. What, then, are the things that have these relations to each other? Must they not have a nonrelational nature if they are to sustain relations? But what is this nature? Physics does not tell us. It is here that the secondary qualities, conceived of as irreducible properties, are thrown into the breach to provide the stuffing for matter.

Reply. Whatever the solution to this difficulty—and it is a central difficulty in that complex of problems that constitute 'the problem of substance'—it is certain that appeal to the secondary qualities cannot solve it. Gregory O'Hair has drawn my attention to the following consideration, which seems quite decisive. I have said, although I have not argued it here, that we must take a Realistic as opposed to an Operationalist or Phenomenalist view of the 'scientific image' of the physical world. Now if we do this, then we must admit that such things as electrons are *individual objects*. But, in that case, the problem just briefly outlined must come up for individual electrons. Yet it seems madness to say that the electron has any of the secondary qualities. It would be plainly contrary to what we know of the physical conditions associated with the existence of the secondary qualities. So the problem of non-relational nature *must* be solved for electrons without bringing in the secondary qualities. And if the problem can be solved for electrons without appealing to the secondary qualities, surely it can be solved for physical objects generally without appealing to the secondary qualities?

What *is* the solution to the problem of the non-relational nature of physical objects? I do not know. In *Philosophy and Scientific Realism* Smart canvasses three suggestions (pp. 74–5). There are other possible solutions. But here we may excuse ourselves further consideration of the difficulty, on the grounds that it is a quite separate problem from the problems considered in this book.

III. EMPIRICAL OBJECTIONS TO IDENTIFYING SECONDARY QUALITIES WITH PHYSICAL PROPERTIES

So much for *a priori* objections to our physicalist doctrine of the secondary qualities. But what actual physical properties of objects are the secondary qualities to be identified with? In the case of the colours, the colour of a surface or the colour of an object such as a piece of amber may be identified with a certain physical constitution of the surface or object such that, when acted upon by sunlight, surfaces or objects having that constitution emit light-waves having certain frequencies. The sound an object emits may simply be identified with the sound-waves it emits. Heat and cold are the mean kinetic energy of the molecules of the hot or cold substance. The exact identification of tastes and smells is still a matter of controversy.

There are, however, still a number of empirical difficulties that can be raised against these identifications. As before, these difficulties centre chiefly around colour.

Objection 8. We have suggested that the colour of a surface is to be contingently identified with that physical constitution of surface which emits light-waves of certain frequencies when acted upon by sunlight. Now under sunlight surfaces assume one colour, under other forms of illumination they assume another. What we call a blue surface looks blue in sunlight, but it looks purple under fluorescent light. Yet we say the surface is blue, not purple. Why do we do this? Why is the colour presented in sunlight said to be the *real* colour? What privilege does sunlight confer, beyond the contingent fact that it is, at present, the natural form of illumination in our life?

Reply. It seems to me that we must admit that a real change in quality occurs at surfaces that, as we *say,* 'appear to change' when conditions of illumination are changed. I can see no ground for saying that such changes are in any way illusory or merely apparent. But it seems that there is room here for two different ways of talking about colours.

In one way of talking, the colour of a surface is determined by, and so can be contingently identified with, the actual nature of the light-waves currently emitted at the surface. In this way of talking, the colour of a surface is constantly changing, really changing, as changes in conditions of illumination occur. Such a way of talking about colours is one that naturally commends itself to those who are concerned with the visual arts.

But in another, more usual, way of talking, colour is determined by the nature of the light-waves created under *normal illumination:* ordinary sunlight. It is therefore a *disposition* of surfaces to emit certain sorts of light-waves under certain conditions. And so, like all dispositions, colour, in this way of talking, can be identified with the state that underlies the manifestation of the disposition: certain physical properties of the surface. In this way of talking, of course, colour does not change very easily, and so this idiom is better suited to the demands of ordinary life.

The former way of talking is, however, less anthropomorphic, because it does not depend upon the conditions of illumination that are normal in the human environment. It is also logically the more fundamental, because we can give an analysis of colour in the second sense in terms of colour in the first sense: viz. colour (in the first sense) assumed under normal illumination. It may be noted that it seems natural to identify sound with the sound-waves being emitted. That is to say, our account of sound is parallel to our account of colour *in the first sense.* There is no way of talking about sound corresponding to the second way of talking about colour, for obvious reasons.

These two ways of talking about colours may be compared with two possible ways of talking about tennis-balls. In one way of talking, tennis-balls are, from time to time, very far from being round. For instance, at the moment of being struck by a racquet they suffer great distortions of shape. They are only round under 'normal conditions': when they are under no particular pressure. But in another, more usual, way of talking, tennis-balls are never anything but round. If they became elliptical they would be discarded. The factory 'makes them round' just as a dyer 'dyes the cloth blue.' Yet we could give an account of this second, more usual, sense of 'round' in terms of the first, less usual, but logically more fundamental sense of 'round.'

This distinction between different ways of talking about colours enables us to solve Locke's problem about porphyry losing its red colour in the dark (*Essay,* Bk. II, Ch. 8, Sect. 19). In the first, or unusual, way of talking porphyry *does* lose its red colour in the dark. In the dark, the surface of the porphyry emits no light-waves at all. So, in this way of talking, porphyry is black in the dark. (Black surfaces emit no wave-lengths.) But in the second, or usual, way of talking the porphyry is still red. For restore normal conditions, that is, restore normal illumination, and the porphyry will reflect 'red' light-waves. It may be noted in passing that there is nothing here that does anything to show that colour is 'subjective,' although this is the conclusion that Locke draws from the case.

Objection 9. But what of the fact that surfaces, etc., under constant illumination may still appear to have different colours in different surroundings and background conditions? The reply to the previous objection will not suffice here. For there may be no change in the light-waves actually emitted by the surface.

Reply. I think we should treat these appearances as mere *appearances.* The sun, or a sodium-vapour lamp, actually *act* on the visible surface, and so it is reasonable to think of them causing different effects at that surface. But the differences in colour exhibited by the same surface placed in different environments are not due, I presume, to the differing causal action of these environments. To some extent, of course, the 'differences' are just a matter of different relations to the environment. A dingy white surface placed against an even dingier background really is, and is seen to be, whiter than its background. Placed against a dazzling white background, it really is, and is seen to be, less white than this new background. There is no sensory illusion here. But where there really is change in the 'colour presented' because of change of background, we can treat this as a change in the *appearances* presented. An obvious analogy is the illusory distortions of visual size and shape that occur in certain sorts of perceptual situation.

Is colour-blindness a matter of being subject to illusions? This is less clear. Colour-blind persons are unable to make all the colour-discriminations that persons with normal sight can make. But mere failure to perceive something is not illusion. There is no necessity to think that any illusion is involved unless the colour-perceptions of the colour-blind are actually *incompatible* with ordinary perceptions. If, however, a surface looks grey to a colour-blind person but looks blue to normal perceivers, then, since grey and blue are incompatible colours, at least one of the perceivers is subject to illusion. The fact that ordinary perceivers make colour-discriminations where colour-blind persons do not (between blue and grey things, say) will then serve as a *reason* for thinking that it is the colour-blind person who is subject to the illusion. For, *in general,* if X perceives a difference between two sorts of thing, but Y perceives no such difference, then there really is a difference. Perception of differences points strongly to the real existence of such differences, failure to perceive differences points much less strongly to the absence of differences.

Objection 10. But what of the difficulties posed by microscopes and perception from a great distance? It is well known that, under these conditions, the colours exhibited by a surface are quite different from, and incompatible with, those exhibited to the unaided eye at an ordinary distance. Yet it is clear that no change in the physical state of the surface is involved. Man might have had microscopic eyes, or have been permanently at a distance from the objects that he sees. What warrant is there for taking the colours exhibited under normal conditions as the real colours? But if the colours exhibited under normal conditions are not the real colours, what are the real colours? Unless we can say what the real colours are we will not know which colour-appearances to correlate with the physical properties. And how then can we identify colour and physical properties?

Reply. In the case of objects at a great distance, the colour exhibited by the objects is largely due to the distorting influence of the air between the object and the eye. The nature of the light-waves that arrive at the eye is not the same as the light-waves *actually emitted at the surface of the object.* It seems reasonable, therefore, to speak of mere appearances, or illusions, in such a case.

But when the same surface presents incompatible colour-properties to the naked eye and to a microscope the problem is not quite so simply dissolved.

Let us begin by returning to the case of objects viewed from a great distance. The hills look blue in the distance, but the surface of the hillside is not really blue. This can be explained by pointing out that the intermediate air between the hills and the viewer filters out all light-waves except those waves or combinations of waves that are emitted by blue surfaces in sunlight. Notice, however, that, although the hills only look blue, this would remain a perfectly good case to use in building up correlations between blueness of surface and emission of certain packets of light-waves. For we could correctly correlate blueness of surface with the pattern of waves that actually enter the eye. For if the waves that get to the eye *and those alone* had been emitted in that pattern at the surface, then the surface would in fact have been blue. The 'information' that enters the eye has been selected and distorted by the intervening atmosphere. But the same 'information,' if unselected and undistorted, would have been that transmitted by a blue surface.

This is relevant to colour-perception in ordinary situations. Even in optimum viewing conditions the eye is visually affected by only a portion of the waves actually emitted by the surface. Correlations can be set up between colour of surface and pattern of light-waves emitted by the surface, but they must be set up on the basis that what enters the eye is a fair sample of what was emitted by the surface. For what enters the eye determines the apparent colour of the surface. There remains the possibility, however, that what enters the eye is an *unsatisfactory sample* of what was emitted by the surface. And, if so, there remains the possibility of deciding that the real colour of the surface is different from the colour a thing looks to have to ordinary observers in ordinary situations. Yet it will be the very correlations between apparent colour of surface in ordinary conditions, and the light-waves that actually affect the eye in these conditions, that will force this revision of our common-sense attributions of certain colours to certain surfaces.

But, by comparison with the naked eye, microscopes do actually cause a more complete sample of the light-waves that leave a certain portion of a surface to be brought to, and to affect, the eye. So it is perfectly possible to favour the evidence of microscopes, rather than the evidence of the naked eye, in deciding what is the true colour of a surface. I have said only that this is 'perfectly possible.' The caution is deliberate. The microscope refracts and scatters rays as well as bringing a larger sample to the eye *per* unit of area. So it distorts as well as reveals. But the way seems open, *if detailed physical considerations should demand it,* to take the microscope as a better guide to the real colour of surface than the naked eye. Further than this a work of philosophy would be unwise to go!

Objection 11. But, even if certain colour-appearances are written off as mere appearances, is it really possible to find one sort of wave-length emitted by all surfaces of the same colour when illuminated by sunlight? In recent years, Smart has emphasized again and again that a huge and idiosyncratic variety of different combinations of wave-length may all present exactly the same colour to the observer. The simple correlations between colour and emitted wave-length that philosophers hopefully assume to exist simply cannot be found. Is this not a bar to an identification of coloured surfaces with surfaces that emit certain wave-lengths under sunlight?

Reply. One possibility here is that all these different combinations of wave-lengths may be instances that fall under some general formula. Such a formula would have to be one that did not achieve its generality simply by the use of disjunctions to weld together artificially the diverse cases falling under the formula. Provided that such faking were avoided, the formula could be as complicated as we please. Such a formula could be tested, at least in principle, by making up new combinations of wave-lengths that nevertheless still obeyed the formula. If the surface from which these wave-lengths were emitted exhibited the predicted colour-appearance, the formula would be at least verified. Under these conditions, it might well be conceded that, because of its complexity and idiosyncratic nature, the physical property involved was not one of any great importance in physics. But it would still be a perfectly real, even if ontologically insignificant, physical property. Now I know of no physical considerations about colour that rule out such a possibility.

A parallel case here is the theory of smell recently put forward in an article in the *Scientific American* ('The Stereochemical Theory of Odor,' John E. Amoore *et al.,* Vol. 210, No. 2, Feb., 1964). According to this view, smell is a matter of molecules of different *shape* fitting into differently shaped receptors in the sense-organ. In this way, the receptors sort out different chemical substances from one another. Now molecular shape is an idiosyncratic property. Chemicals of quite different nature may have the same molecular shape, while chemically similar substances may have different molecular shapes. Yet although molecular shape is not a property of which chemistry need take much account (it is 'ontologically insignificant'), it is a perfectly real property, and there would be no objection to identifying smells with the shape of the molecules of the substance that has the smell. Something similar, although more complicated, may be true of colour.

Suppose, however, that no such unifying formula can be found. Suppose it is simply a matter of *irreducibly* diverse causes in the physical surfaces bringing about identical colour-appearances for human observers. I think we would then have to conclude that colour is a pseudo-quality: a sorting and classifying of surfaces by means of the eye that has no proper basis in physical reality. For the surfaces that we classify together as a result of using our eyes could not be classified together on the basis of physical theory. But what objection is there to this possibility?

A physicalist is in fact already committed to saying something of this sort about heat and cold. Phenomenologically they are distinct qualities, no doubt due to the existence of distinct sets of receptors. But the physicist sees no reason to postulate anything except a *single* physical scale of temperature. So the physicalist must admit that temperature-*perception* involves a measure of illusion here. Why can we not say the same about colour?

Of course, the facts about heat and cold, and the putative facts about colour, might be used by an anti-physicalist to argue for the falsity of the identification of these qualities with physical properties of objects. But the general considerations in favour of physicalism are very strong. They outweigh any doubt created by a failure to produce a positive identification, in terms of the physical properties of objects, for every distinct feature exhibited by the secondary qualities.

Here, then, is a sketch of a physicalist account of the secondary qualities. The account is to be contrasted with the physicalist account put forward by J. J. C. Smart in *Philosophy and Scientific Realism.* There he says of the secondary qualities that they are 'powers to cause differential responses' (p. 88). Earlier he had spoken of giving 'an account of colours which depends on behavioural reactions' (p. 81). I reject this Operationalist view of the secondary qualities. We could say that Smart's view is a Behaviouristic Reductionism, while the view put forward in this chapter is a Realistic Reductionism. Realism about the secondary qualities accords with common sense, while Reductionism accords with findings of physical science, thus doing justice to both manifest and scientific image of the world. There is, indeed, an exact parallel here to the dispute between the Behaviourist and the Central-state account of mental states. I think that Smart's view of the secondary qualities is an unfortunate legacy from an earlier operationalist or behaviourist phase in his thinking.

Reading Questions

1. Armstrong claims that colors "are nothing but physical properties of physical objects or processes. Colours of surfaces, on this view, will be simply physical properties of those surfaces." Yet different observers perceive different colors under the same conditions. Is one observer right and the others wrong? If they are all right, then we can't say that things have any determinate color. Armstrong replies to this objection with the appeal to normal observers: the normal observer is right, and the others wrong. Do you think that this appeal makes the truth about color a fairly subjective and contingent matter of vote?
2. How could Armstrong reply to the following objection? Colors have second-order properties. For example, there is a unique shade of red that contains no hint of another color. By contrast, there is no unique shade of orange; all shades of orange contain red and yellow. Uniqueness is a property of red. It seems unlikely that some physical reflectance-characteristic is "unique" or has a corresponding second-order property. Therefore colors are not physical reflectance-characteristics.
3. Ordinary people know that red is more similar to orange than to blue. Yet if the true nature of color is revealed only through science, as Armstrong claims, then how can a nonscientific layperson know this?
4. The distinction between illusory and genuine colors, according to Armstrong, rests on an appeal to normal observers and normal (or perhaps ideal) conditions of observation. Here is the apparent form of reasoning:

   1. Real colors are those observed under normal conditions.
   2. Normal conditions are white light, X angle, Y distance, Z light amplitude, etc.
   3. These are the normal conditions because
      a. they reveal the real colors
      b. they are statistically the most frequent conditions of observation
      c. ???

   Choosing 3a makes the argument circular. Real colors are those observed under the conditions that reveal real colors. 3b seems arbitrary and contingent. We can't determine the real color of a thing until we conduct a poll or some sort of study to see what the most frequent conditions of observation are. "Normal" becomes no longer normative, but instead just means "average." We run into similar problems when we try to specify what a normal observer is. How could Armstrong fill in 3c to make this a compelling argument?

21 Colour as a Secondary Quality

PAUL A. BOGHOSSIAN AND J. DAVID VELLEMAN

THE GALILEAN INTUITION

DOES MODERN SCIENCE IMPLY, contrary to the testimony of our eyes, that grass is not green? Galileo thought it did:

> Hence I think that these tastes, odors, colors, etc., on the side of the object in which they seem to exist, are nothing else than mere names, but hold their residence solely in the sensitive body; so that if the animal were removed, every such quality would be abolished and annihilated. Nevertheless, as soon as we have imposed names on them, particular and different from those of the other primary and real accidents, we induce ourselves to believe that they also exist just as truly and really as the latter.[1]

The question whether Galileo was right on this score is not really a question about the content of modern scientific theory: aside from some difficulties concerning the interpretation of quantum mechanics, we know what properties are attributed to objects by physics. The question is rather about the correct understanding of colour concepts as they figure in visual experience: how do objects appear to be, when they appear to be green? Galileo seems to have found it very natural to say that the property an object appears to have, when it appears to have a certain colour, is an intrinsic qualitative property which, as science teaches us, it does not in fact possess.

Subsequent philosophical theorizing about colour has tended to recoil from Galileo's semantic intuition and from its attendant ascription of massive error to ordinary experience and thought. Thus, in a recent paper Sydney Shoemaker has written:

> [S]ince in fact we apply color predicates to physical objects and never to sensations, ideas, experiences, etc., the account of their semantics recommended by the Principle of Charity is one that makes them truly applicable to tomatoes and lemons rather than to sense experiences thereof.[2]

Should a principle of charity be applied in this way to the interpretation the colour concepts exercised in visual experience? We think not. We shall argue, for one thing, that the grounds for applying a principle of charity are lacking in the case of colour concepts. More importantly, we shall argue that attempts at giving the experience of colour a charitable interpretation either fail to respect obvious features of that experience or fail to interpret it charitably, after all. Charity to visual experience is therefore no motive for resisting the natural, Galilean response to a scientific understanding of light and vision. The best interpretation of colour experience ends up convicting it of widespread and systematic error.[3]

CHARITABLE ACCOUNTS OF COLOUR EXPERIENCE

According to the principle of charity, the properties that objects are seen as having, when they are seen as coloured, must be properties that they generally have when so perceived. Two familiar interpretations of visual experience satisfy this principle.

THE PHYSICALIST ACCOUNT

The first of these interpretations begins with the assumption that what objects appear to have, when they look red, is the physical property that is normally detected or tracked by that experience. Since

We have benefited from discussing the material in this paper with: Sydney Shoemaker, David Hill, Larry Sklar, Mark Johnston, and participants in a seminar that we taught at the University of Michigan in the fall of 1987. Our research has been supported by the Rackham Faculty Fellowships from the University of Michigan.

From Mind, *vol. xcviii, no. 389, January 1989. © Oxford University Press 1989. Reprinted by permission.*

the physical property that normally causes an object to be seen as red is the property of having one out of a class of spectral-reflectance profiles—or one out of a class of molecular bases for such profiles—the upshot of the present interpretation is that seeing something as red is seeing it as reflecting-incident light in one of such-and-such ways, or as having surface molecules with one of such-and-such electron configurations.[4]

Now, we have no doubt that experiences of an object as having a particular colour are normally correlated with that object's possessing one of a class of spectral-reflectance profiles. But to concede the existence of such a correlation is not yet to concede that membership in a spectral-reflectance class is the property that objects are seen as having when they are seen as having a particular colour. Indeed, the claim that visual experience has this content yields unacceptable consequences.

In particular, this claim implies that one cannot tell just by looking at two objects whether they appear to have the same or different colours. For according to the physicalist interpretation, which colour one sees an object as having depends on which spectral-reflectance class one's visual experience represents the object as belonging to; and which spectral-reflectance class one's experience represents an object as belonging to depends on which spectral-reflectance profiles normally cause experiences of that sort. Hence in order to know whether two objects appear to have the same colour, under the physicalist interpretation, one must know whether one's experiences of them are such as result from similar spectral-reflectance profiles. And the latter question cannot be settled on the basis of the visual experiences alone: it calls for considerable empirical enquiry. The physicalist interpretation therefore implies that knowing whether two objects appear to have the same colour requires knowing the results of empirical enquiry into the physical causes of visual experiences.

But surely, one can tell whether two objects appear similarly coloured on the basis of visual experience alone. To be sure, one's experience of the objects will not necessarily provide knowledge of the relation between their actual colours. But the physicalist account implies that visual experience of objects fails to provide epistemic access, not just to their actual colour similarities, but to their apparent colour similarities as well. And here the account must be mistaken. The apparent colours of objects can be compared without empirical enquiry into the physical causes of the objects' visual appearances; and so the properties that objects appear to have, when they appear coloured, cannot be identified with the physical properties that are detected or tracked by those appearances.

DISPOSITIONALIST ACCOUNTS

We turn, then, to another class of theories that respect the principle of charity in application to colour experience. These theories are united under the name of dispositionalism. All of them are based, in one way or another, on the claim that the concept of colour is such as to yield a priori truths of the following form:

(i) x is red if and only if x appears red under standard conditions.[5]

Different versions of dispositionalism interpret such biconditionals differently and apply them to the vindication of colour experience in different ways.

Applying the Biconditionals: the Direct Approach. Perhaps the most direct way to argue from the dispositionalist biconditionals to the veridicality of colour experience is to point out that the biconditionals assert, as a priori truths, that there are conditions under which things appear to have a colour if and only if they actually have it, and hence that there are conditions under which colour experience is veridical. The possibility of global error in colour experience is thus claimed to be excluded a priori by the very concept of colour.

We think that this version of dispositionalism misappropriates whatever a priori truth there may be in the relevant biconditionals. We are prepared to admit that the concept of colour guarantees the existence of privileged conditions for viewing colours, conditions under which an observer's colour experiences or colour judgements are in some sense authoritative. But colour experiences and colour judgements may enjoy many different kinds of authority, some of which would not entail that objects have the properties that colour experience represents them as having.

Even philosophers who regard colour experience as globally false, for example, will nevertheless want to say that some colour experiences are correct in the sense that they yield the colour attributions that are generally accepted for the purposes of describing objects in public discourse. Of course, such a claim will yield slightly different biconditionals, of the following form:

(ii) *x* is to be described as red if and only if *x* appears red under standard conditions.

Our point, however, is that (ii) may be the only biconditional that is strictly true, and that (i) may seem true only because it is mistaken for (ii). If biconditional (ii) expresses the only genuine a priori truth in the vicinity, then the authority of experiences produced under standard conditions may consist in no more than there being a convention of describing objects in terms of the colours attributed to them in such experiences. As we shall argue at the end of this paper, such a convention may be perfectly justifiable even if all colour experience is, strictly speaking, false. Hence the intuitive support for biconditionals like (i) may not be such as to ground a vindication of colour experience.

In order for the dispositionalist biconditionals to vindicate colour experience, they must mean, not just that convention dictates describing objects in terms of the colours that they appear to have under standard conditions, but also that objects actually have the properties that they thereby appear to have. And we see no reason for regarding this stronger claim as an a priori truth.

Applying the Biconditionals as Content-Specifications. Another way of arguing from dispositionalist biconditionals to the veridicality of colour experience is to interpret the biconditionals as specifying the content of that experience. This argument proceeds as follows.

The first premiss of the argument says that the property that objects are represented as having when they look red is just this: a disposition to look red under standard conditions. The second premiss says that many objects are in fact disposed to look red under standard conditions, and that these are the objects that are generally seen as red. These premisses yield the conclusion that the experience of red is generally veridical, since it represents an object as having a disposition that it probably has—namely, a disposition to look red under standard conditions.

The first premiss of this argument corresponds to a biconditional of the following form:

(iii) *Red* [i.e., the property that objects are seen as having when they look red]	= def	a disposition to appear red under standard conditions

The right side of biconditional (iii) can be interpreted in two different ways, however; and so there are two different versions of the associated argument.

Two Versions of Content-Dispositionalism. The first version of the argument interprets the phrase 'a disposition to look red' on the assumption that the embedded phrase 'to look red' has its usual semantic structure. The entire phrase is therefore taken to mean 'a disposition to give the visual appearance of being red.'[6] The second version interprets the phrase on the assumption that 'to look red' has a somewhat unusual structure. The predicate following 'look' is interpreted as expressing, not a property that a thing is disposed to give the appearance of having, but rather an intrinsic property of the visual appearance that it is disposed to give. The phrase 'a disposition to look red' is therefore taken to mean something like 'a disposition to cause reddish visual appearances.'[7]

Under these two interpretations, (iii) assigns two different contents to colour experience. Under one interpretation, the property that things are seen as having when they look red is defined as a disposition to give the visual appearance of being red; under the other, the property that things are seen as having is defined as a disposition to cause reddish visual appearances. In either case, the content of colour experience is claimed to be true, on the grounds that objects seen as red do have the appropriate disposition.

We regard both versions of the argument as faulty. In the next section, we shall raise an objection that militates against both versions equally. In subsequent sections, we shall consider each version in its own right.

A General Problem in Content-Dispositionalism. Both versions of the present argument are to be faulted, in our opinion, for misdescribing the experience of colour. In assigning colour experience a dispositionalist content, they get the content of that experience wrong.

When one enters a dark room and switches on a light, the colours of surrounding objects look as if they have been revealed, not as if they have been activated. That is, the dispelling of darkness looks like the drawing of a curtain from the colours of objects no less than from the objects themselves. If colours looked like dispositions, however, then they would seem to *come on* when illuminated, just as a lamp comes on when its switch is flipped. Turning on the light would seem, simultaneously, like turning on the colours; or perhaps it would seem like waking up the colours, just as it is seen to startle the cat. Conversely, when the light was extinguished, the colours would not look as if they were being concealed or shrouded in the ensuing darkness: rather, they would look as if they were becoming dormant, like the cat returning to sleep. But colours do not look like that; or not, at least, to us.

More seriously, both versions of (iii) also have trouble describing the way in which colours figure in particular experiences, such as after-images. The colours that one sees when experiencing an after-image are precisely the qualities that one sees as belonging to external objects. When red spots float before one's eyes, one sees the same colour quality that fire-hydrants and maraschino cherries normally appear to have.[8] The problem is that dispositionalist accounts of colour experience must analyse the appearance of colour in after-images as the appearance of a disposition to look red under standard conditions; and after-images simply cannot appear to have such a dispositional property.

This problem would not arise if after-images were full-blown illusions. That is, if seeing an after-image consisted in seeming to see a material object suspended in physical-space, then that object, though in fact illusory, could still appear to have the same colour quality as any other material object. But after-images are not seen as material objects, any more than, say, a ringing in one's ears is heard as a real noise. The items involved in these experiences are not perceived as existing independently of being perceived. On the one hand, the after-image is seen as located before one's eyes, rather than in one's mind, where visual memories are seen; and the ringing is likewise heard as located in one's outer ear, rather than in the inner auditorium of verbal thought and musical memory. But on the other hand, one does not perceive these items as actually existing in the locations to which they are subjectively referred. The ringing is heard as overlaying a silence in one's ears, where there is audibly nothing to hear; and similarly, the after-image is seen as overlaying the thin air before one's eyes, where there is visibly nothing to see. The ringing is thus perceived as a figment or projection of one's ears, the image as a figment or projection of one's eyes: both, in short, are perceived as existing only in so far as one is perceiving them.

Thus, the possibility of a red after-image requires that one see something as simultaneously a figment of one's eyes and red. But how could something that looked like a figment of one's eyes also appear disposed to look a particular way under standard conditions? Because an after-image is seen as the sort of thing that exists only in so far as one is seeing it, it cannot be seen as the sort of thing that others could see nor, indeed, as the sort of thing that one could see again oneself, in the requisite sense. In seeing an after-image as a figment of one's eyes, one sees it as the sort of thing that will cease to exist when no longer seen and that will not be numerically identical to any future after-images, however similar they may be. One does not see it, in other words, as a persisting item that could be reintroduced into anyone's visual experience; and so one cannot see it as having a disposition to present this or any appearance either to others or to oneself on other occasions.

The foregoing, phenomenological problems are common to both versions of the dispositionalist argument currently under consideration. Each version of the argument also has peculiar problems of its own, which we shall now consider in turn. We begin with the first version, which understands a disposition to look red as a disposition to give the visual appearance of having the property red.

Problems in the First Version of Content-Dispositionalism. The problem with this version has to do with the property expressed by the word 'red' in the phrase 'a disposition to appear red under standard conditions'—the phrase constituting the right side of biconditional (iii). Keep in mind that the entire phrase has itself been offered as expressing the property that objects are seen as having when they look red. When things are seen as red, according to the present argument, what they are seen as having is a disposition to appear red under standard conditions. But does the word 'red' here express the same property that the entire phrase purports to express?

Suppose that the answer to our question is no. In that case, what biconditional (iii) says is that the property that things are seen as having when they-look red is a disposition to give the appearance of having some *other* property called red. This other property must naturally be a colour, since the property red could hardly be seen as a disposition to appear as having some property that was not a colour. For the sake of clarity, let us call this other property red*.

Now, in order for objects to have the property red that they appear to have, under the present assumption, they must actually be disposed to give the appearance, under standard conditions, of having the property red*; and in order to have that disposition, they must actually give the appearance of having the property red* under standard conditions. Thus, if the property that things are seen as having when they look red is a disposition to appear red*, then the experience of seeing them as red is veridical, as the dispositionalist wishes to prove, only if they also appear red*. And the question then arises whether red* is a property that things ever do or can actually have. The dispositionalist's argument does not show that the appearance of having red* is ever veridical, since that property is admitted to be different from the disposition whose existence the dispositionalist cites in vindicating the appearance of red. The consequence is that there must be colour experiences that the dispositionalist has failed to vindicate.

Suppose, then, that the dispositionalist answers yes to our question. That is, suppose he says that 'red' expresses the same property on the right side of (iii) as it does on the left. In that case, the dispositionalist's account of colour experience is circular, since in attempting to say what property things appear to have when they look red, he invokes the very property that is at issue.

The dispositionalist may refuse to be troubled by this circularity, however.[9] He may point out that a circular account of a property can still be true, and indeed informative, despite its circularity. For instance, to define courage as a disposition to act courageously is to give a circular definition, a definition that cannot convey the concept of courage to anyone who does not already have it. Even so, courage *is* a disposition to act courageously, and this definition may reveal something important about the property—namely that it is a behavioural disposition. The dispositionalist about colour claims that the circularity in his explication of red is similar.

We grant that circularity alone does not necessarily undermine a definitional equivalence. Yet the circularity in biconditional (iii) is significantly different from that in our circular definition of courage. Our definition of courage invokes courage in an ordinary extensional context, whereas the right side of (iii) invokes red in an intentional context expressing the content of a visual experience, an experience that happens to be the very one whose content (iii) purports to explicate. The result is that the visual experience of seeing something as red can satisfy (iii) only if it, too, is circular, and hence only if it is just as uninformative as (iii). Not only does (iii) fail to tell us which colour red is, then; it also precludes visual experience from telling us which colour an object has. The former failure may be harmless, but the latter is not.

Let us illustrate the difference between an unproblematic circular definition and a problematic one by means of an analogy. Suppose that you ask someone who Sam is and are told, 'Sam is the father of Sam's children.' This answer does not tell you who Sam is if you do not already know. But it does tell you something about Sam—namely, that he has children—and, more importantly, it places Sam in a relation to himself that a person can indeed occupy. In order for Sam to satisfy this assertion, he need only be the father of his own children. Now suppose, alternatively, that your question receives the answer 'Sam is the father of

Sam's father.' This response also identifies Sam by reference to Sam; but it has a more serious defect. Its defect is that it asserts of Sam that he stands to himself in a relation that is impossible for a person to occupy.

These two circular identifications of Sam are analogous to the two circular definitions that we are considering. The definition of courage as a disposition to act courageously is uninformative, but it places courage in a relation to itself that a disposition can occupy. In order to satisfy this definition, courage must simply be the disposition to perform actions that tend to be performed by someone with that very disposition. By contrast, the dispositionalist about colour not only invokes the content of colour experience in explicating that content; he places that content in a relation to itself that is impossible for it to occupy. For his explication says that the content of the visual experience of red must contain, as a proper part, the content of the visual experience of red. To see something as red, according to (iii), is to have an experience whose content is that the thing is disposed to produce visual experiences *with the content that it is red.* The experiential content that something is red is thus embedded within itself, and this is a reflexive relation that no determinate content can occupy. Consequently, (iii) requires that the visual experience of red have an indeterminate content that fails to represent its object as having any particular colour.

Under the terms of (iii), an experience can represent its object as red only by representing it as disposed to produce visual experiences that represent it as red. The problem here is that the experiences that the object is thus represented as disposed to produce must themselves be represented as experiences that represent the object as red, rather than some other colour—lest the object be represented as disposed to appear something other than red. Yet these experiences can be represented as representing the object as red only if they are represented as representing it as disposed to produce experiences that represent it as red. And here the circle gets vicious. In order for an object to appear red rather than blue, it must appear disposed to appear red, rather than disposed to appear blue; and in order to appear disposed to appear red, rather than disposed to appear blue, it must appear disposed to appear disposed to appear red, rather than disposed to appear disposed to appear blue; and so on. Until this regress reaches an end, the object's appearance will not amount to the appearance of one colour rather than another. Unfortunately, the regress never reaches an end.

One might attempt to staunch the regress simply by invoking the relevant colour by name. 'To appear red,' one might say, 'is to appear disposed to appear red—and that's the end of the matter.' 'Of course,' one might continue, 'if you don't already know what red is, then you haven't understood what I've said. But that doesn't impugn the truth of my assertion, nor its informativeness, since you have learned at least that the property things appear to have in appearing red is a disposition to produce appearances.'

This reply cannot succeed. Staunching the regress with the word 'red' can work, but only if the word is not understood in the sense defined in biconditional (iii). We readily agree that red things do appear disposed to look red, and that they appear so without requiring the viewer to run an endless gamut of visual appearances. But what they appear disposed to do is to give the appearance of being red in a non-dispositional sense—the appearance of having a non-dispositional redness. And the way they appear disposed to give that appearance is usually just by giving it—that is, by looking non-dispositionally red.[10] Similarly, objects can appear disposed to look square just by looking square, but only because they look square intrinsically and categorically.

As we have seen, however, the dispositionalist cannot admit an intrinsic and categorical sense of the word 'red' into his formulation. For then he would have to acknowledge that objects appear disposed to look red, and do look red, in a non-dispositional sense. And he would then have acknowledged that an object's being disposed to look red does not guarantee that it is as it looks, in respect to colour, since the redness that it is thereby disposed to give the appearance of having is a different property from the disposition that it admittedly has. The dispositionalist must therefore say that although an object looks disposed to look red just by looking red, this looking red does not involve looking anything except disposed to look red. *In short, the object must look disposed to look a particular way without there being any particular way that it looks, or looks disposed to look, other than so disposed.* And that is why the vicious regress gets started.

Note, once again, that the problem created by the regress is not that we are unable to learn what red is from the statement that red is a disposition to look red. The problem is that, under the terms of that statement, the subject of visual experience cannot see what colour an object has. For he cannot see the particular colour of an object except by seeing the particular way the object tends to appear; and he cannot see the way it tends to appear except by seeing the way it tends to appear as tending to appear; and so on, *ad infinitum*. To be sure, a person can see all of these things if he can just see the object as having a colour, to begin with; but under the terms of dispositionalism, he cannot begin to see the object as having a colour except by seeing these dispositions; and so he can never begin to see it as having a colour at all.[11]

The Second Version of Content-Dispositionalism. The only way to save dispositionalism from its fatal circularity is to ensure that the disposition with which a colour property is identified is not a disposition to give the appearance of having that very property. Christopher Peacocke has attempted to modify dispositionalism in just this way.

According to Peacocke, the property that an object is seen as having when it looks red should be identified as a disposition, not to appear red, but rather to appear in a portion of the visual field having an intrinsic property that Peacocke calls red'. Let us call these portions of the visual field *red' patches*. We can then say that looking red, according to Peacocke, is looking disposed to be represented in red' patches under standard conditions—an appearance that can be accomplished by being represented in a red' patch under recognizably standard conditions, of course, but also in other ways as well, such as by being represented in an orange' patch when illuminated by a yellow-looking light. The upshot, in any case, is that objects often are as they look when they look red, because they both look and are just this: disposed to be represented in red' patches under standard conditions.

Peacocke's qualified dispositionalism eliminates circular experiential contents because it says that appearing to have a colour property is appearing disposed to present appearances characterized, not in terms of that very property, but rather in terms of a different quality, a 'primed' colour. Peacocke can also account for the role of red in the experience of seeing a red after-image, because he can say that the experience consists in a red' patch represented, in the content of one's experience, as a figment of one's eyes.

Peacocke's qualified dispositionalism differs from pure dispositionalism in that it introduces a visual field modified by qualities that—to judge by their names, at least—constitute a species of colour. Peacocke thus abandons a significant feature of the theories that we have examined thus far. Those theories assume that visual experience involves colour only to the extent of representing it. They analyse an experience of red as an experience with the content that something is red—an experience that refers to redness. Because the role of colour in experience is restricted by these theories to that of an element in the intentional content of experience, we shall call the theories intentionalist.

Peacocke's theory is not intentionalist, because it says that visual experience involves colour (that is, primed colour) as a property inhering in the visual field, and not just as a property represented in the content of that experience. We have two points to make about Peacocke's anti-intentionalism. We shall first argue that Peacocke is right to abandon intentionalism and to introduce colours as intrinsic properties of the visual field. But we shall then argue that, having introduced such properties, Peacocke is wrong to remain a dispositionalist about the colours that visual experience attributes to external objects. Peacocke's modification of dispositionalism is unstable, we believe, in that it ultimately undermines dispositionalism altogether.

The Case Against Intentionalism. Peacocke has argued elsewhere, and on independent grounds, for the need to speak about a sensory field modified by intrinsic sensational qualities.[12] We should like to add some arguments of our own.

Our first argument rests on the possibility, noted above, of seeing an after-image without illusion. Consider such an experience, in which an after-image appears to you *as* an after-image—say, as a red spot obscuring the face of a person who has just taken your photograph. Since you suffer no illusion about the nature of this spot, you do not see it as something actually existing in front of the photographer's face. In what sense, then, do you see it as occupying that location at all? The answer is that you see it as merely appearing in that location: you see it as a spot that appears in front of the photographer's face without actually being there. Now, in order for you to see the spot as appearing somewhere, it must certainly appear there. Yet it must appear there without appearing actually to be there, since you are not under the illusion that the spot actually occupies the space in question. The after-image must therefore be described as *appearing in* a location without *appearing to be in* that location; and this description is not within the capacity of any intentionalist theory. An intentionalist theory will analyse the visual appearance of location as the attribution of location to something, in the intentional content of your visual experience. But the intentional content of your visual experience is that there is nothing at all between you and the photographer.

The only way to describe the after-image as appearing in front of the photographer without appearing to be in front of the photographer is to talk about the location that it occupies in your visual field. In your visual field, we say, the after-image overlays the image of the photographer's face, but nothing is thereby represented as actually being over the photographer's face. The after-image is thus like a coffee-stain on a picture, a feature that occupies a location on the picture without representing anything as occupying any location. Similarly, an adequate description of the after-image requires reference to two kinds of location—location as an intrinsic property of features in the visual field, and location as represented by the resulting visual experience.

One might think that this argument cannot be applied to the afterimage's colour, since you may see the after-image not only as appearing red but also as actually *being* red. But then intentionalism will have trouble explaining what exactly your experience represents as being red, given that the experience is veridical. Your experience cannot represent some external object as being red, on pain of being illusory. And if it represents an image as being red, then its truth will entail that colour can enter into visual experience as an intrinsic property of images, which is precisely what intentionalism denies. Hence, there would seem to be nothing that the experience can veridically represent as being red, according to intentionalism. And if the experience represented something as merely appearing red, then our foregoing argument would once again apply. For how could you have a veridical experience that something appeared red unless something so appeared? And if something did so appear, it would have to appear *to be* red, according to intentionalism, which would be an illusion in the present case, unless images can be red.[13]

There are other, more familiar cases that refute intentionalism in a similar way. These, too, are cases in which something is seen without being represented in the content of experience as intentionalism would require. If you press the side of one eyeball, you can see this line of type twice without seeing the page as bearing two identical lines of type. Indeed, you cannot even force the resulting experience into representing the existence of two lines, even if you try. Similarly, you can see nearby objects double by focusing on distant objects behind them, and yet you cannot get yourself to see the number of nearby objects as doubling. And by unfocusing your eyes, you can see objects blurrily without being able to see them as being blurry. None of these experiences can be adequately described solely in terms of their intentional content. Their description requires reference to areas of colour in a visual field, areas that split in two or become blurry without anything's being represented to you as doing so.

The Case Against Peacocke's Dispositionalism. We therefore endorse Peacocke's decision to posit a visual field with intrinsic sensational qualities. What we question, however, is his insistence that the colours of external objects are still seen as dispositions. We believe that once one posits a visual field bearing properties such as red', one is eventually forced to conclude that objects presented in red' areas of that field are seen as red' rather than as possessing some other, dispositional quality.

The reason is that visual experience does not ordinarily distinguish between qualities of a 'field' representing objects and qualities of the objects represented. Visual experience is ordinarily naïvely realistic, in the sense that the qualities presented in it are represented as qualities of the external world. According to Peacocke, however, the aspects of visual experience in which external objects are represented have qualities—and, indeed, colour qualities—that are never attributed by that experience to the objects themselves. Peacocke thus gets the phenomenology of visual experience wrong.

Try to imagine what visual experience would be like if it conformed to Peacocke's model. The visual field would have the sensational qualities red', blue', green', and so on, and would represent various external objects; but it would not represent those qualities as belonging to those objects. Where, then, would the qualities appear to reside? What would they appear to be qualities of? They would have to float free, as if detached from the objects being represented, so as not to appear as qualities of those objects. Or perhaps they would seem to lie on top of the objects, overlaying the objects' own colours—which would be seen, remember, as different, dispositional qualities. The result, in any case, would be that visual experience was not naïvely realistic, but quite the reverse. A veil of colours—like Locke's veil of ideas—would seem to stand before or lie upon the scene being viewed. But one does not continually see this veil of colours; and so visual experience must not conform to Peacocke's model.

The failure of Peacocke's model to fit the experience of colour can be seen most clearly, perhaps, in the fact that the model is a perfect fit for the experience of pain. When one pricks one's finger on a pin, pain appears in one's tactual 'field,' but it is not perceived as a quality of the pin. Rather, the pin is perceived as having a disposition—namely, the disposition to cause pain, and hence to be presented in areas of the tactual field bearing the quality currently being felt. The ordinary way of describing the experience would be to say that by having an experience of pain one perceives the pin as disposed to cause pain. But this description can easily be transposed into Peacocke's notation, in which it would say that one perceives the pin as painful by perceiving it in a painful' patch.

Peacocke's theory is thus ideally suited to describing the experience of pain. Yet the experience of pain is notoriously different from the experience of colour. Indeed, the difference between pain experience and colour experience has always been accepted as an uncontroversial datum for the discussion of secondary qualities. The difference is precisely that pain is never felt as a quality of its apparent cause, whereas colour usually is: the pain caused by the pin is felt as being in the finger, whereas the pin's silvery colour is seen as being in the pin. Hence Peacocke's model, which fits pain experience so well, cannot simultaneously fit colour experience. When applied to colour, that model would suggest that the experience of seeing a rose contains both the flower's redness and the visual field's red'ness, just as the experience of being pricked by a pin contains both the pin's painfulness and the finger's pain.

One might respond that our objection to Peacocke is undermined by an example that we previously deployed against intentionalism. For we have already argued that seeing something blurrily involves a blurriness that is not attributed to what is seen. Have we not already admitted, then, that visual experience contains qualities that it does not attribute to objects, and hence that it is not always naïve?

We have indeed admitted that visual experience is not always naïve, but that admission is consistent with the claim that visual experience is naive most of the time, or in most respects. Seeing blurrily is, after all, unusual, in that it involves seeing, as it were, 'through' a blurry image to a visibly sharp-edged object. It is an experience in which the visual field becomes more salient than usual, precisely because its blurriness is not referred to the objects seen. Peacocke's theory does manage to improve on intentionalism by explaining how one can blurrily see an object as being sharp-edged. But Peacocke goes too far, by analysing all visual experience on the model of this unusual case. He says that every perception of colour has this dual structure, in which the colours that are attributed to objects are seen through colour qualities that are not attributed to them. According to Peacocke, then, the redness of external objects is always seen through a haze of red'ness, just as the sharp edges of an object are sometimes seen through a blur.

THE PROJECTIVIST ACCOUNT

We have argued, first, that visual experience cannot be adequately described without reference to intrinsic sensational qualities of a visual field; and second, that intrinsic colour properties of the visual field are the properties that objects are seen as having when they look coloured. We have thus arrived at the traditional projectivist account of colour experience. The projection posited by this account has the result that the intentional content of visual experience represents external objects as possessing colour qualities that belong, in fact, only to regions of the visual field. By 'gilding or staining all natural objects with the colours borrowed from internal sentiment,' as Hume puts it, the mind 'raises in a manner a new creation.'[14]

Talk of a visual field and its intrinsic qualities may seem to involve a commitment to the existence of mental particulars. But we regard the projectivist view of colour experience as potentially neutral on the metaphysics of mind. The visual field may or may not supervene on neural structures; it may or may not be describable by means of adverbs modifying mental verbs rather than by substantives denoting mental items. All we claim is that, no matter how the metaphysical underpinnings of sense experience are ultimately arranged, they must support reference to colours; as qualities of a visual field that are represented as inhering in external objects.

PROS AND CONS

The projectivist account of colour experience is, in our opinion, the one that occurs naturally to anyone who learns the rudimentary facts about light and vision. It seemed obvious to Galileo, as it did to Newton and Locke as well.[15]

The Principle of Charity as Applied to Visual Experience. Given the intuitive appeal that the projectivist account holds for anyone who knows about the nature of light and vision, the question arises why some philosophers go to such lengths in defence of alternative accounts. The reason, as we have suggested, is that these philosophers are moved by a perceived requirement of charity in the interpretation of representational content. External objects do not actually have the colour qualities that projectivism interprets visual experience as attributing to them. The projectivist account thus interprets visual experience as having a content that would be systematically erroneous. And it therefore strikes some as violating a basic principle of interpretation.

In our opinion, however, applying a principle of charity in this way would be questionable, for two reasons. First, a principle of charity applies primarily to a language, or other representational system, *taken as a whole;* and so, when rightly understood, such a principle is perfectly consistent with the possibility that large regions of the language should rest on widespread and systematic error. Second, what a principle of charity recommends is, not that we should avoid attributing widespread error at all costs, but that we should avoid attributing inexplicable error. And the error that a Galilean view of colour entails is not inexplicable; it can be explained precisely as an error committed through projection—that is, through the misrepresentation of qualities that inhere in the visual field as inhering in the objects that are therein represented.

We therefore think that the usual motives for resisting projectivism are misguided, on quite general grounds. Nevertheless, some philosophers have criticized projectivism for being uncharitable to visual experience in rather specific ways; and we think that these more specific charges deserve to be answered. We devote the remainder of this section to three of these criticisms.

Colours as Visibilia. One argument in this vein comes from the dispositionalists. They contend that failing to see colours as dispositions to look coloured would entail failing to see them as essentially connected with vision, as *visibilia.*[16] But nothing can be seen as a colour without being seen as essentially connected with vision, the dispositionalists continue, and so colours cannot possibly be misrepresented in visual experience.

This version of the argument from charity relies on the assumption that the only way to see colours as essentially connected with vision is to see them as dispositions to cause visual perceptions. We reply that colours can be seen as essentially connected with vision without being seen as dispositions at all. In particular, they can be seen as essentially connected with vision if they are seen as the qualities directly presented in visual experience, arrayed on the visual field. The experience of seeing red is unmistakably an experience of a quality that could not be experienced other than visually. Consequently, red is seen as essentially visual without being seen as a disposition to cause visual perceptions.

A Berkeleyan Objection. Another version of the argument from charity begins with the premiss that qualities of the visual field cannot be imagined except as being seen, and hence that they cannot be imagined as intrinsic and categorical qualities of material objects—qualities belonging to the objects in themselves, whether they are seen or not. This premiss is taken to imply that visual experience cannot possibly commit the error of representing colour *qualia* to be intrinsic and categorical qualities of objects, as projectivism charges, simply because it cannot represent the unimaginable.[17]

Our reply to this argument is that its premiss is false. The colour qualities that modify the visual field can indeed be imagined as unseen. Of course, one cannot imagine a colour as unseen while instantiated in the visual field itself, since to imagine a quality as in the visual field is to imagine that it is seen. But one can imagine a colour as instantiated elsewhere without being seen—by imagining, for example, an ordinary red-rubber ball, whose surface is red not only on the visible, near side but also on the unseen, far side.

What exponents of the present objection are pointing out, of course, is that one cannot imagine the unseen side of the ball as red by means of a mental image whose features include a red area corresponding to that side of the ball. Here they may be correct.[18] To form an image containing a coloured area corresponding to the unseen side of the ball would be to imagine seeing it, and hence not to imagine it as unseen, after all. But one's imagination is not confined to representing things by means of corresponding features in one's mental image. If it were, then one would be unable to imagine any object as being both opaque and three-dimensional; one would be reduced to imagining the world as a maze of backless facades, all artfully turned in one's direction. In actuality, one imagines the world as comprising objects in the round, whose unseen sides are represented in one's image indirectly and, so to speak, by implication. One can therefore imagine unseen colours, despite limitations on how one's imagination can represent them.

Visual experience has the same representational capacity, despite similar limitations. That is, although one cannot visually catch colours in the act of being unseen, one nevertheless sees the world as containing unseen colours—on the far sides of objects, in areas obscured by shadow, and so on. Just as one sees one's fellow human beings as having hair at the back, skin up their sleeves, and eyeballs even when they blink, so one sees them as possessing these unseen features in their usual colours. Thus, one has no trouble seeing colours as intrinsic and categorical properties that exist even when unseen.

Can Experience Commit Category Errors? A third version of the argument from charity alleges that according to projectivism visual experience commits not just a mistake but a *category* mistake, by representing external, material objects as having properties that can occur only within the mental realm.[19] Such a mistake is thought too gross for visual experience to commit.

It is not clear whether it is a necessary or merely contingent fact that external objects do not possess the sorts of property we understand colours to be; hence, it is not clear whether the mistake projectivism attributes to visual experience is categorial or merely systematic. But even if it were a category mistake, why should this necessarily be considered a difficulty for projectivism?

The assumption underlying the objection is that it is somehow extremely difficult to see how experience could commit a category mistake. But as the following remark of Wittgenstein suggests, just the opposite seems true.

> Let us imagine the following: The surfaces of the things around us (stones, plants, etc.) have patches and regions which produce pain in our skin when we touch them. (Perhaps through the chemical composition of these surfaces. But we need not know that.) In this case we should speak of pain-patches just as at present we speak of red patches.[20]

In the normal experience of pain, pain is not perceived as a quality of its cause. As Wittgenstein remarks, however, this seems to be thanks only to the fact that the normal causes of pain constitute such a heterogeneous class. Were pain to be caused solely, say, by certain specific patches on the surfaces of plants, we might well experience pain as being in the plant, much as we now experience its colour. Far from being unimaginable, then, it would seem that nothing but a purely contingent fact about our experience of pain stands between us and a category mistake just like the one that projectivism portrays us as committing about colour.

INTERPRETING COLOUR DISCOURSE

Thus far we have discussed colour concepts as they are exercised in the representational content of colour experience. Let us turn, somewhat more briefly, to the content of ordinary discourse about colour.

We assume that ordinary discourse about colour reports the contents of visual experience. The most plausible hypothesis about what someone means when he calls something red, in an everyday context, is that he is reporting what his eyes tell him. And according to our account, what his eyes tell him is that the thing has a particular visual quality, a quality that does not actually inhere in external objects but is a quality of his visual field. We therefore conclude that when someone calls something red, in an everyday context, he is asserting a falsehood. Indeed, our account of colour experience, when joined with the plausible hypothesis that colour discourse reports the contents of colour experience, yields the consequence that all statements attributing colours to external objects are false.

One would be justified in wondering how we can accept this consequence, for two related reasons. First, we will clearly want to retain a distinction between 'correct' and 'incorrect' colour judgements, distinguishing between the judgement that a fire-hydrant is blue and the judgement that it is red. And it seems a serious question what point we error theorists could see in such a distinction. Second, it seems perfectly obvious that colour discourse will continue to play an indispensable role in our everyday cognitive transactions. Yet how are we error theorists to explain this indispensability, consistently with our claim that the discourse in question is systematically false? We shall begin with the second question.

The Point of Colour-Talk. Consider one of the many harmless falsehoods that we tolerate in everyday discourse: the statement that the sun rises. When someone says that the sun rises, his remark has the same content as the visual experience that one has when watching the horizon at an appropriately early hour. That is, the sun actually looks like it is moving, and that the sun moves in this manner is what most people mean when talking about sunrise. So interpreted, of course, talk about sunrise is systematically false. When someone says that the sun rises, he is wrong; and he usually knows that he is wrong, but he says it anyway. Why?

When one understands why talk about sunrise is false, one also understands that its falsity makes no difference in everyday life. We do not mean that nothing in everyday life would, in fact, be different if the sun revolved around the earth, as it seems to. No doubt, the tides and the phases of the moon and various other phenomena would be other than they actually are. But those differences are not missed by the ordinary person, who does not know and has no reason to consider precisely how the tides and phases of the moon are generated. Consequently, someone who has a normal background of beliefs will find no evidence in everyday life to controvert his belief that the sun revolves around the earth. That belief will not mislead him about any of the phenomena he normally encounters; and it will in fact give him correct guidance about many such phenomena. His judgements about the time of day, the weather, the best placement of crops, the location of glare and of shadows at noon, will all be correct despite being derived from premisses about a stationary earth and a revolving sun. Indeed, he is likely to derive more true conclusions from his belief in a revolving sun than he would from a belief in a rotating earth, for the simple reason that the consequences for earthlings of the former state of affairs are easier to visualize than those of the latter, even though those consequences would be the same, for everyday purposes. Talking about horizon-fall rather than sunrise would thus be downright misleading, even though it would be more truthful. Only an undue fascination with the truth could lead someone to reform ordinary discourse about the sun.

Talk about colours is just like talk about sunrise in these respects. That is, life goes on as if objects are coloured in the way that they appear to be. Experience refutes few if any of the conclusions derived from beliefs about objects' colours; and many true conclusions are derived from such beliefs. Most of those true conclusions, of course, are about how objects will look to various people under various circumstances. And these conclusions are extremely useful in everyday life, since one's ability to communicate with others and with one's future selves about the external world depends on the ability to describe how various parts of that world appear. The point is that such conclusions are more easily and more reliably drawn from the familiar false picture of colours than they would be—by the ordinary person, at least—from the true picture of wavelengths and spectral-reflectance curves. Why, then, should one replace such a useful false picture with a true but misleading one?

Correct vs. Incorrect Colour-Talk. The case of colour differs from that of sunrise in one important respect. The sun never seems to do anything but move in a regular arc across the heavens, whereas objects often seem to have different colours in different circumstances. The ordinary speaker therefore finds himself drawing a distinction between the colours that objects really have and the colours that they only seem to have on some occasions. How can we countenance this distinction between real and illusory colours, given that our theory brands all colours as illusory?[21]

The answer is that classifying an object by the colour that it appears to have under so-called standard conditions is the most reliable and most informative way of classifying it, for the purposes of drawing useful conclusions about how the object will appear under conditions of any kind. Obviously, classifying an object by how it appears in the dark is not at all informative, since all objects appear equally black in the dark, even though they appear to have different colours in the light. Hence one can extrapolate an object's appearance in the dark from its appearance in the light, but not vice versa. The same is true—though to a lesser degree, of course—for other non-standard conditions. For instance, distance tends to lend a similar appearance to objects that look different at close range; coloured light tends to lend a similar appearance to objects that look different in daylight; and so on. The common-sense calculus of colour addition and subtraction therefore enables one to infer an object's appearance under non-standard conditions from its appearance under standard conditions, but not its appearance under standard conditions from that under non-standard conditions. That is why one set of conditions, and the accompanying colour-illusion, are privileged in everyday life.

There are notable exceptions to our claim about the varying informativeness of various colour appearances. But these exceptions actually support our explanation of why particular colour-illusions are privileged in ordinary discourse, because consideration of them leads the ordinary speaker to reconsider the distinction between true and illusory colour.

Some pairs of objects that appear to have the same colour in daylight—say, green—can appear to have different colours under incandescent lighting, where one may appear green and the other brown.[22] In these cases, how an object appears in daylight is not an indication of how it will appear under other less standard conditions.

Yet in these cases, one begins to wonder whether the object has a 'true' or standard colour at all. If an object's apparent colour does not vary, from one set of conditions to the next, in the same way as the apparent colour of objects that share its apparent colour in daylight, then one is tempted to say that the object does not have any one colour at all. Consider the object that looks green in daylight but brown in incandescent light, where most other objects that look green in daylight still look green. Is the object really green? really brown? Does it have any single 'real' colour at all?[23] Here intuitions diverge and ultimately give out. The reason, we think, is precisely that the common-sense notion of an object's real colour presupposes that it is the one apparent colour from which all its other apparent colours can be extrapolated, by fairly familiar rules of colour mixing. When that assumption is threatened, so is the notion of real colour.

NOTES

1. *Opere Complete di G. G.,* 15 vols, Firenze, 1842, IV, p. 333 (as translated by E. A. Burtt in *The Metaphysical Foundations of Modern Science,* Doubleday, Garden City, NY, 1954, p. 85).

2. Sydney Shoemaker, 'Qualities and Qualia: What's in The Mind?' *Philosophy and Phenomenological Research* vol. 50, supplement, 1990, p. 110.

3. One might be tempted to dissolve the conflict between the Galilean view and the charitable view of colour experience by reflecting a presupposition that they share. Both sides of the conflict assume that the properties mentioned in our descriptions of visual experience are properties that such experience represents objects as having. The only disagreement is over the question whether the colour properties that are thus attributed to objects by visual experience are properties that the objects tend to have. One might claim, however, that visual experience does not attribute properties to objects at all; and one might bolster one's claim by appeal to a theory known as adverbialism. According to adverbialism, the experience of seeing a thing as red is an event modified by some adverbial property—say, a seeing event that proceeds red-thing-ly. Not all adherents of adverbialism are committed to denying that such an experience represents an object as having a property; but adverbialism would indeed be useful to one who wished to deny it. For adverbialism would enable one to say that the phrase 'seeing a thing as red' describes a seeing event as having some adverbial property rather than as having the content that something is red. One could therefore contend that the question whether things really have the colour properties that they are seen as having is simply ill-formed, since colour properties figure in a visual experience as adverbial modifications of the experience rather than as properties attributed by the experience to an object.

Our view is that this extreme version of adverbialism does unacceptable violence to the concept of visual experience. Seeing something as red is the sort of thing that can be illusory or veridical, hence the sort of thing that has truth-conditions, and hence the sort of thing that has content. The content of this experience is that the object in question is red; and so the experience represents an object as having a property, about which we can legitimately ask whether it is a property that objects so represented really tend to have.

4. D. M. Armstrong, *A Materialist Theory of Mind,* Routledge & Kegan Paul, London, 1968; J. J. C. Smart, 'On Some Criticism of a Physicalist Theory of Colour,' in *Philosophical Aspects of the Mind-Body Problem,* ed. Chung-yin-Chen, University of Hawaii, Honolulu, 1975 (as cited by Christopher Peacocke, 'Colour Concepts and Colour Experience,' *Synthèse,* 1984, pp. 365–81, n. 5)

5. The final clause of this biconditional is often formulated so as to specify not only standard conditions but a standard observer as well. But the observer's being standard can itself be treated as a condition of observation, and so the distinction between observer and conditions is unnecessary.

6. See John McDowell, 'Values and Secondary Qualities,' in *Morality and Objectivity; a Tribute to L. Mackie,* ed. Ted Honderich, Routledge & Kegan Paul, London, 1985, pp. 110–29; David Wiggins, 'A Sensible Subjectivism?', in *Needs, Values, Truth,* Basil Blackwell, Oxford, 1987, pp. 185–214, p. 189; Gareth Evans, 'Things Without the Mind—A Commentary Upon Chapter Two of Strawson's *Individuals,*' in *Philosophical Subjects; Essays Presented to P. F. Strawson,* ed. Zak van Straaten, Clarendon Press, Oxford, 1980, pp. 76–116, see pp. 94–100, esp. n. 30.
Wiggins and McDowell favour a similar strategy for vindicating our perceptions of other qualities such as the comic and perhaps even the good. See McDowell's Lindley Lecture, 'Projection and Truth in Ethics.'

7. Peacocke, 'Colour Concepts and Color Experience.'

8. Perhaps the best argument for this claim is that no one who can identify the colours of external objects needs to be taught how to identify the colours of after-images. Once a person can recognize fire hydrants and maraschino cherries as red, he can identify the colour of the spots that float before his eyes after the flash-bulb has fired. He does not need to be taught a second sense of 'red' for the purpose of describing the latter experience.

9. See McGinn, *The Subjective View,* Clarendon Press, Oxford, 1983, pp. 6–8; McDowell, 'Values and Secondary Qualities,' n. 6; Wiggins, 'A Sensible Subjectivism?' p. 189; Michael Smith, 'Peacocke on Red and red',' *Synthèse,* 1986, pp. 559–76.

10. See McDowell, 'Values and Secondary Qualities,' p. 112: 'What would one expect it to be like to experience something's being such as to look red, if not to experience the thing in question (in the right circumstances) as looking, precisely, red?'

11. When McDowell discusses dispositionalism about the comic, in 'Projection and Truth in Ethics,' he tries to make the circularity of the theory into a virtue, by arguing that it blocks a projectivist account of humour. He says, 'The suggestion is that there is no self-contained prior fact of our subjective lives that could enter into a projective account or the relevant way of thinking'—that is, no independently specifiable subjective response that we can be described as projecting onto the world (p. 6). We would argue that the same problem afflicts, not just a projectivist account of the comical, but our very perceptions of things as comical, as McDowell interprets those perceptions.

12. *Sense and Content: Experience, Thought, and Their Relations,* Clarendon Press, Oxford, 1983, ch. 1. Other arguments are provided by Sydney Shoemaker in 'Qualities and Qualia: What's in the Mind?'

13. Intentionalism cannot characterize the experience in question as being similar to, or representing itself as being similar to, the experience you have when you see redness as attaching to a material object. Such an experience would have a different content from the one you are now having, and so it would not be like your present experience in any respect that the intentionalist can identify. Of course, once we abandon intentionalism, we can say that your present experience and the experience of seeing a red material object are alike in their intrinsic qualities. But such qualities are denied by intentionalism.

14. David Hume, *Enquiry Concerning the Principles of Morals,* ed. L. A. Selby-Bigge, Oxford University Press, Oxford, 1975, Appendix 1. Of course, this passage is literally about the projection of value, not colour. But surely, Hume chose colour as his metaphor for value, in this context, because he regarded projectivism about colour as an intuitively natural view.

15. Isaac Newton, *Opticks,* Dover Publications, New York, 1979, Book I, part i, definition; John Locke, *An Essay Concerning Human Understanding,* ed. Peter H. Nidditch, Clarendon Press, Oxford, 1975, Book II, ch. viii. Jonathan Bennett has interpreted Locke as a dispositionalist about colour (*Locke,* Berkeley, Hume; Central Themes, Clarendon Press, Oxford, 1971, ch. IV). But the textual evidence is overwhelming that Locke believed colour experience to be guilty of an error, and a projectivist error, at that. Locke was a dispositionalist, in our opinion, only about the properties of objects that actually cause colour experience, not about the properties that such experience represents objects as having.

16. See McDowell, 'Values and Secondary Qualities,' pp. 113-15.

17. See Evans, 'Things Without the Mind,' pp. 99–100. Berkeley carried this argument farther, by claiming that unperceived qualities, being unimaginable, were also inconceivable and hence impossible. Berkeley's willingness to equate imagination with conception was due to his theory of ideas, which equated concepts with mental pictures.

18. We grant this point for the sake of argument; but we think that it, too, underestimates the representational powers of the imagination. For surely one can form a mental image that contains a 'cut-a-way' view, showing how the far side of the ball looks while implying that it is, in reality, unseen.

19. See Shoemaker, 'Qualities and Qualia: What's in The Mind?' p. 10.

20. *Philosophical Investigations,* Blackwell, Oxford, 1974, section 312. We do not necessarily claim that the use to which we should like to put this passage coincides with Wittgenstein's.

21. We should point out that a similar question will confront those who adopt a dispositionalist interpretation of colour discourse. For according to dispositionalism, the colours of objects are their dispositions to present the appearance of colour; and objects are disposed to present the appearance of different colours under different circumstances. Corresponding to every colour that an object ever appears or would appear to have, there is a disposition of the object to give that appearance under the circumstances then prevailing. Now, dispositionalism denominates only one of these innumerable dispositions as the object's real colour, and it does so by defining the object's colour to be that disposition which is manifested under conditions specified as standard. But surely, dispositionalism should have to justify its selection of dispositions—or, what amounts to the same thing, its selection of standard conditions. For if colour is nothing but a disposition to produce colour appearances, one wants to know why a particular disposition to produce colour appearances should be privileged over other such dispositions. And this is, in effect, the same question as why one colour-illusion should be privileged over other colour-illusions, given the assumption that all colours are illusory.

22. This phenomenon is called metamerism. See C. L. Hardin, *Color for Philosophers: Unweaving the Rainbow,* Hackett, Indianapolis, 1988, pp. 28, 45 ff.

23. People who spend much time considering these cases have been known to give up the notion of true colour entirely. We once asked a scientist who performs research on colour vision why people think that most opaque objects have a real colour. His answer was, 'They do? How odd.'

Reading Questions

1. Boghossian and Velleman offer the Knowledge Argument against Physicalism:

    1. A color property is really a physical property like having a particular spectral-reflectance profile. (the physicalist premise)
    2. Thus, two objects have the same color iff they have the same spectral-reflectance profile.
    3. Thus, one knows that two objects have the same color iff one knows that they have the same spectral-reflectance profile.
    4. It is only through considerable empirical research that one can know whether two objects have the same spectral-reflectance profile.
    5. But one can know whether two objects have the same color through visual experiences alone.
    6. Thus, by *reductio,* (1) must be false.

    How could Boghossian and Velleman reply to this argument from logical analogy? Does it show that there must be a flaw in their Knowledge Argument against Physicalism?

    1. A shape property is really a physical property like having a particular molecular structure.
    2. Thus, two objects have the same shape iff they have the same molecular structure.
    3. Thus, one knows that two objects have the same shape iff one knows that they have the same molecular structure.
    4. It is only through considerable empirical research that one can know whether two objects have the same molecular structure.
    5. But one can know whether two objects have the same shape through visual experiences alone.
    6. Thus, by *reductio,* (1) must be false.

2. Boghossian and Velleman reject dispositionalism, namely the view that colors can be defined in this manner: red =df. a disposition to appear red under standard conditions. They raise the question of whether "red" in the *definiens* expresses the same property as "red" in the *definiendum,* and proceed to offer the following argument.

    1. Suppose "red" in the *definiens* expresses the same property as "red" in the *definiendum.*
    2. Thus the dispositionalist's definition is circular—it explains redness in terms of redness.
    3. This is vicious because "red" in the *definiens* can only be understood as a disposition; viz. a disposition to appear red under standard conditions. The occurrence of "red" in this disposition is to be understood in terms of a further disposition, and we are off on an infinite regress.
    4. One can see the color of an object only if one can see this infinity of dispositions.
    5. No one can see such an infinity.
    6. Thus no one can see a color.

    Undoubtedly, this is a counterintuitive consequence for the dispositionalist. But is it more counterintuitive than Boghossian and Velleman's own view that objects are uncolored and that we are in massive error in thinking that they do have colors?

3. Another argument that Boghossian and Velleman marshal against dispositionalism is this one:

    1. If colors are dispositions to appear colored under standard conditions, then turning on a light in a dark room will activate (turn on) the colors.
    2. But colors do not seem activated by illumination; rather, they seem revealed.
    3. Thus colors are not dispositions.

Is this is a good argument? Why won't an analogous one work against Boghossian and Velleman's own view of projectivism? To wit:

1. If colors are properties of the visual field that we project onto things, then turning on a light will cause us to project colors onto essentially uncolored things, like casting paint onto glass objects.
2. But colors do not seem to shoot out of us by the catalyst of illumination; rather, they seem revealed.
3. Thus colors are not projected.

4. Boghossian and Velleman maintain that we project colors onto objects. Why do we so routinely do this? They claim that it is because those objects are the routine causes of color experience. If pain were solely caused by patches on the surfaces of plants, we might experience pain as being in the plant, instead of the plant being a cause of pain. So it is with color. However, pain is very often caused by punctures and abrasions occasioned by external objects. Yet we never think that the pain is in the hammer instead of in one's thumb. If Boghossian and Velleman are right, surely we ought to at least sometimes consider pain as being in the plant, or the hammer, or whatever. Yet we never do this. How could they respond?

22 Color and Illusion

C. L. HARDIN

IMAGINE THE FOLLOWING EXPERIMENT. Before you is a spinning disk, illuminated by an ordinary incandescent lamp. If most people are asked what color they see on the face of the disk, they will unhesitatingly reply that they see a bluish green. But you, ever the skeptical and cagey philosopher, may hesitate, not because what you see doesn't look bluish green, for it very plainly does, but because you suspect a trick. And, indeed, this proves to be a trick of sorts. When the wheel is made to turn very slowly you see a half-black, half-white disk, with a slot through which a red lamp flashes. You saw no red at all before, and you can discern no bluish green now. The bluish green color the disk looked to have was entirely the color of an after-image, one that appeared to be the color of the surface of a physical object rather than the color of a free-floating patch. This particular after-image phenomenon is called Bidwell's ghost, after the early twentieth century psychologist who first discovered it.[1] When you view Bidwell's ghost, it is always open to you to deny that you are seeing bluish green, on the ground that after-images are not physical objects and only physical objects can have colors. But it is then fair to ask you what color you do see. Red? Gray? No color at all? None of these answers is intuitively very appealing.

If you are like most philosophers, you will nevertheless be inclined to say that Bidwell's ghost is a color illusion, and that when the disk is rapidly spinning, you don't see its true colors. But just what is a color illusion? Isn't it a failure of correspondence between the color that an object seems to have and the color that it does have? If it is, to characterize an object's apparent possession of a color as illusory is to presume that one knows what

From C. L. Hardin, "Color and Illusion," in W. Lycan, ed., Mind and Cognition *(1990). Oxford: Blackwell Publishers. Reprinted by permission of the author.*

counts as the object's true color. In ordinary practice this presumption seems natural enough. But it is in fact quite difficult to justify in a principled fashion, especially if you happen to be a physicalist.

I shall argue that the facts about chromatic phenomena[2] make it very hard to construe colors as properties of physical objects or processes outside the body of the perceiver. I shall consider three attempts at a physicalistic reduction of colors: to wavelengths of light as Armstrong (1968) would have it; to the dispositions of objects appropriately to affect normal observers under standard conditions, a thesis defended by Smart (1975) and Lewis;[3] and to spectral reflectances, as proposed by Averill (1985) and Hilbert (1987). We shall have reason to suppose that all such reductions will fail, and thus to question the legitimacy of the conception of a color illusion.

We normally see color because light of certain wavelengths strikes the retina and excites the photoreceptors that dwell there. They in turn hyperpolarize, generating small electrochemical signals in other cells. The photoreceptors that are relevant to color vision are called *cones.* There are three types of cones, each sensitive to a particular range of the visible spectrum. They are often misleadingly labeled the blue, green and red cones. Let us call them instead the shortwave, middlewave and longwave cones. Their sensitivity curves are rather broad and overlap substantially. When a cone absorbs a photon of light of a particular wavelength, it generates a voltage, and the character of this voltage is independent of the wavelength of the photon that the receptor absorbed. Subsequent cells in the visual processing chain can only "know" that a receptor of a particular type has been excited, but they cannot "know" the wavelength of the photon that has caused it to become excited. Information about wavelength can only be gleaned by cells that are able to compare the outputs of cones of different types that are in the same retinal region. So chromatic information about the light in a particular retinal region that is conveyed to higher visual cells takes the form of the ratios of excitations of the three cones types in that region. The vast amount of wavelength information in the optical array that strikes a small retinal region is reduced to a three-termed cone excitation ratio right at the beginning of the visual processing chain. This is a massive information loss, and it has important consequences. In particular, any two stimuli of the same intensity that produce the same cone excitation ratios will be regarded as equivalent by the chromatic visual system. This is one of the most fundamental facts about color vision, since it means that for most perceptible light stimuli, there exist indefinitely many other stimuli, each with a physically distinct wavelength composition, that will evoke precisely the same perceived color. Color vision stimuli that are perceptually equivalent but physically inequivalent are known as *metamers.*

The existence of metamers might be expected to make trouble for a purported reduction of colors to combinations of wavelengths of light. The difficulty arises conspicuously in the case of white. It is often said that white is a combination of light of all colors. But this seems odd on the face of it. Although orange looks reddish as well as yellowish, and purple looks both reddish and bluish, white, far from looking reddish and greenish and yellowish and bluish, looks to have no chromatic colors in it at all. Had he the opportunity to do it all over again, the biblical Joseph would have doubtless preferred his coat of many colors to have been white.

You may reply that this misrepresents the intention of the specification of white, which is not to advance the claim that white is a combination of all other perceived colors, but to assert that perceptions of white are produced by light of all the visible wavelengths put together in the appropriate amounts. Now it is true that light that we call white is most often composed in this fashion, but it is also true that a white light can be generated from the superposition of as few as two monochromatic light sources, and there are infinitely many distinct pairs of such monochromatic sources. Furthermore, one can superimpose as many of these pairs as one likes, and still get light that looks white. On the other hand, each of these white-looking lights has, as we shall see, color-rendering properties that are different from the rest. Which of these, according to the account of color that identifies colors with wavelengths of light, is "real" white, and which is just "apparent" white? And by virtue of what principle does one make such choices?

Let us consider another example. It might seem plausible to identify "pure" yellow with a spectral wavelength that most people see as "pure" yellow—about 577 nm (a *nanometer* is a billionth of a meter) and to suppose that anything that is yellow is such in virtue of sending light to the eye containing a component of 577 nm light. But what are we to say of a spot of light that has just two components: monochromatic 540 nm light (that most people see as green) and monochromatic 670 nm light (that most people see as red)? Such a spot will not only appear yellow, but will exactly match the appearance of a monochromatic yellow, although the one stimulus consists entirely of 577 nm light, whereas the other hasn't a trace of 577 nm light.

The reason that both stimuli look yellow is that they produce the same ratios of excitations in the three cone types. To find out what looks yellow, we obviously must attend to the operating characteristics of human visual systems. But the physicalist who would reduce real colors to wavelengths of light should be able to pick out the *real* colors on the basis of physical considerations alone.

Such physical considerations seem to fail entirely to give us a conceptual grip on the phenomenon of colored shadows, first described in detail by Count Rumford (Thompson 1802). One may illustrate colored shadows in a variety of ways, but a simple and striking way to do it is to arrange two slide projectors so that the light that they project falls on the same area of the screen. First turn them on separately. Let one projector carry a slide that consists of a piece of green celluloid on which is fixed a cross made of two strips of tape. The image that it projects is of a black cross on a green field. Let the second projector carry only the empty frame of a slide, so that it casts a rectangle of incandescent projector light on the screen. What will happen when the two images are superimposed? To the black cross and the green field, the second projector adds only some broadband, approximately white, light. According to the wavelength theorist, you should see nothing particularly remarkable, only a grayish cross on a somewhat washed-out green field. What you will in fact see is quite different: the cross will look bright pink. If you were to bring in a spectrophotometer, it would tell you that the spectrum of light reflected from the area of the screen on which the cross appears is only that which is characteristic of ordinary projector light, and not that which would have been there had you produced the effect by means of a red filter.

"Ah, but this is just another illusion," the wavelength theorist might reply. "What I am concerned to do is to give an account of the real colors of things, not a theory of the colors things seem to have in demonstrations of bizarre effects." Very well. But any theory of color that is to be of any interest must go beyond a set of raw stipulations to the effect that such-and-such wavelength combinations are to count as red, and that so-and-so wavelengths are to be cyan, and so on. Their proponents always claim that materialist theories of color fit into a scientific picture of the world (often The Scientific Picture of the World), so any such theory of color should provide the framework for a scientific theory of the color qualities that we see. At the very least, we can demand of a theory of color that it satisfactorily represent what is going on when we see red and brown and white and black in ordinary life. But in fact, a proper account of our everyday experience of black and brown requires an appeal to one of the fundamental phenomena—namely, simultaneous contrast—that is involved in colored shadows, so this so-called "illusion" is not as far removed from ordinary experience as one might have supposed.

Simultaneous contrast is ubiquitous and easily illustrated. The principle involved is, roughly speaking, that a large area of color tends to induce its complementary color into a neighboring area. Thus, an area of red makes adjacent areas look greener, blue makes a nearby region look more yellow, white induces black, and so on. The effect is rooted in the physiology of the visual system. The biological details are at least roughly understood and quite interesting, but they need not detain us now. The pink that appears on the cross in our colored shadow experiment is, roughly, the complement of the green in the field, and is induced by it.

Simultaneous contrast is consciously manipulated by painters, often to great effect. Delacroix once said "Give me mud, let me surround it as I think fit, and it shall be the radiant flesh of Venus." For examples of simultaneous contrast we do not strictly require either mud or the radiant flesh of Venus. Some experimentation with pieces of colored paper will soon persuade you that two squares cut from the same piece of colored paper can look very different from one another when placed on backgrounds that differ from each other in color.

With certain choices of background, the phenomenon is so strong that often people need to be specially persuaded that the specimen areas will indeed look the same when seen in isolation. When confronted with an effective example of simultaneous contrast, you can undo the effect by using a viewing tube or other device to replace the inducing surround by a neutral one. (It is well to bear in mind that what is "neutral" depends upon the color in question; there is no such thing as a universal neutral surround). It is easy to construct a tolerably useful viewing tube. Just roll up a piece of paper, preferably dark gray, into a tube and peer at the patch you wish to inspect, rolling the paper tightly enough to shut out the view of the ambient light and the surrounding regions. In the colored shadow experiment, if you look at the pink cross through a viewing tube, its pinkness disappears.

Now what does simultaneous contrast have to do with the everyday perception of black and brown? The answer, in brief, is that both blackness and brownness are always the products of simultaneous contrast. Nakedly stated, this seems implausible. But let us examine some of the evidence for it. Take black first, we are commonly told that black is the absence of light, a visual nullity. But in truth, what we see in the absence of visual stimulation is not black, but a dark gray; the blackest blacks arise as a result of contrast. You can see this for yourself by entering at night an unilluminated room containing a collection of objects that, by good light, range from white through the grays to black. Equip yourself with a lamp that is controlled by a dimmer. Go into the darkened room, slowly turn up the dimmer, and look at the contents. Notice that when you look at them under conditions of very dim light, the gray range is tightly compressed, with little visible lightness difference between the lightest and darkest objects. But as the light increases, the gray range expands in both directions: not only do the whites look whiter, the blacks look blacker. An increase in the total amount of light has increased blackness.

Another, more painful, way of seeing this is to watch some daytime television. Before you turn on the set, notice that the screen is, by daylight, a middle gray. Turn on the set, find a clear picture, and stand far enough away from it to minimize most of the remaining visual noise. Look for a good black, and mentally compare its lightness with the middle gray of the turned-off screen. (If you are sufficiently sinful to have two television sets, the comparison could be direct.) The black is obviously darker than the gray. But since television pictures are produced by generating light, not by subtracting it, the blackening of that area of the screen must be the result of contrast.

Browns are, for most people, a distinctive set of colors, as differentiated in character from reds and yellows as reds and yellows are differentiated from each other. But in fact, browns are simply blackened oranges and yellows, and their characteristic (or, to use the technical term, "dominant") wavelengths are the same as those of most orange and yellow objects. The spectral profile of a chocolate bar closely resembles that of an orange, but, under the same lighting conditions, the light reflected from the chocolate bar is of much lower intensity. The characteristic difference in appearance between the two depends entirely upon their perceived relationships to the ambient light.

To see this, you can first project an orange spot on a darkened screen, and then, using a second projector, surround the orange spot with bright projector light. The slides may be prepared in the following way. First, use a paper punch to cut a round hole in a piece of stiff paper, glue a piece of orange celluloid onto the paper, and cut the paper and its attached celluloid so that it will fit inside an empty slide frame. This gives you a projectable orange spot. The second slide, the one that is responsible for the bright surround and blackened center, is produced by gluing onto a piece of transparent celluloid the round piece of paper that was made when you cut out the hole with the punch when you were making the first slide. On the screen, line up the projected (orange) hole with the projected (shadow) disk, and try the experiment. The whiteness of the surround induces blackness into the orange, transforming it into a brown. Here, as before, the action of simultaneous contrast may be undone by the judicious use of a viewing tube. You might also like to use a viewing tube to examine a chocolate bar, or other brown object, in a bright light. It will lose its brownness, and look like a dim orange or yellow. In performing such experiments it is best to use a tube with a blackened interior, and to avoid looking at portions of the surface that contain highlights.

So to write off simultaneous contrast as something that need not enter into one's fundamental theory of colors is also to write off the possibility of giving a proper account of the nature of black and brown. This seems unacceptable, unless one is prepared to think of black and brown as "illusory" rather than as "real" colors.

We also ought to demand that a minimally adequate theory of color lend itself to an account of the elementary laws of color mixing. For example, since orange is visibly yellow-red (notice that it could not *fail* to be yellow-red), it has a red component and a yellow component. Furthermore, when color-normal observers look at *monochromatic* spectral light of 590 nm, they see orange. But how can this be on a wavelength theory that maintains that red is light of a wavelength of, say, 650 nm, and yellow is light of a wavelength of 577 nm? And what of the basic and simple relationships about the relations that colors bear to each other? How is it that we can see reddish blues—the purples—but no reddish greens? One will search the writings of wavelength theorists in vain to find persuasive answers to any of these questions. We might be tolerant of such shortcomings if nobody else had an explanation for color mixing and color compatibilities and incompatibilities—in short, if there were no such discipline as color science. In truth, visual scientists know a great deal about all of these matters. But they do not encumber themselves with the supposition that chromatic phenomena can be accounted for without an essential reference to eyes and brains.

Most philosophers are, indeed, not very sympathetic to a program such as wavelength reductionism. They are aware that a wide variety of distinct physical circumstances can be responsible for producing a given color appearance, and that because of the peculiarities of human perceptual mechanisms, the relationship between external physical conditions and what we see is not a simple one. "No matter," say they, "how physically diverse and, indeed, gerrymandered the class of red things may be, what makes them red is that they are disposed to look red to normal observers under standard conditions." According to the adherents of this position, colors are, to use Locke's term, *powers* of objects to cause us to be in particular perceptual states under particular circumstances. The perceptual states are not themselves to be thought of as colors or as being colored, but, rather, as signs or indices of certain dispositions in physical objects. The human perceptual apparatus is to be regarded as a stalking-horse to pick out and classify physical powers that are of interest to us and to creatures constituted like us, although those powers would not have been picked out or thought to form natural classes on the basis of purely physical considerations.

This way of approaching the problem has much to commend it. For a variety of purposes, the practitioners of that branch of color science known as colorimetry employ a statistically defined Standard Observer whose "receptoral" sensitivities are used in combination with various standard illuminants and viewing conditions to sort objects into classes according to such technical parameters as purity and dominant wavelength. In turn, these parameters are correlated with perceptual variables like saturation and hue. But unlike some philosophers, color scientists are well aware that, for example, hue is a quite different property from dominant wavelength, and that the correlation between the two is only approximate and is well-defined only under certain carefully specified standard viewing conditions. Furthermore, the standard viewing conditions to be employed will depend upon the purpose for which the measurement is being taken. There is, in color science, no set of conditions for determining the "true" or "real" colors of objects. As we shall now see, if they are construed non-pragmatically and in more than a rough-and-ready sense, the notions of "normal observer" and "standard condition" are philosophers' fictions.

Let's look more closely into these matters by returning to the centrally important phenomenon of metamerism. We have previously considered the metameric matches of spots of light. The conception can be extended to reflective surfaces. The wavelength distribution that strikes the eye depends upon the spectral characteristics of both the illumination and the surface that reflects it to the eye. A change in the spectral characteristics of either illumination or surface will often make a difference in what we see. If two spectrally distinct surfaces visually match under a given illuminant for a given observer, the surfaces are said to be metamers for that illuminant and that observer. But we must expect that since the two samples are spectrally different, that difference will be made visually apparent under some illuminant or other. It is not difficult in our age of synthetic colorants to find two color samples that are, for most people, a good match in daylight but when shifted to another illuminant—one or another variety of artificial light—fail to match. Furthermore, when we use first one, then another, illuminant to see a piece of white paper, the illuminants may look to be very similar or even identical, but they may give dramatically different results when they illuminate various pieces of chromatically colored paper.

These effects are well known to people who pay attention to colors. Many people know that it is advisable to see whether the coat and trousers that look so handsome together in the store are equally pleasing when taken into the natural light of the street. Photographers learn to their sorrow that a film that yields a proper color balance when used out of doors gives pictures with a markedly yellow tinge when the same subject is photographed under incandescent light.

It is perfectly true that if you saw the subject of such photographs, first in natural light, then in incandescent light, you would not be aware of such a profound shift in hue. In fact, you might not notice any difference at all if you weren't looking for it. The perceived colors of objects tend to remain relatively stable over a wide variety of changes in illumination. This is partly due to the fact that most people don't attend to relatively small color differences and possess poor color memories for even relatively large differences. But it is also because the eye, unlike a camera's film, adapts automatically to the character of the illuminant and, in large measure, successfully discounts illumination changes. We are more sensitive to the relationships of the colors in a scene than we are to their absolute values. A piece of white paper in shadow looks to us to be lighter than a piece of coal in sunlight, even though the coal sends more light to the eye than the paper does.

This stability across variations in ambient lighting has been called color constancy, and it has frequently been noted, theorized about, and its completeness exaggerated, especially by Land and his followers.[4] Although the phenomenon is robust, constancy is far from complete, even under the range of natural lighting conditions. Inconstancy becomes a very vexing problem with artificial colorants and illuminants, and color technologists wrestle with problems of metamerism every day. For instance, restorers of old paintings are often unable to replicate the original colorants. They create an excellent visual match with the old paint under the illumination of the workshop, only to find that when it is exhibited under the illumination of the gallery, the restoration is plainly visible. So even though adaptation may preserve color appearances for the most part, a change in illuminants that transforms a metameric match into a mismatch—especially a gross mismatch—will always be noticeable.

Let us now see what problems metamerism poses for a theory that would assign colors to objects on the basis of normal observers and standard conditions. First of all, consider two colorants that match metamerically under the standard illuminant. Because the match is metameric, the colorants will have different spectral characteristics and will thus fail to match under some other illuminant. Instead of saying that the two colorants have the same color because they match under the standard illuminant, shouldn't we say that they can't be the same color because under the other illuminant they look different to normal observers?

Although this objection certainly has some force, it is open to the proponent of the normal-observer and standard-condition thesis to stick by her guns, and insist that it is the comparison of samples under the standard illuminant that must decide the issue. But it is now necessary for her to specify the standard illuminant. Two frequently employed standards are sunlight and north daylight. But although some philosophers seem to be unaware of the fact, the spectral characteristics of the two are not the same. So we must expect—and it is in fact the case—that there will be colorants that will match under the one illuminant but not under the other. Then which illuminant is to be the standard? Are there any principled philosophical grounds—as opposed to the pragmatic considerations of color technologists—for choosing one over the other? And shall we let our illuminant have energy outside the visible range and take fluorescence into account, or use a band-limited source so as to exclude it?

There is much more to specifying a set of standard conditions than the choice of illuminant. What are we to do about simultaneous contrast? For many purposes, it makes sense to require that the sample be seen through a viewing tube or other aperture with a "neutral" surround. What counts as "neutral" will depend upon the sample itself, since dark surrounds will brighten light colors, and light surrounds will darken dark colors. There are no all-purpose neutral surrounds, just compromises of various degrees of utility. On the other hand, to insist on using an aperture for all determinations is to forbear categorizing objects as black or brown, since, as we have already seen, these are essentially contrast colors.

The next decision that must be made in assigning standard conditions concerns the angular size of the sample with respect to the eye of the observer. Both a ten-degree standard and a two-degree standard are in use in colorimetric practice. They don't give exactly the same results, and there is no agreed-upon recipe for converting from the one to the other. Color technologists will choose to use the one or the other, depending upon the purpose for which the measurement is to be made, but it never occurs to them to choose one rather than the other because it enables them to determine the "true" colors of material samples. Are we to conclude that color technologists lack a healthy sense of reality? Or do they understand something about standard conditions that philosophers don't?

Then there is the matter of the illuminant-sample-observer viewing angle. The colors we see from all manner of materials depend upon viewing angles, not only because some surfaces are glossy, but because much of the world's color is due to such physical mechanisms as scattering, refraction, interference and polarization, and these are typically angle-dependent. The colors of rainbows, oil films, and iridescent beetles are obvious examples. There are many others. For instance, crumple a piece of transparent cellophane and sandwich it between two sheets of polaroid material. Hold the sandwich up to a strong light, rotate one piece of the polaroid material relative to the other, and enjoy the spectacle of shifting colors. Many objects have transmission colors, which may be quite different from their reflection colors and may interact with them in surprising ways: gold is a notable example. Some objects are translucent, and there do not at the moment exist standards for determining their color characteristics. Then there are fluorescent objects, and self-luminous objects and the like. What are the standard conditions for viewing the colors of stars and bioluminescent fish? North daylight and six inches away?[5]

Still more might be said about viewing conditions, but we must cease beating this moribund horse. However, we should devote a moment to examining the remaining term of the equation, the "normal" observer. About six percent of all males and a much smaller proportion of females are color deficient; doubtless some of the readers of the present volume fall into this category. Color-deficient people can make some visual discriminations that so-called "color normals" can't, a capability used by the military to penetrate camouflage that confuses color normals. Nevertheless, we, the majority, choose not to let them be the arbiters of the colors of things; we reserve this privilege for ourselves.

I have previously referred to the Standard Observer that is used in colorimetric determinations. The Standard Observer (also known as the Average Observer) is actually a standardized set of color matching curves that are based on average values obtained from the color matches made by fifty or so normal—that is, non-color—deficient-observers. The utility of having a standard observer so defined is scarcely to be doubted, but the fact remains that this is only an average taken over a range of people who vary significantly from each other in their visual performance. Indeed, the color matches made by the standard observer would not be fully acceptable to 90 percent of the population, especially if they got more persnickity about the matches than they do in most everyday situations.

You might like to get an intuitive idea of the magnitude of the variation in color perception among normal observers. To do this, it will be helpful to look at a printed hue circle, such as may be found in textbooks on color for students of painting. Notice that all of the hues in the circle look to be either red, or yellow, or blue, or green, or some perceptual combination of two of them. Thus orange is a perceptual mixture of yellow and red, and turquoise is a perceptual mixture of blue and green. Now observe that some of the hues are more elementary than others. For instance, you can locate a red that is neither yellowish nor bluish, but you cannot find a purple that is neither reddish nor bluish; indeed a hue that was not reddish or not bluish could, for this reason alone, not count as purple. Visual scientists refer to hues such as purple and orange as *binary* hues, and to a non-binary hue such as the red that is neither yellowish nor bluish as a *unique* hue. It is easy to see that there are exactly four unique hues: there is a unique red, a unique yellow, a unique green, and a unique blue.

Do color-normal observers see unique hues at the same wavelength locations in the spectrum? Experimental investigations show that they do not. For example, Hurvich et al. (1968) did a study on the spectral location of unique green, a hue that is neither yellowish nor bluish. Under carefully controlled conditions, any individual observer can consistently locate his or her unique green on a spectrum with an error of plus or minus three nanometers. But the average settings for 50 normal observers spanned a range of almost *thirty* nanometers, from 490 run to 520 nm. Most people will see this range of greens as consisting of several distinguishable hues, ranging from a bluish green at one end to a yellowish green at the other. If your library has the *Munsell Book of Color*, you can get some idea of the perceptual breadth of the range. Look at the medium Value, high Chroma color chips in the Hue sequence from 5 Blue-Green to 2.5 Green.

The moral that we can draw from this is that the variability between normal observers is distinctly larger than the accuracy with which any of them can make hue distinctions. Equally large variability holds for the other perceptual dimensions of color. It should not be surprising, then, that just as metameric matches vary with the spectrum of the illumination, they vary from one observer to the next under the same conditions of observation. We may conclude that she who would fix the colors of the surfaces of objects by appealing to the perceptions of a normal observer under standard conditions is obliged not only to specify which normal observer and which set of standard conditions she has in mind, but is also obliged to give us a set of principles that will justify her choices. Needless to say, the philosophical literature contains neither the specifications nor the justifications.

We must now consider the third of the theories we had set out to investigate. This theory maintains that the colors of the surfaces of physical objects are to be identified with the spectral reflectances of such surfaces. Because of the mechanisms of approximate color constancy, reflectance is a physically measurable (though of course non-fundamental) feature of objects that, under ordinary conditions, correlates better with what we see than does the wavelength of the light that strikes the eye. This is because color vision has evolved so that animals can distinguish reflectances from each other without being confused by illuminance changes. Furthermore, reflectance is what is typically picked out by the phrase 'physical color' when that is used by color scientists to refer to an attribute of the surfaces of objects. It is a consequence of the reflectance theory that if objects have distinct spectral reflectances, they must be accounted distinct colors, even though they may not look distinct under any but the most special and bizarre illuminants. So, for the reflectivists, a metameric color match is a match of apparent colors, but not a match of real ones. Therefore, the problems that metamerism poses for the normal-observer, standard-condition theory are not problems for the reflectance theory.

However, there are two tasks that remain to be carried out by the reflectivist before he can claim that his is an adequate theory of color. The first of them is to extend the theory to cover chromatic physical phenomena that do not depend upon the reflection of light. There are many of these, and their number has increased rapidly with the advent of technology. Holograms and color television are obvious examples. The extension of the theory to encompass some of these phenomena will be relatively easy, but rather more difficult in others. For instance, there is more than one basic way to produce color television pictures. One of them, not commercially successful because of ineradicable problems of low saturation and flicker, has the interesting property that it permits the reception of color pictures on "black-and-white" television sets! The picture to be transmitted must first be encoded by a device, the Butterfield encoder (Butterfield 1968), whose effect depends upon the ability of suitably sequenced achromatic pulses to stimulate differentially the color-perception mechanisms in the eye. The same principle is employed on a spinning wheel or top often sold as a novelty item. Psychologists know it as the "Benham disk."[6] The wheel has only a black-and-white pattern on it, but as it spins, you will, if you look at it closely and under a bright incandescent light, see rings of various desaturated colors, the hues of which depend upon the speed and direction of the rotation of the disk. If its inventor had succeeded in circumventing the limitations of the process, the Butterfield encoder might have become the industry standard. Would one then have been so easily tempted to regard these as "illusory" colors?

Let's suppose, though, that the reflectivist has successfully extended his account to cover the wide range of the physical causes of color perceptions. Has he thereby given us a theory of color? Surely he has not until he has told us about red, and green, and yellow, and blue.

These, after all, are what most of us have in mind when we think about colors. By avoiding the problems of metamerism as well as other products of the workings of our visual systems, the reflectivist has no resources within his theory for collecting reflectances into the hue classes that we find in experience. We recall that metamerism comes about because our chromatic information consists entirely of the excitation ratios of three cone types. This trivariant chromatic information is transformed into fourfold hue perception in consequence of the way that the outputs of the cones are subsequently summed and differenced to generate two chromatic channels. One chromatic channel carries information that is registered by the brain as redness or greenness, but not both at once, and the other carries information that is registered by the brain as yellowness or blueness, but not both at once. The four unique hues along with their binary perceptual mixtures arise from this postreceptoral processing, as does the mutual exclusion of color complements. (This is why there are reddish yellows—the oranges—but no reddish greens.) This fourfold color structure has no counterpart in physical structures outside the organism, and any attempt to assign reflectances to fourfold color classes will inevitably appeal to normal observers and standard conditions, with inevitable arbitrariness. But beyond all of that, the colors that we actually see depend upon many more factors than relative spectral reflectance, such as the intensity with which the receptors are stimulated, what is going on in surrounding receptors at the moment, and what went on in the receptors during the previous milliseconds.

Let's look for a moment at just one of these factors, the effect of the intensity of light upon hue. Take an ordinary incandescent bulb and hold it next to a white wall. Since the wall looks white, it ought to reflect pretty faithfully the spectrum of any light that is incident upon it. When it is illuminated by the bulb, the light that the wall reflects will have the same wavelength make-up of the light that comes to your eye directly from the bulb, although the reflected light will be significantly less intense. A piece of red celluloid placed between your eyes and the bulb will serve as a transmission filter that will reduce the intensity of light from both sources. Its wavelength selectivity will be exactly the same for both the direct and the reflected light. Now if hue were to depend only upon the spectrum of the light, the light from the wall should have the same hue as the light that comes directly from the filament of the bulb. But as you will see when you try the experiment, the light from the filament is significantly more yellowish than the light reflected from the wall, although a spectrophotometer would show that the spectral profile is the same for both. Visual scientists explain the effect—a shifting of hues toward yellows and blues as light levels are increased—as a consequence of an increase in sensitivity of the yellow-blue channel relative to the red-green channel as the intensity of the light increases.

So the redness, greenness, yellowness and blueness we see when we look at the surfaces of objects depend upon quite a few more variables than just their wavelength profile. The reflectivist theory, like the wavelength theory, suffers from an irremediable underdetermination: too many of the mechanisms essential to the production of the colors that we see lie within the bodies of perceivers.

This should not be an unwelcome conclusion, even to physicalists. Why should chromatic phenomena not depend essentially upon processes that take place within the confines of the head? The stuffings of the head are, after all, material, and the whole process of color perception is physical, determinate, and lawlike from beginning to end. Physical objects need not have colors of their own, in some special, elitist manner, in order to look colored. The world need contain only objects and "looks," and sometimes just the looks will do. In a spirit of chromatic democracy, we should be willing to embrace Bidwell's ghost, for its origins are not supernatural, but only out of the ordinary. It is no more, but also no less, illusory than all the rest of the world's colors.

NOTES

1. See Bidwell (1901).

2. An excellent source for these facts about color and color vision is Hurvich (1981). Many of the chromatic phenomena likely to be of interest to philosophers are discussed in Hardin (1988).

3. David Lewis's view is described in Smart (1975).

4. For a brief discussion of the advantages and difficulties of Edwin Land's retinex theory of color vision, see the appendix to Hardin (1988).

5. See Austin (1962).

6. See Benham (1894).

REFERENCES

Armstrong, D. M. (1968). *A Materialist Theory of the Mind*. London: Routledge and Kegan Paul.

Austin, J. L. (1962). *Sense and Sensibilia*. Oxford: Oxford University Press.

Averill, E. W. (1985). "Color and the Anthropocentric Problem." *Journal of Philosophy* 82, 281–303.

Benham, E. C. (1894). "Notes." *Nature* 51, 113–114.

Bidwell, S. (1901). "On Negative After-Images and Their Relation to Certain Other Visual Phenomena." *Proceedings of the Royal Society of London* B 68, 262-269.

Butterfield, J. F. (1968). "Subjective (Induced) Color Television." *Society of Motion Picture and Television Engineers Journal* 77, 1025–1028.

Hardin, C. L. (1988). *Color for Philosophers.* Indianapolis: Hackett.

Hilbert, D. (1987). *Color and Color Perception: A Study in Anthropocentric Realism*. Chicago: University of Chicago Press.

Hurvich, L. M. (1981). *Color Vision*. Sunderland, MA: Sinauer Associates.

Hurvich, L. M., D. Jameson, and J. D. Cohen (1968). "The Experimental Determination of Unique Green in the Spectrum." *Perceptual Psychology* 4, 65–68.

Smart, J. J. C. (1975). "On Some Criticisms of a Physicalistic Theory of Colors." In C.-Y. Cheng, ed., *Philosophical Aspects of the Mind-Body Problem*. Honolulu: University of Hawaii Press.

Thompson, B. (Count Rumford) (1802). *Philosophical Papers,* vol. 1. London: Cadell and Davies.

Reading Questions

1. What are metamers and what, if anything, does their existence imply for the view that colors are light wavelengths?
2. What is simultaneous contrast, and how can one use it to make a black thing blacker by increasing the total amount of light? What does Hardin claim that this shows about the view that black is the absence of color?

3. How does Hardin argue that the existence of metamers undermines the dispositionalist view that red =df. a disposition to appear red under standard conditions?
4. What is the color of a (lit) firefly, according to the view that colors are the spectral reflectances of physical objects? Does it have a color?

Further Readings

Books

Byrne, Alex, and David R. Hilbert, eds. 1997. *Readings on Color.* 2 vols. Cambridge, MA: MIT Press [A Bradford Book].

Clark, Austen. 1993. *Sensory Qualities.* Oxford: Oxford University Press.

Hardin, C. L. 1986. *Color for Philosophers: Unweaving the Rainbow.* Indianapolis: Hackett.

Hilbert, David R. 1987. *Color and Color Perception: A Study in Anthropocentric Realism.* Stanford: Center for the Study of Language and Information.

Jackson, Frank. 1977. *Perception: A Representative Theory.* Cambridge: Cambridge University Press.

Landesman, Charles. 1989. *Color and Consciousness: An Essay in Metaphysics.* Philadelphia: Temple University Press.

McGinn, Colin. 1983. *The Subjective View: Secondary Qualities and Indexical Thoughts.* Oxford: Oxford University Press.

Maund, Barry. 1995. *Colours: Their Nature and Representation.* Cambridge: Cambridge University Press.

Thompson, Evan. 1995. *Colour Vision.* New York: Routledge.

Westphal, Jonathan. 1991. *Colour: A Philosophical Introduction.* Oxford: Blackwell.

Articles

Averill, Edward Wilson. 1982. "The Primary-Secondary Quality Distinction." *Philosophical Review* 91: 343–362.

———. 1985. "Color and the Anthropocentric Problem." *The Journal of Philosophy* 82 (6): 281–303.

———. 1992. "The Relational Nature of Color." *Philosophical Review* 101 (3): 551–588.

Bigelow, John, John Collins, and Robert Pargetter. 1990. "Colouring in the World." *Mind* 99 (394):2 79–288.

Boghossian, Paul A. 1991. "Physicalist Theories of Color." *Philosophical Review:* 67–106.

Campbell, John. 1993. "A Simple View of Color." In *Reality, Representation, and Projection,* ed. J. Haldane. Oxford: Oxford University Press.

Goldstick, D. 1987. "Secondary Qualities." *Philosophy and Phenomenological Research* (48): 145–146.

Grandy, Richard E. 1989. "A Modern Inquiry Into the Physical Property of Colors." In *Mind, Value and Culture: Essays in Honor of E. M. Adams,* ed. D. Weissbord. Atascadero: Ridgeview.

Hacker, P. M. S. 1986. "Are Secondary Qualities Relative?" *Mind* 95: 180–197.

Hardin, C. L. 1989. "Could White Be Green?" *Mind* 98 (390): 285–288.

Harvey, J. 1992. "Challenging the Obvious: The Logic of Colour Concepts." *Philosophia* 21 (34): 277–294.

Hilbert, David. 1992. "What is Color Vision?" *Philosophical Studies* 68 (3): 351–370.

Jackson, Frank, and Robert Pargetter. 1987. "An Objectivist's Guide to Subjectivism About Colour." *Revue Internationale de Philosophie* 41: 127–141.

Jackson, Frank. 1996. "The Primary Quality View of Color." In *Metaphysics,* ed. J. E. Tomberlin. Vol. 10, *Philosophical Perspectives.* Cambridge: Blackwell.

Johnston, Mark. 1992. "How to Speak of the Colors." *Philosophical Studies* 68 (3): 221–263.

Kraut, Robert. 1992. "The Objectivity of Color and the Color of Objectivity." *Philosophical Studies* 68 (3): 265–287.

Levin, Janet. 1987. "Physicalism and the Subjectivity of Secondary Qualities." *Australasian Journal of Philosophy* 65: 400–411.
Levine, Joseph. 1991. "Cool Red." *Philosophical Psychology* 4 (1): 27–40.
McGilvray, James A. 1983. "To Color." *Synthèse* 54: 37–70.
———. 1994. "Constant Colors in the Head." *Synthèse* 100 (2): 197–239.
McGinn, Marie. 1991. "On Two Recent Accounts of Colour." *Philosophical Quarterly*: 316–324.
Nathan, Nicholas. 1986. "Simple Colours." *Philosophy* 61: 345–353.
O'Shaughnessy, Brian. 1986. "Secondary Qualities." *Pacific Philosophical Quarterly* 67: 153–171.
Peacocke, Christopher. 1984. "Colour Concepts and Colour Experience." *Synthèse* 58: 365–382.
Shoemaker, Sidney. 1990. "Qualities and Qualia: What's in the Mind?" *Philosophy and Phenomenological Research* 50 (supplement): 109–131.
Smith, A. D. 1990. "Of Primary and Secondary Qualities." *Philosophical Review* 99 (2): 221–254.
Thompson, Evan. 1992. "Novel Colours." *Philosophical Studies* 68 (3): 321–349.
Valberg, E. 1980. "A Theory of Secondary Qualities." *Philosophy* 55: 437–453.

Part VI

Events

JONATHAN BENNETT

Introduction to Events

Events Are Tropes

WHAT SORT OF THINGS ARE EVENTS? The only real answer to this was perhaps first given in the work of Locke and Leibniz, and was rediscovered in our century by Kim. It holds that events are property-instances, in a sense I now explain. According to many philosophers down the ages, the fact that this pebble is round has involved not only *the pebble* (a concrete particular) and *roundness* (an abstract universal) but also *the roundness of this pebble,* which is an abstract particular. Unlike the universal property roundness it is particular, pertaining only to this pebble; and unlike the pebble it is abstract, involving no property except roundness. Down the centuries property instances (in recent years called "tropes," for short) have entered into various theories: that in sense perception tropes travel from objects to the percipient's mind; that causation involves the transfer of tropes from one thing to another; that things are really bundles of tropes; and—coming to our topic—that events are tropes. Locke often referred to tropes (property instances) as "modes" and in one place said that most "mixed modes" are "actions which perish in their birth [and] are not capable of a lasting duration" *(Essay* III.vi.42); which seems to imply that events are tropes. Leibniz, reporting and commenting on this passage, made it clear that he took Locke's "modes" to be property instances and said explicitly that they include events (*New Essays* III.vi.42).

That view about the nature of events seems right. If a sparrow's fall is a particular instance of the property *falling,* that would explain why the fall is so intimately linked with the sparrow yet not identical with it, how the fall is related to the universal property *falling,* why there cannot be a fall unless some thing falls, and so on. Everything that we know for sure about events flows from their being tropes.

Kim has espoused this view about what events are. He puts it by calling them "property exemplifications," meaning they are tropes.[1] But this insight was not widely accepted because Kim drew from it an implausible conclusion, arguing like this:

This essay was commissioned especially for this volume and appears here for the first time.

> Kicking is a different property from assaulting; so an instance of kicking differs from an instance of assaulting; so when he kicks her, at least two events occur, one an instance of kicking and the other an instance of assaulting.

That seems wrong, and I now offer an argument against it. Suppose that *he assaulted her once, which he did by kicking her, and at no other time did he either assault her or kick her.* That, I contend, makes the following answers to these questions inevitable:

> How many kicks did he give her? One.
> How many assaults did he make on her? One.
> Was that kick that he gave her a joke? No, it was an assault.

This is not a vague intuitive matter; knowing that those answers are correct is part of basic competence with this part of our language. If a theory has to say that any of the answers is not strictly true, that must count heavily against it. But if all three answers are true, then his kick was his assault, and Kim's conclusion is false.

Kim's Inference

His premise, however, is true: events are tropes. I now explain what is wrong with Kim's inference. Although each event is a trope, an event name such as "the sparrow's fall" and "his assault on her" need not wear on its face every detail of the trope or property instance that it names. In this respect, names of events resemble names of physical objects: "the green book on the table over there" is silent about many features of the book in question; to know more about it, you must turn from the name to the book. Analogously, "his assault on her" is silent about many features of the assault; you learn whether it was a kick or a punch not by staring at the phrase through which you referred to it but by investigating the event itself. In conclusion: events are tropes, and standard event names like "the kick that he gave her" tell you *something but not everything* about what property instance the event is. They tell you one of the properties of which it is an instance, but not all of them. What else should we expect, given that events are contingently existing particulars?

In his essay in Part III of this volume, Kim tentatively suggests something like this accounts for certain troublesome cases. But his suggestion seems designed only for event names using an adjective or adverb: it could save Kim from identifying *his assault on her* with *his fierce assault on her,* but not from identifying it with *the kick that he gave her.* In this and other ways, the proposal looks arbitrary, and Kim himself does not confidently endorse it.

Kim confidently stands his ground, not even considering a way out, for a range of examples in which his views about "event identity" seem to him intuitively plausible. When she asked him, "Do you want to get out of this relationship?" he shouted "*Yes!*" He produced an answer, and also a shout; most of us would say that the shout was the answer—that is, that only one event occurred, he performed only one act. Kim discusses such cases in different words, however, saying things like, "His shouting at her is not the same as his answering her." Now, that seems right, doesn't it? Then is Kim right, after all, in at least some cases?

Distinguishing Events from Facts

No. We can (i) distinguish his shouting at her from his answering her without (ii) distinguishing his shout from his answer; for (ii) concerns events while (i) has nothing to do them. The phrases "his shouting at her" and "his answering her" refer not to events but to facts. Consider these two statements:

(a) The fact that he answers her is not the same as the fact that he shouts at her.
(b) His answering her is not the same as his shouting at her.

Nobody would dispute the trivial and obvious (a). Most people find (b) plausible, which explains why Kim uses it in argument; but not everyone sees the source of (b)'s plausibility—namely, that it is equivalent to (a). Their equivalence shows in the fact that "his answering her" and "that he answers [or answered or will answer] her" can be interchanged in all contexts, as can "his shouting at her" and "that he shouts at her."

It surprised me that he shouted at her, but not that he answered her;
His shouting at her surprised me, but not his answering her;

and so on. "His answering her" is a so-called *imperfect nominal.* It is a nominal, a noun phrase, which can serve as the subject of a sentence, as it does in several of the preceding examples. It is imperfect because in it the gerund "answering" retains many of the features of the verb from which it comes. Compare:

direct object: he answers her—his answering her
adverb: he loudly answers her—his loudly answering her
tense: he has answered her—his having answered her
modals: he has to answer her—his having to answer her.

In all these ways the gerund "answering" ("having answered," "having to answer," etc.) behaves like a verb.

None of this holds for *his answer* (meaning by this his action, not the word(s) that he uttered). The noun "answer" takes adjectives not adverbs; it cannot be modified by tenses or modalities; it cannot only have an indirect object—we cannot say "his answer her" but only "his answer to her." It is perfectly a noun, with no lingering grammatical traces of its parent verb; and, consistently with that, we use it to refer not to his answering her but to the answer that he made, not to a fact but to an event. So his answer can be a shout: it is just false to say that his answer was one event and his shout another; nobody would entertain such a thought for a moment if some philosophers had not conflated his answer with his answering her, confusing an event with a fact.

Many writers on events have failed to grasp that *imperfect* gerundial nominals stand for facts, not events; they have been helped to do so by the fact that *perfect* gerundial nominals stand for events, not facts. I shall explain this effect through an example of someone who pushes a rock, thereby dislodging it from the hole in which it lay half-buried. The fact that he pushed the rock is distinct from the fact that he dislodged it: neither entails the other; and their relations to surprise, belief, expectation, gladness, regret, and so on can be quite different. So his pushing the rock is one fact, his dislodging it is another; his pushing it was legal, his dislodging it criminal; and so on.

Now the phrase "his pushing *of* the rock" is a perfect nominal, in which the gerund bears no grammatical marks of its origin in a verb. The word "of" indicates this: the object is now genitive, not direct. Whereas "his pushing the rock" is a natural partner of "He pushes the rock," "his pushing of the rock" is grammatically like "the surface of the rock." That difference brings others with it. If he pushed the rock strenuously, that can be reported by putting an adjective into the perfect nominal: "his strenuous pushing of the rock." We cannot use the adverb "strenuously" here. Also, perfect nominals have plural forms and can take definite and indefinite articles: "pushings of the rock," "a pushing of the rock," "the pushing of the rock." Try those with the imperfect "pushing the rock" and you will find that it cannot be done.

So the perfect gerundial "pushing of the rock" behaves exactly like the noun "push," as in "push that he gave the rock"; and you can verify for yourself that "his pushing of the rock" and "the push that he gave the rock" can be interchanged in all contexts. The case for regarding perfect nominals as names of events is overwhelming. With that in mind, consider something Davidson writes in this volume:

> I turn . . . to Kim's remark that it is not absurd to say that Brutus's killing Caesar is not the same as Brutus's stabbing Caesar. The plausibility of this is due, I think, to the undisputed fact that not all stabbings are killings. . . . But [this does not show] that this particular stabbing was not a killing. Brutus's stabbing of Caesar did result in Caesar's death; so it was in fact, though not of course necessarily, identical with Brutus's killing of Caesar.

Then notice Kim's report on this (near the end of section II of his paper): "Davidson and I disagree about . . . whether Brutus's stabbing Caesar is the same as Brutus's killing Caesar." Kim's original imperfect nominals were switched by Davidson to perfect ones; now Kim switches them back again. That is what enables Kim to say true things about facts and Davidson to respond by saying true things about events. The audible *click!* as the change occurs seems to have passed unheard by both writers.

Event-Identity Statements

When he answered very loudly, his shout was his answer. When he dislodged the rock by pushing it, the push that he gave it was his dislodgement of it. Once we stop confounding events with facts, we are free to hold that an event can be referred to by several phrases each of which gives a different selection from the whole truth about it; and so we can have such contingent truths as that the shout was the answer, the kiss was the greeting, and so on. Can we lay down any general principles that constrain what event identities of this kind can be true?

Only two significant answers to this question have been offered, and both are included here. One is Davidson's thesis that no two events can have exactly the same causes and effects. That could secure that (say) the kiss is the greeting if the causes (effects) of the kiss were all and only the causes (effects) of the greeting. Davidson points out that the formula expressing this principle has an identity sign on the left and none on the right, from which he infers that it is not circular, and so might really help to determine the truth values of some event identity statements. For it to give such help, though, we would have to be able to discover that the causes (effects) of the kiss were exactly those of the greeting while still being agnostic about whether the kiss was the greeting. I agree with the critics of Davidson who hold that this is impossible.

The other general proposal is Lombard's, which is addressed to one special kind of situation where event identity questions arise. When a cannonball arcs its way over the wall into the city, an event occurs that I shall call JO (for journey). Now consider this proposal:

(1) JO is a composite event, made up of two simpler ones: EW, which is the horizontal east-to-west component of JO, and UD, its vertical up-and-down component. EW and UD are distinct events, though they have the same subject (the ball), and occur in the same place at the same time—namely, in the spatio-temporal track of JO.

With that at the back of your mind, now consider this:

(2) While undergoing JO, the cannonball also rotates on its axis, this being the event ROT. It has the same subject as JO, and occurs in the same region of space-time; but JO and ROT are distinct events, though they are parts of a more complex event—namely TOT, which is the total movement of the ball at that time.

These two proposals raise several questions, the answers to which are controversial. Among the views that have been defended are these:

There is such an event as JO, but no such events as EW and UD.
There are such events as JO and ROT, but no such event as TOT.
Every event named in either proposal exists as a distinct event.

In section 6 of his essay in this volume, Lombard offers a causal principle that he think can guide our decisions on questions like these. This is an honorable attempt, which I have and discussed respectfully and at length elsewhere. Here I can only report my conclusion that it fails.[2] My own guess is that there are no objectively right answers to these questions, and that people's intuitions about them are mainly guided by what *event names* are available (other than artificial ones like "EW"). Because we have "the ball's journey into the city" and "the ball's rotation on its axis," we are tolerant of the idea that JO and ROT are distinct events. We are less tolerant about EW and UD, preferring to view them not as two events but only as two aspects of a single event, because we have no short idiomatic ways of referring to them.

Language also calls the tune, though in a different way, over questions about whether two events that do not exactly coincide in space-time are parts of a single more extensive event. The armies clashed on Monday and on Tuesday: were these parts of a single battle? Was there a single fire of which one part burned down my house on Tuesday and another burned down yours on Monday? Were the synchronous events in the two adjacent valleys on Monday parts of a single battle (or: parts of a single fire)? We answer such questions by consulting our semantic conventions governing phrases like "same fire" and "same battle." It cannot be the same fire, we hold, unless some continuous spatio-temporal zone linking the two incinerations of houses is fiery throughout; but we allow that it can be the same battle even if the two episodes are not linked by a spatio-temporal zone that is actively combative throughout (the armies can sleep and then resume their battle). This difference is purely conventional; we can imagine handling "same battle" differently. Nothing of philosophical interest is going on here.

Differentiating Events from Other Tropes

It has been maintained that all events must be changes. (1) That entails that each event must involve the instantiation of one property and then later of a different one, which means that each event must stretch through time. That debars starts and finishes—construed as instantaneous—from counting as events, though they are clearly property instances. (2) It also implies that, although when a monument decays over centuries there occurs a protracted event which we might call *its decay,* no corresponding event occurs when a monument remains unchanged for centuries. You may find one or both of these plausible; I have no strong views about either, and do not want any. Each case involves a property instance; and questions about whether a given property instance counts as an event is not metaphysically interesting.

Contrast this with the metaphysical theory that a physical object is an aggregate of spatio-temporal zones. Someone who finds that plausible, as Newton and Spinoza did, will not say that every aggregate of zones is a physical object; he will want to understand what it takes for an aggregate to satisfy the stern constraints that our concept of a physical object lays down. Our evidence about these constraints consists not in shapeless intuitions of verbal propriety but in plain hard structural facts about what inferences are valid, what statements are self-contradictory, and so on. There are such facts because the physical object concept does hard, central, disciplined work for us. Not so our event concept. We use it to give small, vague gobbets of information about what goes on—the storm lasted for three days, the battle raged fiercely, he has been through two divorces—but when we want precision and detail we break away from the event concept and work with other parts of our conceptual repertoire. That is why the issue about which property instances are events is thin and boring.

NOTES

1. Jaegwon Kim, "On the Psycho-Physical Identity Theory," *American Philosophical Quarterly* 3 (1966): pp. 277–85; "Events and Their Descriptions: Some Considerations," in N. Rescher et al. (ed.), *Essays in Honor of Carl G. Hempel* (1969), pp. 198–215; "Causation, Nomic Subsumption, and the Concept of an Event," *Journal of Philosophy* 70 (1973), pp. 217–36; "Events as Property Exemplifications," in this volume, pp. 336–347.

2. Jonathan Bennett, *Events and Their Names* (Indianapolis: Hackett, 1988), section 56.

The Individuation of Events

23

DONALD DAVIDSON

WHEN ARE EVENTS IDENTICAL, when distinct? What criteria are there for deciding one way or the other in particular cases?

There is a familiar embarrassment in asking identity questions of this sort that comes out clearly if we rephrase the question slightly: when are two events identical? Or, when is one event identical with another? It seems only one answer is possible: no *two* events are identical, no event is ever identical with *another*. It is hopeless to try to improve matters by asking instead, when is an event identical with itself? For again, only one answer is possible: always.

The difficulty obviously has nothing special to do with events, it arises in relation to all identity questions. The only move I know for circumventing this conundrum is to substitute for questions about identities questions about sentences about identities. Then instead of asking when events are identical, we may ask when sentences of the form '*a* = *b*' are true, where we suppose '*a*' and '*b*' supplanted by singular terms referring to events.

We have no sooner to restate our problem in this standard way, however, than to realize something scandalous about events. Events, even in the best philosophical circles, lead a double life. On the one hand, we talk confidently of sentences that 'describe' or 'refer to' events, and of cases where two sentences refer to the same event; we have grown used to speaking of actions (presumably a species of event) 'under a description.' We characterize causal laws as asserting that every event of one sort is followed by an event of another sort, and it is said that explanation in history and science is often of particular events, though perhaps only as those events are described in one way rather than another. But—and this is the other hand—when we turn to the sentences, formalized in standard ways or in our native dialect, that are so familiarly interpreted as describing or referring to events, or as making universal claims about events, we generally find nothing commonly counted as singular terms that could be taken to refer to events. We are told, for example. that on occasion 'He raised his arm' and 'He signalled' describe the same action; yet where are the singular terms in these sentences that could do the describing? 'Whenever a piece of metal is heated it expands' is normally taken as quantifying over physical objects and perhaps times; how could we analyse it so as to justify the claim that it literally speaks of events?

Quine has quipped: 'No entity without identity' in support of the Fregean thesis that we ought not to countenance entities unless we are prepared to make sense of sentences affirming and denying identity of such entities. But then more obvious still is the motto: 'No identity without an entity.' and its linguistic counterpart: 'No statements of identity without singular terms.'

Our problem was to determine when sentences formed by flanking an identity sign with singular terms referring to events are true; at this point the problem seems to invite the response that there are no such sentences because there are no such singular terms. But of course this is too strong; there are singular terms that apparently name events: 'Sally's third birthday party,' 'the eruption of Vesuvius in A.D. 1906,' 'my eating breakfast this morning,' 'the first performance of *Lulu* in Chicago.' Still, the existence of these singular terms is of uncertain relevance until we can firmly connect such singular terms with sentences like 'Vesuvius erupted in A.D. 1906' or 'I ate breakfast this morning,' for most of our interest in identity sentences about events depends upon the assumption that the singular terms that appear in them refer to entities that are needed for the analysis of more ordinary sentences. If the only pressure for adopting an ontology of

From Essays in Honor of Carl G. Hempel, *ed. N. Rescher, pp. 216–234. Dordrecht, Holland: D. Reidel, 1969. Reprinted by permission of the publisher and author.*

events comes from such phrases as 'Sally's third birthday party,' we would probably do better to try and paraphrase these away in context than meddle with the logical form of sentences like 'Brutus killed Caesar' or 'Bread nourishes' so as to show singular terms referring to events or variables ranging over them.

Are there good reasons for taking events seriously as entities? There are indeed. First, it is hard to imagine a satisfactory theory of action if we cannot talk literally of the same action under different descriptions. Jones managed to apologize by saying 'I apologize'; but only because, under the circumstances, saying 'I apologize' *was* apologizing. Cedric intentionally burned the scrap of paper; this serves to excuse his burning a valuable document only because he did not know the scrap was the document and because his burning the scrap was (identical with) his burning the document. Explanation, as already hinted, also seems to call for events. Last week there was a catastrophe in the village. In the course of explaining why it happened, we need to redescribe it, perhaps as an avalanche. There are rough statistical laws about avalanches: avalanches tend to occur when a heavy snow falls after a period of melting and freezing, so that the new snow does not bind to the old. But we could go further in explaining this avalanche—why it came just when it did, why it covered the area it did, and so forth—if we described it in still a different and more precise vocabulary. And when we mention, in one way or another, the cause of the avalanche, we apparently claim that though we may not know such a description or such a law, there must *be* descriptions of cause and avalanche such that those descriptions instantiate a true causal law. All this talk of descriptions and redescriptions makes sense, it would seem, only on the assumption that there are *bona fide* entities to be described and redescribed. A further need for events springs from the fact that the most perspicuous forms of the identity theory of mind require that we identify mental events with certain physiological events; if such theories or their denials are intelligible, events must be individuals. And for such theories to be interesting, there must be ways of telling when statements of event-identity are true.[1]

The reasons just canvassed for accepting an explicit ontology of events rest upon the assumption that one or another currently accepted or debated philosophical position or doctrine is intelligible when taken at face value; so it remains possible to resist the conclusion by rejecting the relevant doctrines as unintelligible, or by attempting to reinterpret them without appeal to events. The prospects for successful resistance are, in my opinion, dim: I do not believe we can give a cogent account of action, of explanation, of causality, or of the relation between the mental and the physical, unless we accept events as individuals. Each of these claims needs detailed defence.[2]

There remains, however, a more direct consideration (of which the others are symptoms) in favour of an ontology of events, which is that without events it does not seem possible to give a natural and acceptable account of the logical form of certain sentences of the most common sorts; it does not seem possible, that is, to show how the meanings of such sentences depend upon their composition. The situation may be sketched as follows. It is clear that the sentence 'Sebastian strolled through the streets of Bologna at 2 a.m.' entails 'Sebastian strolled through the streets of Bologna,' and does so by virtue of its logical form. This requires, it would seem, that the patent syntactical fact that the entailed sentence is contained in the entailing sentence be reflected in the logical form we assign to each sentence. Yet the usual way of formalizing these sentences does not show any such feature: it directs us to consider the first sentence as containing an irreducibly three-place predicate 'x strolled through y at t' while the second contains the unrelated predicate 'x strolled through y.' It is sometimes proposed that we can mend matters by treating 'Sebastian strolled through the streets of Bologna' as elliptical for 'There exists a time t such that Sebastian strolled through the streets of Bologna at t.' This suggestion contains the seed of a general solution, however, only if we can form a clear idea of how many places predicates of action or change involve. But it is unlikely that we can do this since there appear to be ways of adding indefinitely to the number of places that would be required. Consider, for example, 'The shark devoured Danny by chewing up his left foot, then his left ankle, then his left knee, then . . . ,' or, 'The fall of the first domino caused the fall of the last by causing the fall of the second, which caused the fall of the third, which caused. . . .[3]

Ingenuity may conceive more than one way of coping with these and associated puzzles, but it is impressive how well everything comes out if we accept the obvious idea that there are things like falls, devourings, and strolls for sentences such as these to be about. In short, I propose to legitimize our intuition that events are true particulars by recognizing explicit reference to them, or quantification over them, in much of our ordinary talk. Take as an example, 'Sebastian strolled': this may be construed along lines suggested by 'Sebastian took a stroll.' 'There is an x such that x is a stroll and Sebastian took x' is more ornate than necessary, since there is nothing an agent can do with a stroll except take it; thus we may capture all there is with 'There is an x such that Sebastian strolled x.'

In this way we provide each verb of action or change with an event-place; we may say of such verbs that they take an *event-object*. Adverbial modification is thus seen to be logically on a par with adjectival modification: what adverbial clauses modify is not verbs, but the events that certain verbs introduce. 'Sebastian strolled through the streets of Bologna at 2 a.m.' then has this form: 'There is an event x such that Sebastian strolled x, x took place in the streets of Bologna, and x was going on at 2 a.m.' Clearly, the entailments that worried us before go through directly on this analysis.

We recognize that there is no singular term referring to a mosquito in 'There is a mosquito in here' when we realize that the truth of this sentence is not impugned if there are two mosquitos in the room. It would not be appropriate if, noticing that there are two mosquitos in the room, I were to ask the person who says, 'There is a mosquito in the room,' 'Which one are you referring to?' On the present analysis, ordinary sentences about events, like 'Doris capsized the canoe yesterday,' are related to particular events in just the same way that 'There is a mosquito in here' is related to particular mosquitos. It is no less true that Doris capsized the canoe yesterday if she capsized it a dozen times than if she capsized it once; nor, if she capsized it a dozen times, does it make sense to ask, 'Which time are you referring to?' as if this were needed to *clarify* 'Doris capsized the canoe yesterday.' We learned some time ago, and it is a very important lesson, that phrases like 'a mosquito' are not singular terms, and hence do not refer as names or descriptions do. The temptation to treat a sentence like 'Doris capsized the canoe yesterday' as if it contained a singular term referring to an action comes from other sources, but we should be equally steadfast in resisting it.

Some actions are difficult or unusual to perform more than once in a short or specified time, and this may provide a specious reason in some cases for holding that action sentences refer to unique actions. Thus with 'Jones got married last Saturday,' 'Doris wrote a cheque at noon,' 'Mary kissed an admirer at the stroke of midnight.' It is merely illegal to get married twice on the same day, merely unusual to write cheques simultaneously, and merely good fortune to get to kiss two admirers at once. Similarly, if I say, 'There is an elephant in the bathtub,' you are no doubt justified in supposing that one elephant at most is in the bathtub, but you are confused if you think my sentence contains a singular term that refers to a particular elephant if any. A special case arises when we characterize actions in ways that logically entail that at most one action so characterized exists: perhaps you can break a certain piece of news to a particular audience only once; a man can assassinate his enemy only once; a woman can lose her virtue only once. 'Brutus killed Caesar' is then arguably equivalent to 'Brutus killed Caesar exactly once' which is arguably equivalent (by way of Russell's theory of descriptions) to 'The killing of Caesar by Brutus occurred.' This last certainly does contain a description, in the technical sense, of an action, and so we could say that 'Brutus killed Caesar' refers to or describes the killing of Caesar by Brutus in that it is logically equivalent to a sentence that overtly refers to or describes the killing of Caesar by Brutus. By parity of reasoning we should, of course, maintain that 'There exists a prime between 20 and 28' refers to the number 23. There is a good reason against taking this line, however, which is that on this view someone could be uniquely referring without knowing he was using words that imputed singularity.

Confusion over the relation between ordinary sentences about actions, and particular actions, has led some philosophers to suppose or to suggest that these sentences are about *generic* actions, or *kinds* of actions. Von Wright, for example, says that 'Brutus killed Caesar' is about a particular action, while 'Brutus kissed Caesar' is about a generic action.[4] It is true that we can paraphrase 'Brutus kissed Caesar' as 'There is at least one event belonging to the genus, a kissing of Caesar by Brutus'; but we can equally well paraphrase 'Brutus killed Caesar' as 'There is at least one event belonging to the genus, a killing of Caesar by Brutus.' In neither case does the sentence refer to a generic action. Analogous remarks apply to the idea that 'Lying is wrong' is about a kind of action. 'Lying is wrong' may be rendered. 'For all x if x is a lie then x is wrong' or even, 'The class of lies is included in the class of wrong actions,' but neither of these says that a kind of action is wrong, but rather that each action of a kind is wrong.

Failure to find an ordinary singular term referring to an event in a sentence like 'Caesar died' is properly explained by the fact that such sentences are existential and general with respect to events: we do not find a singular term referring to an event because there is none. But many philosophers, not doubting that 'Caesar died' refers to or describes an event, have confusedly concluded that the sentence *as a whole* refers to (or perhaps 'corresponds to') an event. As long ago as 1927, Frank Ramsey pointed out this error, and how to correct it; he described it as the error of conflating facts (which in his view are what sentences or propositions correspond to) and events.[5] And certainly there are difficulties, of a kind more general than we have indicated, with the idea that whole sentences refer to events. For suppose we agree, as I think we must, that the death of Scott is the same event as the death of the author of *Waverley:* then if sentences refer to events, the sentence 'Scott died' must refer to the same event as 'The author of *Waverley* died.' If we allow that substitution of singular terms in this way does not change the event referred to, then a short and persuasive argument will lead to the conclusion that all true sentences refer to the same event. And presumably only true sentences refer to an event; the conclusion may therefore be put: there is exactly one event. Since the argument is essentially the argument used by Frege to show that all sentences alike in truth-value must name the same thing, I spare you the details.[6]

The mistaken view that a sentence like 'Doris capsized the canoe yesterday' refers to a particular event, whether or not tied to the idea that it is the sentence as a whole that does the referring, is pretty sure to obliterate the difference between 'Doris capsized the canoe yesterday' and 'Doris' capsizing of the canoe occurred yesterday.' Yet without this distinction firm in our minds I do not believe we can make good sense of questions about the individuation of events and actions, for while the second sentence does indeed contain a singular description (the sentence as a whole meaning 'There is an event identical with the capsizing of the canoe yesterday by Doris'), the first sentence merely asserts the existence of at least one capsizing. If we are not alert to the difference, we are apt to ask wrongheaded questions like: if Jones apologized by saying 'I apologize,' do 'Jones apologized' and 'Jones said "I apologize"' describe the same action? The right response is, I have urged, that neither sentence describes an action. We may then add, if we please, that at least one, or perhaps exactly one, action accounts for the truth of both sentences; but both sentences could be true although no apology by Jones was made by his saying, 'I apologize .'[7]

To see how not appreciating the generality in 'Jones apologized' can lead to mistakes about the individuation of events, consider a suggestion of Kim's.[8] Kim assumes that sentences such as 'Brutus killed Caesar' and 'Brutus stabbed Caesar' refer to events, and he asks under what conditions two such sentences describe or refer to the same event. He proposes the following criterion: two sentences are about the same event if they assert truly of the same particulars (i.e., substances) that the same properties (or relations) hold of them. Kim has a rather complicated doctrine of property identity, but it need not delay us since the point to be made depends only on a simple principle to which Kim agrees: properties differ if their extensions do. The effect is to substitute for what I think of as particular, dated events classes of such, and thus to make identities harder to come by.

Where I would say the same event may make 'Jones apologized' and 'Jones said "I apologize"' true, Kim is committed to holding that these sentences describe different events. Nor can Kim allow that a stabbing is ever a killing, or the signing of a cheque the paying of a bill. He must also hold that if psychological predicates have no coextensive physical predicates, then no psychological event is identical with a physical event.

Kim recognizes these consequences of his criterion, and accepts them; but for reasons I find weak. He writes:

> Brutus' killing Caesar and Brutus' stabbing Caesar turn out, on the proposed criterion of event identity. to be different events, and similarly, 'Brutus killed Caesar' and 'Brutus stabbed Caesar' describe different events. Notice, however, that it is not at all absurd to say that Brutus' killing Caesar is *not the same as* Brutus' stabbing Caesar. Further, to explain Brutus' killing Caesar (why Brutus killed Caesar) is not the same as to explain Brutus' stabbing Caesar (why Brutus stabbed Caesar). . . .[9]

Certainly Brutus had different reasons for stabbing Caesar than for killing him; we may suppose he went through a little piece of practical reasoning the upshot of which was that stabbing Caesar was a good way to do him in. But this reasoning was futile if, having stabbed Caesar, Brutus has a different action yet to perform (killing him). And explanation, like giving reasons, is geared to sentences or propositions rather than directly to what sentences are about: thus an explanation of why Scott died is not necessarily an explanation of why the author of *Waverley* died. Yet not even Kim wants to say the death of Scott is a different event from the death of the author of *Waverley.* I turn last to Kim's remark that it is not absurd to say that Brutus's killing Caesar is not the same as Brutus's stabbing Caesar. The plausibility in this is due, I think, to the undisputed fact that not all stabbings are killings. We are inclined to say: *this* stabbing might not have resulted in a death, so how can it be identical with the killing? Of course the death is not identical with the stabbing; it occurred later. But neither this nor the fact that some stabbings are not killings shows that this particular stabbing was not a killing. Brutus's stabbing of Caesar did result in Caesar's death; so it was in fact, though of course not necessarily, identical with Brutus's killing of Caesar.

Discussions of explanation may also suffer from confusion about how sentences are related to events. It is sometimes said, for example, that when we explain the occurrence of an event, we can do so only under one or another of its sentential descriptions. In so far as this remark reminds us of the essential intensionality of explanation, it is unexceptionable. But a mistake may lurk. If what we are to explain is why an avalanche fell on the village last week, we need to show that conditions were present adequate to produce *an* avalanche. It would be confused to say we have explained only an aspect of 'the real avalanche' if the reason for saying this lies in the fact that what was to be explained was itself general (for the explanandum contained no mention of a particular avalanche). We might instead have asked for an explanation of why *the* avalanche fell on the village last week. This is, of course, a harder task, for we are now asking not only why there was at least one avalanche, but also why there was not more than one. In a perfectly good sense the second explanation can be said to explain a particular event; the first cannot.

An associated point may be made about causal relations. Suppose it claimed that the lighting of this match was caused by the striking of the match. The inevitable comment (since the time of Mill anyway) is that the striking may have been *part* of the cause, but it was hardly sufficient for the lighting since it was also necessary for the match to be dry, that there be enough oxygen, etc. This comment is, in my opinion, confused. For since this match was dry, and was struck in enough oxygen, etc., the striking of this match was identical with the striking of a dry match in enough oxygen. How can one and the same event both be, and not be, sufficient for the lighting? In fact, it is not *events* that are necessary or sufficient as causes, but events as *described* in one way or another. It is true that we cannot infer, from the fact that the match was struck, and plausible causal laws, that the match lit; we can do better if we start with the fact that a dry match was struck in enough oxygen. It does not follow that more than the striking of this match was required to cause it to light.

Now that we have a clearer idea what it is like to have singular terms, say '*a*' and '*b*,' that refer to events we may return to our original question when a sentence of the form '$a = b$' is true. Of course we cannot expect a general method for *telling* when such sentences are true. For suppose '$(\iota x)(Fx)$' describes some event. Letting '*S*' abbreviate any sentence,

$$(\iota x)(Fx) = (\iota x)(Fx \,\&\, S)$$

is true just in case '*S*' is true. Since '*S*' is an arbitrary sentence, a general method for telling when identity sentences were true would have to include a method for telling when any sentence was true. What we want, rather, is a statement of necessary and sufficient conditions for identity of events, a satisfactory filling for the blank in:

If *x* and *y* are events, then $x = y$ if and only if ______.

Samples of answers (true or false) for other sorts of entities are: classes are identical if and only if they have exactly the same members; times are identical if and only if they are overlapped by exactly the same events; places are identical if and only if they are overlapped by exactly the same objects; material objects are identical if and only if they occupy exactly the same places at the same times. Can we do as well as this for events? Here follows a series of remarks that culminate in what I hope is a satisfactory positive answer.

(1) Many events are changes in a substance. If an event *a* is a change in some substance, then $a = b$ only if *b* is also a change in the same substance. Indeed, if $a = b$, every substance in which *a* is a change is identical with a substance in which *b* is a change. To touch on such necessary conditions of event-identity is to do little more than reflect on what follows if events really do exist; but that is to the present point. And of course we will not alter the event, if any, to which a description refers if in that description we substitute for the name or description of a substance another name or description of the same substance: witness the fact that the death of Scott is identical with the death of the author of *Waverley*. This is an example of a sufficient condition of identity.

We very often describe and identify events in terms of the objects to which they are in one way or another related. But it would be a mistake to suppose that, even for events that are naturally described as changes in an object, we *must* describe them (i.e., produce unique descriptions of them) by referring to the object. For in fact any predicate of any event may provide a unique description: if an event *a* is *F*, *a* may turn out also to be the only event that is *F*, in which case 'the event that is *F*' uniquely refers to *a*. One important way to identify events without explicit reference to a substance is by demonstrative reference: 'that shriek,' 'that dripping sound,' 'the next sonic boom.'

These last points are well made by Strawson.[10] Strawson also remarks that the possibilities for identifying events without reference to objects are limited, because, as he puts it, events do not provide 'a single, comprehensive and continuously usable framework' of reference of the kind provided by physical objects.[11] This claim is made by Strawson in support of a grander thesis, that events are conceptually dependent on objects. According to Strawson we could not have the idea of a birth or a death or a blow without the idea of an animal that is born or dies, or of an agent who strikes the blow.

I do not doubt that Strawson is right in this: most events are understood as changes in a more or less permanent object or substance. It even seems likely to me that the concept of an event depends in every case on the idea of a change in a substance, despite the fact that for some events it is not easy to say what substance it is that undergoes the change.

What does seem doubtful to me is Strawson's contention that while there is a conceptual dependence of the category of events on the category of objects, there is not a symmetrical dependence of the category of objects on the category of events. His principle argument may, I think, be not unfairly stated as follows: in a sentence like 'There is an event that is the birth of this animal' we refer to, or quantify over, events and objects alike. But we can, if we please, express exactly the same idea by saying, 'This animal was born' and here there is no reference to, or quantification over, events. We cannot in the same way eliminate the reference to the object.[12] This is supposed to show that objects are more fundamental than events.

A closely related argument of Strawson's is this: the sentence 'The blow which blinded John was struck by Peter' presupposes, for its truth, that John exists, that Peter exists, and that there is a striking of John by Peter. But the last presupposition may also be expressed simply by saying that Peter struck John, which does not treat the blow as an entity on a par with Peter and John. Strawson again concludes that events are dispensable in a sense in which objects are not.[13] It is hard to see how the evidence supports the conclusion.

If 'Peter struck John' and 'There was a striking of John by Peter' express the same presupposition, how can they require different ontologies? If 'This animal was born' and 'There is an event that is the birth of this animal' are genuine paraphrases one of the other, how can one of them be about a birth and the other not? The argument proves either too much or too little. If every context that seems to refer to, or to presuppose, events may be systematically rephrased so as not to refer to events, then this shows we do not need an ontology of events at all. On the other hand if some categories of sentence resist transformation into an eventless idiom, then the fact that we can apparently banish events from other areas cannot suffice to relegate events to a secondary status; indeed it does not even serve to show that the sentences we know how to parse in superficially event-free terms are not about events. It was in fact in just this vein that I have been urging that we cannot give acceptable analyses of 'This animal was born' and 'Peter struck John' without supposing that there are such things as births and blows. In Strawson's view, if I understand him, 'The blow which blinded John was struck by Peter' entails 'Peter struck John.' But a theory about what these sentences mean that justifies the entailment must, or so I have argued, acknowledge an ontology of events. Thus if my interpretation of the evidence is correct, there is no reason to assign second rank to events; while if, contrary to what I have maintained, total reducibility is possible, then again events do not take a back seat, for there are no events.

In my view, a sentence like 'John struck the blow' is about two particulars, John and the blow. The distinction between singular terms and predicates is not abolished: rather, striking is predicated alike of John and of the blow. This symmetry in the treatment of substances and their changes reflects, I think, an underlying symmetry of conceptual dependence. Substances owe their special importance in the enterprise of identification to the fact that they survive through time. But the idea of survival is inseparable from the idea of surviving certain sorts of change—of position, size, shape, colour, and so forth. As we might expect, events often play an essential role in identifying a substance. Thus if we track down the author of *Waverley* or the father of Annette, it is by identifying an event, of writing, or of fathering. Neither the category of substance nor the category of change is conceivable apart from the other.[14]

(2) Should we say that events are identical only if they are in the same place? Of course if events have a location, same events have same locations; but here is a puzzle that may seem to cast a doubt on the project of assigning a clear location to events. Perhaps those events are easiest to locate that are obviously changes in some substance: we locate the event by locating the substance. But if one substance is part of another, a change in the first is a change in the second. Every substance is a part of the universe: hence every change is a change in the universe. It seems to follow that all simultaneous events have the same location. The error lies in the assumption that if an event is a change in a substance, the location of the event is the entire space occupied by the substance. Rather, the location of the event at a moment is the location of the smallest part of the substance a change in which is identical with the event.

Does it make sense to assign a location to a mental event such as remembering that one has left a zipper open, deciding to schuss the headwall, or solving an equation? I think we do assign a location to such an event when we identify the person who remembered, decided, or solved: the event took place where the person was. Questions about the location of mental events are generally otiose because in identifying the event we have usually identified the person in whom the event was a change, so no interesting question about the location of the event remains that is not answered by knowing where the person was when the event occurred. When we do not know who the relevant person is, queries about the location of mental events are perfectly in order: 'Where was the infinitesimal calculus invented?'

Mental events (by which I mean events described in the mental vocabulary, whatever exactly that may be) are like many other sorts of events, and like material objects, in that we give their locations with no more accuracy than easy individuation (within the relevant vocabulary) demands. Aside from a few dubious cases, like pains, itches, pricks, and twitches, we have no reason to locate mental events more precisely than by identifying a person, for more than this would normally be irrelevant to individuation. Similarly, we uniquely identify a mountain by giving the latitude and longitude of its highest summit, and in one good sense this gives the location of the mountain. But a mountain is a material object, and so occupies more than a point; nevertheless, convention decrees no formula for defining its boundaries.

An explosion is an event to which we find no difficulty in assigning a location, although again we may be baffled by a request to describe the total area. The following quotation from an article on locating earthquakes and underground explosions illustrates how smoothly we operate with the concept of the place of an event:

> Information on the accuracy with which a seismic event can be located is not as complete as could be wished. . . . if data from stations distant from the event are used, it seems realistic to estimate that the site can be located within a circular area whose radius is about eight kilometers. Stations that are 500–2,000 kilometers from the event may give much larger errors. . . .[15]

(3) No principle for the individuation of events is clearer or more certain than this, that if events are identical, they consume identical stretches of time. Yet even this principle seems to lead to a paradox.

Suppose I pour poison in the water tank of a spaceship while it stands on earth. My purpose is to kill the space traveller, and I succeed: when he reaches Mars he takes a drink and dies. Two events are easy to distinguish: my pouring of the poison, and the death of the traveller. One precedes the other, and causes it. But where does the event of my killing the traveller come in? The most usual answer is that my killing the traveller is identical with my pouring the poison. In that case, the killing is over when the pouring is. We are driven to the conclusion that I have killed the traveller long before he dies.

The conclusion to which we are driven is, I think, true, so coping with the paradox should take the form of reconciling us to the conclusion. First, we should observe that we may easily know that an event is a pouring of poison without knowing it is a killing, just as we may know that an event is the death of Scott with knowing it is the death of the author of *Waverley.* To describe an event as a killing is to describe it as an event (here an action) that caused a death, and we are not apt to describe an action as one that caused a death until the death occurs; yet it may be such an action before the death occurs. (And as it becomes more certain that a death will result from an action, we feel less paradox in saying, 'You have killed him.')[16]

Directness of causal connection may also play a role. To describe the pouring as a killing is to describe it as the causing of a death; such a description loses cogency as the causal relation is attenuated. In general, the longer it takes for the effect to be registered, the more room there is for a slip, which is another way of saying, the less justification there is for calling the action alone the cause.

Finally, there may be a tendency to confuse events described (partly or wholly) in terms of terminal states and events described (partly or wholly) in terms of what they cause. Examples of the first sort are 'the rolling of the stone to the bottom of the hill' (which is not over until the stone is at the bottom of the hill) or 'his painting the barn red' (not over until he has finished painting the barn red); examples of the second sort are 'the destruction of the crops by the flood' (over when the flood is, which may be finished before the crops are) and 'Jones inviting Smith to the party' (which Jones does only if Smith gets invited, but has finished doing when he drops the card in the mail).[17]

It is a matter of the first importance that we may, and often do, describe actions and events in terms of their causal relations—their causes, their effects, or both. My poisoning of the victim must be an action that results in the victim being poisoned; my killing of the victim must be an action that results in the death of the victim; my murdering of the victim must be an action that results in the death of the victim and also an action that was caused, in part, by my desire for the victim's death. If I see that the cat is on the mat, my seeing must be caused, in part, by the cat's being on the mat. If I contract Favism, I must contract haemolytic anaemia as a consequence of eating, or otherwise coming in contact with, the Fava bean. And so forth. This tendency to identify events in terms of their causal relations has deep roots, as I shall suggest in a moment. But it should not lead to a serious difficulty about the dates of events.

(4) Do place and time together uniquely determine an event; that is, is it sufficient as well as necessary, if events are to be identical, that they occupy exactly the same time and the same place? This proposal was made (somewhat tentatively) by John Lemmon;[18] of course the same proposal has often been made for physical objects. I am uncertain both in the case of substances and in the case of events whether or not sameness of time and place is enough to insure identity. Doubt comes easily in the case of events, for it seems natural to say that two different changes can come over the whole of a substance at the same time. For example, if a metal ball becomes warmer during a certain minute, and during the same minute rotates through 35 degrees, must we say these are the same event? It would seem not; but there may be arguments the other way. Thus in the present instance it might be maintained that the warming of the ball during *m* is identical with the sum of the motions of the particles that constitute the ball during *m;* and so is the rotation. In the case of material objects it is perhaps possible to imagine two objects that in fact occupy just the same places at all times but are different because, though never separated, they are separable.

(5) We have not yet found a clearly acceptable criterion for the identity of events. Does one exist? I believe it does, and it is this: events are identical if and only if they have exactly the same causes and effects. Events have a unique position in the framework of causal relations between events in somewhat the way objects have a unique position in the spatial framework of objects. This criterion may seem to have an air of circularity about it, but if there is circularity it certainly is not formal. For the criterion is simply this: where x and y are events,

$$x = y \text{ if and only if } ((\forall z)\ (z \text{ caused } x \leftrightarrow z \text{ caused } y) \text{ and } (\forall z)\ (x \text{ caused } z \leftrightarrow y \text{ caused } z)).$$

No identities appear on the right of the biconditional.

If this proposal is correct, then it is easy to appreciate why we so often identify or describe events in terms of their causes and effects. Not only are these the features that often interest us about events, but they are features guaranteed to individuate them in the sense not only of telling them apart but also of telling them together. It is one thing for a criterion to be correct, another for it to be useful. But there are certainly important classes of cases at least where the causal criterion appears to be the best we have. If we claim, for example, that someone's having a pain on a specific occasion is identical with a certain complex physiological event, the best evidence for the identity is apt to be whatever evidence we have that the pain had the same causes and the same effects as the physiological change. Sameness of cause and effect seems, in cases like this one, a far more useful criterion than sameness of place and time.[19]

Perhaps sameness of causal relations is the only condition always sufficient to establish sameness of events (sameness of location in space and time may be another). But this should not be taken to mean that the only way of establishing, or supporting, a claim that two events are identical is by giving causal evidence. On the contrary, logic alone, or logic plus physics, or almost anything else, may help do the job, depending on the descriptions provided. What I do want to propose is that the causal nexus provides for events a 'comprehensive and continuously usable framework' for the identification and description of events analogous in many ways to the space-time coordinate system for material objects.

This paper may be viewed as an indirect defence of events as constituting a fundamental ontological category. A defence, because unless we can make sense of assertions and denials of identity we cannot claim to have made sense of the idea that events are particulars. Indirect, because it might be possible to make such needed sense, and to provide clear criteria for identity, and yet to have made no case at all for the need to posit events as an independent category. In other places I have tried to make good on the question of need; here I have not much more than summarized the arguments. But I have found that even those who are impressed with the arguments often have a residual doubt that centres on the apparent intractability of the question when events are identical.

I have tried to banish this doubt as far as I could. The results are not, it must be allowed, overwhelming. But how much should one expect? Can we do any better when it comes to giving criteria for individuating material objects? It should be noticed that the subject has been the individuation of events quite generally, not kinds of events. The analogous problem for material objects would be to ask for conditions of identity of equal generality. At this level, there is individuation without counting. We cannot answer the question, 'How many events occurred (since midnight, between Easter and Christmas)?' but neither can we answer the question, 'How many material objects are there (in the world, in this room)?' We do equally badly on counting classes, points, and intervals of time. Nor are there very good *formulas* for individuating in some of these cases, though we make good enough sense of assertions and denials of identity.

Individuation at its best requires sorts or kinds that give a principle for counting. But here again, events come out well enough: rings of the bell, major wars, eclipses of the moon, and performances of *Lulu* can be counted as easily as pencils, pots, and people. Problems can arise in either domain. The conclusion to be drawn, I think, is that the individuation of events poses no problems worse in principle than the problems posed by individuation of material objects; and there is as good reason to believe events exist.

NOTES

1. This point is well stated by Jaegwon Kim, 'On the Psycho-Physical Identity Theory,' *American Philosophical Quarterly,* vol. 3 (1966) pp. 277–285.

2. See Essays 1, 6, 7, and 11 in Donald Davidson, *Essays on Actions and Events* (Oxford: Oxford University Press, 1980).

3. The difficulty discussed here is raised by Anthony Kenny in *Action, Emotion and Will,* Ch. VII (London: Routledge and Kegan Paul, 1963). In Essay 6 in *Essays on Actions and Events* I devote more space to these matters and to the solution about to be outlined.

4. Georg Henrik von Wright, *Norm and Action,* 23 (London: Routledge and Kegan Paul, 1963).

5. 'Facts and Propositions,' 140, 141. Also see the reply to Martin in Essay 6 in *Essays on Actions and Events.*

6. See Essays 6 and 7, ibid.

7. F. I. Dretske in 'Can Events Move?' *Mind* vol. 76 (1967) pp. 479-492, correctly says that sentences do not refer to or describe events, and proposes that the expressions that do refer to events are the ones that can properly fill the blank in 'When did ——— occur (happen, take place)?' This criterion includes (as it should) such phrases as 'the immersion of the paper' and 'the death of Socrates' but also includes (as it should not) 'a discoloration of the fluid.'

8. In 'On the Psycho-Physical Identity Theory.' Essentially the same suggestion is made by Richard Martin in 'On Events and Event-Descriptions,' in *Facts and Existence* ed. J. Margolis (Oxford: Basil Blackwell, 1969) pp. 63–73.

9. Op. cit., 232 (footnote).

10. In *Individuals* (London: Methuen, 1959), 46ff. I am not sure, however, that Strawson distinguishes clearly among: pointing out an entity to someone; producing a unique description of an entity; producing a description guaranteed to be unique.

11. Ibid., 53.

12. Ibid., 51ff.

13. Ibid., 200.

14. The same conclusion is reached by J. Moravscik, 'Strawson and Ontological Priority.' In *Analytical Philosophy,* second series, ed. R. J. Butler (New York: Barnes and Noble, 1965) pp. 106–119.

15. E. C. Bullard, 'The Detection of Underground Explosions,' 24. *Scientific American* vol. 215 (1966) pp. 19–29.

16. Harry Levin, *The Question of Hamlet* (Oxford: Oxford University Press, 1959), 35, says in effect that the poisoned Hamlet, in killing the King, avenges, among other murders, his own. This he could not do if he had not already been murdered.

17. I discuss this issue at greater length in Essay 3 in *Essays on Actions and Events.*

18. E. J. Lemmon. 'Comments on D. Davidson's "The Logical Form of Action Sentences."' In *The Logic of Decision and Action* ed. N. Rescher (Pittsburgh: University of Pittsburgh Press, 1967) pp. 96–103. Lemmon goes further, suggesting that '. . . we may invoke a version of the identity of indiscernables and identify events with *space-time zones.*' But even if there can be only one event that fully occupies a space-time zone, it would be wrong to say a space-time zone *is* a change or a cause (unless we want to alter the language).

19. Thomas Nagel suggests the same criterion of the identity of events in 'Physicalism,' 346. *Philosophical Review* vol. 74 (1965) pp. 339–356.

Reading Questions

1. Davidson argues that an ontology of events is required if certain philosophical projects are to be intelligible. What projects are these? Why can't "event" just be taken as a primitive by those pursuing these projects?
2. What, according to Davidson, is the difference between "Doris capsized the canoe yesterday" and "Doris's capsizing of the canoe occurred yesterday"? Why does he think that this difference shows that it is a mistake to think that whole sentences refer to events?
3. Davidson claims that events are identical if and only if they have exactly the same causes and effects. Imagine that two photons (α and β) spontaneously come into existence in different parts of our galaxy. There is no cause for this in any usual sense, other than that according to quantum physics, there was a certain probability that this would happen. The photons exist for a nanosecond and then go out of existence *in nihilum.* Their lifespan was so short that their existence had no causal consequences. Intuitively we would say that there were two events that transpired: the life of photon α (call it A) and the life of photon β (call it B). Yet Davidson's view seems to entail that there was only one event, since A and B have exactly the same causes (none) and the same effects (none). How could Davidson answer this challenge?
4. Davidson maintains that he is offering a very general individuation condition for events, a criterion that does not give us a way of properly counting events. He also claims that "individuation at its best requires sorts or kinds that give a principle for counting." Do you see any way Davidson's account could be expanded or augmented to provide a principle for counting?

24 Events as Property Exemplifications

JAEGWON KIM

I

THE TERM 'EVENT' ORDINARILY IMPLIES CHANGE, and most changes are changes in a substance. Whether coming into being and passing away can be construed as changes in substances is a question we shall not consider here. A change in a substance occurs when that substance acquires a property it did not previously have, or loses a property it previously had. Whether fissions and fusions of substances can be considered as cases of losing or acquiring properties is, again, a question we shall not discuss in this paper. By 'substance' I mean things like tables, chairs, atoms, living creatures, bits of stuff like water and bronze, and the like; there is no need here to associate this notion with a particular philosophical doctrine about substance.

Besides events, we also speak of "states." If "events" signal changes, "states" seem to be static things, "unchanges," to use a term of C. J. Ducasse's;[1] some examples of states would be my body's weighing 140 pounds, the earth's being nearly spherical in shape, and the presence of oxygen in this room. There are, however, good reasons for not taking this dichotomy of changes and unchanges, or of events and states, too seriously at the initial stage of developing a theory of events. For one thing, there are cases that are hard to classify; e.g., the whirring of my typewriter, having a throbbing pain in the right elbow. Then there are "conditions," which, it seems, can be either events or states depending on essentially pragmatic contextual factors. And what of "processes"? A deeper analysis may reveal subtle and important differences among these entities, but I think that can wait until we have a good enough grasp of them as a distinct ontological category. Of course, this may turn out to be a wrong move; there may not be a single, unitary ontological category of interest comprising all, or even most, of them. But if we are wrong here, it would be philosophically profitable to find out that we are.

Moreover, it is a philosophical commonplace to use the term 'event' in a broad sense, not only to refer to changes but also to refer to states, conditions, and the like. When universal determinism is formulated as "Every event has a cause" or "the aim of science" is said to be the explanation and prediction of events in nature, it surely is not intended that states, narrowly so-called, escape the net of causal relations or that it is not the business of science to explain why certain states obtain, e.g., why the sky looks blue or why the earth is pear-shaped. To give one more reason for playing down the differences between events and states: some properties already imply changes in the substance that has them; for example, fading in color, falling, and freezing. This means that a change need not necessarily be characterized as a losing or acquiring of some property; it may simply be the *having* of some property at a time.

Just as changes are changes of properties in substances—again leaving aside such difficult cases as coming into being, passing away, fusion and fission—states and conditions are states and conditions *of* or *in* substances or systems of substances. Add this to our earlier reasons for underplaying the differences between changes and unchanges, and we naturally arrive at a conception of events and states as *exemplifications by substances of properties at a time*. This account can be called 'the property-exemplification account' of events; it has also been

I have benefited from discussions with, or unpublished materials furnished by, the following persons: David Benfield, Richard Cartwright, Roderick Chisholm, Donald Davidson, Fred Feldsman, Michael A. Slote. Ernest Sosa, and Ed Wierenga.

From Action Theory, *ed. M. Brand and D. Walton. Dordrecht, Holland: D. Reidel, 1976. Reprinted by permission of the publisher and author.*

called a theory of events as "structured complexes," since it attributes to an event a complex structure: an event (or state) is a structure consisting of a substance (an n-tuple of substances), a property (an n-adic relational attribute), and a time. This in essence is the view of events I have advocated in several earlier papers.[2]

This view of events has been criticized from many quarters, notably by Donald Davidson. The present paper aims at providing further clarifications of the theory, in part in light of some of these criticisms, and also raises some further issues concerning events and actions. In order to do this we need to state a few more details of the property-exemplification account. According to this account, each individual event has three unique constituents: a substance (the "constitutive object" of the event), a property it exemplifies (the "constitutive property" or "generic event"), and a time. An event is a complex of these three, and I have used the notation $[x, P, t]$, or variants thereof, as a canonical notation for events in general. There are two basic principles in the theory, one stating the conditions under which an event exists (occurs, if you like) and the other stating the conditions under which events are identical.

Existence condition: Event $[x, P, t]$ exists just in case substance x has property P at time t.

Identity condition: $[x, P, t] = [y, Q, t']$ just in case $x = y$, $P = Q$, and $t = t'$.

(For simplicity's sake we won't bother with dyadic and higher-place events, although these will show up later as examples. For details see my 'Causation, Nomic Subsumption, and the Concept of Events,' Essay 1 of *Supervenience and Mind*.) We shall sometimes use the expression 'event structure'[3] when we want to refer specifically to entities satisfying these conditions, i.e., events under the property-exemplification account.

As far as monadic events are concerned, i.e., events involving nonrelational, one-place attributes as constitutive properties, the theory can easily be developed along a different line: dispense with the existence condition and define the *predicate* 'is an event' over ordered triples of substances, properties, and times. An ordered triple $\langle x, P, t\rangle$ would be an event just in case the substance x has the property P at time t. The existence of the triple would be guaranteed by the principles of set theory, provided x, P, and t exist, whether or not x has P at t. And the identity condition for events would merely be a special case of the identity condition governing n-tuples. For dyadic and higher-place events, this approach of defining an event predicate within set theory introduces some complexities in regard to the identity condition, complexities which are by no means insuperable. In any case this approach has the advantage of using the familiar set-theoretic apparatus and of doing away with a special operator '[, ,]', which some people seem to find mysterious (but given the identity condition, '[, ,]', may be taken as a special case of the familiar definite description operator, and in this regard it is not different from the set-abstraction operator '{v| . . . v . . . }'). It would also allow us to speak of "possible events," i.e., the ordered triples $\langle x, P, t\rangle$, whether or not x has P at t, which might be useful for certain philosophical purposes.[4]

What is essential is that we are assuming as primitives the three functions on events: 'is the constitutive property of,' 'is the constitutive object of,' and 'is the time of the occurrence of.' The theory states that just in case a substance x has property P at t, there is an event whose constitutive object is x, whose constitutive property is P, and whose time of occurrence is t (the existence condition), and that events are identical just in case they have the same constitutive property, object, and time (the identity condition). This is the core of the account of events under discussion. The introduction of the notation '[, ,]' is merely abbreviatory; the use of the set-theoretic machinery *may* have certain metaphysical consequences, depending on one's metaphysical views of sets, as regards, for example, the essential properties of events. But I regard these as peripheral issues pertaining largely to the mode of presentation of the theory; the basic elements of the account are not essentially altered thereby.

The account so far presented is not an "eliminative" or "reductive" theory of events; that is, it does not attempt to show that events are in some eliminative sense "reducible" to substances, properties, and times. (It may be remarked, though, that a better case for the elimination or reduction of events might be made if we take the ordered triple approach sketched above.) I do not know exactly when a metaphysical theory is "reductive"; the account, however, attempts to tell us something about the metaphysical nature of events by relating them to such other ontological categories as substances, properties, and times. And I have tried to show, in several earlier papers, how this view of events can provide a useful framework within which to develop and discuss theories of causation and explanation, and the round-body problem; I believe it also provides a framework in which an account of the relation between micro-events and macro-events can be developed.[5]

I have said little about what properties are allowable as constitutive properties of events; namely, what "generic events" are. It clearly will not do to count as an event the exemplification of any arbitrary property by an object. This becomes obvious if one thinks, as many do, that there is a property expressed by any open sentence, or if one thinks of properties in the way modal logicians do nowadays, namely as functions from possible worlds to sets of individuals. There is also the problem, a difficult and important one, of properties ordinarily considered generic events, e.g., becoming a widow, which give rise to "Cambridge events."[6] It will only beg the issue to try to explain 'generic event' in terms of such notions as 'change' and 'alteration.' And it may be tempting, but no less question-begging, to try to define it in terms of overtly causal concepts, for "real changes" or "real events" seem to be just those that make a causal difference, and generic events seem to be just those properties whose possession by an object bestows upon it a causal power or potency, or whose possession by an object indicates its being subjected to such powers.

This causal approach, I think, may turn out to be the correct one—but in a roundabout way: the basic generic events may be best picked out relative to a scientific theory, whether the theory is a common-sense theory of the behavior of middle-sized objects or a highly sophisticated physical theory. They are among the important properties, relative to the theory, in terms of which lawful regularities can be discovered, described, and explained. The basic parameters in terms of which the laws of the theory are formulated would, on this view, give us our basic generic events, and the usual logical, mathematical, and perhaps other types of operations on them would yield complex, defined generic events. We commonly recognize such properties as motion, colors, temperatures, weights, pushing, and breaking, as generic events and states, but we must view this against the background of our common-sense explanatory and predictive scheme of the world around us. I think it highly likely that we cannot pick out generic events completely a priori. If generic events are understood along these lines, not all of the Boolean combinations of generic events can be relied on to yield generic events; for example, if two generic events are from different theories or rival theories about the same subject matter. It is even clear that if *F* is a generic event, non-*F* is also a generic event in every case.

There is also the following problem: generic events are often picked out by verbs and predicates. Now there is a group of words that modify them—adverbs and, generally, predicate modifiers. The question arises: If '*F*' is a predicate or verb designating a generic event and α is a predicate modifier, under what conditions does '$\alpha(F)$' designate a generic event? The answer will of course depend on the particular properties of 'α' and of '*F*.' If walking is a generic event, walking slowly seems to be one also. What about walking while chewing gum, walking toward the Eiffel Tower, and walking exactly two thousand years after the death of Socrates? Are they *kinds of events*? Or should we treat the modifiers as indicating properties *of* the individual events arising from the generic event of walking—e.g., treat '(being done) while chewing gum' as designating a property of the event of my walking at a particular time *t*? We shall briefly recur to this problem below.

II

A metaphysical theory of events of the sort just sketched must be distinguished from a theory of the "logical form" of event and action sentences—

a theory that attempts to exhibit the relevant logical and semantical structures of sentences about events—of the sort initiated essentially by Donald Davidson in an influential series of papers.[7] To call attention to this distinction is not to say there are no important connections between the two. Davidson has made ontological claims based on his work on the logical form of event and action sentences; most notably, he has claimed that his investigations have shown that events and actions must be admitted into our ontology as values of bound variables, and that they are "particulars" that can be described and referred to in various nonequivalent ways. However, Davidson has also emphasized a distinction between a logical and semantical theory of event discourse and a metaphysical theory of events:[8]

> On the score of ontology, too, the study of logical form can carry us only a certain distance. . . . Given this much, a study of event sentences will show a great deal about what we assume to be true concerning events. But deep metaphysical problems will remain as to the nature of these entities, their mode of individuation, their relation to other categories.

Davidson did go beyond a theory of event sentences: in his paper 'The Individuation of Events'[9] he has given us a principle of individuation for events. It is this: events are the same just in case they have the same causes and the same effects. This criterion has been criticized as covertly circular, since causes and effects themselves are events.[10] If the criticisms are correct, it may be unsound as a "criterion" of individuation; nonetheless, it may be true that events having the same causes and same effects are in fact one and the same, although one wonders how the criterion would fare in an indeterministic, causally irregular world (this world could be such a world). Further, it may in fact turn out that my criterion of event identity is coextensive with Davidson's: that is, for events x and y, $x = y$ under the identity condition of the property-exemplification account of events if and only if $x = y$ under Davidson's criterion.[11]

Let us now look into the question whether the property-exemplification account of events is incompatible with Davidson's theory of event sentences and his metaphysical claims based on that theory. The two are often considered as competing theories,[12] and it is a matter of some interest to see what differences, if any, exist between them.[13]

Central to Davidson's theory of event sentences is the point that a sentence like

(1) Flora dried herself with a towel on the beach at noon,

which is just the sort of sentence often said to "describe" or "represent" an event, contains a covert existential quantification over concrete events, and its logical form should be brought out thus:

(2) There is an event *e* such that *e* is a drying of Flora by Flora, *e* was done with a towel, *e* occurred on the beach, and *e* occurred at noon.

Now there seems to be no reason why the variable '*e*' cannot take as its values the event structures of the property-exemplification account: in fact, no reason why the particular event structure [(Flora, Flora), ① dries ②, noon] isn't just the value of '*e*' that makes (2) true. As (2) affirms, this event—an action, as it happens—has the property of being done with a towel, the property of occurring on the beach, and so on. Notice, by the way, that the first clause in the matrix of (2) says '*e is a drying* of . . .'; this 'is a (verb)-ing' construction and other verb nominalizations are good clues for identifying the generic events involved in Davidsonian paraphrases of event sentences. To cite two of his own examples:[14]

(3a) The boiler exploded in the cellar.

(3b) There exists an x such that x was an explosion and x was in the cellar and x was of the boiler

(4a) Jack fell down . . .

(4b) There is an event *e* such that *e* is a falling down of Jack . . .

On my account exploiting, falling, and the like are generic events in the intended sense; the boiler and Jack, in the above examples, are the constitutive substances of the two events, respectively.

Obviously, my events can be quantified over; and there is no problem about quantifying *into* the event structures unless of course there happen to be other barriers to quantification such as psychological modalities. My events are "particulars" and "dated." That they are dated is obvious. I am not clear what "particulars" are; but events in my sense have locations in space, namely the locations of their constitutive substances (if mental substances have no spatial location, then mental events would have no spatial location either, which presumably is what some dualists want to claim). And my events are not "eternal" objects; they do not exist in all possible worlds; they exist only if the existence condition is met, which is a contingent matter of fact. If this doesn't show that something is "concrete" or "particular," what does?[15]

Davidson has considered it an important mistake to regard a sentence like

(5) Doris capsized the canoe yesterday

as picking out a unique event, for she may have capsized the canoe more than once yesterday. Generally speaking, it is a mistake, according to him, to think of such sentences as playing the role of singular terms for events. Now my account does not compel us to render (5) into

(6) The event [Doris, capsized the canoe, yesterday] occurs.

(Here we disregard the fact that a dyadic event may be involved; we also disregard the tense.) For we may put (5) thus:

(7) $(\exists t)$([Doris, capsizes the canoe, t] exists and t belongs to yesterday).

But we are not quite through with Davidson on this point. According to the existence condition, as I intended it, if an object x exemplifies P *at* t in the sense of *throughout t,* then the existence of a *unique* [x, P, t] is guaranteed by the identity condition. Davidson writes:[16]

> Some actions are difficult or unusual to perform more than once in a short stretch of time, and this may provide a specious reason in some cases for holding that action sentences refer uniquely to actions. Thus with 'Jones got married last Saturday,' 'Doris wrote a check at noon,' 'Mary kissed an admirer at the stroke of midnight.' It is merely illegal to get married twice on the same day, merely unusual to write checks simultaneously, and merely good fortune to get to kiss two admirers at once.

Let us assume that kissing some admirer or other is a generic event. My two conditions, then, imply that there is the unique event of Mary's kissing an admirer at the specified time. From the existence of this event, however, nothing follows as to how many persons she kissed at the time, although ordinarily, it would be safe enough to assume she kissed one person. Suppose she in fact kissed two admirers, Steve and Larry. If we take the dyadic kissing, x's kissing admirer y, as the generic event involved, the two conditions entail the existence of two unique dyadic kissings, Mary's kissing Steve and her kissing Larry. Thus, there are three kissings here, which some might find a bit disconcerting; but once it is realized that they are one monadic kissing and two dyadic kissings, the situation need no longer strike us as implausible or incoherent. In fact, it seems to me that that is what we should say to describe Mary's kissings.[17]

Another point of some importance, though obvious, is this: there is nothing in my account that implies that from any sentence about an event we can read off what the event's constitutive components are. From the sentence 'A momentous event occurred yesterday' we can only approximately locate the time of the event; we can tell nothing about its constitutive property or substance. From the sentence 'The momentous event that occurred yesterday caused the event now under discussion by the regents of the university' we can say nothing about the constituents of these events, except, again, the time of the first event. This is as it should be. The situation is quite similar with sentences about physical objects. In a sense knowing what the constitutive object, property, and time of an event are *is* to *know what that event is.* Although we are here treading on uncertain grounds, my canonical description of an event, I believe, gives an "intrinsic description" of an event (assuming that the three components are given "intrinsic descriptions"), in the sense in which such descriptions as 'the momentous event yesterday' and 'the event now under discussion' are "extrinsic." I am not here prepared to explain, much less define, what is to be meant by 'intrinsic' and 'extrinsic'; perhaps they are explainable in terms of a combination of modal and epistemic concepts.

There are other points of apparent disagreement between Davidson's views and mine, some of which will be taken up in succeeding sections. But overall it seems to me that there are no irreconcilable *doctrinal* differences between Davidson's theory of event discourse as a semantical theory and the property-exemplification account of events as a metaphysical theory. True enough, Davidson and I disagree about particular cases of individuation of events; for example, whether Brutus's stabbing Caesar is the same event as Brutus's killing Caesar. But most of these differences about particular cases seem traceable to possible differences in our views about causation, explanation, and intensionality. Where Davidson says, with regard to a sentence like

(8) The collapse was caused, not by the bolt's giving way, but the bolt's giving way so suddenly,

that here 'was caused' should be understood in the sense of 'is causally explained,' and that explanations "typically relate statements, not events,"[18] I would take (8) more literally and be inclined to take it as evidence for saying that in virtue of their different causal properties, the bolt's giving way and the bolt's giving way suddenly are different events, though one is "included" in the other. But here we are coming dangerously close to some difficult problems about the relationship between causation and explanation, and the intensionality of causal and explanatory relations, problems well beyond the scope of the present paper.

III

One of the most frequently voiced objections to the theory of events as property exemplifications is the point that this theory multiplies events beyond necessity. Not only is Brutus's stabbing Caesar distinct from his killing Caesar and also from his assassinating Caesar; but in fact no stabbings are killings, and no killings are assassinations.[19] What seems worse, Brutus's stabbing Caesar is also a different event from Brutus's stabbing Caesar with a knife, since stabbing and stabbing with a knife presumably are different properties; and neither of these events is the same as Brutus's stabbing Caesar in the heart; and so on. These considerations seem to have led some philosophers to think that the property-exemplification account does not permit redescriptions of events,[20] since any addition or deletion from a given description would alter the constitutive property of the event in question.

Let us first examine the problem of redescribing an event. It is true that if an event description is altered so that a different generic event is picked out, then the resulting description, on my view, would pick out a different event. That much is clear enough. And the same applies to the names and descriptions of the constitutive objects and times of events. On the other hand, it is not part of the account in question that the use of different predicates—nonsynonymous, logically inequivalent predicates—invariably leads to a multiplicity of properties. 'Is blue' and 'has the color of the sky' pick out the same property, namely the color blue.[21] Moreover, as noted earlier, events themselves *have* (exemplify) properties; Brutus's stabbing Caesar has the property of occurring in Rome, it was intentional, it led to the death of Caesar and caused Calpurnia to grieve, and so on. Needless to say, the properties an event exemplifies must be sharply distinguished from its constitutive property (which is exemplified, not by the event, but by the constitutive substance of the event). It is also a property of Brutus's stabbing Caesar that its constitutive property is stabbing. Thus, events can be redescribed by the use of different predicates expressing the properties *of* (exemplified by) them; what cannot be done is to redescribe them by tampering with their constitutive properties. The point I am making should be obvious if we consider such "extrinsic" descriptions of events as 'the event we are talking about' and 'the most unforgettable event in David's life.' What the theory implies is that if 'the most unforgettable event in David's life' refers, then the event thus referred to must have a structure of the sort the theory attributes to events; for example, the event could have been David's falling off a horse at age five.

But the foregoing isn't likely to satisfy the critics as allowing us a full range of describing and redescribing events. 'Brutus stabbing Caesar' and 'Brutus killing Caesar,' they insist, are redescriptions of the same event; and what may seem even more obvious, 'Brutus's stabbing Caesar' and 'Brutus's stabbing Caesar with a knife' *are* two descriptions of the same event, one being somewhat more detailed and more informative than the other. Similarly, for such examples as 'Sebastian's stroll,' 'Sebastian's leisurely stroll,' and 'Sebastian's limping stroll.' Here we return to the initial objections mentioned at the outset of this section.

I do not want to discuss here the question of whether Brutus's stabbing Caesar is the same event as Brutus's killing Caesar; for I have little to add to the existing arguments in favor of their distinctness.[22] Also, intuitively, it is more plausible to deny identity in cases like it than in cases like Sebastian's stroll and Sebastian's leisurely stroll (where, we suppose, Sebastian did stroll leisurely).

So what of Sebastian's stroll and Sebastian's leisurely stroll? First of all, there is the question whether being leisurely is to be taken as a property exemplified by the event of Sebastian's stroll, or as modifying the generic event of strolling, thereby issuing in another generic event, namely strolling leisurely. If the former line is taken, there is no special problem—no more problem here than there is in the case of 'this red rose on the table' and 'this withered red rose on the table' where there is one unique red rose on the designated table which is withered. So on this approach Sebastian's stroll, after all, turns out to be the very same event as Sebastian's leisurely stroll, i.e., Sebastian's stroll, which, as it happens, was leisurely.

Thus, the general strategy is this: we deny that strolling leisurely or stabbing with a knife are generic events, although strolling and stabbing are. The modifiers 'leisurely' and 'with a knife' are taken, not as modifying 'strolling' and 'stabbing,' but rather as indicating properties of the individual events which arise from the exemplifications of the generic events designated by 'strolling' and 'stabbing.' We could say, somewhat more generally, that predicate modifiers indicating means-manners-methods, may be construed in this way.[23] Taking this way out, however, is not entirely appealing, for at least two reasons: first, it would place a very severe and urgent burden on us to produce an account of generic events and of the modifiers of expressions designating them, although this is a problem that one has ultimately to face in any case. Second, this approach neutralizes one of the initial motivations for developing the structured complex view of events. Whatever else events might be, they were intended to be entities that enter into causal relations with one another, and that can be objects of explanations. But it is clear that we may want to explain not only why Sebastian strolled, i.e., Sebastian's stroll, but also why he strolled leisurely, i.e., his leisurely stroll. Under the approach being considered, the second explanation would be of why Sebastian's stroll was leisurely; we would be explaining why a certain event had a certain property, not why a certain event occurred. But perhaps it was a mistake to bring very broad and general considerations about explanations into a theory of events, to begin with. The desire to have events as the relata of causal relations could, I believe, be accommodated within this approach, although some of the specific things I have said in earlier articles about causation would have to be retracted (especially, the claim that for Humean causation there must be a lawlike connection between the generic events of any two causally connected individual events).

The other strategy for dealing with Sebastian's stroll and his leisurely stroll, which one might call "the official line" of the property-exemplification account, is to affirm that these are different, if not entirely distinct, events. Not entirely distinct since the latter *includes* the former.[24] I will not try to give a characterization of inclusive for events here; a completely general characterization gets, as far as I know, to be very complicated without being philosophically interesting; also, various different kinds of "inclusion" have to be distinguished (obviously, the sense in which an assassination *includes* a killing or strolling leisurely *includes* strolling is very different from the sense in which, say, my walking to the door *includes* my moving my left foot to take the first step, or the burning of the barn *includes* the burning of the roof of the barn). But I assume that it's intuitively plausible to say there is some relation here that can be called "inclusion."

Difference need not be total distinctness or absence of any significant relation whatever. Once this is granted, there being two events (actions) here, and not one, impresses us as not such an extravagant claim after all. Take this table: the top of the table is not the same thing as the table. So there are two things, but of course one table—in fact, there are lots of things here if you include the legs, the molecules, the atoms, etc., making up the table.

Unfortunately, we are not through with the proliferating events. The new difficulty I have in mind is this: Granted there are two events here, of which one is included in the other. Now, Sebastian's strolling is a strolling—a stroll event, if you like—and Sebastian's strolling leisurely is also a stroll event. You say they are two events, not one; so it follows that there are two stroll events, both strolled by Sebastian on that memorable night through the streets of Bologna. In fact, given such generic events as strolling with a cane in hand, strolling with a limp, and so on, there were indefinitely many strolls strolled by Sebastian that night! And of course indefinitely many stabbings administered by Brutus on Caesar!

The analogy with tables and other sundry physical objects may still help us here. We normally count this as *one* table; and there are just so many (a fixed number of) tables in this room. However, if you believe in the calculus of individuals,[25] you will see that included in this table is another table—in fact, there are indefinitely many tables each of which is a proper part of this table. For consider the table with one micrometer of its top removed; that is a table different from this table; and so on.

It would be absurd to say that for this reason we must say there are in fact indefinitely many tables in this room. What I am suggesting is merely that the sense in which, under the structured complex view of events, there are indefinitely many strolls strolled by Sebastian may be just as harmless as the sense in which there are indefinitely many tables in this room. The proliferation of events with which my account of events is often charged is not in itself serious; for "the number of *events*" is very much like "the number of *things*" or "the number of *facts*"; 'event' isn't an ordinary run-of-the-mill count noun. What is bothersome is the seeming fact that the number of stabbings or strollings seems to go beyond any bound. 'Stabbing' and 'stroll' seem to be as good count nouns as 'table' and 'apple.' In any case I hope that I have succeeded in mitigating this difficulty. If I have not, the earlier strategy of handling the proliferation problem would merit more serious consideration.

IV

The question has been raised whether my account of events has implausible consequences concerning the essential properties of events.[26] Take Sebastian's leisurely stroll at midnight. According to the structured complex account, it may be thought, there are three essential properties of that event: one, that the stroll was strolled by Sebastian; two, that it was a leisurely stroll; and three, that it occurred at midnight. More generally, it is alleged that the account is committed to the thesis that the three constituents of an event constitute the essential properties of the event. It is then argued that, at least, the time of the occurrence of an event is not an essential property of it. Sebastian's stroll could have taken place five minutes before or after midnight. And perhaps its being a leisurely stroll isn't an essential property of the stroll either; if Sebastian had been pressed for time, the stroll would have been a brisk one. Similarly, the stroll could have been taken by someone else. Suppose that the midnight stroll was done as some sort of ritual by a member of a secret society chosen by lottery, and that it so happened that Sebastian was so chosen. If Mario, Sebastian's friend, had been chosen, then Mario would have strolled that stroll.[27]

It isn't clear to me what, if anything, an analysis or metaphysical theory of something implies about the essential properties of that thing. There is a metaphysical theory of physical objects, which is of respectable vintage and tradition, that asserts that a physical object is a "congeries of properties" or something like that. So this table is a "congeries" of such properties as brown color, the mass it has, and so on. But presumably it is not a consequence of the theory that the table has essentially the properties it actually has, that the brown color of the table is an essential property of it. Why should it be thought, then, that the structured complex view of events is saddled with the essentialist consequences mentioned above?

But perhaps it is my identity condition for event structures that is the chief focus of the objections. Here, too, analogy with other cases makes it difficult to see how any essentialist consequences necessarily follow from identity criteria. It is at least a respectable identity criterion for physical objects that they are the same just in case they are completely coincident in space and time. From this it does not follow that a physical object is essentially where and when it in fact is. To give another, possibly controversial, example, the extensionality criterion of set identity does not entail that a given set has its members essentially. It seems at least arguable that the set of the planets could have comprised eight planets rather than nine; even if this is wrong, it's not easy to see how the extensionality criterion (or any part of the usual mathematical theories of sets) shows it; we would need an independent metaphysical argument.

On the other hand, I don't want to claim that the essentialist consequences attributed to my account are in themselves false. At least, I find it plausible to think of the constitutive substance of an event as essential to the identity of that event. The fact that someone other than Sebastian could have taken a stroll in his place does not make it the case that the very stroll that Sebastian took could have been taken by someone else. If Mario had been chosen to stroll that night, then there would have been another stroll, namely Mario's. It has been remarked by some philosophers that, although you could have a pain that is qualitatively identical with the pain I am now having, you could not, logically or metaphysically, have the very same, numerically identical pain that I have.[28] The event of my strolling could not, logically or metaphysically, occur to anyone else any more than the event of my being in pain could. Only Socrates could have died *his* death. It seems not implausible to think that events and states are essentially individuated with respect to their constitutive substances.

The essentiality of the constitutive property to the identity of an event is less certain. For one thing, the question seems to depend on some of the issues earlier raised concerning generic events. If strolling leisurely is a generic event, there seems to be a case for saying that the generic event is not essential to the identity of an event which involves it. But it is highly dubious that Sebastian's leisurely stroll could have been a run or a crawl, and it certainly could not have been a coughing or dozing, although Sebastian could have stayed home that night with a cold, coughing and dozing. The case seems still weaker for the essentiality of the time of occurrence: it seems correct to say that the stroll could have occurred a little earlier or later than it actually did. The stroll, we suppose, could have taken place five minutes later than it actually did, but could it—the very same stroll—have occurred five months later? Five years? In any case, caution is required: we should not infer, from the mere fact that Sebastian could have strolled at a different time, the conclusion that this very stroll Sebastian took could have occurred at that different time.

Some of these issues may have important bearings on other philosophical problems, such as the identity theory of mind; also, what we want to say about the bearing of generic events on the essential properties of events may in turn constrain what we want to pick as generic events. And what I said earlier about "knowing what a given event is" and an "intrinsic description of an event" is likely to have a bearing on these issues. There is at present only a mass of intuitions, some conflicting with others, which need to be sorted out by a theory. We don't have such a theory, and in any case, events don't seem to be much worse off than anything else with respect to these problems about essences.

There is an essentialist consequence I am willing to accept: events are, essentially, structured complexes of the sort the theory says they are. Thus, events could not be substances, properties, and so on. But this should not be confused with the assertion that *each* event structure has *its* constituents essentially. This assertion is at least partially true, as I argued; but the general problem is still open.

V

Actions are usually taken as a subclass of events. How to characterize this subclass is a problem considered very important, but we shall not be concerned with it here. Killings are actions—at least, those that involve agents (I assume falling rocks and lightnings can also kill)—and thus events as well. But what is a killing? As has frequently been observed of late, 'kill' is a near synonym of 'cause to die.' Since killing presumably isn't a basic action, not for humans at any rate, it must involve two events, one an action performed by the killer and the other the death caused by the action. Thus, Brutus's killing Caesar seems to be nothing other than some action of Brutus causing the death of Caesar. The action event of Brutus's killing Caesar thus threatens to turn into a *relation,* a *causal* relation, between two events. And Brutus's stabbing Caesar, the cause event in this causal relation, itself may turn into a causal relation between two events, in the same way. Thus, killings so analyzed don't seem to fit the model of events under the property-exemplification account; they do not seem to have the complex event structure it attributes to events; instead, they seem to be relations between events.

This feature isn't limited to action events. As noted some time ago by C. J. Ducasse, many transitive verbs are implicitly causal; e.g., 'pull,' 'push,' 'break,' 'shatter.' When the wind blows the door open, this involves a causal relation: the pressure of the wind on the door causes the opening of the door. So the event of the wind's blowing open the door appears to turn into a causal relation between two events, the wind's pressure on the door and the door's opening. The question arises: are we to accept these causal relations themselves, i.e., one event's causing another, as events?[29] Or should we fit them into some other ontological category, say, facts?

One argument for treating, say, killings as events may be this: they are just the sort of thing that can have causes and effects, and just the sort of thing that can be given causal explanations. Brutus's killing Caesar may have been caused by Brutus's political ambitions and personal jealousies; it in turn caused Calpurnia's grief and caused Caesar to be absent from the Roman Senate the next day. It is of the essence of events that they can enter into causal relations. So why not treat killings and other actions as events?

This argument isn't decisive, however. As earlier noted, there are two events involved in Brutus's killing Caesar: Brutus's action, which was his stabbing Caesar, and Caesar's death. When we cite Brutus's motives and beliefs as causes of the killing, we do not seem to be saying that they are the causes of the stabbing's causing the death; rather, we seem to be saying that they are causes—or among the causes—of Brutus's undertaking the action, namely the stabbing of Caesar, which he believed would result in Caesar's death. I would venture the hypothesis that what we normally take to be a cause of the killing will ultimately turn out to be a cause—or among the causal conditions—of the basic action which was undertaken by Brutus in the endeavor that Caesar be dead and which in fact did cause the death.

What of the effects of the killing? Calpurnia's grief may very well have been caused by her *belief* that Caesar was dead, or that Caesar was so brutally murdered, or that it was Brutus who killed him. As for Caesar's absence from the Senate the following day, we can attribute it to his death as one of its effects. I think that what we normally take as an effect of a killing is often attributable to the death of the person killed or someone's cognitive attitude, such as belief, toward some aspects of the killing.

I believe similar things can be said of events that do not involve agents. The rock shatters the window. This we normally call an event. But it involves a causal relation: the rock's impact on the window caused it to shatter. What is the cause of the rock's shattering the window? Well, Johnny threw the rock. But we can take Johnny's throwing the rock as the cause of the rock's impact on the window, namely the first of the two events in the causal relation. The rock's shattering the window caused a cut on my hand. Again, the cut can be construed as an effect of the shattering of the window, namely the second of the two events in the causal relation, and not as the effect of the rock's shattering the window. One might object: But what of the fragility of the window glass? Why isn't that a cause of the rock's impact's causing the shattering? We do say: If the glass in the window had not been so fragile, the rock's impact would not have caused the window to shatter. Furthermore, the fragility of the window glass is not a cause of the rock's impact on the window. My reply is this: we still need not say that the fragility is a cause of one event's causing another; it is a cause, along with the rock's impact and perhaps other things, making up the complete cause of the window's shattering.

So the thesis I am suggesting is this: the causes and effects of actions and events exhibiting the causal features under discussion are attributable to the events in the causal relation that constitute such an action or event. (I leave aside here effects like Calpurnia's grief that may be caused by beliefs about such actions and events.) The thesis has two interpretations, one stronger than the other: (1) all causes of, say, a killing are among the causes of the action that caused the death, and all effects of the killing are among the effects of the death; and (2) all causes of the killing are among the causes of the action that caused the death or of the death, and all effects of the killing, too, are among the effects of the action or of the death. The stronger thesis, (1), appears to be false; suppose that as a result of the vigorous wielding of the knife, Brutus dislocated his right shoulder. It would be correct to say that Brutus's dislocating his right shoulder was caused by his killing Caesar, but clearly it is not caused by Caesar's death. The weaker interpretation (2) of course accommodates this sort of example. In any case, if the thesis is correct in either interpretation, we can block the argument that killings must be treated as events since they enter into causal relations.

If we decide not to regard killings and such as events, then it would be open to us to regard them as *facts* (which should not preclude us from taking events simpliciter as a special subclass of facts): Brutus's killing Caesar is the fact that some action of Brutus caused Caesar to die, and the rock's shattering the window is the fact that the rock's impact caused the window to shatter. Such events and actions turn out to be causal facts. Treating them in this way may affect the ontology of action theory, theory of explanation, and the analysis of causation. And it may lead us to the talk of "basic events," namely those events not involving causal and other relations among events.

But the above is not the only course open to us. If we are prepared to accept causal properties as generic events, that is, if we are prepared to allow causal relations between events to appear in generic events, then we could accommodate killings and their ilk within our scheme. For we can render

(9) Brutus's doing some action which caused Caesar's death

into

(10) [(Brutus, Caesar) for some generic action event *P* and times t^* and t'[(①, ②), P^{①②}, t^*] caused [②, dies, t'], t].[30]

Which way is better? I think that the second way leads to a messy situation with regard to the problem of characterizing generic events, and creates complications in the theory of causation, explanation, and so forth. The first way is largely unexplored at this stage, but I would look upon it more favorably; I think it presents us with interesting possibilities to explore.[31]

NOTES

1. In Ducasse, C. J., *Causation and the Type of Necessity*, Univ. of Washington Press, Seattle, 1924.

2. 'On the Psycho-Physical Identity Theory.' *American Philosophical Quarterly* 3 (1966), 231–32; 'Events and Their Descriptions: Some Considerations,' N. Rescher, *et al.* (eds.), *Essays in Honor of Carl G. Hempel*, Reidel, Dordrecht-Holland, 1969; 'Causation, Nomic Subsumption, and the Concept of Event,' Essay 1 of Jaegwon Kim, *Supervenience and Mind* (Cambridge: Cambridge University Press, 1993). A similar account of action was given by Alvin Goldman in *A Theory of Human Action*, Prentice-Hall, Englewood Cliffs. N.J., 1970; an account of events very much like mine is found in R. M. Martin's 'On Events and Event-Descriptions,' J. Margolis (ed). *Fact and Existence*. See also N. L. Wilson, 'Facts, Events and Their Identity Conditions.' *Philosophical Studies* 25 (1974), 303–21.

3. This expression was suggested by Richard Cartwright.

4. For a treatment of "possible facts" somewhat along these lines see Bas van Fraassen, 'Facts and Tautological Entailments,' *Journal of Philosophy* 66 (1969), 477–87.

5. Interesting results have been obtained along these lines by Terence Horgan in his doctoral dissertation. *Microreduction and the Mind-Body Problem,* at the University of Michigan, 1974.

6. See my 'Noncausal Connections,' Essay 2 of *Supervenience and Mind.* The term 'Cambridge change' comes from Peter Geach, *God and the Soul,* Routledge & Kegan Paul, London, 1969, p. 71.

7. To cite a few: 'The Logical Form of Action Sentences.' N. Rescher (ed.), *The Logic of Decision and Action,* Univ. of Pittsburgh Press, Pittsburgh, 1967; 'Causal Relations,' *Journal of Philosophy* 64 (1967), 691–703; 'Truth and Meaning,' *Synthèse* 17 (1967), 304–23.

8. 'Action and Reaction,' *Inquiry* 13 (1970), 140–48.

9. In N. Rescher (ed.), *Essays in Honor of Carl G. Hempel.*

10. E.g. by N. L. Wilson in 'Facts, Events and Their Identity Conditions'; and by George Sher in 'On Event-Identity," *Australasian Journal of Philosophy* 52 (1974), 39–47.

11. In 'On Kim's Account of Events and Event-Identity,' *Journal of Philosophy* 71 (1974), 327–36, Alexander Rosenberg claims that, with a slight revision in my account of events, Davidson's criterion and my criterion are equivalent under the Humean constant-conjunction view of causation.

12. Davidson himself refers to my account as a "rival" account, in his 'Events as Particulars,' *Noûs* 4 (1970), 25–32, p. 26, footnote 4.

13. I shall not discuss here Roderick M. Chisholm's very different theory of events as "states of affairs" in his sense of abstract intensional entities, developed in his *Person and Object,* Open Court Publishing Co., 1976. See also his 'Events and Propositions,' *Noûs* 4 (1970), 15–24.

14. The first pair comes from his 'Eternal vs. Ephemeral Events,' *Noûs* 5 (1971), 335–49, p. 337; the second from 'Causal Relations,' 696.

15. Chisholm refers to both Davidson's account and mine as variants of "the concrete event theory" in *Person and Object.*

16. 'The Individuation of Events,' 220.

17. Especially if we keep in mind the fact that there being three different kissings does not entail that there can be no intimate and significant relations between them.

18. 'Causal Relations,' 703. (8) is a slightly altered version of Davidson's own example.

19. Davidson in his 'Comments' on Martin's 'On Events and Event-Descriptions,' Margolis (ed.,), *Fact and Existence,* 81. Also Rosenberg in 'On Kim's Account of Events and Event-Identity.'

20. E.g. Carl G. Hedman claims this in his 'On When There Must Be a Time-Difference Between Cause and Effect,' *Philosophy of Science* 39 (1972), 507–11.

21. On property identity, see Peter Achinstein, 'The Identity of Properties,' *American Philosophical Quarterly* 11, 1974, 257–75.

22. I have in mind: Lawrence H. Davis, 'Individuation of Actions,' *Journal of Philosophy 67* (1970), 520–30; Judith Jarvis Thomson, 'The Time of a Killing.' *Journal of Philosophy* 68 (1971), 115–32; Alvin I. Goldman, 'The Individuation of Action,' *Journal of Philosophy* 68 (1971), 761–74.

23. Such a view is suggested by Judith Jarvis Thomson in her 'Individuating Actions,' *Journal of Philosophy* 68 (1971), 774–81.

24. Goldman would say that the former 'level-generates' the latter; see *A Theory of Human Action,* Chapter 2.

25. In the sense of Nelson Goodman, *The Structure of Appearance,* Harvard University Press, Cambridge, 1951.

26. Ed Wierenga has raised this question in his doctoral dissertation, *Three Theories of Events,* University of Massachusetts at Amherst, 1974.

27. This is substantially what Davidson says in 'Eternal vs. Ephemeral Events' to answer a question raised by Chisholm.

28. Jerome Shaffer in 'Persons and Their Bodies,' *Philosophical Review* 75 (1966), 59–77.

29. From similar considerations N. L. Wilson concludes ". . . 'alerting,' 'killing' and all the other causative verbs do not refer to events" in 'Facts, Events and Their Identity Conditions,' 318.

30. The question of the relationship between t^*, t', and t is discussed by Judith Jarvis Thomson in 'The Time of a Killing.'

31. The problem of generic events that contain causal relations is related to Bernard Berofsky's problem of characterizing "R-sentences" in his *Determinism,* Princeton Univ. Press, Princeton, 1971, Chapter V, esp. 157ff.

Reading Questions

1. Kim rejects a dichotomy between events (typically understood to involve changes in a substance) and states (typically understood to be static). Why?

2. Suppose a property realist (cf. Part IV, Abstracta) watches a painter paint a blue sky and says "The property blue has a new instance." Kim claims that events are the dated exemplifications of properties by *substances*. Therefore it seems that the dated exemplifications of properties by other properties couldn't be an event. Is this a problem for Kim's theory?
3. Kim denies that strolling leisurely or stabbing with a knife are generic events, although strolling and stabbing are. What problem is he trying to avoid with this approach?
4. Suppose Sebastian takes a leisurely stroll at midnight. What are the reasons, pro and con, for thinking that only Sebastian could have taken that stroll, and that that very stroll had to have occurred leisurely and at midnight?

25 Events

LAWRENCE BRIAN LOMBARD

IN THIS ESSAY, I want eventually to get around to proposing a criterion of identity for events which are changes in physical objects, where events are construed as comprising a distinct metaphysical category of thing. The proposal will be preceded by a discussion of what I take to be a mistaken suggestion for such a criterion; I will do that because I think that seeing what it takes to show why that suggestion fails helps to motivate a theory about what it is to be an event; and that theory will supply the conceptual foundations for my proposal concerning the criterion of identity for events. Before that suggestion is discussed, however, I want to discuss briefly an aspect of the question, Why do we have to give a criterion of identity for events, or for objects of any sort whatsoever? I want to have a brief look at the connection between identity criteria and the idea of a kind of object. And I want to say something which bears on the idea that metaphysicians, when wondering about what there is, are not interested in the existence of tigers, bachelors, or prime numbers, but are interested in the existence of sets, properties, physical objects, and events. The sorts of objects whose existence is, I believe, of interest to metaphysicians form what I shall call "metaphysical categories" of thing.

I

I shall presume that if x and y are any objects whatsoever, then x and y are the very same object if and only if they share all the same properties. This principle, Leibniz's law, constitutes a kind of criterion of identity for objects, irrespective of the sorts to which objects belong. But what is it that distinguishes objects of one sort from objects of another? What is it that distinguishes, say, physical objects and sets? Of course, the fact that the set of bicycles, for example, has properties not had by the Eiffel Tower is enough to show, *via* Leibniz's Law, that that set is distinct from that physical object. But surely, that sort of remark misses entirely the point of the question. It is, presumably, not as if those two things just happen to be discernible and, hence, distinct. No physical object could be a set; that's the upshot of saying, in the first place, that sets and physical objects form two distinct categories of existent.

The bachelors do not form a distinct metaphysical category of thing. This is, I think, connected up with the fact that no bachelor is necessarily a bachelor; any individual who belongs to the class of bachelors could have failed to so belong. That is, while it is necessary that any object which is a

From the Canadian Journal of Philosophy, *Volume IX, Number 3, September 1979. Reprinted by permission of the author and publisher.*

bachelor is an object which has certain, bachelor-making properties, it is not the case that any object which is a bachelor is an object which necessarily has certain, bachelor-making properties. Bachelors may, in some loose sense, comprise a sort of person, but not a kind of thing. But physical objects do form a kind of thing; and they do so, in part, because any thing which is a physical object could not fail to be one, and could not have failed to be one, except by failing to exist, I want to make an attempt to make this a bit more precise. I want to get hold of the idea of a "metaphysical category" of existent, and to connect up that idea with the task of giving criteria of identity. The intuition behind all this is that physical objects, events, and sets are kinds of things which do comprise metaphysical categories of existent, but that bachelors, prime numbers, tigers, things, and abstract things are not.

By and large, any property determines a sort of objects insofar as it will determine a class whose members are just those objects which have that property. I shall say, however, that such a property, ϕ, is an *essence* of some class of objects if and only if

(1) it is necessarily true, that if some entity has ϕ, then it is necessary that if that entity exists, then it has ϕ, and

(2) it is possible that there are entities which have ϕ.[1]

Condition (1) rules out as essences properties of things which things which have them have only contingently; being a bachelor and being blue are not essences. However, (1) allows universal properties, e.g., being an existent thing, to be essences; and the property of being an abstract entity is an essence (if it also meets (2)). Condition (2) rules out inconsistent properties; being a round square is not an essence of any class of objects. For a property to be an essence, it must be a property which things can have. The notion of essence, as defined by (1) and (2), is different from that of essential property, as defined, say, by Plantinga (in "World and Essence," *Philosophical Review* 79 (1970)). For according to Plantinga, essential properties are properties which some objects may have essentially (in every world in which they exist), but which others may have only accidentally (e.g., being either prime or prim). My essences, however, are had essentially by every object which has them at all. And I am interested in the notion of essence and not in that of essential property, because I am interested, here, in *kinds* of things and in the differences between things *qua* members of different kinds; and that, it seems to me, requires not a notion of essential property, but rather a notion of essence.[2]

Conditions (1) and (2) together do not constitute a sufficient, but only a necessary, condition for a property to be an essence which determines a class of entities whose members constitute a metaphysical category of existent. For one thing, the conditions are met by the property of being a prime number and by the property of being a tiger; and the prime numbers and the tigers do not form metaphysical categories of thing. The intuition behind that is that a prime number is a number which is so-and-so (and, perhaps, numbers are sets which are thus-and-so), and that a tiger is an animal which is such-and-such.

For another thing, the conditions are met by the property of being an abstract entity. And I want to suggest that the abstract entities should not be construed as comprising a single metaphysical category, simply because that category includes such diverse sorts of things as sets, propositions, and properties. However, if, for example, it were to turn out that properties and propositions were just sets, or if necessarily sets were the only sort of abstract entity, then I would have no objection to treating the property of being an abstract entity as an essence determining a metaphysical category of thing. What irks about treating that property as an essence determining a metaphysical category of thing (when it includes those different sorts of abstract entity) and convinces me that it should not be so treated is that there is no possibility of giving a criterion of identity which is *stronger* than Leibniz's Law for abstract entities construed simply as such. A criterion of identity for a class of objects is, as I shall say, *stronger* than Leibniz's Law, if it picks out from among all the properties which the members of that class can have some proper subset which is such that if any members of that class of objects are alike with respect to the possession and non-possession of the properties in that subset, then they are guaranteed to be alike with respect to all their other properties as well, and hence, by Leibniz's Law, are guaranteed to be identical. We shall want a criterion of identity to be stronger than Leibniz's Law, because, as I shall suggest in section II, only in that way will we have any clear way of knowing what "kind" of object is in question. In the case of the abstract entities, we have no hope (and this is not a matter of giving up in desperation) of producing a true formula, stronger than Leibniz's Law, of the form, "if x and y are abstract entities, then x = y if and only if ______," except, perhaps, by filling in the blank with a disjunction, each of whose disjuncts is a formula which gives a criterion of identity, stronger than Leibniz's Law, for the entities which comprise each of the species of abstract object. What that suggests is that the class of abstract objects really consists of a number of importantly distinct, and distinguishable, metaphysical categories of existent. Of course, the members of those categories do have something important in common which justifies their being subsumed under the super-categorical heading "Abstract Entity"; but no unique, distinct metaphysical category of existents such that it has the property of being an abstract entity as its essence. So, to rule out such properties as being an abstract entity, being an existent thing, and, perhaps, being a spatio-temporal thing (if there is more than one kind of spatio-temporal thing), we add condition (3):

(3) we can, at least in principle, give a (non-disjunctive) criterion of identity, stronger than Leibniz's Law, for the things which have ϕ.[3]

Now, any property which meets conditions (1) and (2) is an essence of a class of objects. But any property which meets conditions (1), (2), and (3) will be an essence which will pick out a class of objects whose members we might be inclined to say form a "kind." If a property, ϕ, is an essence determining a kind, and the objects which have ϕ are biological creatures, then ϕ determines a biological kind (e.g., tiger); if ϕ is an essence determining a kind, and the things which have ϕ are physical, though not necessarily biological, in character, then ϕ determines a physical kind (e.g., gold, water, if ϕ is an essence determining a kind, and the things which have ϕ are numbers, then ϕ determines a numerical kind (e.g., prime number). On this conception, the kinds are just those classes of entities which have an essence and for which we can give, at least in principle, a (non-disjunctive) criterion of identity stronger than Leibniz's Law.

But the classes of objects which form kinds are not necessarily classes which form metaphysical categories of thing. The class of all abstract entities (if there could be such a class) forms neither a metaphysical category nor a kind of thing, for it includes too much. The kinds do not necessarily form metaphysical categories, for they may not include enough; the three-membered sets are just sets which are so-and-so, and water is just a physical substance which is such-and-such. Intuitively, many kinds are just species of entities of certain other kinds. We can, however, rule them out and zero in on just those classes of entity whose members comprise kinds which constitute the distinct metaphysical categories of thing by adding a fourth condition:

(4) there is no essence ψ which is such that
   (a) necessarily, anything which has ϕ has ψ (but not *vice versa*), and
   (b) there is a (non-disjunctive) criterion of identity, stronger than Leibniz's Law, for the things which have ψ.

Any property which meets conditions (1)–(4) will be an essence which, I conjecture, picks out a class of objects which constitutes a metaphysical category of existent. The metaphysical categories are just the *broadest* kinds of thing for which we can, in principle, give non-disjunctive criteria of identity stronger than Leibniz's Law.[4]

"No entity without identity." The point of this dictum of Quine's may be this. If it were to turn out, as a matter of fact, to be the case that no two physical objects ever had the same shape, we would not, for all that, be satisfied with a criterion of identity for physical objects which ran as follows: for any objects, x and y, if x and y are physical objects, then x = y if and only if x and y have the same shape. We would not be satisfied because the claim, even if true, would be true only contingently. We insist, I think, that acceptable identity criteria for objects should be, in some sense, true necessarily. And it is, in part, because we take it to be part of the very idea of a physical object that physical objects are impenetrable that we find sameness of spatio-temporal location to be an acceptable criterion of identity for such objects. Such a criterion captures and articulates our beliefs about what the essence of a physical object is, and, in that way, satisfies our demand for necessity. To lack a criterion of identity, stronger than Leibniz's Law, for a class of entities, then is to lack a clear idea of what it is to be an entity of that kind, of what kind of entity is in question. For to be a kind is for there to be a certain criterion of identity for the members of that kind. So, if we do not have a criterion of identity, we do not even know that we have a kind of entity on our hands at all, as the discussion of (1)–(4) suggests. And, thus, to lack a criterion of identity is, in a way, to fail to know the first thing about those entities. Our lacking a criterion of identity for a class of objects might indicate any one of several possibilities. First, that there just couldn't be any such entities; hence, such entities could not, by condition (2), have an essence, and there would be nothing about those entities to articulate in a criterion of identity. Secondly, that the class of entities does not constitute a kind, because its members belong to several different kinds. And, of course, one could not give a criterion of identity for, say, propositions, if it were to turn out that some propositions were properties and others were sets, for example. And thirdly, that we have not yet discovered the essence of what it is to be a member of that kind, supposing that the class does constitute a kind, and so we would have nothing, as yet, on which to hang a criterion of identity.[5] In each of these three cases, we just do not know the sort of thing we need to know about the entities in question to justify serious metaphysical talk about them. So, of course, one has a right to be suspicious.

Thus, if we are to count *events* as objects which constitute a metaphysical category of existent, we must be satisfied that a criterion of identity for such objects can be given which captures and articulates, in some sense, an essence of events not shared by the members of any other kind which we suspect to be a distinct category of thing. We cannot, of course, demand that such a criterion be epistemologically useful by giving a way of finding out, for every case, when a sentence of the form '$e_1 = e_2$,' where the terms pick out events, is true. For if a criterion with such epistemic import could be given, then, since for every event, e, and any true sentence, s, e = (ιx = e and s is true), we would have a criterion which would tell us when any sentence is true.[6] Still, we must insist that a criterion of identity be essence-articulating, non-disjunctive, and stronger than Leibniz's Law; and we might also ask that it be the strongest criterion one could give, in the sense that it make use of the fewest properties the sharing of which by events is sufficient to insure their numerical identity. If a criterion does do all that, it will perforce have some epistemological bite, since it will tell us, in general, what sort of investigation is especially and essentially relevant to settling questions concerning identity. This is what sameness of spatial and temporal properties is said to do for physical objects. And we can be satisfied with no less for events, for if we fail to develop a similar theory for events, we fail to understand just what kind of thing an event is.

Now, despite whatever unclarities there may be in the notions of the time and the place of an event, it is clear, if events are particulars, that occurrence at the same time and in the same location by events is a necessary condition for their numerical identity. This follows simply from the fact that events, construed as particulars, have spatial and temporal properties. But, is sameness of spatial and temporal properties (spatio-temporal identity, for short) a *sufficient* condition as well? That is, can two or more events occur simultaneously in the same place?

From a metaphysical point of view, a great deal hangs on our answers to these questions. How the issue of whether or not spatio-temporal identity constitutes a criterion of identity for events is settled will determine whether or not events and physical objects constitute separate and distinct metaphysical categories of thing. For if spatio-temporal identity is a criterion of identity for events—just as it is for physical objects—then the apparently two categories of spatio-temporal thing will collapse into one, the category of spatio-temporal chunks. Cars and the crashings of them, checks and the signings of them, and muggers and their muggings will all be the same kind of thing. This much is, I take it, obvious; for, as the discussion of (1)–(4) suggests, the differences between kinds of objects is to be found in differences in the identity criteria for objects of those kinds. If spatio-temporal identity is a criterion of identity for events, then since it can be the case that some event can have the same spatio-temporal properties as some physical object, it would follow that that event just *is* that physical object. And that result can be generalized for all events, if all events are changes in physical objects. Each event would be identical with some temporal part of some physical object, and each physical object would be identical with some sequence of events; if physical objects are constantly changing (by undergoing events), then every physical object will be identical with the change it undergoes during its existence (if sequences of events are events). Thus, one who thinks, as I do, that events constitute a metaphysical category of existent distinct from that of physical objects cannot regard spatio-temporal identity as a criterion of identity for events. Of course, to say that does not count against that criterion of identity for events all by itself; it only specifies the price one must, either gladly or not, pay for it.

In the rest of this paper, I want to do several things: (a) describe a picture of what I think the answer to the question, Is spatio-temporal identity sufficient, as well as necessary, for the numerical identity of events? depends on; (b) suggest that, on that picture, the answer is that it is not; (c) attempt to refine that picture so as to get a clearer idea of what an event is; and (d) say, on the basis of that refined picture, what the criterion of identity for events is.

III

In his "Comments on D. Davidson's 'The Logical Form of Action Sentences,'"[7] the late E. J. Lemmon suggested spatio-temporal identity as a criterion of identity for events, and a collapsing of the categories of events and physical objects into one category of spatio-temporal particulars; but he offered no argument for that criterion. In his reply to Lemmon, Davidson said that he was not sure that Lemmon wasn't right; but he expressed the desire for an argument which would allay suspicion towards that criterion generated by what seem to be counterexamples.[8] If we locate the things which happen to a person, as well as the things he does, at the body of the person, then when Jones thinks of Vienna and catches a cold during the entire period in which he swims the Channel, the thinking, the catching, and the swimming all seem to be occurring in the same place simultaneously. If those events are really not three but one, then we had better come up with an argument, in view of the counter-intuitiveness involved in identifying those events. In "The Individuation of Events," Davidson still appears undecided. First, he suggests that spatio-temporal identity is not sufficient for the numerical identity of events, and hence cannot constitute a criterion of identity for them:

> . . . it seems natural to say that two different changes can come over the whole of a substance at the same time. . . . For example, if a metal ball becomes warmer during a certain minute, and during that time rotates through 35 degrees, must we say that these are the same event? It would seem not. (p. 230)

But then, though we still have no *general* argument in favor of the spatio-temporal criterion of identity for events, Davidson warns that there may be arguments in particular cases:

> . . . it might be maintained that the warming of the ball during *m* is identical with the sum of the motions of the particles that constitute the ball during *m*; and so is the rotation. (pp. 230–31)

And the dialectic can continue almost indefinitely.[9]

What is going on here, and why do none of the examples seem to be decisive? It seems as if we might always be able to say, in favor of Lemmon's criterion, one of the following two things in any particular case where we seem to have two or more events occurring simultaneously in the same place. First, that the appearance is mere and that the apparently distinct events really are identical. Secondly, that they really are distinct, but have different locations. It is, we are reminded, simply incorrect to identify the location of an event just by reference to *the* object which changes, for a change in any object is a change in any other object of which the first is a part. We need, therefore, to define the notion of the *minimal* location of an event, and ask whether two or more simultaneous events can have the same minimal location.[10] Here, the aim is to retain our intuitions about the identity and distinctness of particular events, while retaining spatio-temporal identity as the criterion of identity for events. We retain, for example, the distinctness of the cold-catching, the thinking, and the swimming, by arguing that not all changes which come over a person have that person's body as their minimal location.

However, we do, I submit, have these intuitions about the distinctness of thinkings, cold-catchings, and swimmings quite apart from any considerations regarding the minimal locations of such events. But what is troubling is that these intuitions may be grounded in considerations expressed in the form of rhetorical questions like, How can an event which is an instance of the type "catching a cold" be identical with an event which is an instance of the type "thinking of Vienna"? Now such intuitions may be correct, and I think they are; but we must look for deeper foundations which show why such questions have the answers that they do. In the next section, I want to present a picture of what the foundations for judgments in particular cases about whether or not more than one event can occur in the same place at the same time must be like.

IV

An object is the subject of some change if and only if it has a property at one time which it lacks at another.[11] Now some properties are such that their being possessed at a particular time by an object does not imply that that object has changed, is changing, or will change; such properties can be called "static" properties, and include such properties as that of being blue and that of being located at place p_1. If an object has at some time some static property, P, then at that time that object can be said to be in the state of being P. Other properties are such that if an object has such a property at a particular instant, then it is true that that object is changing at that instant; being a presently shrinking thing and having instantaneous acceleration are properties of that sort, and we can call them "instantaneous dynamic" properties. It should be noted that if an object has an instantaneous dynamic property at a particular instant, t, then there must be an interval which includes t during which that object has and then lacks some static property. Now, if an object has some instantaneous dynamic property, at an instant t, then it will also have at an *interval,* t', which includes t, a property, which I shall call a "dynamic" property, the possession of which at that interval implies that at that interval the object is changing from having one to having another static property; indeed, it just is the property of first having one and then having another static property. It is a property such that at instants, in the interval during which the object has that dynamic property, the object has some instantaneous dynamic property. Dynamic properties are had by objects only at times which are intervals; that is, change takes time.[12] The property of reading a book from cover to cover is a dynamic property had by the reader at a time which is an interval including both the time he starts to read the book and the time he finishes reading the book; the property of being in the process of reading a book from cover to cover is, however, an instantaneous dynamic property, had by the reader at each instant (and collection thereof) in that interval.[13]

I shall call any set, S, of simple static properties, $\{P_0, P_1, \ldots, P_n, \ldots\}$, a *quality* space[14] when it meets the following two conditions:

(i) if at any time, t, any object, x, has $P_i \varepsilon S$, then at t, for every $j \neq i$, it is not the case that x has $P_j \varepsilon S$,

(ii) if any object, x, which has $P_i \varepsilon S$ at t, fails by t' ($t' \neq t$) to have P_i as a result of some change, then x changes in S, that is, by t', x has, for some j ($j \neq i$), $P_j \varepsilon S$.

What (i) says is that a quality space consists of mutually exclusive, static properties of objects. The import of (ii) is that quality spaces consist of sorts or kinds of properties, and that if any object changes with respect to any of its static properties, then it must come to have another property of the same sort. The idea behind this is that no object can be said without further comment to change, for example, from being red to being square. The further comment might be that it is a law of nature that red objects are round and blue objects square, and that the object has changed from being red to being blue; but some further comment there must be. As Aristotle points out (*Physics,* Bk. 1, Chap. 5, 188a32–189a10):

> Our first presupposition must be that in nature nothing acts on, or is acted on by, any other thing at random, nor may anything come from anything else, unless we mean that it does so in virtue of a concomitant attribute. For how could 'white' come from 'musical', unless 'musical' happened to be an attribute of the not-white or of the black. . . . It is clear then that our principles must be contraries.

So, a quality space is just a set of static properties of objects which is such that when an object changes one of its static qualities, one which belongs to some quality space, at least one result of that change is that the object acquires another property from that same space. Which properties belong to which quality spaces is a question which cannot be answered *a priori*. Such a question, if it arises at all, can be answered only after we observe what the results of various changes which can come over an object are; and clearly observation won't really turn the trick, unless observation is colored and determined by scientific theories which tell us how to describe those changes.[15] And even after such questions are answered, it will still be the case that not all static properties can be fitted neatly in quality spaces, if those spaces are already partially filled, for they may not meet the condition of mutual exclusivity.

If we have the static properties divided into quality spaces and we assign numbers to the properties in each space, we can represent each element of a quality space as a point on a line or a plane. And then by representing times on another line, we can represent each change which comes over an object in the form of a *graph* which plots the "movement" of the object through a given quality space against time. [And, if the properties in a given quality space are tightly packed, that is, if for every real number there is a property in the space assigned to it, then we can define a *continuous* change by an object, x, in that quality space, S, as follows: a change in x, which consists in x's moving from having P_i at t to its having P_k at t'(where P_i, $P_k \varepsilon S$, $i \neq k$, and $t \neq t'$) is continuous if and only if at each t* between t and t', x has some $P_j(P_j \varepsilon S)$ which is such that the real number assigned to P_j is equal to the real number assigned either to P_i or to P_k or is between those two real numbers, and at each time during every interval which is included in the period t–t', the same condition is met (also, every temporally contiguous sequence of continuous changes in the same space by the same object is a continuous change).]

Can two or more simultaneous changes have the same minimal location? It would seem so. Each change on the picture just described is a movement during a stretch of time through at least part of some quality space. And though during a particular stretch of time there cannot be more than one movement in each minimal location through each quality space—since no object can possess all over mutually exclusive properties at the same time—there are numerous quality spaces. And there seems to be no reason to suppose that an object cannot possess all over properties belonging to different quality spaces which change simultaneously. But is this clearly true?

Consider a particle moving during the period from a time t to a time t' from a point p to a point p' along a diagonal. How shall we graph this change? One suggestion would be to plot the particle's movement during that period of time through a location-space whose elements are the properties of being located at such-and-such a point in two-dimensional space. The graph of this change will be three-dimensional, with moments of time represented on one axis and location properties represented on a plane. A second suggestion for graphing the particle's movement would be to construe the properties of being located at points on the horizontal, of having such-and-such a horizontal coordinate, and the properties of being located at points on the vertical, of having such-and-such a vertical coordinate, as constituting different quality spaces. Here, there will be two graphs, one plotting the particle's movement during the period from t to t' through a horizontal-location space and another plotting the particle's movement during the period from t to t' through a vertical-location space.

What difference do these two ways of graphing the particle's diagonal movement make? Since each of the two graphs is a graph of a distinct change, the second suggestion would have us view the diagonal movement as a *composite* event, consisting of a horizontal movement and a vertical movement, both of which occur during each moment of the period from t to t' at the place of the particle at that moment. The first suggestion, however, views the particle's movement as, in the requisite sense, non-composite. What appear on the second construal as distinct horizontal and vertical movements appear on the first construal as no more than distinct *vectors* of a single movement; and vectors of movements are not movements, they are aspects of movements. The property of having such-and-such a vertical vector is a property of a movement; it is not a property of a thing which moves. What the second suggestion does is take (what on the first appear as) vectors of movements and make them movements; it reconstrues properties of events as properties of the subjects of events. And graphs of events plot properties of things which change, not properties of changes, against time. On the second suggestion, there are two movements, one horizontal and one vertical, taking place simultaneously in the same location; and the diagonal movement is an event composed of the two, just as a party might be said to consist at a certain time of dancing and eating, though here the dancing and the eating will be likely to have different minimal locations. On the first suggestion, the diagonal movement can, in a sense, be said to be composed of movements; during the first half of the period from t to t', the particle moves halfway from p to p', and covers the rest of the distance in the remaining time. But, the diagonal movement is not composed of horizontal and vertical movements. The movement along the diagonal has horizontal and vertical vectors; but, again, vectors of movements are not movements.

In the case of movement across space, my inclination is to collapse all the location-spaces into one, and not to make vectors into movements. The reasons for being so inclined will emerge later on. But in any event, if one does collapse the location-spaces into one, then it will be true to say that each particle can be the subject of only one movement through space at a time.

Consider, now, the case of a young, adolescent boy. Let us construct a graph plotting the lowering of his voice from ages twelve to sixteen, and a graph plotting the growth of facial hair during the same period; and let us ignore the question of the minimal locations of these changes. It seems reasonable to suppose that the lowering of the boy's voice and the growth of his facial hair are two distinct changes which the boy is undergoing during those years; and the two graphs, plotting movements through two different quality spaces, reflect that. The maturing of the boy would, then, be a composite event, consisting, in part, of these two changes. But we can collapse the two quality spaces, and some others as well, into one *maturation*-space. Now, the lowering of the voice and the growth of facial hair would appear, not as distinct changes, not as events of which the boy's maturation is composed, but as distinct vectors or aspects of the boy's maturation. In this case, my inclination is not to collapse the quality spaces into one maturation-space, but to make changes out of vectors of changes (and, again, the reasons for this will emerge later on).

The upshot of the foregoing is this. The more divided the properties of things into distinct quality spaces the more the distinct changes there can be which can come over the whole of an object simultaneously. The more the properties of things can be compressed into fewer and fewer spaces, the fewer the number of distinct simultaneous changes will be to which an object can be subject. If there were only one, universal quality space in which things change, then—and only then—only one change could come over an object at a time. So, the issue of whether or not sameness of spatial and temporal properties constitutes an adequate criterion of identity turns on whether there is only one or more than one quality space in which things change. And I, for one, cannot see a reason for thinking that there is exactly one such space; thus, I see, in the end, no reason to believe that spatiotemporal identity constitutes an adequate criterion of identity for events.

V

In the last section, a number of suggestions were made. I suggested that it was of the essence of an event to be a change in a physical object; and change was understood as a "movement" (a having of one and then another quality) by an object through (some portion of) a quality space during a stretch of time. I also suggested, in a rough way, a starting point for a criterion of identity for events. This consisted in suggesting that since one proposal for graphing a certain event involved the use of two different quality spaces, we were construing, on that proposal, that event as really composed of two other distinct events. I should like now to make this somewhat more precise.

We can begin to refine this picture of the relation between events and quality spaces by asking why it is that we are, in some cases, inclined to make vectors of movements into movements, and, in other cases, inclined to relegate putative movements to the status of a vector. Let us consider the examples from section IV. Why did it seem right to collapse all the location-spaces into one, so that the diagonal movement of the particle was construed as an event which had horizontal and vertical vectors, and not as an event composed of horizontal and vertical movements? I think that the reason has to do with the fact that we have a physical theory of movement according to which *all* movements through space, regardless of their directions, are the results of the same sorts of forces. If, for example, the horizontal movements of objects were the results of impartings of momentum by other objects, but vertical movements were the results of the will of God, then it would, I think, be appropriate to say that movements through two-dimensional space were composed of (possibly null) horizontal and vertical movements, and we would be justified in dividing the location-space into distinct horizontal and vertical ones. In such a situation, there may be a very good reason to think that horizontal and vertical movements were movements, and hence events, of different kinds. But we do not believe that anything like this is true; we believe that the sorts of forces which can produce horizontal movements can also produce vertical movements.

Why did it seem right to divide the maturation-space into several distinct quality spaces, including a voice-tone-space and a facial hair-length-space, so that the maturation of the boy would be construed as an event which was composed, in part, of voice lowering events and facial hair growing events, and not as a simple event with voice and facial hair vectors? Again, I think that the reason has to do with the fact that we believe that an adequate physiology of adolescence shows that the growth of facial hair can be traced to factors to which the lowering of the voice cannot (and *vice versa*). And that provides us with a reason for thinking that a boy's maturation is an event composed of other events which are jointly brought about by the conjunction of several different sorts of forces. Such a physiological theory tells us that when a boy matures, he really undergoes a lowering of his voice, etc., etc.[16]

Perhaps one more example is in order of the manner in which scientific theories affect the way properties of changing things are sorted into quality spaces, and hence affect the way events are identified. Let it be the case an object is grue* if and only if it is green before some specified time, t, and blue thereafter. Has an object changed if it is green before t and blue after t? It was, after all, grue* all along. It seems true to say that a decision on this matter cannot be made independently of a decision as to what to count as an object. If our best available geology were to claim that there are emerires—gems which are emeralds before t and sapphires thereafter—then it would be the case that some things were grue*, and they would change color, or fail to do so, accordingly. What the properties are with respect to which things can change depends, at least in part, on what sorts of objects there are; and that sort of issue falls, at least in part, within the purview of science.

On the basis of the examples adduced above, I want to suggest what it is that scientific theories tell us concerning events and quality spaces. Scientific theories tell us what objects are really made of; they tell us what the ultimate constituents of objects are. And they tell us what sorts of properties these ultimate objects have in virtue of which objects, constituted of such ultimate objects, have the properties they have. And they tell us what sorts of changes ultimate objects can undergo in virtue of which objects, constituted of such ultimate objects, undergo the changes which they do. And they tell us what those changes in ultimate objects consist in. For example, our science tells us, when water is heated, that water is a bunch of molecules and the heating of the water is an increasing of the mean kinetic energy of the molecules; and that the molecules consist of such-and-such particles, and that increasing of the molecules' mean kinetic energy consists in increasing the movement of those particles, and so on. This process of scientific reduction (in some loose sense) stops when the science in question reaches objects which it takes to be such that their changes are not to be construed as composed of changes in other objects of which the original is constituted. When this sort of story is given, we can understand it as saying that a conceptualization of an event (say, the heating of water) as an event with many vectors has given way to a conceptualization of that event as an event composed of other events which are changes in objects of which the subject of the original event (say, the water) is composed. In short, scientific theories are theories about what the ultimate quality spaces through which ultimate objects move when they change are. I propose, in light of this, the following definitions:[17]

(D1) An object, x, is an *atomic object* for a theory, T, if and only if it is the case, in T, that x exists and there are no objects, y, which are distinct from x, such that they are what x consists of;[18]

(D2) A set, S, is an *atomic quality space* for a theory, T, if and only if S is a quality space whose members are properties which atomic objects (in T) can have;

(D3) An event, e, is an *atomic event* for a theory, T, if and only if (a) e is a movement of some object, x, which is atomic (according to T), which consists in x's having P_i and then having P_k, at some interval of time, t, where P_i and P_k are distinct properties belonging to some quality space, S, which is atomic (according to T), and (b) if there is any P_j (in S), distinct from P_i and P_k, which x has during t, then it is of the essence of e in T that its subject, x, have P_j during t.[19]

It is, of course, the case that which the atomic objects, spaces, and events are will be determined by the scientific theory in question together; one cannot settle the question of which entities satisfy any of the definitions for a given scientific theory independently of settling the question of which entities satisfy the others.

I now offer the following hypothesis about the things we ordinarily think of as events on the basis of which I intend to go on to discuss descriptions of events and a criterion of identity for events:

(H) Every event is either
- (a) an atomic event, or
- (b) a temporal sequence of atomic events (which may, under certain circumstances, itself be an atomic event), or
- (c) a non-atomic event, i.e., an event which is composed of atomic events all of which occur at the same time, or
- (d) a temporal sequence of non-atomic and (perhaps) atomic events.[20]

VI

Each atomic event is a movement by an atomic object which consists in that object's first having one and then having another property in a particular atomic quality space (within the limits imposed by the restriction in D3). Now, for each pair of static properties within a given quality space, which are such that if an atomic object were to move at some time from having the one to having the other then that change would be an atomic event, there will be a dynamic property which the object will have at the time (an interval) at which it is so changing. That dynamic property will just *be* the property of first having the one and then having the other static property. Sometimes there will be a verb already in the language which expresses such a property; and if there isn't one, one can always be introduced. 'Rots' might be thought of as such a verb were it not for the fact that a rotting of wood is not an atomic event; but in a theory which construed medium-sized, not-so-dry goods as atomic objects, it might well be.[21] Be that as it may, a verb will be called an "atomic event verb" when it means the same as, or is equivalent on the theory in question to, 'exemplifies the property of first having P_i and then having P_j', where P_i and P_j are properties belonging to an atomic quality space and where any atomic object's having that dynamic property (at some interval of time) constitutes an atomic event (in the theory T). Such verbs and the dynamic properties of atomic objects which they express are associated with properties of atomic events which are *atomic event types.* An atomic event is an event which has the property of being a ϕing, where ϕing is an atomic event type, just in case that atomic event consists of the atomic event verb 'ϕ' 's being true of the atomic object involved at the time (an interval) of that atomic event. Thus, for example, if the rotting of some wood were an atomic event, and 'rots' were an atomic event verb true of the wood at the interval of time in which the wood was rotting then the atomic event undergone by the wood would be a rotting and would be an event of the atomic event type "rotting." For an event to be of the atomic event type which in a canonical language for the theory T in question is called a "ϕing," it must be an atomic event which consists in some atomic object's exemplifying the dynamic property expressed by the verb 'ϕ,' where 'ϕ' is an atomic event verb, at some interval t. Each atomic event is an instance of some atomic event type.[22]

The *canonical description* of an atomic event will be a singular term of the form '[x, ϕ, t],' where 'x' is to be replaced by a name or description of the atomic object which is the subject of that atomic event, 't' is to be replaced by a name or description of the interval of time at which the event occurs, and 'ϕ' is to be replaced by the atomic event verb which expresses the dynamic property the having or exemplifying of which (by the object referred to by whatever replaced 'x') at the interval referred to by whatever replaces 't') is that atomic event. Such a term may be read as: x's exemplifying ϕ at t. However, it must be noted that atomic events may be referred to by a phrase of the form 'x's exemplifying ϕ at t' (or 'x's ϕing at t'), where that phrase is *not* canonical. For 'x's exemplifying ϕ at t' to be a canonical description of an atomic event, and hence for it to be capable of being re-written as '[x, ϕ, t],' 'ϕ' must be an atomic event verb. Canonical descriptions of atomic events seem to have the same structure as the event-descriptions which figure so prominently in the writings of Kim and Goldman.[23] It is to be noted that the appearance of no canonical description of an atomic event logically insures that there is an atomic event which satisfies it; that is an empirical matter. But it does seem to be the case that if there is an atomic event which satisfies such a description, then there will be at most one that does; but more of that a bit later. It should also be emphasized that there is no systematic way to generate canonical descriptions of events from atomic-event-describing sentences or from atomic-event-referring terms, for such sentences, say of the form 'x ϕed at t,' and such terms, say of the form 'x's ϕing at t,' though they may describe or refer to some atomic event, need not describe or refer to it by employing an atomic event verb. That a description of an atomic event is canonical or not will be determined not only by the description's form, but also by its content (the event must be described by means, in part, of an atomic event verb).

The basic idea behind this characterization of the canonical descriptions of atomic (and, as we shall see, other) events is that such descriptions should, in their atomic event verb-place, draw only upon the resources afforded by the atomic quality spaces movements in which constitute the events so described. This idea can be extended, for purposes of easy speech, to allow us to construe some events, which we know full well are not atomic, for we accept a theory in which they are not, as atomic and to give descriptions of them in the style of a canonical one. However, it must be pointed out that the descriptions which are merely for all practical purposes canonical may lead one to draw certain conclusions, if taken to be actually canonical, which we would not be tempted to draw, if one did not take them to be canonical; more of this below.

Non-atomic events come in two sorts. One sort consists of events which are composed of atomic events each of which is an atomic change in the same atomic object and all of which occur over the same interval; such events can be called simple non-atomic events. The other sort consists of events which are composed of atomic events some of whose subjects are different from each other but all of which occur over the same interval; those are the complex non-atomic events. A non-atomic event will have for its canonical description a description of the form, 'the event which is composed of $[x_0, \phi_0, t], \ldots, [x_1, \phi_1, t]$ and $[x_n, \phi_n, t]$,' where each of the terms following 'of' is a canonical description of each of the non-atomic event's compositional parts, that is, of each of the atomic events of which the non-atomic event is composed. If $x_0 = x_1 = \ldots = x_n$, then we have a simple non-atomic event; if not, then the non-atomic event in question is complex; of course, all the t's (which are intervals of time) are the same. Some events will be temporal sequences of atomic and/or non-atomic events; and their descriptions will be canonical just in case they describe the events they do solely in terms of the canonical descriptions of their atomic and non-atomic temporal parts (and the order in which those parts occur).

Canonical descriptions of events describe events only in terms of the atomic objects involved in the event's compositional and temporal parts, the intervals of time at which those parts occur, and the dynamic properties, expressed by atomic event verbs, which those objects exemplify. A description of an event will be non-canonical when it describes the event it does in such a way that the description's holding implies, apart from the way the involved object(s) and time(s) are referred to, that some event, other than the event in question or any of its compositional or temporal parts, occurred, is occurring or will occur, or implies that some entity, other than the ones involved in the event or any of its parts and other than any which exist necessarily, existed, exists, or will exist. That is, a description of an event will be non-canonical when the fact that that event is an instance of the event type which that description says it is implies the existence of an event or other entity which is not involved in the event itself or any of its parts (necessary existents not included). A description of an event is canonical just in case that description would still describe that event even if that event and its compositional and temporal parts and the atomic objects involved in those parts were the only contingently existing things.

Events aggregate into kinds. The class of events divides into sorts which are characterizable by essences which meet conditions (1)–(3) of section I. It seems to me that there are properties of events which are such that if an event has such a property, it could not fail to have it except by not occurring. Of course, the property of being an event is one such; but this property is had by all events and does not divide events into kinds. The properties which I take to meet (1)–(3) and which divide events into kinds are, in the case of atomic events, properties of the sort "being an instance of the atomic event type ϕing." That is, it is of the essence of an atomic event that it be an instance of the atomic event type which it in fact is, that it be an atomic object's exemplifying of the property which is in fact expressed by the atomic event verb which that object in fact exemplifies. If, for example, being a movement through a particular region of space were an atomic event type, on some theory, then if some event is a movement through that region of space, it could not have failed to be a movement through that region except by failing to occur. And this seems reasonable; for how could an atomic event which was such a movement have failed to have been such a movement? Surely, it could not have been, instead, a change in color! In short my conjecture here is that if being an instance of an atomic event type ϕing is a property of some atomic event, e, then necessarily if e occurs then e is an exemplifying by some object at sometime of ϕ (where 'ϕ' is an atomic event verb). So, while events may have lots of properties essentially (e.g., the property of being other than a number), what I want to call "*the* essence of an event," in the case of atomic events, is its property of being an instance of the atomic event type of which it in fact is an instance. Such properties do divide the events into species which constitute kinds of events. (The meeting of condition (3) is trivial, if a criterion of identity can be given for events generally.) The essence of an atomic event can be "read off" its canonical description; if some event's canonical description is '$[x, \phi, t]$,' then the essence of that event is that it be an event of the atomic event type ϕing. And similarly, the essences of events which are not atomic can be read off their canonical descriptions; it is the essence of an event which is not atomic to be an event which is composed (compositionally and temporally) of events which are instances of the atomic event types instances of which in fact compose the event in question.

So, although it is a contingent matter whether or not an event with a certain essence (which belongs, that is, to a certain kind) actually occurs, it is not a contingent matter whether or not an event which actually occurs has the essence (belongs to the kind) which it in fact does.[24] It is not a contingent matter that an event which actually occurs is an instance of the event type which can be read off its canonical description. But it *is* a contingent fact, if it is a fact, that an event is describable by the non-canonical descriptions which in fact describe it. This is so, because the correctness of a non-canonical description clearly depends on the existence of some entity whose existence is implied by the fact that description holds, but whose existence is not implied by the holding of that event's canonical description, whose existence is not implied by the fact that that event has a certain property as its essence (again, I am not interested in entities whose existence is implied by the ways in which the involved object(s) and interval(s) of time are referred to). For example, being an instance of the type "being an event which causes an explosion" cannot be the essence of any event, and 'did something which causes an explosion' (and 'causes an explosion') cannot occupy the event-property place in the canonical description of any event, for the holding of that description by any event clearly implies the existence of some *other* event which is an explosion, and the holding of no canonical description of any event can have such an implication. No event which is in fact an event of that sort has to be an event of that sort; such an event could have occurred and yet not have caused an explosion. Events which are causally related are only contingently so related, despite the fact that if e caused f, then 'the cause of f caused f' is true and necessary. However, the event which in fact caused the explosion could not have been other than a ϕing, if being a ϕing is the essence of the event which was in fact an event which caused an explosion. Properties of events which do not correspond to event verbs which can appear in canonical descriptions (or combinations of them) are contingent properties of the events which have them, and are not essences of events; hence they do not divide events into kinds. Only the essences of events, the properties which can be read off their canonical descriptions, do that.

VII

It is clear now, I think, what the criterion of identity for events, construed as movements in quality spaces by objects at intervals of times, should be. As I argued in section IV, it is possible for an object to move in more than one quality space at the same time. But it is *not* possible for an object to move more than once in the same quality space at the same time; for that would amount to an object's having mutually incompatible properties simultaneously. Indeed, the very idea of such multiple movements by the same object only barely, if at all, makes sense, for the *raison d'être* of dividing qualities into spaces is to be able to say what change in property by an object at a time a particular, individual event consists in.

The essence of an atomic event is its being an instance of the atomic event type which the subject of that event exemplifies; and that atomic event type is the property of moving from having one to having another property in a particular atomic quality space. The essence of an atomic event, of course, determines only that that event belongs to a certain kind. What individuates events of that kind, that is, what makes an event of that kind this or that particular event of that kind, is the fact that this or that event is a change of that kind involving some particular object which occurred at some particular interval of time. If matter is what individuates entities of a certain kind, then the matter of an event belonging to a certain kind is the object and interval of time involved. If, for example, x were an atomic object, and moving from point p to point p' were an atomic event type, according to some theory, then what could possibly show that there could be two such movements by x from p to p' both of which occur at a certain interval of time?[25] Nothing could show that, and that suggests that canonical descriptions of atomic events refer at most to just one event; the occurrence of an atomic event with a certain canonical description guarantees the uniqueness of that description.[26] Thus, if e_1 is an atomic event whose canonical description is '[x, ϕ, t]' and e_2 is an atomic event whose canonical description is '[y, ϕ', t'],' then $e_1 = e_2$ if and only if x = y, ϕ = ϕ', and t = t'. Atomic events are identical if and only if they are atomic events of the same kind which are simultaneous changes in the same object, if and only if they are simultaneous movements by the same atomic objects through the same portion of the same atomic quality space. ϕ' must be identical with ϕ, for any event which is identical with an event whose essence is being a ϕing must itself be an event whose essence is being a ϕing.

The extension to events which are not atomic is straightforward; non-atomic events are identical just in case they are composed of the same atomic events, and temporal sequences of atomic and nonatomic events are identical just in case they are temporal sequences of the same atomic and non-atomic events which occur in the same order. Since all events are either atomic events or composed (either compositionally or temporally) of atomic events, and since the canonical descriptions of events describe the events they do in terms of the atomic events which constitute them, and since the canonical descriptions of events both give their essences and individuate them, the foregoing may be summarized in the following criterion of identity for events:

(E) For any objects, e and e', if e and e' are events, then e = e' if and only if e and e' have the same canonical description.

VIII

One task which a criterion of identity for events should perform is that of getting at the roots of the disputes concerning the truth of particular identity statements concerning events; it should be able to perform that task because it states what kind of fact is especially relevant to settling such disputes concerning events. It cannot be expected to settle, by itself, those disputes; but it can be expected to discover the reasons why they arise and to say what it would, in principle, take to resolve them.

The theory of events which I have tried to sketch out in this paper is a theory which construes events as particulars, that is, as concrete, datable, non-repeatable occurrences. Among the philosophers who understand events in this way are Kim, Goldman, and Davidson; and the disagreements between the first two, on the one hand, and the third, on the other, have been both frustrating and legion. Goldman, in *A Theory of Human Action,* devotes the first half of the first chapter to providing counterexamples to event-identity claims made by Davidson, and later develops a theory of the relationship between the events which he thinks cannot be identified. And Davidson, commenting on a paper by R. M. Martin in which he puts forward a view concerning event-identity similar to Kim's and Goldman's, writes:

> . . . by Martin's account no meeting is identical with an encounter, though between the same individuals and the same time. . . . No stabbing can be a killing and no killing can be a murder, no arm-raising a signalling, and no birthday party a celebration. I protest.[27]

Goldman has denied the possibility of identity claims similar to the ones Martin denied, as well as one asserting the identity of a particular strolling and a particular leisurely strolling; and Kim has done likewise. The view which I am advocating provides us, I believe, with a way of getting to the bottom of these disagreements.

At first glance, the criterion of identity for events advanced by Kim and Goldman seems much like (E). For a certain class of cases, the proposals give the same results; and for atomic events, the proposals even look the same. But there are crucial differences. Kim and Goldman derive their "standard" descriptions of events from sentences of the form 'x ϕed at t,' where 'ϕ' is a verb of change (or unchange). The standard description derived from such a sentence is '[x, ϕ, t],' which is to be read as 'x's exemplifying ϕ at t.'[28] And their criterion of identity for events is this: if e_1 = [x, ϕ, t], and e_2 = [y, ϕ', t'], then $e_1 = e_2$ if and only if x = y, $\phi = \phi'$, and t = t'. And $\phi = \phi'$ only if every ϕing is a ϕ'ing and *vice versa*. For this reason, no shooting is a killing because there are shootings which are not killings, no arm-waving is a signalling because there are arm-wavings which are not signallings, and so on. And thus Davidson protests. These consequences all result from the idea that identical events must be events of the same type, and that for types to be identical all their instances must be identical, and from the idea that the type of which an event is an instance can be read off a sentence of the form 'x ϕed at t,' where a sentence of that form reports the occurrence of an event. So what is the difference between the Kim-Goldman criterion of identity for events and (E)?

My canonical descriptions of events can *not* be derived from just any event-reporting sentence of the form 'x ϕed at t' (even when a sentence of that form is made true by there being exactly one ϕing by x at t). For me, in order for a term of the form 'x's ϕing at t' to be a canonical description of an event, and hence for it to be re-writable as '[x, ϕ, t],' being a ϕing must be the *essence* of the event described. If so, then it is clear why it is the case that if an event whose essence is the property of being a ϕing is identical with an event whose essence is the property of being a ϕ'ing, then every event whose essence is the property of being a ϕing must be an event whose essence is the property of being a ϕ'ing. For identical events must have the same essence; so the essence which is the property of being a ϕing just is the property of being a ϕ'ing; and the property of being a ϕing cannot be the property of being a ϕ'ing unless every ϕing is a ϕ'ing and *vice versa*. An event, e, is a ϕing if and only if there is an object, x, and an interval of time, t, such that e is x's exemplifying ϕ at the interval t. But not every term of the form 'x's exemplifying ϕ at (the interval) t' is a canonical description of e; for that, 'ϕ' must, in the case of atomic events, be an atomic event verb.[29] Thus, from the fact that e = [x, ϕ, t] and the fact that e is also a ϕ'ing, though it does follow that e is x's exemplifying ϕ' at t, it does not follow that e = [x, ϕ', t]. For it to follow, it would have to be the case that being a ϕ'ing is the essence of e. And if that were true, then, of course, $\phi = \phi'$, and every event which is ϕing would have to be a ϕ'ing as well. Thus, the claim that it is necessary that no event which is a ϕing can be an event which is a ϕ'ing unless every ϕing is a ϕ'ing and *vice versa* is a claim which, though Kim and Goldman are willing to endorse quite generally, I can endorse only in case being a ϕing and being a ϕ'ing are the essences of the events of which those events are instances.

But, when being a ϕing and being a ϕ'ing are not essences of the events of which they are instances, this glaringly does not go. The reason for this is that the non-essential properties of events are only contingently properties of the events which have them; an event's having such a property is contingent upon the contingent existence of entities whose existence is logically independent of the existence of the event (and its event parts and involved objects) which has such a property. So, any event which has such a non-essential property could have failed to have had that property, and would have failed to have had it in any situation in which the independent and contingent entities, whose existence is entailed by the event's having that property, fail to exist. Hence, this ϕing could be identical with that ϕ'ing, even though not every ϕing is a ϕ'ing and not every ϕ'ing a ϕing, if either or both being a ϕing and being a ϕ'ing are not the essences of the events which have those properties. I am inclined then to think that the cases of alleged event-identity over which there has been so much dispute are cases in which the events involved are not described in terms of their essences. Let us consider a few such cases.

Some events are described by the use of what are called "causal" verbs; 'a's shooting of b at t' and 'c's closing the door at t' would count as such descriptions. Now, if such causal verbs can be given analysis so that 'x ϕed y at t,' where 'ϕ' is a causal verb, is to be understood, roughly, as 'x did something at t which causes y's being ϕed,'[30] then it becomes clear that being a ϕing, where 'ϕ' is a causal verb, cannot be the essence of any event which is in fact a ϕing. For the having of that property by any event is contingent upon the occurrence of y's being ϕed, and that is arguably not a part of, but is a result of, the event which is the ϕing. If such a view can be sustained, then one cannot argue that, for example, no shooting can be a killing (or a moving of one's finger) on the grounds that there are shootings which are not killings (or finger-movings which are not shootings), or that some shooting (or finger-moving) which in fact resulted in a death (or in a shooting) need not have so resulted. For such an argument is germane only in connection with events described in terms of their essences. So, although this does not show that any shooting is a killing, what is shown is that it is not impossible, despite the obvious fact that not every shooting results in a death, that some shootings are identical with some killings.

Can someone's extending his arm out the car window ever be his signalling for a turn? Again, it might be argued that such events cannot be identical for there are arm stickings which are not signallings. It is then suggested that such events are intimately related, though distinct, and an account may get offered in which it is suggested that a signalling occurs because an arm sticking occurs within a set of circumstances which includes a rule such as "extending one's arm out the car window while driving counts as signalling for a turn."[31] But, it is countered, the arm sticking event is an event which occurs in such a set of circumstances, and so is, on that occasion, the signalling. What seems to be going on is this. Being a signalling is not an essence of events, for to describe an event as a signalling is to describe it in terms of one of that event's causes, perhaps, an intending to obey some law. Being a signalling, then, is a property which an event can have, but only if some other event, distinct from the signalling occurs. Hence, it is not the case that any event which is a signalling must be a signalling; and, hence, not every arm sticking out a car window need be a signalling in order for some such arm stickings to be signallings.

In a similar way, it cannot be shown that Jones's running the mile in three and a half minutes and Jones's breaking the world's record cannot be identical, even when he breaks the record with that running, by insisting that not every such run is a record breaking one. For any event which is a breaking of the world's record for the mile is so only because, in part, there once occurred some other event which was both a setting of the latest world's record for the mile and a running of the mile in more than three and a half minutes. Being a breaking of the world's record for the mile is a property of events such that events which have it have it only contingently; it is not a property which can be the essence of a kind of event. Thus, it is not necessary that every running of the mile in three and a half minutes be a breaking of the world's record for the mile in order for one such running to be a record breaking one.[32]

In each of the three cases just discussed, what seems to stand in the way of saying that the appropriate events are identical and leads to disagreement is the same thing. And that is the tendency to treat each of the event "types" in question (e.g., shooting, killing, signalling, breaking the world's record) as if they were, on my account, the essences of the events which are of that "type." But, in each case, it would be clearly wrong to treat them so. And that is, in effect, admitted by those who would insist that such identity claims are false. For what is claimed about such properties (e.g., being a killing), in the defense of the falsity of those identity claims, is that they are properties of the events which have them (indeed, the events which have them occur) only because other things, quite independent of the event itself, are in fact the case. But it is for precisely that reason, as I see the matter, that such properties cannot be the essences of the events which have them. Identical events must have the same essence. They must, of course, share all their other properties as well. But their sharing those other properties in common will be a matter of contingent fact only. If being a ϕing is an essence of events, but being a ϕ' is not, then every event which is identical with an event which is a ϕing and a ϕ'ing must be a ϕ'ing as well as a ϕing. But not every ϕing need be a ϕ'ing; so not every event which is identical with a ϕing must be a ϕ'ing as well. None of this shows for certain that the pairs of events discussed are indeed identical; such certain judgments await reduction of those events to their atomic constituents. But in advance of such a reduction, we can, and we do, make some good guesses, and back them up with some good reasons.

So we can, I believe, have our cake, eat it, and have some left over. We can, that is, have a theory which explains what kind of thing an event is, which explains what the essence of an event is, and which explains what must be the case in order for an identity statement concerning events to be true. That, in conjunction with a belief in the power of an ontology of events, construed as particulars, to aid in the explanation and clarification of a great deal of what we think needs to be explained and clarified, constitutes as powerful a reason as I can imagine for thinking that there are indeed such things as events.

APPENDIX ON RELATIONAL CHANGE

It has been contended that there are relational changes.[33] Xanthippe's becoming a widow and Sam's becoming an uncle are examples of relational, or as they are sometimes called, (merely) Cambridge, changes. A relational change which an object undergoes is not, it is said, a real alteration in the object which undergoes it. Now all change consists of some object's having and then lacking some property; but a relational change consists in an object's having and then lacking a property solely in virtue of the fact that that object bears some relation to an object which "really" changed or altered. Xanthippe's becoming a widow consisted entirely of her being the last wife of Socrates when he died. At one time, I suggested that relational changes were not events, and the reason for that was that relational changes did not seem to be changes whose occurrences are caused (for their alleged causes would cause them simultaneously and at a distance), though events were changes whose occurrences are caused.[34] Now, I do still think that all this true, though of course the claim that all events are caused and all relational changes are not is contentious. But, inasmuch as events and relational changes are all changes in objects, it seemed to me[35] reasonable that a single, nondisjunctive criterion of identity for all changes should be given. It now seems to me that I was wrong about that.

To be an event, according to the theory which I have been advancing in this paper, is to be a movement by an object (or objects) in a quality space (or spaces) at an interval of time, where that movement is either a movement by an atomic object in an atomic quality space or is compounded (either compositionally or sequentially or both) of such atomic movements. But any such event must have a canonical description which specifies a property which that event, if it occurs, must have (its essence). But in order for any property to be the essence of any event, it must be a property which that event can have independently of the occurrence of any other event (other than its parts) and independently of the existence of any object other than ones involved in the event (or its parts), necessary existents not included.

It is clear, then, that no relational change can have an essence of that sort. For it is of the essence of a relational change that the following constitutes a criterion for distinguishing relational changes from among all the changes that there can be:

> For all c, x, and t, c is a *relational change* in an object, x, which occurs at a time, t, if and only if c is a change in x which occurs at t and it is not possible for c to occur and for no other change (apart from changes which are parts of c) to occur at t.[36]

For example, Xanthippe could not have become a widow, that is, Xanthippe's becoming a widow could not have occurred, if there were not some change, namely a death, which the person to whom she was married underwent. Of course, relational changes have essences; but the essences of relational changes are relational properties. Hence, there can be no resolution of a relational change into its atomic parts, for it has none, in the sense of 'atomic' operative in this paper.

One must be careful to distinguish relational changes, which occur only because other changes occur, from non-relational changes with non-canonical descriptions, which have those descriptions only because some entity (distinct from that change, or its parts, or its involved objects) exists. The distinction is this. In the case of some non-relational change (an event), e, the failure of some entity, whose existence makes it possible for e to have some non-canonical description, d, to exist implies only that e is not, in such a situation, describable by d. But, e would still have occurred. However, in the case of a relational change, c, the failure of some change, whose occurrence c depends on, to occur implies that c fails to occur. Consider these two cases. Case (1): at t, object a is 40°F and object b is 50°F, and at t', a, by being heated, is 60°F, and b, by being cooled, is 45°F. Here, it is true to say that b has become cooler with respect to a. But that change in b is a non-relational one, an event. For, although if a had not existed, b could not have gotten cooler with respect to a, b's dropping 5°F would still have occurred. And b's dropping 5°F is just what its becoming cooler with respect to a consists in, when a does exist and has its temperature increased by 20°F. Case (2): at t, a is 40°F and b is 50°F, and at t', a, by being heated, is 60°F and b is still 50°F. Here, it is also true to say that b has become cooler with respect to a. But that change in b is, in this case, a relational change. For while it is the case that if a's increase in temperature had not occurred, b could not have become cooler with respect to a, it is also the case, in such a situation, that *no* change in b could have occurred which would have been its getting cooler with respect to a had a existed and had its temperature increased. Thus, one cannot, in general, tell, just by looking at a description of a change, whether it is a description of a relational change or a non-canonical description of an event (a non-relational change). One tells that by discovering whether or not the change actually described by that description could have occurred, if it were the universe's only change, however that change would be described in such circumstances.

This shows the sense in which it is true to say that relational changes are "dependent" entities. For there could not be relational changes in objects unless there were other changes. But there could be non-relational changes (events) without relational ones, say in a universe which consists of only one contingent, partless, changing thing. This is a deeper sense, I think, than the sense in which it is sometimes claimed that events are dependent entities, dependent for their existence on objects whose changes are those events; for it might be argued that the objects whose changes are those events could not have existed unless they changed; it might be part of the concept of a physical object that physical objects are the subjects of events.

In any event, it is clear that the criterion of identity for relational changes cannot be the same as that for events, for relational changes do not have the same sort of canonical descriptions that events have. It also seems clear that there cannot be a criterion of identity which will do for all changes which is non-disjunctive and stronger than Leibniz's Law, for events and relational changes do not share, in the requisite sense, a common essence. And it seems clear what the pattern for a criterion of identity for relational changes must be; it must draw on what the essence of relational change is, and, in so doing, reveal the dependent character of relational changes on events. In short, it must look something like this

> (R) For all c and c', if c and c' are relational changes, then c = c' if and only if the occurrence of c and the occurrence of c' are dependent on the occurrence of exactly the same events.

What all this suggests is that although there are both events and relational changes, and although relational changes are dependent on events, they do not belong to the same metaphysical category of existent. The class of entities which are changes in things, like the class of entities which are abstract, is just too broad for that.[37]

NOTES

1. Several things should be said about (1). (a) I am not much concerned, here, with whether existence is a property. (1) can be read either as '$\Box(x)(\phi x \supset \Box(x \text{ exists} \supset \phi x))$' or as '$\Box(x)(\phi x \supset \Box(\exists y)(y = x) \supset \phi x])$.' (b) The sense of necessity operant here is the sense of necessity in quantified S5 given a Kripkean semantics in which the Barcan formula fails. (c) I prefer (1) as it is, i.e., '$\Box(x)(\phi x \supset \Box(x \text{ exists} \supset \phi x))$' to '$\Box(x)(\phi x \supset \Box \phi x)$,' because the latter commits one, on a natural interpretation, either to the view that all objects which exist exist in all possible worlds or to the view that objects have their essences in worlds in which those objects do not exist. To avoid confronting this issue, I adopt the weaker former over the latter (which implies the former).

2. Every property which is an essence, in my sense, will be an essential property in Plantinga's (except perhaps for existence, if it's a property at all), though not every essential property is an essence. Tautological properties, like being either green or non-green, are essences for me; but I don't mind that, for I am interested in what I shall call kinds and metaphysical

categories; and those concepts will require the addition to (1) and (2) of condition (3), below, which will rule out tautological properties as being essences of kinds or metaphysical categories (if there is more than one kind of thing—and that I am, in this essay, taking for granted).

3. What I mean here is that if there is more than one kind of abstract entity, that is, abstract entities which are, say, propositions, sets, properties, then we could get, for a criterion of identity for abstract entities construed as such, nothing better than

> if x and y are abstract entities, then x = y if and only if x and y are propositions and R(x,y), or x and y are sets and R'(x,y), or x and y are properties and R''(x,y), or. . . ,

where the expressions of the form 'R(x,y),' 'R'(x,y),' 'R''(x,y),' etc. each give a criterion of identity for the abstract entities which are propositions, sets, properties, etc., respectively. Criteria of identity of the form displayed I wish to call "disjunctive," and I mean to rule out any class of objects, as forming a metaphysical category of thing or a kind of thing, whose members can have nothing better than a disjunctive criterion of identity. Of course, an acceptable criterion of identity for a class having an essence ϕ must meet other conditions as well (e.g., it must not contain, after 'if and only if,' the identity sign flanking terms whose references are ϕs), but non-disjunctiveness is the only one that really concerns me here,

4. So, if the ϕ is a metaphysical category, then ϕ is a kind (but not necessarily *vice versa*), and if ϕ is a kind, then ϕ is an essence (but not necessarily *vice versa*).

5. A fourth possibility is that we've not been clever enough. This is different from the third case, for in this case, we might know perfectly well that we've got a kind on our hands and know what that kind's essence is, but just not have been smart, lucky, or diligent enough to hit on the right criterion of identity. This possibility is, from a metaphysical point of view, uninteresting. And attacks on entities, based on Quine's dictum, when this possibility describes the actual state of the situation, are similarly uninteresting, though it might be difficult to say when that is the case.

6. This argument is Davidson's and it appears in his paper, "The Individuation of Events," in this volume, p. 330.

7. In N. Rescher (ed.), *The Logic of Decision and Action* (Pittsburgh: University of Pittsburgh Press, 1967), pp. 96–103. Davidson's paper is to be to found in that volume as well, pp. 81–95.

8. Ibid., pp. 116–17.

9. Myles Brand has continued it in his paper, "Particulars, Events, and Actions," in Brand and Walton (eds.), *Action Theory* (Dordrecht: D. Reidel, 1976).

10. If we say (1) that an event, e, is located at a place, p, at a time, t, if and only if all objects, o, which are involved in e at t are in p at t, and (2) that an object, o, is involved in e at t if and only if it is the case that if e occurs (or is occurring) at t, then o changes (or is changing) at t, and a change in o at t is identical with e at t, then we can define 'the minimal location of e at t' as 'the location of the smallest object a change in which is identical with e at t.' See "The Individuation of Events," p. 331.

11. I am excluding, here, changes such as coming into existence and going out of existence. And I would also like a restriction placed in the choice of properties such that it will not be the case that something changes just because it has and then lacks a property the having and then lacking of which is just what that object's persisting consists in. Also, it should be noted that not every object which is the subject of some change, according to the criterion of change just employed, is *ipso facto* the subject of some event. This distinction is discussed in the appendix to this paper. But, so far as the main body of the paper is concerned, one should understand talk of changes as talk of events.

12. A change, say, from being F to being G, takes place *during* t, if t is an interval of long enough duration to include the time at which the changing thing was F and the time at which it was G. A change takes place *at* t, if t is the shortest interval during which it takes place.

13. So, when I later speak of an object's exemplifying or having some dynamic property *at* a time t, t must be construed as an interval of time, not as an instant. Of course, an object can exemplify a static property or an instantaneous dynamic property at successive instants (and, hence, over an interval). And so, some property-expressions may be ambiguous with respect to its picking out a dynamic or an instantaneous dynamic property. But, no object can have a dynamic property at an instant; for to have a dynamic property at t is to have and then lack a static property, and that takes "two" times at least.

14. I want, here, to acknowledge my thanks to David Kaplan, for it was in discussion with him that the idea of a quality space in which things change arose. I do not know, however, whether or not he would approve of what I've done with this idea, or even how I have explicated it.

15. My thanks go to Alexander Rosenberg for this last observation which was made in the course of his comments on my paper, "Events and Quality Spaces," read at the APA, Western Division, Meetings, 1 May 1976. The effects of this observation are felt in the second and third paragraphs of section V which were motivated by an example of Rosenberg's. Sections III and IV of this present paper are revisions of parts of my APA paper.

16. This and the previous paragraph might show what it is that is so plausible about, irrespective of the eventual outcome of, a criterion of identity for events given in terms of sameness of causes and effects.

17. The definitions which follow, particularly (D3), are motivated in addition by my interest in giving an account of events as the exemplifyings by objects of dynamic properties at times (which are intervals). This account comes in Section VI, and is ultimately motivated by my sketch in Section IV of the idea that events are movements through quality spaces by objects, where I take that idea to capture the idea that events are changes.

18. The objects which are to serve, in my view, as atomic are objects which are extended in time and have no temporal parts. Thus, when I speak of an object's exemplifying a property at a time (either an instant or an interval), I do not mean that some object, x-at-t, has timelessly some property P. Nor do I mean that the object, x, has the property of being P-at-t. I take 'has the property P at t' to express a two-place relation holding between objects and times.

19. The complication in (D3), which begins with (b), is needed because we will not want to say that two events, one consisting of a movement by an object from having P_i to having P_k "directly," and one consisting of a movement by an object from having P_i to having P_j to having P_k, are two events of the same type. With the complication, we can have an atomic event which consists of an atomic object's movement from having P_i to having P_j to having P_k. But, if a movement is one such that if its subject passes through P_j in getting from having P_i to P_k, and it does so only contingently, then that movement cannot be atomic and must be construed as a sequence of atomic movements. One price which must be paid for this is that some atomic events will be construable as temporal sequences of atomic events as well. But with the complication, though it may be the case that some atomic events have atomic events among their parts, atomic events "of the same type" must always have exactly the same atomic event part. As an example, no movement (in a flat two-dimensional space, say) from a point p_1 to a point p_2 can be atomic, if one instance of that "type" can be straight and another curved. The restriction (b) in (D3) makes the "directionality" (in general) of a movement (change) part of the essence of such movements (changes). The result of all this, as will be clear, is that some events may have more than one canonical description; this, however, will not imply that some events may have more than one essence, in the sense of 'essence' to be discussed. So, in what follows, I shall speak of *the* canonical description of an event; but, though some events can have more than one, this simplification will be harmless, since from a canonical description of an atomic event construed as a sequence we can, by consulting the relevant quality space, derive the canonical description of the event construed as not being a sequence. For if we know that an atomic event is being construed as a sequence, we know automatically what that sequence must be. The restriction in (D3) shows us that, for it shows that the only sequences which can be atomic events are those events which must (according to T) pass certain points in the quality space in getting from P_i to P_k.

20. I suspect that not every combination of simultaneous atomic events will be a non-atomic event; there seems to be no event which consists of this pot of water's boiling at t and an eruption of a volcano on Jupiter at t. Similarly, not every group of atomic and non-atomic events occurring over a stretch of time counts as a sequence; there seems to me to be no event which consists of this pot of water's boiling at t and then Jupiter's turning on its axis at t'. Surely, there must be some restrictions dealing with which combinations of events constitute events. But it is not my intention, here, to delve into this question.

21. 'Rots' also might pick out an instantaneous dynamic property (if it were an atomic event verb), for it would be true of the wood at each instant during which the wood is rotting, and its being true of the wood at any such instant would imply that at different surrounding instants the wood had different static properties. But then it would also have a dynamic sense, in which it picks out a property of the wood which the wood would have at the time of the whole interval of time at which the wood was rotting (viz. the property of first being wholly unrotten and then completely rotten). And it is the latter, dynamic, property that is of concern here. Of course, the fact that the wood has the dynamic property of rotting is not independent of the fact that it has at instants in the interval of the rotting the instantaneous dynamic property of rotting.

22. The event types to which events which are not atomic belong can be derived from the atomic event types to which their atomic constituents belong.

23. See, for example, Kim's "Events and Their Descriptions," in *Essays in Honor of Carl G. Hempel*, pp. 198–215, his "Events as Property Exemplifications," in this volume, pp. 336–347, and Goldman's *A Theory of Human Action* (Englewood Cliffs: Prentice-Hall, 1970). It might be noted here that my canonical descriptions cannot be descriptions of states, but only of events. I am inclined not to lump events and states into one category of thing, since, it seems to me, there are important differences between events and states, and I don't see any overriding motive for ignoring those differences. But this is not the place to go into this issue.

24. It is, of course, to be understood here that what is contingent or not must be relativized to the theory

against the background of which events are given their canonical descriptions.

25. Of course, two atomic events of the same type involving the same subject can occur *during* a certain period of time, but not *at* a certain period of time. An event occurs *at* t when t is the shortest interval of time during which that event occurs.

26. Of course, two or more events of the same type which are not atomic could occur simultaneously; but for that to be the case, at least some of their atomic constituents must be different.

27. In "On Events and Event-Descriptions," *Fact and Experience,* ed. J. Margolis, (Oxford: Blackwell, 1969), p. 81.

28. I am not especially concerned here with the fact that 'x ϕed at t' is general with respect to ϕings by x at t, while 'x's exemplifying ϕ at t occurred' is not.

29. Thus, one can define 'e is a ϕing by x at t' as follows: an event, e, is a ϕing by x at t if and only if there is an object, x, and an interval of time, t, such that either (a) e is x's exemplifying ϕ at t, where being a ϕing is not the essence of e, or (b) e is x's exemplifying ϕ at t, where being a ϕing is the essence of e. Note that if e is an atomic event and being a ϕing is the essence of e, then e = [x, ϕ, t], but not otherwise. Also, it seems as if the Kim-Goldman definition of 'e is a ϕing by x at t' would delete alternative (a).

30. See my paper, "Actions, Results, and the Time of a Killing," *Philosophia* 8 (1978), for a defense of a version of this analysis.

31. See Goldman, op. cit., pp. 25–26.

32. Another class of identity claims, typified by 'Sebastian's stroll = Sebastian's leisurely stroll,' gets dealt with in a different way. The issue here, it seems to me, has to do with events and vectors of events. It seems unlikely that being a leisurely stroll should be the essence of any event, even if being a stroll were. Being leisurely seems to be better construed as a property of events (rather than being a leisurely stroll being construed as a property of strolling things); and being a leisurely one seems clearly to be a contingent property of such events.

33. See Kim's "Noncausal Connections," *Noûs* 8 (1974), pp. 41–52, and my "Events, Changes, and the Non-extensionality of 'Become,'" *Philosophical Studies* 28(1975), pp. 131–36.

34. See my just cited paper for the suggestion, and Kim's for the reasons.

35. In "Events and Quality Spaces."

36. This criterion is motivated and defended in my paper, "Relational Change and Relational Changes," *Philosophical Studies* (1978).

37 1 would like to express my gratitude to Michael McKinsey with whom I spent a great deal of time (a lot of his patience) talking about the issues discussed in this paper. He made some very valuable suggestions (especially in section I, but elsewhere as well), and tried to make me less muddled. I am certain that his suggestions were valuable; but I am not certain that he succeeded in making me less muddled, though that was not his fault. And my thanks also go to Lawrence Powers for some helpful suggestions. I am also indebted to the editors and referees at the *Canadian Journal of Philosophy* whose suggestions and criticisms forced me to make this essay better than it would otherwise have been. I am, of course, solely responsible for what is in this essay.

Reading Questions

1. Lombard states that he wants to provide a criterion of identity for events that is more robust than Leibniz's Law. What is Leibniz's Law? Why does Lombard think it too weak to be a completely satisfactory criterion of identity?
2. Lombard claims that if we lack a criterion of identity stronger than Leibniz's Law for a given class of entities, we do not have a clear idea of what it is to be an entity of that kind. Is this right? Suppose we don't know the necessary and sufficient conditions for a plot of land to be a garden (when does a garden become a farm? are gardens essentially cultivated or not? etc.). Does this mean that we don't know a garden when we see one? If we do, why couldn't we similarly know an event when we see one without having identity criteria?
3. Lombard accepts a dichotomy between events and states. What is his reasoning? Imagine an eternally existing, eternally unchanging object. We might say that nothing (no event) happened to such an object, and so its existence is rather dull. But should we say that its existence, or lifespan, is itself an event? Is there an event of the object's unchanging duration? Or is Lombard right in thinking that the existence of such an object is strictly uneventful?
4. How does Lombard use the appeal to the essences of events to distinguish his account of events from Kim's?

Further Readings

Books

Bennett, Jonathan. 1988. *Events and Their Names.* Indianapolis: Hackett.

Casati, Roberto, and Achille C. Varzi. 1997. *Fifty Years of Events: An Annotated Bibliography 1947 to 1997.* Bowling Green: The Philosophy Documentation Center.

Davidson, Donald. 1980. *Essays on Actions and Events.* Oxford: Oxford University Press.

Lombard, Lawrence B. 1986. *Events: A Metaphysical Study.* London: Routledge and Kegan Paul.

Thomson, Judith Jarvis. 1977. *Acts and Other Events.* Ithaca, NY: Cornell University Press.

Articles

Bach, Kent. 1980. "Actions Are Not Events." *Mind* 89:114–120.

Chisholm, Roderick M. 1990. "Events Without Times: An Essay On Ontology." *Noûs* 24 (3): 413–427.

Cleland, Carol. 1991. "On the Individuation of Events." *Synthèse* 86 (2): 229–254.

Gill, Kathleen. 1993. "On the Metaphysical Distinction Between Processes and Events." *Canadian Journal of Philosophy* 23 (3): 365–384.

Hacker, P. M. S. 1981. "Events and the Exemplification of Properties." *Philosophical Quarterly* 31:242–247.

______. 1982. "Events and Objects in Space and Time." *Mind* 92: 1–19.

Hughes, Christopher. 1994. "The Essentiality of Origin and the Individuation of Events." *Philosophical Quarterly* 44 (174): 26–44.

Katz, Bernard D. 1983. "Perils of an Uneventful World." *Philosophia* 13: 1–12.

Kim, Jaegwon. 1973. "Causation, Nomic Subsumption, and the Concept of Event." *The Journal of Philosophy* 70: 217–236.

Levison, Arnold. 1983. "Might Events be Propositions?" *Philosophy and Phenomenological Research* 44: 169–188.

Lewis, David. 1986. "Events." In *Philosophical Papers,* ed. D. Lewis. Vol. 2. Oxford: Oxford University Press.

Lombard, Lawrence B. 1995. "Sooner or Later." *Noûs* 29 (3): 343–359.

Peterson, Philip L. 1989. "Complex Events." *Pacific Philosophical Quarterly* 70: 19–41.

Schmitt, Frederick F. 1983. "Events." *Erkenntnis* 20: 281–294.

Stern, Cindy D. 1988. "The Prospects for Elimination of Event–Talk." *Philosophical Studies* 54: 43–62.

Part VII

Concreta: Substance

E. J. LOWE

Introduction to Substance

THEORIES OF SUBSTANCE CANNOT EASILY BE UNDERSTOOD without some reference to their history—and for our purposes that history begins with Aristotle. Of Aristotle's many works, two have a particular importance for theories of substance: the *Categories* and the *Metaphysics*, of which the former is commonly thought to be the earlier.[1] Commentators disagree about the extent to which Aristotle's views about substance differ between these two works, though most agree that there is some tension between them. Of course, the very word 'substance' is of Latin origin and thus postdates the Greek word 'ousia,' which it is used to translate, and it is a matter of some dispute how good a translation 'substance' provides. But, setting aside such linguistic difficulties, the chief features of Aristotle's theory of substance may be stated as follows.

In the *Categories* (though not in the *Metaphysics*), Aristotle distinguishes between *primary* and *secondary* substances. What he there takes to be primary substances are such items as an individual horse or an individual house, that is, what modern philosophers would call particular concrete things, or 'continuants.'[2] By 'secondary substances,' he means the kinds or species which such things instantiate, such as the (natural) kind *horse* and the (artifactual) kind *house*. However, our main interest in what follows will lie with the primary substances, so henceforth I shall omit the adjective 'primary' in speaking of them. For Aristotle, substances have certain distinctive ontological characteristics, notably the following. First, substances are bearers of qualities, such as color and shape, and these qualities are ontologically dependent upon their bearers: a quality can only exist as the quality of some substance, whereas substances enjoy an independent kind of existence. Second, substances persist through time, very often undergoing qualitative change as they do so, so that one and the same substance can, at different times, be the bearer of contrary qualities (as when a green banana becomes yellow). Qualitative change of this sort is to be distinguished from *substantial* change, which occurs when a substance either comes into existence or ceases to be (as, for example, when an animal is born or dies).

This essay was commissioned especially for this volume and appears here for the first time.

The phenomenon of substantial change presents a problem, however, as Aristotle recognizes in the *Metaphysics*. The problem is one of reconciling this phenomenon with the deeply held conviction of many philosophers, Aristotle included, that nothing can come from nothing or entirely pass away into nothing. When a substance is created or perishes, something must precede and follow it that somehow survives the processes of creation and destruction. It is this requirement, it would seem, that motivates the most striking new feature of Aristotle's account of substance in the *Metaphysics:* his introduction of the distinction between *matter* and *form*. In the *Metaphysics*, Aristotle treats particular concrete things, such as an individual horse or house—the primary substances of the *Categories*—as being, in some sense, combinations of matter and form. Very roughly, a thing's matter is what it is composed of and its form is the way its matter is so organized as to confer upon it the properties characteristic of a thing of its kind. Thus, the matter of a house is the bricks and beams of which it is composed and its form is the structural arrangement of those bricks and beams that gives the house its characteristic shape and enables it to serve its characteristic function of providing human shelter. These bricks and beams exist prior to the creation of the house and, typically, survive its subsequent destruction. The same might be said of the organic molecules composing an animal or the bronze composing a statue.

A thing's form is *essential* to it, in the sense that loss of that form brings about its destruction (as when the bricks and beams of a house are taken apart), but other features of a thing (such as the color of a house) are only *accidental*, so that alteration in respect of them constitutes merely qualitative change in that thing. Of course, items like the bricks and beams of a house may themselves be seen as combinations of matter and form, so that the Aristotelian picture envisages a hierarchy of composition, which terminates (on some interpretations) in so-called 'prime' matter, an undifferentiated basic stuff of which every material thing is ultimately composed.

However, having introduced the distinction between matter and form, Aristotle is forced to reconsider what items are truly most fundamental, from an ontological point of view: individual concrete things (which he took to be fundamental in the *Categories* but now conceives to be combinations of matter and form), the matter of which those things are composed, or the forms which that matter receives. His verdict, according to many commentators, is that the forms are truly most fundamental and therefore most properly deserve to be called 'substances,' but in this few subsequent philosophers would agree with him. By the seventeenth century, indeed, Aristotelian metaphysics, after a long period of ascendency during medieval times, was generally on the retreat and with it Aristotle's views about substance, though various ingredients of his account survived in modified forms. Thus, for example, John Locke speaks of individual concrete things as being particular substances, but suggests that, because we think of the qualities of such things as being ontologically dependent items incapable of existing on their own, we have to conceive of the things themselves as possessing, in addition to their qualities, a material 'substratum' that acts as the bearer or support of those qualities but that has no positive characteristics of its own—an echo, it would seem, of Aristotle's notion of prime matter.[3] In modern times, this notion resurfaces as that of the 'bare particular,' the somewhat mysterious item which supposedly serves to individuate each particular thing uniquely, differentiating it from any other thing which is exactly like it in respect of all its qualities.[4]

It is only relatively recently that the term 'substance' has been restored to widespread use amongst metaphysicians, almost always to denote the sort of item Aristotle referred to as a 'primary substance' in the *Categories*, that is, a particular concrete thing, or 'continuant.'[5] (There is also, of course, the use of the term 'substance' to denote a kind of *stuff*—such as gold or water—which has long since entered both everyday language and the specialist vocabulary of chemistry; but this use does not directly concern us here.) Restored confidence in this use of the term 'substance' by philosophers no doubt reflects the general resurgence of metaphysics in recent years. Two distinct but related questions concerning substance have been of particular concern to modern metaphysicians. One is the question of how to define the term 'substance,' or how to explicate the concept it expresses. Let us call this the *analytical* question of substance. The other is the question of how, if at all, we are to accommodate substances within a general account of what does or could exist, that is, within a comprehensive system of ontology. Let us call this the *ontological* question of substance.

I have already remarked that most modern metaphysicians use the term 'substance' to denote particular concrete things or 'continuants,' things such as horses, trees, tables, stars, and molecules. But this is only to identify the category of substance by way of example: it doesn't provide us with a clear criterion for membership of that category. To provide such a criterion would, in effect, be to answer the analytical question of substance. One problem here, however, is that, historically speaking, many *different* characteristics have been taken to be definitive of the category of substance. We have already met four in our discussion of Aristotle's views. Substances are variously taken to be (1) entities that are bearers of qualities, (2) entities that enjoy an independent kind of existence, (3) entities that persist through time and are capable of surviving change, and (4) entities that are, somehow, ontologically more fundamental than anything else. Unfortunately, as we saw in our discussion of Aristotle's views, it is debatable whether any single class of entities exhibits all four of these characteristics. Thus, Aristotle himself apparently came to believe that the entities that are bearers of qualities and that persist through time and undergo change—things like horses and tables—are *not* ontologically more fundamental than anything else, since they are combinations of matter and form. So there is no guarantee that the items commonly cited by modern philosophers as examples of 'substances' really possess all the characteristics traditionally associated with the term—and this then raises the question of whether it is not simply misleading to call them 'substances.'

Another problem is that, even if we could agree that one of the characteristics traditionally associated with the term 'substance' is somehow more truly definitive of it than any of the others, these characteristics themselves stand in need of explication. For example, when it is said that substances are entities that enjoy an independent kind of existence, we have to consider what 'independent' means in this context. Do we mean that a substance would have to be something which could exist even if it were the only existing entity? If so, then this raises some further questions. First, what kind of possibility is being expressed by 'could' here? Presumably, either logical or so-called 'metaphysical' possibility (if one distinguishes between the two): and there are, of course, difficult issues that can be raised about what grounds this kind of possibility and how we can have knowledge of possibilities of this kind.[6] Second, there may be a danger that, in defining substance in this way, we are condemning the category of substance to being necessarily empty, since it may be that nothing whatever—not even God—could be the *only* entity in existence. (Even God, it may be argued, must have attributes, which are not simply identical with Himself.) Certainly, it does not appear to be possible for something like a *horse* or a *table* to be the only entity in existence, if only because such a thing necessarily occupies a spatial position or place, which is not identical with it. (Such things also have proper parts, that are distinct from the wholes which they compose.) A converse danger is that, if David Hume was right in maintaining, as he sometimes does, that *everything* that exists is 'distinct and separable' from everything else, then everything will qualify as a substance' and so the term will mark no useful distinction.[7] The essay by Gary Rosenkrantz and Joshua Hoffman addresses many of these problems in the course of presenting a new 'independence' criterion of substance, which very arguably captures the central core of the intuitive notion of substance as that which possesses an independent kind of existence.

Let us turn now to what I earlier called the *ontological* question of substance. Suppose we could hit upon a satisfactory answer to the analytical question of substance which licensed us to describe as 'substances' those items that modern philosophers typically cite as examples of the category—things like horses and tables. Then the question arises as to how we should accommodate things of this kind within a broader ontological scheme. One's answer to this question will, of course, depend on what else one wants to include within one's ontological scheme and which items one takes to be ontologically 'basic.' One may discern three different sorts of answer to this question: (1) eliminativist answers, (2) reductionist answers, and (3) nonreductionist answers. The eliminativist says, quite simply, that *there are no substances*, that is, that items such as horses and tables, as we ordinarily conceive of them, are at best convenient fictions, not to be included in a comprehensive account of what really exists. An eliminativist may adopt this view because, for instance, he espouses a pure event ontology, according to which the only concrete entities that really exist are events, construed as 'basic' items in their own right rather than as, say, changes in the properties or relations of substances. Clearly, though, the eliminativist position is not one that can hold much interest for a substance ontologist, other than as a target of attack. (Typically, the attack will take the form of an attempt to show that the eliminativist's ontology is rendered inadequate by its omission of substances: for instance, it might be argued that an adequate account of time—necessary for an event ontology—demands appeal to the existence of substances persisting through time and capable of undergoing change.[8])

Reductionist answers to the ontological question of substance may take many different forms. A reductionist may adopt the same basic ontology as an eliminativist, but simply disagree with the eliminativist on the question of whether substances can be accommodated within that ontology. Thus, a pure event ontologist might hold that substances—things like horses and tables—*just are* complex events or processes, extended through time (though to most substance ontologists this proposal looks like a straightforward category mistake). One particularly interesting reductionist position is that taken by those ontologists who take substances to be 'bundles' or 'complexes' of compresent or coexemplified properties. This position is further divisible in various ways—for instance, some who espouse it take properties to be universals while others take them to be particulars, that is, *tropes*.[9] The latter view brings with it certain advantages, but also certain disadvantages, as far as the ontlogical question of substance is concerned. On one hand, if substances are taken to be bundles of tropes rather than bundles of universals, then it seems relatively easy to make sense of the idea that two different substances—two bronze spheres, say—could be qualitatively exactly similar (and even that two such spheres could be the sole material occupants of space in some possible world), thereby avoiding commitment to an implausibly strong version of Leibniz's principle of the identity of indiscernibles.[10] On the other hand, when properties are conceived of as particulars—such as the particular redness and roundness of a certain apple—one is apparently constrained to regard them as ontologically dependent entities, which depend for their existence and their identity upon the substances whose properties they are. And then it is difficult to see how, on pain of circularity, those substances can simply be reduced to—that is, identified with—mere 'bundles' of such properties.

In this volume, bundle theories are critically examined and found wanting in the paper by James Van Cleve, while the essay by Peter Simons presents and defends a sophisticated version of the trope-bundle theory. Simons's account recognizes the ontologically dependent character of tropes, but argues that the tropes within the sort of trope-bundle that can be identified with a substance all depend for their existence only upon other tropes within the bundle, thus avoiding (at least in part) the charge of circularity. However, this still leaves unanswered the question of how tropes are to be individuated—that is, what determines their *identity*—given that it would be circular to identify a particular redness, say, as the redness of a certain apple, while simultaneously identifying the apple as a bundle of tropes including this particular redness.

If eliminativist and reductionist answers to the ontological question of substance are both found wanting, all that remains are nonreductionist answers, though these too are not without their problems. One view that might variously be interpreted as reductionist or as nonreductionist is the 'substratum' view, earlier attributed to Locke (though even this is in dispute amongst commentators). On one version of the view, the things we call 'substances'—things like horses and tables—consist of various qualities or properties (conceived of either as universals or as particulars, though in Locke's case certainly as particulars), tied together by a single underlying entity, their substratum, which acts as their 'bearer' or 'support.' This version of the theory would appear to be, strictly speaking, a reductionist account, because neither qualities nor substrata are themselves *substances*, but only the composite entities that consist of a substratum together with the qualities which it supports. But a grave difficulty with this version of the theory is that it is difficult to see what a 'substratum' could *be* and how it could serve the function demanded of it by the theory. For, not being either qualities or substances, substrata on this view would appear to have no positive characteristics of their own, but are necessarily condemned to remain, as Locke himself suggests, 'something we know not what.'

However, there is another possible version of the substratum theory which escapes the foregoing difficulty.[11] On this version, a substratum just *is* a substance—something as familiar to us as a horse or a table. For recall that the putative role of a substratum is to act as the 'bearer' or 'support' of a substance's qualities: but why not say, quite simply, that *the substance itself* is the bearer of its qualities? Then, indeed, we must not say, as in the previous version of the substratum theory, that a substance is composed of a substratum together with the various qualities borne by that substratum, since nothing can be *composed* of itself together with certain other items. What we have, rather, is a genuinely nonreductionist view of substance—what Michael Loux has called the 'substance' theory of substance[12]—which takes substances to be members of a basic ontological category that is perfectly intelligible in its own right. Understandably, though, opponents of this view charge its proponents with complacency for taking as basic and inexplicable a feature of their ontological scheme which demands some sort of explanation, namely, how it is possible for there to be such things as substances—that is, things that 'bear' qualities while not being qualities themselves. However, all explanation must find a terminus somewhere and the only reliable sign that such a terminus has been reached is our persistent failure to find a further explanation. The nonreductionist may urge that, after two thousand years of failure, we have a reliable sign that a terminus has indeed been reached.

NOTES

1. See *Aristotle's Categories and De Interpretatione*, trans. J. L. Ackrill (Oxford: Clarendon Press, 1963) and *The Works of Aristotle*, Vol. 8, *Metaphysica*, trans. W. D. Ross (Oxford: Clarendon Press, 1928).

2. The term 'continuant' was coined by W. E. Johnson: see his *Logic, Part III* (Cambridge: Cambridge University Press, 1924), ch. 7.

3. See John Locke, *An Essay Concerning Human Understanding*, ed. P. H. Nidditch (Oxford: Clarendon Press, 1975), bk. II, ch. 23. For a fuller account of Locke's views on substance, see my *Locke on Human Understanding* (London: Routledge, 1995), ch. 4.

4. See Gustav Bergmann, *Realism* (Madison: University of Wisconsin Press, 1967).

5. See, especially, David Wiggins, *Sameness and Substance* (Oxford: Blackwell, 1980).

6. See further Saul Kripke, *Naming and Necessity* (Oxford: Blackwell, 1980).

7. See David Hume, *A Treatise on Human Nature*, ed. L. A. Selby-Bigge and P. H. Nidditch (Oxford: Clarendon Press, 1978), bk. I, part IV, sect. V, and especially p. 233.

8. For an attempt to argue along such lines, see my "Substance, Identity and Time," *Proceedings of the Aristotelian Society*, supp. vol. 62 (1988): 61–78.

9. For a comprehensive treatment of tropes, or (as they are also sometimes called) property instances, see Keith Campbell, *Abstract Particulars* (Oxford: Blackwell, 1990).

10. For discussion, see Dean W. Zimmerman, "Distinct Indiscernibles and the Bundle Theory," *Mind* 106 (1997): 305–9.

11. Cf. C. B. Martin, "Substance Substantiated," *Australasian Journal of Philosophy* 58 (1980): 3–10.

12. See Michael J. Loux, *Substance and Attribute* (Dordrecht: D. Reidel, 1978); see also Wiggins, *Sameness and Substance*, for an articulation of this point of view.

26 Three Versions of the Bundle Theory

JAMES VAN CLEVE

'A THING (INDIVIDUAL, CONCRETE PARTICULAR) is nothing but a bundle of properties.' If we take it as it stands, this traditional metaphysical view is open to several familiar and, to my mind, decisive objections. Sophisticated upholders of the tradition, such as Russell and Castañeda, do *not* take it as it stands, but I shall argue that even their version of it remains open to some of the same objections. Then I shall suggest a third version of the view that avoids *all* the standard objections, but only at a price I think most people would be unwilling to pay.

I

Let us begin by setting what is wrong with the bundle theory in its crudest version. There are several subversions here, depending on how one unpacks the 'bundle' metaphor. For example, it could be said that a thing is a set of which properties are members, or that it is a *whole* of which properties are parts. Perhaps there are other possibilities, too, but the idea in any case would be (i) that a thing is a complex entity of which properties are the sole constituents, and (ii) that for a thing to

Philosophical Studies *47 (1985) 95–107. © 1985 by D. Reidel Publishing Company. Reprinted by kind permission of Kluwer Academic Publishers.*

have or exemplify a property is for that property to be a constituent of it.

The bundle theory in this form is open to at least six objections.[1] The statement of them below assumes the theory holds a thing to be a *set* of properties, but parallel objections apply to the other alternatives as well.

Objection 1. If a thing were nothing more than a set of properties, any set of properties would fulfill the conditions of thinghood, and there would be a thing for every set. But in fact there are many sets without corresponding things—e.g., the set {being an alligator, being purple}.

Objection 2. If a thing were a set of properties, it would be an eternal, indeed, a necessary, being. For properties exist necessarily, and a set exists necessarily if all its members do.

Objection 3. Exemplification cannot be analyzed simply as the converse of membership. Redness is a member of {redness, roundness}, but it would be absurd—a category mistake—to say that that set is red.

Objection 4. If a thing were a set of properties, it would be incapable of change. For a thing could change its properties only if the set identical with it could change its members, but that is impossible; no set can change its members.[2]

Objection 5. Similarly, if a thing were a set of properties, all of its properties would be *essential* to it: not only could it not change its properties, but it could not have had different properties to start with. This is because it is essential to a set that it contains the very members it does.[3]

Objection 6. If a thing were a set of properties, it would be impossible for two things to have all the same properties, since it is impossible for two sets to have all the same members. Thus, the bundle theory requires the Principle of the Identity of Indiscernibles (PII for short) to be a necessary truth. But PII is not a necessary truth; exceptions to it are conceivable.

This last objection requires elaboration. Anyone who countenances 'impure' properties (properties such as *being identical with individual A*) could maintain that PII is a necessary truth after all, since such properties are obviously unshareable. But not much reflection is needed to see that this defense is not available to proponents of the bundle theory. Impure properties, if such there be, are ontologically derivative from individuals; individuals, if the bundle theory is true, are ontologically derivative from properties. One cannot have it both ways. Hence, the bundle theory cannot admit impure properties, and is committed to the consequence that no two individuals can have all the same *pure* properties.[4] It is to PII in this strong form that counterexamples are conceivable.[5]

So go the objections. Some readers may wonder whether certain of them, especially Objections 4 and 5, are equally applicable if bundles are taken to be wholes rather than sets. For is it not possible for a whole to change its parts, or to have had different parts originally? That depends. If a whole is a mereological *sum,* the answer is no. Indeed, if wholes are sums, the part-whole relation is analogous to the member-set relation in the following ways: wholes are individuated by their parts; they necessarily exist if their parts do; and they have whatever parts they do essentially. So I presume that those who believe a whole can change its parts would deny that a whole is a sum. But if wholes are not sums, what are they? I do not see what else they can be except *logical constructions* out of their parts.[6] In the case at hand, this would mean that individuals are logical constructions out of their properties—a rather different form of the bundle theory, and one to which I shall return in section III.

II

Sophisticated defenders of the bundle theory do not say that a thing is *nothing but* a bundle of properties; they say that it is a bundle whose elements all stand to one another in a certain very important relation. Let us call the relation *co-instantiation.* (Russell speaks of 'compresence,' Goodman of 'togetherness,' and Castañeda of 'consubstantiation.'[7]) The informal explanation of co-instantiation is generally this: it is the relation that relates a number of properties just in case they are all properties of one and the same individual.

This makes it sound very much as though co-instantiation either is or is derivative from a relation that properties bear to an entity in some other ontological category, namely, the category of individuals or things, in which case the bundle theorist's analysis would be circular. He must therefore insist that the informal explanation is merely a ladder to be kicked away, and that co-instantiation is really a relation among properties and nothing else. In Bergmann's language, it must be a *homogeneous tie,* connecting properties with properties, not a heterogeneous tie, connecting properties with things.[8] To make this more plausible, the bundle theorist could perhaps cite the relation of simultaneity, which one might informally explain as the relation that relates two events just in case they occur at the same time, but which it is plausible to regard nonetheless as a dyadic relation holding directly between two events, rather than as a triadic relation among two events and a time.[9] I am not entirely satisfied with the analogy, but since my main concerns with the bundle theory lie elsewhere, I shall simply give the bundle theorist his relation of co-instantiation.

It is convenient to regard co-instantiation as a variably polyadic and possibly infinitary relation—one into which two, three, or infinitely many properties may enter. But this assumption is neither essential to the theory nor presupposed by the objections I shall raise against it.

The cardinal point about co-instantiation is that it is a *contingent* relation.[10] That is, if two or more properties are co-instantiated, it is not in general necessary that this have been so. Redness is co-instantiated with roundness in a ripe tomato, but the two properties might not have been instantiated at all (i.e., each might not have been co-instantiated with *anything* else), and in any case the two need not have been instantiated together.

By introducing co-instantiation into his world, the bundle theorist neatly avoids the first three objections. He need not say that there is a thing for every set of properties, since a collection of properties will yield a thing only if its members are mutually co-instantiated.[11] Nor need he say that a thing exists eternally and necessarily, since it will cease to exist if the properties constituting it cease to be co-instantiated. (The *set* of these properties will still exist, of course, but the thing is not the set; it is something that exists just when the properties in the set are all co-instantiated.[12]) Nor, finally, is he committed to the absurdity that the doubleton {redness, roundness} is red. For he can say that for a bundle to be red it is not enough that it have redness as a constituent; in addition, its members must be co-instantiated, and it must be *complete,* i.e., it must contain every property that could be added to it without generating inconsistency.[13]

But what of the remaining three objections? In so far as the new view identifies a thing with a complex of properties that exists just when its constituents are co-instantiated, it seems to me that they apply with as much force as before. Consider first the objection about change. It is true that in the bundle theorist's world there can be plenty of change of one sort, namely, change in the relational characteristics of properties; a given property or group of them can be co-instantiated now with one property, now with another. But this is not to say that any *individual* can change. If *F* and *G* are coinstantiated first with *H* and later with *K,* so that the complex *FGH* is superseded by the complex *FGK,* what we have is replacement of one individual by another, not change in the properties of one and the same individual. *FGH* is simply not identical with *FGK.*

Consider next the objection about accidental predication. It is true that in the bundle theorist's world there is room for a good deal of contingency. It can be contingent, for example, that snub-nosedness is co-instantiated with wisdom, and that whatever is co-instantiated with being an emerald is also co-instantiated with being green. Moreover, of any individual it will be true that it might not have existed at all, since the properties constituting it might not have been co-instantiated. But it will *not* be true of any individual that it might have existed with properties other than the ones it actually has: we cannot suppose that a complex whose constituents are *F, G,* and *H* might have existed with *F, G,* and *K* as its constituents instead. Thus the bundle theorist's world, though not a Spinozistic one in which every truth is a necessary truth, is nonetheless a Leibnizian one in which every individual has just the properties it does necessarily.

Adam need not have existed at all, but once in existence could not have done otherwise than eat the apple.

Loux has tried to free the bundle theory from this objection by criticizing the assumption that the user of a name must "know in advance all of the properties associated with [the substance bearing the name]."[14] Russell seems to have tried a similar strategy, maintaining that "although '*W*' is, in fact, the name of a certain bundle of qualities, we do not know, when we give the name, *what* qualities constitute *W*."[15] But the objection as I have presented it does not depend on any semantic or epistemological doctrines about the use of names; it depends solely on the nature of the constituent-whole relation. I cannot see, therefore, that either of these maneuvers gets around it.

A more promising way to avoid the objection would be to divide each complete bundle of mutually co-instantiated properties into two sub-bundles, an inner core and an outer fringe, and then to identify individuals with cores rather than with complete bundles. One could then say that an individual has *essentially* just those properties that belong to its core and *accidentally* just those properties that belong to its fringe. More formally, the suggestion would be that an individual X has a property F iff there is a complete bundle of mutually co-instantiated properties Y such that (i) X is a sub-bundle within Y and either (iia) F is an element of X (in which case X has F essentially) or (iib) F is not an element of X, but is an element of Y (in which case X has F accidentally).

This suggestion avoids the objection, but has difficulties of its own. To accommodate the conviction that the vast majority of a thing's properties are accidental to it, we would have to select a very small sub-bundle as the core—in the case of a human being, perhaps the sub-bundle {animality, rationality}. But surely no human being is identical with *that!* The core would not have to be this impoverished, of course, but add whatever other properties you think essential to a given thing, and I think you will still find it difficult to regard the result as an individual.[16] Moreover, if we identify an individual with anything short of a complete bundle, we get the consequence that it is possible for an individual to have several incompatible properties at once, since there is nothing to prevent the same core's occurring within several complete bundles whose fringes contain mutually incompatible elements. For example, the core {animality, rationality} may occur within one bundle whose fringe contains wisdom and simultaneously within another bundle whose fringe contains foolishness; on the theory of predication suggested above, this would mean that one and the same individual is both wise and foolish.

The last-mentioned difficulty would not arise if core properties could not occur in more than one complete bundle, but how is the bundle theorist to prevent this? We have already seen that he has none but pure properties at his disposal, and these, it seems, are always capable of multiple occurrence.[17]

I should like to consider one more attempt to free the bundle theory from the consequence that all of a thing's properties are essential to it. In an unpublished manuscript, Paul Bowen and Ted Schick have suggested that the bundle theorist should identify things not with bundles of ordinary properties, but with bundles of *world-indexed properties (WIPs),* such as *being snub-nosed in world 322.* Obviously, from the fact that a thing had *this* property essentially it would not follow that it had *being snub-nosed* essentially. (Compare: from the fact that someone has the property *being drunk on New Year's Eve, 1982,* as long as he lives, it does not follow that he is never sober.[18])

Leaving aside misgivings about the very idea of a world-indexed property, I think it is questionable that a bundle theorist can make use of them. What, after all, is a world? Some philosophers apparently think of them as concrete particulars in their own right, but a bundle theorist obviously would not share this conception. It would be more in keeping with his theory to construct worlds, too, out of properties. Bowen and Schick propose one way of doing this: let a possible world be the totality of all those properties that are indexed to the same world. But this has the appearance of being circular. If worlds are to be built out of properties, the properties in question must not involve worlds in their own constitution, and WIPs appear to do just that. Bowen and Schick are aware of this objection, and seek to meet it by maintaining that the appearance of circularity is mere appearance; it derives from the fact that we can only identify a WIP by referring to its index, but this fact does not imply that WIPs are relational properties incorporating worlds as terms. I must say in reply that if WIPs are *not* relational properties incorporating worlds as terms, I lose my grasp of what they are, and can no longer see how the inference from '*S* has *F*-in-*W* essentially' to '*S* has *F* essentially' is to be blocked.

There is a further problem with the bundle theorist's having recourse to WIPs. For a thing *A* to have the WIP of being *F* in *W*, it must be such that *W*'s being actual would entail *its* being *F*. But what must a world be like in order to sustain such an entailment? It seems clear to me that it would have to contain either an irreducibly singular state of affairs with *A* as constituent or else an irreducible haecceity instantiable only by *A*. Neither of these alternatives is something a bundle theorist can permit. (Compare what was said earlier about impure properties.)

Let us come around finally to the objection that the bundle theory implies a dubious version of PII. This objection applies to the second version no less than it did to the first, since according to both versions individuals are complexes whose only constituents are properties, and it can scarcely be denied that complexes differ only if their constituents do.[19] In assessing the force or the objection against either version, however, we should stop and reconsider what it is that gets bundled. The elements of bundles, a defender might say, are not *universals,* as I have been supposing so far, but such items as 'this particular redness' or 'the redness of *x*,' so conceived of as to be necessarily distinct from the redness of *y* if *x* and *y* are distinct. Such items are known in the literature variously as 'property tokens,' 'particularized properties,' 'perfect particulars,' 'abstract particulars,' and 'tropes.'[20] From the supposition that things are bundles of items of this sort, PII still follows, of course (two things could not share a *single* particularized property, let alone all of them), but it is not thereby implied that two things could not be perfectly alike. As a further benefit, particularized properties would enable the bundle theorist to avoid the difficulty raised above about the repeatable cores.

My objection to this strategy is that when I read accounts of what 'particularized properties' are supposed to be, I cannot help thinking that they belong to the category of *particulars* rather than to the category of properties. A 'particular redness' seems really to be a special kind of red particular. (Perhaps it is a particular that exemplifies just one property, redness, and that one essentially.[21]) But if this is so, the bundle theorist who resorts to such items is not reducing particulars *tout court* to properties; he is reducing ordinary complex particulars to more basic particulars.

III

To get around Objections 4, 5, and 6, I think one must advance to a third version of the bundle theory, a version that to my knowledge has never been held, but one that comes naturally to mind when one considers the two forms historically taken by another reductionist doctrine, phenomenalism. The phenomenalists of the previous two centuries tended to put their view by saying that a material thing is a clump, collection, family, or *some* kind of complex of sense data (or impressions or whatever). A consequence, as Berkeley was willing to acknowledge, is that that 'we eat and drink ideas [sense data], and are clothed in ideas.'[22] The phenomenalists of the present century, on the other hand, have generally taken the linguistic turn, maintaining that sentences ostensibly about material things can be translated into sentences that mention only sense data. Material things are logically constructed from sense data, not literally composed of them.

The importance of this difference was unfortunately obscured by Carnap's doctrine of the material and the formal modes. According to Carnap, what we have here is not *two* versions of phenomenalism, but only one, expressed once in the confused and misleading material mode and again in the more perspicuous formal mode. This is wrong. Old-style phenomenalism may be a bad view, but it is not merely a bad way of saying what new-style phenomenalists say better.

What for my purposes is the most important difference between the two views may be brought out by considering an observation of G. E. Moore's. By way of characterizing a view he attributed to Mill and Russell, he said this:

> Though there are plenty of material things in the Universe, there is nothing in it of which it could truly be asserted that it is a material thing.[23]

Now at first glance this has an air of contradiction about it. How can there be material things if there is nothing of which *it* is true that it is a material thing? The air can be dispelled, however, if we understand the Mill-Russell view as follows.[24] The existential statement 'There are material things' is true, but only because material things are logical constructions out of sense data; the statement is made true by the fact that sense data exist and occur in patterns definitive of the existence of material things. But the sense data are the only ultimate constituents of the world; none of them singly is a material thing; *nor is any clump, collection, or family of them a material thing.* Thus our existential statement is true *only as a whole;* there is nothing to which its predicate, 'is a material thing,' truly applies. This is in direct contrast to old style phenomenalism, according to which the predicate 'is a material thing' truly applies to certain groups of sense data.[25]

We can thus reconcile the two halves of Moore's puzzling remark if we treat 'There are material things' and 'There is something such that *it* is a material thing' unequally, ignoring the quantificational structure of the first while taking seriously that of the second. I think there is good point in doing this, but do not wish to argue the matter here. So if anyone insists that 'There are material things' and 'There is something such that *it* is a material thing' must stand or fall together, I will say fine, *provided* he recognizes that for latter-day phenomenalism *they both fall.* According to old-style phenomenalism, by contrast, they both stand. If the terms 'reductive' and 'eliminative' were not already in use in a somewhat different way, one might say that what the older view reduces, the newer one eliminates.

From now on I shall lump together the first two versions of the bundle theory under the heading 'old bundle theory.' The old bundle theory is analogous to the old phenomenalism: for each individual thing it finds some complex of properties with which to identify it. Since it is precisely this feature that makes it vulnerable to the objections about change, accidental predication, and indiscernibility, the strategy recommends itself of adopting instead the form of the bundle theory that would be analogous to the new phenomenalism. This version would decline to *identify* individuals with complexes of properties, offering instead to *translate* any statement ostensibly about individuals into a statement exclusively about properties. For example, it might translate 'There is a red, round thing here' as 'Redness and roundness are here co-instantiated.'[26] But it would not, to repeat, identify the red, round thing with the complex of properties co-instantiated at the place in question; indeed, it would not identify the red, round thing with *anything*. 'Red, round thing' would be a non-referring phrase, susceptible only of contextual definition.

It should now be apparent both how the new bundle theory escapes the objections to the old and at what cost. Unlike the old theory, it does not populate the world with individuals that are incapable of change, devoid of accidental properties, and qualitatively unique; but that is only because it does not populate the world with individuals at all. Or if you prefer to put the point Moore's way, the statement 'there are individuals' is true, but there is nothing of which it is true that *it* is an individual; hence, there is nothing of which it is true that it is an individual and incapable of change, etc.

What the new bundle theory amounts to is a purely Platonic ontology in which properties are the only ultimate logical subjects. An appropriate language for this ontology would consist simply of names of properties plus a sign for instantiation, say an exclamation mark.[27] Instead of '$\exists x(Fx)$,' which suggests that there is some *thing* that instantiates F, we could have '$!(F)$' (F is instantiated); instead of '$\exists x(Fx \,\&\, Gx)$' we could have '$!(FG)$' (F is co-instantiated with G), and instead of '$\exists x \exists y (Fx \,\&\, Fy \,\&\, \sim(x \approx y))$' we could have '$!!(F)$' ($F$ is instantiated at least twice).[28] This notation highlights the fact that although properties are instantiated, they are not instantiated *by* anything—not even by bundles of properties.[29]

The new bundle theory may be used in an interesting way to circumvent a difficulty that arose for Leibniz. We have seen that the old bundle theory rules out something that seems plainly possibly, namely, there being two individuals with all the same pure properties. The new bundle theory can admit this possibility, or at least a facsimile of it: it allows that the same maximal intersection of pure properties can be instantiated twice, and this seems to be a reasonable sense in which there could be a world containing two indiscernibles. Now according to Leibniz, a world containing two indiscernibles would automatically have a *twin* world in which the indiscernibles had switched places, and between two such worlds God would have no grounds for choice. Finding this consequence repugnant, Leibniz declared worlds containing indiscernibles to be impossible, thus affirming PII in its problematic form. But a proponent of the new bundle theory can avoid the embarrassing consequence without going to Leibnizian lengths. He can admit the possibility of a world containing two indiscernibles, *yet deny that this would generate a second world indiscernible from the first.* There would not be a second world with the two things switched, for there are not in the first world two things to *be* switched; there is just one set of properties instantiated at two different places.[30] Thus the new bundle theorist can admit indiscernibility *within* worlds, yet at the same time deny it *between* them.[31]

IV

Is there any philosopher who has explicitly advocated the new bundle theory? Not that I know of, though A. J. Ayer has come close: he once said that he could not 'see how asserting that an individual exists can be to assert anything more than that some predicate, or set of predicates, is instantiated.'[32] In the same paragraph, however, he confessed himself inclined as a result to uphold PII in its strong form as a necessary truth, and we have seen that there would be no call for this unless one thought of individuals as identical with complexes of properties in the fashion of the old bundle theory.[33]

Given its success in dealing with Objections 4, 5, and 6, why hasn't the new bundle theory been more widely adopted? Perhaps it is owing to the realization that anyone who held it would be in the following predicament: since properties would be the building blocks of his universe, and since he would not be identical with any property or any complex of them, he would have to believe that there is nothing with which he is identical—or in other words, that there is no such thing as himself.

Anyone who wants to believe that there is such a thing as *himself,* therefore, must reject the new bundle theory; and anyone who wants to allow for change, accidental predication, and indiscernibility must reject the old one. What is the alternative? In a word, it is *substance:* an individual is something over and above its properties, something that *has* properties without being constituted by them.[34] But the elaboration and defense of this alternative must be left for another occasion.[35]

NOTES

1. The third objection below can be found in J. M. E. McTaggart, *The Nature of Existence* (Cambridge: The University Press. 1921), Vol. 1, pp. 66–67. 'The others or near variants of them are all discussed by Michael Loux in *Substance and Attribute* (Dordrecht, Holland: D. Reidel Publishing Company, 1978). pp. 115–39.

2. See Richard Sharvy, 'Why a Class Can't Change Its Members,' *Noûs* 2, (1968), pp. 303–314.

3. See my paper 'Why a Set Contains Its Members Essentially,' *Noûs* 19 (1985), pp. 585–602.

4. This point is also made by Loux on p. 133 and by D. M. Armstrong in *Universals and Scientific Realism* (Cambridge: Cambridge University Press, 1978), Vol. 1, pp. 94–95.

5. E.g., Max Black's universe consisting of nothing but two spheres perfectly alike in color, size, composition, etc. (Max Black, 'The Identity of Indiscernibles,' *Mind* 61 (1962); reprinted in *Universals and Particulars,* ed. by Michael Loux (Garden City. N.Y.: Doubleday Anchor Books. 1970), pp. 204–16.) There are those who object that to suppose such a universe possible is to beg the question, but in so far as the objectors can find nothing wrong with the universe except that it conflicts with their principle, it seems to me it is *they* who beg the question. Leaving aside the issue of who begs the question, it should be pointed out that PII in its strong form would preclude even a universe with a single homogeneous sphere, since any two of its hemispheres would be indiscernible in respect

of pure properties. Yet what is more easily conceivable than such a universe?

6. In the manner, perhaps, of what Chisholm calls *entia successiva*. See R. M. Chisholm, *Person and Object* (La Salle, Illinois: Open Court Publishing Company. 1976), pp. 97–104.

7. Bertrand Russell, *An Inquiry into Meaning and Truth* (Baltimore: Penguin Books, 1967), pp. 89–101 and 121–123, and *Human Knowledge: Its Scope and Limits* (New York: Simon and Schuster, 1948), pp. 292–308; Nelson Goodman, *The Structure of Appearance* (2nd ed., Indianapolis: The Bobbs-Merrill Company, Inc., 1966), pp. 200–211: Hector-Neri Castañeda, 'Thinking and the Structure of the World,' *Critica* 6 (1972), pp. 43–81. It is not really one and the same relation that these authors introduce under their various names, but their relations all play the same role, and for our purposes it does not matter which is chosen.

8. Gustav Bergmann, *Realism* (Madison: The University of Wisconsin Press, 1967), p. 26.

9. The Special Theory of Relativity introduces a third term here, but it is not a *time*.

10. Castañeda ('Thinking and the Structure of the World,' p. 54) calls it "the fundamental, the number one, contingent relation," and adds "in a world deprived of thinking it would be the only one."

11. This does not mean merely that any two members of the set are co-instantiated, for to impose this requirement alone would beget what Goodman calls "the problem of imperfect community." Rather, it means that *all* the members of the set stand in one 'big' co-instantiation relation. If co-instantiation is not indefinitely polyadic there are other ways of avoiding this problem; see Goodman, *The Structure of Appearance,* pp. 204–11.

12. To put the matter this way is to take a long step in the direction of the third version of the bundle theory, to be discussed in section III. Indeed, I sometimes wonder whether there really is any ground to occupy between the first version and the third, but I shall suppress these doubts in order to bring out other difficulties with the second version.

13. Note this peculiarity, however: The needed refinement in the definition of predication merely adds a condition on the side of the subject; it says nothing new about the *relation* between subject and predicate. And it must be added that McTaggart, from whom Objection 3 was taken, would find an absurdity in the idea that a set or aggregate of properties of any kind, however large and whatever the relation among its members, could have a color.

14. *Substance and Attribute,* p. 154.

15. *Inquiry,* p. 122.

16. A similar objection is noted by Panayot Butchvarov on pp. 233–34 of *Being Qua Being* (Bloomington, Ind.: Indiana University Press, 1979), but it does not prevent him from advocating a version of the bundle theory. Owing to his systematic distinction between objects and entities, Butchvarov's theory is unlike any I consider here.

17. I shall consider a reason for denying this presently.

18. Indeed, Schick and Bowen also require the properties in bundles to be *time-indexed,* thus avoiding in analogous fashion the objection that the bundle theory does not allow for change.

19. According to Loux (*Substance and Attribute,* p. 157), this principle "defines for the ontologist the very notion of the constituent-whole relation."

20. For a nice exposition and defense of this tradition see Keith Campbell, 'The Metaphysics of Abstract Particulars,' in *Midwest Studies in Philosophy,* Volume VI, ed. by Peter A. French, T. I. Uehling, Jr., and Howard K. Wettstein (Minneapolis: University of Minnesota Press, 1981), pp. 477–88.

21. Such seems to be Sellars' conception of a 'basic particular.' See Wilfrid Sellars, "Particulars," in *Science, Perception, and Reality* (London: Routledge and Kegan Paul, 1963), pp. 282–97.

22. George Berkeley, *A Treatise Concerning the Principles of Human Knowledge,* section 38.

23. G. E. Moore, 'Some Judgments of Perception,' *Proceedings of the Aristotelian Society,* XIX (1918–19); reprinted in *Perceiving, Sensing. and Knowing,* ed. by Robert J. Swartz (Garden City, N.Y.: Doubleday Anchor Books, 1965), pp. 1–28.

24. I am not sure that Mill really held it, but that is by the way.

25. See W. V. Quine, *Ontological Relativity and Other Essays* (New York: Columbia University Press, 1969), pp. 98–99.

26. The difficulties introduced by 'here' are discussed in note 30.

27. Here I follow a suggestion of Ayer's in *The Origins of Pragmatism* (San Francisco: Freeman, Cooper & Company, 1968), p. 300.

28. Even if we give the new bundle theorist this much, how will he be able to say that a given property is instantiated exactly n times?

29. There is a partial analogy here with Chisholm's theory of states of affairs. According to this theory, a state of affairs is an abstract entity that can occur or obtain without being embodied by a concrete event or fact, and the same state of affairs can occur any number of times. Similarly, according to the present theory, a property is an abstract entity that can occur or be instantiated without being embodied in a concrete individual or instance, and the same property can be instantiated any number of times. The analogy is imperfect, however, since on Chisholm's view states of

affairs are 'concretised by' sets of concrete individuals. See *Person and Object,* Chapter IV.

30. But what is the status of places in the bundle theory? Theories of space may be either relational or absolute and, if absolute, either adjectival or substantival. (The latter subdivision is due, I believe, to C. D. Broad.) The new bundle theorist cannot adopt a relational theory, since he has not got individuals to be the terms of spatial relations. Nor in the present context can he adopt the adjectival form or the absolute theory (which posits 'pure positional properties'), since it would then be false after all that the same maximal intersection of pure properties can be instantiated twice. So it appears that the new bundle theorist must adopt the substantival form of the absolute theory, which makes places individuals in their own right. Though perhaps not inconsistent with his theory, this is hardly a result he will find appealing.

31. For a version of PII like this see N. L. Wilson, 'Individual Identity, Space, and Time in the Leibniz-Clarke Correspondence,' in *The Philosophy of Leibniz and the Modern World,* ed. by Ivor Leclerc (Nashville: Vanderbilt University Press, 1973): pp. 189–206.

32. The Identity of Indiscernibles,' p. 224 in Loux, *Universals and Particulars.*

33. Others may have committed themselves to the new bundle theory more or less tacitly; one such is N. L. Wilson, mentioned in note 31.

34. Does it follow that an individual is a 'bare particular' or 'featureless substratum'? Not at all; rather than following from the premise ('an individual is something that *has* properties. . . '), this astonishing doctrine flatly contradicts it. On this point see Sellars, 'Particulars,' pp. 282–83, and Chisholm, *Person and Object,* p. 43.

35. For comments on earlier drafts I wish to thank Diana Ackerman, Paul Bowen, Roderick Chisholm, Eli Hirsch, Philip Quinn, Ernest Sosa, and my audience at a University of Miami Philosophy Department colloquium. My research was supported by a grant from the American Council of Learned Societies.

Reading Questions

1. What is the first version of the bundle theory? What exactly gets bundled?
2. Van Cleve lists six objections to the view that things are nothing but bundles of properties. He claims that the more sophisticated view that things are nothing but bundles of co-instantiated properties escapes three of these objections. What is co-instantiation? Which objections is the more sophisticated view supposed to elude? How does the theory do it?
3. What is it for an object to be a "logical construction," as required by the third version of the bundle theory?
4. Why does Van Cleve assert that the third version of the bundle theory entails that there are no selves? What are the premises of his argument?

27 The Independence Criterion of Substance

GARY ROSENKRANTZ AND JOSHUA HOFFMAN

According to a traditional view, an individual substance is that which could exist all by itself or which in some sense is "independent." In this paper, we construct a new version of an analysis of the notion of substance in terms of independence, and argue for its adequacy.

It should be noted that our project is to analyze the concept of individual substance as ordinarily

Philosophy and Phenomological Research, *Vol. LI, No. 4, December, 1991. Reprinted by permission of the authors.*

understood, paradigm instances of which seem to be particular material objects and persons. In one of its ordinary senses, the term 'thing' means individual substance. For example, the term 'thing' is being used in this sense in the following sentences:

> 'Wisdom is not a thing, it is a quality of a thing';
>
> 'Surfaces and holes are not things, they are limits and absences of them, respectively'; and
>
> 'A chameleon's turning color is not a thing, it is a change in one.'[1]

Our project is to construct an adequate philosophical analysis of this intuitive notion of thinghood. For the purposes of our analysis we shall assume (plausibly, we think) that a thing in this ordinary sense, i.e., an individual substance, is not reducible to or identifiable with an entity of another kind or ontological category, e.g., a set or collection of either properties, ideas, sense-data, or events.[2] (This does not rule out the possibility that a substance can be ***eliminated*** in favor of an entity of another kind or ontological category.[3])

Since there is considerable disagreement among philosophers about what kinds of entities could exist, and since such disagreement is difficult to resolve, there is an advantage, epistemically speaking, in providing an analysis of substance which is ontologically neutral. Accordingly, we aim to provide an analysis of substance which is ontologically neutral in the sense that it is compatible with the existence of entities of any intelligible sorts, given some plausible view about the natures, existence conditions, and interrelationships of entities of those sorts. The epistemic advantage of this procedure is that we can put forward and defend an analysis of substance without having to argue (questionably) that certain kinds of entities could not exist. As we shall see, such an ontically neutral analysis of substance provides an adequate criterion by which objects of discourse that would be nonsubstantial entities if they were to exist, e.g., events, after-images, properties, times, places, surfaces, and shadows, can be distinguished from genuine substances.

However, it seems that entities of indefinitely many kinds could be advocated, and there is sometimes disagreement among philosophers over whether or not an entity of a given kind is intelligible. In the light of this, it does not seem reasonable to expect a single paper to provide both an analysis of substance and a complete argument that this analysis is ontologically neutral in the specified sense. Accordingly, in this paper we will only attempt to show that our analysis of substance is at least neutral with respect to a wide range of apparently intelligible ontologies encountered in philosophical literature.

I THE PROBLEM AND A PROPOSED SOLUTION

Pivotal figures who have defended an independence criterion of individual substance include Aristotle and Descartes. Aristotle wrote as follows.

> Some things can exist apart, and some cannot, and it is the former that are substances.[4]

In one place, Descartes states his criterion in this way.

> Really, the notion of *substance* is just this—that which can exist an by itself, without the aid of any other substance.[5]

This definition seems to suffer from the fatal flaw of conceptual circularity, since it explicates the notion of substance in terms of the notion of substance.[6] However, Descartes also wrote:

> By substance, we can understand nothing else than a thing which so exists that it needs no other thing in order to exist.[7]

This definition is noncircular if 'thing' means entity. However, there is a general problem facing this and related attempts to analyze the notion of substance in terms of the possibility of substance existing all by itself or in terms of some other form of independence. This general problem is that it would seem that if there is a substance, then there must be other entities too. There are a number of different sorts of examples of this problem, each of which presents a different aspect of the problem.

Firstly, suppose that there is a substance, for instance, a stone (call this stone *b*). It is arguable that *b* is necessarily such that there exist many other entities as well. These other entities include some substances, e.g., *b*'s parts, and some nonsubstances, e.g., *b*'s surface, *b*'s properties, *b*'s location in space and time, occurrences involving *b* (such as *b's* having a certain shape at a particular time), and propositions about *b*. Moreover, theists would add God (a substance) to this list.

Secondly, consider the class, ϕ, of all kinds of torus-shaped material objects, examples of such objects being certain bagels and doughnuts. Arguably, in ϕ there is a kind of substance such that: any substance of this kind would be necessarily such that there is a nonsubstance, i.e., a hole.

Thirdly, it has been argued that any human being is necessarily such that he or she originated from certain other temporally prior substances, i.e., a certain sperm and egg.

Finally, husbands are substances, as are both widowers and husbands-to-be. However, if a husband (widower, husband-to-be) exists, then this entails that another substance exists (did exist, will exist), i.e., a wife.

Each one of the four examples above suggests that independence is not a logically necessary condition of substancehood. However, a Humean can argue that independence is not a logically sufficient condition of substancehood. To see this, assume for the sake of argument a neo-Humean ontology in which the only existents are instantaneous concrete events (inspired by Hume's *impressions*), none of which is necessarily connected in any manner to another. Clearly, such an event is not a substance, but on Humean assumptions it is possible for one such entity to exist all by itself.[8]

In what follows, we develop an analysis of substance in terms of a notion of independence. This analysis will be both ontologically neutral and compatible with objections of the aforementioned sorts. According to our analysis, a substance is an entity of a certain kind, i.e., of a certain ontological category. The basic idea of our analysis is that this category, substance, is one whose instances meet certain independence conditions *qua* being instances of that category. This notion of an ontological category needs to be explained, since every entity is of many different kinds or categories of varying degrees or levels of generality or specificity. Thus, if we are to develop our analysis we must specify the degree of generality of the ontological categories we have in mind. This is a kind of generality problem. Below, we provide a solution to this problem by giving informal and formal accounts of the appropriate degree of generality of an ontological category or kind of entity.

To begin, there is an intuitive notion of a hierarchy of levels of generality among ontological categories. At the highest level of generality (*level A*) is the category of being an entity (being an existent) which everything instantiates and which is therefore a kind of limiting case. At a lower level of generality (*level B*) are the categories of being a concrete entity, and being an abstract entity (which we take to be equivalent to being a nonconcrete entity).[9] At a yet lower level of generality (which we shall call *level C*) are the ontological categories which are the various types of *concreta,* and the various types of *abstracta,* just provided that each of these ontological categories could be instantiated or is *instantiable*. Thus, each one of the following categories of concrete entity is at level *C* (just in case such a category is instantiable): being a substance, being a (concrete) event, being a trope, being a time, being a place, being a limit, being a privation, and being a collection. Likewise, each

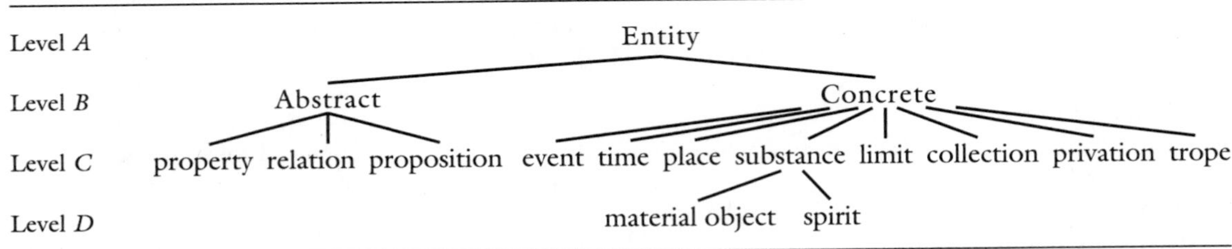

Figure 1

one of the following categories of abstract entity is at level *C* (just provided that such a category is instantiable): being a property, being a relation, and being a proposition (state of affairs). At a level of generality lower than *C* (call it *level D*) are those instantiable ontological categories which are the various types of the categories at level *C*. For instance, at level *D* we find types of substance, e.g., material object, or spirit; types of event, e.g., material event, or spiritual event; types of limit, e.g., surface, or line, or instant; and types of privation, e.g., shadow, or hole. More specific types are at lower levels of generality.

In what follows, we argue that by using the notion of a category of concrete or abstract entity at level *C*,[10] together with standard modal, logical, and temporal notions, an adequate analysis of substance can be formulated in terms of certain independence conditions. We begin by formally defining certain fundamental features and relationships of categories that will be employed both in our formal account of independence and in our formal account of a category at level *C*, viz., category equivalence, instantiation, instantiability, and subsumption, respectively.

(D1) A category *being an F* and a category *being a G* are *equivalent* =df. $\Box(\forall x)\ (Fx \leftrightarrow Gx)$.[11]

For example, being an event and being an occurrence are equivalent categories. Any two equivalent categories are at the same level of generality.

(D2) A category *being an F* is *instantiated* =df. $(\exists x)\ (Fx)$.

(D3) A category *being an F* is *instantiable* =df. $\Diamond\ (\exists x)\ (Fx)$.

(D4) A category *being an F subsumes* a category *being a G* =df. (i) $\Box\ (\forall x)\ (Gx \rightarrow Fx)$, and (ii) $\Diamond\ (\exists x)\ (Fx\ \&\ {\sim}Gx)$.[12]

For instance, being an animal subsumes being a dog. (If *A* subsumes *B*, then *A* is at a higher level of generality than *B*.) Notice that in this technical or logician's sense of subsumption a noninstantiable category is subsumed by any instantiable category, and a category that must be universally instantiated subsumes any category that need not be universally instantiated.

In what follows, we first clarify further the intuitive notion of an ontological category at level *C* by providing an informative logically necessary and sufficient condition for this intuitive notion. We then use the notion of a level *C* category to formulate an adequate analysis of substance in terms of independence. This informative set of truth conditions for the intuitive notion of a level *C* category will qualify either as a philosophical analysis which enhances our understanding of that intuitive notion or as a criterion of application which provides a decision procedure for determining the extension of that intuitive notion. We do not think that it is incumbent upon us to provide such a set of truth conditions. In the light of our earlier account of the intuitive notion in question, we believe that this notion is sufficiently clear for our purposes without our providing a philosophical analysis or criterion of application for it. However, the discovery of a set of truth conditions of this kind answers anyone who claims that the intuitive notion of an ontological category *at level C* and our earlier account of it are unacceptably vague or unclear.

The first step in stating our formal account of the truth conditions for an ontological category being at level *C* is to compile a list, *L*, of typical or core categories that are at level *C* (just provided that they are instantiable).[13]

List *L:* being a (concrete) event, being a trope, being a time, being a place, being a limit, being a privation, being a (concrete) collection, being a property, being a relation, and being a proposition.[14]

We also presuppose the truth of the following apparently plausible proposition about level *C:*

(A*) There are at least two (nonequivalent) instantiable categories of *concreta* at level *C* (at least one of which is on *L*), and there are at least two (nonequivalent) instantiable categories of *abstracta* at level *C* (at least one of which is on *L*).

Our formal account can now be stated as follows.

(D5) A category *C*1 is at level *C* if and only if either (i) *C*1 is on *L*, and *C*1 is instantiable, or (ii) [(a) *C*1 is not on *L*, and *C*1 does not subsume an instantiable category on *L*, and no category on *L* subsumes *C*1, and (b) there is no category *C*2 which satisfies the conditions in (ii)(a) and which subsumes *C*1].[15]

Notice that the category of being a substance is not on *L* but is at level *C* (assuming it is instantiable). A category of this kind satisfies (D5) by virtue of satisfying clause (ii) of (D5). This clause has two parts (a) and (b). Let us see why being a substance (if it is instantiable) satisfies both of these parts. First of all, the category of substance satisfies (ii)(a) because that category is not on *L* and neither subsumes nor is subsumed by a category on *L*. In Aristotelian terms, the category of substance is neither a genus nor a species of a category on *L*.[16] In addition, the category of substance appears to satisfy clause (ii)(b), since it seems that every category that subsumes substance also subsumes an instantiable category on *L*. For instance, given (A*), being concrete is a category that subsumes substance. Moreover, given (A*), being concrete subsumes some instantiable category on *L*, i.e., being a time, or being a place, or being an event, etc. It seems that parallel considerations apply to any category that subsumes substance.

It should also be observed that a category *C** not on *L* which is at a *higher* level than *C* both fails to satisfy (i) of (D5), and fails to satisfy (ii)(a) of (D5) (because *C** subsumes some instantiable category on *L*). Thus, such a category *C** does not meet (D5). (An example is the category of being concrete.) Furthermore, a category *C** (at a level *lower* than *C*) that is subsumed by a level *C* category on *L* fails to satisfy both (i) of (D5) (inasmuch as *C** either will not be on *L* or else will not be instantiable) and (ii)(a) of (D5) (because *C** is subsumed by some instantiable category on *L*). Hence, a category *C** of this kind does not satisfy (D5). (An example might be the category of being a material event.) In addition, a category *C** (at a level *lower* than *C*) that is subsumed by a level *C* category *not* on *L* both fails to meet (i) of (D5) (since *C** will not be on *L*) and fails to meet (ii)(b) of (D5). Therefore, such a category *C** does not satisfy (D5). (An example might be the category of being a material object.)

As we noted at the beginning of this section, the instantiation of properties such as being a husband and being a torus have certain troublesome existential entailments. Recall that these existential entailments create problems for an independence criterion of substance because they suggest that independence is not a logically necessary condition of substance. Because the category of substance (if instantiable) is at level *C*, and because the instantiation of this category does not have the aforementioned troublesome existential entailments, these problems can be solved by stating an independence criterion of substance in terms of a category variable that ranges only over ontological categories at level *C* of generality. Moreover, being a substance subsumes more specific properties like being a husband and being a torus (thereby ensuring that the latter properties are not level *C* categories). This is the strategy which we shall pursue in formulating our analysis of substance in terms of independence. Our way of avoiding the problems created by lower level kinds of substantial entities shows that it is not *qua* substance that there being a husband or a torus entails that there are certain other entities, but *qua* husband or torus.

We are now prepared to state our analysis of substance, which we do in two steps.

(D6) A level *C* category *C*1 is *capable of having an independent instance* =df. (i) ◊ [there is a

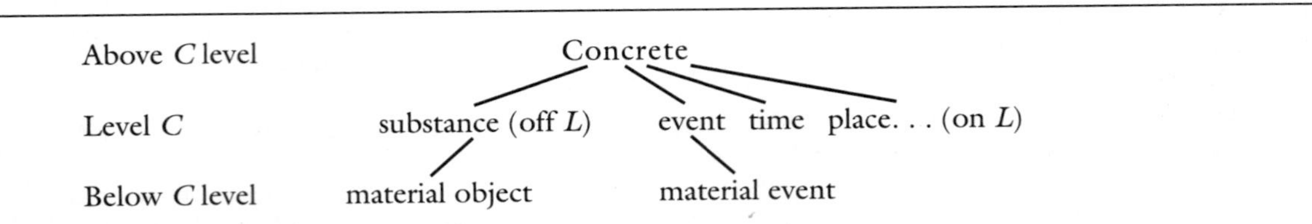

Figure 2

temporal interval t and an x such that x instantiates $C1$ throughout t & $(\forall y)$ ((in t y instantiates $C1$ and in t y is not a part of $x) \rightarrow y{=}x)$], & (ii) $\Diamond(\exists z)$ [(z instantiates $C1$) & $\sim(\exists x)$ (x instantiates a level C category $C2$ which satisfies (i) and which is not equivalent to $C1$)], & (iii) $\sim \Diamond$ $(\exists x)$ $(\exists y)$ ((x instantiates $C1$) & (y is a part of x) & (y instantiates a level C category (other than a category equivalent to being a proper part) that is not equivalent to $C1$)).

(D7) x is a substance =df. x instantiates a level C category which is capable of having an independent instance.

(D6) makes use of the generic concept of parthood, a concept we take as a primitive. Species of generic parthood include spatial parthood, temporal parthood, and logical parthood. Entities of different kinds may have different kinds of parts, e.g., spatial parts, temporal parts, or logical parts. But in the generic sense of 'part' that we shall employ throughout this paper, entities of different kinds have parts in the very same sense.

In (D6) and (D7), we understand the independence of an entity as something derivative upon a level C category instantiated by that entity. Intuitively, and without reference to category instantiation, there are at least two senses in which it can be said that an entity is independent of certain other entities. The first sense is that the existence of an entity does not entail the existence of those other entities. Accordingly, if an entity could not exist in the absence of certain other entities, then there is a sense in which that entity depends upon those other entities. The second sense is that it is possible for an entity not to have certain other entities as parts. Correspondingly, there is a sense in which certain complex entities depend upon their parts, viz., when it is impossible for such a complex to exist without those parts.[17] Related senses of independence explicable in terms of level C category instantiation include the following three, which correspond to the three clauses of (D6), respectively.

Firstly, an entity, x, that instantiates a level C category, $C1$, is independent of other entities of category $C1$ (other than parts of x) if the instantiation of $C1$ by x does not entail that there is an instance of $C1$ other than x or a part of x. An entity of such a category will be said to be *independent within its kind*. In virtue of clause (i) of (D6), (D7) implies that an entity which instantiates the category of substance is independent within its kind.

Secondly, an entity, x, that instantiates a level C category, $C1$, is independent of any other entity that is independent within its kind if the instantiation of $C1$ by x does not entail the instantiation of a nonequivalent level C category by another entity that is independent within its kind. In virtue of clause (ii) of (D6), (D7) entails that an entity which instantiates the category of substance is independent of any other entity of a different level C category that is independent within its kind.

Finally, if it is impossible that a level C category, $C1$, be instantiated by an entity having as parts entities instantiating another level C category, $C2$, then this is a sense in which an entity of category $C1$ is independent of any such entities of category $C2$. In virtue of clause (iii) of (D6), (D7) implies that an entity which instantiates the category of substance is in this sense independent of entities of other level C categories.

Notice that in virtue of clause (i) of (D6), (D7) allows that if a substance must have parts, then it must in a sense be dependent upon them. However, this general dependence of any complex or extended entity upon its parts is *not* the sort of dependence which distinguishes other sorts of entities from substance. On the other hand, as we shall see, a substance is distinguished from some other sorts of entities by not depending on parts that are not of the same level C category as itself. This is the point of clause (iii) of (D6).

Below, we shall argue that individual substances possess a type of independence which no other type of entity possesses, viz., the conjunction of the three forms of independence explained above. Unlike some previous accounts, our account does not claim that other kinds of entities depend on substance, but not *vice-versa*. Thus, our account does not assert that substances possess a *dyadic* asymmetric independence of all other sorts of entities. Rather, our account asserts the more complex asymmetric independence of substance explicated above.

II DEFENSE OF SOLUTION

In what follows, we confirm the adequacy of (D7) by arguing that even if it is granted that there could exist abstract and concrete entities of a variety of categories at level *C*, it is impossible for such an entity to instantiate a level *C* category that is capable of having an independent instance, except for one which is a substance.

Let us begin with a type of abstract entity, properties. In what follows, we argue that since it is impossible for a property to instantiate a level *C* category that satisfies clause (i) of (D6), (D7) implies that a property could not be a substance. In the first place, the level *C* category of being a property satisfies clause (i) of (D6) only if it is possible that there exists a property and no other properties except for that property's parts. However, it is controversial whether a property could have parts. If a property could not have parts, then all that needs to be shown in order to demonstrate that the category of being a property does not satisfy clause (i) of (D6) is that there could not be one and only one property. That there could not be one and only one property can be shown as follows.

To begin with, if there is a property, then there must be a *first-order property,* a property (such as being blue) that could only be exemplified by a concrete individual. Hence, it is impossible that every property is self-instantiating. Furthermore, there could not be a first-order property unless there were another property, viz., a *second-order property,* a property of a first-order property that could only be exemplified by a first-order property. For example, being blue exemplifies the second-order property of being a first-order property. The notions of a *third-order property,* a *fourth-order property,* and so on, *ad infinitum,* can each be defined in a fashion parallel to the way in which a second-order property was defined above. For instance, a third-order property, e.g., being a second-order property, is a property of a second-order property that could only be exemplified by a second-order property.

As the foregoing discussion shows, there could not be one and only one property. It follows that if it is impossible for a property to have parts, then the category of being a property does not satisfy clause (i) of (D6). On the other hand, suppose it is possible for a property to have parts. Only if a logically complex property has other properties as logical parts do we need to consider the idea that properties have parts. The idea here would be that a conjunctive property has each of its conjuncts as a logical part, a disjunctive property has each of its disjuncts as a logical part, and so forth. If it is possible for a property to have parts of this kind, then we need to determine whether there could be a logically complex property, e.g., a "huge" disjunctive property, that has every other property as a logical part. If there could be such a huge property, then there could be a property which except for its parts is the only property, and our analysis of substance would falsely imply that properties are substances. Below, we argue that there could *not* be a logically complex property of this kind.

In the first place, since it is a necessary truth that an entity is not a proper part of itself, there could not be a logically complex property which had as a logical proper part every property, including itself. Furthermore, we will argue that for any property, *P*1, there must be another property, *P*2, such that *P*2 is not a logical part of *P*1, and *P*1 is not a logical part of *P*2. To begin with, if there is a first-order property, say, being blue, then this entails that blueness has the property of being a first-order property, and that being a first-order property has the property of being a second-order property, and that being a second-order property has the property of being a third-order property, and so on, *ad infinitum.* Each property in such an infinite hierarchy is *not* a logical part of either any of its predecessors or successors in the hierarchy, since it is not possible for a property of a given order to have as a logical part a property of a different order. For instance, being blue (a first-order property) is not a logical part of being a first-order property (a second-order property), and *vice-versa.* Clearly, a parallel argument applies to any pair of properties belonging to an infinite hierarchy of the kind under discussion. It follows that there could not be a property which except for its logical parts is the only property, *unless* there is a logically complex property which has *all* of the properties in such an infinite hierarchy as logical parts. An example of such a logically complex property would be the "infinite" disjunctive property (call it P^*) of being either blue, or a first-order property, or a second-order property, or a third-order property, or . . . If P^* exists, then this entails that P^* has the property, P^{**}, of being a disjunctive property having an infinite number of disjuncts, the first of which is a first-order property, the second of which is a second-order property, the third of which is a third-order property, and so on, *ad infinitum*. Inasmuch as P^{**} is of a higher order than P^*, P^* *is not* a logical part of P^{**}, and *vice-versa*.

An argument of the foregoing kind applies to every infinite hierarchy of properties and to every logically complex property having infinitely many logical parts. It follows that it is impossible for there to be a property which except for its logical parts is the only property. Consequently, the category of being a property fails to satisfy clause (i) of (D6). Parallel arguments apply to other categories of abstract entity such as relation and proposition: either an entity of such a kind does not have parts and there cannot be an entity of that kind which is the only entity of that kind, or else there cannot be an entity of such a kind which, except for its parts, is the only entity of that kind. Inasmuch as none of these various general categories of *abstracta* at level *C* of generality satisfy (D6), none of these categories of *abstracta* is capable of having an independent instance. Moreover, as far as we can tell, there is no other level *C* category which is capable of having an independent instance and which could be instantiated by an abstract entity of any of these kinds. Thus, (D7) has the desirable implication that neither a property, nor a relation, nor a proposition could be a substance.

Turning to *concreta,* let us consider the category of tropes, i.e., concrete properties such as the particular wisdom of Socrates or *that* particular redness. If a trope has parts, then it is has either spatial, or temporal, or logical parts. However, if there is a trope, *P*1, then this entails that there are other tropes of a higher order than *P*1 such that *P*1 is not a part of them and none of them is a part of *P*1. For example, if there is the first-order trope, *that* particular redness, then there must be the second-order trope, *that* particular being a trope, and so forth. Surely, the former is not a spatial or temporal part of the latter, and *vice-versa*. And for reasons parallel to those advanced with respect to abstract properties, the former is not a logical part of the latter, and *vice-versa*. Since an argument of this kind implies that if there is a trope, *P*1, then there must be another trope which is not a part of *P*1, the level *C* category of being a trope does not satisfy clause (i) of (D6).[18] And it would seem that there is no other level *C* category which is capable of having an independent instance and which could be instantiated by a trope. Consequently, (D7) has the welcome consequence that a trope could not be a substance.

Other categories of *concreta* include being a place, being a time, and being a limit. We will argue below that these categories also fail to satisfy clause (i) of (D6). To begin, it is plausible that if there is an entity of one of these three kinds, then this entails that there is a dense continuum of entities of that kind containing both minimum or zero-dimensional entities of that kind, i.e., point-positions, instants, and point-limits, respectively, and extended entities of that kind. But such minimum entities cannot be parts of extended places, temporal intervals, or nonzero-dimensional limits. This is because the sum of even an infinite number of minima of these kinds does not add up to an extended place, a temporal interval, or a nonzero-dimensional limit, but the sum of the proper *parts* of an entity must add up to that entity. Thus, there cannot be a place and no other place other than its parts. Likewise, for times and limits. Hence, the level *C* categories of being a place, being a time, and being a limit do not satisfy clause (i) of (D6). In addition, as far as we can see, there is no other level *C* category which is capable of having an independent instance and which could be instantiated by a place, a time, or a limit. Thus, (D7) has the happy consequence that neither a place, a time, nor a limit could be a substance.

A parallel argument also applies to (concrete) events provided that there could be events which are temporally extended. This is true for the following reasons. An event is what happens or occurs at a time. Given the density of time, if there is a temporally extended event, *E,* occurring at a temporal interval, *T,* then there must also be instantaneous events occurring in *T,* viz., instantaneous "slices" of *E*. Moreover, for reasons parallel to those given above in the cases of places, times, and limits, an instantaneous event cannot be part of a temporally extended event. Hence, there could not be a temporally extended event, *E*, occurring throughout an interval, *T*, unless there were other events in *T* that are not parts of *E*. Therefore, the category of being an event does not satisfy clause (i) of (D6). And as in the case of places, times, and limits, an event fails to satisfy (D7) because it is impossible for there to be an event that instantiates a level *C* category which satisfies clause (i) of (D6).

On the other hand, if there could only be events that are instantaneous, then an event does not satisfy (D7). This is because it would not be possible for an event to instantiate a level *C* category, *C*1, that satisfies clause (i) of (D6)'s requirement that it be possible for *C*1 to be instantiated by an entity *throughout an interval of time*.[19] Thus, (D7) has the desirable consequence that such instantaneous events would not be substances.

It is plausible that either there could only be events that are instantaneous or there could be both such events and ones that are temporally extended. In either case, the foregoing argument implies that (D7) has the desired consequence that an event is not a substance.

In what follows, we shall argue that the level *C* category of being a privation does not satisfy clause (iii) of (D6). To begin with, recall that clause (iii) of (D6) requires that it be impossible for an entity of a level *C* category to have as a part an item which instantiates a nonequivalent level *C* category (other than a category equivalent to being a proper part). But it is possible for there to be a privation which has as a part an item that instantiates a nonequivalent category of this kind. For example, consider a privation such as a hole in a bagel, or a silence between two temporally separated noises. It would seem that if a hole exists, then it has as a part each one of the extended places inside that hole. For instance, the hole has a certain volume of space as its right half, and another volume of space as its left half. Similarly, it is plausible that if a silence exists between two temporally separated noises, then that silence has as a part each one of the temporal intervals between the noises, i.e., the periods of time through which that silence endures. These two examples illustrate the fact that it is possible for some privations to have places or times as parts. But the categories of being a place and being a time are at level *C* and neither one of these categories is either equivalent to being a proper part or equivalent to being a privation. It follows that the level *C* category of being a privation does not satisfy clause (iii) of (D6). Additionally, as far as we can tell, there is no other level *C* category which is capable of having an independent instance and which could be instantiated by a privation. Hence, (D7) has the desired consequence that a privation could not be a substance.

Next, let us consider the category of being a (concrete) collection. We will argue that this level *C* category fails to satisfy clause (iii) of (D6). This clause of (D6) requires that it be impossible for an entity of a level *C* category to have as a part an item which instantiates a nonequivalent level *C* category (other than being a proper part). However, a member of a collection is a part of that collection, and it is possible for some collections to have as members items which instantiate a level *C* category that is equivalent neither to being a proper part nor to the category of being a collection, e.g., items such as substances, events, times, places, etc. Hence, the level *C* category of being a collection does not satisfy clause (iii) of (D6). Moreover, as far as we can tell, there is no other level *C* category which is capable of having an independent instance and which could be instantiated by a collection. Therefore, (D7) has the intuitively plausible consequence that a collection could not be a substance.

We are now prepared to discuss the category of being a substance. This level *C* category appears to satisfy clause (i) of (D6) because it seems possible that there be a substance, *x*, which exists throughout some interval of time, *t*, without any other substance existing in *t*—except for any parts that *x* has in *t*.[20] For example, there could exist throughout *t* a material object, *x*, when no substance other than *x* exists except for any parts that *x* has in *t*. Also, there could exist throughout *t* a spirit, when no other substance exists.[21]

Moreover, the following line of reasoning shows that the category of substance also satisfies clause (ii) of (D6). First of all, it may be supposed that if there is a substance, then this entails that there are in addition entities of one or more of the following other kinds: properties, or times, or concrete occurrences, or propositions, or places, or limits.[22] However, as we have argued above, the level *C* categories that these other entities instantiate do not satisfy clause (i) of (D6). We contend that any level *C* category the instantiation of which is entailed by the instantiation of the category of being a substance is either not a level *C* category that satisfies clause (i) of (D6), or else is equivalent to the level *C* category of being a substance. It follows that the category of being a substance satisfies clause (ii) of (D6), a clause requiring the possibility of a level *C* category being instantiated without there existing an entity of a nonequivalent level *C* category that satisfies clause (i) of (D6).

Finally, the category of substance satisfies clause (iii) of (D6). To see this, consider that this clause requires that it be impossible for an entity which is an instance of a category, *C*1, to have a part that instantiates a level *C* category (other than a category equivalent to being a proper part) not equivalent to *C*1. So, let *C*1=being a substance. Is it possible for a substance to have a part that instantiates a level *C* category (other than a category equivalent to being a proper part) not equivalent to substance? For example, is it possible for a material thing or a spirit to have as a part either an event, a property, a time, a place, a privation, or a limit, or a proposition? Clearly not, since a part of a material substance could only be a material substance or a portion of matter, and a spirit is a simple.[23] Hence, it appears to be impossible for a substance to have a part that instantiates a level *C* category (other than a category equivalent to being a proper part) not equivalent to substance. Thus, the category of substance seems to satisfy clause (iii) of (D6).

Since the category of substance satisfies (D6), this category is capable of having an independent instance. Thus, an instance of this category, viz., a particular individual substance, must satisfy (D7), our analysis of substance.

As we have seen, the category of substance satisfies clause (i) of (D6). However, clause (ii) of (D6) requires that a category at level *C* could be instantiated even if there did not exist an entity of a nonequivalent category at level *C* that satisfies clause (i) of (D6). Therefore, if the instantiation by an entity, *x*, of a level *C* category, *C*1, not equivalent to substance, entails the instantiation of the category of substance, then *C*1 fails to meet clause (ii) of (D6). Thus, *C*1 is not capable of having an independent instance. And assuming that there is no other level *C* category which is capable of having an independent instance and which *x* instantiates, (D7) implies that *x* is not a substance. An Aristotelian would argue that the instantiation of *any* level *C* category not equivalent to substance entails the instantiation of the category of substance. Such an argument implies that every level *C* category instantiated by a nonsubstance fails to satisfy clause (ii) of (D6), and hence that any nonsubstance fails to satisfy (D7). Although an argument of this kind lends further support to our analysis of substance, and has some attractions, we do not need or want to appeal to it. Still, it is arguable that at least *some* categories of concrete entities other than substance could not be instantiated unless the category of substance were instantiated, e.g., being an event, being a trope, and being a privation. Thus, it is arguable that entities of these categories are not substances because of the failure of these categories to satisfy clause (ii) of (D6).

III OTHER CATEGORIES

Notice that our account of a level *C* category in terms of *L* and (D5) generates a "list" of categories of being that is *open-ended*. In other words, (D5) is logically compatible with two things. Firstly, that there are one or more level *C* categories which are *not* on *L*. Secondly, that one or more of the categories on *L* are *not* at level *C* (because they are not instantiable). Hence, (D5) differs from Aristotle's list of the categories of being, which has a *fixed membership*.[24]

Of course, it is extremely plausible that some categories on *L* are at level *C*. In addition, it is tempting to argue (*á la* Aristotle) that there is no category at level *C* that is not on *L* except for a category equivalent to substance. Nevertheless, since (D5) is open-ended, we can allow that there are level *C* categories not on *L* other than ones equivalent to being a substance. Some representative candidates for examples of such categories are being a sense-datum, being a nation, and being a sentence-type. However, it seems that each of *these* candidates is a species of a category at level *C*. For example, it can be argued plausibly that nation is a species of collection, that sense-datum is a species of event, and that sentence-type is a species of property. If so, then (D5) implies that the categories of nation, sense-datum, and sentence-type are *not* at level *C*, and that these categories are too specific to be values of the category variable in (D6).

On the other hand, assume for the sake of argument that these categories *are* at level *C*. We contend that on this assumption these categories fail to satisfy (D6). For example, if there is a nation, then it is possible for a nation to have a city as a part. Moreover, if being a nation is at level *C*, then being a city is also at level *C*. Finally, being a nation and being a city are nonequivalent, and being a city is not equivalent to being a proper part. Consequently, being a nation does not satisfy clause (iii) of (D6).

Furthermore, as we stated earlier, we presuppose that an individual substance is not reducible to or identifiable with an entity of another ontological category. Given this presupposition, and assuming that the categories of nation and sense-datum are at level *C*, it is extremely plausible to suppose that the instantiation of either one of these two categories entails that the category of substance is instantiated, viz., that there is a piece of territory or a person, or that there is a sensing organism or creature, respectively. For reasons explained earlier, this entailment, together with the fact that neither the category of nation nor the category of sense-datum is equivalent to the category of being a substance, implies the conclusion that the categories of being a nation and being a sense-datum fail to satisfy clause (ii) of (D6). Hence, we infer the truth of this conclusion.

On the other hand, being a sentence-type fails to satisfy clause (i) of (D6). This is because if there is a sentence-type, then there must be another sentence-type that is not a part of the former one.

Thus, if the categories of nation, sense-datum, and sentence-type are at level *C*, then none of these categories is capable of having an independent instance. In addition, it appears that if the categories of nation, sense-datum, or sentence-type are at level *C*, then there is no other level *C* category which is capable of having an independent instance and which could be co-instantiated with one of the former categories. Therefore, (D7) has the welcome implication that neither a nation, nor a sense-datum, nor a sentence-type could be a substance.

Arguments parallel to the foregoing ones seem to apply to any other candidate for being a level *C* category, e.g., to categories of *concreta* such as being a rainbow, being a reflection, being a storm, etc., and to categories of *abstracta* like being a set, being a number, being a fact, etc. In other words, either such a category is a species of a category at level *C* (e.g., set and number are a species of property, fact is a species of proposition, and rainbow, reflection, and storm are a species of concrete event), or else such a category is at level *C* and there is no level *C* category that could be co-instantiated with it which is capable of having an independent instance (e.g., the categories, of set, number, and fact do not satisfy clause (i) of (D6), and if the categories of rainbow, reflection, and storm are at level *C*, then these categories do not satisfy clause (ii) of (D6)). Thus, it seems that there is no counter-example to the sufficiency of (D7) in which a nonsubstance instantiates a level *C* category not on *L*.[25]

NOTES

1. Accordingly, it is impossible for a thing or an object in this ordinary sense either to *occur* (as an event does) or to be *exemplified* (as some properties are). To suppose otherwise is to commit what Ryle called a category mistake. This is the source of the apparent absurdity of saying, for example, that George Bush occurs or is exemplified by something.

2. We call a theory that identifies a substance with a set or collection of either properties, ideas, sense-data, or events a *collectionist* theory. Such theories face two difficulties, sketched below. (1) There is the unity of qualities problem. Consider the collection of the greenness of an apple, the taste of a pickle, the sound of a ball being dropped, the shape of an orange, the smell of an onion, and so forth. (Alternatively, consider a collection of diverse psychological qualities of different

persons.) Collections of this kind are *not* substances, but it is not clear that a collectionist or a bundle theorist can provide an adequate account of this fact. Notice that since such an account should distinguish a nonsubstantial collection from a substance in any *possible* case, it appears that it ought do this *both* in the case of material objects and spirits. (2) There is the problem of excessive essentialism. It seems that there could be individual substances that have accidental qualities and endure through changes in some of their intrinsic qualities. However, since it is extremely plausible that a collection has its parts or elements essentially, it is hard to see how a collectionist can satisfactorily account for the full range of such accidental qualities and changes.

3. If an entity, *e*, is *reduced to* or *identified with* an entity, e^*, then necessarily, *e* exists if and only if e^* exists. If *e* is eliminated in favor of e^*, then *e* fails to exist.

4. *Metaphysics,* Book XII, Chapter 5; 1070b–1071a.

5. *The Philosophical Works of Descartes.* Vol. I and II. trans. Haldane and Ross (Cambridge, 1931). Vol. II, p. 101.

6. However, this definition might be read as putting forward the condition that a substance is an entity of an ontological category that could have one and only one instance. Notice that a definition of substance in terms of such an independence condition is clearly not conceptually circular. As we shall see, our definition of substance will incorporate a condition of this kind.

7. *The Principles of Philosophy,* Part I, LI.

8. Hume gives an argument of this kind in his *Treatise Concerning Human Nature,* ed. Selby-Bigge (Oxford, 1888), Part IV, Section V, p. 233.

9. The distinction between concrete entities and abstract entities that we are employing is an intuitive one. This intuitive distinction may be difficult to analyze, but it is serviceable nonetheless. The distinction in question seems indispensable in ontology, and is presupposed by realists and antirealists in their debates about the problem of universals.

10. Henceforth, we shall abbreviate the expression 'a category of concrete or abstract entity at level *C*', as 'a category at level *C*'.

11. In (D1)–(D4), the letters '*F*' and '*G*' are schematic, and are to be replaced with an appropriate predicate expression. The modalities employed here, and elsewhere in the paper, are metaphysical ones.

12. For the purposes of (D1)–(D4), 'category' may be understood in the generic sense of a *property,* as opposed to the narrower sense of a genuine ontological kind, which we employ in all other contexts. Although the intuitive concept of a genuine ontological kind may be hard to analyze, it is necessary to use this notion both in the study of ontology in general, and in the framing of a particular ontology—enterprises involved in any attempt to provide a comprehensive understanding of the world.

13. Note that if two categories are at the same level of generality, e.g., level *C,* then neither one of these categories subsumes the other.

14. We employ ordinary or intuitive conceptions of the categories on *L,* and presuppose (plausibly, we think) that given such intuitive conceptions, not every instance (actual or possible) of one of these categories is identifiable with an instance of another ontological category. (The *irreducibility* of a category on *L* that this implies is consistent with the *eliminability* of an entity of such a category in favor of an entity of another ontological category.) While we do not have the space to defend this presupposition in detail, such a defense would in a general way parallel the one we suggested (in notes 1 and 2) of the proposition that a substance is not reducible to or identifiable with an instance of another ontological category. If the foregoing presupposition is mistaken, then the categories that make it so should be removed from *L.* The only limitation which we place on this process of removal is the following: that (A*) below is true, and that whatever categories satisfy (A*) are compatible with the above presupposition.

15. For the purposes of (D5), 'category' means an ontological category in the intuitive sense of the term. Although all ontological categories are properties, many properties are not ontological categories, e.g., redness, squareness, being a torus, being a husband, and (the disjunctive property of) being a substance or a surface. Thus, if a property is not an ontological category, then *ipso facto* that property does not satisfy (D5).

16. It might be objected that substance is a species of *collection,* viz., that, necessarily, a substance is a collection of other substances (its parts). In reply, we would argue that it is impossible for a material substance to be a collection of this kind, since it is essential to a material substance that its parts have some principle of unity, e.g., physical bonding, whereas it is inessential to a collection that its parts have any such principle of unity.

17. We assume only that possibly, there exists a complex entity that has its parts essentially. A stronger doctrine of mereological essentialism has been maintained, viz., that necessarily, any complex entity has its parts essentially. Such a doctrine is controversial, but nevertheless merits serious consideration.

18. If species-genus or determinate-determinable relationships are part-whole or whole-part relationships, our conclusions about abstract and concrete properties stand, since neither of the first two relationships can hold between properties of different orders.

19. It should be noted that our analysis of substance is not stated in terms of a notion of bare independence,

but rather in terms of an enriched notion of independence, viz., independence through an interval of time. Because of this feature, our analysis has the desirable consequence that an entity of an instantaneous sort, e.g., an instantaneous event, is not a substance, even if them being such in entity does not entail that there is any other entity.

20. Notice that our claim that the category of substance satisfies clause (i) of (D6) is compatible with the view that every human being is necessarily such that he originated from certain other *temporally prior* substances i.e., a certain sperm and egg.

21. It appears that if the following plausible assumption is true, then (D6) can be simplified by deleting the phrase, 'in *t*, *y* is not a part of *x*,' from clause (i) of (D6). This simplifying assumption is that it is possible that there is a substance that has no other substance as a part, e.g., either a spirit, or a spatially extended material atom, or a spatially located Boscovichian point particle. The simplified version of (D6), call it (D6*), would consist of the following first clause:

> ◊ [there is a temporal interval t and an x such that x instantiates Cl throughout t and $(\forall y)$ (in t y instantiates $Cl \rightarrow y = x$)],

and a second and third clause which would be identical in wording with clauses (ii) and (iii) of (D6). (D6*) has certain advantages. In particular, clause (i) of (D6*) expresses a simplified sense of an entity's being *independent within its kind*. And as a result, fewer assumptions are needed in the case of (D6*) than in the case of (D6) to show that properties, relations, propositions, tropes, times, places, limits, and events do not satisfy clause (i).

22. However, there being a substance does not entail that there is a privation. But, there being a torus does entail this. This contrast is indicative of how (D6) provides the solution we promised to the problem of existential entailments, in this case in terms of the distinction between *x qua* substance and *x qua* torus.

23. A substance can have an entity of another (level *C*) kind as a part only if a substance is reducible to or identifiable with an entity of that kind or a collection of such. Since we presuppose that a substance is not reducible to or identifiable with an entity of another kind or ontological category, we conclude that a substance cannot have as a part an entity of another (level *C*) kind.

24. See Aristotle's *Categories,* Chapter 4.

25. We would like to express our gratitude to Roderick Chisholm, who is the source of our interest in the independence criterion of substance. Thanks are also due to Michael Zimmerman for his helpful comments.

Reading Questions

1. Rosenkrantz and Hoffman claim that their analysis of substance precludes holes, surfaces, and shadows from being genuine substances. Do you think that it is reasonable to rule these out as substances *tout court,* or would it be better to allow them to be dependent substances, if not independent ones? Think about this again after you read the articles in Part VIII, Dependent Particulars.
2. What are the four examples Rosenkrantz and Hoffman examine that are designed to show that independence is not a logically necessary condition of substancehood? How do these examples work?
3. Are the categories at level *C* really discrete, as Rosenkrantz and Hoffman maintain? Recall what Van Cleve said about tropes (property instances) in the last chapter. Would they be better classified as a species of substance? Rosenkrantz and Hoffman claim not, but what is their argument?
4. Why are doughnuts substances but not a level *C* category?
5. If parts are essential to the wholes that have them, does this show that no wholes are substances? That is, if the parts of a certain table are essential to it, then the table could not exist independently of those parts. On the Rosenkrantz and Hoffman criteria, is the table then not a substance? Or can they answer this objection?

Particulars in Particular Clothing: Three Trope Theories of Substance

28

PETER SIMONS

> *[W]hen we talk or think of any particular sort of corporeal Substances, as* Horse, Stone, *etc. though the* Idea, *we have of either of them, be but the Complication, or Collection of those several simple* Ideas *of sensible Qualities, which we find united in the thing called* Horse *or* Stone, *yet because we cannot conceive, how they should subsist alone, nor one in another, we suppose them existing in, and supported by some common subject;* which Support we denote by the name Substance, *though it be certain, we have no clear, or distinct* Idea *of that* thing *we suppose a Support.*
>
> *(John Locke,* An Essay Concerning Human Understanding, *Book II, Chapter XXIII, §4.)*

1 INTRODUCTION

I PROPOSE TO TRY AND PICK a safe path through part of that ontological minefield, the problem of particulars and universals. Of those forms of nominalism which hold out any promise of success in the ontological assay of corporeal substances like horses and stones, two especially clamor for attention. Both use the notion of a trope or individual property instance. The bundle theory is perhaps at present the more popular. It has been strongly supported by Donald Williams and Keith Campbell, and says that a concrete particular is nothing but a bundle of tropes. The second is the *substratum* theory, which asserts that a concrete particular requires, besides its tropes, a nontrope ingredient which we may call a *substratum.* Substrata are sometimes called *bare particulars.* Perhaps the most famous substratum theorist is Locke (cf. the quote above), though there are similar tendencies in Aristotle and Thomas. A prominent contemporary supporter of Locke and the substratum theory is C. B. Martin. Each of these views has points in its favor and other points against, which I shall discuss. In the end I shall prefer a third theory, which I call the *nuclear* theory, which is neither a bundle theory nor a substratum theory, but combines the advantages of both without, I hope, the disadvantages of either.

It is gratifying that discussion of the old problem of universals has advanced in recent years to a point where the alternatives have seemingly been more or less canonically charted and many standard moves in the debate have been codified. Foremost among those contributing to this advance has been David Armstrong. It is interesting to compare Armstrong's positions in his two works, *Universals and Scientific Realism* of 1978 and *Universals, an Opinionated Introduction* of 1989. The most prominent change concerns precisely the sort of position I think is correct, which is nowadays generally called *trope nominalism.* Armstrong's change of mind shows nicely how trope nominalism has come to be more widely known and accepted. Whereas in the earlier book he is fairly brief in dismissing the position, for what

To the memory of Col. Marcus J. Gravel (1930–1992).

Philosophy and Phenomenological Research, *Vol. LIV, No. 3, September 1994. Reprinted by permission of the author.*

even he now accepts were bad reasons, his present view is that a kind of trope nominalism is the most promising rival to his own kind of *a posteriori* realism, and that while realism has a slight edge, the final decision between the two theories is probably awaiting arguments which have yet to be given. In a nutshell, and leaving personalities out of it, the inherent strengths of trope nominalism have found increasing recognition, and Armstrong, honest as ever, has not failed to call attention to these, despite their reflecting against his own view.

I shall not attempt to set out all the advantages of the trope theory over nominalism without tropes, or its advantages over theories replacing universals by tropes. These have been capably set forth both in Armstrong's later book and, with more personal conviction, in Keith Campbell's book *Abstract Particulars* (1990).

2 WHY TROPES HAVE BEEN SO IGNORED

Tropes are now a relatively familiar, if still not popularly accepted category in ontology. Most philosophers raised on standard analytical fare in the English-speaking world probably on first acquaintance considered them as somewhat exotic creatures in the ontological zoo. By contrast, those with a more thorough grounding in medieval philosophy will have found them familiar as the individual accidents of Aristotle and the Scholastics. That they should have been thought exotic, and that they have been cursed with a plethora of unlovely names as numerous philosophers came across the need for them more or less independently, are perhaps due to the way analytic philosophy has been developed and taught in much of the world in this century, and more especially to the influence of Russell and Moore. Russell, in his discussion of properties and relations, never even raises the issue whether these are universals or particulars, assuming simply that they are universals. Moore rather effectively drove people away from tropes in a famous criticism of Stout's trope theory, making realism about universal properties seem the only reasonable view.

Even a quite brief look at the relevant passages of famous philosophers from the past suggests that belief in tropes, under whatever name, has been the exception rather than the rule. Apart from the Aristotelian-Scholastic tradition, we have the (not unconnected) modes of Locke, the properties of monads in Leibniz, and (with qualifications) the ideas of Berkeley and Hume. Tropes are also prominent in the main tradition of scientific philosophy on the European continent around 1900, the pupils of Brentano. When Meinong spoke of properties and relations in his early work on the empiricists, he assumed without question that they were particulars, not universals.[1] A deepening of the analysis of tropes was effected by Husserl in his *Logical Investigations*.[2] Husserl extended the idea of a dependent content or idea, which he had found in Stumpf, from the psychological to the ontological sphere, and called dependent objects *moments*. Brentano likewise developed the idea of an object only one-sidedly separable from another. It is conceivable that Stout, whose *Analytical Psychology* was influenced by the Brentano school, also received impulses to his theory of abstract particulars from this direction.

My own route to tropes was somewhat deviant: not via Stout or the Scholastics but as Husserl's *moments*. In that context they do not feature as possible pieces in the game of universals, since Husserl also believed in universals, which he called *ideal species*. The first suggestion I found that tropes could be of use to nominalists was in Guido Küng's *Ontology and the Logistic Analysis of Language*, which was influenced by the nominalists Goodman and Leśniewski, and appeared in English translation in 1967. It was no accident that Küng was knowledgeable about both Husserl and the Scholastic tradition. Ignacio Angelelli's *Studies on Frege and Traditional Philosophy* (also 1967) showed how modern views had consistently suppressed the individual accidents from the "ontological square" of Aristotle's *Categories*, and from then onwards I was hooked. Tropes were put to use, again under the name *moments*, in the theory of truth-makers of Kevin Mulligan, Barry Smith and myself (1984).

Institutional and accidental historical reasons do not seem sufficient to account for the recent widespread ignoring of tropes, and Küng, in his book, offers three more systematic reasons:[3]

(1) *We are accustomed to say two things are equal because they are the same with respect to some properties. so we are inclined to think there must always be some reason why two numerically distinct things are alike.*

So if properties are equal, i.e., exactly resembling in themselves, yet possibly numerically distinct, then they are either identical, or are alike in virtue of some properties of properties. The first answer relieves us of tropes, the second is unsatisfying because either it gives us second-order universals supposedly explaining what could be better done by first-order ones, or else it threatens an infinite regress. Küng's answer to this point, which is surely the only one a trope theorist can accept, is that the equality of tropes is a basic relation in need of no further justification. In more recent works on tropes, the same view is explicated by saying that exact resemblance of tropes (Küng's equality) is an internal relation, entailed by the nature of the tropes, or that the fact that two tropes are equal is supervenient on their being the two individuals they are. Internal relations do not constitute ontological additions and arrest infinite regresses. Supervenience is ontologically innocuous.

(2) *The usual logistic languages contain no names for tropes, and we do not usually quantify over them.*

It may be added that natural languages also do not exactly thrust tropes under our noses. I think this can be given a pragmatic explanation. We largely use tropes as mere means to help us recognize and identify particulars which are of greater interest to us and so merit their own proper names. While numerous non-substantial individuals have their own singular terms, some may even be considered to have proper names (like battles, whose names are derived from but distinct from those of the places they occurred (*Trafalgar, Gettysburg*), I cannot think of a single proper name of a trope, and very few tropes attain such prominence in their own right that they merit a definite description. Candidate examples might be aesthetic, e.g. the shape of the Mona Lisa's mouth, the way Ingrid Bergman asked Sam to play "As Time Goes By" in *Casablanca,* or of historical moment, e.g. the trajectory of the movement of John F. Kennedy's head after the last head shot.

(3) *Tropes may be rejected out of fear of an infinite regress.*

If we have three exactly resembling or equal tropes, then the three consequent relations of equality must be equal (or else we smuggle in a universal, as in Russell's argument against resemblance nominalism), and these equalities must be equal, and so on. There are two ways out of this. One uses the supervenience or internality of equality to block further ontological addition. We do not have two tropes and a relation of equality, but two tropes, and given these two, they are equal. This is the way chosen by Campbell. Küng does not however mind the regress: for him, an infinity of relations of equality is not necessarily a barrier to their acceptance. The regress is not a hindrance to talking about things, since it is stopped in any language at the level where equality is pictured rather than represented, he says.

3 TERMINOLOGY

Since the term 'trope' has now more or less established itself, and since it is at least opaque enough to be free from misleading connotations, I shall continue to use it. In earlier writings I used the term 'individual accident.' This is both longer and potentially misleading, as some accidents may be essential to their bearers. I still like Husserl's term 'moment,' but apart from its other use for a temporal instant, it is really a German import and does not set the nice connotations jangling in English that it does in German.

The terms 'nominalism' and 'realism' are more damagingly equivocal. The denial that there are universals I shall call *particularism,* while their acceptance I call *universalism.* The defining characteristic of universals is that they may be multiply exemplified. This is usually taken to entail, via arguments about the occupation of spatio-temporal positions, that universals are abstract entities. We do not need to decide on this question, though I think such arguments deserve re-examination. So I shall distinguish the denial that there are abstract objects, *concretism*, from their acceptance, *abstractism*. The terms 'abstract' and 'concrete' have been used in two incompatible ways in connection with particulars and universals. The way I have used so far is the one according to which abstract objects have neither spatial nor temporal location, whereas concrete objects have at least temporal location, if not spatial location as well. This is distinguished from the use whereby concrete objects are those particulars which can exist of themselves, whereas abstract ones arc incapable of independent existence. This is the sense used by Keith Campbell in his book *Abstract Particulars*. The equivocation had been noted as early as 1901 by Husserl.[4] The discomfort involved in calling tropes "concrete" is lessened if we distinguish between dependent and independent particulars. Since we have the term 'dependent particular,' we best do to describe tropes as a kind of dependent concrete particular. This leaves open both that there can be other sorts of dependent concrete particular, such as events and boundaries, and that an abstractist might want to talk of abstract individuals or particulars, such as sets, which, if there are any, need not be universals. Also, such a set theorist might want to distinguish between independent abstract particulars, such as the null set, and dependent abstract particulars, such as the singleton set, which only exists if its member does. To have a convenient term for independent concrete particulars, I shall call them *substances*. I do not think this is very far away from the classical idea: at any rate, since my focus is not on substances, it is close enough for present purposes.

4 BUNDLE THEORIES

The idea that independent particulars are simply collections or bundles of tropes is a most tempting one. Berkeley essayed it for physical individuals, Hume for selves. Donald Williams espoused the view in his pioneering "The Elements of Being"[5] that ordinary substances are swarms or bundles of tropes related by an equivalence relation of compresence. Keith Campbell, following Williams, writes, "An ordinary object, a concrete particular, is a total group of compresent tropes. It is by being the complete group that it monopolizes its place as ordinary objects are ordinarily thought to do."[6]

The attraction of the bundle theory is undeniable. It holds out the promise of, in Campbell's words, a one-category ontology. It is elegantly Ockhamist. It dispenses with an unknowable substratum or bare particular. But it has its problems. The first group of problems concern the relation of compresence. Is it unanalysable? Does this not lead to a vicious infinite regress? What is to stop several tropes of the same kind, e.g. rednesses, from being compresent in one bundle? Do we not then need some further modal relation of spatio-temporal exclusion among co-specific tropes? The second group of problems concerns the objection that tropes are too insubstantial to give rise to substantial individuals by bundling, that they remain a collection and not an individual.

Consider first the relation of compresence. It is not clear whether this should be a two-place relation binding two tropes, or a three-place one linking a place with two tropes, or a relation of many more places binding the whole lot into a system. Consider the first alternative. Since normal substances have many tropes, there must be many compresences all of which are compresent in order to build up a single substance. So we account for the bundling of the initial tropes by bundling of the compresence relations, which raises exactly the same problem we had to start with, but at a more rarefied level. The arithmetic also gets worse: with four compresent tropes there are six compresences, with five there are ten, and in general with *n* tropes there are ${}^{n}C_2$ compresences. It might be answered that we have no more a vicious regress here than we do in the case of resemblance. But I think the case is not as favorable. In the case of resemblance, it was plausible that the resemblance (exact or not) between two tropes is an internal relation, deriving from the separate natures of the tropes themselves. But the compresence of two tropes is not always of this kind. There may be some cases where two or more tropes have to co-occur; but in substantial particulars many of the tropes are only contingently in that bundle: not that *they* could be elsewhere, but that *that substance* might be otherwise, and indeed can change. Suppose a certain bundle of tropes, corresponding to a sheet of paper, say, has at a given time a certain shape trope S and a certain temperature trope T (it is not important whether the examples are wholly acceptable, the point is not dependent on that). Now we may envisage the object changing shape without changing temperature (bend the paper slowly) or changing temperature without changing shape. On the standard trope account of real change, change of a substance consists in the replacement of one trope by another. So S may continue to exist and be in the bundle with a new temperature trope T', or T may continue to exist compresent with a new shape trope S'. In either case, the compresence relation between S and T lapses, suggesting that it is not because of the natures of S and T alone that S and T were compresent. Where two or more tropes essentially occur together, it is more plausible that their compresence is internal, but we surely do not want this to apply to all tropes.

Primitive internal relations serve to put a stop to vicious infinite regresses, and the regress of unification was known to Husserl. He criticised a view of Twardowski, relevant to what we have been discussing, according to which the unity of any two items in a whole is guaranteed by a third item which links them.[7] Obviously, Husserl says, this leads to a vicious infinite regress: not only do we have infinitely many items, but at no stage is unification achieved. Husserl's way out was to concoct a special relation, which he called a *foundation relation,* which serves to bind things into a unity without requiring any further glue. In fact he distinguishes two distinct kinds of foundation. An individual A is *weakly founded* on an individual B iff A is necessarily such that it cannot exist unless B exists. An object is weakly founded on its essential proper parts. But there is another sense of foundation, more appropriate here, which says that A is *strongly founded* on B iff A is weakly founded on B and B is not a part of A. Husserl's idea is to use foundation as a formal relation to secure unity without regresses: he explicitly says, "All things that truly unify are relations of foundation."[8] But does this suffice? Suppose that A and B are strongly mutually founding, that is, neither is part of the other, and neither can exist without the other. We may now ask, what is it about A and B that makes this so? Husserl's answer is that an object of one sort (a color trope, say) requires an object of another (an extension trope) by virtue of the kind, or ideal species, to which they belong. Foundation is primarily a relation at the species level, and is as it were inherited by the instances. But this answer works only for cases of essential compresence. We may admit that any extension trope requires some color trope, but it does not follow that *this* extension trope E requires just *this* color trope C, since E may continue to exist while C is replaced by another color trope C' of a different kind. This standardly happens when a stationary object changes color. Husserl is careless about the distinction between foundation relations holding in virtue of a dependence at the species level, like *Any pitch (of a tone) requires an intensity,* and those holding at the individual instance level: *This pitch requires this intensity.* Specific foundation is compatible with individual flexibility. Incidentally, it is misleading to describe the two kinds of foundation or dependence as *de dicto* for the specific and *de re* for the individual. Both are *de re.* Rather one should distinguish *de specie* dependence from *de individuo* dependence. The result is that Husserl's idea of using foundation as the cement of groups of tropes into more substantial wholes will only work for tropes which are individually founded on one another. Between contingent or accidental tropes (even though they be of kinds, of each of which an instance is required) there is no foundation relation.

It would seem that what we need to link two accidentally compresent tropes is their common relation of dependence to the larger bundle of which both are elements. But this cannot serve as the definition of compresence, since it presupposes what the relation of compresence is supposed to itself accomplish, namely the welding of a collection of tropes into a whole.

Another suggestion which might seem useful is to explicate the relation of compresence between two tropes in terms of a three-placed relation between these and the place where they both are: A and B are compresent in the place P. Then A and B are compresent in the old binary sense iff there is *some* place P in which they are compresent. This has three drawbacks. One is that it presupposes places can properly be the terms of relations. That is a form of absolutism about places which it would be nicer not to have to presuppose if possible. Another objection is that the relation in effect makes places substrata, since a number of tropes will all be compresent (in the two-placed sense) iff there is a place P with which they are all compresent, so that it is the identity of P which secures the integrity of the whole bundle. This is a substratum theory, not the bundle theory. It differs from the standard substratum theory only in not making the place P the bearer or support of the tropes A, B, etc. The third objection is that the theory makes the motion of substances more mysterious than it should be. If places were bearers, tropes could not move, since the moment a trope ceased to occupy the place it was in, it would cease to be, even if replaced next door by an exactly similar one. If tropes could not move, neither could bundles thereof, and the identity of substances over time would be lost. The present theory is not quite so badly off, since A can remain compresent with B although they are compresent with more than one place in succession, so tropes can genuinely move. When a substance moves, its tropes move with it. If a substance is the compresence bundle associated with a place P, then for the bundle to move is for the whole series of 3-place compresence relations with P to be replaced by a similar series with other places P', P'' etc. What explains the fact that all of these compresence relations with P', P'' etc. not only affect all the same tropes, but that they are all generated at the same time and all lapse together, in perfect harmony? What keeps the tropes from wandering off in different directions? If we can account for the bundlehood of the bundle in some other way, these facts are easily explained in one sweep by the fact that the bundle as a whole moves. Otherwise we are faced with a mystery or a miracle. Notice that this objection does not apply to the version of the substratum theory which makes substrata something other than places, since the togetherness of the motion of a bundle of tropes in a substance is explained by their all being bound to the same substrate. That theory has the further advantage of being neutral with respect to the question whether a relational theory of space is true or not.

The final possibility for compresence is that compresence is neither a binary nor a ternary relation but one with many more terms, as many as there are tropes in the bundle. We may not know what arity this relation has—it might even be infinite—and there might be different arities for different types of concrete independent particular, but there will be such a relation nevertheless. This has two drawbacks that I can see. In the first place, it is hard to see what explanatory force it has. All we are saying is that a bundle of tropes is held together by whatever relation holds it together. This is really giving up. The other objection is that again it is difficult to see how contingency and change can be explained. If some tropes are essential to their substances, and others are accidental, this is not marked in the huge relation binding them all together. And the relation does not of itself explain why when a substance changes, part of the bundle remains fixed, while other tropes of similar kind slip into the slots just vacated by their expiring colleagues. For these reasons, it seems to me that it is a despairing move to adopt this alternative. One point worth retaining from it though is that we might look for different kinds of concrete independent particular to have not just different kinds of trope, but perhaps also different numbers of tropes.

The second group of objections concern the apparently insubstantial nature of tropes and their consequent inability to make a substance by being bundled. Martin says, "An object is not a collectable out of its properties or qualities or properties as a crowd is collectable out of its members. For each and every property of an object has to be had by that object to exist at all. The members of a crowd do not need to be had by that crowd in order to exist at all."[9] Levinson, Seargent, and Armstrong think of tropes as individualized ways. It is hard to see how a substance can be composed of a bunch of ways. Tropes are supposed to be dependent entities: that I take it is the common thrust of both Martin's and Armstrong's objection to them if substances are to be composed of them. That, says Armstrong, is why trope theorists try to "build tropes up into something more substantial."[10] Well, of course they do, since they are trying to account for appearances, which are of complex individuals. Perhaps however the idea is that no amount of collecting or tying together of dependent entities will result in anything but a dependent entity, or a collection of dependent entities. So the existence of an independent entity, at least one of which must exist if anything at all exists is not accounted for.

Martin's comparison of trope bundles with crowds of people is not completely apt. Trope bundles are not meant to be mere collections, and certainly not collections of self-subsistent individuals which could first exist and then be assembled into a whole like an army is built by putting men together, or a ship is built out of divers bits of steel etc. A sensitive account of the relationship holding tropes together will not only take account of their dependence. It will also try to show why having a large number of dependent tropes together can yield something, whether it be a collection or an individual, which has the emergent property of independence. To find such an account, we can look again to Husserl. Husserl distinguishes a number of concepts of whole. The most important one for our purposes is what he calls that of a *whole in the pregnant sense,* what I shall call simply an *integral whole.*[11] The following explanation is based on Husserl's, but uses more modern terminology.[12] Firstly, two particulars are said to be *directly foundationally related* if either is founded, whether weakly or strongly, on the other. Two particulars are then *foundationally related* iff they bear the ancestral of the relation of direct foundational relatedness to one another. A collection forms a *foundational system* iff every member in it is foundationally related in it to every other, and none is foundationally related to anything which is not a member of the collection. An object is an *integral whole* iff it can be partitioned into parts which form a foundational system.

Notice how the relation of foundational relatedness is defined in terms of dependence or foundation. The definition of a foundational system requires that the dependence needs of each member of the collection is met within the collection, and further requires that the whole system be fully connected. Thus while two substances would be independent, their joint collection of tropes would not form a foundational system, since there is no dependence relation crossing between the two collections of tropes. The tropes would fall into two (or perhaps more?) disjoint foundational systems. Can the presence of a foundational system ensure independence? It would seem so, provided we add the supplementary principle: A *collection of particulars, all of whose foundational needs are met within the collection, is itself independent.* This principle seems difficult to contradict. So independence can emerge from dependence. But notice that we have spoken only of the independence of a collection, whereas the substance is supposed to be not a collection but an individual. I am not sure this is a severe objection. A foundational system is not just a mere collection or plurality of things, but a connected system. In a similar way, while an army is in some sense a collective entity, it is not a mere collection or plurality of soldiers. Not just any plurality of soldiers makes an army. And, to recall Martin's example, not just any plurality of people makes a crowd: they have to be all the people who are close together and not separated by physical barriers: someone too far away or separated from the rest is not in the crowd, and anyone close enough to another in the crowd and not physically separated by a barriers is in the crowd. A crowd is a kind of "spatial proximity system." We even use the singular: *a* crowd. That we do not regard some kinds of substance, such as physical bodies, as collectives, may simply be due to our not perceiving their constitutive elements, and registering only their aggregative or Gestalt qualities rather than the relationships among their elements.

There are however two disquieting aspects about this Husserlian solution. The first is that again it overlooks the distinction between essential and accidental tropes in a substance. And secondly, whether substances are individuals or collective systems, it treats tropes as parts of substances. Husserl is quite open about this: for him, a part is anything that goes into the actual make-up or constitution of an individual. What we standardly call 'parts' are a special kind, *independent* parts or *pieces:* the other sort, *dependent parts,* are what he calls *moments.*[13] Now it seems to me quite implausible to think of tropes as *parts* of their substances. If Seargent and Armstrong are right that tropes are individualized *ways* a thing is, it is surely wrong to think of them as parts. *How* something is is something about it, but not a part of it. Examine all the parts of a complex artifact, like an airplane. You will find its wings, its radar systems, its engines, its ailerons, etc., down to smaller parts like bolts, rivets, transistors, and bits of cable. You will not find its being 10.5 tonnes in weight among them. Parts is one thing, properties another (and properties of parts something else again). The temptation to think of tropes as parts (whether in a straightforward sense or in some analogous sense to the usual one) seems to me to arise, if not from the bundle theory itself, from considerations about spatial position. Where else can the redness of the red glass cube be if not where the cube itself (or at least its outer surface) is? So if the location of the redness is part or all of the location of the cube, in the same way that the location of a spatial chunk of the cube is part of the location of the whole cube, surely, one might reason, it does not hurt to say the redness is part (in some sense) of the cube. But the temptation should be resisted, for then we think of substances as being made up of their tropes instead of other (smaller) substances standing in relation to one another.

Levinson has argued, and Seargent and Armstrong have seconded him,[14] in the view that universals are best construed as not things at all, no matter how tenuous, but ways something can be. Now this is universal talk: a particularist cannot accept ways as such, but only instances of ways. But this is subject to the same remarks about naturalness that we made for tropes above, so is not an obstacle: we just talk of "particularized ways." I have another, linguistically motivated reservation about calling all tropes "ways." Think of how we standardly talk about things. We use nouns for the things we talk about, saying what they are, adjectives for their qualities, saying what they are like, whereas adverbs (sc. of *manner)* describe not things but events or actions: he spoke quietly, she walked briskly, etc. The term *way* is not tailored to first-order tropes, that is tropes of substances, at all, but to second-order ones. Another way (!) to see this is to consider an old way (!) of considering the Aristotelian categories. Aristotle had no category of ways, and there is a reason why. As Aristotle himself doubtless intended, and as commentators on the *Categories* at least from Averroes and Ockham onwards have emphasized, the Aristotelian categories are closely related to the different basic kinds of question one can ask about a substance, and only those questions of the form "What is it?" invite a nominal answer. Answers like "red," "twelve yards," "kicking," "being kicked," "older than Alfred" and "under the tree" are not names. Grouping the kinds of answer and nominalizing to name what the groups are about would in honest Saxon yield abstract terms of frequently rude barbarousness such as *howness, howmuchness, doing, undergoing, bearing-to-ness* and *wherehood,* which would lend our philosophy an almost Heideggerian earthiness, were it not that we can already use noble Norman nominals like *quality, quantity, action, passion, relation, place* for the same purpose. The terms *way* (Saxon) and *manner* (Norman) do not readily occur here, and the reason is not hard to find: they refer to *how* something is *done* or *takes place* or perhaps how it is *arranged* rather than what it is *like,* how much it is, what is being done etc. If an action is an accident, the mode or manner or way of doing it is an accident of an accident, and Aristotle did not accept such things except as accidents of their original substances. Describing all tropes as ways of *being* distorts this aspect of the term, at the same time as riding in on the back of that most unsubstantial nominalization *being,* which, since *be* describes no state or activity, has not even the secondary decency of an honest gerund like *kicking.* At the same time, since a trope of a trope is more remote from being a substance, calling tropes *ways* highlights their non-substantiality. A description of a way is a natural answer to a "How?" question, which most naturally tells us what actions and other events are like, and not what substances are like. So while I accept that some tropes are particularized ways, i.e. that ways are natural kinds of such tropes, not all tropes are ways.

The point of seeing tropes as particularized ways is to ensure that they are as unsubstantial as possible. This move, and the use of *way,* once again recall Ockham. When Ockham wanted to stress that a certain way of speaking did not commit one to entities, he tended to use an oblique Latin case. Rather than say that a substance has a particular way or mode of being *(modus se habendi, modus essendi)*, he speaks of its being thus or so, somehow, *alio et alio modo, aliquo modo*.[15] The temptation to reify so-nesses or somehows or thusses is meagre to say the least. Nevertheless, our natural tongues constrain us to talk *about* things by putting noun phrases in subject position and predicating. Provided we are not inclined to think of tropes as parts of substances, there is no need to artificially raise the barrier to so thinking of them by regarding them all as particularized ways.

We should not however take seriously the view that tropes, whether they are ways or not, are not entities at all. Clearly a bundle theorist cannot, because then he would be building entities out of non-entities. Ways and other tropes are not nothing, hence they are something, hence they are entities. But they are not THING-like, if by that we mean substance-like. They are not *res*, they are *rei* or *rerum*. But bundle theorists are forced to be less conservative than substratum theorists about substances, and when we look at what is said to happen on a microscopic scale, the substantiality of substances starts to look much thinner. It is prudent not to be too dogmatic about the gulf in being between substances and tropes.

The main unresolved objection from this section on bundle theories is that the most promising version of the theory, based on Husserl's concept of foundation, has difficulty accounting for anything like the distinction in status between accidental and essential tropes of a substance.

5 SUBSTRATUM THEORIES

Substratum theories claim that there is more to a substance than a bundle or collection of tropes: there is a further something, the substratum, which both bears the tropes (and hence accounts for their dependent status), and also accounts for the unity of the class of tropes borne, since they are all borne by one and the same substratum. Of course, substratum theories are also found among universalists, who invoke substrata as individuators to yield individual substances from what would otherwise be bundles of universals. But we shall be concerned only with particularist versions. We find the beginnings of substratum theory in Aristotle (not a universalist in my view), who in *Metaphysics Z* talks about stripping away the properties of a substance and arriving at the common bearer of these properties, which of itself has no properties except *in potentia*, and this bearer is the *materia prima*: "When all else is stripped off evidently nothing but matter remains [...] the ultimate substratum is of itself neither a particular thing nor of a particular quantity nor otherwise positively characterized nor yet is it the negations of these, for negations will belong to it only by accident."[16] Whether this was Aristotle's considered view or not, it finds its echo in Thomas, who lets non-substantial forms be predicated of substance, but substantial form is predicated of matter. In its inherent formlessness, lack of properties, supporting function and role of ultimate subject of predication, *materia prima* lacks only one thing which would convert it into the bare particular of Bergmann: individuality.

Bergmann's bare particulars are principally individuators: he expressly admits that if we "assay" an individual into a complex of universal properties, we cannot distinguish individuals having the same properties, and need bare particulars, whereas a nominalist already has individuality and so "In strict logic, a nominalist is therefore [...] not forced to search for further constituents [of a substance beyond its tropes]."[17] But some of the standard objections to bare particulars in the context of a universalist theory[18] also apply in a particularist context: bare particulars cannot be objects of acquaintance, they appear to be inconsistent in that it is essential to them that they have no properties (tropes) essentially, and essential that they be not in more than one substance at once. Another objection is that if a bare particular has no properties essentially, it is indestructible except by the kind of miracle Leibniz ascribed to the destruction of monads. None of these objections is perhaps lethal, but taken together they provide a strong incentive to look for another account of substrata.

A genuine alternative appears to be provided by Charlie Martin, whose theory is the one Armstrong prefers. Martin argues that "If properties are not to be thought of as parts of an object, and the object is not then to be thought of as a collection of properties, as its parts may be, then there must be something *about* the object that is the bearer of properties that under any description need to be borne. And *that* about the object is the substratum."[19] And again, "When we are thinking in the most general possible way of the attribution of properties *(each* and *every* one) to an object, we are thinking of, or partially considering, the object [...] simply *qua* or simply in its role as, the bearer, not itself borne, of its properties without at the same time considering it in terms of the actual properties it undoubtedly bears."[20] There is no question here that we have a strange kind of particular which has no properties and yet cannot survive the loss of certain properties by its associated substance. Nor is the substratum, so considered, a part or constituent of its substance. But the very innocuousness that Martin claims for substrata robs them of their *raison d'être*. That about a bearer of properties (i.e. here, tropes), that it is a bearer of tropes, is either not itself a trope, or, more plausibly, it is a second-order trope, supervening upon there being first-order tropes the substance has. In either case, it does not explain how it comes about that there is something other than the bundle of tropes that bears the tropes, nor does it help to explain what this relation of bearing is. Martin's substratum is ineffective as a trope-gatherer. If we want to talk about this second-order trope, well and good, but the problem of the relation of tropes to substance is not carried forward. Rather the account of substratum as a substance *qua* non-borne bearer of tropes, whether there are genuine items called *qua* objects or rather there are just different ways of partially viewing substances, presupposes we have a satisfactory account of what it is to be a substance and of the notion of bearing. Martin's account then refers us back to the original problem: we have a substance, and we have its tropes, and it bears its tropes, that is, they depend on it and not vice versa. If no further explanation is forthcoming, we have not a substratum theory but a particularist equivalent of what Loux calls a *substance theory of substance*. That is to say, the notion of substance remains basic. Now it may be that the notion of substance has indeed to remain basic, but we had already made some progress along the path of explaining what bearing is with the idea of foundation or dependence, which we needed for the bundle theory. Can we do better?

6 A NUCLEAR THEORY

Consider the following view. Rather than a bare something as bearer or tie for the bundle of tropes, and rather than take the whole bundle, neglecting the distinction between essential and accidental tropes, consider a two-stage approach. In the first stage, we have a collection of tropes which must all co-occur as individuals. These form an essential kernel or *nucleus* of the substance. For them we could have a substratum tying them together, but in view of the problems mentioned in the last section, which carry over, I prefer a bundle theory in the style of Husserl. Since these tropes are all directly or indirectly mutually founding as the individuals they are, they form a foundation system in the sense discussed above. Such a nucleus forms the *individual essence* or *individual nature* of a substance, but will usually not be a complete substance, since there are further, non-essential properties that the substance has. The nucleus will require supplementation by tropes of certain determinable kinds, but not require particular individual tropes of these kinds: its dependence will be specific, not individual. The other tropes it has, and which may be replaced without the nucleus ceasing to exist, may be considered as dependent on the nucleus as a whole as bearer (they will then be dependent on each necessary trope in the nucleus, by the transitivity of necessary dependence). Their dependence is partly one-sided, for while these accidental tropes depend on the nucleus for their existence, it does not depend on theirs, though it requires some trope from that family. The nucleus is thus itself a tight bundle that serves as the substratum to the looser bundle of accidental tropes, and accounts for their all being together. The nuclear theory thus combines aspects of both bundle theory and substratum theory. If we had a separate substrate for the nucleus instead of accepting a bundle theory, we would arrive at a theory rather like that of Aristotle or Thomas, where matter is the substratum, the substantial form corresponds to the nucleus, and serves as the bearer for further, non-substantial tropes. The theory I have suggested is simpler in that it dispenses with an ultimate substratum.

Obviously if I had thought of lots of objections to this theory (ones which at any rate are not shared by any other trope theory), I should have preferred one of the others. So let me leave it to you to come at me with objections, while I mention one or two advantages, apart from those which are evident in view of the theory's avoiding the major difficulty of each of the other theories.

One is that the theory is in fact rather flexible. It allows nuclei of different sizes and complexities. Perhaps there are substances without a peripheral cloud of accidental tropes, ones which are all nucleus. These would be like Leibnizian monads: each of their properties would be *de individuo* necessary to the substance. It might be that the most basic building blocks of the physical universe are like this, that all their non-relational properties are essential, that they can only be destroyed by total annihilation, and that all contingent complexity into which they enter is a matter of contingent external relations between them, or between them and other things. Then again, perhaps there are substantial collections of tropes without a nucleus. This does not mean that there could be free single tropes, but it might mean that which particular tropes an individual trope is associated with in the course of its career is always a matter of accident. While such a trope could not perhaps exist alone, it might change all its partners in its life, and that even if it originally had to consort with some particular others at the beginning. Finally, we might have a single nuclear trope, which required a periphery of tropes from particular families, but which could survive the loss of each of them, provided it was replaced by another from the same determinable family. Such a trope would be a genuine substratum to the others, and its destruction would annihilate all those dependent on it.

Among the tropes in the periphery of a substance, we may want to distinguish those which are of kinds that are required from those that are optional extras. Perhaps a given substance might gratuitously acquire a few extra tropes. I cannot think of any example, but it might be prudent not to rule the possibility out *a priori*.

Another source of flexibility is that the periphery may consist not of single tropes but of clumps, each of which has its own subnucleus satisfying most of its needs, but having some member in the nucleus or periphery which needs to be appended to another nucleus. So some properties may themselves be complex. Or we might have clumps of almost-free, almost substantial tropes, which hold together via a narrow bridge of one or two relations.

Yet another possibility is that among the peripheral tropes of one substance are relational tropes which require that two or more substances be related, yet because each could be replaced by another, the relationship is not essential to either. Here I am envisaging the possibility of relational tropes, that is, tropes requiring more than one nucleus for their existence. While numerous philosophers have tried to rule out such things *a priori*, most notoriously Leibniz in his correspondence with Clarke, it is a likelihood I take seriously, and intend to examine at greater length elsewhere.

In general then, I think the nuclear theory shares with the bundle theory the merit of openness and flexibility which ought to characterize a scientifically acceptable ontology. This is a point which has been stressed for the bundle theory by Campbell. It should be evident that I prefer what is known as a sparse theory of tropes, by analogy with Armstrong's sparse theory of universals: not just any old predicate we happen to use corresponds to a kind of trope. Which kinds of trope there really are is in general a matter for empirical investigation rather than armchair pronouncement.

7 FERMIONS, BOSONS, AND IDENTITY

It is a good test of a such a would-be scientific ontology to see whether it can be smoothly applied to areas outside the medium-sized world with which we are familiar, in particular to the objects of advanced physical science. This is an area into which fools rush at their own risk, since the physical facts and their interpretation are themselves frequently the subject of controversy among the scientists as well as the philosophers of that science.

One can be little more foolhardy than to rush into a look at tropes in the context of quantum theory. If there is one thing on which all commentators on quantum physics agree, it is that the explanations quantum physics offers for numerous observed phenomena require a radical departure from our previous, "classical" way of thinking about things. The kinds of object for which trope theory was framed are those for which other theories of particulars and universals were framed, namely medium-sized objects of acquaintance like cabbages and kings. I shall be just a little foolish. There is not the space, and I have not the competence, to launch into a comprehensive discussion of quantum theory, but I want to discuss a small issue whose standard terminology makes philosophers blanch, namely what physicists call "identical particles," which can be numerically distinct. Much of the discussion on tropes, bundles and the like is concerned with issues of identity, so it is to be expected that this will have repercussions for the theory of tropes. The authorities I lean on are Richard Feynman,[21] Bas van Fraassen,[22] and Peter Mittelstaedt,[23] all of whom have discussed the issue.

There is a reprehensible way in which physicists talk about "identical particles" which is easily avoided: elementary particles have a number of nuclear or essential properties like rest mass, charge, and quantum of spin.[24] Physicists sometimes call elementary particles whose nuclear properties are the same, e.g. all electrons, "identical." This is loose talk: they are in our terminology particles whose nuclei or, as I shall temporarily also say to avoid ambiguity in the context of microphysics, *kernels*, are exactly alike. No problem for the nuclear theory here. But particles also have contingent properties, e.g. their relative position, kinetic energy, momentum, direction of spin (all *at a time*) and so on.[25] It turns out that it is physically possible for certain kinds of particle for two particles with equal kernels to have also exactly resembling peripheries, that is, for all of their tropes to be exactly resembling, including those having to do with relative position. In this case physicists describe such particles as being in the same state, and then it is more philosophically understandable to call them "identical," since the particles are thus indiscernible by their (absolute and relational) tropes, and since no other means are available for distinguishing them are given, they are indiscernible, period. Yet they are numerically distinct: the physics of the situations described requires us to assume the presence of more than one particle. Thus Feynman: "By *identical particles* we mean things like electrons which can in no way be distinguished from one another."[26] Now the talk of being able to distinguish particles is epistemological, not ontological. It does not rule out that the particles are distinct in fact, though we are unable to tell which is which. But there are two kinds of fundamental particles which differ radically in their interactions with their own kind. *Fermions,* which include electrons, are characterized by tropes which obey the *Pauli Exclusion Principle:* no two fermions can be in exactly the same state. Thus the reason that a helium atom may have two electrons in its innermost shell is that their spins are in opposite directions, so they differ in one trope (maybe a second-order trope: spin-*direction*). Since electron spin direction of two superposed electrons is quantized so that it can only be in one of two opposite directions, the Exclusion Principle requires that a lithium atom must have its third electron in a second shell at a different energy level from the innermost ones.[27] The other sort of particles are *bosons.* They do not obey the Pauli Principle, and so two or more bosons can be in the same state at the same time, in particular they can both be in the same place at once and not differ in any trope at all. If electrons were bosons they could all three occupy the same space around a lithium nucleus. The most familiar bosons are photons, and it is their superposability in large numbers that makes lasers possible.

Now if we have three electrons around a lithium nucleus, they occupy what are called mutually orthogonal states. This is physicists' jargon for their differing in at least one of the relevant properties. The electrons seem to be *in principle* distinguishable at a given time, if not in practice: though we have no way of distinguishing one from the other, they are *in fact* distinct: Van Fraassen puts the point in a more technically grounded way by saying that, in an aggregate of fermions, "each particle is in the same reduced state, which is a mixture of at least N mutually orthogonal pure states."[28] And, for all his reservations, van Fraassen is prepared for pragmatic reasons to look favorably on the "ignorance" interpretation of the (reduced) indiscernibility of fermions.[29] Feynman, on the other hand, runs epistemology into ontology when he says, "The third electron can't go near the place occupied by the other two, so it must take up a special condition in a different kind of state farther away from the nucleus [...] (We are speaking only in a rather rough way here, because in reality all three electrons are identical; since we cannot really distinguish which one is which, our picture is only an approximate one.)" (4–13) This is double-talk: the electrons are the same because they are indistinguishable, yet different because they occupy different quantum states. What we cannot do is to trace the histories of fermions across different interactions. If two electrons settle down into a helium shell and then leave again, we have no way to say which one is which, even though they were in principle distinguishable while superposed.

The way in which aggregates of bosons behave is different. Since they may be superposed in the same state, they sometimes cannot even be distinguished at a time, even in principle, by their tropes. In collisions between bosons (e.g. photons) which scatter "identical" particles, there is no way even in principle of telling which of two apparent outcomes takes place, so again no way of tracing the life-histories of "identical" bosons. So we cannot really talk about individual particles which enter into interactions and then go their separate ways. For both bosons and fermions, van Fraassen recommends, following Mittelstaedt, that "re-identification over time has no empirical significance in quantum mechanics."[30] The difference between fermions and bosons is then that while fermions can in principle be distinguished *at a time* if not over time, bosons cannot always even be distinguished at a time.

This suggests (though it does not entail) that the idea that we are talking about distinct particles is misleading. Where there is no procedure by which a wedge can be driven ontologically between two particulars we have a choice: there are two distinct particulars with the same properties (rejecting Leibniz's Law) or there are not two distinct particulars. What then exists in that place where like particles are superposed? A realist might say that electronhood is multiply exemplified in a certain way in a given region.[31] Apart from wanting to avoid universals, I do not find this description at all helpful, because it seems to require more than one substrate. Nor would I want to make the region the subject or substrate of electronnish properties. I prefer another account. It has often been noted in opposition to trope theories (as distinct from realist theories of properties) that there appears to be no logical or metaphysical reason why an individual cannot have two or more tropes of the same kind, e.g. two exactly like shape or color tropes. This problem does not arise for the realist of course, since he or she only has the one universal. Trope theorists tend to dismiss this objection rather out of hand, as I think they can do if it is taken as a general point in favor of realism (why cannot an individual exemplify an universal doubly?) But suppose we consider the nuclear double bundle of tropes making up the nature of an electron: its essential ones, making up the kernel, and its accidental ones. When an electron is physically isolated from others, it is a substance. When two electrons with opposite spin are superposed, e.g. in a helium atom, the electrons cease to be substances, but their tropes retain their identity, and are modified by their proximity. This is not electronhood twice, but two electron trope-bundles in one substance. Pauli's Exclusion Principle is a constraint on how bundles can be combined to produce a larger bundle with doubling up of some kinds of trope. The same consideration also applies to the more recently postulated quarks.[32]

The same thing happens when bosons are superposed. What is called an aggregate of bosons is then a complex substance in which several of the relevant bosonic trope packages are superposed. Indeed, even this may be too optimistic a description. In the case of boson interaction not only the particle but also the tropes that constitute it cannot be ascribed identity across the interaction. Perhaps what happens is that two or more trope packages, when they get into proximity, expire in favor of new trope packages, some of whose own properties are derived from those of the originals, or in favor of a single trope package whose properties are not really, but only apparently inherited from their predecessors. The differences between fermions and bosons can be interpreted as imposing different kinds of constraint on how the combination or replacement may occur. In neither case are we called upon to describe several individual particles which are somehow indiscernible. Since the identity over time of "identical" particles is not defined except when they do not interact, it must be seen as an advantage to have a bundle theory, since a substratum theory thrusts an identifier upon us. Some theory along these lines at any rate seems to me to be a way out of the conceptual *impasse* created by the problems of "identical particles." I incline to think trope theory can also cope without gross upheaval with the problems of non-localization predicted in quantum theory and now experimentally confirmed.

While I have the impression that trope theory can provide the ontological tools to solve problems the others cannot reach, let me leave you with a puzzle which applies to trope theories as much as property theories, though I suspect the revisions required again cause less of an upheaval for trope theorists than for realists about properties. Of course physicists tend not to use scholastic or philosophical terminology, but that is not to say they do not recognize properties, so they can just as well be understood as talking about tropes. Particles have measurable properties (or something approximately measurable) which are vector and scalar magnitudes.[33] An electron for instance has spin in some direction (whose magnitude 1/2 is constant). Then there is momentum. But the magnitudes needed in quantum theory are essentially and necessarily complex ones (complex in the sense of requiring complex functions for their mathematical formulation). In fact a particle does not in quantum mechanics actually *have* a certain definite momentum, rather it has a momentum with a probability, or, as Feynman says, has a (complex) probability *amplitude* to have a momentum. The exact momenta are what Feynman calls the *base states,* i.e. what we use in conjunction with probability to describe the state of the system, so they need not in fact be realized by any individual. "The complete description of an electron, *so far as we know,* requires only that the base states be described by the *momentum* and the *spin.*"[34] The actual state of an electron is given by an amplitude distribution over momenta and spins. (The probability of finding a given particle is proportional to the absolute value or modulus of the probability amplitude.) Because hydrogen atoms have internal structure, there is a further factor caused by the interaction of the electron and the proton: a hydrogen atom may or may not be in an excited internal energy state (having an electron not in the ground state). No such internal structure has been detected in electrons. But it is unclear to me at present what the superposition of probability amplitudes means in ontological terms. Is a particular exact momentum a trope of an electron, or is exact momentum a theoretical construct we bring to bear on much more ethereal tropes, namely probability amplitudes to have momenta? Trope theory to date does not help us to decide; more work needs to be done. Which reminds me of an admonition of Donald Williams: "We are only beginning to philosophize till we turn from the bloodless proposition that things in any possible world must consist of tropes to specific studies of the sorts of tropes of which the things in this world actually consist."[35] It is sobering to reflect that this was written almost forty years ago.

NOTES

1. Cf. Grossmann 1974, p. 5.
2. Husserl 1970, Investigation III, "On the Theory of Wholes and Parts." For a commentary, see Simons 1982 (1992).
3. Küng 1967, pp. 166–68.
4. Husserl 1970, p. 426,
5. Williams 1953 (1966).
6. Campbell 1990, p. 21.
7. Husserl 1970, pp. 478–79. The regress is of course related to one made famous by Bradley.
8. Cf. Husserl 1970, p. 478.
9. Martin 1980, p. 8.
10. Armstrong 1989, p. 115.
11. Husserl 1970, p. 475.
12. See the accounts in my 1982 and 1987, Chapter 9, for more details.
13. Husserl 1970, p. 437. Among moments he recognizes, besides qualities, also intensities, extensions, boundaries and relational forms (ibid., p. 456).
14. Levinson 1978, Seargent 1985, Armstrong 1989.
15. See Adams 1985, pp. 181–82.
16. 1029a 10–25.
17. Bergmann 1967, pp. 22–23.
18. For which see Loux, 1978, chapter 8.

19. Martin, op. cit., pp. 7–8.

20. Ibid., p. 9.

21. Cf. Feynman *et al.* 1965.

22. Van Fraassen 1991, chapters 11–12.

23. Cf. Mittelstaedt 1986.

24. It might seem anachronistic to use the old essentialist vocabulary of *essential* vs. *accidental* to talk about fundamental particles, but I discovered after using it that Mittelstaedt 1986, p. 146 does the same.

25. Note incidentally that for elementary particles the determinables of their essential and accidental properties are finite in number. This is not a source of disquiet for a sparse trope theory, since there is no reason for there to be a one-to-one correspondence between tropes a thing has and predicates true of it.

26. Feynman. op. cit., p. 4–1.

27. That electrons are fermions has far-reaching consequences: it means that matter as we know it is stable, and hence that we can be here, e.g., to find this out.

28. Van Fraassen, op. cit., p. 386.

29. Ibid.

30. Ibid., p. 430.

31. Van Fraassen talks in a similar way. He says: suppose we could understand *The species COW is multiply instantiated* in such a way that it does not imply *there is more than one cow.* Could we have a world in which there is multiple cowhood without individual cows? (Ibid., p. 436.)

32. Campbell. op. cit., p. 68, suggests (following Armstrong), that an electron might contain three charge-tropes of magnitude $e/3$ inherited from their "constituent" quarks. The physics is wrong here: only hadrons are composed of quarks, while electrons are leptons. But the general idea is right: a proton is supposed to consist of two up quarks, each with charge $+2e/3$, and one down quark, with charge $-e/3$. Incidentally, the fact that quarks may not be isolable is easy to accommodate for trope theorists: perhaps quarks are just non-independent trope clusters within larger substantial bundles. An adequate trope theory will have to provide a satisfactory account of scalar and vector magnitude tropes.

34. Feynman *et al.,* op. cit., p. 8–5.

35. Williams 1966, p. 108.

REFERENCES

Adams, M. M. 1985. "Things versus 'Hows,' or Ockham on Predication and Ontology." In J. Bogen & J. E. McGuire, eds., *How Things Are. Studies in Predication and the History of Philosophy and Science.* Dordrecht: Kluwer, pp. 175–88.

Angelelli, I. 1967. *Studies on Gottlob Frege and Traditional Philosophy.* New York: Humanities Press.

Armstrong, D. M. 1978. *Universals and Scientific Realism.* Cambridge: Cambridge University Press.

______1989. *Universals: an Opinionated Introduction,* Boulder: Westview.

Bergmann, G. 1967. *Realism: A Critique of Brentano and Meinong.* Madison. University of Wisconsin Press.

Campbell, K. 1990. *Abstract Particulars.* Oxford: Blackwell.

Feynman, R. P., Leighton, R. B., & Sands, M. 1965. *The Feynman Lectures in Physics Vol. 3: Quantum Mechanics.* Reading: Addison-Wesley.

Grossmann, R. 1974. Meinong. London: Routledge & Kegan Paul.

Husserl, E. 1970. *Logical Investigations.* London: Routledge & Kegan Paul.

Küng, G. 1967. *Ontology and the Logistic Analysis of Language.* Dordrecht: Reidel.

Levinson, J. 1978. "Properties and Related Entities." *Philosophy and Phenomenological Research* 39, 1–22.

Loux, M. J. 1978. *Substance and Attribute. A Study in Ontology.* Dordrecht: Reidel.

Martin, C. B. 1980. "Substance Substantiated." *Australasian Journal of Philosophy* 58, 3–10.

Mittelstaedt, P. 1986. "Naming and Identity in Quantum Logic." In P. Weingartner & G. Dorn, eds., *Foundations of Physics.* Vienna: Hölder-Pichler-Tempsky, pp. 139–61.

Mulligan, K., Simons, P. M. & Smith, B. 1984. "Truth-Makers." *Philosophy and Phenomenological Research* **44**, 287–322.

Seargent, D. A. J. 1985. *Plurality and Continuity. An Essay in G. F. Stout's Theory of Universals.* The Hague: Nijhoff.

Simons, P. M. 1982. "The Formalisation of Husserl's Theory of Wholes and Parts." In B. Smith, ed., *Parts and Moments.* Munich: Philosophia, pp. 113–59. Reprinted in Simons 1992.

______ 1987. *Parts. A Study in Ontology.* Oxford: Clarendon.

______ 1992. *Philosophy and Logic in Central Europe from Bolzano to Tarski.* Dordrecht: Kluwer.

Van Fraassen, B. C. 1991. *Quantum Mechanics: an Empiricist View.* Oxford: Clarendon.

Williams, D. C. 1953. "On the Elements of Being." *Review of Metaphysics* 7, 3–18, 171–92. Reprinted as "The Elements of Being" in his *Principles of Empirical Realism,* Springfield: Thomas, 1966, pp. 74–109.

Reading Questions

1. Simons characterizes tropes as "a kind of dependent concrete particular." He subsequently states that substances are "independent concrete particulars." How then could tropes alone comprise substances? How could something independent be built out of dependent things? Do Simons's definitions make any theory that attempts to bundle tropes into substances a non-starter?
2. What does Simons consider to be the most serious problem facing the traditional bundle theory of tropes?
3. What is the foundational relatedness relation, and how is it supposed to hold tropes together into a bundle?
4. Simons claims that sometimes an electron is a substance and sometimes it is not. What is the basis for this unusual view?

Further Readings

Books

Hoffman, Joshua, and Gary S. Rosenkrantz. 1997. *Substance: Its Nature and Existence.* London: Routledge.

______. 1994. *Substance Among Other Categories.* Cambridge: Cambridge University Press.

Lowe, E. J. 1998. *Substance, Identity and Time.* Oxford: Oxford University Press.

Wiggins, David. 1980. *Sameness and Substance.* Cambridge: Harvard University Press.

Articles

Allaire, Edwin B. 1963. "Bare Particulars." *Philosophical Studies* 14: 1–7.

Ayers, Michael. 1991. "Substance: Prolegomena to a Realist Theory of Identity." *The Journal of Philosophy* 88 (2): 69–90.

Casullo, Albert. 1988. "A Fourth Version of the Bundle Theory." *Philosophical Studies* 54: 125–139.

Clark, Ralph W. 1976. "The Bundle Theory of Substance." *New Scholastic* 50: 490–503.

Denkel, Arda. 1992. "Substance Without Substratum." *Philosophy and Phenomenological Research* 52 (3): 705–711.

————. 1997. "On the Compresence of Tropes." *Philosophy and Phenomenological Research* 57 (3): 599–606.

Forbes, Graeme. 1981. "An Anti-Essentialist Note on Substances." *Analysis* 41: 32–37.

Glouberman, M. 1975. "The Substance of Bundles." *The Personalist* 56: 38–46.

Gram, Moltke S. 1983. "The Skeptical Attack on Substance: Kantian Answers." In *Contemporary Perspectives on the History of Philosophy,* ed. P. A. French, T. E. Uehling and H. K. Wettstein." Vol. 8, *Midwest Studies in Philosophy.* Indianapolis: University of Minnesota Press.

Gyekye, Kwame. 1973. "An Examination of the Bundle Theory of Substance." *Philosophy and Phenomenological Research* 34: 51–61.

Hacker, P. M. S. 1979. "Substance: The Constitution of Reality." In *Studies in Metaphysics,* edited by P. A. French, T. E. Uehling and H. K. Wettstein. Vol. 4, *Midwest Studies in Philosophy.* Minneapolis: University of Minnesota Press.

LaBossiere, Michael C. 1994. "Substances and Substrata." *Australasian Journal of Philosophy* 72 (3): 360–369.

Losonsky, Michael. 1987. "Individuation and the Bundle Theory." *Philosophical Studies* 52: 191–198.

Lowe, E. J. 1988. "Substance, Identity and Time." *Proceedings of the Aristotelian Society* 62 (supplement): 61–78.

______. 1991. "Substance and Selfhood." *Philosophy:* 81–99.

______. 1994. "Primitive Substances." *Philosophy and Phenomenological Research* 54 (3): 531–552.

Martin, C. B. 1980. "Substance Substantiated." *Australasian Journal of Philosophy* 58: 3–10.
O'Leary-Hawthorne, John. 1995. "The Bundle Theory of Substance and the Identity of Indiscernibles." *Analysis* 55 (3): 191–196.
Unwin, Nicholas. 1984. "Substance, Essence, and Conceptualism." *Ratio* 26: 41–54.
Wilson, N. L. 1959. "Substances Without Substrata." *Review of Metaphysics* 12: 521–539.
Zimmerman, Dean W. 1997. "Distinct Indiscernibles and the Bundle Theory." *Mind* 106: 305–309.

Part VIII

Dependent Particulars: Holes, Boundaries, and Surfaces

H. SCOTT HESTEVOLD

Introduction to Dependent Particulars

I. Introduction

THE FOLLOWING STATEMENTS seem perfectly coherent:

(a) The edge of a marble-cube paperweight scratched the surface of the table.
(b) As it moved toward the shoreline, the large wave overturned a surfer.
(c) The shadow of the ship's bow crossed the Equator before the ship did.
(d) The perimeter of the hole in a doughnut's shadow is much smaller than the perimeter of the hole in the tractor-tire's shadow.
(e) Looking at her reflection, the grandmother decided that her wrinkles gave her smile character.

If these statements are true, they would seem to imply that there do exist edges, scratches, surfaces, shorelines, waves, shadows, lines of latitude, holes and their boundaries, reflections, wrinkles, and smiles. Such things, however, apparently *depend* on other things such as marble cubes, tables, bodies of water, ships, doughnuts, tires, mirrors, and faces. Though a cube's left half could exist without being conjoined with any other object, no edge of the cube can obviously exist detached from all other three-dimensional objects. A body of ocean water could exist without a wave, but no ocean wave could exist without the water. A tire can exist without its shadow, but the shadow cannot exist without the tire nor can the shadow exist without some other object that it shadows. The grandmother's reflection depends, in some sense, both on a reflective surface and on the face reflected; and the grandmother's smile and wrinkles depend on her face, which existed years ago independently of that smile and those wrinkles.

This essay was commissioned especially for this volume and appears here for the first time.

Scratches, surfaces, waves, edges, shadows, reflections, and holes are apparently particular things that are *dependent* on other things. But in what sense are these things *particulars*? And in what sense are they *dependent*? *Do* such dependent particulars exist, or is talk about such things merely disguised talk about particulars that are *not* dependent?

After discussion of the nature of universals in Part II, particulars are identified in Part III as those entities that are not universals. In Part IV, dependent particulars are characterized as constituentive particulars that are in a specified sense *dependent* on other constituentive particulars. Introductions to this chapter's essays on holes and boundaries are found in Parts V and VI. Finally, there is a brief discussion of whether talk of dependent particulars *is* reducible to talk of particulars that are not dependent.

A Word of Caution. Philosophers disagree about the existence of universals and about what sorts of things universals are if they do exist. Philosophers also disagree about which entities are to count as particulars and about what makes a particular a *particular*. Although what is said in this essay about the nature of universals and particulars is controversial, it should prove adequate for introducing the intriguing philosophical problems that involve dependent particulars.

II. Universals

Substantial things such as animals, fruit, and tables are said to have and lack various qualities: some animals are cats, but no animal is a unicorn; ripe strawberries are red, ripe bananas are not; some tables are round, some are not. Qualities such as catness, redness, and roundness do not themselves seem to be substantial things, but are the sorts of things *had* by substantial things.[1]

What qualities *are* is a topic addressed in Part IV of this anthology. (See in particular the essay by David M. Armstrong.) According to some, there are truths about qualities such as catness and unicornicity that are true regardless of whether cats and unicorns exist. For example, both qualities involve animalness, but neither involves square-rootness. On one traditional view, then, such qualities are *universals* (properties), which are construed as abstract entities that necessarily exist that cannot possibly fail to exist.[2] This traditional view allows that some universals are *exemplified* while others are not. For example, although catness and unicornicity both exist, many substantial things (e.g., cats) exemplify catness, but nothing exemplifies unicornicity.

How can universals be distinguished from other things? One obvious suggestion is this: any given universal *could* exist at multiple places at a time, but no substantial thing can (wholly) exist at more than one place at a time. Redness can exist simultaneously in both a jar of jam and a strawberry pie, but no strawberry can (wholly) exist simultaneously both in a jar of jam and in a pie.

Characterizing universals as entities that are exemplifiable at multiple locations would not be accurate. If numbers are abstract entities that lack spatial location, then numbers 3 and 5 (and infinitely many other numbers) would exemplify oddness, but they would not exemplify it *at* a location. Moreover, the possibility should be left open that there exist universals—for example, *being the time at which Socrates died, being Socrates, being President of the U.S.*—that cannot be multiply exemplified by more than one thing or by more than one thing at a time.[3]

More simply, then, universals can be characterized as those entities that are *exemplifiable*—entities that *could* be exemplified by at least one thing.[4] Oddness hereby counts as a universal: though not exemplifiable *at* multiple locations as is redness, oddness *is* nonetheless exemplifiable. Unicornicity is not exemplified by anything, but *could* be exemplified (and perhaps *will* be exemplified by some animal that has yet to evolve).[5] Particular things exemplify universals, but how are particulars and universals to be distinguished?

III. Particulars

Rocks, bodies of water, raindrops, trees, kidneys, doughnuts, and whatever constituents such entities may have are to count as particulars. If there exist surfaces, waves, shadows, and holes, then they, too, are particulars. What, though, is the difference between particulars and nonparticulars?

One should not characterize particulars as those things that exemplify universals because universals themselves exemplify universals, but are not *ipso facto* particulars.[6] Dinosaurness, for example, is a universal even though it exemplifies the universal of being no longer exemplified.[7]

Particulars are characterized very broadly as those entities that are not universals. That is, particulars are those entities that are *nonexemplifiable*. A particular can *be* the exemplification of a universal, but nothing can *be* the exemplification of a particular. A particular animal may exemplify catness, but nothing can exemplify a particular cat.[8]

If events, God, monads, numbers, and souls all exist, they would all count as particulars because none is exemplifiable. These particulars, however, are not the sorts of particulars that could be *dependent* particulars.

IV. Dependent Particulars

If surfaces, boundaries, waves, shadows, holes, and reflections *are* dependent particulars, then they are particulars that in some sense *depend* on *independent* particulars. What kind of particular, however, could *be* a dependent particular, and in what sense would it be dependent? First, unlike universals construed as *necessary* things, dependent particulars are *non*necessary—they are things that *could* fail to exist. Thus, if God exists necessarily, then God is a particular, but could not be a *dependent* particular. Any wave, surface, or hole, however, *could* fail to exist in *some* possible scenario. For example, the wholes of which a particular wave, surface, and hole are constituents might never have existed or may someday all cease to exist.

Second, events (if they exist) are particulars that occur, but dependent particulars are *non*occurrable particulars.[9] There is a difference between a cube's surface and the surface's moving through space with the cube: the latter particular is an event, which is the sort of thing that *begins, happens* (or *occurs*), and *ends;* the surface, however, is not itself an event. Surfaces and other dependent particulars may come into being, endure, and cease to be, but they cannot begin, happen, and end.

Third, dependent particulars are (spatially) *constituentive*[10]—they can *be* (spatial) constituents of other particulars.[11] A (constituentless) corner of a cube can be a constituent of the cube's edges and faces, a wave can be a constituent of an ocean, and a hole can be a constituent of a piece of fried sweet dough. In this sense, dependent particulars resemble certain independent particulars: independent particulars such as small marble spheres, small quantities of water, and doughnut halves are also constituentive: they can be constituents of other particulars such as, respectively, large marble cubes, oceans, and uneaten doughnuts.

Cubes and their corners, oceans and their waves, and doughnuts and their holes are all particulars that are nonnecessary, nonoccurrable, and constituentive. Unlike bodies of cubes, water, and doughnuts, however, corners, waves, and holes are *dependent* on other particulars. One cannot isolate a "point of matter" by gradually obliterating every part of a cube except one of its corners. No ocean wave can exist independently of a larger body of water of which it is a wave. By consuming a doughnut, one cannot leave behind a free-standing hole. Among nonnecessary, nonoccurrable, constituentive particulars, what is the difference between those that are dependent and those that are not? In what sense, *are* dependent particulars *dependent* on independent particulars?

Körner's suggestion. Stephen Körner characterizes a sense in which dependent particulars are dependent on other particulars:

> [A] particular *d* [is] existentially dependent on a particular *i* if, and only if, *d* cannot exist (in logic or in fact) without *i*'s existing, but *i* can exist without *d*'s existing. A particular *i* can then be defined as an existentially independent particular *in a certain universe of fact and discourse* if, and only if, *i* belongs to a class of particulars . . . none of whose members is existentially dependent on any particular.[12]

Körner's suggestion is too loose because it implies that a cube of marble would count as a *dependent* particular. The marble cube's left half could exist without the rest of the cube, but the cube could not exist without a left half.[13] Though Körner's account of existential dependence is satisfied, a marble cube is not a dependent particular—it *can* exist without being a constituent of some other particular.

Brentano's insight. Writing about spatial continua and their boundaries (i.e., non-three-dimensional constituents), Franz Brentano explicates a sense in which dependent particulars are dependent on other particulars:

> . . . a point depends on something to which it belongs as a boundary. And this is a part of the nature of a point. . . . One cannot say of any specific continuum that its existence is required for the existence of a particular point. . . . For one and the same individual point to exist, what is necessary is not a certain specific continuum, but rather a continuum in general.[14]
>
> If something continuous is a mere boundary then it can never exist except in connection with other boundaries and except as belonging to a continuum which possesses a larger number of dimensions. Indeed this must be said of all boundaries, including those which possess no dimensions at all such as spatial points and moments of time and movement: a cutting free from everything that is continuous is for them absolutely impossible.[15]

What Brentano writes about continua and their non-three-dimensional constituents can be construed more broadly as an account of what makes dependent particulars dependent: a particular is dependent, if and only if, it cannot exist in any possible scenario without there being some other particular of which it is a constituent. *Independent* particulars are those particulars that are not in this sense dependent. Though a marble cube cannot itself exist without its left half, neither the cube nor its left half is a dependent particular: the cube can exist without itself being a constituent of something else; and by obliterating the cube's right half, the left half could exist without being a part of anything else. If the cube's boundaries (e.g., its faces, surfaces, midlines) cannot exist without being constituents of *something*, then such boundaries are dependent particulars.

An implication of this characterization of dependent particulars is that although a dependent particular may be a constituent of another dependent particular, every dependent particular *must* be a constituent of an independent particular. Suppose, for example, that (non-three-dimensional) boundaries are dependent particulars on grounds that such entities cannot exist apart from three-dimensional objects. A cube's bottom front edge would be a constituent of the cube's front face, but these boundaries would be dependent particulars that *ipso facto* would *have* to be constituents of a three-dimensional object. Given that three-dimensional objects are *independent* particulars, the boundaries would *have* to be constituents of an independent particular. Similarly, if shadows are dependent particulars, then a shadow's outer boundary may be a constituent of the shadow, but the outer boundary must also be a constituent of that independent particular (viz., the shadowed three-dimensional object) on which the shadow is dependent.

The characterization of dependence inspired by Brentano's insight appears to capture the sense in which waves, wrinkles, scratches, holes,[16] smiles, and shadows are dependent, if such entities *are* dependent particulars. One would assume that no wave or wrinkle can possibly exist apart from an independent particular that is waved or wrinkled, that no scratch or hole can exist apart from an independent particular that is scratched or perforated, and that no shadow can exist apart from an independent particular that is shadowed.

V. Holes

Holes are candidates for inclusion in the class of dependent particulars: they seem to be constituents of things that cannot exist independently of those things. One cannot obliterate a tooth, leaving behind just the cavity. Consider the following philosophical questions about holes:

(f) What *are* holes? Are holes, ontologically speaking, *sui generis*? In addition to matter and perhaps universals, must the metaphysician admit that *holes,* too, exist? Or, are holes identical with more familiar particulars—with regions of space or with the matter or boundaries that surround "empty areas"?

(g) Which sorts of things count as holes? Is the train tunnel through a mountain a hole? If so, is there also a hole through an empty ten-foot length of plumbing pipe? If what a dog digs in the ground is a hole, then is a dent in a car's fender a hole? If a sculptor produces a large glass orb that is solid with the exception of a small empty bubble in the center, is there also a hole inside the orb? If so, is there a hole inside an empty capped pill bottle? Are there holes in the orb and bottle if there are a loose glass bead inside the bubble and a pill in the bottle? If a hoop is made of a hollow tube, is there thereby a large circular hole surrounded by a round tubular hole? If the hoop is tossed over an empty pipe, is there a hole within a hole that is itself within a hole? If one spins the hoop around the pipe, is there also a hole that spins around the pipe?

David and Stephanie Lewis are responsible for the recent philosophical interest in holes. More concerned with addressing questions (f) than questions (g), the Lewises argue (in the 1970 philosophical dialogue reprinted in this volume) that a hole is identical with a *hole lining,* and a hole lining is that material part of a material object that "defines" or "surrounds" the "empty space" that one would ordinarily think of as the hole.

Inspired by the Lewises' essay, Roberto Casati and Achille C. Varzi published in 1994 a delightful treatise on holes and other "superficial particulars." They defend a comprehensive theory of holes, providing answers to questions (f) *and* (g). In the chapter reprinted here, Casati and Varzi offer objections to the Lewises' hole-lining view and then defend their thesis that holes are "*immaterial bodies,* 'growing' parasitically, like negative mushrooms, at the surfaces of material bodies." Claiming that "space is to holes what matter is to material objects," Casati and Varzi argue that holes are not regions of space, but are "superficial particulars" that are "*made of*" space. Their view implies that if one moves a doughnut, then its hole moves with it, but the hole may be composed of different regions of space as it moves with the doughnut.

VI. Boundaries and Surfaces

Leonardo Da Vinci wrote that "[a] body is something of which the boundaries form the surface."[17] Ordinarily, there is thought to be nothing puzzling about the boundary that separates the United States from Canada or about two spheres whose surfaces touch. Consider, however, some troubling questions. How thick *is* the boundary between the United States and Canada? And to which country does it belong? If it is part of both, then how could it be the boundary *between* the two countries? About the contact of solid objects with gases or liquids, Leonardo writes: "The surface is not part of the body nor part of the air or water that surround it, but it is a common boundary . . . in which the body ends in contact with the air. . . ."[18] Aristotle claims that "the extremities of things may be '*together*' without necessarily being *one:* but they cannot be one without being necessarily together."[19] Presumably, Leonardo (and perhaps Aristotle) would claim that there exists a "common boundary" between the United states and Canada that is a *part* of neither country. If there is such a "common boundary," is there yet another boundary between the "common boundary" and the United States and between the "common boundary" and Canada? What would happen to the "'common boundary" if an earthquake were to cleave cleanly one country away from the other?

Imagine a circle with quadrants each of a different color. What color is the *center* of the circle? Citing Galileo's claim that *the* center of the circle has as many parts as its periphery,[20] Brentano suggests that if a red and blue quadrant are in contact, then an outermost line of the red quadrant spatially coincides with an outermost line of the blue quadrant.[21] Though surprising enough that a dimensionless center could have color at all, could the circle's center exemplify *four* colors simultaneously? If not, then which one of the four colors *is* the circle's center, and why is the center *that* color rather than one of the other three?

If a sculpture is composed of a red sphere and blue sphere that touch, is it possible that, as Galileo would allow, the spheres touch at a single point?[22] If so, would this point be red, blue, or colorless? Could the spheres be subdivided until this non-three-dimensional constituent is isolated?[23] Moreover, how can infinitely many non-three-dimensional entities ever *compose* a three-dimensional object?[24] If dimensionless constituents *are* colorless, then how can red and blue spheres be composed of such constituents?

In his essay in this volume, Roderick Chisholm develops Brentano's view that there are two kinds of constituents: (non-three-dimensional) boundaries and (three-dimensional) parts. Chisholm argues that boundaries are dependent particulars that are (nonphysical[25]) *constituents* but not *parts* of objects. This view is consistent with the Leonardo-type claim that the boundary between the United States and Canada is a *constituent* of both countries but a *part* of neither country.

Avrum Stroll defends a radically different concept of surfaces, claiming that an object's surface is its outermost layer of atoms. Insofar as atoms are three-dimensional physical objects, Stroll rejects Chisholm's view that surfaces are non-three-dimensional, nonphysical constituents.

VII. Are *There Any Dependent Particulars?*

If Casati and Varzi are right about holes or if Chisholm is right about boundaries, then a complete ontology must include at least some dependent particulars because there *would* exist some entities that are essentially "parasitic" on independent particulars. If, however, the Lewises and Stroll are right, then truths about holes and boundaries do not obviously imply that *dependent* particulars exist. If, as the Lewises claim, all talk about holes can be reduced to talk about hole linings that are proper parts of material objects, then holes are not dependent particulars given that an object that is a proper part can exist without being a proper part of any object. Similarly, following Stroll, if all talk about boundaries and surfaces can be reduced to talk about layers of atoms, then boundaries and surfaces are *independent,* not dependent, particulars: there are possible scenarios in which a given layer of atoms is a part of no other particular.

Are there any entities that are obviously *dependent* particulars? Statements (b)–(e) at the beginning of this introductory essay suggest that waves, shadows, reflections, wrinkles, and smiles may be dependent particulars. Are they? Consider the following:

(h) The cat's shadow is on the wall.

Does (h), if true, imply that there exist dependent particulars that are shadows? Presumably, a shadow cannot exist unless there also exist a particular that casts the shadow and a particular that is shadowed. One might argue, however, that (h) can be reduced to a statement that refers only to independent particulars:

(h') There is a cat-shaped proper part of the wall that is not illuminated because a cat blocks the light source that illuminates the proper parts of the wall that surround the cat-shaped proper part.

Are there any truths about shadows that cannot be similarly reduced? If so, then regardless of the outcome of the disputes about holes and boundaries, shadows would require the inclusion of dependent particulars in one's ontology.

Are waves, reflections, wrinkles, and smiles dependent particulars? *Must* a thing that is an ocean wave be a constituent of an independent particular? Or could that thing exist apart from the ocean (though it might not then be a wave)? Are reflections particulars that *must* be constituents of independent particulars? Or can all talk of reflections be reduced to talk about certain independent particulars and ways that they can appear? Are wrinkles and smiles dependent on independent objects that are faces? Or are wrinkles and smiles facial proper parts that could exist independently of any object? Could a plastic surgeon excise a piece of skin that is a wrinkle? Though the skin on the tip of the surgeon's scalpel may have ceased to be a wrinkle, could the skin not exist independently of any other particular?

This introductory essay leaves to the reader the task of determining whether all talk of holes, boundaries, shadows, waves, reflections, and the like can be reduced to talk about *independent* particulars. Thus, left open is the question of whether there is good reason to believe that dependent particulars exist.[26]

NOTES

1. For a clear, succinct introduction to metaphysical problems involving qualities and substantial things, see W. R. Carter, *The Elements of Metaphysics* (New York: McGraw-Hill, 1990), pp. 45–62. See also Bruce Aune, *Metaphysics: The Elements* (Minneapolis: University of Minnesota Press, 1985), Chapters 3–6. For more advanced work, see D. M. Armstrong, *Universals: An Opinionated Introduction,* Focus Series (Boulder, CO: Westview Press, 1989) and D. H. Mellor and Alex Oliver, eds., *Properties* (Oxford and New York: Oxford University Press, 1997).

2. So construed, universals are what Roderick M. Chisholm calls *properties* or *attributes.* Chisholm offers a defense of attributes in *A Realistic Theory of Categories: An Essay on Ontology* (Cambridge and New York: Cambridge University Press, 1996), pp. 4, 11–21. See also Michael J. Loux, *Substance and Attribute* (Dordrecht, Holland: D. Reidel, 1978), pp. 89–104. Not every philosopher is as friendly toward universals; for example, see Michael Devitt, "'Ostrich Nominalism' or 'Mirage Realism'?" in Mellor and Oliver's *Properties.*

3. Cf. Armstrong, *Universals: An Opinionated Introduction,* p. 16.

4. This working characterization of universals is controversial. For example, it implies that there are no impossible universals (e.g., round-squareness)—no existing universals that cannot possibly be exemplified. Chisholm's theory of attributes includes impossible attributes; see *A Realistic Theory of Categories,* pp. 11-12, 18. To allow for impossible universals, one could claim instead that universals are the sorts of entities that can bear the relation *involves* to other entities (where involvement is a primitive logical relation that can obtain only between universals). For example, squareness would count as a universal because it involves rectangularity; though a particular square table top may exemplify rectangularity, the table top cannot itself involve anything.

5. Cf. Saul A. Kripke, *Naming and Necessity* (Cambridge, MA: Harvard University Press, 1980), pp. 23–24, 156–57.

6. That substances are those things that have accidents is the view that Franz Brentano attributes to Aristotle. See Brentano, *The Theory of Categories,* trans. Roderick M. Chisholm and Norbert Guterman (Boston: Martinus Nijhoff, 1981), p. 101.

7. Cf. Brian Carr, *Metaphysics: An Introduction* (London: Macmillan Education, 1987), p. 45.

8. Philosophers who insist that qualities require not a theory of necessary universals but a theory of tropes might characterize a trope as something that is *compresentable*—something that can exist *compresent* with something else (i.e., another trope). Then, instead of suggesting that an identifying feature of particulars is nonexemplifiability, one could suggest instead that a particular is a thing that is *non*compresentable or that a particular is a thing constituted by compresentable entities sharing a common location. For an introductory discussion of tropes, see Keith Campbell, *Metaphysics: An Introduction,* The Dickenson Series in Philosophy (Encino and Belmont, CA: Dickenson, 1976), pp. 206–19, and see Armstrong's *Universals: An Opinionated Introduction,* pp. 113–33.

9. Among those who characterize particulars more narrowly, some would claim that events are not particulars. Cf. Carr, *Metaphysics: An Introduction,* pp. 51–52. See also Peter van Inwagen, *Material Beings* (Ithaca: Cornell University Press, 1990), p. 82; cf. van Inwagen, *Metaphysics,* Dimensions of Philosophy Series (Boulder, CO: Westview Press, 1993), p. 25.

10. How spatial constituents should be characterized is controversial. Informally, one could claim that a thing is a *spatial* constituent of a whole if it bears spatial relations to other constituents of the whole. Spatial relations would include *is to the left of, is longer than,* and *is continuous with.* How spatial relations are to be distinguished from nonspatial relations is yet another matter.

11. Cf. van Inwagen's *Material Beings,* pp. 81-97. *If* there exist monads that *cannot* be a part of any whole, then such monads could not be *dependent* particulars.

12. Stephan Körner, *Metaphysics: Its Structure and Function* (Cambridge: Cambridge University Press, 1984), p. 17.

13. Cf. Aune, *Metaphysics: The Elements,* p. 77.

14. Brentano, *The Theory of Categories,* pp. 157–58. Chisholm makes much use of Brentano's insight in his essay on boundaries that appears in this anthology.

15. Brentano, *Philosophical Investigations on Space, Time and the Continuum,* trans. Barry Smith (London, New York, Sydney: Croom Helm, 1988), p. 10. See also Brentano's *Psychology from an*

Empirical Standpoint, ed. Oscar Kraus; English edition, ed. Linda L. McAlister; trans. Antos C. Rancurello, D. B. Terrell, and McAlister (New York: Humanities Press, 1973), p. 356.

16. Cf. Roberto Casati and Achille C. Varzi, *Holes and Other Superficialities* (Cambridge, MA: MIT Press, 1994), pp. 17–19.

17. *The Notebooks of Leonardo Da Vinci,* vol. 1, trans. Edward MacCurdy (New York: Reynal & Hitchcock, 1938), p. 627.

18. Ibid.; see also p. 81.

19. Aristotle, *Physics,* trans. R. P. Hardie and R. K. Gayle, in *The Basic Works of Aristotle,* ed. Richard McKeon (New York: Random House, 1941), V.3.227a2O.

20. Galileo Galilei, *Dialogues Concerning Two New Sciences,* trans. Henry Crew and Alfonso De Salvio (New York: The Macmillan Co., 1914), pp. 26–29.

21. Cf. Brentano, *Psychology from an Empirical Standpoint,* p. 357 and *Philosophical Investigations on Space, Time and the Continuum,* p. 41.

22. Cf. Galileo Galilei, *Concerning the Two Chief World Systems,* trans. Stillman Drake, 2nd ed. (Berkeley and Los Angeles: University of California Press, 1967), p. 206.

23. Cf. Galileo, *Dialogues Concerning Two New Sciences,* pp. 30–31.

24. Cf. Aristotle, *Physics,* III.6.206a15–20: "When we speak of the potential existence of a statue we mean that there will be an actual statue. It is not so with the infinite. There will not be an actual infinite."

25. In later work, Chisholm explains clearly why his view implies that boundaries are nonphysical constituents of physical objects. See *A Realistic Theory of Categories,* pp. 95–96. Cf. *The Notebooks of Leonardo,* vol. 1, p. 654: "The line has not in itself any matter or substance but may more readily be called an incorporeal thing than a substance, and being of such condition it does not occupy space."

26. For their many helpful objections and suggestions, I thank W. R. Carter, Russell Daw, Steven Hales, Nita Hestevold, Kipp McMichael, James Otteson, and Norvin Richards.

Holes 29

DAVID LEWIS AND STEPHANIE LEWIS

Argle. I believe in nothing but concrete material objects.

Bargle. There are many of your opinions I applaud; but one of your less pleasing characteristics is your fondness for the doctrines of nominalism and materialism. Every time you get started on any such topic. I know we are in for a long argument. Where shall we start this time: numbers, colors, lengths, sets, force-fields, sensations, or what?

Argle. Fictions all! I've thought hard about every one of them.

Bargle. A long evening's work. Before we start, let me find you a snack. Will you have some crackers and cheese?

Argle. Thank you. What splendid Gruyère!

Bargle You know, there are remarkably many holes in this piece.

Argle. There are.

Bargle. Got you!

Bargle. You admit there are many holes in that piece of cheese. Therefore, there are some holes in it. Therefore, there are some holes. In other words,

From Australasian Journal of Philosophy, *vol. 48, 1970, pp. 206–212. Reprinted by permission of the*

holes exist. But holes are not made of matter; to the contrary, they result from the absence of matter.

Argle. I did say that there are holes in the cheese; but that is not to imply that there are holes.

Bargle. However not? If you say that there are A's that are B's, you are committed logically to the conclusion that there are A's.

Argle. When I say that there are holes in something, I mean nothing more nor less than that it is perforated. The synonymous shape-predicates '. . . is perforated' and 'there are holes in . . .'—just like any other shape-predicate, say '. . . is a dodecahedron'—may truly be predicated of pieces of cheese, without any implication that perforation is due to the presence of occult, immaterial entities. I am sorry my innocent predicate confuses you by sounding like an idiom of existential quantification, so that you think that inferences involving it are valid when they are not. But I have my reasons. You, given a perforated piece of cheese and believing as you do that it is perforated because it contains immaterial entities called holes, employ an idiom of existential quantification to say falsely 'There are holes in it.' Agreeable fellow that I am, I wish to have a sentence that sounds like yours and that is true exactly when you falsely suppose your existential quantification over immaterial things to be true. That way we could talk about the cheese without philosophizing, if only you'd let me. You and I would understand our sentences differently, but the difference wouldn't interfere with our conversation until you start drawing conclusions which follow from your false sentence but not from my homonymous true sentence.[1]

Bargle. Oh, very well. But behold: there are as many holes in my piece of cheese as in yours. Do you agree?

Argle. I'll take your word for it without even counting: there are as many holes in mine as in yours. But what I mean by that is that either both pieces are singly-perforated, or both are doubly-perforated, or both are triply-perforated, and so on.

Bargle. What a lot of different shape-predicates you know! How ever did you find time to learn them all? And what does 'and so on' mean?[2]

Argle. Let me just say that the two pieces are equally-perforated. Now I have used only one two-place predicate.

Bargle. Unless I singly-perforate each of these crackers, how will you say that there are as many holes in my cheese as crackers on my plate? Be so kind as not to invent another predicate on the spot. I am quite prepared to go on until you have told me about all the predicates you have up your sleeve. I have a good imagination, and plenty of time.

Argle. Oh, dear . . . (ponders)

Argle. I was wrong. There are holes.

Bargle. You recant?

Argle. No. Holes are material objects.

Bargle. I expected that sooner. You are thinking, doubtless, that every hole is filled with matter. silver amalgam, air, interstellar gas, luminiferous ether or whatever it may be.

Argle. No. Perhaps there are no truly empty holes; but I cannot deny that there might be.

Bargle. How can something utterly devoid of matter be made of matter?

Argle. You're looking for the matter in the wrong place. (I mean to say, that's what you would be doing if there were any such things as places, which there aren't.) The matter isn't inside the hole. It would be absurd to say it was: nobody wants to say that holes are inside themselves. The matter surrounds the hole. The lining of a hole, you agree, is a material object. For every hole there is a hole-lining; for every hole-lining there is a hole. I say the hole-lining *is* the hole.

Bargle. Didn't you say that the hole-lining surrounds the hole? Things don't surround themselves.

Argle. Holes do. In my language, 'surrounds' said of a hole (described as such) means 'is identical with.' 'Surrounds' said of other things means just what you think it means.

Bargle. Doesn't it bother you that your dictionary must have two entries under 'surrounds' where mine has only one?

Argle. A little, but not much. I'm used to putting up with such things.

Bargle. Such what?

Argle. Such dictionary entries. They're made of dried ink, you recall.

Bargle. Oh. I suppose you'll also say that ' . . . is in . . . ' or ' . . . is through . . . ' said of a hole means ' . . . is part of . . . '.

Argle. Exactly so, Bargle.

Bargle. Then do you still say that 'There are holes in the cheese' contains an unanalyzed shape-predicate synonymous with ' . . . is perforated'?

Argle. No; it is an existential quantification, as you think it is. It means that there exist material objects such that they are holes and they are parts of the piece of cheese.

Bargle. But we wouldn't say, would we, that a hole is made out of cheese?

Argle. No; but the fact that we wouldn't say it doesn't mean it isn't true. We wouldn't have occasion to say, unless philosophizing, that these walls are perpendicular to the floor; but they are. Anyhow we *do* say that caves are holes in the ground and that some of them are made out of limestone.

Bargle. Take this paper-towel roller. Spin it on a lathe. The hole-lining spins. Surely you'd never say the hole spins?

Argle. Why not?

Bargle. Even though the hole might continue to be entirely filled with a dowel that didn't spin or move at all?

Argle. What difference does that make?

Bargle. None, really. But now I have you: take a toilet-paper roller, put it inside the paper-towel roller, and spin it the other way. The big hole spins clockwise. The little hole spins counter-clockwise. But the little hole is part of the big hole, so it spins clockwise along with the rest of the big hole. So if holes can spin, as you think, the little hole turns out to be spinning in both directions at once, which is absurd.

Argle. I see why you might think that the little hole is part of the big hole, but you can't expect me to agree. The little hole is inside the big hole, but that's all. Hence I have no reason to say that the little hole is spinning clockwise.

Bargle. Consider a thin-walled hole with a gallon of water inside. The volume of the hole is at least a gallon, whereas the volume of the hole-lining is much less. If the hole is the hole-lining, then whatever was true of one would have to be true of the other. They could not differ in volume.

Argle. For 'hole' read 'bottle'; for 'hole-lining' also read 'bottle.' You have the same paradox. Holes, like bottles, have volume—or, as I'd rather say, are voluminous or equi-voluminous with other things—in two different senses. There's the volume of the hole or bottle itself, and there's the volume of the largest chunk of fluid which could be put inside the hole or bottle without compression. For holes, as for bottles, contextual clues permit us to keep track of which we mean.

Bargle. What is the volume of the hole itself? How much of the cheese do you include as part of one of these holes? And how do you decide? Arbitrarily, that's how. Don't try saying you include as little of the cheese as possible, for however much you include, you could have included less.

Argle. What we call a single hole is really many hole-linings. Some include more of the cheese, some include less. Therefore I need not decide, arbitrarily or otherwise, how much cheese is part of the hole. Many different decisions are equally correct.

Bargle. How can a single hole be identical with many hole-linings that are not identical with one another?

Argle. Really there are many different holes, and each is identical with a different hole-lining. But all these different holes are the same hole.

Bargle. You contradict yourself. Don't you mean to say that they all surround the same hole—where by 'surround' I mean 'surround,' not 'be identical with'?

Argle. Not at all. I would contradict myself if I said that two different holes were identical. But I didn't; what I said was that they were the same hole. Two holes are the same hole when they have a common part that is itself a hole.

Bargle. You agreed before that there were as many holes in my cheese as crackers on my plate. Are there still?

Argle. Yes; there are two of each left.

Bargle. Two crackers, to be sure, but how can you say there are two holes?

Argle. Thus: there is a hole, and there is another hole that is not the same hole, and every hole in the cheese is the same hole as one or the other.

Bargle. Be so kind as to say 'co-perforated,' not 'same,' and stop pretending to talk about identity when you are not. I understand you now: co-perforation is supposed to be an equivalence relation among hole-linings, and when you say there are two holes you are trying to say that there are two non-identical co-perforation-classes of hole-linings. Really you identify holes not with hole-linings but with *classes* of hole-linings.

Argle. I would if I could, but I can't. No; holes are hole-linings; but when I speak of them as holes, I find it convenient to use 'same' meaning 'co-perforated' wherever a man of your persuasion would use 'same' meaning 'identical.' You know my reason for this trickery: my sentences about sameness of holes will be true just when you wrongly suppose your like-sounding sentences to be. The same goes for sentences about number of holes, since we both analyze these in terms of sameness.[3]

Bargle. You still haven't told me how you say there are as many holes in my cheese as crackers on my plate, without also saying how many there are.

Argle. Here goes. There exist three things X, Y, and Z. X is part of the sum of the crackers, Y is part of the cheese, and Z is part of Y. Every maximal connected part of Y is a hole, and every hole in the cheese is the same hole as some maximal connected part of Y. X overlaps each of the crackers and Z overlaps each maximal connected part of Y. Everything which is either the intersection of X and a cracker or the intersection of Z and some maximal connected part of Y is the same size as any other such thing. X is the same size as Z.[4]

Bargle. Your devices won't work because co-perforation is not an equivalence relation. Any two overlapping parts of my cheese have a common part that is a hole-lining, though in most cases the hole-lining is entirely filled with cheese. To be co-perforated is therefore nothing more than to overlap, and overlapping is no equivalence relation. The result is that although, as you say, you can find two hole-linings in this cheese that are not co-perforated, you can find another one that is co-perforated with both of them.

Argle. If you were right that a hole made of cheese could be entirely filled with the same kind of cheese, you could find far more than two non-co-perforated hole-linings; and there would be no such thing as cheese without holes in it. But you are wrong. A hole is a hole not just by virtue of its own shape but also by virtue of the way it contrasts with the matter inside it and around it. The same is true of other shape-predicates; I wouldn't say that any part of the cheese is a dodecahedron, though I admit that there are parts—parts that do not contrast with their surroundings—that are *shaped like* dodecahedra.

Bargle. Consider the paper-towel roller. How many holes?

Argle. One. You know what I mean: many, but they're all the same.

Bargle. I think you must say there are at least two. The left half and the right half are not the same hole. They have no common part, so no common part that is a hole.

Argle. They're not holes, they're two parts of a hole.

Bargle. Why aren't they holes themselves? They are singly-perforated and they are made of matter unlike the matter inside them. If I cut them apart you'd have to say they were holes?

Argle. Yes.

Bargle. You admit that a hole can be a proper part of a bigger—say, thicker-skinned-hole?

Argle. Yes.

Bargle. You admit that they are shaped like holes?

Argle. Yes, but they aren't holes. I can't say why they aren't. I know which things are holes, but I can't give you a definition. But why should I? You already know what hole-linings are. I say the two halves of the roller are only parts of a hole because I—like you—would say they are only parts of a hole-lining. What isn't a hole-lining isn't a hole.

Bargle. In that case, I admit that co-perforation may be an equivalence relation at least among singly-perforated hole-linings.

Argle. All holes are singly-perforated. A doubly-perforated thing has two holes in it that are not the same hole.

Bargle. Are you sure? Take the paper-towel roller and punch a little hole in its side. Now you have a hole in a hole-lining. You'd have to say you have a hole in a hole. You have a little hole which is part of a big hole; the big hole is not singly-perforated; and the little hole and the big hole are the same hole, since the little hole is a common part of each.

Argle. I think not. You speak of the big hole; but what we have are two big holes, not the same, laid end to end. There is also the little hole, not the same as either big hole, which overlaps them both. Of course we sometimes call something a hole, in a derivative sense, if it is a connected sum of holes. Any decent cave consists of many holes that are not the same hole, so I must have been speaking in this derivative sense when I said that caves are holes.

Bargle. What peculiar things you are driven to say when philosophy corrupts your mind! Tell me the truth: would you have dreamt for a moment of saying there were two big holes rather than one if you were not suffering under the influence of a philosophical theory?

Argle. No; I fear I would have remained ignorant.

Bargle. I see that I can never hope to refute you, since I no sooner reduce your position to absurdity than you embrace the absurdity.

Argle. Not absurdity; disagreement with common opinion.

Bargle. Very well. But I, for one, have more trust in common opinions than I do in any philosophical reasoning whatever. In so far as you disagree with them, you must pay a great price in the plausibility of your theories.

Argle. Agreed. We have been measuring that price. I have shown that it is not so great as you thought; I am prepared to pay it. My theories can earn credence by their clarity and economy; and if they disagree a little with common opinion, then common opinion may be corrected even by a philosopher.

Bargle. The price is still too high.

Argle. We agree in principle; we're only haggling.

Bargle. We do. And the same is true of our other debates over ontic parsimony. Indeed, this argument has served us as an illustration—novel, simple, and self-contained—of the nature of our customary disputes.

Argle. And yet the illustration has interest in its own right. Your holes, had I been less successful, would have punctured my nominalistic materialism with the greatest of ease.

Bargle. Rehearsed and refreshed, let us return to—say—the question of classes.[5]

NOTES

1. *Cf.* W. V. Quine, "On What There Is." *From a Logical Point of View,* 2nd ed. (Cambridge, Mass: Harvard University Press, 1961), p. 13.

2. *Cf.* Donald Davidson, "Theories of Meaning and Learnable Languages," in Y. Bar-Hillel, *Logic, Methodology and Philosophy of Science,* Proceedings of the 1964 International Congress (Amsterdam, 1965), pp. 383–94.

3. *Cf.* Quine's maxim of identification of indiscernibles in "Identity, Ostension, and Hypostasis," *From a Logical Point of View,* p. 71; P. T. Geach, "Identity," *Review of Metaphysics* 21 (1967): 3–12.

4. This translation adapts a device from Nelson Goodman and W. V. Quine, "Steps toward a Constructive Nominalism," *Journal of Symbolic Logic* 12 (1947): 109–10.

5. There would be little truth to the guess that Argle is one of the authors and Bargle is the other. We thank Charles Chastain, who is also neither Argle nor Bargle, for many helpful comments.

Reading Questions

1. Argle allows that "a single hole is really many hole linings." A doughnut's single hole is both its eighth-inch thick hole lining and also the quarter-inch thick hole lining that contains the former. Suppose that one digs a hole in an otherwise spherical planet. Does the Argle's view imply that, by digging the hole, the entire planet is a hole? If so, does this counterintuitive implication pose a serious problem for the hole-lining view?
2. Argle would agree that to scoop the small quantity of membrane and seeds from half a cantaloupe is to create a hole in the melon half. If, however, one slices a one-half-inch wedge from the melon half, is the indentation in the large remaining melon wedge a hole? If one continues to slice one-half-inch wedges until one has exactly one quarter of the melon left, is the indentation in that melon quarter a hole? Is there a hole in one of the half-inch slices? How might Argle respond to these questions?

3. If Argle's hole-lining view is correct, holes are material objects that are indeed particulars, but would they be dependent particulars?

30 Immaterial Bodies

ROBERTO CASATI AND ACHILLE C. VARZI

LUDOVICIAN HOLES

In their 1970 paper "Holes," David and Stephanie Lewis distinguished clearly—and tried to solve—the major difficulties surrounding a nominalist *cum* materialist account of holes. Their reasoning goes as follows: We easily talk of, refer to, or quantify over holes; however, holes do not seem to be made of matter, and we seem unable satisfactorily to paraphrase talk about holes into talk about perforated material objects. The suggestion, then, is that holes *are* material things. They are not, as one might think, the "fillers" (the airy plugs that fill up every hole); rather, they are the hole-linings (figure 1). "The matter isn't inside the hole. It would be absurd to say it was: nobody wants to say that holes are inside themselves. The matter surrounds the hole. The lining of a hole, you agree, is a material object. For every hole there is a hole-lining; for every hole-lining there is a hole. I say the hole-lining *is* the hole." (p. 424)

Several bizarre consequences of this account are discussed by the Lewises. Here are some of them, together with the Lewises' own replies.

(1) We accept that holes cannot be hole-fillers, for they cannot be inside themselves. Now, if holes are hole-linings, and if hole-linings surround holes, then holes surround themselves. Reply: 'Surrounds' has two different meanings: when said of ordinary things, it has its ordinary meaning; when said of a hole, it means 'is identical with.'

(2) Holes cannot be made of cheese, but hole-linings can. Reply: "We *do* say that caves are holes in the ground and that some of them are made out of limestone."

(3) If you were to take a paper-towel roller, spin it clockwise, put a toilet-paper roller inside it, and spin it counterclockwise, then something would spin in one way when a part of the same thing spins in the opposite way. Reply: The little hole inside the big hole is *not* a part of it.

(4) The volume of a hole could be less than the volume of a hole-lining. Reply: "For 'hole' read 'bottle'; for 'hole-lining' also read 'bottle.' You have the same paradox.... Contextual clues permit us to keep track of which we mean."

(5) The hole's volume is arbitrary, depending on which hole-lining we choose. Reply: "What we call a single hole is really many hole-linings."

(6) "How can a single hole be identical with many hole-linings that are not identical with one another?" Reply: *a* and *b* are the same hole "when they have a common part that is itself a hole."

(7) Then a hole is really two, at least: the left half and the right half of a paper-towel roller are not the same hole, as they have

From Holes and Other Superficialities *by Roberto Casati and Achille C. Varzi. Cambridge, MA: MIT Press, 1994. Reprinted by permission of MIT Press.*

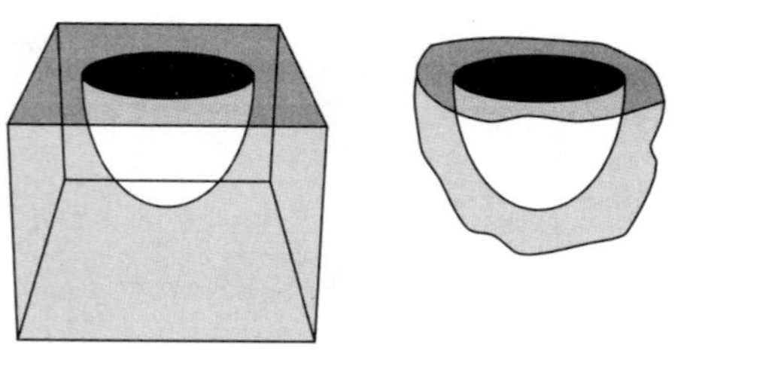

Figure 1
A hole (left); one of its hole-linings (right), i.e., a hole *tout court* according to the Lewises: a material body.

> no part in common. If you were to cut the two halves apart, you would say that they are holes, since they are shaped like holes. Thus there are two holes here, and not one. Reply: these are parts of a hole, but they are not holes. "I can't say why they aren't. I know which things are holes, but I can't give you a definition."

DANGEROUS AMBIGUITIES

We have indulged in reporting these objections and replies because they are indicative of the difficulties involved in the proposed account. The Ludovician identification of holes with hole-linings does provide an appealing way of treating holes as (parts of) material objects, yet it gives rise to numerous puzzles whose alleged solutions seem in some cases to be hardly tenable.

Note in particular that the given identification implies a radical change in the meaning of certain predicates. For instance, 'surrounds' becomes 'is identical with' (or, better, it becomes a reflexive relation; as Jerzy Perzanowski pointed out to us, the Lewises' account here is stronger than it need be). This and similar changes are required; insofar as a hole-lining surrounds a hole, if the hole *is* a hole-lining it will surround itself. A revisionary proposal is not in itself unacceptable. Yet some predicates seem to require special care—their translations become very problematic. If holes are hole-linings, 'inside' turns out to be ambiguous when its second argument is a hole. It means both what 'inside' ordinarily means (the internal part of the hole-lining, which is material) and also 'outside' (the empty part that, on the common-sense understanding, corresponds to the hole). But there are two outsides here. In figure 2, let *h* be what we would ordinarily take as a hole, let *l* be one of its hole-linings, and let *o* be whatever is not inside *l* (in the previous sense) and does not overlap *h*. In the revisionary account, 'inside' means 'outside.' But now, does 'outside *l*' refer to *o* or to *h*? "Look," one could say, "'outside' means *the smaller outside*. *h* is smaller than *o*. Therefore 'outside' means *h*." Surely this is not an acceptable answer.

Or, imagine cutting the profile of a fish out of a sheet of paper, as in figure 3. Look at the sheet. If somebody asks you what profile you see, you will naturally speak of a fish outline, though *that* is actually the shape of the hole. Now, if somebody asks you to put something outside the hole's profile, where will you put it? We believe you will not put it inside the hole (in *A*). Yet this is precisely what would be required by the identification of holes with hole-linings.

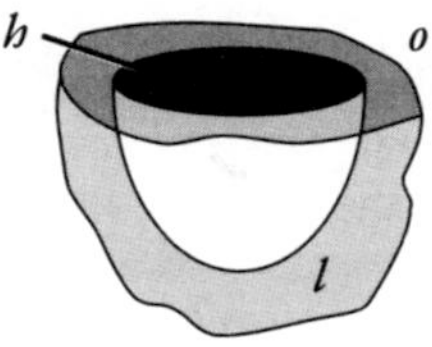

Figure 2
If holes are hole-linings, 'inside' and 'outside' can be ambiguous.

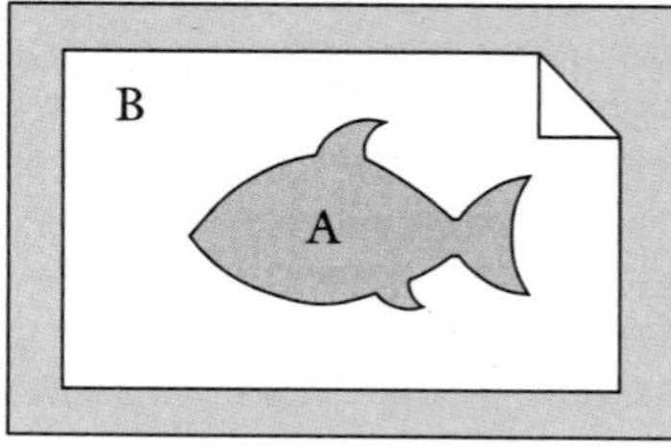

Figure 3
A fishy hole.

A much more problematic predicate is 'to enlarge.' To enlarge a hole is not necessarily to enlarge its hole-linings; sometimes it is exactly the opposite! In figure 4, for instance, the hole on the right is bigger than the one on the left, but it definitely has a smaller hole-lining. In this case, not only cannot the predicate preserve its ordinary meaning, but it receives different interpretations with no apparent uniform translation algorithm. Sometimes to enlarge a hole is to enlarge the hole-lining, but not always. The Lewises would insist here on the importance of contextual clues. Nevertheless, one could doubt whether context is always sufficient to disambiguate. Suppose you are asked to enlarge the hole in the left object of figure 4. The context is clear. But what does the question amount to? If holes are hole-linings, the question is really a request to enlarge the hole-lining. But does that determine an enlargement of what *we* take to be the hole (as in case *a* of figure 5), or an enlargement that does not affect our hole (as in case *b*)? The context is clear, but there is no way to resolve the ambiguity without somehow relying on our pre-Ludovician notion of a hole.

And, finally, one would prefer some systematicity, even if one does not see any objection to constant implicit reference to the context—a preference whose plausibility is especially dramatic if we keep in mind that we are dealing here with some basic spatial and material predicates which provide the stuff for our more metaphorical (and surely more contextual) thoughts. From this point of view, the account we are pursuing can claim to be not only more intuitive but also more systematic, and therefore preferable.

Other worries could be added to the list. It sounds bizarre, for instance, to affirm that explosions produce hole-linings. (*Don't* say now that 'produce' really means 'enlarge.') And in ordinary discourse it makes little sense to speak of a hole's being "removed" (unless this is taken to mean that a hole is destroyed or eliminated); by contrast, one can certainly remove a hole-lining (an operation which, however, would likely produce a *bigger* hole than the original, not a smaller one).

Further, one must address the basic question of *how* one can identify holes with their linings, since it seems that a hole may have indefinitely many linings. Here the Ludovician answer is that one need not decide: "Really there are many different holes, and each is identical with a different hole-lining. But all these different holes are the same hole." As was mentioned above, the intended solution here is to draw a distinction between identity and the relation of "being the same hole as," the latter amounting to "having a common part that is itself a hole." But this can be quite odd. For instance, with reference to figure 6 we may consistently hold that (a) every part of l_1, that *prima facie* qualifies as a lining of h_1 is the same hole as l_1, (b) every part of l_2 that *prima facie* qualifies as a lining of h_2 is the same hole as l_2, and (c) l_1 is not the same hole as l_2, for they do not have any common parts. On the other hand, l_3 has many parts in common with l_1 which are themselves holes, hence it must be the

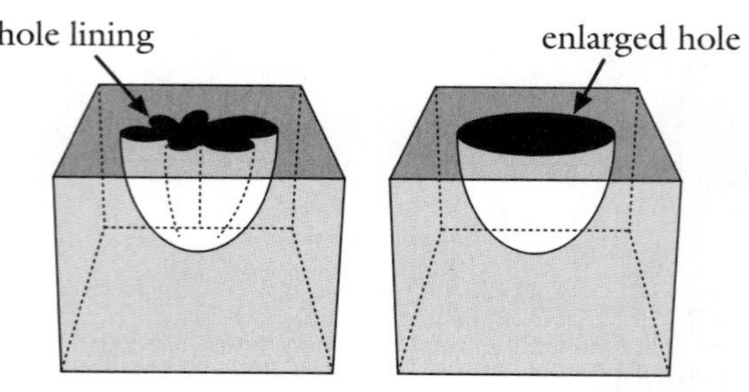

Figure 4
An enlarged hole with a smaller hole-lining.

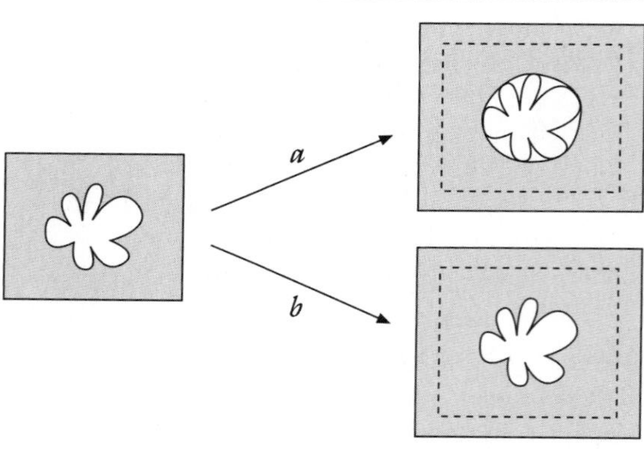

Figure 5
Enlarging a Ludovician hole—but how?

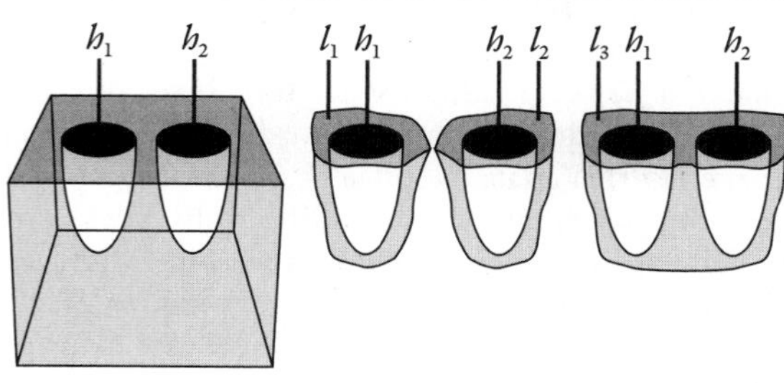

Figure 6
If being the same hole is having a common part that is a hole, then l_1 is not the same hole as l_2, though they are both the same hole as l_3.

same hole as l_1; and it has many parts in common with l_2 which are themselves holes, hence it must be the same hole as l_2. In view of (c) above, this means that the relation is-the-same-hole-as is not transitive, at least on the usual understanding of part-whole relations. But then the basic question remains: How many holes are there in the cube? Two or three? The Ludovician account seems to yield the second answer—and that is hardly tenable.

There is, finally, some ontological question left open by the very notion of a hole-lining when this is different from the entire host. A hole-lining is in such a case a proper part of the host, and a *potential* part only. Therefore, if we do not have complete clarity about the ontological status of potential parts, we should avoid ontological commitment to them, and the whole project of explaining away holes by reference to hole-linings becomes at least suspicious. Moreover, if holes are anything, they are actual—one cannot detect potential holes in an object.

A RADICAL ALTERNATIVE

Such difficulties also arise with other attempts to explain away holes in terms of linings. For instance, Frank Jackson has argued that there is another response available, not considered by the Lewises: "Holes are not hole-surrounds [i.e., hole-linings], for they are nothing at all; nor can statements 'about' holes in things be translated in terms of unstructured one-place predicates like 'is perforated' or 'has four holes'; but what can be done is to translate statements putatively about holes in terms of statements about hole-surrounds, 'There are many holes in that piece of cheese' just says that it contains many hole-surrounds; 'There are the same number of holes in *A* as in *B*' just says that *A* and *B* have the same number of hole-surrounds; *and so on and so forth*." (*Perception*, p. 132, our italics)

One might well agree that "to offer these translations is not to identify holes and hole-surrounds anymore than to translate statements about the average family in the usual way is to identify the average family with the families that are there" (ibid.). But how should one fully spell out the details of the clause "and so on and so forth"? Surely this is not a matter of trivial details needing only to be routinely worked out. The systematic feasibility of such a treatment is far from obvious, and some of the above-mentioned difficulties prove just as threatening in this approach as in the materialist account of the Lewises. Although hole-linings are no longer being asserted to coincide with holes, some effective way of relating our putative holes with their linings is still wanted. We need a definite notion of what a hole-lining is, and it is not clear how one should define that. In fact it is not even clear whether such a notion can be adequately characterized, as our argument referring to figure 6 suggests.

TWO THEORIES, AND MORE

We have seen that there are at least two different ways to construe holes. First there is the possibility of relying heavily on the suggestion that holes are superficial parts—parts of an object's surface. The properties of a hole are all the properties of that part of an object's surface (theory 1; we may call this the Superficial Theory). Then there is the Ludovician idea that holes are parts of material objects—they are hole-linings (theory 2).

These two theories do not, of course, exhaust the matter. For example, one can combine them. According to the resulting variant (which we label theory 2^{-}), holes are *superficial* hole-linings. They are the surface of any hole in the sense of theory 2; i.e., they are any part of the object's surface that comprises what, in theory 1, is a hole. Moreover, there exist some interesting relationships between these three theories. For instance, holes in the sense of theory 1 are *minimal* holes both in the sense of theory 2^- and in the sense of theory 2. One could also consider the radical view according to which the hole coincides with the entire host. Such a view—call it theory 2^+—can be kept separate from the philosophical position of *reism,* which would say that holes do not exist at all insofar as only material objects exist. Rather, according to theory 2^+, holes exist: they are *maximal* hole-linings and coincide spatially with the entire holed object.

All these theories (see figure 7) rest on a very strong relation tying holes to their hosts, or at least to material parts thereof (a relation that in theories 2 and 2^+ is so strong as to become identity). We shall now introduce an entirely different account that conceptually frees holes from their hosts. As we shall see, such a theory bears some interesting relations to any of the theories above. But let us address the matter indirectly.

WHAT ARE HOLES MADE OF?

Consider the following hypothesis: Holes are *made of* space. They are not identical with some region of space, but they are constituted by space. Space is, in a sense, the matter of holes—or, if you prefer, space is to holes what matter is to material objects.

The analogy is far-reaching. Just as we have flux of matter for material objects, we have flux of space for holes. And just as portions of matter can coincide with objects, portions of space can coincide with holes. However, the analogy need not be complete, and we need not accept all the implications. Some questions then arise immediately. Are material objects made of space too? If so, they are made of *two* different matters: ordinary matter and space. Is that plausible at all? And if objects are made of space, how do they differ from holes?

The answer to the last question is not difficult: Both holes and material objects are made of space; however, unlike material objects, holes are made of space *only.* This raises the further question of the difference between holes and regions of space, for one can say that regions of space, too, are made of space. But again the solution is not difficult: Holes are things that can both (i) be made of space only and (ii) be not identical with some region of space. (Remember that holes can move, whereas regions of space cannot.)

In fact, one could wonder whether holes are *the only* things satisfying conditions i and ii, in which case one could even consider taking this as a sort of definitory axiom for holes. One could be tempted here to think of a counterexample. Imagine some qualitatively filled region of space (say, a volume of pinkish expanse), and imagine that a shadow—a colorless floating spot—finds its way into it. There is no quality exemplified at that region; thus, it is made of space only. That is, condition (i) is satisfied. And the region is not identical with a region of space, for it can move. Hence, condition (ii) is also satisfied. Yet what we have here is a shadow, not a hole. The counterexample nevertheless suggests a way out. Floating expanses are indeed metaphysically floating; they enjoy independence, whereas holes would be lost if they did not have a sustaining material object. There is no object the floating expanse is parasitic upon, whereas holes are always closely tied to something they are holes in.

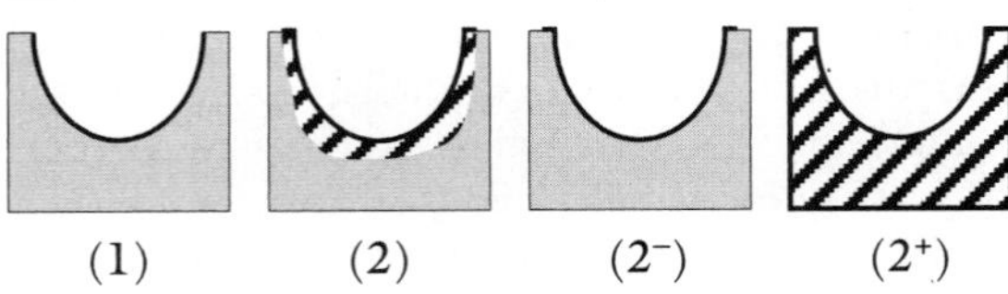

Figure 7
Four different ways of construing holes.

MATTER AND SPACE

In regard to the first question above (are material objects made of space too?), common sense does not forbid us to treat space as a kind of stuff. And according to some theorists it would be reasonable to consider matter as *qualified space.* For instance, Jonathan Bennett has suggested that "we can be helped to understand the notion of a thing *in* space if we analyze it in terms of qualitative variation of space. The basic idea is that for there to be an atom in a given region of space is for that region to be *thus* rather than *so*." *(Events and Their Names,* p. 117) Indeed, the idea can be traced back to Plato's account of the Receptacle or empty space in the *Timaeus,* a notion that has sometimes been defended as a basis for the "explanation of the ultimate grounds of individuation of spatio-temporal (concrete) individuals" and of their objectivity (Richard Gale, *Negation and Non-Being,* p. 63).

Even without being pushed that far, this way of looking at things would provide a coherent solution to the puzzle. We would avoid having two kinds of stuff (space and ordinary matter) constituting a material object; space only—qualified space—constitutes material objects. Space, on this view, is not another sort of matter alongside ordinary matter (and with some special properties: it could be *penetrated* by ordinary matter); it is the only stuff objects are made of. If one accepts this piece of metaphysics, one may properly regard holes as being made of *unqualified matter* (that is, "bare" matter)—which is what space, according to this view, really is. To fill a hole would then be to qualify or requalify the matter (space) inside it; to empty a hole would be to requalify or dequalify that matter.

HOLES AS IMMATERIAL BODIES

This, then, is how the new account goes: Holes are spacious; they are made of space; they consist *of* "bare," unqualified matter. They are—we shall say—*immaterial bodies,* "growing" parasitically, like negative mushrooms, at the surfaces of material bodies.

Figure 8
Holes can be construed as "immaterial bodies" complementary to their material hosts. (Compare figure 7.)

This way of looking at things, which we will label the Immaterial Theory, or simply theory 3, shares with theories 1 and 2^- the idea that holes are superficial particulars (they are located at the surfaces of material objects). However, it also provides a way of modeling our pre-analytical intuition that holes are somehow *complementary* to material objects (see figure 8). It does not detach holes from their hosts (the ontological link remains), but it provides a means of *conceptually* unchaining them from the things they are in. It draws our attention not to the hole's actual host but to its actual or possible guests—to what is or could be hosted *by* the hole.

Of course this new theory needs to be further scrutinized. Our putative "immaterial bodies" threaten to turn out to be a sort of philosophical phlogiston, another—to come closer to their real nature—ether. Are they so ethereal as to vanish altogether? Let us consider some more objections and basic puzzles.

ACTUALITY VS. POTENTIALITY

"Holes," one could argue, "are actual. But the immaterial bodies they are identical with are not always completely delimited by actual surfaces, and are therefore not actual. Thus holes are both actual and not actual."

The answer to this objection is that if we accept regions of space we also accept immaterial bodies, be they actual or not. But are we saying that immaterial bodies are individuals proper in other worlds only? We are *not* saying that immaterial bodies are material bodies in some other world—though it is obviously true that they are penetrated by material bodies in other worlds. Holes are fillable, therefore they are filled in other worlds.

There is, however, an important difference here. Consider the case of potential parts of material bodies. One can say that it is *not,* for them, the same as for regions of space. The latter are all actual. They do not need any real surface to get individuated (though we could use surfaces to indicate them). The surface of the hole's potential filler, including those parts of it that are not actual, can be regarded as the actual surface of the hole.

GUESTS, HOSTS, AND IMMATERIAL GHOSTS

Someone could say: "Holes are just their own potential fillers—the imaginary plugs that could be used to fill them up completely. After all, holes and fillers coincide spatially."

The answer to this objection is, of course, that the identity between holes and fillers is unwarranted, insofar as holes can exist unfilled. Even if all holes could be filled in our world, there will be possible worlds in which they are not. The relation between a hole and its possible "guests" is indeed a crucial one, and we shall try to investigate it more closely later on. It is not, however, a relation of identity.

Likewise, consider the objection that holes are necessarily dependent on having an actual host—that immaterial bodies can exist even outside and in the absence of material objects, but holes cannot. The reply is simply that to regard holes as immaterial bodies does not mean that the converse should also hold: not every immaterial body is identical with some hole. (Think, for instance, of the metaphysical shadow discussed above.) Holes are only a subclass of immaterial bodies, those that "grow" inside material objects or at their surfaces.

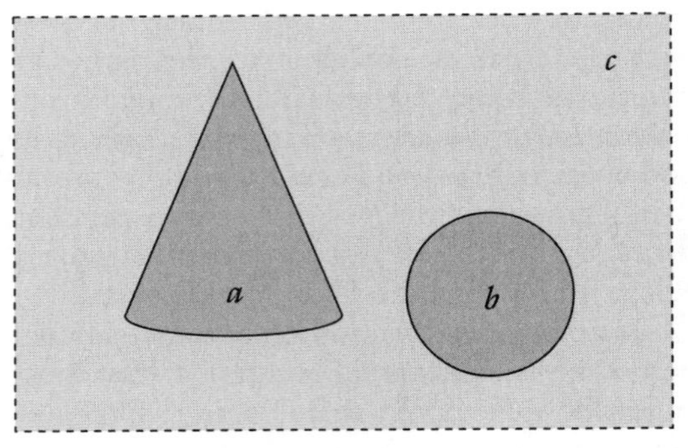

Figure 9
Three immaterial bodies, two of which (*a* and *b*) are penetrated by material bodies.

And this subclass of bodies cannot exist outside or in the absence of material objects. They are, as we saw in the previous chapter, superficially dependent entities.

More objections could be raised at this point, for it seems as if we are going to be left with lots of immaterial bodies of different sorts. We know that penetration is exclusive: an immaterial body can be penetrated by a material body (as when you fill up a hole). But how can such a body be limited by a host? Immaterial bodies do not interact. It is not as if you pushed an immaterial body inside a material one, thereby creating a hole. Perhaps, in a world nomologically different from ours, immaterial objects *could* be responsible for annihilation of stuff? Well, then, in such a world holes would be unfillable, or else our concepts of filling and impenetrability would have to be changed.

Be it as it may, an account is available which claims that when two holes (and, in general, two immaterial bodies) penetrate each other they share space—up to the point where they are made of exactly *the same* space.

A MINIMAL THEORY OF IMMATERIAL BODIES—AND ALL PROBLEMS SOLVED

In a minimal theory there are just as many immaterial bodies as material ones, plus (maybe) the complement of all the latter taken together. In figure 9, for instance, there are three immaterial bodies: *a*, *b*, and complement *c*. Bodies *a* and *b*, but not body *c*, are occupied by material bodies. Note that the complement of a body *a* and the complement of a body *b* are not objects contemplated by this theory, as opposed to their joint complement *c*; the minimal theory does not allow for partial penetration. Moreover, according to this theory, only cavities among holes (along with occupied immaterial bodies) are immaterial bodies proper (they are internal complements). Other types of holes, such as superficial hollows and perforations, would be *parts of* immaterial bodies (parts of the object's complement). In figure 10, hollow *h* is part of body *c*. Moreover, body *a* can be moved in its complement. Body *a* will stay unchanged, and body *c* will continuously change its shape as body *a* moves. In the

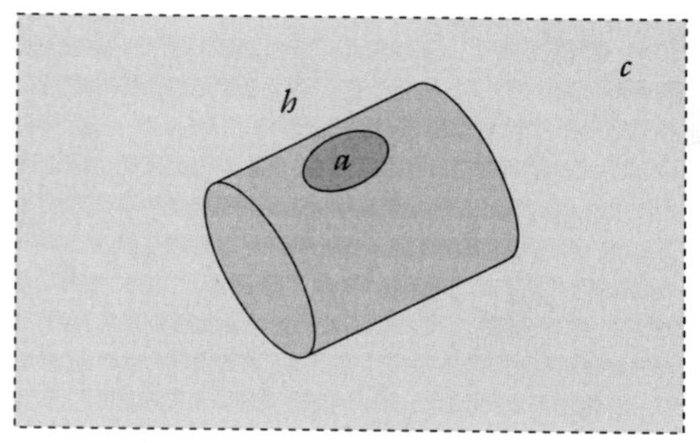

Figure 10
Two immaterial bodies, *a* and its complement *c*, and a hole, *h*, which is part of *c*.

minimal theory, immaterial bodies do not occupy, though they could be occupied by, material bodies.

Thus, the correct expression of theory 3 seems to be as follows: Holes are either immaterial bodies proper (cavities) or parts of immaterial bodies (hollows and perforating tunnels). In the latter case, when a hole is perfectly filled, it gets separated from the immaterial body it was part of; it becomes an immaterial body proper. Holes can be made of space only, without having to be identical to any region of space, and they live an intrinsically parasitic life.

SUMMARY

Our inquiry into holes led us to a discussion of different *theories* of holes, different ways of construing them: as superficial parts (theory 1); as material parts, viz. hole-linings (theory 2); or as immaterial bodies located at the surfaces of material bodies (theory 3). (Look again at figures 7 and 8.) We suggested that the first theory is too reductive, and we argued against the second theory (including various possible *variations sur le thème)* on account of its counterintuitiveness. By contrast, theory 3 (the Immaterial Theory) provides what seems to be a natural way of modeling our pre-analytical intuition that holes are in some way complementary to material objects, and it does so by drawing our attention from what is hosting a hole to what could be hosted by the hole.

Reading Questions

1. Casati and Varzi write that "[h]oles are either immaterial bodies proper (cavities) or parts of immaterial bodies (holes and perforating tunnels)." How might Casati and Varzi go about distinguishing cavities, hollows, and tunnels? What exactly is the difference between a cavity and a hollow? Between a hollow and a tunnel?
2. Casati and Varzi claim that a hole is "made of space only," but is "not identical with some region of space." If Casati and Varzi are right, then what are holes? What exactly is the relationship between the thing that is a hole and the space that constitutes the thing? If a hole is something other than the space that constitutes it, must one also believe that a dining table is something other than the wood that constitutes it? Are there two things in one's dining room—a table and the wood that constitutes it? If not, then is it plausible to claim that a doughnut contains both a hole and the space that constitutes that hole?
3. If Casati and Varzi are right that holes are composed of (but not identical with) regions of space, must they thereby agree that "absolute space" exists—that there are "fixed spatial locations" that exist independently of any material objects that might occupy such locations? Casati and Varzi claim that they need not posit "two kinds of stuff"—both matter and space. Rather, they suggest that material objects are constituted by space, distinguishing "qualified" space (matter) from "unqualified" space (holes). Is this view plausible if coherent? Does this view commit Casati and Varzi to the existence of space that is, in some sense, absolute? If there are compelling objections to their view regarding space, must their view regarding holes be rejected?

4. If the Lewises are mistaken that holes are proper parts of material objects, and Casati and Varzi are mistaken that holes are immaterial things, could it be that holes are particular kinds of boundaries?

31 Boundaries as Dependent Particulars

RODERICK M. CHISHOLM

INTRODUCTION

STEPHAN KÖRNER HAS NOTED that one way of drawing up a theory of categories will divide all particulars "into (a) a class of independent particulars, i.e. particulars which are ontologically fundamental, and (b) a class of dependent particulars, i.e. particulars which are not ontologically fundamental."[1] The dependent particulars might be said to be "parasitical upon" the fundamental particulars.

I shall here discuss the nature of spatial boundaries, viewing them as dependent particulars.

WHAT ARE BOUNDARIES?

Frege observes: "One often calls the equator an imaginary (*gedachte*) line, but it would be wrong to call it a line that has merely been thought up (*erdacht*). It was not created by thought as the result of a psychological process, but is only apprehended or grasped by thought. If its being apprehended were a matter of its coming into being, then we could not say anything positive about the equator for any time prior to this supposed coming into being."[2] Suarez had said, of the outer surfaces of a body, that they are genuine entities distinct from the body itself. And evidently he held that God could preserve the boundaries of a thing in separation from the thing (and also that God could preserve the thing in separation from its boundaries).[3]

Are boundaries parts of things? To avoid a mere verbal question, we will introduce the word "constituent" and say that things may have two types of constituent—parts and boundaries. And we will say that a part of a thing is a constituent which is not a boundary.

Why assume, then, that there *are* boundaries? The concept is needed for the description of physical *continuity.*

CONTIGUITY AND CONTINUITY

What is it for two things to be continuous with each other?

Let us recall an ancient problem. "Consider two discrete physical bodies thought to be continuous with each other; the east side of body A, say, is continuous with the west side of body B. How is this possible? Either (i) the eastmost part of A is in the same place as is the westmost part of B or (ii) no part of A occupies the same place as does any part of B. In the case of (i), we would have two discrete things in the same place. But this is impossible. In the case of (ii), since A and B occupy different places, there is a place between the place where A is and the place where B is. But if there is a place between A and B, then A and B are not continuous."

From Grazer Philosophische Studien, *vol. 20, 1983. Reprinted by permission of the journal.*

Shall we say that, if two things are continuous with each other, then nothing can be put between them unless at least one of the two things is moved? This would be true, but it is too broad to capture the concept of continuity. For it holds of things that are merely *contiguous* with each other but which are not *continuous* with each other (for example, two blocks pushed together). A similar objection applies to the suggestion that, if two bodies are continuous with each other, then there is no space between them.

The problem requires that we make reference to the *boundaries* of things.

Aristotle had said:

> The *continuous* is a species of the contiguous. I call two things continuous when the limits of each, with which they touch and by which they are kept together, become one and the same, so that plainly the continuous is found in the things out of which a unity naturally arises in virtue of their contact.[4]

If the continuous object is cut in half, then does the one boundary become two boundaries, one thing thus becoming two things? This is suggested by the passage from Aristotle. But how can one thing—even if it is only a boundary—become two things? And does this mean that when two things become continuous, then two things that had been diverse *become identical with each other,* two things thus becoming one thing?

Or should we say that when two things become continuous, then one of the outer boundaries ceases to be—*in nihilum.* This view has been attributed to Bolzano.[5] If we took this view, then we would have to say, of the thing that is cut in half, that one of the two severed halves keeps the boundary and that a new boundary comes into being which is then the boundary of the other half. This would seem to be a clear case of coming into being *ex nihilo.* And what is to determine which half gets the new boundary and which half keeps the old one?

Or could it be that one of the halves retains the old boundary and the other half is open-ended, having a side without a boundary—though not a side that is boundless? But what determines which side is to be the one without the boundary? If it is possible for a thing to exist without a boundary, why assume that either half has a boundary? And why assume that there is a boundary separating the two halves of the continuous object?

Or could it be that, if two things are in contact, then their boundaries *coincide* or overlap? Descartes, in speaking of the relation between a surrounding body and the body that it surrounds, speaks of "the common surface which is a surface that is not a part of one body rather than of the other."[6] This would mean that distinct boundaries can occupy precisely the same place at the same time. And it would also mean that, strictly speaking, more than one straight line can be extended between two points. This is the view that Brentano suggests.

Let us try to develop the suggestion further.

BOUNDARIES, PARTS AND CONSTITUENTS

We will make use of the concepts of *constituent,* of *de re* necessity and of *coincidence.*[7] We presuppose that there is no actual concrete infinite—and hence that there cannot be lines that are infinitely long or bodies that extend infinitely in space. The expression "x is discrete from y" is an abbreviation for "there is nothing that is a constituent both of x and of y."

There are two ways of defining *boundary.* We could appeal to the fact that a boundary is a dependent particular—a thing which is necessarily such that it is a constituent of something. Or we could appeal to the fact that a boundary is a thing that is capable of coinciding with something that is discrete from it. One of these should be a definition and the other an axiom.

Let us take the first course and say that a boundary is a dependent particular:

> D1 x is a boundary in y =Df x is a constituent of y; and every constituent of x is necessarily such that there is something of which it is a constituent

Why not say simply that a boundary is a thing which is necessarily such that it is a constituent of something? In such a case, we would have to count as a boundary such a hybrid object as the sum or heap consisting of Venus and the top surface of a certain table.

It should be noted that we have defined "x is a boundary *in* y," and not "x is a boundary *of* y." The latter expression would normally be taken in such a way that it applies only to the outer boundaries of y. Thus, the expression "x bounds y" would normally be taken to abbreviate "x is a boundary of y." Any boundary *in* y is a boundary *of* a proper part of y.[8]

I have said, following Brentano, that the concept of a boundary is closely related to that of *total coincidence*. I suggest that the relation is this:

A1 For every x, x is a boundary, if and only if, x is possibly such that there is something with which it wholly coincides

We will consider the logic of total coincidence below.

If we take as our primitive concept, that of being a (proper) *constituent*, then, as I have noted, we may define the concept of a (proper) *part* as follows:

D2 x is a part of y =Df x is a constituent of y; and x is not a boundary in y

If we replace "constituent" for "part" in the usual axioms for the concept of (proper) part, we can retain the axioms of transitivity and irreflexivity, as well as that of mereological essentialism (for every x and y, if x is a constituent of y, then y is necessarily such that x is a constituent of it). But although we can say that every part has a (proper) part, we cannot say that every constituent has a (proper) constituent. For a point may be a constituent without having a constituent.

The following axiom reflects the fact that boundaries are essentially dependent entities:

A2 For every x, y and z, if x is a boundary in y, and if z is a part of y in which x is not a boundary, then there is a part of y discrete from z in which x is a boundary

This principle implies that every constituent of every boundary is a constituent of something that is not a boundary. It is thus inconsistent with Suarez' suggestion, referred to above, according to which God could remove just the surface of a three dimensional object. The principle does not preclude our saying that there are hybrid objects such as the sum of Venus and a certain surface which is not a surface of Venus; but it does imply that, if there are such objects, then there are individual things which are discrete from such objects.

Could God preserve any of the boundaries of a thing apart from the thing? We could say that, for any thing having boundaries, God could destroy the thing and preserve the boundaries—by destroying some part of the thing such that the part did not contain any of those boundaries. But he couldn't preserve the boundaries except by retaining *some* part of the original thing.

COINCIDENCE

We have taken as primitive the concept of *total coincidence*. Let us now express this concept by "x wholly coincides with y" ("xWy").

One axiom for this locution is A1 above:

A1 For every x, x is a boundary, if and only if, x is possibly such that there is something with which it wholly coincides

In formulating additional axioms, we will use the abbreviations: "xCy" ("x is a constituent of y"); "xDy" ("x is discrete from y") and "xBy" ("x is a boundary in y").

The relation of total coincidence is symmetrical and irreflexive:

A1.1 $xWy \rightarrow yWx$

A1.2 $xWy \rightarrow \neg(xWx)$

Hence "xWy" is not transitive. But if one thing wholly coincides with a second thing and if the second thing wholly coincides with still a *third* thing, then the first thing wholly coincides with the third thing. In other words:

$[xWy \ \& \ yWz \ \& \ \neg(x=z)] \rightarrow xWz$

We may also affirm that, if x wholly coincides with y, then every constituent of x wholly coincides with a constituent of y:

A1.3 $xWy \rightarrow \{(\forall z)(zCx) \rightarrow [(\exists v)(vCy \ \& \ vWz)]\}$

And if two boundaries wholly coincide, then they are constituents, respectively, of two things having no *parts* in common:

A1.4 $xWy \rightarrow [(\exists u)(\exists v)(uDv \ \& \ xBu \ \& \ yBv)]$

Total coincidence may hold between surfaces, or between lines, or between points, but it may not hold between two things of different dimensions or between solids. In terms of the undefined concept of total coincidence, we may now define the broader concept of coincidence:

D3 x coincides with y =Df Either (a) x wholly coincides either with y or with a constituent of y or (b) a constituent of x wholly coincides with a constituent of y

The first clause of this definition insures that coincidence, unlike total coincidence, may obtain between points and lines, between points and surfaces, and between lines and surfaces; the second clause insures that coincidence—but not total coincidence—may obtain between three-dimensional things.

What, then, of dimensionality?

DIMENSIONALITY

We now define dimensionality—assuming that things may have either no spatial dimensions, or one such dimension, or two, or three. Thus we take it to be a necessary truth that there are exactly three spatial dimensions.[9]

We will not equate solids with what is 3-dimensional. That sum consisting of Venus and the top surface of the table is 3-dimensional, but not a solid. We will say, analogously, that there are no "broken surfaces"; hence that 2-dimensional object which is the sum of the front and back surfaces of a certain cube will not be a surface. And analogously there will be no "broken lines." Surfaces are like solids and unlike lines in that they may have holes.

We now set forth the following definitions:

D4 x is 0-dimensional (a point) =Df x is a boundary and x has no constituents

D5 x is 3-dimensional =Df x has constituents and is not a boundary

We have thus defined 0-dimensionality and 3-dimensionality. Let us now consider 2-dimensionality.[10]

Shall we say that a 2-dimensional object is a boundary which is possibly such that the only things of which it is a constituent are 3-dimensional? No; for, if there cannot be things that are infinitely extended, then any part of the surface of a thing must also be a part of that 2-dimensional sum composed of it and some other part of the surface of the thing.[11] Thus the front surface of a cube must be a part of that 2-dimensional sum consisting of its front surface and back surface. Our conception, of coincidence, moreover, requires that solids have "inner surfaces"; hence the entire outer surface of a solid as necessarily such that it is a constituent of 2-dimensional wholes consisting of it and an inner surface.

The concept of coincidence, however, presents us with one feature that is peculiar to 2-dimensional boundaries. A point is capable of coinciding with any number of points at a time; and a line is capable of coinciding with any number of lines at a time; but a surface can coincide only with one surface at a time. Let us say, then:

D6 x is 2-dimensional =Df x is a boundary; and for all y and for all z, if x wholly coincides with y and x wholly coincides with z, then y = z

(This definition, as well as the others here, should be taken to be in the present tense. If the definitions are interpreted "tenselessly," then a temporal variable should be taken to be implicit throughout.)

And now we may define 1-dimensionality:

D7 x is 1-dimensional =Df x is neither 0-dimensional, 2-dimensional nor

3-dimensional; and x is necessarily such that it is a (proper) constituent of something that is 2-dimensional

CONTINUITY

Two three-dimensional things are said to be discrete when they have no parts in common. It is convenient to introduce analogous concepts for 2-dimensional things and for 1-dimensional things. And so let us distinguish among three subspecies of discreteness: as a relation between 3-dimensional things; as a relation between 2-dimensional things; and as a relation between 1-dimensional things.

D8 x and y are 3-dimensionally discrete =Df x and y are 3-dimensional; and nothing 3-dimensional is a part of both

D9 x and y are 2-dimensionally discrete =Df x and y are 2-dimensional; and nothing 2-dimensional is a constituent of both

D10 x and y are 1-dimensionally discrete =Df x and y are 1-dimensional; and x is other than y

We may now distinguish three types of contact: that between 3-dimensional things ("touching"); that between 2-dimensional things; and that between 1-dimensional things.

D11 x is in 3-dimensional contact with y (x touches y) =Df is 3-dimensionally discrete from y; and x coincides with y

D12 x is in 2-dimensional contact with y =Df x is 2-dimensionally discrete from y; and x coincides with y

D13 x is in 1-dimensional contact with y =Df x is 1-dimensionally discrete from y; and x coincides with y

We may say, then, that a thing x is *in contact with* a thing y, provided only that x is either in 1-dimensional, 2-dimensional or 3-dimensional contact with y. And now we may say that x is *continuous* with y, provided only that x is in contact with y.[12]

NOTES

1. Stephan Körner, *Categorical Frameworks,* Oxford: Basil Blackwell, 1970, p. 4.

2. Gottlob Frege, *Foundations of Arithmetic,* Oxford: Basil Blackwell, 1950, p. 35.

3. See Hugo Bergmann, *Das Philosophische Werk Bernard Bolzano,* Halle: Max Niemeyer, 1909, p. 207. Bergmann refers to Suarez's *Metaphysicae Disputationes,* XL, 5, Sections 37 and 41.

4. Aristotle, *Metaphysics,* 1069a.

5. Compare Bernard Bolzano, *Paradoxes of the Infinite,* New Haven: Yale University Press, 1950. See paragraph 67 (p. 168). Bolzano speaks here of certain things but not others "being devoid of limiting atoms."

6. Descartes *Principles of Philosophy,* Part II, Principle XV; in E. S. Haldane and R. T. Ross, *Philosophical Works of Descartes,* Vol. 1, Cambridge: Cambridge University Press, 1931, p. 261.

7. The concept of coincidence is used by Franz Brentano, in *Philosophische Untersuchungen zu Raum, Zeit und Kontinuum,* ed., Stephan Körner and Roderick M. Chisholm, Hamburg: Felix Meiner Verlag, 1976. Compare also Brentano's *Psychology from an Empirical Standpoint,* London: Routledge & Kegan Paul, 1973; pp. 351–358; *Psychologie vom empirischen Standpunkt,* Band II, Hamburg: Felix Meiner Verlag, 1971, pp. 259–262.

8. Brentano discusses inner and outer boundaries, *Raum, Zeit und Kontinuum,* p. 15.

9. One can, of course, construe time as a "fourth dimension." But it is not a fourth *spatial* dimension. The "four dimensional" things that relativity theory speaks about are *events* of a certain sort—not *bodies* having four spatial dimensions.

10. Brentano discusses dimension in: *Philosophische Untersuchungen zu Raum, Zeit und Kontinuum,* p. 13ff. He appears to assume, mistakenly, that the only boundaries found in surfaces are lines (but smaller surfaces will also be boundaries *in* any surface); and analogously for lines and points.

11. This point was made by Michael Zimmerman.

12. I am indebted to Stephan Körner, who introduced me to this topic when we were preparing Brentano's *Philosophische Untersuchungen zu Raum, Zeit und Kontinuum* for publication. I am also indebted to Robert Frederick, Richard Potter, James Van Cleve, and Michael Zimmerman.

Reading Questions

1. Chisholm presupposes that if two half cubes are pushed together to form a cube, a surface of the cube's left half "wholly coincidences" ("overlaps") with a surface of the cube's right

half. This concept of total coincidence is, however, left undefined. Is it plausible that two discrete objects can share a common constituent—that a constituent of one thing and a constituent of another can come to occupy the same place?

2. If two half cubes form a cube when they have wholly coinciding surfaces, what would Chisholm say about the status of the cube's proper parts? If there is a place occupied by the overlapping surfaces, what matter occupies that place? matter that belongs to the cube's left half? to the cube's right half? (Or, are such questions ill-formulated?)
3. Chisholm writes that "[Suarez] evidently. . . held that God could preserve the boundaries of a thing in separation from the thing (and also that God could preserve the thing in separation from its boundaries)." On this view, non-three-dimensional boundaries are not *dependent* particulars. Is there philosophical reason to prefer Suarez's view to the Brentano/Chisholm view that a boundary cannot exist without being a constituent of something that is not a boundary?
4. Chisholm cites Bolzano's view that "when two things become continuous, then one of the outer boundaries ceases to be—*in nihilum*." This view implies that a non non-three-dimensional boundary can "wholly coincide" with another. Is there philosophical reason to prefer Bolzano's view to Chisholm's?
5. Chisholm offers a theory of boundaries and surfaces of continuous wholes, but common objects such as tables, apples, and fingers are not continuous wholes—they are "gappy" objects whose atomic parts are "scattered." Do tables, apples, and fingers have boundaries? If so, what are they?
6. Does Chisholm's view regarding spatial boundaries have implications for puzzles regarding temporal boundaries? For example, if Socrates died at time T, what was the first moment of Socrates's nonexistence? If time is continuous, there was no particular time that immediately followed time T. Is there, then, no moment of time that marks the beginning of Socrates's nonexistence? Was T both the last moment of Socrates's existence and the first moment of his nonexistence?

Two Conceptions of Surfaces 32

AVRUM STROLL

IN THIS PAPER I SHALL RAISE and try to answer some questions about surfaces: What are they? Are they things? Can they be parts of things? Do they have depth? Can one scratch the surface of an object without scratching the object? Does everything have a surface? There are some related questions, concerned with the *seeing* of surfaces, that I shall not discuss. For example, can one see an object without seeing its surface? Can one see its surface without seeing the object? What exactly is it that one is seeing in such cases? In what follows I shall argue that the answers to all such questions depend on which of two quite different conceptions of surfaces one has in mind, or presupposes, in discussing them.

From Midwest Studies in Philosophy. Vol. 4, Studies in Metaphysics, *1979 (Minneapolis: University of Minnesota Press). Reprinted by permission of* Midwest Studies.

I

What are the two conceptions? An elegant expression of one of them is to be found in the writings of Leonardo da Vinci; for this reason I shall call it "The Leonardo Conception." In Part II I shall describe the second conception which I shall call "The Somorjai Conception," naming it after a contemporary scientist. Let us begin with Leonardo. I quote the passage dealing with surfaces in its entirety:

> The contact of the liquid with the solid is a surface common to the liquid and to the solid, and the lighter liquids with the heavier have the same.
>
> All the points are equal to one and one to all.
>
> Nothingness has a surface in common with a thing, and the thing has a surface in common with nothingness, and the surface of a thing is not part of this thing. It follows that the surface of nothingness is not part of this nothingness; it must needs be therefore that a mere surface is the common boundary of two things that are in contact; thus the surface of water does not form part of the water nor consequently does it form part of the atmosphere, nor are any of the bodies interposed between them. What is it, therefore, that divides the atmosphere from the water? It is necessary that there should be a common boundary which is neither air nor water but is without substance, because a body interposed between two bodies prevents their contact, and this does not happen in water with air because they are in contact without the interposition of any medium.
>
> Therefore they are joined together and you cannot raise up or move the air without the water, nor will you be able to raise up the flat thing from the other without drawing it back through the air. Therefore a surface is the common boundary of two bodies which are not continuous, and does not form part of either one or the other, for if the surface formed part of it, it would have divisible bulk, whereas, however, it is not divisible and nothingness divides these bodies the one from the other.[1]

The main (though not all) the points being made by Leonardo may be summarized as follows:

(i) When a liquid and a solid (no doubt Leonardo would say "any two media") come in contact, the point where they meet is a surface. An example: The interface of air and water.

(ii) Clearly, water and air are juxtaposed—you cannot raise up or move the air without the water; and conversely—and yet they are divided or separated from one another.

(iii) What, then, divides the atmosphere from the water? Answer: it must be a common boundary which is neither air nor water.

(iv) Such a boundary is not part of either medium. The surface of the water is not part of the water, the surface of the air is not part of the air.

(v) Such a common boundary must be without substance. For if it had substance or divisible bulk, it would be a body interposed between the two media, and thus would prevent their contact. But they are in contact; therefore what separates them cannot have divisible bulk.

(vii) Therefore the surface is not a thing.

The notion that surfaces are not things, that they lack divisible bulk, is the essence of the Leonardo conception. The same notion can be expressed in a number of different idioms. It has been said of surfaces, for example, that they are "conceptual entities only" or "logical abstractions," or "mere outsides," or "the outermost boundary of a thing," or "an outermost aspect." Of course, these same phrases may be given, as we shall see, other interpretations as well; but they are often used to express just the conception that Leonardo has in mind. When they are, it is implied that surfaces, being nothing at all, cannot be parts of objects either. If, for instance, one were to list the parts of an apple (and on the assumption, perhaps incorrect, that apples can be truly said to have surfaces), then the surface of an apple, according to this view, would not be part of it in the way that its skin and core are. This conception tends, furthermore, to assimilate surfaces to boundaries: A surface is not unlike the equatorial boundary that separates the northern and southern hemispheres of the earth. The equator is not a thing, has no bulk, cannot be seen, even in good light, by the weary traveler who crosses it; and it is not part of either hemisphere. Just so with the common surface that separates water from air: It is not a thing, has no bulk, and is not a part of either medium.

The Leonardo conception has a solid foothold in both science and common sense; in this respect it is like the Somorjai conception. But it also has implications which though acceptable to science may not be to common sense. Its common basis derives from a process of reflection about the nature of surfaces; there is thus a sense in which this conception is not part and parcel of the ordinary man's pre-analytical or unreflective acceptance of the world, but rather the outcome of some conscious thinking about it. As such it could, in principle, be reconstructed as a formal argument, having premises and a conclusion. But to do so is not necessary for our purposes here. The intuitive idea is that of a progressive thinning out of a surface, and this can be illustrated by examples. Consider the following. Suppose a person believes that a particular surface is a thing having some physical bulk: Say a certain depth. One might believe this of a road that had just been resurfaced with macadam, or of the uppermost stratum of the water of a large lake. In the latter case, one might think that the surface of the lake has a specific depth on the ground that, as a surface, it has properties that the mass of water beneath it does not have: For example, being rough, being of a light green color, and so forth. It might be possible if one scrutinizes the lake to see just how deep this layer goes: Suppose such properties hold of the water to a depth of one foot. One might thus say of the surface that it is a foot deep.

But, so the process of thinking runs, suppose now that one sees a fish swimming in the lake six inches below the point where the uppermost layer of water meets the air. Could we say that the fish is swimming below the surface? Obviously not if the surface is a foot deep. Yet it clearly makes sense to say that the fish is swimming just below the surface, even that it is swimming *six inches* below the surface. Yet how could this make sense if the surface is a foot deep? Well, then, shall we say it is six inches deep? Clearly if the fish were swimming three inches below the interface of water and air, we could still sensibly say it is swimming below the surface. Take any supposed depth and we obtain exactly the same result. If that is so, it follows that the surface cannot have *any* depth; it cannot be identified with a discernibly different layer of water that is a foot deep. In Leonardo's phrase, it cannot have bulk or "divisible substance." Moreover, as he says, it cannot be a part of the water; since any part of water will have *some* depth. The surface thus ultimately turns out to be no thing at all, but is a mere boundary between water and air. This process of "thinning out x," where x is the surface of y, will always result in the kind of progressive emasculation of x that turns it into a mere limit, an abstraction or logical entity, lacking physical properties and dimensions.

The Leonardo conception is employed both in ordinary discourse and in scientific talk about surfaces. Both scientists and ordinary persons arrive at the conception via the "thinning out process" I have characterized. One can say it is a concept both of common sense and of science. Yet when it is unpacked, it has implications that common sense, but not science, would find paradoxical. For while both common sense and science are in agreement that surfaces—on this interpretation—lack divisible bulk, they are not in agreement that wherever one has two media in contact the boundary separating them is a surface. This seems to be a view held only by science.

For science a cube-shaped, wooden tank of water, open at the top, has five (not six) interior surfaces. The water in the tank has six surfaces, five of them impinging against the wooden walls of the tank, the other against the open air. But ordinary speakers, left to their own devices and without special guidance, would be hesitant to say that the water in the tank has six surfaces. They would probably be equally hesitant to say that the tank itself, even if filled with water, has five interior surfaces; they might be more willing to say this if the tank were empty. If later the tank were carefully filled with water to the top, and then enclosed, thus forming a perfect wooden cube, filled with water, and with no interior air bubbles, science would say that both the tank and the water have six surfaces, while common sense would be likely to say that neither the interior of the tank nor the water in it has any surfaces. If the tank were then opened, so that one dimension were exposed to the air, a scientist might not find it odd to say that a heavy object inserted into the tank is sinking to a surface. Common sense would find this way of speaking confusing. It, instead, would say of the object that it is sinking to the bottom of the tank and would deny that insofar as it is doing so it is sinking to a surface. This is in part because it would presuppose that there is just one surface involved, and it is located where the water and the air intersect (that is, at the open end of the tank, and not at its bottom). It would find it bizarre, without some special instructions, to say for example that a swimmer is sinking to the surface or a surface. Again this would be in part a function of the logic of 'to sink,'[2] and in part a function of holding that there exists only one surface in this particular case, and it is to be found where the water and the air come in contact.

Without relinquishing the Leonardo conception, common sense and science disagree about what the conception entails. Science feels no special tension in accepting the notion that surfaces can be thought of as boundaries that divide contiguous media. Insofar as it does, it accepts the Leonardo position that it is a *façon de parler* to speak as if each medium itself has a surface; no such attribution is to be taken literally. Thus, if one juxtaposes two solid billiard balls, what separates or divides them is a common boundary without substance or bulk. But such a boundary does not belong to either medium.

Common sense, however, would find Leonardo's question "What separates the two media when they are in direct contact?" puzzling. It would say that if they are in direct contact, nothing separates them. To be sure this is also explicitly what Leonardo says, but he adds, nevertheless, that what separates them is a surface belonging to neither medium. Common sense, unlike science, would be reluctant to add Leonardo's tag. Instead, it believes that each of the billiard balls has its own surface, a surface that exists before they are brought together, which they are not thought to lose while they are in contact. Common sense would be hesitant to assert that there is anything they have in common while in contact though of course not denying that their surfaces are touching at some point. Common sense might agree that this "point" represents a "common boundary," but if it made this concession, it would not go on to agree that this entails that either ball has lost the surface it originally had. Accordingly, common sense would seem to say that there is a sense, consistent with the Leonardo conception but not otherwise specified, in which each surface is "part of" the billiard ball of which it is the surface. This sense of 'part' would not, of course, entail that the surface *per se* had any divisible bulk; but it would entail that it somehow belonged to the particular billiard ball whose surface it is.

Science and common sense would differ in other ways, especially in terms of what each would partake of the Leonardo conception. Unlike science, which might be inclined to attribute surfaces indiscriminately to any sort of physical object or phenomenon, common sense would withhold such an attribution from whole classes of "entities." With respect to some of them, it would agree that they have boundaries which serve to mark them off from other items in their environments, but it would deny that such boundaries are surfaces. In yet other cases, it would maintain that though such entities are full-fledged physical objects, it would deny that surface talk was applicable to them, thus, in effect, denying that they have surfaces. In an earlier paper,[3] I described some of these cases in detail and the supporting arguments for these inferences. Rather than repeating the arguments here, I shall simply summarize the main findings.

One might begin by drawing a distinction between physical phenomena and physical objects. Shadows, rainbows, lightning (the list is, of course, much larger) fall into the former category, and, in ordinary discourse such entities are not thought to have surfaces. Take shadows, for example. One can draw an outline around a shadow; in that sense it might be said that the shadow has a boundary. Yet it would seem odd to say that the shadow has a surface. No properties or features are attributable to the *surface itself* of a shadow. It cannot be said to be dark or light, thick or thin, smooth or rough, wet or damp; nor does it have depth or mass. It cannot be removed from the shadow, polished, washed, or sanded down. Though the locution "the surface area of a shadow" is sometimes used in ordinary speech, this expression would normally be taken to be referring to the surface area of the ground, earth, or water that is covered by the shadow, not to the surface of the shadow itself. And this is so because for common sense, as expressed in everyday speech, shadows do not have surfaces and are not the sorts of things that could have. Similar comments apply to the other items belonging to this category, such as flashes of lightning, rainbows, and so on.

Moreover, many things belonging to the class of full-fledged physical objects ("material things") are not normally said to have surfaces. Among these are included mountains, trees, persons, and animals. How do we speak about clouds, for example? Unlike a submarine, which may be described as coming to, floating upon, breaking through or just gliding beneath the surface of the sea, an airplane is not described in these ways with respect to clouds: it does not break through the surface, rest upon it, and so on. Why the difference? In my earlier paper I suggested that objects to which surfaces are ascribed must have a certain density or compactness, and reasonably determinate boundaries. As a medium, clouds stand intermediate between water (that is, a lake) which clearly satisfies these criteria and a medium such as air which does not; it is less dense than the former and more dense than the latter. But for ordinary speakers it is probably considered insufficiently dense and as lacking sufficiently determinate boundaries for surface talk to apply. It is for similar reasons that surface talk is held to be inapplicable to afro wigs, trees, deep grass. Why we withhold such talk from living persons (though not from statues of them) and from animals is more complicated; and in my previous article I suggested some reasons why this might be so. Whether those reasons are good ones or not I do not wish to debate here; my main point is that in ordinary speech surface talk is withheld from variety of physical phenomena and objects.

I have, however, chosen to talk specifically about clouds because the considerations that apply to them enable us to identify another respect in which the Leonardo model would not be acceptable *in toto* by ordinary speakers. For, to take his specific example, we find that ordinary speakers would not describe both *the air* and the water as having a surface, but only the water. And even in such a case surface talk would apply to water only when it is in a fairly stable configuration, where the qualities of determinateness of outline, density, and compactness are apparent. So though surface talk is applicable to water in a lake (in fact, actually to the lake taken as a body of a certain density), it probably would not be applicable to water rapidly running out of a faucet. In accordance with this principle, ordinary speakers do not describe the interface of lake and air as the *surface of the air.* This may be because it is difficult to see air, and thus to ascribe to it the determinate boundaries that surface talk requires. It may also be that surface talk requires that an object be relatively localizable, and thus have a discernible autonomy, characteristics that air discernibly lacks. But in the end this may be simply another way of saying that unless something his reasonably determinate boundaries, surface talk will not be applicable to it.

So though common sense may, in some of its postures, accept the Leonardo model, it does not accept all of its consequences.

II

The Somorjai Conception of surfaces is also to be found in scientific talk and in ordinary discourse; yet it seems not only different from but actually incompatible with the Leonardo Conception. Since science and common sense make use of both concepts, are they each internally inconsistent? Let us defer consideration of this question until we have a clearer picture of this second notion.

A typical statement of it is to be found in a recent paper by the scientist G. A. Somorjai.[4] Like many scientists who talk about surfaces, Somorjai sometimes seems to have the Leonardo model in mind; for example, he speaks about the difficulties involved in studying "solid-liquid, and solid-solid *interfaces.*" But the substance of the paper is concerned with examples of surfaces where surfaces are taken to be "things" (or in his parlance "systems"). He speaks, for example, about the coral reef, the leaf, and other photosynthetic "systems" with a high surface area, or as having a high surface-to-volume ratio (A/V) (p. 489). In one place he writes:

> Defining the surface to be studied as the topmost layer of atoms, one must obtain detectible signals from 10^{15} atoms or molecules in the background of 10^{22} atoms or molecules to obtain surface information. (p. 489)

A layer of atoms—perhaps the uppermost layer of atoms—is not so different from a last layer of water; this conception seems similar to that which common sense and science rejected in espousing the Leonardo Conception. There it thinned the latter out to the point where it became an abstraction or mere limit. But there is no doubt that Dr. Somorjai does not think of surfaces in this way. In his paper there are schematic representations, that is, actual drawings of what a surface looks like on the atomic scale. With his kind permission, I reproduce such a drawing from his article in *Science*.

The surface depicted in Figure 1 looks surprisingly familiar; it contains various topological features analogous to those one might find in a well-tended garden or orchard. Some of these he calls "terraces," "steps," "kinks," "vacancies," and so on. He states further that these features have been identified by experiments. Some of the features "Adatoms," look like ivory cubes, say like six-sided dice, except, of course, that they are writ much smaller. One committed to the Leonardo model might be tempted to ask of such features whether they themselves do not have surfaces, and where their surfaces begin. The thinning out process seems almost irresistible; yet Dr. Somorjai does resist it. The surface is the whole system which includes these features.

To a great extent his paper is a description of the physical and chemical properties of the kind of surface we see in Figure 1; for example, he holds that the surface of an ordinary solid is heterogeneous on the atomic scale (having just such different features as "steps" and "terraces") and that different types of surface features ("sites") have different chemistries (p. 490).

It seems clear that Somorjai takes surfaces to be things of a complex sort, having specific physical and chemical properties. It is also obvious that this is how common sense, as exhibited in ordinary ways of talking, sometimes conceives of surfaces. Indeed, depending on what one is speaking about, common sense holds not only that surfaces are things but even that they are physical objects. The Somorjai Conception is thus grounded in both science and common sense. But what is this conception that they both accept?

It begins from what it takes to be a fact, namely that surfaces have properties and are subject to various kinds of operations. Marbles are the kinds of things that have surfaces. Their surfaces can be described as rough, smooth, slippery, chipped, sticky, blemished, pitted, or damaged; one can speak about sanding, polishing, painting, wiping, or waxing their surfaces. In Somorjai's parlance, a marble is a "solid." It will indeed have a surface, which Somorjai will identify with its outermost layer of atoms. Corresponding to ordinary predicates such as "rough" or "pitted," Somorjai's vocabulary will speak about the surface as having "steps"

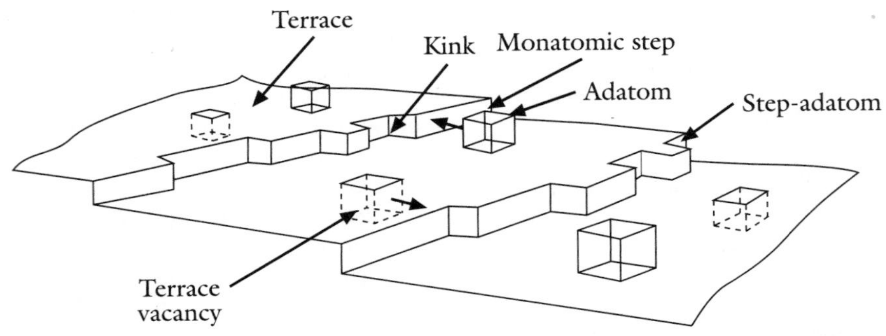

Figure 1
Schematic representation of the heterogeneous surface on the atomic scale. Terrace, step, and kink atoms as well as point defects (adatoms and vacancies) have been identified by experiments. From G. A. Somorjai, "Surface Science," *Science,* vol. 201, No. 4355 (11 Aug. 1978, pp. 489–97). Reproduced with permission of author and publisher. Copyright 1978 by the American Association for the Advancement of Science.

or "kinks," or being "heterogeneous." Thus with respect to conceiving of surfaces as kinds of things, the views of common sense and Somorjai do not substantially differ.

But both views differ from the Leonardo Conception. For if, as Leonardo contends, a surface is a "mere common boundary," having no substance or divisible bulk, how is it possible that some surfaces can be correctly depicted as being rough or slippery, or as requiring painting or wiping? Surely if a surface were like the equator, a mere conceptual entity, none of the predicates would be applicable. The difference comes out most strikingly when we speak, as we did earlier, of a surface's having depth (or divisible bulk in Leonardo's phrase). For Leonardo, a surface being nothing cannot have depth; the surface boundary that separates water from air has no thickness or density or depth, and is not made up of layers. But according to Somorjai it would at least be one atomic layer thick. Or to vary the example, common sense would aver that when a road is resurfaced with a macadam covering, one could say either that the macadam is three inches thick or that its surface is three inches thick. Moreover, if the job were performed ineptly, one could remove the surface by removing the macadam. To do the one is to do the other. For common sense surfaces are often identified with such covering material as paint, lacquers, glosses; and it is these that are scratched or pitted or removed when the surface is said to be scratched or pitted or removed. But even when the surface is not taken to be a covering material—as, for example, the surface of a solid steel marble—its surface can still be said to be pitted or scratched. And this would only be possible if surfaces were things having depth or divisible bulk. According to this conception none of these ascriptions would be possible if surfaces were, as Leonardo states, "mere common boundaries," having no substance.

III

It does appear, on the basis of the preceding discussion, as if the two conceptions are different from each other. Yet the matter is not as simple as it looks. In the following two sections I wish to investigate the question of whether they are different from one another; in the end I shall decide that they are.

We have seen that the Somorjai Conception holds surfaces to be things and that the Leonardo Conception denies this. Put in this simple way the two views seem incompatible. Yet there are some complications arising from how the notion of being a "thing" is unpacked.

One of the grounds that both common sense and science have for holding that surfaces are things is that surfaces can truly be said to have properties and be subject to certain sorts of operations or procedures. But though Leonardo denies that surfaces are things, it is consistent with his conception of them as common boundaries that they can have properties and are subject to certain operations. If so, the mere possession of properties and susceptibility to operations may not be a sufficient condition for distinguishing the two conceptions from each other.

To illustrate the point, let us return to the equator analogy. Though the equator is, to be sure, nothing that one can scratch or pick up, and is not the kind of thing that reflects light, nevertheless it is true to say that it is equidistant from the north and south poles. A surface considered as a common boundary may well be equidistant from two arbitrarily selected points in the media that it divides. So the analogy seems close. Most such properties, such as that of being equidistant from x and y, would be relational properties rather than what might be called intrinsic properties. It thus might be argued that one can distinguish surfaces as boundaries from surfaces as things on the ground that the former have only relational properties and lack such intrinsic properties as length, mass, color, etc. But promising though this line seems, it probably will not do. It can be said of the equator, for example, that it is curved or that it has a measurable length at any given time, and, if so, one would be attributing some intrinsic properties to it. Generally speaking, there is nothing paradoxical about attributing intrinsic properties to boundaries; we do it all the time. The French-Spanish border, for example, belongs neither to France nor to Spain, yet it has a definite length. Clearly, we can measure the surface area of one face of a die, and so on. One can generalize beyond surfaces to see that the point is not decisive. Even nonexistent entities can have intrinsic properties; Pegasus, for example. Thus it is not the case that all things lacking substance or divisible bulk lack intrinsic properties. Tempting though this route may be, I do not think it will lead us to a distinction between the two conceptions of surfaces.

A second approach might take the following line. According to Leonardo, a common boundary is not only not a thing but it is not a part of anything either. So a surface for him is not a property either of the water or of the air that it divides. On the other hand, the Somorjai Conception allows the surfaces to be properties of things. An ivory die can be said to have the property of having six surfaces. Thus the difference between the two conceptions would be that one of them, the Somorjai, would allow surfaces to be properties themselves, while the other would not.

Unfortunately, this suggestion will not do either. For though Leonardo speaks as if surfaces cannot be parts of the media that ordinarily might be said "to have" them, they still might be regarded as being properties of those media. In particular, a given surface might be regarded as a common property that two media jointly have. This response would hold that "not being a part of x" does not entail "not being a property of x." There is a sense in which "the French border" and "the Spanish border" are different borders, even when one is speaking about points where they coincide. For example, the French border is manned by French police while the Spanish border is not. But there is a sense in which the two terms denote exactly the same border. In such a case, one might say that the two countries have a common property, that of having the same border.

Even more to the point, the border that France shares with Spain exactly defines a property that France has, that is, of being a certain width, for example. There is thus a kind of isomorphism between common boundaries and properties possessed by their associated media. The surface shared by air and water, even on the Leonardo conception, may exactly define the surface area of a given lake. Though even if one granted that the "surface" in Leonardo's sense was not made of water and hence was not part of the lake, it gives rise to certain derivative properties that are.

Yet despite these difficulties, I still believe that there is a fundamental difference between the two conceptions. So let us make another effort to see where it may be found. The key clearly will lie in how the Somorjai Conception unpacks the notion that surfaces are things. As we have seen, it will not be sufficient to maintain that surfaces have properties and are subject to various kinds of operations: What is at stake must turn on what kinds of properties and operations are involved.

These properties and operations cannot be what I called in my earlier paper "intensional" properties and operations. These are concerned with imagining, believing, thinking, intending, and so forth. One can imagine, for example, a given surface to be larger than it is, to be detached from the object that has it, to be bent in space when it is in fact not, and so forth. What is characteristic of such intensional properties and operations is that they may apply both to actual things and to nonactual ones; to things having divisible bulk and to things lacking substance. One can imagine Secretariat and Pegasus as being the same color; Breshnev with snakes in his hair and Medusa as bald; one can imagine the equator as a kind of elastic band, brown in color, tightly wound around the earth, itself conceived of as a golden ball set in an orrery. So one could imagine Leonardo's surfaces, those "mere boundaries," as having thickness and depth, as being of a certain color, or as made of fine-spun gossamer. Since both things having divisible bulk and things not having divisible bulk are capable of "possessing" such intensional properties and of being subject to such conceptual operations, we cannot distinguish surfaces in Leonardo's sense from surfaces in Somorjai's by saying that one type will have such properties while the other will not.

But there are sets of properties and operations that differ from the preceding, and can be used to distinguish between the two conceptions. I shall call them "physical" properties and operations. Examples of the first sort are being sticky, damp, pitted, rough; examples of the second kind are sanding, polishing, painting, wiping, waxing.

It is these kinds of properties and operations that do not apply to surfaces as characterized by

Leonardo, but that do apply to surfaces as characterized by Somorjai. For if, as Leonardo claims, surfaces have no substance or divisible bulk, then how would it be possible to paint, wax or wipe them, or sand them down and refinish them; and how would it be possible for a "mere boundary" to be rough, smooth, slippery, damp, sticky, and pitted? Surely, if a surface were, as Leonardo suggests, like the equator, a mere conceptual entity, none of these operations or predicates would apply to it. But since they do have application, then what they apply to cannot merely be a boundary in Leonardo's sense.

Though it is difficult to specify in general the criteria that properties and operations must satisfy to be members of the class of "physical" properties and operations, the examples we have cited seem (and I stress the word 'seem') sufficient to enable us to distinguish the Leonardo and Somorjai Conceptions from each other.

IV

Why do I say "seem" sufficient, rather than "are" sufficient? As I mentioned earlier, there remains one major difficulty that must be overcome before we can conclude that there are two irreducibly different conceptions here. The reason for this is that the Somorjai Conception may in some important sense not be about *surfaces* after all, but rather about the objects that have such surfaces.

Let me quickly summarize the situation as it now appears from the preceding discussion. We have seen that Leonardo tends to "thin" out surfaces so that they become mere abstractions, having neither substance nor bulk. But we have also seen that Somorjai tends to assimilate surfaces to physical objects; and the question we must now ask is: Has this assimilation been carried so far that so-called surface talk is just talk about objects or parts of objects?

Somorjai produces representations of surfaces in which they look like landscapes. They have terraces, steps, kinks, holes, and various irregular protrusions. One could say that it is the object that has such terraces, steps, kinks. So, for example, to say that the surface of a mirror is chipped or pitted, or that the surface of the mirror has been wiped, or needs cleaning, is just to say that the mirror itself is chipped and has been wiped. One can say both that the road is rough and that its surface is rough; one can say that it is the table that needs refinishing and that its surface does. In applying these terms and predicates both to surfaces and to the objects that have them, are we not simply saying the same thing twice over; is it not the case that the terms are being applied to exactly the same thing in both cases? Is surface talk merely talk about the object, so that on the Somorjai Conception the distinction between a surface and the object that has it is a distinction without a difference, or at least without an ontological difference? The question at stake is: Are surfaces, considered as things, entities in their own right, somehow autonomous and different from the objects that have them? By this question I do not merely mean that a surface differs from the object that has it in the way that a scratch differs from the object that is scratched. What I do mean is: is the surface of a road really identical with the macadam that covers it; is the surface of a refinished table really identical with the new paint that has been applied to it? And how are we to characterize how surfaces differ from their corresponding objects when we are talking about the surfaces of solid steel marbles or ball-bearings, for example? What is the surface identical with in such cases, since they possess no "covering materials" such as macadam or paint, but are homogeneous throughout?

It may be possible to distinguish surfaces from their corresponding objects in two ways: First, by showing that objects have properties their surfaces do not have; and then by showing that surfaces have properties their objects do not have. The kinds of properties (and operations) involved will have to be "physical" properties and operations, of the kind depicted above.

There are obviously some properties (and operations) that are applicable only to the objects and not to their surfaces. We can say of a particular table that it weighs 200 pounds, that it has four legs, and that it folds down the middle. None of these things can sensibly be said of its surface. But, of course, to show this is not yet to show that surfaces are autonomous things, or that they exist in their own right. For object-talk could simply be about the same object as surface-talk, but richer: Objects may simply have some properties that their surfaces do not have; and indeed the existence of such properties is consistent with surfaces having no physical properties at all. So in order to show that the Somorjai Conception really does differ from the Leonardo Conception, one would have to show that surfaces themselves have properties their objects do not have. If one can find the right properties, this should show that surfaces are, in some important sense, independent entities.

This sort of model we want could be described as follows: A leg of a table is part of the table. Yet it is an autonomous thing in its own right. It can have properties the table does not have, and is subject to some operations that the table is not. We can say of the leg that it is round or cylindrical, while saying of the table that it is rectangular or square. It is not clear that we could say that we can sand down the leg while denying that we are sanding down the table, but surely we can say that we have removed the leg without saying that we have removed the table.

Now, using this example as a guide, can we say of the surface of the table that it has properties and operations that are not applicable to the table itself?

It looks as if we can find some such properties and operations. We can, for example, remove the (old) surface of a table without removing the table; this seems a direct analogue of what we could do with the leg. If someone were asked to paint the surface of a table, he would understand this request to mean that he paint the top of the table. If that were so, he could not paint the surface without painting the table; and he could not scratch the surface without scratching the table. But one could measure the surface of the table without measuring the table, and one could cover the surface with a well-fitting plastic cover without covering the table. In such a case, one would be treating the surface as a part of the table in just the sense that the leg was. For one could fit it with a plastic cover and measure its dimensions, without fitting the table with a plastic cover or measuring its dimensions. Moreover, when one removes the leg of a table, say by unscrewing it, so that the leg remains intact and undamaged, one will have a recognizable entity, something that has not lost its identity as a table leg (this remark is subject to qualification, of course). When one scrapes the paint off a table in the process of resurfacing it, one might end up with an irregular pile of chips. In such a case, it is doubtful that a person would refer to the pile as the surface even if he knew that it had been removed from a particular table and could have been described as the surface before removal. If the paint had been taken off the table in such a way that it remained intact, then one seeing it off the table might well refer to it as "the old surface." This sort of case is not unfamiliar in the art world. In Florence at the present time, some scientists suspect that underneath a Vasari painting that covers a wall there is a Leonardo da Vinci "lost masterpiece," and there is evidence, based on sonar research, to this effect. These scientists plan to strip the surface of the wall containing the Vasari in order to expose the Leonardo. They will do it by an intricate masking process that takes off the surface of the wall in one long roll. This they can then transfer to a new wall. This will amount to transferring the Vasari intact to a new wall. In effect, then, they will be removing the surface of the wall by removing the paint (the Vasari); one might properly describe the result by saying that the Vasari was the old surface.

Of course, such examples are very context dependent; one can remove the surface of a wall without removing the wall, but one cannot remove the surface of an onion (if it has one) without peeling the onion.

Other examples might be the following: If we identify the surface of a table as "the top" of the table, then it is possible for the top to have a property not possessed by the whole table. For instance, it could be red, but the table could be multicolored; its surface could be dull, but the table might not be describable as either dull or not dull; its surface could be described as "flat" when this epithet would not apply to the table as a whole.

With respect to such "mantel covering" examples, therefore, it does appear as if surfaces have passed the two tests that certify them as autonomous entities: The objects that have them possess properties that the surfaces do not, and the surfaces possess properties that the objects do not.

But it may be queried whether objects without mantels—that is, lacking coverings, such as finishes, layers of material, and so on—could pass such tests. Take a solid steel ball, for example. It has no covering that is of a different material from the ball. It makes no sense to speak about removing its surface, though it does make sense to speak of sanding it down, for there is nothing to remove. Do objects of this sort provide an exception to the claim that their surfaces are autonomous entities?

I do not think so. Let us look again at the schematic representation in Figure 1. Suppose that what Dr. Somorjai has depicted is the surface of a homogeneous solid steel marble. Then it is clear that we can ascribe properties to it that we cannot ascribe to the ball. We can say of the surface that it has kinks, terraces, steps, is not smooth, and so on. But none of these ascriptions would be true if applied to the ball, taken as a macroscopic object. It follows that the surface has properties that the ball does not possess and, accordingly, that it is an autonomous object. And if so, it follows that the difference between objects having mantels and objects lacking them is not a significant difference with respect to the question of the autonomy of surfaces.

On the basis of such considerations, I conclude that the Leonardo and Somorjai Conceptions are irreducibly different from each other. The former regards surfaces as non-things, incapable of having physical properties; the latter regards them as things, capable of possessing such properties. Leonardo denies that surfaces can be parts of things, while Somorjai affirms the opposite. The conceptions are thus different from each other.

V

Let me conclude with two brief comments about the need for future research in this domain.

1. I had hoped to address the question of whether both common sense and science are internally inconsistent insofar as they embody both the Leonardo and Somorjai conceptions. The answer clearly depends on whether the two conceptions are not merely different but are in some strong sense logically inconsistent with one another. Obviously, logical incompatibility in this sense does not follow from mere difference. From the fact that 'statement' may be used on some occasions to denote the first presentation of a musical theme, and on others a written summary by a bank of one's financial standing, it does not follow that these uses of 'statement' are logically inconsistent. It can be held that words like 'statement' and 'bank' are homonyms, expressing different but not incompatible concepts.

One major issue here, then, is whether 'surface' is a homonym having differing uses (two of which we have described) that are not necessarily incompatible. I have not pursued the subject in this paper because of the complexities in deciding what a homonym is. One of the most difficult aspects of this question is whether 'surface' expresses a "paronymous concept" (to use Austin's term); that is, whether there is some common meaning strain that all uses of 'surface' embody—such as "being an outer aspect"—though the application of the term may be to different things. In such a case, we might find differing uses of 'surface' but no inconsistency among them.

My own intuition—I offer it without having done the necessary research for a positive answer—is that 'surface' is not homonymous in the way that 'bank' and 'statement' are. This intuition is partly based upon the fact that we cannot find the Somorjai and Leonardo Conceptions expressed as distinct entries in dictionaries in the way in which the various homonyms of 'bank' are, and partly on the observed fact that both in common sense and in science users of the term 'surface' seem to wobble between the two uses in a way in which they never do for real homonyms. But the matter is tricky and requires further study. Nevertheless, suppose that it does turn out that the two conceptions are logically incompatible; does it then follow that both science and common sense which employ, and which vacillate between these conceptions, can each of them be convicted of inconsistency?

2. As I mentioned at the beginning, these "ontological" investigations into the nature of surfaces have their inevitable "epistemological" coun-

terparts, including, I believe, important consequences for the theory of perception. I indicated that I would not in this paper follow up these leads; but I should like to mention one that I think is worth pursuing.

Earlier in the paper I distinguished "intensional" properties and operations from "physical" ones. The question worth investigating is whether *seeing* is an intensional operation, a physical one, or neither.

On the basis of what has already been discovered, there is some reason for thinking that it is neither an intensional nor a physical operation. Let us take the example of seeing a solid steel marble to illustrate why.

I have already pointed out that intensional operations—believing, imagining, etc.—apply to surfaces on either the Leonardo or the Somorjai Conception, but that physical operations apply only to the latter. With respect to the marble, for instance, we can wash or wipe its surface; we cannot wash or wipe a "mere boundary." What is interesting about some of the physical operations that apply to certain objects is that there is no way of performing an operation on the surface without performing it on the object that has the surface, and conversely. There is thus no way of wiping or waxing the surface of a solid steel marble (intact of course) without wiping or waxing the marble—and most important, conversely.

In my earlier paper, I produced some compelling examples to show that it is possible to see a physical object without seeing its surface. I also believe, though the matter is very tricky, that there may be some cases where we could properly say that we see the surface but deny that we see the object that has it. The mere fact that we can say we see the object without seeing its surface shows that the logic of 'see' must be different from the logic of 'wipe,' 'wash,' and 'scratch,' which are cases *par excellence,* of physical operations. It would be very interesting if it could be shown that we could see the surface without seeing the object that has it. If we could, this would show that *seeing* is not a physical operation in the sense previously defined; and that would have interesting and important consequences for epistemology.

NOTES

1. *The Notebooks of Leonardo da Vinci,* 1, ed. Edward MacCurdy, (New York, 1958), 75–76.

2. The point is especially perspicuous in Italian. "Affondare" shows its sense in a way in which "to sink" does not; it means "to sink to the bottom" (fondo).

3. "Talk about Talk about Surfaces," (co-authored with Robert Foelber), *Dialectica* 31, Fasc. 3–4 (1977) especially 426–28.

4. G. A. Somorjai, "Surface Science," *Science* 201 (1978): 489–97.

Reading Questions

1. If Stroll is right about the nature of surfaces, then surfaces are particulars. But are they *dependent* particulars?
2. Stroll suggests that by stripping an artist's painting from the wall on which it was painted, scientists can thereby remove the surface of the wall. If Stroll is right, then what is left behind? A surfaceless wall? A wall with a surface that came into being when the painting was removed?
3. If a one-atom thick painting is stripped from a wall and if Stroll is right that surfaces are outermost layers of atoms, then does Stroll's view imply that the detached painting is a three-dimensional object that lacks a surface?
4. Can Stroll's conception of surfaces be a complete theory of surfaces? If a common object's surface is its outermost layer of atoms, then what about the components of such layers of atoms? Do they not have surfaces? If so, must Stroll expand his view? How might he do this?

Further Readings

Books

Casati, Roberto, and Achille C. Varzi. 1994. *Holes and Other Superficialities.* Cambridge: MIT Press.

Stroll, Avrum. 1988. *Surfaces.* Minneapolis: University of Minnesota Press.

Articles

Adams, Ernest W. 1984. "On the Superficial." *Pacific Philosophical Quarterly* 65: 386–407.

———. 1986. "On the Dimensionality of Surfaces, Solids, and Spaces." *Erkenntnis* 24: 137–201.

Factor, R. Lance. 1992. "Regions, Boundaries, and Points." In *Logic, God and Metaphysics,* ed. J. Harris. Dordrecht, Holland: Kluwer.

Hestevold, H. Scott. 1986. "Boundaries, Surfaces, and Continuous Wholes." *The Southern Journal of Philosophy* 24 (2): 235–245.

Karmo, Toomas. 1977. "Disturbances." *Analysis* 37: 147–148.

Martin, C. B. 1996. "How It Is: Entities, Absences and Voids." *Australasian Journal of Philosophy* 74 (1): 57–65.

Simons, Peter. 1991. "Faces, Boundaries, and Thin Layers." In *Certainty and Surface in Epistemology and Philosophical Method,* ed. A. P. Martinich and M. J. White. Lampeter: Edwin Mellen Press.

Smith, Barry. 1997. "Boundaries: An Essay on Mereotopology." In *The Philosophy of Roderick M. Chisholm,* ed. L. E. Hahn. Vol. 25, *The Library of Living Philosophers.* Carbondale: The University of Southern Illinois Press.

Smith, Barry, and Achille C. Varzi. 1997. "The Formal Ontology of Boundaries." *The Electronic Journal of Analytic Philosophy* 5. http://www.phil.indiana.edu/ejap/

Stroll, Avrum. 1985. "Faces." *Inquiry* 28: 177–194.

———. 1987. "Counting Surfaces." *American Philosophical Quarterly* 24: 97–101.

———. 1989. "On Surfaces: A Rejoinder." *Inquiry* 32: 223–231.

———, and Robert Foelber. 1977. "Talk About Talk About Surfaces." *Dialectica* 31: 409–430.

Varzi, Achille C. 1997. "Boundaries, Continuity, and Contact." *Noûs* 31 (1): 26–58.

Zimmerman, Dean. 1996. "Indivisible Parts and Extended Objects: Some Philosophical Episodes from Topology's Prehistory." *The Monist* 79 (1): 148–180.

Part IX

Mereology

PETER SIMONS

Introduction to Mereology

Brief History

MEREOLOGY IS THE THEORY OF PART AND WHOLE. The name was invented in the 1920s by Stanislaw Lesniewski, and derives from Greek *meros,* 'part'. Often the name is reserved for formalized theories of part and whole expressed in a logical language with symbolic notation.

The concept of part is one that applies in all domains, so while it is not a logical concept, it is the nearest thing: a formal ontological concept. Because of this ubiquity, the concept of part is one of the most commonly used but was taken for granted and not analyzed until the twentieth century.

Ancient philosophers used the concept in various ways. The Greek atomists conjectured that material bodies were made of small invisible parts, atoms, that are neither physically divisible nor generable nor destructible, and whose shapes and changing configurations determined the macroscopic properties of larger bodies.

Plato uses the concept of part in his dialogue *Parmenides,* where he discusses the question of whether being or the one has parts and presents arguments on both sides. In the *Theaetetus* Plato discusses a hypothetical theory, similar to that of Ludwig Wittgenstein in the *Tractatus Logico-Philosophicus* according to which the world consists of simple objects without parts, which yield all other things by their combination. Simples are merely nameable; nothing can be said about them, only about the complexes they form. Thus quality and quantity arise out of the combinations of simples.

Aristotle noted that the term 'part' was used in various ways. It can mean a physical part, such as an animal's limb, but also a quantity that is either smaller than another (as a gram is part of a kilogram) or a factor or aliquot part (as 2 is part of 6 but 5 is not). It can also mean that the species is part of the genus in one sense and the genus is part of the species in another sense. The matter and substantial form of a concrete individual are both parts of it, and Aristotle calls such individuals "composite." He discusses in detail the conditions that must obtain for a whole to exist, and which parts a thing may lose and still

This essay was commissioned especially for this volume and appears here for the first time.

exist as a whole. A man may lose a leg and be called 'mutilated,' he may lose his hair when going bald, but he cannot lose his head or heart and survive as a living organism. In Aristotle's biological works attention is paid to the question of which parts are characteristic of certain kinds of animal, what their functions are, which parts are materially uniform or *homeomerous* (e.g. muscle) and which are materially varied or *heteromerous* (e.g., the eye). He applies considerations of part and whole to the analysis of tragedy in the *Poetics*. In short, very little in Aristotle's writings is remote from some meaning or other of 'part.'

Ancient geometry is mereological. Euclid defines a point as that which has no part, and his fifth Common Notion states that the whole is greater than the part. Plutarch tells us of a dispute that gripped the philosophers of Athens: whether the ship that brought back Theseus from his exploits and was reverently preserved by replacing its parts remained the same ship.

In the Middle Ages Peter Abelard pondered the problem of increase—whether a thing can grow—and distinguished two kinds of whole: a distributive whole, as humankind is a distributive whole of humans, and a collective or conjunctive whole, one literally made up of several things (e.g., the whole of all human flesh).

Whenever some form of atomism or analysis into parts is in question, mereology is in play. Leibniz defines monads as true atoms, objects without parts, and complexes he declared to be mere aggregates. Here he failed to apply Abelard's distinction, but in his analysis of ideas Leibniz followed Raymond Llull in assuming complex ideas could be analyzed into simple ones, the elements or letters of thought. The simple ideas of the empiricists are the psychological counterparts of the corpuscles of Newtonian physics, while the logical atoms of Bertrand Russell and Wittgenstein are the elements guaranteeing truth and the terminus of analysis.

In the nineteenth century it gradually became apparent that the intuitive notions of part could no longer be taken for granted. In his investigations of the ontology of number, Bernard Bolzano distinguished several of different kinds of collection, some of them clearly mereological. Bolzano's ideas stimulated Georg Cantor and the development of set theory. In the anti-atomistic psychology of Franz Brentano's school it was held that some parts of mental acts are inseparable, that in the perception of a colored object the aspects of shape, extension and color are mutually inseparable parts.

Brentano and Bolzano both influenced Edmund Husserl, who proclaimed the need for a formal theory of part and whole, distinguished independent parts (pieces) from dependent parts (moments), and offered some theorems of such a theory. Husserl applied his distinctions to grammar—distinguishing semantic categories by the supplementary parts that meanings need when composing a coherent grammatical whole—and to his phenomenology or theory of consciousness, with its analysis of mental acts into their essential components. Much of Husserl's phenomenology is mereology applied to the mental.

Mereology as a formalized theory begins around 1914 with the works of Alfred North Whitehead and Stanislaw Lesniewski. The motivations of these two philosophers were different. Whitehead used notions of part in the analyses of geometry that were to have gone into the fourth volume of *Principia Mathematica*. They figured thereafter in his mathematical analyses of the physical world. Lesniewski, concerned to analyze and avoid Russell's antinomy, was led to construe classes as collective wholes. In his *Enquiry* of 1919, Whitehead gave a mereology of events and used this notion with that of an ultrafilter in the method of extensive abstraction to define geometrical notions such as point and line in terms of concrete elements of experience. Whitehead's efforts were later taken up by

Jean Nicod. Lesniewski developed his theory of (collective) class, which he came to call 'mereology,' as part of an antinomy-free, intuitively motivated foundation for mathematics compatible with nominalism. Lesniewski's ideas were presented in more familiar logical guise in Henry Leonard and Nelson Goodman's calculus of individuals.

Modern formal mereology has gradually played a greater part in ontological and metaphysical discussions, and it is now an established area of ontology, with applications not only in philosophy but also in cognitive science and in software engineering. Many of the distinctions and concerns of mereology's long prehistory have reemerged as ontology has reestablished itself at the heart of philosophy.

The Formal Theory of Part and Whole

Modern mereology is given as a formal theory using a logic perhaps with some set theory. We shall assume a free predicate logic, allowing unbound singular terms to be empty. The most natural basic concept of mereology is that of a (proper) part to its (larger) whole. Define the following auxiliary concepts:

COINC *a* coincides with *b* =Df. *a* and *b* both exist and either *a* = *b* or *a* and *b* both have parts and *a* has the same parts as *b*

INGR *a* is an ingredient of *b* =Df. either *a* is part of *b* or *a* coincides with *b*

OV *a* overlaps *b* =Df. something is an ingredient of both *a* and *b*

DISJ *a* is disjoint from *b* =Df. *a* and *b* both exist and *a* does not overlap *b*

SUM the Sum of the *F*s =Df. the *x* such that everything which overlaps *x* overlaps some *F*

PROD the Product of the *F*s = Df. the sum of the objects which are ingredients of every *F*

ATOM *a* is an atom = Df. *a* exists and nothing is part of *a*

UNIV the (mereological) Universe = Df. the Sum of everything

The standard minimum conditions governing the part concept are

EXIST If *a* is part of *b*, then both *a* and *b* exist

ASYM If *a* is part of *b*, then *b* is not part of *a*

TRANS If *a* is part of *b* and *b* is part of *c*, then *a* is part of *c*

SUPPL If *a* is part of *b*, then there is *a* part of *b* which is disjoint from *a*

Few theories of part and whole fail to fulfill these principles, an exception being that of the later Brentano, who postulated the existence of objects having parts without supplements in their whole. For Brentano, a soul seeing something red is a whole with the soul as its part, but no supplement (in particular, no "seeing red" part).

Very often it is assumed that things with the same parts are identical, guaranteed by

EXT If *a* is an ingredient of *b* and *b* is an ingredient of *a*, then *a* = *b*

A mereology satisfying EXT is called *extensional.* Extensional mereologies have many algebraic advantages. In an extensional mereology, coincident objects are always identical; without EXT the definitions of sum, product and universe fail to guarantee uniqueness.

So extensional theories are simpler and are the rule. A further condition that many mereologies respect is an axiom of conditional sum existence

EXSUM If there exists at least one *F*, then the sum of *F*s exists.

An extensional mereology satisfying EXSUM is a *classical* mereology. The mereologies of Lesniewski, Leonard, and Goodman are classical. That of Whitehead is not. Whitehead's mereology fulfills principles of anti-atomism and anti-universism:

ANTIATOM Every object has some (other) object as a part
ANTIUNIV Every object is part of an (other) object

Since Whitehead disallows points (atoms), he must construct them logically using apparatus stronger than in employment here. Whitehead's anti-universism entails the falsity of EXSUM, since the Universe is an object that is not part of any other. Classical extensional mereology (CEM) is the most widely known and used mereology. Algebraically it is modeled by any complete Boolean algebra minus the null element, and is therefore a consistent theory.

CEM entails that there is a unique universe (provided at least one thing exists), but it does not pronounce either way on atomism, the antithesis of Whitehead's view:

ATOM Every object is either an atom or has an atom as part

Atomic mereologies are simpler: they may be finite, whereas anti-atomic ones have only uncountable standard models. Anti-atomic mereologies are appropriate in modeling the mereology of continua (where we do not assume there are points), which is precisely what Whitehead used them for.

The logical work of mereologists, most particularly from the schools of Lesniewski and his students, have shown that there is a wide range of possible primitive concepts and axioms for CEM. Our focus here is on clarity and intuitive simplicity rather than axiomatic elegance.

Extensions

Mereology as so far expounded is rather neutral. It does not pronounce, for example, on the question of whether ordinary objects like tables and organisms are three-dimensional continuants (without a temporal extension) or four-dimensional occurrents (with temporal extension), though its very use as given here tends to predispose to the latter view. The very expression of the distinction draws on mereological notions that go beyond what we have so far—namely, on the question of whether or not an object has *temporal* parts, in the way, for example, that a football match has periods or a symphony has movements. To express the distinction, we need to develop mereological concepts appropriate to time. If we favor continuants, we need a temporally modified part relation: *a* is part of *b* at time *t*, or (if we prefer tense logic to 'at-*t*' logic) *a* is part of *b* (now). Temporally modified versions of the axioms for part tell us only about the parts of a thing at a single time: they say nothing about how it may or may not develop mereologically over time. In general, it is hard to discern any general principles about this, because it seems that different things may metabolize or change their parts in different ways. The dispute about the ship of Theseus, given to us by Plutarch and intensified by Hobbes in his story of reassembling a ship from the original parts while a repaired ship still exists, turn on the lack of precise criteria for continued or renewed existence of ships in the face of part replacement.

Careless treatment of such issues can easily lead to paradoxes—for example, that there can be more than one ship in one place at a time, or that one ship can be multiply present at different places. One simple and radical position to adopt is that, strictly speaking, nothing changes its parts. This view was formulated by Leibniz and was presaged by Abelard. It is the Principle of Mereological Constancy

CONST At all times at which a thing exists, it has the same parts

from which it follows that no thing can gain or lose parts. This position is metaphysically extreme, since ordinary objects seem quite happily to change their parts. The only sensible way to reconcile the two is to introduce two tiers: one of prime objects keeping their parts constant, and another of derivative objects parasitic upon them and migrating like waves from one constant object to another. Roderick Chisholm, who has formulated this view, calls the prime objects *entia per se* and the derivative ones *entia successiva*. The difficulties of change are one reason that it has been popular to plump for a four-dimensional ontology of occurrents, since then objects are continually gaining parts by mere temporal accumulation.

Aristotelian questions about what parts are essential to an object are beyond CEM, and the language of mereology has to be modally strengthened to encompass them. How to do this is a matter of dispute: one might simply mix propositional modal operators with mereology, or one might introduce the notion of an essential property of an individual. There are advantages either way, but we shall attempt to finesse the issue. As with temporal mereology, modal mereology, beyond the obvious modal strengthenings of standard principles, offers little formal guidance, and the variety of modal mereological behavior appears wide. One difficulty is fixing the strength of the modality involved when we say an object *a* has a part *b* essentially. Sometimes the necessity is merely analytic: it is analytically necessary of any helium atom that it have as parts two protons and if either of these becomes detached from the nucleus, the atom ceases to exist. Any object of which this were false would simply not be termed a helium atom. But consider the heart of a human being, taken by Aristotle and Aquinas to be an essential and permanent part. Modern transplant surgery shows them to have been wrong. Whether we discover in the future that the brain is not essential is hostage to medical advance rather than a matter of metaphysical pronouncement.

As with temporal mereology, there is an extreme doctrine of mereological rigidity that goes under the name of Mereological Essentialism. This states that

ESS If *b* is part of *a* then it is not possible for *a* to exist and not have *b* as part

This is usually accepted along with CONST, but the two are distinct and to some extent independent. Like CONST, it is contrary to common sense. It implies that, for example, a certain carbon atom currently part of me could not have failed to be part of me. But it seems accidental that I ate the food containing it or breathed it in. The move to a four-dimensional ontology is less help here, because ESS is almost as counterintuitive for events. Consider an event such as a war or a football game and one tiny and insignificant incident within it. We are to suppose that the incident is essential to the larger event just as much as the most considerable part.

Applications

Applications, like extensions, introduce nonmereological concepts, but their interest is in use rather than analysis of mereological concepts. An example is the theory of temporal extension and order (chronology). Here the idea of one event's being temporally wholly before another interacts with mereology (no part of an event is wholly before it) but requires its own principles. Mereology can be used as a basis, alternative to set theory, for a geometry (in the old-fashioned sense of a theory of space, or stereology), or more generally as a basis for topological notions. The lead was given here by Whitehead, whose mereology already incorporated topological presuppositions such as the connectedness of each event, and who could therefore define topological notions such as interior. The situation was clarified in Whitehead's *Process and Reality,* whose basic notion, that of connection of two regions, is overtly "mereotopological." Mereotopology has become one of the principal areas of application for mereological concepts, as it is more natural and less ontologically extravagant than using set theory.

Aristotle, Abelard, Bolzano, and Lesniewski all gave as one interpretation of the relation of part to whole the subclass relation. This interpretation is exploited by David Lewis to propose a "harmless" justification of set theory. Standard mereology, however, deliberately fails to distinguish a unit class or singleton from it sole member, whereas set theory must do this. Thus Lewis needs to supplement his mereology of class-containment with a theory of singletons, that is both nonmereological and controversial.

The ubiquity of part-whole relations guarantees the relevance of mereology to all domains, but the actual use of mereological principles becomes crucial once one needs to formulate principles governing items in these domains, as in cognitive science and in the software required to define, represent and even (robotically) manipulate objects that are parts of other objects. Attempts to standardize product definitions in industry, to automate the managing of manufacture and maintenance of complex artifacts with their manifold associated parts lists or bills of materials, and to provide general knowledge bases for realistic attempts at artificial intelligence all require that complex representation systems be mereologically informed. The widespread applications of mereology are as yet in their infancy, but they are sure to be legion.

BIBLIOGRAPHY

Baumgartner, W. and P. M. Simons. 1994. "Brentano's Mereology." *Axiomathes* 5: 55–76.

Chisholm, R. M. 1976. *Person and Object. A Metaphysical Study.* London: Open Court.

Husserl, E., 1970. "On the Theory of Wholes and Parts." In *Logical Investigations,* 2 vols. London: Routledge and Kegan Paul.

Krickel, F. 1995. *Teil und Inbegriff. Bernard Bolzanos Mereologie.* St. Augustin: Academia.

Leonard, H. S. and N. Goodman. 1940. "The Calculus of Individuals and Its Uses." *Journal of Symbolic Logic* 5: 45–55.

Lesniewski, S. 1992. "On the Foundations of Mathematics." In *Collected Works,* pp. 174–382. Dordrecht, Holland: Kluwer.

Lewis, D. K. 1991. *Parts of Classes.* Oxford: Blackwell.

Simons, P. M. 1987. *Parts: A Study in Ontology.* Oxford: Oxford University Press.

______, and Dement, C. W. 1996. "Aspects of the Mereology of Artifacts." In R. Poli and P. M. Simons, eds., pp. 255–276. *Formal Ontology,* Dordrecht, Holland: Kluwer.

Whitehead, A. N. 1919. *An Enquiry Concerning the Principles of Natural Knowledge.* Cambridge: Cambridge University Press.

______. *Process and Reality.* 1978. Corrected ed., New York: The Free Press.

Identity, Ostension, and Hypostasis 33

W. V. QUINE

1

IDENTITY IS A POPULAR SOURCE of philosophical perplexity. Undergoing change as I do, how can I be said to continue to be myself? Considering that a complete replacement of my material substance takes place every few years, how can I be said to continue to be I for more than such a period at best?

It would be agreeable to be driven, by these or other considerations, to belief in a changeless and therefore immortal soul as the vehicle of my persisting self-identity. But we should be less eager to embrace a parallel solution of Heracleitus's parallel problem regarding a river: "You cannot bathe in the same river twice, for new waters are ever flowing in upon you."

The solution of Heracleitus's problem, though familiar, will afford a convenient approach to some less familiar matters. The truth is that you *can* bathe in the same *river* twice, but not in the same river stage. You can bathe in two river stages which are stages of the same river, and this is what constitutes bathing in the same river twice. A river is a process through time, and the river stages are its momentary parts. Identification of the river bathed in once with the river bathed in again is just what determines our subject matter to be a river process as opposed to a river stage.

Let me speak of any multiplicity of water molecules as a *water.* Now a river stage is at the same time a water stage, but two stages of the same river are not in general stages of the same water. River stages are water stages, but rivers are not waters. You may bathe in the same river twice without bathing in the same water twice, and you may, in these days of fast transportation, bathe in the same water twice while bathing in two different rivers.

We begin, let us imagine, with momentary things and their interrelations. One of these momentary things, called *a,* is a momentary stage of the river Caÿster, in Lydia, around 400 B.C. Another, called *b,* is a momentary stage of the Caÿster two days later. A third, *c,* is a momentary stage, at this same latter date, of the same multiplicity of water molecules which were in the river at the time of *a*. Half of *c* is in the lower Caÿster valley, and the other half is to be found at diffuse points in the Aegean Sea. Thus *a, b,* and *c* are three objects, variously related. We may say that *a* and *b* stand in the relation of river kinship, and that *a* and *c* stand in the relation of water kinship.

Now the introduction of rivers as single entities, namely, processes or time-consuming objects, consists substantially in reading identity in place of river kinship. It would be wrong, indeed, to say that *a* and *b* are identical; they are merely river-kindred. But if we were to point to *a,* and then wait the required two days and point to *b,* and affirm identity of the objects pointed to, we should thereby show that our pointing was intended not as a pointing to two kindred river stages but as a pointing to a single river which included them both. The imputation of identity is essential, here, to fixing the reference of the ostension.

These reflections are reminiscent of Hume's account of our idea of external objects. Hume's theory was that the idea of external objects arises from an error of identification. Various similar impressions separated in time are mistakenly treated as identical; and then, as a means of resolving this contradiction of identifying momentary events which are separated in time, we invent a new nonmomentary object to serve as subject matter of our statement of identity. Hume's charge of erroneous identification here is interesting as a psychological

From The Journal of Philosophy, *vol. 47, 1950, pp. 621–632. Reprinted by permission of the journal and the author.*

conjecture on origins, but there is no need for us to share that conjecture. The important point to observe is merely the direct connection between identity and the positing of processes, or time-extended objects. To impute identity rather than river kinship is to talk of the river Caÿster rather than of *a* and *b*.

Pointing is of itself ambiguous as to the temporal spread of the indicated object. Even given that the indicated object is to be a process with considerable temporal spread, and hence a summation of momentary objects, still pointing does not tell us *which* summation of momentary objects is intended, beyond the fact that the momentary object at hand is to be in the desired summation. Pointing to *a*, if construed as referring to a time-extended process and not merely to the momentary object *a*, could be interpreted either as referring to the river Caÿster of which *a* and *b* are stages, or as referring to the water of which *a* and *c* are stages, or as referring to any one of an unlimited number of further less natural summations to which *a* also belongs.

Such ambiguity is commonly resolved by accompanying the pointing with such words as 'this river', thus appealing to a prior concept of a river as one distinctive type of time-consuming process, one distinctive form of summation of momentary objects. Pointing to *a* and saying 'this river'—or ὅδε ὁ ποταμός, since we are in 400 B.C.—leaves no ambiguity as to the object of reference if the word 'river' itself is already intelligible. 'This river' means 'the riverish summation of momentary objects which contains this momentary object.'

But here we have moved beyond pure ostension and have assumed conceptualization. Now suppose instead that the general term 'river' is not yet understood, so that we cannot specify the Caÿster by pointing and saying 'This river is the Caÿster.' Suppose also that we are deprived of other descriptive devices. What we may do then is point to *a* and two days later to *b* and say each time, 'This is the Caÿster.' The word 'this' so used must have referred not to *a* nor to *b*, but beyond to something more inclusive, identical in the two cases. Our specification of the Caÿster is not yet unique, however, for we might still mean any of a vast variety of other collections of momentary objects, related in other modes than that of river kinship; all we know is that *a* and *b* are among its constituents. By pointing to more and more stages additional to *a* and *b*, however, we eliminate more and more alternatives, until our listener, aided by his own tendency to favor the most natural groupings, has grasped the idea of the Caÿster. His learning of this idea is an induction: from our grouping the sample momentary objects *a*, *b*, *d*, *g*, and others under the head of Caÿster, he projects a correct general hypothesis as to what further momentary objects we would also be content to include.

Actually there is in the case of the Caÿster the question of its extent in space as well as in time. Our sample pointings need to be made not only on a variety of dates, but at various points up and down stream, if our listener is to have a representative basis for his inductive generalization as to the intended spatio-temporal spread of the four-dimensional object Caÿster.

In ostension, spatial spread is not wholly separable from temporal spread, for the successive ostensions which provide samples over the spatial spread are bound to consume time. The inseparability of space and time characteristic of relativity theory is foreshadowed, if only superficially, in this simple situation of ostension.

The concept of identity, then, is seen to perform a central function in the specifying of spatio-temporally broad objects by ostension. Without identity, *n* acts of ostension merely specify up to *n* objects, each of indeterminate spatio-temporal spread. But when we affirm identity of object from ostension to ostension, we cause our *n* ostensions to refer to the same large object, and so afford our listener an inductive ground from which to guess the intended reach of that object. Pure ostension plus identification conveys, with the help of some induction, spatiotemporal spread.

2

Now between what we have thus far observed and the ostensive explanation of *general* terms, such as 'red' or 'river,' there is an evident similarity. When I point in a direction where red is visible and say 'This is red,' and repeat the performance at various places over a period of time, I provide an inductive basis for gauging the intended spread of the attribute of redness. The difference would seem to be merely that the spread concerned here is a conceptual spread, generality, rather than spatiotemporal spread.

And is this really a difference? Let us try shifting our point of view so far as to think of the word 'red' in full analogy to 'Caÿster.' By pointing and saying 'This is Caÿster' at various times and places, we progressively improve our listener's understanding as to what portions of space-time we intend our word 'Caÿster' to cover; and by pointing and saying 'This is red' at various times and places, we progressively improve our listener's understanding as to what portions of space-time we intend our word 'red' to cover. The regions to which 'red' applies are indeed not continuous with one another as those are to which 'Caÿster' applies, but this surely is an irrelevant detail; 'red' surely is not to be opposed to 'Caÿster,' as abstract to concrete, merely because of discontinuity in geometrical shape. The territory of the United States including Alaska is discontinuous, but it is none the less a single concrete object; and so is a bedroom suite, or a scattered deck of cards. Indeed every physical object that is not subatomic is, according to physics, made up of spatially separated parts. So why not view 'red' quite on a par with 'Caÿster,' as naming a single concrete object extended in space and time? From this point of view, to say that a certain drop is red is to affirm a simple spatio-temporal relation between two concrete objects; the one object, the drop, is a spatiotemporal part of the other, red, just as a certain waterfall is a spatio-temporal part of Caÿster.

Before proceeding to consider how it is that a general equating of universals to particulars breaks down, I want to go back and examine more closely the ground we have already been over. We have seen how identity and ostension are combined in conceptualizing extended objects, but we have not asked why. What is the survival value of this practice? Identity is more convenient than river kinship or other relations, because the objects related do not have to be kept apart as a multiplicity. As long as what we may propose to say about the river Caÿster does not in itself involve distinctions between momentary stages *a, b,* etc., we gain formal simplicity of subject matter by representing our subject matter as a single object, Caÿster, instead of a multiplicity of objects *a, b,* etc., in river kinship. The expedient is an application, in a local or relative way, of Occam's razor: the entities concerned in a particular discourse are reduced from many, *a, b,* etc., to one, the Caÿster. Note, however, that from an over-all or absolute point of view the expedient is quite opposite to Occam's razor, for the multiple entities *a, b,* etc., have not been dropped from the universe; the Caÿster has simply been added. There are contexts in which we shall still need to speak differentially of *a, b,* and others rather than speaking indiscriminately of the Caÿster. Still the Caÿster remains a convenient addition to our ontology because of the contexts in which it does effect economy.

Consider, somewhat more generally, a discourse about momentary objects all of which happen still to be river stages, but not entirely river-kindred. If it happens in this particular discourse that whatever is affirmed of any momentary object is affirmed also of every other which is river-kindred to it, so that no distinctions between stages of the same river are relevant, then clearly we can gain simplicity by representing our subject matter as comprising a few rivers rather than the many river stages. Diversities remain among our new objects, the rivers, but no diversities remain beyond the needs of the discourse with which we are occupied.

I have been speaking just now of integration of momentary objects into time-consuming wholes, but it is clear that similar remarks apply to integration of individually indicable localities into spatially extensive wholes. Where what we want to say about certain broad surfaces does not concern distinctions between their parts, we simplify our discourse by making its objects as few and large as we can—taking the various broad surfaces as single objects.

Analogous remarks hold, and very conspicuously, for conceptual integration—the integrating of particulars into a universal. Suppose a discourse about person stages, and suppose that whatever is said about any person stage, in this particular discourse, applies equally to all person stages which make the same amount of money. Our discourse is simplified, then, by shifting its subject matter from person stages to income groups. Distinctions immaterial to the discourse at hand are thus extruded from the subject matter.

In general we might propound this maxim of the *identification of indiscernibles:* Objects indistinguishable from one another within the terms of a given discourse should be construed as identical for that discourse. More accurately: the references to the original objects should be reconstrued for purposes of the discourse as referring to other and fewer objects, in such a way that indistinguishable originals give way each to the same new object.

For a striking example of the application of this maxim, consider the familiar so-called propositional calculus. To begin with, let us follow the lead of some modern literature by thinking of the '*p*', '*q*', etc. of this calculus as referring to propositional concepts, whatever they may be. But we know that propositional concepts alike in truth value are indistinguishable within the terms of this calculus, interchangeable so far as anything expressible in this calculus is concerned. Then the canon of identification of indiscernibles directs us to reconstrue '*p*', '*q*', etc., as referring merely to truth values—which, by the way, was Frege's interpretation of this calculus.

For my own part, I prefer to think of '*p*', '*q*', etc., as schematic letters standing in place of statements but not referring at all. But if they are to be treated as referring, the maxim is in order.

Our maxim of identification of indiscernibles is relative to a discourse, and hence vague in so far as the cleavage between discourses is vague. It applies best when the discourse is neatly closed, like the propositional calculus; but discourse generally departmentalizes itself to some degree, and this degree will tend to determine where and to what degree it may prove convenient to invoke the maxim of identification of indiscernibles.

3

Now let us return to our reflections on the nature of universals. Earlier we represented this category by the example 'red,' and found this example to admit of treatment as an ordinary spatio-temporally extended particular on a par with the Caÿster. Red was the largest red thing in the universe—the scattered total thing whose parts are all the red things. Similarly, in the recent example of income groups, each income group can be thought of simply as the scattered total spatio-temporal thing which is made up of the appropriate person stages, various stages of various persons. An income group is just as concrete as a river or a person, and, like a person, it is a summation of person stages. It differs from a person merely in that the person stages which go together to make up an income group are another assortment than those which go together to make up a person. Income groups are related to persons much as waters are related to rivers; for it will be recalled that the momentary object *a* was part in a temporal way both of a river and of a water, while *b* was a part of the same river but not of the same water, and *c* was a part of the same water but not of the same river. Up to now, therefore, the distinction between spatio-temporal integration and conceptual integration appears idle; all is spatio-temporal integration.

Now let me switch to a more artificial example. Suppose our subject matter consists of the visibly outlined convex regions, small and large, in this figure. There are 33 such regions. Suppose further that we undertake a discourse relatively to which any geometrically similar regions are interchangeable. Then our maxim of identification of indiscernibles directs us for purposes of this discourse to speak not of similarity but of identity; to say not that x and y are similar but that $x = y$, thus reconstruing the objects x and y as no longer regions but shapes. The subject matter then shrinks in multiplicity from 33 to 5: the isosceles right triangle, the square, the two-to-one rectangle, and two forms of trapezoid.

Each of these five is a universal. Now just as we have reconstrued the color red as the total spatio-temporal thing made up of all the red things, so suppose we construe the shape square as the total region made up by pooling all the five square regions. Suppose also we construe the shape isosceles right triangle as the total region made up by pooling all the 16 triangular regions. Similarly suppose we construe the shape two-to-one rectangle as the total region made up by pooling the four

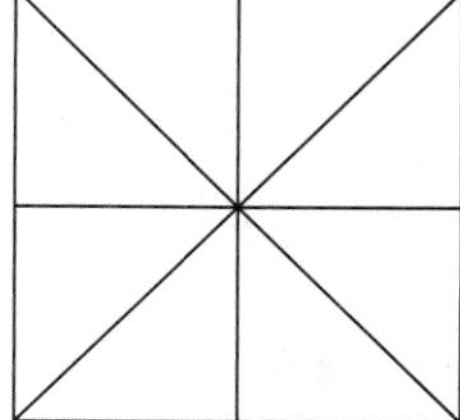

two-to-one rectangular regions; and similarly for the two trapezoidal shapes. Clearly this leads to trouble, for our five shapes then all reduce to one, the total region. Pooling all the triangular regions gives simply the total square region; pooling all the square regions gives the same; and similarly for the other three shapes. We should end up, intolerably, by concluding identity among the five shapes.

So the theory of universals as concrete, which happened to work for red, breaks down in general.[1] We can imagine that universals in general, as entities, insinuated themselves into our ontology in the following way. First we formed the habit of introducing spatio-temporally extended concrete things, according to the pattern considered earlier. Red entered with Caÿster and the others as a concrete thing. Finally triangle, square, and other universals were swept in on a faulty analogy with red and its ilk.

Purely as philosophical sport, without supposing there to be any serious psychological or anthropological import in our reflections, let us now go back to Hume's theory of external objects and carry it a step further. Momentary impressions, according to Hume, are wrongly identified with one another on the basis of resemblance. Then, to resolve the paradox of identity among temporally disparate entities, we invent time-consuming objects as objects of the identity. Spatial spread, beyond what is given momentarily in an impression, may be supposed introduced in similar fashion. The entity red, call it a universal or a widespread particular as you please, may be viewed as entering by the same process (though we are now beyond Hume). Momentary localized red impressions are identified one with another, and then a single entity red is appealed to as vehicle of these otherwise untenable identities. Similarly for the entity square, and the entity triangle. Square impressions are identified with one another, and then the single entity square is imported as vehicle for the identity; and correspondingly for triangle.

So far, no difference is noted between the introduction of particulars and universals. But in retrospect we have to recognize a difference. If square and triangle were related to the original square and triangular particulars in the way in which concrete objects are related to their momentary stages and spatial fragments, then square and triangle would turn out to be identical with each other—as lately observed in terms of our artificial little universe of regions.

Therefore we come to recognize two different types of association: that of concrete parts in a concrete whole, and that of concrete instances in an abstract universal. We come to recognize a divergence between two senses of 'is': 'This is the Caÿster' versus 'This is square.'

4

Interrupting this speculative psychology, let us return to our analysis of ostension of spatio-temporally extended objects, and see how it differs from what may be called the ostension of irreducible universals such as square and triangle. In ostensively explaining the Caÿster we point to *a*, *b*, and other stages, and say each time 'This is the Caÿster,' identity of indicated object being understood from each occasion to the next. In ostensively explaining 'square,' on the other hand, we point to various particulars and say each time 'This is square' *without* imputing identity of indicated object from one occasion to the next. These various latter pointings give our listener the basis for a reasonable induction as to what we might in general be willing to point out as square, just as our various former pointings gave him the basis for a reasonable induction as to what we might willingly point to as the Caÿster. The difference in the two cases is merely that in the one case an identical indicated object is supposed, and in the other case not. In the second case what is supposed to be identical from pointing to pointing is not the indicated object, but, at best, an attribute squareness which is *shared by* the indicated objects.

Actually there is no need, up to this point, to suppose such entities as attributes at all in our ostensive clarification of 'square.' We are clarifying, by our various pointings, our use of the words 'is square'; but neither is an object squareness supposed as object pointed to, nor need it be supposed available as reference of the word 'square.' No more need be demanded, in explication of 'is square' or any other phrase, than that our listener learn when to expect us to apply it to an object and when not; there is no need for the phrase itself to be a name in turn of a separate object of any kind.

These contrasts, then, have emerged between general terms and singular terms. First, the ostensions which introduce a general term differ from those which introduce a singular term in that the former do not impute identity of indicated object between occasions of pointing. Second, the general term does not, or need not, purport to be a name in turn of a separate entity of any sort, whereas the singular term does.

These two observations are not independent of each other. The accessibility of a term to identity contexts was urged by Frege as the standard by which to judge whether that term is being used as a name. Whether or not a term is being used as naming an entity is to be decided, in any given context, by whether or not the term is viewed as subject in that context to the algorithm of identity: the law of putting equals for equals.

It is not to be supposed that this doctrine of Frege's is connected with a repudiation of abstract entities. On the contrary, we remain free to admit names of abstract entities; and, according to Frege's criterion, such admission will consist precisely in admitting abstract terms to identity contexts subject to the regular laws of identity. Frege himself, incidentally, was rather a Platonist in his own philosophy.

It is clearest, I think, to view this step of hypostasis of abstract entities as an additional step which follows after the introduction of the corresponding general terms. First we may suppose the idiom 'This is square,' or 'x is square,' introduced—perhaps by ostension as previously considered, or perhaps by other channels, such as the usual geometrical definition in terms of prior general terms. Then as a separate step we derive the attribute *squareness,* or, what comes to much the same thing, *the class of squares.* A new fundamental operator 'class of,' or '-ness,' is appealed to in this step.

I attach much importance to the traditional distinction between general terms and abstract singular terms, 'square' versus 'squareness,' because of the ontological point: use of the general term does not of itself commit us to the admission of a corresponding abstract entity into our ontology; on the other hand the use of an abstract singular term, subject to the standard behavior of singular terms such as the law of putting equals for equals, flatly commits us to an abstract entity named by the term.

It is readily conceivable that it was precisely because of failure to observe this distinction that abstract entities gained their hold upon our imaginations in the first place. Ostensive explanation of general terms such as 'square' is, we have seen, much like that of concrete singular terms such as 'Caÿster,' and indeed there are cases such as 'red' where no difference need be made at all. Hence the natural tendency not only to introduce general terms along with singular ones, but to treat them on a par as names each of a single entity. This tendency is no doubt encouraged by the fact that it is often convenient for purely syntactical reasons, reasons, for example, of word order or cross-reference, to handle a general term like a proper name.

5

The conceptual scheme in which we grew up is an eclectic heritage, and the forces which conditioned its evolution from the days of Java man onward[2] are a matter of conjecture. Expressions for physical objects must have occupied a focal position from the earliest linguistic periods, because such objects provided relatively fixed points of reference for language as a social development. General terms also must have appeared at an early stage, because similar stimuli tend psychologically to induce similar responses; similar objects tend to be called by the same word. We have seen, indeed, that the ostensive acquisition of a concrete general term proceeds in much the same way as that of a concrete singular term. The adoption of abstract singular terms, carrying with it the positing of abstract entities, is a further step and a philosophically revolutionary one; yet we have seen how this step in turn could have been made without conscious invention.

There is every reason to rejoice that general terms are with us, whatever the cause. Clearly language would be impossible without them, and thought would come to very little. On the admission of abstract entities, however, as named by abstract singular terms, there is room for divergent value judgments. For clarity it is important in any case to recognize in their introduction an additional operator, 'class of' or '-ness.' Perhaps, as just now suggested, it was failure to appreciate the intrusion of such an additional unexplained operator that engendered belief in abstract entities. But this genetic point is independent of the question whether abstract entities, once with us, are not a good thing from the point of view of conceptual convenience after all—happy accident though their adoption may have been.

Anyway, once abstract entities are admitted, our conceptual mechanism goes on and generates an unending hierarchy of further abstractions as a matter of course. For, it must be noted to begin with that the ostensive processes which we have been studying are not the only way of introducing terms, singular or general. Most of us will agree that such introduction is fundamental; but once a fund of ostensively acquired terms is at hand there is no difficulty in explaining additional terms discursively, through paraphrase into complexes of the terms already at hand. Now discursive explanation, unlike ostension, is just as available for defining new general terms applicable to abstract entities, for example, 'shape' or 'zoölogical species,' as for defining general terms applicable to concrete entities. Applying then the operator '-ness' or 'class of' to such abstract general terms, we get second-level abstract singular terms, purporting to name such entities as the attribute of being a shape or zoölogical species, or the class of all shapes or zoölogical species. The same procedure can be repeated for the next level, and so on, theoretically without end. It is in these higher levels that mathematical entities such as numbers, functions of numbers, etc., find their place, according to the analyses of the foundations of mathematics which have been usual from Frege onward through Whitehead and Russell.

The fundamental-seeming philosophical question, How much of our science is merely contributed by language and how much is a genuine reflection of reality? is perhaps a spurious question which itself arises wholly from a certain particular type of language. Certainly we are in a predicament if we try to answer the question; for to answer the question we must talk about the world as well as about language, and to talk about the world we must already impose upon the world some conceptual scheme peculiar to our own special language.

Yet we must not leap to the fatalistic conclusion that we are stuck with the conceptual scheme that we grew up in. We can change it bit by bit, plank by plank, though meanwhile there is nothing to carry us along but the evolving conceptual scheme itself. The philosopher's task was well compared by Neurath to that of a mariner who must rebuild his ship on the open sea.

We can improve our conceptual scheme, our philosophy, bit by bit while continuing to depend on it for support; but we cannot detach ourselves from it and compare it objectively with an unconceptualized reality. Hence it is meaningless, I suggest, to inquire into the absolute correctness of a conceptual scheme as a mirror of reality. Our standard for appraising basic changes of conceptual scheme must be, not a realistic standard of correspondence to reality, but a pragmatic standard.[3] Concepts are language, and the purpose of concepts and of language is efficacy in communication and in prediction. Such is the ultimate duty of language, science, and philosophy, and it is in relation to that duty that a conceptual scheme has finally to be appraised.

Elegance, conceptual economy, also enters as an objective. But this virtue, engaging though it is, is secondary—sometimes in one way and sometimes in another. Elegance can make the difference between a psychologically manageable conceptual scheme and one that is too unwieldy for our poor minds to cope with effectively. Where this happens, elegance is simply a means to the end of a pragmatically acceptable conceptual scheme. But elegance also enters as an end in itself—and quite properly so as long as it remains secondary in another respect; namely, as long as it is appealed to only in choices where the pragmatic standard prescribes no contrary decision. Where elegance doesn't matter, we may and shall, as poets, pursue elegance for elegance's sake.

NOTES

1. *Cf.* Goodman, *The Structure of Appearance* (Cambridge: Harvard University Press, 1951) pp. 46–51.

2. The unrefined and sluggish mind
Of *Homo javanensis*
Could only treat of things concrete
And present to the senses.

3. On this theme see Duhem, *La Théorie Physique: son objet et sa Structure* (Paris, 1906) pp. 34, 280, 347; or Lowinger, *The Methodology of Pierre Duhem* (New York: Columbia University Press, 1941) pp. 41, 121, 145.

Reading Questions

1. Quine defends the view that objects are composed out of temporal parts. Each momentary time slice of the Caÿster River is what Quine calls a water stage (note that not all sums of river stages are rivers). The Caÿster River in 400 B.C. and the Caÿster River now are not identical rivers, but are river-kindred. According to Quine, we couldn't truly say "that's the same river we saw yesterday." Why exactly is this?
2. How are we to identify something like the Caÿster as an object? Does this presuppose that we are legitimately persisting things that must continue to reify parts at different times into the Caÿster? Is Quine committed to the view that there is at least a kind of primitive unity of consciousness over time?
3. If things are four-dimensional timeworms, as Quine thinks, do things really *change?* It doesn't seem that the Caÿster, for example, could lose parts, since it will always have the part *water-stage-x-at-time-t*. Does it really have that part right now? Sure, just as we might view a film at its denouement and ask whether the film continues to contain its beginning frames. We can't see the part now, but it is still there. Is this right? Is it a problem for Quine's position?
4. Quine thinks that the four-dimensional view helps with ostension. However, one can't point to the same river stage or even the same water stage that one pointed to five minutes ago. So what exactly is the subject of ostension?

34 Temporal Parts of Four-Dimensional Objects

MARK HELLER

PROBABLY THE BEST OBJECTION to there being so-called temporal parts is that no one has adequately made sense of what a temporal part is supposed to be. Such phrases as "temporal part," "temporal phase," and "temporal slice" have been used in ways that suggest such varied purported objects as processes, events, ways things are, sets, and portions of careers or histories. The account which comes closest to making sense of temporal parts is Judith Jarvis Thomson's in 'Parthood and identity

My thanks to Jonathan Bennett, Mark Brown, Jan Cover, Paul Hrycaj, Carl Matheson, Judith Jarvis Thomson, and Peter van Inwagen.

Philosophical Studies *46 (1984) 323–334.*

across time.'[1] Consider an object *O* which exists from time t_0 to t_3. On Thomson's account, a temporal part of *O*, call it *P*, is an object that comes into existence at some time $t_1 \geq t_0$ and goes out of existence at some time $t_2 \leq t_3$ and takes up some portion of the space that *O* takes up for all the time that *P* exists.[2] Her account has the strength of being reasonably explicit about what she means by "temporal part." Furthermore, as she explains them, temporal parts do, at least on the face of it, seem to be parts. Her account, however, has the weakness of, as Thomson claims, making the existence of temporal parts fairly implausible. I shall offer an account which is at once explicit and supportive.

The basic problem with Thomson's account is that it is developed against the background of an unhelpful presupposition about the nature of physical objects. She thinks of physical objects as being three dimensional and enduring through time. I admit from the outset that this is our normal philosophical way of thinking of physical objects. But it is this way of thinking that makes temporal parts seem implausible. I see nothing in favor of it other than the fact that it is our standard view, and I put very little weight on this advantage. Furthermore, this view leads to having to choose between what I take to be unpleasant alternatives. The alternatives are:

(a) there is no such physical object as my body.

(b) there is no physical object in the space that we would typically say is now exactly occupied by all of me other than my left hand.

(c) no physical object can undergo a loss of parts (in the ordinary sense of "parts").

(d) there can be distinct physical objects exactly occupying the same space at the same time.

(e) identity is not transitive.

To deny each of these alternatives and to accept three dimensional enduring objects would lead to a contradiction. To show this I present an abbreviated, slightly altered version of an argument of Peter van Inwagen's.[4] If we deny alternative *a*, then there is such an object as my body. Call it Body. If we deny alternative *b*, then there is an object that is all of me other than my left hand. Call that object Body-minus. Now consider some time *t* at which my left hand is cut off. This does not affect Body-minus, so:

(1) the thing, before *t*, is Body-minus = the thing that, after *t*, is Body-minus.

If we also deny alternative *c*, then my losing my hand does not end my body's existence, so:

(2) the thing that, after *t*, is Body = the thing that, before *t*, is Body.

Further, if we deny *d*, it *seems* to follow that:

(3) the thing that, after *t*, is Body-minus = the thing that, after *t*, is Body.

If we can deny *e*, by transitivity of identity it follows that:

(4) the thing that, before *t*, is Body-minus = the thing that, before *t*, is Body.

But since Body was bigger before *t* than Body-minus was before *t:*

(5) the thing that, before *t*, is Body-minus ≠ the thing that, before *t*, is Body.

and (5) contradicts (4).

In the end, Thomson's preferred way of avoiding this contradiction is to accept *d*.[5] In contrast, van Inwagen avoids the contradiction by accepting *b*.[6] Roderick Chisholm instead accepts *c*.[7] And Peter Geach seems to accept *e*.[8] My way of avoiding the contradiction is to claim the (3) does not follow from the denial of *d* unless we accept the additional thesis that physical objects are three dimensional and endure through time. I will deny this additional thesis. Doing so will allow me to claim that Body and Body-minus are distinct objects that, even after *t*, do not occupy the same space at the same time. It is incumbent upon me, then, to offer a reasonable alternative to the three dimensional view of physical objects.

I propose that a physical object is not an enduring spatial hunk of matter, but is, rather, a spatiotemporal hunk of matter. Instead of thinking of matter as filling up regions of space, we should think of matter as filling up regions of spacetime. A physical object is the material content of a region of spacetime. Just as such an object has spatial extent, it also has temporal extent—it extends along four dimensions, not just three. To see the contrast clearly, consider an object that is created at noon and destroyed at one. If we think of the object as three dimensional and enduring though time, it would be appropriate to say that the object exists at different times; the same object exists at noon and at one. Such an object has boundaries along only three dimensions. The whole object is that hunk of matter which entirely fills up those boundaries. The whole object, therefore, exists at noon and still exists at one. A four dimensional object, on the other hand, has boundaries along an additional dimension. The whole object must fill up all its boundaries and, therefore, does not exist at a single moment. If we accept that physical objects are four dimensional, the appropriate thing to say about the object under consideration is that it takes up more than an instantaneous region of time. It does not exist *at* noon *and* one; rather, it exists *from* noon *until* one. Instead of thinking of an object as existing at various times, we should think of it as existing within regions of time.

In so far as time is just one more dimension, roughly alike in kind to the three spatial dimensions, we should expect that our claims about an object's spatial characteristics have analogues with respect to its temporal characteristics. For instance, just as we might talk about the distance between two points along a line in space, we can also talk about the distance between two points in time. This allows us to understand the notion of temporal boundaries as analogous to that of spatial boundaries. Furthermore, there is an analogy with respect to the part-whole relationship. Just as a spatial part fills up a sub-region of the space occupied by the whole, a temporal part fills up a subregion of the time occupied by the whole. Another important analogy is that, for both spatial and temporal parts, we can, loosely speaking, point at or perceive or name a whole by pointing at, perceiving, or indicating a part. It should be noted that an object's temporal characteristics are not completely analogous to its spatial characteristics. This is because time is not completely alike in kind to the three spatial dimensions. Time, for instance, seems to have a direction. Also, our perception along the temporal dimension is only one directional (memory) and is discontinuous (I can remember what happened on my third birthday without remembering anything that happened between my third and fourth birthdays). Furthermore, temporal units of measurement are not of the same kind as spatial units of measurement. These disanalogies will not affect our present discussion.

One question that arises is whether it is possible to have zero extent along the temporal dimension. I do not have a strong opinion on this issue, although I tend towards the view that zero extent is impossible. What should be noted is that this is no more an issue with respect to the temporal dimension than with any of the spatial dimensions. Could there be any such thing as the surface of a cube? I do not know the answer. Thinking according to our standard three dimensional picture such an object would have zero extent along one of the spatial dimensions and could, therefore, be called a two dimensional object. According to our new four dimensional picture such an object would still have zero extent along one of the spatial dimensions. It could, therefore, be called a three dimensional object, one of the three being the temporal dimension. I shall, for convenience's sake, simply assume that zero extent along the temporal dimension, and along each of the other dimensions, is possible.

Now that we have some understanding of the notion of a four dimensional object, let us turn our attention to the parts of such objects. A four dimensional object is the material content of a filled region of spacetime. A spatiotemporal part of such an object is the material content of a sub-region of the spacetime occupied by the whole. For instance, consider a particular object *O* and the region *R* of spacetime that *O* fills. A spatiotemporal part of *O* is the material content of a sub-region of *R*. A spatiotemporal part, as long as it has greater than zero extent along every dimension, is itself a four dimensional physical object.[9] A spatiotemporal part is not a set or a process or a way something is at a place and time. It, like the object it is part of, is a hunk of matter. If Heller is a physical object, then so is Heller's-left-hand-from-(1:00 P.M., January 3, 1980)-to-(1:01 P.M., January 3, 1980). This spatio-temporal part of me could have, between 1:00 P.M., and 1:01 P.M. on January 3, 1980, been felt, seen, heard, smelled, and, if need be, tasted. It had weight and volume. Thinking of spatio-temporal parts as physical objects corresponds to the way we ordinarily think of parts on our old three dimensional picture. When not being swayed by philosophical considerations we have no doubt that my hand is a physical object. Accepting the account of four dimensional objects presented in this paper, we may continue to hold the general principle that a part of a physical object is itself a physical object.

It should be noted that the fact that any part of *O* is the material content of a sub-region of *R* does not entail that every filled sub-region of *R* contains a part of *O*. I happen to believe that this is true, but it is not a feature of the concept of a spatiotemporal part. One could consistently accept all three of the following:

(i) there are four dimensional objects and spatiotemporal parts of such objects,

(ii) not every filled region of spacetime contains a physical object,

(iii) even for a region of spacetime that does contain a physical object, not every sub-region contains a spatiotemporal part of that object.

I take it that typically someone who accepts all three of these would be accepting (iii) because he accepts (ii). Someone might accept (ii) if he thought that there is good reason to reject scattered objects. Or (ii) might be accepted if independent grounds could be found for some claim like "every object must contain its principle of unity within itself" (whatever that might mean). My goal here is not to supply a means of answering every question of the form "is there a spatiotemporal part here?", but rather to make clear the concept of spatiotemporal parthood.

It is now easy to understand the notion of a temporal part. Any proper part of a four dimensional object is smaller than the whole object along at least one dimension. A proper temporal part is smaller along just one dimension, the temporal dimension. A temporal part of *O* is a spatiotemporal part that is the same spatial size as *O* for as long as that part exists, though it may be a smaller temporal size. Let us suppose that object *O* exactly fills the temporal region from t_0 to t_3. That is, the region of spacetime filled by *O*, namely region *R*, has the temporal boundaries t_0 and t_3. Now consider a certain sub-region of *R* the temporal boundaries of which are $t_1 \geq t_0$ and $t_2 \leq t_3$ and the spatial boundaries of which are just the spatial boundaries of *R* from t_1 to t_2. Call this sub-region *S*. If the material content of *S* is an object, then it is a temporal part of *O*. In general, using the single letters in variables rather than names, a temporal part of *O* is the material content—a temporal sub-region of *R*. "Temporal sub-region of *R*" means spatiotemporal sub-region that shares all of *R*'s spatial boundaries within that sub-region's temporal boundaries. A temporal part of me which exists from my fifth birthday to my sixth is the same spatial size I am from age five to age six.

One matter of detail that is particularly important for temporal parts specifically and four dimensional objects in general is how to understand such phrases as "_______ exists in region _______" or "_______ exists at time _______." Physical objects are four dimensional hunks of matter. They, therefore, have precise spatiotemporal boundaries. Consider a particular physical object, this piece of paper.[10] Call it Whitey. Whitey has certain spatiotemporal boundaries—there is a region which it exactly occupies. But we also think that it is true to say that Whitey now exists. This way of talking may be misleading. If Whitey exists now and existed a minute ago, then it is the same object which exists at both times. But this suggests the old three dimensional picture that we have been denying.

This confusion is easily avoided. When we say that Whitey exists now this should be taken as a loose way of saying that part of Whitey exists now. If we meant strictly that Whitey exists now we would be saying something false. "Whitey" names the whole piece of paper,[11] and that object does not exist now. Strictly speaking, Whitey is temporally too large to exist now. Only a part of Whitey exists now. This, then, is the major difference between the three dimensional and four dimensional pictures. On the three dimensional picture if we said that Whitey exists now and really meant Whitey, the whole piece of paper, we would be saying something true. It is Whitey which exist at different times. On the other hand, on the four dimensional picture Whitey does not, strictly speaking, exist at different times. Whitey's parts exist at different times (different parts at different times), and, in virtue of this fact, we say that Whitey exists at those times.

This can be made clearer by considering a spatial analogy. Put Whitey mostly in a drawer, but leave a small corner sticking out. Now if asked where Whitey is you will answer that it is in the drawer. Strictly speaking, however, your answer would be false. Even on the three dimensional picture, part of Whitey is not in the drawer. But "Whitey" names the whole piece of paper, so if it is not the whole piece in the drawer, then it is not Whitey in the drawer. We say that Whitey is in the drawer because a part of Whitey is in there. Notice also that with some rewording it can be seen that how large a portion of the paper is in the drawer is not crucial. If only a corner of the paper were inside we would be less likely to say that Whitey is in the drawer when asked where Whitey is. But if asked "Does Whitey exist inside that drawer?" I think we would all say "yes." For another case consider Alice's mother screaming at her "Now, Alice, you stay out of that cookie jar!"

Recognizing that we have this loose way of speaking even when using our three dimensional picture, it is not surprising that we also have this loose way of speaking when using our four dimensional picture. Recognizing that such a phrase as "Whitey exists now" is just loose speaking, we see that, strictly speaking, Whitey only exists within the spatiotemporal region which it exactly fills and regions of which that one is a sub-region. To loosely say that Whitey exists now is to strictly say that the present time is within Whitey's temporal boundaries, and thus is equivalent to saying that Whitey has a temporal part that exists now (assuming that there are instantaneous temporal parts).

One nice ramification of these considerations is that an object and a proper part of that object do not, strictly speaking, exist in the same space at the same time. An object is not coincident with any of its proper parts. Intuitively, the problem with coincident entities is that of overcrowding. There is just not enough room for them. But an object and a part of that object do not compete for room. There is a certain spatiotemporal region exactly occupied by the part; the whole object is not in that region. There is only as much of the object there as will fit—namely, the part. This intuitive understanding of the relationship between part and whole is what I intended to capture with my discussion of our loose way of talking. When we say that Whitey is in the drawer, that is just a loose way of saying that part of Whitey is there. When we say Whitey exists now we are only saying that a part of Whitey exists now. Keeping this in mind allows us to avoid being committed to coincident entities.

Let us consider a spatial case. Even adopting a three dimensional picture, we are not tempted to say that Heller and Heller's left hand are coincident entities. These are not two distinct entities in one place at one time. Strictly speaking, there is only one entity in that hand shaped region of space—my hand. Whatever truth there is in saying that I am in that region can be wholly captured by saying that a part of me is there. The relation between my hand and me is not that of coincidence, but, rather, that of part to whole. Similar points are relevant to cases of spatial overlap. My living room and dining room share a common wall. But this does not entail that there is a wall shaped region of space occupied by both my living room and my dining room. That region is occupied by the wall, and that wall happens to be part of both rooms.

If we adopt the four dimensional view of physical objects, then similar points can be made about the relation between an object and its temporal parts. Heller is not coincident with Heller-during-1983. The only truth there is in saying that I occupy the year long region of time is that I have a part that occupies that region. Strictly speaking, there is only one entity in the relevant spatiotemporal region—my 1983 part. Also, analogous to the case of spatial overlap, there may be cases of temporal overlap. If I were to undergo fusion next year, that should not tempt us to say that prior to 1984 there were two objects in the same space at the same time.[12] Rather, we should say that two four dimensional objects overlapped prior to 1984—they shared a common temporal part. Perhaps a less controversial case would be a hunk of gold that is shaped into a ring. The ring then undergoes a gradual replacement of matter until it is entirely composed of silver. Many would be tempted to say that the ring and the hunk of gold were, for a period of time, coincident entities. However adopting the four dimensional view, we can say that the gold and the ring temporally overlap. The gold has a ring shaped temporal part, the ring has a golden temporal part, and the gold's part is identical to the ring's part. The relationship of the part of the one and the part of the other is identity, not coincidence. The relationship between the gold and the ring is that they share a common part, they overlap.[13]

In contrast, trying to make sense of temporal parts without shifting to a four dimensional picture would require a commitment to coincident entities. On Thomson's account, Heller and Heller-now are, in the strictest sense, two distinct entities occupying the same space at the same time.[14] Heller is, at any given time between his birth and his death, complete. Right now I exactly fill all of my three dimensional boundaries. But that supposed temporal part of me called Heller-now also exactly fills those same boundaries. Yet the two entities are distinct because I have a much longer career than Heller-now. Thomson cannot claim that strictly speaking I am temporally too big to be coincident with my instantaneous temporal part, because she avails herself of only three dimensions along which to measure. Along those dimensions I am now exactly the same size as Heller-now.

In fact Thomson's problem of coincident entities is a symptom of a much deeper problem with trying to explain temporal parts without rejecting the old three dimensional picture. Let us return to Whitey, the piece of paper. On the old picture it is, strictly speaking, true that Whitey exists now. It is the same three dimensional object which exists at different times. "Whitey" names the whole piece of paper. So it is true that the whole piece of paper does exist now. So even though Whitey will continue to exist for the next several hours, "Whitey-from-(now + one hour)-to-(now + two hours)" does not pick out a part of Whitey unless that part exists now. But if there were such a temporal part it would not yet have come into existence. So Whitey has no temporal parts other than the one which exists now. Indeed, it does not even have that temporal part, since Whitey (all of it) existed an hour ago, and the temporal part which supposedly exists now did not exist then. If one holds the three dimensional view of physical objects it is perfectly reasonable to think of an ontology including temporal parts as a "crazy metaphysic."[15]

Of course, this is not Thomson's reason for calling it a crazy metaphysic. She does not draw attention to the three dimensional/four dimensional distinction at all, Thomson writes:

> I said this seems to me a crazy metaphysic. It seems to me that its full craziness only comes out when we take the spatial analogy seriously. The metaphysic yields that if I have had exactly one bit of chalk in my hand for the last hour, then there is something in my hand which is white, roughly cylindrical in shape, and dusty, something which also has a weight, something which is chalk, which was not in my hand three minutes ago, and indeed, such that no part of it was in my hand three minutes ago. As I hold the bit of chalk in my hand, new stuff, new chalk keeps constantly coming into existence *ex nihilo*. That strikes me as obviously false.[16]

I suggest that this attack on temporal parts depends on accepting the thesis that physical objects are three dimensional.

Why does Thomson think that temporal parts would come into existence *ex nihilo*? It is obviously not because nothing exists before the temporal part. It is not even because everything that exists before the temporal part continues to exist, for there are prior temporal parts that go out of existence at just the moment that the part in question comes into existence. I suggest that Thomson's claim is founded on the belief that there is no significant material change occurring at the time that the temporal part is supposed to be coming into existence. The piece of chalk does not undergo any alteration. No molecules need be altering their internal structure or their relationships to other molecules. No matter from outside the chalk is added, nor is any matter that was part of the chalk released into the surrounding atmosphere. In short, nothing has occurred that would be enough to bring an object into existence. The temporal part just seems to pop into existence without any sufficient cause.

But this argument ignores one significant change that takes place—the passage of time. It is this change which is responsible for the temporal part's coming into existence. Of course, this passage of time does not provide the whole causal explanation for why the temporal part exists. To give the full explanation we would have to account for why there is matter at that place at that time. It is this passage of time, however, that explains why that matter's being there at that time constitutes a new object's coming into existence. At t_0 the temporal part in question did not exist. At t_1 it did exist. The change which brought this object into existence was just the change in time from t_0 to t_1. Some philosophers—Thomson, for instance—will undoubtably feel that this kind of change is too superficial to bring an object into existence. But this feeling is based on an unwarranted prejudice in favor of the spatial over the temporal. This prejudice, in turn, is founded upon the thesis that physical objects are three dimensional and enduring. Once we surrender this thesis, adopting instead the four dimensional view, I can find no defense for the claim that temporal parts would have to come into existence *ex nihilo*.

To support temporal parts and the four dimensional view of physical objects, recall that earlier in this paper I argued that thinking of objects as three dimensional and enduring would commit us to one of the following five unpleasant alternatives:

(a) there is no such physical object as my body,

(b) there is no physical object in the space that we would typically say is now exactly occupied by all of me other than my left hand,

(c) no physical object can undergo a loss of parts (in the ordinary sense of "parts"),

(d) there can be distinct physical objects exactly occupying the same space at the same time,

(e) identity is not transitive.

We are now in a position to see how viewing objects as four dimensional allows us to avoid all of these alternatives. Once we adopt the four dimensional picture, we can deny all five alternatives without having to be committed to:

(3) the thing that, after *t*, is Body-minus = the thing that, after *t*, is Body.

The objects claimed to be identical in (3) are distinct and do not occupy, except in a loose sense, the same space at the same time.

Body and Body-minus are distinct four dimensional objects, since they have different spatial shapes before *t*. But then, it might be objected, they seem to be distinct but coincident entities—co-occupying a single spatiotemporal region *R* which begins at *t*. The response is that *strictly speaking* neither of them is in *R*. They are both temporally too big. They each take up a spatiotemporal region that is temporally larger than R, since their regions begin before *t*. Of course, each has a temporal part that is in *R*, but that does not entail that either Body or Body-minus is in that region. They overlap in *R*, but neither one exactly fills *R*.

Perhaps there may be another way of generating the difficulty. Instead of comparing Body with Body-minus, let us compare that part of Body which does exactly fill *R* with that part of Body-minus which also exactly fills *R*. It might be claimed that here we have an example of two distinct objects in the same space at the same time. But this again would be a mistake, for these temporal parts are not two distinct objects but, rather, one object under two descriptions. Body and Body-minus have a common temporal part, just as my living room and my dining room have a common spatial part.

I have tried to expound a metaphysic for temporal parts that is at least plausible. I have also tried to give one reason why it might be desirable to adopt such a metaphysic. Still, there is much work left to be done. We will have to develop an understanding of change as a relationship between temporal parts of a four dimensional whole. This will have effects on our understanding of causation and, in particular, of an agent's bringing about change. For instance, Paul Bunyan's cutting down a tree should be seen as a relationship between certain of Bunyan's spatiotemporal parts and certain of the tree's spatiotemporal parts. There is also other important work to be done with respect to the question of whether four dimensional objects have their spatiotemporal parts essentially. Still one more relevant task would be to see how issues concerning the relationship between the mental and physical might affect our considerations of four dimensional objects. These are just some of the chores left undone. At least now that we have a better understanding of what four dimensional objects and temporal parts are, we have a solid basis for carrying out these and other future projects.

NOTES

1. Judith Jarvis Thomson. 'Parthood and identity across time,' *The Journal of Philosophy* 80 (April 1993), pp. 201–220.

2. Thomson would have been better off calling this a spatiotemporal part of *O*, since it may be spatially part of *O* at some of the times at which it exists. She also defines "cross-sectional temporal part," and this could appropriately be called a temporal part.

3. She calls it "a crazy metaphysic" on pp. 210 and 213.

4. Peter van Inwagen, 'The doctrine of arbitrary undetached parts,' *Pacific Philosophical Quarterly* 62 (April 1981), pp. 123–137.

5. Thomson *op. cit.*

6. van Inwagen, *op. cit.*

7. Roderick Chisholm: 'Parts as essential to their wholes,' *Review of Metaphysics* 26 (1973), pp. 581–603.

8. Peter Geach: 'Identity,' *Review of Metaphysics* 21 (1967–1968), pp. 3–12.

9. I am using "object" to pick out the broadest ontological category. To be is to be an object. To be physical is to be a physical object.

10. Assuming that this piece of paper does have precise boundaries.

11. Notice that my claims here are not presupposing a description theory of names. On a causal theory of names "Whitey" refers to the whole piece of paper if and only if it was the whole piece which was originally baptised when the reference of "Whitey" was fixed.

12. Compare this to David Lewis's discussion in 'Survival and identity,' *The Identity of Persons,* ed. Amelie Oksenberg Rorty (Berkeley: University of California Press, 1976), pp. 17–40.

13. Compare this to John Perry's discussion in 'The same F,' *The Philosophical Review* 79 (April 1970), pp. 181–200, esp. pp. 198–199.

14. See Thomson, p. 211.

15. See note 3.

16. Thomson, p. 213.

Reading Questions

1. What is the difference Heller draws between enduring through time by means of three-dimensional parts and perduring through time by means of four-dimensional temporal parts?
2. How does Heller address the ostension issue? That is, how at some given time can one point to an entire four-dimensional object?
3. Heller defines a material object as the material content of a filled region of space-time. He seems to take "filled" as a primitive notion. What could it be to fill a region?
4. How does Heller use the doctrine of temporal parts to answer the ancient puzzle of whether a given ring is identical to the gold that makes it up? (The puzzle: There can't be two objects in the same place at the same time, therefore it must be the case that the ring = the gold, but you can destroy the ring without destroying the gold, therefore the ring ≠ the gold.)

35 Four-Dimensional Objects

PETER VAN INWAGEN

IT IS SOMETIMES SAID THAT THERE ARE two theories of identity across time. First, there is "three-dimensionalism," according to which persisting objects are extended in the three spatial dimensions and have no other kind of extent and persist by "enduring through time" (whatever exactly that means). Secondly, there is "four-dimensionalism," according to which persisting objects are extended not only in the three spatial dimensions, but also in a fourth, temporal, dimension, and persist simply by being temporally extended.

In this paper, I shall argue that there are not two but three possible theories of identity across time, and I shall endorse one of them, a theory that may, as a first approximation, be identified with what I have called "three-dimensionalism." I shall present these three theories as theories about the ways in which our names for persisting objects are related to the occupants (or the alleged occupants) of certain regions of spacetime.

I

Let us begin by considering some object that persists or endures or exhibits identity across time. I will use Descartes as an example of such an object. Let us draw a spacetime diagram that represents Descartes's "career." In order to confer on this diagram maximum powers of accurate representation, let us pretend two things: (1) that the diagram is three-dimensional—made of wire, say, with the z-axis perpendicular to the page—and, (2) that Descartes was a "flatlander," that he had only two spatial dimensions.

The outlined three-dimensional region in the diagram—or, since we are imagining that the "diagram" sticks out of the page and is made of wire, let us call it a model—represents a 2 + 1-dimensional region of spacetime called R. (We represent the dimensionality of regions of spacetime, and of objects that are extended in time as well as in space, by expressions of the form 'n + 1.' In such expressions, 'n' represents the number of spatial dimensions included in the region or exhibited by the object.) R is the region that some will say was occupied by the 2 + 1-dimensional Descartes; others will call it the union of the class of regions successively occupied by the always two-dimensional Descartes in the course of his career. R_1 and R_2 are subregions of R of zero temporal extent. Some will describe R_1 as the region occupied by the largest part of Descartes that is wholly confined to t_1; others will say that R_1 is the region that Descartes occupied at t_1. But, however R, R_1, and R_2 are to be described in terms of their relations to Descartes, it's clear which spacetime regions—that is, which sets of spacetime points—they *are*.

We may now present three theories about how the name 'Descartes' is semantically related to the occupants of R and of subregions of R like R_1 and R_2. (Two of these theories, the second and the third, are reflected in the disagreements I have noted about how to describe R and R_1.)

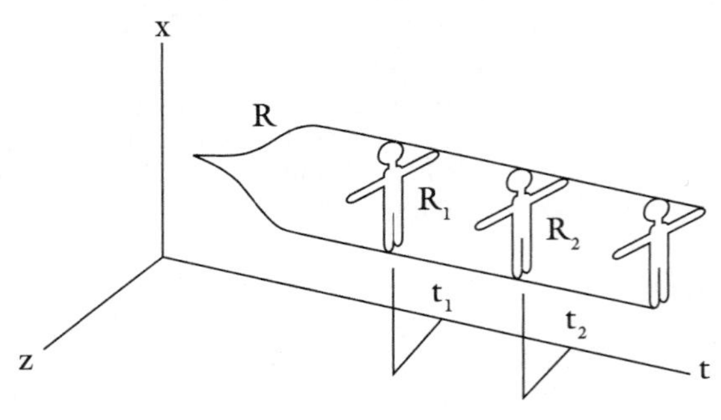

Noûs 24 (1990) 245–255. © 1990 by Noûs Publications. Reprinted by permission of Blackwell Publishers.

THEORY 1

If you say, "Descartes was hungry at t_1," you refer to, and ascribe hunger to, a two-dimensional object that occupies (fits exactly into) R_1 and no other spacetime region. If you say, "Descartes was thirsty at t_2," you refer to a *distinct* two-dimensional object, one that occupies R_2, and ascribe thirst to *it*. Let us suppose that both of the descriptions 'the philosopher who was hungry at t_1' and 'the philosopher who was thirsty at t_2' denote something. It is evident that they cannot denote the *same* thing. It is therefore evident that the sentence 'the philosopher who was hungry at t_1 = the philosopher who was thirsty at t_2' cannot be true. Thus, if those sentences of ordinary English that *appear* to assert that one and the same person (building, river . . .) existed at two different times are ever to be true, what looks like the 'is' of identity in them must be interpreted as standing for some other relation than identity—call it gen-identity.

THEORY 2

When you use the name 'Descartes' you always refer to the 2 + 1-dimensional whole that occupies R. When you say "Descartes was hungry at t_1," you are referring to this whole and ascribing to it the property of having a t_1-part that is hungry. Thus, this sentence is exactly analogous to 'Water Street is narrow at the town line': in saying *that,* you refer to the whole of Water Street and ascribe to it the property of having a narrow town-line-part' What occupies R_1 is not what anyone, ever, even at t_1, refers to as 'Descartes'; it is, rather, a proper temporal part of the single referent that 'Descartes' always has.

THEORY 3

All of the regions like R_1 and R_2—instantaneous "slices" of R—are occupied by the very same two-dimensional object. When we say that Descartes was hungry at t_1, we are saying either (take your pick) that this object bore the relation *having* to the time-indexed property *hunger-at-t_1*, or else that it bore the time-indexed relation *having-at-t_1* to hunger.

The proponent of Theory 3, then, agrees with the proponent of Theory 2 that 'The philosopher who was hungry at t_1 = the philosopher who was thirsty at t_2' can be a genuine identity-sentence and be true; and he agrees with the proponent of Theory 1 that each of the terms of this sentence refers to a two-dimensional object—or, in the real world, a three-dimensional object. (But this second parallel should not be pressed too far. The "Oneist" holds that the terms of this sentence refer to objects that have non-zero extent in the spatial dimensions, but zero temporal extent: in *that* sense they are two-dimensional in our imaginary world, and three-dimensional in the real world. The "Threeist," on the other hand, is probably not going to want to talk about temporal extent at all, not even temporal extent of zero measure. I shall presently return to this point.)

I am a proponent of Theory 3. In this paper, I can't hope to say even a fraction of what there is to be said about the questions raised by these three theories. I want to do just two things. First, to address some arguments for the conclusion that Theory 3 is incoherent, and, secondly, to present an argument for the conclusion that Theory 2 commits its adherents to a counterpart-theoretic analysis of modal statements about individuals. That hardly constitutes a refutation of Theory 2, of course, but, if true, it is an important truth: and it does seem that most philosophers, including, I suppose, many adherents of Theory 2, find counterpart theory rather unattractive. (I will not further discuss Theory 1, except in relation to one very special point. I doubt that anyone would prefer Theory 1 to Theory 2.)

II

In this section, I shall reply to four arguments for the conclusion that Theory Three is incoherent. I shall also attempt to answer two pointed questions that my replies to these arguments are likely to raise.[1]

Argument A What exactly fills one region of spacetime cannot be what exactly fills another.

Reply Any plausibility that this assertion may have arises from an illegitimate analogy with the clearly true principle:

> What exactly fills one region of *space* at a given time cannot be what exactly fills a distinct region of *space* at that time.

This is valid for a space of any number of dimensions. Suppose spacetime is 9 + 1-dimensional, as in "superstring" theories. Then space is nine-dimensional and what occupies any, e.g., four-dimensional region of space at t is not what occupies any other four-dimensional region at t—much less any two- or seven-dimensional region. But the corresponding *spacetime* principle is wrong, or at least not self-evident, and would be wrong, or not self-evident, for any number of dimensions.

The spacetime principle may get an illusory boost from our three-dimensional physical model of a 2 + 1-dimensional spacetime. The two-dimensional region of space that represents R_1 in the physical model, and the two-dimensional region of space that represents R_2 in the model, cannot, of course, be simultaneously occupied by the same two-dimensional physical object. But it no more follows that R_1 and R_2 must have different occupants than it follows from the fact that two photographs are in different places at the same time that they are not photographs of the same object. Our model occupies a three-dimensional region of space; one axis of the model has been arbitrarily assigned the task of representing the temporal dimension of a 2 + 1-dimensional spacetime. But this three-dimensional region of space is simply *not* a 2 + 1-dimensional region of spacetime, and the properties of a 2 + 1-dimensional region of spacetime can be read from the model only with caution. In my view, at least, any support that the physical model seems to give to the spacetime principle is an "artifact of the model." We could perhaps imagine a universe—call it Flatland—associated with a 2 + 1-dimensional spacetime, a universe whose spatial dimensions at different times coincided with those of appropriate cross-sections of the model. If the speed of light in Flatland were low enough, time-like intervals in the spacetime of Flatland might even be made to coincide in a non-arbitrary way with appropriate spatial intervals in the model. Nevertheless, the space the model occupies would not be a *duplicate* of the spacetime of Flatland, but only a representation of it.

Argument B (The "Twoist" speaks.) "Do you say that only a part of Descartes occupies R_1, or that all of him does? In the former case, you agree with me—in the latter, well it's just obvious that you haven't got all of him in there."

Reply I cannot yet answer this question because the appropriate senses of 'part of' and 'all of' have not yet been defined. I shall return to this question. For the nonce, I will say that my position is that *Descartes* occupies both R_1 and R_2, and that if you understand 'part of Descartes' and 'all of Descartes,' then you understand 'Descartes.'

Argument C Theory 3 must employ either time-indexed properties or the three-term relation "x has F at t." But how are these properties, or this relation, to be understood? Take the case of the relation. We are familiar with the relation "x has F," the relation that holds between an object and its properties. If we are to understand the three-term relation, we must be able to define it using the two-term relation and other notions we understand. (We cannot simply take "x has F at t" as primitive, for that would leave the logical connections between the two-term and the three-term relation unexplained.) The "Twoist" has such a definition:

> x has F at t =df the t-part of x has F.

But the "Threeist" has no such definition. He must leave the relationship between *has-at-t* and *has* a mystery—and a wholly unnecessary mystery, at that. One might as well postulate a mysterious, inexplicable connection between "x has F" and "x has F at the place p." Just as it is obvious that 'The U.S. is densely populated in the Northeast' means 'The northeastern part of the U.S. is densely populated' it is obvious that 'The U.S' was sparsely populated in 1800' means 'The 1800-part of the U.S. was sparsely populated.'

Reply One may say both that the relation "x has F at t" is primitive and that its connection with "x has

F" is not inexplicable. One need only maintain that "x has F" is the defined or derived relation, and "x has F at t" the undefined or primitive relation. (Such cases are common enough. Consider, say, "x is a child of y" and "x is a child of y and z.") And I do maintain this. To say that Descartes had the property of being human is to say that he had that property at every time at which he existed. To say that he had the property of being a philosopher is to say that he had that property at every member of some important and salient class of moments—his adult life, say. I concede that "x has F" is primitive and "x has F at the place p" is derived (or, more exactly, that "x has F at t" is primitive and "x has F at t at p" is derived). But I see no reason why I should take the interaction of place and predication as a model for the interaction of time and predication. It may be that both space and time are abstractions from the concrete reality of spacetime. But they are *different* abstractions, and may be differently related to many things, including predication.

Argument D What occupies R_1—call it D_1—is clean-shaven. What occupies R_2—call it D_2—is bearded. Hence, D_1 is not identical with D_2.

Reply R_1 and R_2 are *indices.* Descartes is clean-shaven at R_1 and bearded at R_2. Let R_3 be a region of spacetime that was occupied by Mark Brown at some instant in 1973. 1 could point at Brown and say (correctly), "See that bearded man over there? He is cleanshaven at R_3."

Pointed Question 1 So "that man over there" occupies R_3, a region that fell within 1973. *When* does he occupy it?

Answer When is the proposition that Descartes was born on March 31st, 1596 true? Say what you like: that it's timelessly true, that the question is meaningless, that it's always true, that, strictly speaking, there is no *time* at which it's true. . . . and I'll obligingly adopt the corresponding answer to your question.

Pointed Question 2 So Descartes occupies both R_1 and R_2. What occupies *R*? And what properties does it have? Please describe them carefully.

Answer Well, it's not clear that I'm forced to say that *anything* occupies R. But let's assume that something does. It seems plausible to suppose that if something occupies R_1 and R_2 then, if anything occupies $R_1 \cup R_2$, it must be the mereological sum of what occupies R_1 and what occupies R_2. And it seems plausible to generalize this thesis: if something occupies the union of a class of regions of spacetime, and if each member of that class is occupied by something, then the thing that occupies the union must be the mereological sum of the things that individually occupy the members of the class.

Now the region R is the union of an infinite class of regions that includes R_1 and R_2 and indenumerably many other regions much like them. Each of these regions, *I* say, is occupied by, and only by, Descartes. It follows from this and our "plausible supposition" that it is *Descartes* that occupies R.

You ask me to describe carefully the properties of this object. An historian of early modern philosophy could do this better than I, but I can certainly tell you that it was human, that it was French, that it was educated by the Jesuits, that it wrote the *Meditations on First Philosophy,* that it believed that its essence was thinking, that it died in Sweden, and many things of a like nature.

Of course, the question is a little imprecise, since the occupant of R had different properties at different indices—it was, for example, hungry at R_1 and full at many other regions. If you insist on treating R as an index, and ask what properties the occupant of R had *at* R, it seems most reasonable to say: only those properties that it had at *all* the "momentary" indices like R_1 and R_2: *being human,* say, or *having been born in 1596.*

We may note that if Descartes occupies R as well as R_1 and R_2, this explains why the adherent of Theory 3 and the adherent of Theory 1 cannot mean quite the same thing by saying that the referent of, e.g., 'the philosopher who was hungry at t_1' is—in the real world and not in our simplified 2 + 1-dimensional world—a three-dimensional object. The "Oneist" means by a three-dimensional object (at least in this context) one that has a greater-than-zero extent in each of the three spatial dimensions, and zero extent in the temporal dimension. But the "Threeist," if he takes the option we are now considering, believes that Descartes occupied R_1, which is of zero temporal extent, and *also* occupied *R* which has a temporal extent of fifty-four years—and, presumably, that he occupies regions having extents whose measures in years correspond to every real number between 0 and 54. Therefore, in his view, Descartes did not have a unique temporal extent. That is to say, he didn't have a temporal extent at all; the concept of a temporal extent does not apply to Descartes or to any other object that persists or endures or exhibits identity across time. Thus, in saying that the philosopher who was hungry at t_1 was a three-dimensional object, the "Threeist" means that he had a greater-than-zero extent in each of the three spatial dimensions—and that's all.

This completes my attempt to meet the most obvious arguments for the incoherency of Theory 3. I now turn to the promised argument for the conclusion that Theory 2 commits its adherents to a counterpart-theoretical understanding of modal statements about individuals.

III

Theory 2 entails that persisting objects, objects like Descartes, are sums of *temporal parts*. That is, the "Twoist" holds that persisting objects are extended in time, and are sums of "briefer" temporally extended objects. Descartes, for example, extended from 1596 to 1650, and, for any connected sub-interval of that fifty-four year interval, that sub-interval was occupied by a temporal part of Descartes. (He may also have had discontinuous or "gappy" temporal parts, but, if so, we shall not need to consider them.)

Now it does not seem to be the case that Descartes had a temporal extent of fifty-four years essentially: his temporal extent might have been one year or fifty-five years or even a hundred years. But how will the Twoist understand this modal fact, given his thesis that Descartes is an aggregate of temporal parts? He will almost certainly not say *this:* If Descartes had had a different, temporal extent from his actual temporal extent, he would have been composed of exactly the same temporal parts that composed him in actuality, but some or all of those parts would have had a different temporal extent from their actual temporal extent. For example, it is not likely that the Twoist will say that if Descartes had had a temporal extent of eighty-one years, he would have been composed of exactly the same temporal parts, each of which would have had a temporal extent half again as great as its actual temporal extent. No, the Twoist will want to say that if a temporally extended object like Descartes has different temporal extents in different possible worlds, it must accomplish this feat by being the sum of different (although perhaps overlapping) sets of temporal parts in those worlds. And the Twoist will want to say this because he will want to say that temporal parts (i.e., objects that are temporal parts of something) have their temporal extents *essentially*. The Twoist will want to say that it would make no sense to say of the temporal part of Descartes that occupied the year 1620 that it might have had an extent of a year and a half: any object in another possible world that has a temporal extent of a year and a half is some other object than the object that in actuality is the 1620-part of Descartes. We may summarize this point by saying that the Twoist will want to maintain that temporal parts are "modally inductile" (and "modally incompressible" as well). And I am sure that the Twoist is right to want to say these things. If there are objects of the sort the Twoist calls temporal parts, then their temporal extents must belong to their essence.

But then the argument against Theory 2 is almost embarrassingly simple. If Theory 2 is correct, then Descartes is composed of temporal parts, and all temporal parts are modally inductile. But Descartes himself is one of his temporal parts—the largest one, the sum of all of them. But then Descartes is himself modally inductile, which means he could not have had a temporal extent greater than fifty-four years. But this is obviously false, and Theory 2 is therefore wrong.

We may also reach this conclusion by a slightly different route. If Theory 2 is correct, then there is an object, a temporal part of Descartes, that we may call his "first half." Now suppose that Descartes had been annihilated halfway through his actual span: then Descartes would have *been* the object that is in actuality his "first half." (At least I think so. In a possible world in which

Descartes ceased to exist at the appropriate moment, Descartes would have existed—we have so stipulated—and so would the object that is, in actuality, his first half. At least I *think* it would have. How not? But if they both existed in such a world, what could the relation between them be but identity?) But if Descartes and a numerically, distinct object could have been identical, then they conspire to violate the very well established modal principle that a thing and another thing could not have been a thing and itself.

There seems to me to be only one way for the Twoist to reply to these arguments. The Twoist must adopt a counterpart-theoretic analysis of modal statements about individuals. And he must suppose that there are two different counterpart relations that figure in our modal statements about the object X that is both the person Descartes and the largest temporal part of Descartes: a *personal* counterpart relation and a *temporal-part* counterpart relation. According to this view of things, an object in some other world will count as a temporal-part counterpart of X only if it has the same temporal extent as X—anything that lacks this feature will be *ipso facto* insufficiently similar to X to be a counterpart of X under that counterpart relation. But an object in another world will count as a personal counterpart of X only if, like X, it is a maximal aggregate of temporal parts of persons. (That is, only if it is a temporal part of a person and its mereological union with any temporal part of a person that is not one of its own parts is not a temporal part of a person.) This device will allow us to say that X, which is both a temporal part and a person, could not have had a greater temporal extent *qua* temporal part and could have had a greater temporal extent *qua* person. That is: while every temporal-part counterpart of X has the same temporal extent as X, some personal counterparts of X have greater temporal extents than X. (As to the second argument: (i) counterpart theory allows world-mates to have a common counterpart in another world; (ii) this liberality is irrelevant in the present case, for if an object Y in another world is a maximal aggregate of temporal parts of persons that is an intrinsic duplicate of the first half of X, Y will not be a counterpart of *both* X and the first half of X under either counterpart relation.)

This reply to our two arguments is certainly satisfactory—provided that one is willing to accept counterpart theory. (It is important to realize that, as Stalnaker has pointed out, one can accept counterpart theory without accepting the modal ontology—David Lewis's "extreme" or "genuine" modal realism—that originally motivated it.[2]) I can see no other satisfactory reply to these arguments. I conclude that the proponents of Theory 2 are committed to a counterpart-theoretic analysis of modal statements about individuals.[3]

NOTES

1. Three of the arguments—A, B, and D—and the pointed questions are taken from letters I have received from, and conversations I have had with, various philosophers. I am particularly grateful to David Armstrong, Mark Heller, Frances Howard, Michael Levin, David Lewis, and Michael Patton. Argument C is an adaptation of some points that have been made by David Lewis. See his discussion of "the problem of temporary intrinsics" in *On the Plurality of Worlds* (Oxford: Basil Blackwell, 1986), pp. 202–204, and 210.

2. Robert Stalnaker. "Counterparts and Identity," *Midwest Studies in Philosophy* 11 (1986), pp. 121–140.

3. Versions of this paper were read at departmental colloquia at the University of Massachusetts, Amherst, Virginia Polytechnic Institute and State University, Wayne State University, and York University. I am grateful to the audiences at these colloquia for their useful comments and questions. Special thanks are due to David Cowles, Fred Feldman, Edmund Gettier, Toomas Karmo, Cranston Paul, Larry Powers, and Jonathan Vogel.

Reading Questions

1. Van Inwagen presents three theories of objects. The second theory is the temporal parts view familiar from Quine and Heller. Theories 1 and 3 are variants of a three-dimensional view. The first theory describes objects in a kind of Heraclitean flux. What is the salient distinction between it and the third theory?

2. To what extent does van Inwagen's reply to Argument A depend on insisting that the temporal dimension is vitally different from spatial dimensions? In his answer to Argument A, does he merely reject all analogies between the two? If so, is he just begging the question against arguments for temporal parts that rely on such analogies?
3. Van Inwagen advocates the following three theses: (1) Descartes is wholly within space-time regions R_1 and R_2 (the temporal parts theorist thinks only a part of Descartes was within each of these regions), (2) the occupant of region R is the mereological sum, or physical combination, of regions R_1, R_2, etc., and (3) it is Descartes that occupies the entire region R. How are these three consistent? How can Descartes be both a mereological sum and each part of that sum?
4. What is "modal inductility"? How does van Inwagen move from the claim that all of Descartes's temporal parts are modally inductile to the claim that a combination of these parts, Descartes himself, is modally inductile? Could a similar argument be made that three-dimensional parts are also modally inductile?

36 Mereological Essentialism, Mereological Conjunctivism, and Identity Through Time

JAMES VAN CLEVE

MEREOLOGICAL ESSENTIALISM IS the doctrine that no whole can change its parts; mereological conjunctivism is the doctrine that any two objects form a whole. In what follows I shall say something about how the two doctrines are related, defend at least a limited version of each, and draw morals for the problem of identity through time.

I. THREE GRADES OF MEREOLOGICAL ESSENTIALISM

Let us begin by distinguishing three grades of mereological essentialism.

1. A whole cannot survive the *destruction* of a part.
2. A whole cannot survive the *removal* of a part.
3. A whole cannot survive the *rearrangement* of its parts.

Since the rearrangement of a thing's parts is generally a less drastic operation than the removal of one part, and since removal in turn is less drastic than destruction, these doctrines may appear to be progressively stronger. Whether they are really so is a question I shall take up in section III.

As stated, 1–3 are merely temporal versions of essentialism, telling us what changes are compatible with the persistence or identity of a whole through time. A full-blooded essentialist doctrine also has modal force, telling us what "changes" are compatible with the "persistence" or identity of an object through various possible worlds. The full-strength versions of 1-3 would be as follows:

1'. If *x* is part of *y*, then *x* exists in every possible world in which *y* exists. (Or: If *x* is part of *y*, then *y* is necessarily such that *x* exists if *y* does.)

2'. If *x* is part of *y*, then *x* is part of *y* in every possible world in which *y* exists. (Or: If *x* is

From Midwest Studies in Philosophy XI: Studies in Essentialism, *eds. P. A. French, T. E. Uehling, and H. K. Wettstein (Minneapolis: University of Minnesota Press, 1986). Reprinted by permission of the publisher.*

part of *y*, then *y* is necessarily such that *x* is part of it.)[1]

3'. If *x* and *y* are parts of *z* related by *R*, then *x* and *y* are parts of *z* related by *R* in every possible world in which *z* exists. (Or: If *x* and *y* are parts of *z* related by *R*, then *z* is necessarily such that *x* and *y* are parts of it related by *R*.)

My concern is with the full-strength doctrines, but for the sake of convenience in discussing them, I shall often use the temporal versions. What I have to say should carry over, *mutatis mutandis,* to the modal versions.

Mereological essentialism of the second grade has been espoused by a number of the great philosophers, including Locke, Leibniz, and Hume. In recent times, it has been defended by Chisholm but has found few other adherents.

II. CONJUNCTIVISM, ANTICONJUNCTIVISM, AND EXTREME ANTICONJUNCTIVISM

Before I can explain these doctrines, I must provide several preliminary definitions. An object *z* is *composed of x* and *y* (or, *x* and *y* compose *z*) iff *x* and *y* are parts of *z*, and every part of *z* has a part in common either with *x* or with *y*. An object *z* is *exactly composed* of *x* and *y* iff *z* is composed of *x* and *y*, and *x* and *y* have no parts in common. A *sum* of *x* and *y* is any object composed of them; if there is just one such, let us denote it by '*x* + *y*.'[3] An object with parts is *continuous* iff any two parts of it that exactly compose it are in contact with each other.[4] (The idea is that a continuous object is "all in one piece.") Finally, an object is *scattered* iff it has parts and is not continuous.

The three doctrines listed above may now be described. *Conjunctivism* is the doctrine that for any two concrete objects, there is a third that is composed of them.[5] As a corollary, for any two *nonoverlapping* objects, i.e., objects having no part in common, there is a third that is *exactly* composed of them. It will readily be seen that conjunctivism countenances scattered objects, e.g., objects such as that object exactly composed of the Eiffel Tower and the Statue of Liberty. *Anticonjunctivism* is the direct contradictory of conjunctivism; it denies that any two objects compose a third. Finally, *extreme anticonjunctivism* is the doctrine that two objects *never* compose a third unless they are at least in contact. (Perhaps more than mere contact would be required.) Although anticonjunctivism permits the existence of *some* scattered objects, extreme anticonjunctivism rules out scattered objects altogether.

Among the proponents of conjunctivism have been Brentano, Tarski, and Goodman; among the proponents of anticonjunctivism have been Broad, Wiggins, and Chisholm.[6] I do not know of anyone who has explicitly advocated extreme anticonjunctivism.

III. LOGICAL RELATIONS AMONG THE DOCTRINES

I said earlier that the three grades of essentialism appear to be successively stronger, but whether this is really so depends on what one assumes in regard to the conjunctivism issue.

If we understand 'removal' to cover both the destruction of a part and the detachment of it without destruction, it is clear that grade 2 implies grade 1. (This is clearer yet in the modal versions.) Does 1 imply 2? The answer is that it would be possible for 1 to be true and 2 false *provided* conjunctivism were true, but not if extreme anticonjunctivism were true. To see this, consider the following diagram.

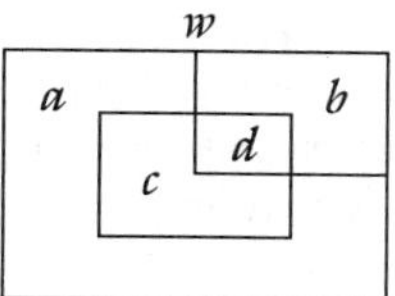

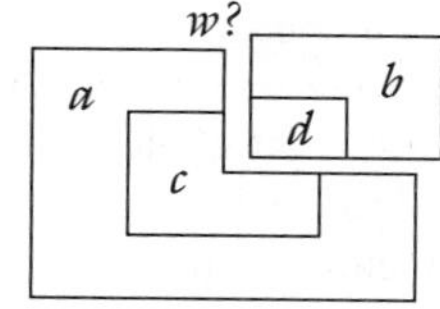

We start with the whole *w*, composed of *a* (which has *c* as a part) and *b* (which has *d* as a part). We then remove part *b*. Does *w* still exist? Conjunctivists can say yes, for they can hold that no part has been destroyed in the process. The part *c* + *d*, which was continuous before the removal of *b*, is now scattered; but it still exists.

Extreme anticonjunctivists, on the other hand, *cannot* say that $c + d$ exists any longer. Assuming that it *did* exist before *b* was removed,[7] they must say that the removal of *b* has destroyed a part of *w*. But we are assuming that *w* cannot survive the destruction of a part; hence, it cannot survive the removal of a part either. QED.

The reader may wonder why I did not use this shorter argument from extreme anticonjunctivism to the nonsurvival of *w*: *w* is scattered after the removal of *b;* hence, it no longer exists. The reason is that my adversaries in this argument—extreme anticonjunctivists who seek to affirm 1 while denying 2—would not accept the implicit identification of *w* with the scattered object $a + b$. They would maintain that although *w* was formerly composed of *a* and *b,* it was not then and is not now identical with their sum. That sum may be scattered, but *w* is not.[8]

This response by grade-2 inessentialists may provoke a further question. If they can evade the shorter argument by refusing to identify a whole with the sum of its parts, why can't they evade my longer argument in the same way? That is, why can't they say that just as the part formerly composed of *a* and *b* is not identical with the sum $a + b$, so the part formerly composed of *c* and *d* (call it George) is not identical with the sum $c + d$? This would enable them to say that George is still intact after the removal of *d*, from which one might conclude that no part of *w* has been destroyed by the removal of *b* after all.

But this maneuver will not suffice to evade my argument. *George* may have survived the removal of *b* from *w*, but that does not alter the fact that $c + d$ did *not* survive. Assuming that $c + d$ was a part of *w* to begin with (temporarily coinciding with George in material extent), we still have the result that at least one part of *w* has been destroyed. Grade-1 essentialism then requires us to conclude that *w* itself has been destroyed.[9]

So extreme anticonjunctivists who affirm grade 1 of mereological essentialism will also have to affirm grade 2. I want to argue next that they will be driven all the way to grade 3.

Typically, rearranging the parts of a thing involves removing some of them and reattaching them elsewhere. If all rearrangement were like this, our result would be immediate: no rearrangement without removal of a part, no removal without destruction of a part; hence, no rearrangement without destruction of a part (and therefore of the whole).[10] But not all rearrangement is like this. A blacksmith might move the head from one end of a nail to the other by bending the nail into a loop, fusing the head to the other end, snipping at the original junction, and then straightening the whole thing out again—a procedure in which no part is ever detached. Moreover, the modal version of grade-3 essentialism rules out *transworld* differences in arrangement, which are not the outcome of any process of rearrangement.

Nonetheless, we can still argue that 2 implies 3 and that 2' implies 3' if extreme anticonjunctivism is true. The strategy is the same as that used above in arguing that 1 implies 2. If a whole *w* differs in arrangement from a whole *w*', there will be parts that are adjacent in *w* but not in *w*'. For the extreme anticonjunctivist, this means that all those parts that straddled the plane of adjacency in *w* will no longer exist in *w*'. Hence, *w* itself will no longer exist. QED.[11]

So extreme anticonjunctivists cannot affirm grade 1 without affirming the other grades as well. What about conjunctivists? I said above that they can affirm 1 while denying 2. I should say now that although this combination is possible for them so far as logic alone goes, I don't think it is a reasonable one. When we detach a part from a whole, have we "removed" it in the sense of making it no longer a part of that whole? Not if the resulting scattered object is identical with the original whole, for the detached part is certainly a part of the scattered object. It begins to appear that for a conjunctivist, there can be no such thing as mere detachment; the only way to remove a part would be to destroy it.[12] In that case, grade 1 would imply grade 2 after all. The only way to avoid this result would be to refuse to identify the scattered object with the original whole—to reject the principle that anything having all the same parts as *w* must be *w*. But anyone who rejects this principle loses any rationale I can see for affirming grade 1 to begin with. So any conjunctivist who affirms 1 ought also to affirm 2.

Matters are otherwise with grade 3, however. The conjunctivist, unlike the extreme anticonjunctivist, can affirm both 1 and 2 while rejecting 3. This seems to me to be the *right* combination. It is also the combination advocated by Locke:

> If two or more atoms be joined together into the same mass . . . the mass, consisting of the same atoms, must be the same mass, or the same body, let the parts be ever so differently jumbled. But if one of these atoms be taken away, or one new one added, it is no longer the same mass or the same body.[13]

He goes on to make exception for living creatures: "in them the variation of great parcels of matter alters not the identity." I shall discuss attempts to limit the scope of mereological essentialism in section VII.

IV. THE CASE FOR CONJUNCTIVISM

To argue for conjunctivism, I shall use the following strategy: first I shall argue that extreme anticonjunctivism is false, i.e., that there are at least *some* scattered wholes; then I shall argue that once some scattered wholes have been admitted, there is no principled way of excluding the rest.

One argument against extreme anticonjunctivism is already afforded us by the results of the last section. We saw there that grade 1 together with extreme anticonjunctivism implies grade 3. I also asserted there that 1 is true, 3 false. (I assume the reader will agree with me that 3 is false; in section VI, I will say what needs to be said in defense of 1.) It follows, by the principle of antilogism, that extreme anticonjunctivism is false.

Another way to argue against extreme anticonjunctivism is simply to cite examples of scattered objects: the land mass of the state of Michigan, tokens of the letter 'i,' and, for that matter, almost any of the familiar objects around us. Physics tells us that even such a paradigm of continuity as my desk is really a scattered swarm of atoms, and that the atoms themselves are scatterings of subatomic particles. Those who would exclude all scattered objects would thus be left with nothing but the basic particles. If what motivates extreme anticonjunctivists is allegiance to common sense, they have joined the wrong camp.

Suppose, then, that we agree to admit at least some scattered objects into our ontology. Does there remain any way to exclude the rest of the objects that the conjunctivist believes in? I doubt that we can find any principle for doing this that is not either vague, arbitrary, or a matter of degree.

Shall we say that scattered objects are permitted only if they are parts of some continuous object? (I mention this proposal because the antilogism above forces upon us only scattered things meeting this restriction.) If we accept what physicists say, this proposal won't get us anything larger than subatomic particles. If we modify the proposal by saying scattered objects are permitted only if they are parts of objects that are not *perceptibly discontinuous,* we will be letting in objects as bizarre as any we keep out. For example, if you and I are standing on the same planet, we will be letting in the sum of my left leg and yours, both limbs being parts of all those not-perceptibly-discontinuous objects that are composed of our two bodies and various connecting tracts of earth.[14]

Shall we say that a collection of objects forms a single object only if the objects can be moved together as a unit? That would admit a house of brick and mortar, but not one of carefully piled stone; and it would admit a pond with its fish in winter (when all are frozen into one block), but not the pond in summer.

Shall we say that a single object must contrast with its environment? That would rule out a ball of cotton if it is packed tightly with others in a bag; it would rule in the contents of the bag if they are scattered about the floor.

One could go on seeking further criteria and trying out various combinations and weightings of them, but I am convinced that the task is bootless. Even if one came up with a formula that jibed with all ordinary judgments about what counts as a unit and what does not, what would that show? Not, I take it, that there exist in nature such objects (and only such) as answer to the formula. The factors that guide our judgments of unity simply do not have that sort of ontological significance.[15]

The position I am contending for can be clarified by comparison with the following passage from Leszek Kolakowski:

> The picture of reality sketched by everyday perception and by scientific thinking is a kind of human creation (not imitation) since both the linguistic and the scientific division of the world into particular objects arise from man's practical needs. In this sense the world's products must be considered artificial. . . . In abstract nothing prevents us from dissecting surrounding material into fragments constructed in a manner completely different from what we are used to. Thus speaking more simply, we could build a world where there would be no such objects as 'horse,' 'leaf,' 'star,' and others allegedly devised by nature. Instead, there might be, for example, such objects as 'half a horse and a piece of river,' 'my car and the moon,' and other similar products of a surrealist imagination.[16]

With its mention of such objects as 'my ear and the moon,' this passage has an unmistakably conjunctivist ring. But conjunctivists, unlike Kolakowski, do not say that such objects *might* have existed *instead* of the more familiar ones; they say that such objects *do* exist in *addition* to the familiar ones.[17] By suggesting that what objects there are depends on our conceptual practices, Kolakowski intimates a form of idealism or conceptualism that is quite foreign to conjunctivism.

V. ARE MINDS EXCEPTIONS TO CONJUNCTIVISM?

One sometimes encounters the suggestion that the mental and the physical realms are governed by different principles of unity. In the physical realm, so the suggestion goes, things may be compounded and divided as you please, but in the mental realm this is not so. Even if conjunctivism is true of all physical things, it is not true of minds or persons.

This contention might be bolstered by appeal to Kant's principle of *the unity of apperception*. If a subject of consciousness S is to be genuinely *one* subject of consciousness, S must have the following property: if S is aware of p and also aware of q, S must be at least potentially aware of p & q. We could tarry over the exact formulation of this principle, but the application of it is clear. If Smith is aware of seeing lightning and Jones is aware of hearing thunder, it does not follow that anyone is aware (even potentially) of *both* seeing lightning and hearing thunder. (Maybe Smith is deaf and Jones is blind.) Hence, it would be a mistake to fuse Smith and Jones together into one person, as conjunctivism apparently bids us do.[18]

This argument against conjunctivism rests on a confusion. Conjunctivism does indeed imply that two minds or persons must add up to a third *thing*, but it does not imply that two minds must add up to a third *mind*. Conjunctive entities such as Smith + Jones, though composed of minds, are not themselves minds, and for that reason the principle of unity of apperception does not apply to them. (No one would apply that principle to a team or a committee.) There is simply no conflict between unity of apperception and unbridled conjunctivism.

Having seen this, let us go on to consider whether there is anything to the argument for dualism hinted at in the first paragraph of this section. One possible version of the argument would be this:

1. Any two physical things compose a third thing.
2. It is *not* the case that any two *minds* compose a third thing. Therefore,
3. Minds are not physical things.

This argument is valid, provided the conclusion is read as '*Some* minds are not physical things.' But the second premise is not true, or at any rate is not supported by the unity of apperception—that is what we just saw.

Here is another version of the argument:

1. Any two physical things compose a third physical thing.
2. It is not the case that any two minds compose a third *mind*. Therefore,
3. Some minds are not physical things.

This time the second premise is true; in denying it, we *would* run afoul of unity of apperception.[19] But the argument employing it is invalid. Two shoes seldom if ever compose a third *shoe*, but we could not combine that fact with the first premise to conclude that some shoes are not physical things. All that follows from our premises is that it is not the case that for any *x*, *x* is a mind iff *x* is a physical thing—but that could be true simply because not all physical things are minds.[20]

VI. THE CASE FOR MEREOLOGICAL ESSENTIALISM

There is at least one class of entities to which the application of mereological essentialism (by which hereafter I mean mereological essentialism of the second grade) is not in much dispute—namely, mereological sums, or what Locke calls masses of matter. Mereological essentialism in regard to such entities is highly intuitive. After all, if one particle in a mass of matter is removed, how can it be the very same mass that remains? What is controversial (and usually controverted) is the application of mereological essentialism to entities of other kinds—artifacts, living creatures, and (especially) persons.

My purposes do not require me to affirm mereological essentialism in regard to anything but masses of matter; that is all that is involved in my argument against extreme anticonjunctivism.[21] I should nonetheless like to take the opportunity to argue in the remainder of this section that mereological essentialism should be adopted in regard to artifacts and nonliving things in general.

As an example of an artifact, let us use a plastic letter *T*, such as might be used in a movie marquee. I take it that this is as good an artifact as any, and that our conclusions in regard to it can be extended to coffee cups, sailing ships, and so on.

I am assuming, as noted, that mereological essentialism holds in regard to aggregates of matter. If it does *not* hold in regard to our *T*, this must be because the *T* is something *other* than the aggregate of its matter. It is composed of this matter or constituted out of it, but it is not identical with it. Let us pursue the consequences of denying this identity.

I see only two further possibilities. The first is that the *T* is not identical with *anything*, because it does not really exist. That is to say, it exists only as a logical construction or in a manner of speaking; to say that a *T* exists is simply to say that two bars are related in a certain way. The other alternative is that the *T* exists as a logical subject in its own right, distinct from but coincident with a certain parcel of matter. The "coincidence" I speak of involves being in exactly the same place and sharing exactly the same matter. Without any pretense of historical fidelity, let me label the first alternative as "atomist" and the second as "Aristotelian."[22]

One difference between the alternatives may be brought out by asking what happens when two bars cease to be *T*-related. The Aristotelian would say that something has genuinely ceased to be, namely, a certain *T*, whereas the atomist would say that the passing away of the *T* is only nominal, that it is merely a way of describing an alteration in the bars. Another difference is this: although both parties can accept the *de dicto* statement "necessarily, every *T* is *T*-shaped," only the Aristotelian can accept the *de re* statement "every *T* is necessarily *T*-shaped."

Atomism can be developed in a way that accommodates ordinary talk of a thing's gaining and losing parts. For example, the statement that the *T* on the marquee has lost one of its corners since yesterday could be accepted as meaning that the *T* that is there now was a proper part of the *T* that was there yesterday. Such matters are worked out in Chisholm's theory of *entia successiva*.[23]

I have no quarrel with the atomist alternative; I wish simply to point out that it does not give us exceptions to mereological essentialism. At one level, this is because what exists only in a manner of speaking cannot be an exception to any ontological principle. (The average plumber is not an exception to the rule that no one has a fractional number of children.) At another level, it is because the change of parts that is possible on the atomist alternative is only nominal change: it is really a matter of a thing with one set of parts being superseded by a thing with a different set of parts. There is nothing such that *it* first had one set of parts and then another.

For genuine exceptions to mereological essentialism, we must turn to the Aristotelian alternative, which provides us with a real "it" or abiding subject that has different parts at different times. What can be said against this view?

Let us imagine that there is language whose alphabet contains the letter *schmee*. A token of *schmee* consists of a vertical bar joined at right angles to the underside of a horizontal bar; it is like our *T*, except that the upright may be attached at any point along the length of the crossbar. Suppose now that we begin with a *T* and move the upright gradually to the left. At some point in this operation, the *T* will cease to be, but the *schmee* will still remain. This shows that the *T* and the *schmee* must have been two distinct things to start with, since they have different essential properties or persistence conditions. And, of course, each of them must be distinct from the matter of which both are composed.

We have just seen that by the reckoning of the Aristotelian, there are at least three entities sharing the space of our *T*: the *T* itself, the *schmee*, and the underlying matter. From there it is but a short step to the recognition that the Aristotelian must admit that there are *infinitely many* distinct objects inhering in any parcel of matter. In the case at hand, there are the *T*, the *schmee*, the *squee*—a separate object for each range of displacement (of the upright from the midpoint of the crossbar) that could be used to define a letter.

Perhaps some readers will be tempted to say at this point that there are only *possible* objects corresponding to all these ranges of displacement, and that none of them have actual existence except those actually adopted as letters by some linguistic group. But that would make the number of material beings in the universe a function of human fertility in devising alphabets. Such an attitude is comparable to Kolakowski's and is to be deprecated for the same reason.

Atomists are not implicated in any similar proliferation of entities. In their view, the leftward passage of the upright involves a continuous series of alterations but no infinite number of passings-away.

This, then, is my objection to Aristotelianism: if impartially carried out, it forces us to believe that millions of entities coexist in any parcel of matter. What I find objectionable about this is not the sheer number of entities that are generated; conjunctivism in its own way generates entities aplenty. It is rather that all these entities must occupy exactly the same place and share exactly the same matter, thus violating two plausible philosophical principles: "Two things cannot be in the same place at the same time" and "There cannot be difference of entities without difference of content."[24]

To be sure, these principles probably cannot be accepted without qualification. In stating the first, Locke found it necessary to put it this way: there cannot be two entities of the same *kind* in the same place at the same time." He recognized three kinds of entities: finite souls, bodies, and God; his version thus leaves open the possibility of a soul sharing space with a body or of God sharing space with everything. But even if the list of kinds were much longer than Locke's, a *T* and a *schmee* would surely belong to the same kind, so even the qualified principle would be violated.

Another proposed qualification of the first principle might be this: two things cannot be in the same place at the same time unless one of them is constituted out of the other. But this principle is still violated by the *T* and the *schmee*, which are constituted out of the same third thing but not, presumably, out of each other.[26]

To sum up the case for extending mereological essentialism from aggregates to artifacts and nonliving things generally: the only alternative is Aristotelianism, which involves us in an objectionable multiplication of entities.

VII. LIMITING THE SCOPE OF MEREOLOGICAL ESSENTIALISM

Can mereological essentialism be affirmed for aggregates (or for aggregates and artifacts) without being affirmed for living things and persons? I think so, but combining these positions consistently turns out to be trickier than one might expect. I shall illustrate this by considering the views of Locke and Wiggins, both of whom affirm mereological essentialism for aggregates but make exception for living creatures. (Wiggins also makes exception for artifacts.)

Let us begin by noting that unless they are qualified in some way, the two principles I cited above against Aristotelianism can be used to show that mereological essentialism holds for entities of any sort whatever, including organisms. Take any entity with parts: it must surely share space and matter with some mereological sum. If things that share space and/or matter are held to be identical, it will follow that everything with parts is a mereological sum; so if mereological essentialism holds for sums, it will hold for all entities with parts. To avoid this result without giving up the case against Aristotelianism, we would have to qualify the two principles somehow. For example, we might say "There can be no difference in *inanimate* things without difference in content" and "There cannot be two *inanimate* things in the same place at the same time."

Let us now see what happens to the attempts of Locke and Wiggins to affirm mereological essentialism for aggregates while denying it for organisms. If this position is to be tenable, one must be able to say that an organism and the aggregate of its matter are two different things. Locke and Wiggins both say this, but both also fall into inconsistency.

Locke says that an oak tree and the small plant from which it grew are the same oak but not the same mass of matter. Some have seen in this an anticipation of the doctrine of "relative identity" (x and y can be the same F without being the same G—even when both are G's), but I think such an interpretation is ruled out because Locke explains further that in this case "identity is not applied to the same thing."[27] I take this to mean: identity is not applied to the same *relata*. So there are two things before us, a certain parcel of matter and a tree composed of it; the tree is identical with a plant that was here twenty years ago, but the matter is not identical with the matter that was here then. Locke's inconsistency arises because he is required to *identify* the tree and its matter by his principle that two things of the same kind exclude each other from the same place. For unless Locke wants to classify a tree as an intelligent spirit, it comes under his category of body and is thus of the same kind as a mass of matter. To avoid this inconsistency, he should either have given up the exclusion principle or added living things to his list of kinds.

Wiggins runs into similar inconsistency. Having argued that mereological essentialism holds for sums, he denies that it need also hold for the cat Tibbles, insisting that Tibbles is not identical with Tib + Tail (i.e., the tail of Tibbles plus the rest of Tibbles) or any other sum of its bodily parts.[28] Conformably with this, he also denies that community of all parts is sufficient for identity, since Tibbles has the same parts as any sum of its parts. The inconsistency arises because a crucial part of Wiggins's case for mereological essentialism for sums is Postulate II of Tarski's mereology, which runs as follows:

> For every non-empty class a of individuals there exists exactly one individual x which is a sum of all elements of a.[29]

Well, if there is exactly *one* sum, there cannot be *two* things with all the same parts. Tibbles must be identical with Tib + Tail after all.

Perhaps Wiggins would want to reply to this difficulty as follows: "Postulate II just says there is a unique *sum* having a given set of parts; it does not say there is a unique *thing* having them. There is therefore nothing to prevent two things from having all the same parts so long as one of them is not a sum." This reply would be correct so far as Postulate II by itself is concerned, but it overlooks what happens when the postulate is combined with Tarski's definition of 'sum.' This definition, which is also part of Wiggins's argument for mereological essentialism, runs as follows:

> An individual X is called a *sum* of all elements of a class a of individuals if every element of a is a part of X and if no part of X is disjoint from all elements of a.[30]

By this definition, Tibbles is a sum of the set {Tib, Tail}. So, of course, is Tib + Tail. But Postulate II says there is only one such sum; hence, Tibbles = Tib + Tail. More generally, we can point out that this definition counts anything with parts as a sum and thus, in conjunction with Postulate II, implies that there can never be two entities with all the same parts.

If mereological essentialism has the basis Wiggins says it does, it holds for any entities whatever that have parts. If he wants to avoid mereological essentialism for cats while keeping it for sums, he will have to reject as too broad Tarski's definition of sum. But what could he put in its place? Could he say that Tarski's definition, while not giving a sufficient condition by itself, is part of an axiom system (including Postulate II) that implicitly defines the notion of sum? This would raise the following question: what independent characterization of sums is there that will determine whether a given entity with parts is a sum, and therefore subject to the axioms, or a nonsum and exempt from them?

VIII. TEMPORAL CONJUNCTIVISM AND IDENTITY THROUGH TIME

A common approach to the problem of identity through time is to conceive of persisting objects as four-dimensional entities with *temporal* parts as well as spatial ones.[31] The temporal parts, or the ultimate ones anyway, are strictly momentary; they themselves do not persist through time. Things that *do* persist through time do so in this conception by having different temporal parts at different times. Questions about identity through time then get recast as questions about diachronic or cross-temporal unity: how must parts or stages existing at different times be related in order to be parts of one and the same continuing object?

I think this question should be answered as follows: *any* two or more nonsimultaneous temporal parts are *automatically* parts of a continuing whole, no matter *how* they are related. In other words, if objects have temporal parts, *temporal* conjunctivism is just as reasonable in regard to them as spatial conjunctivism is in regard to spatial parts.[32]

Quine, who is one of the leading proponents of temporal parts, makes no bones about accepting the conjunctivist thesis I have enunciated. An object, he says, "comprises simply the content, however heterogeneous, of sonic portion of space-time, however disconnected and gerrymandered."[33] Among the objects thus countenanced are "the monetary content of my pocket," a temporally scattered object consisting sometimes of nickel and sometimes of copper,[34] and *the President,* a temporally continuous but spatiotemporally discontinuous object that has undergone many changes of political party and may one day undergo nonsurgical change of sex.[35]

My impression is that Quine has few followers in the matter of temporal conjunctivism. I do not see how it can be avoided, however, if one has already taken the first step of admitting temporal parts.[36] Once you allow that things can be chopped up in the temporal dimension, you will have to allow that the pieces can be reassembled as you please.

The doctrine of temporal parts is, in my view, not only sufficient for the existence of entities such as *the President,* but necessary as well. Let me illustrate this point with an example from Eli Hirsch. Hirsch has described an "identity scheme," called Contacti, in which persons "switch identities" during any interval when they are in contact. More accurately: if Smith and Jones are what we would normally regard as two persons who come together at $t1$, maintain contact until $t2$, and then go their separate ways, then according to Contacti there is one person corresponding to the shaded portion of the diagram below, and another corresponding to the unshaded portion.[37]

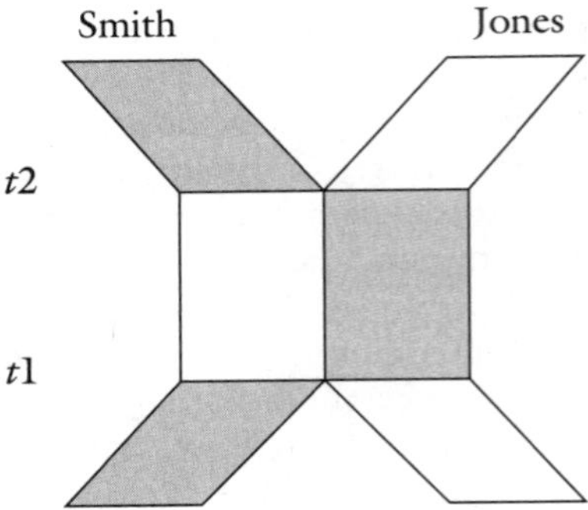

Now if Smith and Jones have temporal parts, I cannot see any objection to there being a person (or at any rate an object[38]) having some of Smith's parts and some of Jones's. If objects do *not* have temporal parts, however, then it seems to me simply a mistake to suppose that there could be objects such as the Contacti persons—as much a mistake as supposing that there could be an object composed of the left half of A and the right half of B if A and B are metaphysical atoms, i.e., entities without spatial parts.

Of course, one could devise some sort of logical construction answering to the shaded portion of the diagram. One could name it Smones and propose that Smones is *F* at *t* iff (i) Smith and Jones are touching at *t* and Jones is *F*, or (ii) Smith and Jones are not touching at *t* and Smith is *F*. But it would be wrong to think that this construction represents a genuine entity. For example, from the fact that Smones was smiling one moment and frowning the next, it would not follow that anything had changed its facial expression. (Maybe all that happened is that a smiling Smith shook hands with a frowning Jones.)[39]

Let us now return to temporal conjunctivism and its consequences. If any two things belong to indefinitely many temporal sums, then the answer to the question "is there a continuant to which *x* and *y* both belong?" is ***automatically yes***, no matter what *x* and *y* may be. By the same token, the answer to the question "Do *x* and *y* belong to the same continuant?" is ***automatically no***, no matter what *x* and *y* may be. If we want to ask a question to which the answer is not already settled ahead of time, we must indicate what sort of continuant we are interested in. We must ask, "Do *x* and *y* belong to the same ***F-continuant***?" The answer to this may be yes or it may be no, depending on the unity conditions incorporated in the concept of an *F*. Without such a "covering concept," statements of diachronic unity are vacuous.

We get a further consequence (as Quine has noted[40]) that is reminiscent of the doctrine of relative identity. 'Reminiscent' is the right word, since it is ***unity*** that is relative, not identity: *x* and *y* may be parts of the same *F*, but not of the same *G*. For example, if *x* and *y* are person-stages, they might be parts of the same lineage (or something more bizarre), but not parts of the same person.

There is also something in all of this akin to the doctrine that identity is conventional. As before, it is not identity that has the feature in question, but unity. Convention enters as follows: out of all the indefinitely many temporal sums that are there, some only are singled out for recognition in our conceptual scheme, and it is with reference to these that questions about diachronic unity get asked and answered. One might say that the role of convention is to specify the covering concepts that are understood when (as is often the case) none are stated.[41]

It should be clear in light of the foregoing that if temporal conjunctivism is true, many questions about identity have no unique answer as typically stated. Or rather, they have an automatic answer if no covering concept is supplied, and as many nonautomatic answers as there are covering concepts. For example, consider the question "Will I still be around in the year 2000—will any object existing then be identical with me?" Before we can answer this, we must restate it as a question about unity, and if we are not to give the automatic answer, we must supply a covering concept. Different covering concepts will yield different answers.

I cannot help thinking to the contrary that the original question has a unique and nonautomatic answer as it stands, and am therefore led to reject the doctrine of temporal parts.[42]

It might be said in reply that the hypothesis of temporal parts does, after all, permit a unique answer to my question, the question being equivalent to this one: "Is my current stage part of any person-continuant that will have stages in the year 2000?" But why are ***person***-continuants more pertinent than continuants of any other sort in answering my original question?

In conclusion, then, I should like to put forth the following argument:[43] (1) if objects had temporal parts, temporal conjunctivism would be true: (2) if temporal conjunctivism were true, questions about identity through time would be relative and conventional in the oblique way I have noted; (3) but questions about identity through time are not thus relative: therefore, (4) objects do not have temporal parts.[44]

NOTES

1. I take this formulation from R. M. Chisholm. *Person and Object* (La Salle, Ill., 1976). 145. Note that 2' implies that a whole cannot survive the ***addition*** of a part, since it implies that a whole with a new part could not have existed as that very whole previously.

2. For Chisholm's defense, see Chisholm, ibid., 145–58; for references to Leibniz and Hume, see ibid., 221, n. 2. For references to Locke, see below, n. 13.

3. What we really need here is the notion of the sum of an arbitrary number of elements, not just two. Such a notion is defined in section VII.

4. This definition was first suggested to me by Richard Potter; it also occurs in Eli Hirsch. *The Concept*

of Identity (Oxford, 1982), 97. Note that for an object to be continuous, it is not enough that *some* two parts of it that exactly compose it be in contact; *any* two such parts must be in contact.

5. And more generally, for *any* number of objects, there is a further object composed of them. I take the term 'conjunctivism' from lectures by Chisholm.

6. Proponents of conjunctivism: Franz Brentano, *The Theory of Categories,* translated by Roderick M. Chisholm and Norbert Guterman (The Hague, 1981), 45–46; Alfred Tarski, "Foundations of the Geometry of Solids," in *Logic, Semantics and Metamathematics* (Oxford, 1956), 24–29; Nelson Goodman, *The Structure of Appearance,* 2nd ed. (Indianapolis, 1966), 51. The mereologies of Tarski and Goodman both derive from Lesniewski.

Proponents of anticonjunctivism: C. D. Broad, *Examination of McTaggart's Philosophy* (New York, 1976: reprint of 1933 edition, Cambridge), Vol. 1, 292; David Wiggins, *Sameness and Substance* (Cambridge, Mass., 1980), 138–39; Chisholm, *Person and Object,* 151 (A4).

7. This assumption seems perfectly reasonable to me, but I should acknowledge that some have questioned it. See Peter van Inwagen, "The Doctrine of Arbitrary Undetached Parts," *Pacific Philosophical Quarterly,* 62 (1981): 123–37.

8. Instead of saying that $a + b$ is scattered, the extreme anticonjunctivist would say that a is separated from b.

9. Note that anyone who distinguishes George from $c + d$ cannot speak of the part composed of c and d, for there are at least two such.

10. Presupposed in this argument is Locke's principle (*An Essay Concerning Human Understanding,* II, xxvii, 4) that nothing can have two beginnings of existence; otherwise the original whole could be said to come back into being upon reassembly.

11. Is it possible to *bend* or *stretch* an object without disturbing any adjacency relations? If so, we must limit the class of rearrangements to which this argument applies.

12. Furthermore. the only way to destroy a part would be to *annihilate* it—or at least to annihilate one of its own parts.

13. Locke, *Essay,* II, xxvii, 4.

14. Perhaps someone will object that your leg, my leg, and the tract of earth between do not make a continuous object because they do not make an *object* at all. But this objection presupposes a criterion of objecthood, which is just what we are seeking.

15. The most detailed discussion of this issue I know of is Hirsch, *The Concept of Identity,* 105–12 and 236–63. Hirsch identifies six "articulation-making" factors (109). But his task is expressly psychological, not ontological; he is asking what induces us to *treat* a portion of matter as a unit, not what *makes* it a unit.

16. Leszek Kolakowski, *Towards a Marxist Humanism* (New York, 1968), 47–48; quoted (with disapproval) in Wiggins, *Sameness and Substance,* 138.

17. Strictly speaking, conjunctivism only says there is such an object as 'my car and the moon' *if* there are such objects as my car and the moon separately. To affirm the proviso, we would need something like the doctrine of arbitrary undetached parts. (See n. 7.)

18. When I speak here of two persons being fused into one, I am not referring to the phenomenon (so much discussed in the literature on personal identity) of two persons becoming amalgamated into one: I am referring instead to two persons composing a third. In the first case, we start with two persons and end up with one; in the second, we have three all along.

19. Or at any rate, we would run afoul of unity of apperception if we made this further assumption: a composite of two minds is aware of whatever either component is aware of.

20. Perhaps a similar criticism is applicable to the following argument for dualism in Descartes's Sixth Meditation: any physical thing may be divided in two, but no mind may be divided in two, so no mind is a physical thing. If the second premise says that a mind cannot be divided into two *minds,* the argument is invalid, and if it says that a mind cannot be divided into two entities of *any* kind, it is problematic.

21. In "Why a Set Contains Its Members Essentially." *Noûs* 19 (1985), 585–602, I have stated premises from which mereological essentialism may be derived. I do not appeal to this derivation in the present paper because one of its premises is conjunctivism. The only other attempt I know of to provide an axiomatic basis for mereological essentialism (that of Wiggins, cited in n. 28 below) also makes use of conjunctivism.

22. The term 'atomism' is meant to suggest something of Greek atomism and something of logical atomism. As for Aristotelianism, good examples are Baruch Brody, *Identity and Essence* (Princeton, 1980), especially 70–73, and Wiggins, *Sameness and Substance.*

23. See Chisholm, *Person and Object,* 89–113, and Chisholm's replies to criticisms in Ernest Sosa, ed., *Essays on the Philosophy of Roderick M. Chisholm* (Amsterdam, 1979), 384–88.

24. For the latter principle, see Goodman, *The Structure of Appearance,* 36.

25. Locke, *Essay,* II, xxvii, 4.

26. Some of this dialectic occurs in classical Indian philosophy. Members of the Nyaya school maintained that a cloth or a pot is something different from the threads or the clay of which it is composed. Their Buddhist opponents objected that this would permit two things to be in the same place at the same time,

thus violating the principle of the impenetrability of matter. The Nyaya reply was that it is all right for two things to be in the same place, provided that there is a one-way relation of ontological dependence or subordination between them. (In their view, the cloth was dependent on the threads, but not vice versa.) For an account of all this, see Bimal K. Matilal, *Epistemology, Logic, and Grammar in Indian Philosophical Analysis* (The Hague, 1971), 55–58, 75.

In connection with the Nyaya point, let me note that although *T*'s could perhaps be said to be subordinate to *schmees* (every *T* implying a *schmee,* but not conversely), one could easily define a character whose permissible range of shapes overlapped the *T* range without containing it; here, there would be cohabitation without subordination.

27. Locke, *Essay,* II, xxvii, 4.

28. David Wiggins, "Mereological Essentialism: Asymmetrical Essential Dependence and the Nature of Continuants," in Sosa, *Essays on the Philosophy of Roderick M. Chisholm,* 297–315, at 309.

29. Ibid, 302.

30. Ibid.

31. "A body is thus visualized eternally as a four-dimensional whole, extending up and down, north and south, east and west, hence and ago." W. V. Quine, *Philosophy of Logic* (Englewood Cliffs, N.J., 1970), 30.

32. Chisholm has impressed upon me that the plausibility of temporal conjunctivism may depend on "spatializing time" in a way that goes beyond dividing things into temporal parts: one must also credit past and future parts with some mode of tenseless existence. (Otherwise, they would not come within the range of our quantifiers.) Temporal parts and tenseless existence usually come together in a package deal, but a philosopher who accepted only the first half of the package could perhaps avoid temporal conjunctivism. I do not think, however, that such a one could avoid the *consequences* of temporal conjunctivism I elicit below.

33. W. V. Quine, *Word and Object* (Cambridge, Mass., 1960), 171.

34. W. V. Quine, *Theories and Things* (Cambridge, Mass., 1981), 125.

35. Quine, *Theories and Things.* 13. Another somewhat similar object, Quine adds, "is the Dalai Lama, an example that has been invigorated by a myth of successive reincarnation. But the myth is unnecessary."

36. And tenseless existence; see n. 32.

37. Hirsch, *The Concept of Identity,* 287–93.

38. Perhaps a cross-temporal version of the unity of apperception could be used to show that no such object is a person.

39. On this point, see what Sydney Shoemaker has to say about tables and "klables" on page 339 of "Identity, Properties, and Causality," in *Midwest Studies in Philosophy IV,* edited by Peter A. French, Theodore E. Uehling. Jr., and Howard K. Wettstein (Minneapolis, 1979), 321–42.

I should note that Hirsch himself apparently does not construe the Contacti example in either of the two ways I have suggested—in terms of temporal parts or logical constructions. He says that the issue of whether there are temporal parts is *verbal* (189–92). And he denies that Contacti is necessarily just a code for other statements that better reveal the true logical forms of facts (296).

40. Quine, *Theories and Things,* 125.

41. Compare Shoemaker. "Identity, Properties, and Causality," 322.

42. For criticisms of arguments *for* the doctrine of temporal parts, see Chisholm, *Person and Object,* 138–47.

43. Shoemaker ("Identity, Properties, and Causality") has advanced a view at first sight at odds with what I say here. Despite holding that the problem of identity through time is the problem of specifying the relation that unites momentary thing-stages, and despite holding (or at least not disputing) that arbitrary sums of stages exist, he maintains that not all sums of stages are ontologically on a par: some constitute the histories of continuants, and others do not. It emerges, however, that there is no disagreement between Shoemaker and me. His "thing-stages" are not parts of continuants, but parts of their histories.

The point is worth elaborating. Shoemaker says his thing-stages are *property instantiations* (or, more accurately, sets of property instantiations that are closed under the relation of synchronic unity, but that does not affect my point). He does not tell us what a property instantiation is, but three possibilities come to mind: a property instantiation might be (a) a "particularized property," or (b) an event of a thing's having a property, or (c) an ordered triple $<x, F, t>$, in case this is different from (b). I don't think it matters which alternative we choose—let it be (c). Shoemaker's project is then to seek a relation between $<x, F, t>$ and $<y, G, t'>$ that will guarantee that they belong to the history of the same continuant, i.e., that $x = y$. He is correct in maintaining that two such triples or events do not automatically belong to the history of the same continuant, even if they do belong to many of the same sums or sequences.

In contrast, a proponent of temporal parts who talks of thing-stages is talking of momentary particulars or slices of substances. A sum of *these* automatically determines the history of a continuant, because it *is* a continuant.

I note in passing that Shoemaker finds no relation of diachronic unity that does not conceptually presuppose identity. His favored relation is "immanent causality," which by its very definition holds between $<x, F, t>$ and $<y, G, t'>$ only if $x = y$.

44. I wish to thank Diana Ackerman, Roderick Chisholm, and Ernest Sosa for helpful discussions of the material in this paper.

Reading Questions

1. Van Cleve defines continuous objects and scattered objects in terms of whether their parts are in contact. However, he leaves "being in contact" as an undefined primitive relation. What could this relation be? Given what you know of microphysics, are any two things in contact?
2. Van Cleve argues that unless you think there are at least some scattered objects, you are committed to the view that nothing could survive the rearrangement of its parts. This consequence he claims is false and, by *modus tollens,* concludes that there are at least some scattered objects. But why is the consequent false?
3. Aside from conjunctivism, what are some other principles of unity that Van Cleve considers? Why does he reject these others?
4. Van Cleve considers the issues of temporal parts and temporal conjunctivism, and argues that if the former doctrine is true, then so is the latter. He then raises various questions about how temporal parts belong to *continuants.* Does Van Cleve's discussion of continuants implicitly depend on a three-dimensional picture of objects? That is, are continuants just objects that exist wholly at any moment and persist (continue) through time? If so, then they are not really four-dimensional entities built out of temporal parts. How could Van Cleve reply?

Further Readings

Books

Chisholm, Roderick M. 1976. *Person and Object.* La Salle, Illinois: Open Court Publishing.
———. 1989. *On Metaphysics.* Minneapolis: University of Minnesota Press.
Goodman, Nelson. 1966. *A Structure of Appearance.* 2nd ed. Indianapolis: Hackett Publishing Co.
Heller, Mark. 1990. *The Ontology of Physical Objects: Four-Dimensional Hunks of Matter.* Cambridge: Cambridge University Press.
Henry, Desmond Paul. 1991. *Medieval Mereology.* Amsterdam: J. Benjamins.
Lewis, David. 1991. *Parts of Classes.* Oxford: Basil Blackwell.
Simons, Peter. 1987. *Parts: A Study in Ontology.* Oxford: Oxford University Press.
Van Inwagen, Peter. 1990. *Material Beings.* Ithaca: Cornell University Press.

Articles

Chisholm, Roderick M. 1973. "Parts as Essential to Their Wholes." *Review of Metaphysics* 26: 581–603.
Dau, Paolo. 1986. "Part-Time Objects." In *Studies in Essentialism,* ed. P. A. French, T. E. Uehling, and H. K. Wettstein. Vol. 11, *Midwest Studies in Philosophy.* Minneapolis: University of Minnesota Press.
Fine, Kit. 1994. "Compounds and Aggregates." *Noûs 28* (2): 137–158.
Lesniewski, Stanislaw. 1983. "On the Foundations of Mathematics." *Topoi* 2: 3–52.
Plantinga, Alvin. 1975. "On Mereological Essentialism." *Review of Metaphysics* 28: 468–476.
Price, Marjorie S. 1988. "On a Paradox of Mereological Change." *Philosophical Studies* 54: 109–124.
Scaltsas, Theodore. 1990. "Is a Whole Identical to its Parts?" *Mind:* 583–598.
Sider, Theodore. 1997. "Four-Dimensionalism." *Philosophical Review* 106 (2):197–231.
Thomson, Judith Jarvis. 1983. "Parthood and Identity Across Time." *The Journal of Philosophy* 80:201–219.
Van Inwagen, Peter. 1987. "When Are Objects Parts?" In *Metaphysics,* ed. J. E. Tomberlin. Vol. 1, *Philosophical Perspectives.* Atascadero, CA: Ridgeview.
Wiggins, David. 1979. "Mereological Essentialism: Asymmetrical Essential Dependence and the Nature of Continuants." *Grazer Philosophische Studien* 7/8: 297–315.
Zimmerman, Dean. 1996. "Persistence and Presentism." *Philosophical Papers* 25 (2): 115–126.